THE AMERICAN MARKETPLACE

Demographics and Spending Patterns

THE
AMERICAN
MARKETPLACE

Demographics and Spending Patterns

BY THE EDITORS OF NEW STRATEGIST PUBLICATIONS

New Strategist Publications, Inc.

Ithaca, New York

New Strategist Publications, Inc.
P.O. Box 242, Ithaca, New York 14851
800/848-0842; 607/273-0913
www.newstrategist.com

ISBN 978-1-935114-28-4
ISBN1-935114-28-X

Printed in the United States of America

Table of Contents

Introduction 1

Chapter 1. Attitude Trends

Highlights 3
Only about One-Third of Americans Are "Very Happy" 4
One in Eight Americans Is a Business Owner 9
One in Five Think Their Income Is above Average 13
Many Think Their Standard of Living Is Falling 18
The Two-Child Family Is Most Popular 22
Religion Is Important to Most Americans. 28
Growing Tolerance of Same-Sex Relationships 35
Television News Is Most Important 38
Most Support Right to Die, Gun Permits 41

Chapter 2. Education Trends

Highlights 47
Many Americans Are Well Educated 48
Most Asian Men Have a College Degree 52
Educational Attainment Varies Widely by State 55
More than One in Four Americans Are in School 59
Parents Are Involved in Their Children's Education 64
Most Parents Are Satisfied with Their Child's School 67
School Enrollment Is Projected to Rise 69
Fewer Students Are Dropping Out of High School 73
Stability in High School Graduates. 75
SAT Scores Vary by Income and Parent's Education 77
College Enrollment Rates Are at a Peak 79
College Costs Have More than Doubled in Three Decades 83
More Americans Attend College 87
More than 30 Percent of College Students Are Minorities 92
Earning a Bachelor's Degree Often Takes More than Five Years. 95
Women Earn Most Degrees 98
Many Participate in Adult Education 104

Chapter 3. Health Trends

Highlights 107
Most Americans Feel "Very Good" or "Excellent" 108
Weight Problems Are the Norm 110
Fewer than One-Third of Americans Are Physically Active 113
Forty-Six Percent of the Nation's Newborns Are Minorities 116
More Have Hypertension 120
One in Five Americans Smokes Cigarettes. 123
Millions of Americans Lack Health Insurance 127
Asthma and Allergies Affect Many Children 132
Health Problems Are Common among Older Americans 136
Many People Are Disabled 140
Women Account for Most Doctor Visits 142
Many Americans Turn to Alternative Medicine 146
One in Twelve Had a Hospital Stay 151

Nearly 1 Million Have Been Diagnosed with AIDS. 153
Heart Disease and Cancer Are the Biggest Killers 155
Life Expectancy Is at a Record High 157

Chapter 4. Housing Trends

Highlights 159
Homeownership Is Near Its Record High 160
Homeownership Rises with Income 165
Homeownership Is Highest in the Midwest 169
Most Americans Live in Single-Family Homes 176
American Households Are Well Equipped 182
Most Are Satisfied with Home and Neighborhood 186
Many People Live near Open Space, Woodlands 189
Few Americans Live in Gated Communities 192
Monthly Housing Costs Are Higher for Homeowners 194
Median Value of Owned Homes Topped $190,000 in 2007 197

Chapter 5. Income Trends

Highlights 201
Peak Affluence in 2007 202
Income Inequality Is Down Slightly 204
Rich and Poor Have Unique Characteristics 206
Median Household Income Fell between 2000 and 2007 209
Many Household Types Lost Ground between 2000 and 2007 211
Asians, Blacks, and Hispanics Have Lost Ground 213
The Median Income of Middle-Aged Married Couples Tops $88,000. 215
The Median Income of Black Married Couples Tops $62,000. 217
Householders Aged 45 to 54 Have the Highest Incomes 219
Income Peaks in Middle Age for Blacks, Hispanics, and Non-Hispanic Whites 221
The Median Income of Married Couples Exceeds $72,000 224
From Young to Old, Incomes Vary by Household Type 226
Dual-Earner Couples Have the Highest Incomes 233
Single Parents Have Low Incomes 236
Older Women Who Live Alone Have Low Incomes 238
College-Educated Householders Have the Highest Incomes 240
Women's Incomes Are Growing, Men's Are Shrinking 242
Between 2000 and 2007, Asian and Non-Hispanic White Men Lost Ground 245
The Incomes of Men and Women Peak in the 45-to-54 Age Group 248
Women Have Been Gaining on Men 251
The Income Gap between Men and Women Is Smallest among Young Adults 253
Education Boosts Earnings 255
Among Wage and Salary Workers, Women Earn 80 Percent as Much as Men 258
Incomes Are Highest in the Suburbs 263
Wages and Salaries Rank Number One 266
Minorities Account for Most of the Poor 268

Chapter 6. Labor Force Trends

Highlights 273
Labor Force Participation Has Declined. 274
Sixty-Six Percent of Americans Are in the Labor Force 276
Labor Force Participation Varies by Race and Hispanic Origin 278
Working Mothers Are the Norm 283
More than Half of Couples Are Dual Earners 286
Most Preschoolers Are in Day Care 288
Eighteen Percent of Workers Are Part-Timers 291

Occupations Differ by Sex 294
Job Tenure among Middle-Aged Workers Has Decreased 304
Self-Employment Rises with Age 307
Few Workers Are Represented by Unions 309
More than 2 Million Earn Minimum Wage or Less 312
Fifteen Million Workers Have Alternative Jobs 314
Millions Work at Home 316
Most Workers Drive to Work Alone 318
Many Workers Lack Benefits 320
Number of Older Workers Will Expand Rapidly 322
Number of Asian and Hispanic Workers Will Grow the Fastest 324
Biggest Gains Forecast for Registered Nurses 327
Management, Scientific, and Technical Consulting Services Industry
Projected to Grow the Fastest 332

Chapter 7. Living Arrangement Trends

Highlights 335
Married Couples Account for Half of Households 336
Number of Households Headed by 55-to-64-Year-Olds Growing Rapidly 338
Lifestyles Change with Age 340
Big Differences in Household Type by Race and Hispanic Origin 342
Most Households Are Small 344
More than Eight Million Elderly Women Live Alone 346
Household Numbers Are Growing Fastest in the South and West 348
More than 80 Percent of Households Are in Metropolitan Areas. 350
Nearly One in Four Children Lives with Mother Only 352
Most Married Couples Do Not Have Children under Age 18 at Home 360
Most Moms Are in the Labor Force 363
Most Americans Live in Family Households 365
More than Three out of Four Women Aged 20 to 24 Are Single 368
Most Men and Women Are Currently Married. 372
Husbands and Wives Are Alike in Many Ways 377
Divorce Is Highest among Men and Women in Their Fifties 380

Chapter 8. Population Trends

Highlights 385
More Women than Men 386
Number of Older Americans Will Soar. 389
The Non-Hispanic White Population Is Growing Slowly 391
Number of Asians and Hispanics Will Grow the Fastest 396
The South Is the Most Populous Region 398
Nevada Was Growing the Fastest 402
Four States Have Minority Majorities 405
Most People Live in Metropolitan Areas 408
Americans Are Moving Less 412
Legal Immigration Adds Millions to the Population 417
Many U.S. Residents Are Foreign-Born 421
Millions of U.S. Residents Speak Spanish at Home 425

Chapter 9. Spending Trends

Highlights 427
Average Household Spending Increased between 2000 and 2007 428
Householders Aged 35 to 54 Spend the Most 433
Spending Rises with Income 444
Couples with Children Spend the Most 464

Asians Spend the Most 475
Spending Is Highest in the West 486
College Graduates Spend More 497

Chapter 10. Time Use Trends

Highlights 509
Americans Spend More than One Hour a Day Eating and Drinking 510
Women Aged 25 to 44 Have the Least Amount of Leisure Time 519
Hispanic Men Spend the Most Time Working 523
Time Use Differs on Weekends and Weekdays 526

Chapter 11. Wealth Trends

Highlights 533
Net Worth Climbed Sharply during the Housing Bubble 534
Two-Thirds of Household Assets Are Nonfinancial 536
Financial Asset Values Rose between 2004 and 2007 538
Stock Values Fell between 2004 and 2007 542
Nonfinancial Assets Are the Foundation of Household Wealth 545
Many Households Are in Debt 549
Two Out of Three Workers Have Access to a Retirement Plan 553
Retirement Worries Are Growing 556

Glossary   559

Bibliography 565

Index   569

List of Tables

Chapter 1. Attitude Trends

1.1	General Happiness, 1998 and 2008	5
1.2	Happiness of Marriage, 1998 and 2008	6
1.3	Life Exciting or Dull, 1998 and 2008	7
1.4	Trust in Others, 1998 and 2008	8
1.5	How People Get Ahead, 1998 and 2008	10
1.6	Geographic Mobility since Age 16, 1998 and 2008	11
1.7	Business Ownership, 2008	12
1.8	Social Class Membership, 1998 and 2008	14
1.9	Family Income Relative to Others, 1998 and 2008	15
1.10	Satisfaction with Financial Situation, 1998 and 2008	16
1.11	How Has Pay Changed, 2008	17
1.12	Parents' Standard of Living, 1998 and 2008	19
1.13	Standard of Living Will Improve, 1998 and 2008	20
1.14	Children's Standard of Living, 1998 and 2008	21
1.15	Ideal Number of Children, 1998 and 2008	23
1.16	Spanking Children, 1998 and 2008	24
1.17	Better for Man to Work, Woman to Tend Home, 1998 and 2008	25
1.18	Working Mother's Relationship with Children, 1998 and 2008	26
1.19	Should Government Help the Sick, 1998 and 2008	27
1.20	Attitude toward Science, 2008	29
1.21	Attitude toward Evolution, 2008	30
1.22	Religious Preference, 1998 and 2008	31
1.23	Degree of Religiosity, 1998 and 2008	32
1.24	Belief in the Bible, 1998 and 2008	33
1.25	Bible in the Public Schools, 1998 and 2008	34
1.26	Premarital Sex, 1998 and 2008	36
1.27	Homosexual Relations, 1998 and 2008	37
1.28	Main Source of Information about Events in the News, 2008	39
1.29	Political Leanings, 1998 and 2008	40
1.30	Favor or Oppose Death Penalty for Murder, 1998 and 2008	42
1.31	Favor or Oppose Gun Permits, 1998 and 2008	43
1.32	Support for Legal Abortion by Reason, 1998 and 2008	44
1.33	Allow Patients with Incurable Disease to Die, 1998 and 2008	45

Chapter 2. Education Trends

2.1	Educational Attainment by Age, 2008	49
2.2	Educational Attainment of Men by Age, 2008	50
2.3	Educational Attainment of Women by Age, 2008	51
2.4	Educational Attainment of Men by Race and Hispanic Origin, 2008	53
2.5	Educational Attainment of Women by Race and Hispanic Origin, 2008	54
2.6	High School Graduates by Region, Sex, and Age, 2007	56
2.7	College Graduates by Region, Sex, and Age, 2007	57
2.8	Educational Attainment by State, 2007	58
2.9	School Enrollment by Age, 2007	60
2.10	School Enrollment by Grade and Year of College, 2007	61
2.11	Enrollment in Public Elementary and Secondary School by State, Race, and Hispanic Origin, 2006	62
2.12	Parental Involvement in School Activities, 2006–07	65

2.13   Parental Involvement in Child's Homework, 2006–07 66
2.14   Parental Satisfaction with School, 2006–07 68
2.15   Projected Enrollment in Prekindergarten through 12th Grade, 2007 and 2017 70
2.16   Projected Enrollment in Prekindergarten through 12th Grade in Public Schools
        by State, 2007 and 2017 71
2.17   High School Dropouts by Sex, Race, and Hispanic Origin, 1990 to 2007 74
2.18   Projections of High School Graduates, 2007–08 to 2017–18 76
2.19   SAT Scores by Selected Characteristics, 2007–08 78
2.20   College Enrollment Rates by Sex, 1990 to 2007 80
2.21   College Enrollment Rates by Race and Hispanic Origin, 1990 to 2007 81
2.22   College Enrollment Rate by Sex and Type of Institution, 1990 to 2006 82
2.23   College Costs, 1977–78 and 2007–08 84
2.24   College Enrollment Rate by Family Income, 1990 to 2006 85
2.25   College Enrollment Rate by Parents' Education, 1992 to 2006 86
2.26   College Enrollment by Type of College and Attendance Status, 2000 to 2007 88
2.27   Number of Undergraduates Enrolled Full-Time in Four-Year Colleges by
        Control of School, 2000 to 2007 89
2.28   College Students by Age and Sex, 2007 90
2.29   College Students by Age, Type of School, and Attendance Status, 2007 91
2.30   College Students by Race, Hispanic Origin, and Type of Institution, 2000 and 2007 93
2.31   Degrees Conferred by Race and Hispanic Origin, 2006–07 94
2.32   Average Years to Complete Associate's Degree, 2004 96
2.33   Average Years to Start and Complete a Bachelor's Degree, 2004 97
2.34   Associate's Degrees Earned by Field of Study and Sex, 2006–07 99
2.35   Bachelor's Degrees Earned by Field of Study and Sex, 2006–07 100
2.36   Master's Degrees Earned by Field of Study and Sex, 2006–07 101
2.37   Doctoral Degrees Earned by Field of Study and Sex, 2006–07 102
2.38   First-Professional Degrees Earned by Field of Study and Sex, 2006–07 103
2.39   Participation in Adult Education, 2005 105

Chapter 3. Health Trends

3.1   Health Status, 2007 109
3.2   Average Measured Weight by Age and Sex, 2003–06 111
3.3   Overweight and Obesity by Selected Characteristics, 2007 112
3.4   Participation in Leisure-Time Physical Activity, 2007 114
3.5   Sports Participation of People Aged 7 or Older, 2007 115
3.6   Births by Age, Race, and Hispanic Origin, 2007 117
3.7   Characteristics of Births by Race and Hispanic Origin, 2007 118
3.8   Births to Unmarried Women by Age, 2007 118
3.9   Births by Age of Mother and Birth Order, 2007 119
3.10   Hypertension by Sex and Age, 1988–94 and 2003–06 121
3.11   High Cholesterol by Sex and Age, 1988–94 and 2003–06 122
3.12   Percent Distribution of People Aged 18 or Older by Cigarette Smoking Status, 2007 124
3.13   Percent Distribution of People Aged 18 or Older by Alcohol Drinking Status, 2007 125
3.14   Illicit Drug Use by People Aged 12 or Older, 2007 126
3.15   Health Insurance Coverage by Age, 2007 128
3.16   People without Health Insurance by Age, 2000 to 2007 129
3.17   People without Health Insurance by Race and Hispanic Origin, 2002 to 2007 130
3.18   Reason for Lack of Health Insurance Coverage by Selected Characteristics, 2007 131
3.19   Health Conditions among Children by Selected Characteristics, 2007 133
3.20   Distribution of Health Conditions by Selected Characteristics of Children, 2007 134
3.21   Percent of Children with Health Conditions by Selected Characteristics, 2007 135
3.22   Number of Adults with Health Conditions by Age, 2007 137

3.23   Distribution of Health Conditions among Adults by Age, 2007 138
3.24   Percent of Adults with Health Conditions by Age, 2007 139
3.25   Difficulties in Physical Functioning among Adults by Age, 2007 141
3.26   Health Care Visits by Sex, Age, and Race, 2006 143
3.27   Number of Visits to a Doctor or Other Health Care Professional by
        Selected Characteristics, 2007 145
3.28   Use of Alternative and Complementary Medicine by Type, 2007 147
3.29   Characteristics of Adults Who Use Complementary and Alternative Medicine, 2007 148
3.30   Characteristics of Children Who Use Complementary and Alternative Medicine, 2007   150
3.31   Number of Overnight Hospital Stays by Selected Characteristics, 2007 152
3.32   Cumulative Number of AIDS Cases by Sex and Age, through 2006 154
3.33   Cumulative Number of AIDS Cases by Race and Hispanic Origin, through 2006 154
3.34   Leading Causes of Death, 2006 156
3.35   Life Expectancy by Age, 1950 to 2006 158
3.36   Life Expectancy by Age and Sex, 2006 158

Chapter 4. Housing Trends

4.1   Homeownership Rates by Age, Household Type, Race, and
        Hispanic Origin, 2000 and 2008 161
4.2   Age of Householder by Homeownership Status, 2008 162
4.3   Type of Household by Homeownership Status, 2008 163
4.4   Race and Hispanic Origin of Householders by Homeownership Status, 2007 164
4.5   Household Income by Homeownership Status, 2007 166
4.6   Educational Attainment of Householder by Homeownership Status, 2007 167
4.7   Nativity of Householder by Homeownership Status, 2007 168
4.8   Region of Residence by Homeownership Status, 2008 170
4.9   Metropolitan Residence by Homeownership Status, 2007 171
4.10   Homeownership Rate by State, 2000 and 2008 172
4.11   Homeownership Rate by Metropolitan Area, 2008 174
4.12   Units in Structure by Homeownership Status, 2007 177
4.13   Size of Housing Unit by Homeownership Status, 2007 178
4.14   Year Unit Built by Homeownership Status, 2007 179
4.15   Fuels Used by Homeownership Status, 2007 180
4.16   Main Heating Fuel Used by Homeownership Status, 2007 181
4.17   Kitchen, Laundry, and Safety Equipment by Homeownership Status, 2007 183
4.18   Amenities of Home by Homeownership Status, 2007 184
4.19   Air Conditioning by Homeownership Status, 2007 185
4.20   Opinion of Housing Unit by Homeownership Status, 2007 187
4.21   Opinion of Neighborhood by Homeownership Status, 2007 188
4.22   Characteristics of Neighborhood by Homeownership Status, 2007 190
4.23   Neighborhood Problems by Homeownership Status, 2007 191
4.24   Public Services in Neighborhood by Homeownership Status, 2007 191
4.25   Characteristics of Community by Homeownership Status, 2007 193
4.26   Monthly Housing Costs by Homeownership Status, 2007 195
4.27   Monthly Utility and Property Insurance Costs by Homeownership Status, 2007 196
4.28   Homeowners by Housing Value and Purchase Price, 2007 198
4.29   Homeowners by Mortgage Characteristics, 2007 200

Chapter 5. Income Trends

5.1   Distribution of Households by Income, 1990 to 2007 203
5.2   Distribution of Aggregate Household Income, 1990 to 2007 205
5.3   Distribution of Households by Income Quintile, 2007 207
5.4   Characteristics of Households within Income Quintiles, 2007 208
5.5   Median Household Income by Age of Householder, 1990 to 2007 210

5.6   Median Household Income by Type of Household, 1990 to 2007 212
5.7   Median Household Income by Race and Hispanic Origin of
        Householder, 1990 to 2007 214
5.8   Median Household Income by Household Type and Age of Householder, 2007 216
5.9   Median Household Income by Household Type and Race and
        Hispanic Origin of Householder, 2007 218
5.10   Household Income by Age of Householder, 2007: Total Households 220
5.11   Household Income by Age of Householder, 2007: Asian Households 222
5.12   Household Income by Age of Householder, 2007: Black Households 222
5.13   Household Income by Age of Householder, 2007: Hispanic Households 223
5.14   Household Income by Age of Householder, 2007: Non-Hispanic White Households 223
5.15   Household Income by Household Type, 2007: Total Households 225
5.16   Household Income by Household Type, 2007: Householders under Age 25 227
5.17   Household Income by Household Type, 2007: Householders Aged 25 to 34 228
5.18   Household Income by Household Type, 2007: Householders Aged 35 to 44 229
5.19   Household Income by Household Type, 2007: Householders Aged 45 to 54 230
5.20   Household Income by Household Type, 2007: Householders Aged 55 to 64 231
5.21   Household Income by Household Type, 2007: Householders Aged 65 or Older 232
5.22   Income of Married Couples by Presence of Children, 2007 234
5.23   Income of Dual-Earner Married Couples by Presence of Children, 2007 235
5.24   Income of Female- and Male-Headed Families by Presence of Children, 2007 237
5.25   Household Income of Men Who Live Alone, 2007 239
5.26   Household Income of Women Who Live Alone, 2007 239
5.27   Household Income by Education of Householder, 2007 241
5.28   Median Income of Men by Age, 1990 to 2007 243
5.29   Median Income of Women by Age, 1990 to 2007 244
5.30   Median Income of Men by Race and Hispanic Origin, 1990 to 2007 246
5.31   Median Income of Women by Race and Hispanic Origin, 1990 to 2007 247
5.32   Income of Men by Age, 2007 249
5.33   Income of Women by Age, 2007 250
5.34   Median Income of Full-Time Workers by Sex, 1990 to 2007 252
5.35   Median Income of Full-Time Workers by Selected Characteristics and Sex, 2007 254
5.36   Earnings of Men Who Work Full-Time by Education, 2007 256
5.37   Earnings of Women Who Work Full-Time by Education, 2007 257
5.38   Median Weekly Earnings of Full-Time Workers by Occupation and Sex, 2007 259
5.39   Median Household Income by Metropolitan Status and Region of Residence, 2007 264
5.40   Median Household Income by State, 2005–07 265
5.41   Sources of Income, 2007 267
5.42   People in Poverty, 1990 to 2007 269
5.43   People in Poverty by Age, Race, and Hispanic Origin, 2007 270
5.44   Families in Poverty by Family Type, Race, and Hispanic Origin, 2007 271
5.45   Families with Children in Poverty by Family Type, Race, and Hispanic Origin, 2007 . . . 272

Chapter 6. Labor Force Trends

6.1   Labor Force Participation by Sex and Age, 1990 to 2008 275
6.2   Employment Status by Sex and Age, 2008 277
6.3   Employment Status of Asians by Sex and Age, 2008 279
6.4   Employment Status of Blacks by Sex and Age, 2008 280
6.5   Employment Status of Hispanics by Sex and Age, 2008 281
6.6   Employment Status of Whites by Sex and Age, 2008 282
6.7   Labor Force Status of Women by Presence of Children, 2007 284
6.8   Labor Force Status of Families with Children under Age 18, 2007. 285
6.9   Labor Force Status of Married-Couple Family Groups, 2008 287

6.10   Day Care Arrangements of Preschoolers, 2005 289
6.11   Before- and After-School Activities of Children, 2005 290
6.12   Full- and Part-Time Workers by Age and Sex, 2008 292
6.13   Part-Time Workers by Age, Sex, and Reason, 2008 293
6.14   Workers by Occupation and Sex, 2008 295
6.15   Workers by Occupation, Race, and Hispanic Origin, 2008 296
6.16   Workers by Detailed Occupation, Sex, Race, and Hispanic Origin, 2008 297
6.17   Job Tenure by Sex and Age, 2000 and 2008 305
6.18   Long-Term Employment by Sex and Age, 2000 and 2008 306
6.19   Self-Employed Workers by Age, 2008 308
6.20   Workers Represented by Unions by Sex, Race, and Hispanic Origin, 2008 310
6.21   Workers Represented by Unions by Occupation, 2008 311
6.22   Workers Earning Minimum Wage by Selected Characteristics, 2008 313
6.23   Workers in Alternative Work Arrangements, 2005 315
6.24   People Who Work at Home, 2007 317
6.25   Journey to Work, 2007 319
6.26   Employee Benefits by Occupation, 2008 321
6.27   Projections of the Labor Force by Sex and Age, 2006 and 2016 323
6.28   Labor Force Participation by Race and Hispanic Origin, 2006 and 2016 325
6.29   Distribution of the Labor Force by Race and Hispanic Origin, 2006 and 2016 326
6.30   Employment by Major Occupational Group, 2006 and 2016 328
6.31   Fastest-Growing Occupations, 2006 and 2016 329
6.32   Occupations with the Largest Job Growth, 2006 to 2016 330
6.33   Occupations with the Largest Job Decline, 2006 to 2016 331
6.34   Employment by Major Industry, 2006 to 2016 333
6.35   Industries with the Fastest Wage and Salary Employment Growth, 2006 to 2016 334

Chapter 7. Living Arrangement Trends

7.1   Households by Type, 2000 and 2008 337
7.2   Households by Age of Householder, 2000 and 2008 339
7.3   Households by Household Type and Age of Householder, 2008 341
7.4   Households by Household Type, Race, and Hispanic Origin of Householder, 2008 343
7.5   Households by Size, 2000 and 2008 345
7.6   People Living Alone by Sex and Age, 2008 347
7.7   Households by Region, 2000 and 2008 349
7.8   Households by Region, Race, and Hispanic Origin, 2008 349
7.9   Households by Metropolitan Status, Race, and Hispanic Origin, 2008 351
7.10   Living Arrangements of Children, 1970 to 2008 353
7.11   Living Arrangements of Children, 2008: Total Children 354
7.12   Living Arrangements of Children, 2008: Asian Children 355
7.13   Living Arrangements of Children, 2008: Black Children 356
7.14   Living Arrangements of Children, 2008: Hispanic Children 357
7.15   Living Arrangements of Children, 2008: Non-Hispanic White Children 358
7.16   Fathers' Living Arrangements with Children, 2002 359
7.17   Total Families by Presence and Age of Children, 2008 361
7.18   Families by Number of Children under Age 18, 2008 362
7.19   Stay-at-Home Parents among Married Couples, 2008 364
7.20   Living Arrangements by Sex, 2008 366
7.21   Living Arrangements of People Aged 65 or Older by Sex, 2008 367
7.22   Never-Married People by Age and Sex, 2008 369
7.23   Cohabitation Experience of Women, 2002 370
7.24   Cohabitation Experience of Men, 2002 371
7.25   Median Age at First Marriage by Sex, 1890 to 2008 373

7.26   Marital Status by Sex, 2008 374
7.27   Current Marital Status of Women, 2002 375
7.28   Current Marital Status of Men, 2002 376
7.29   Age Difference between Husbands and Wives, 2008 378
7.30   Earnings Difference between Husbands and Wives, 2008 378
7.31   Educational Difference between Husbands and Wives, 2008 379
7.32   Race and Hispanic Origin Differences between Husbands and Wives, 2008 379
7.33   Marital History of Women by Age, 2004 381
7.34   Marital History of Men by Age, 2004 381
7.35   Cumulative Percentage of Women Whose First Marriage Has Dissolved, 2002 382
7.36   Cumulative Percentage of Men Whose First Marriage Has Dissolved, 2002 383

Chapter 8. Population Trends

8.1   Population by Age and Sex, 2008 387
8.2   Population by Age, 2000 and 2008 388
8.3   Population by Age, 2008 to 2025 390
8.4   Total Population by Race, 2000 and 2008 392
8.5   Hispanics and Non-Hispanics by Race, 2008 393
8.6   Population by Age, Race, and Hispanic Origin, 2008 394
8.7   Population by Race and Hispanic Origin, 2008 to 2025 397
8.8   Population by Region, 2000 and 2008 399
8.9   Population by Region, Division, Race, and Hispanic Origin, 2008 400
8.10   Population by State, 2000 and 2008 403
8.11   Population by State, Race, and Hispanic Origin, 2008 406
8.12   Population by Metropolitan Status, 1950 to 2000 409
8.13   Population of Metropolitan Areas, 2000 and 2008 410
8.14   Geographical Mobility, 1950 to 2008 413
8.15   Geographic Mobility by Age and Type of Move, 2007–08 414
8.16   Movers by Age and Type of Move, 2007–08.. 415
8.17   Place of Birth, 2007 416
8.18   Legal Immigration to the United States, 1901 to 2008 418
8.19   Legal Immigrants by Country of Birth and State of Intended Residence, 2008 419
8.20   Unauthorized Immigrant Population, 2000 and 2008 420
8.21   Foreign-Born by Citizenship Status, Year of Entry, and World Region of Birth, 2007 ... 422
8.22   Foreign-Born Population by Age, 2007 423
8.23   Ancestry of the U.S. Population, 2007 424
8.24   Language Spoken at Home, 2007 426

Chapter 9. Spending Trends

9.1   Household Spending Trends, 2000 to 2007 430
9.2   Average Spending by Age of Householder, 2007 435
9.3   Indexed Spending by Age of Householder, 2007 438
9.4   Market Shares by Age of Householder, 2007 441
9.5   Average Spending by Household Income, 2007 446
9.6   Indexed Spending by Household Income, 2007 449
9.7   Market Shares by Household Income, 2007 452
9.8   Average Spending of High-Income Households, 2007 455
9.9   Indexed Spending by High-Income Households, 2007 458
9.10   Market Shares of High-Income Households, 2007 461
9.11   Average Spending by Household Type, 2007 466
9.12   Indexed Spending by Household Type, 2007...................................... 469
9.13   Market Shares by Household Type, 2007 472
9.14   Average Spending by Race and Hispanic Origin of Householder, 2007 477

9.15 Indexed Spending by Race and Hispanic Origin of Householder, 2007 480
9.16 Market Shares by Race and Hispanic Origin of Householder, 2007 483
9.17 Average Spending by Region, 2007 488
9.18 Indexed Spending by Region, 2007 491
9.19 Market Shares by Region, 2007 494
9.20 Average Spending by Education of Householder, 2007 499
9.21 Indexed Spending by Education of Householder, 2007 502
9.22 Market Shares by Education of Householder, 2007 505

Chapter 10. Time Use Trends

10.1 Total Time Use and Percent Reporting Activity, 2007. 511
10.2 Men's Time Use and Percent Reporting Activity, 2007. 513
10.3 Women's Time Use and Percent Reporting Activity, 2007 515
10.4 Time Use by Sex, 2007 517
10.5 Time Use by Age, 2007 520
10.6 Men's Time Use by Age, 2007. 521
10.7 Women's Time Use by Age, 2007 522
10.8 Time Use of Men by Race and Hispanic Origin, 2007 524
10.9 Time Use of Women by Race and Hispanic Origin, 2007. 525
10.10 Average Time Use on Weekdays and Weekends, 2007 527
10.11 Percent Participating in Activity on Weekdays and Weekends, 2007 529
10.12 Average Time Spend by Participants in Activity on Weekdays and Weekends, 2007. 531

Chapter 11. Wealth Trends

11.1 Net Worth of Households, 2004 and 2007 535
11.2 Distribution of Household Assets and Debts by Type, 2004 and 2007 537
11.3 Ownership and Value of Financial Assets, 2004 and 2007 539
11.4 Percent of Households Owning Financial Assets by Type of Asset, 2007 540
11.5 Median Value of Financial Assets by Type of Asset, 2007 541
11.6 Stock Ownership of Households by Age of Householder, 2004 and 2007 543
11.7 Stock Ownership by Household Income Percentile, 2004 and 2007. 544
11.8 Ownership and Value of Nonfinancial Assets, 2004 and 2007 546
11.9 Percent of Households Owning Nonfinancial Assets by Type of Asset, 2007 547
11.10 Median Value of Nonfinancial Assets by Type of Asset, 2007 548
11.11 Debt of Households, 2004 and 2007 550
11.12 Percent of Households with Debt, 2007 551
11.13 Median Value of Debt Owed by Households, 2007. 552
11.14 Workers with a Retirement Plan by Type, 1988 to 2006 554
11.15 Workers with Retirement Benefits, 2008 555
11.16 Retirement Outlook, 2000 and 2009 557

List of Illustrations

Chapter 1. Attitude Trends

Few young adults trust others...4
Blacks lag in business ownership...9
Dissatisfaction with personal finances has been growing...............................13
Children will be better off..18
Hispanics believe in traditional sex roles...22
Half of Americans are Protestants..28
Most still disapprove of same-sex relationships......................................35
Newspapers have fallen into third place as the source for news.......................38
When abortion should be legal..41

Chapter 1. Education Trends

Among young people under age 55, women are better educated than men 48
Blacks are better educated than Hispanics..52
West Virginia's population is least likely to be college educated 55
The number of people in college now surpasses the number in high school 59
Educated parents are most likely to attend their children's class events 64
Blacks are least likely to be "very satisfied" with their child's school.............67
School enrollment is projected to climb the most in the South 69
Non-Hispanic whites have the lowest dropout rate 73
Little change is forecast in the number of high school graduates.....................75
Parent's education influences child's test score 77
Enrollment rates were higher in 2007 than in 1990 79
College enrollment rate increases with family income.................................83
Among undergraduates at four-year schools, women outnumber men by nearly 1 million...87
Blacks, Hispanics, and Asians account for a significant share of college students ...92
Nearly half of college graduates spent at least five years earning their bachelor's degree..........95
Men earn fewer degrees than women at every level but first-professional..............98
The middle aged are most likely to participate in work-related adult education 104

Chapter 3. Health Trends

The majority of people under age 65 say their health is very good or excellent 108
The overweight dominate every age group...110
Physical activity increases with education 113
The nation's newborns are diverse 116
Women are more likely than men to have high blood pressure 120
Men are more likely than women to drink alcoholic beverages..........................123
One in six Americans lacks health insurance 127
Boys are more likely than girls to have attention deficit hyperactivity disorder 132
Most people aged 75 or older have arthritis 136
The percent of people with physical difficulties rises with age 140
Many without health insurance do not go to the doctor 142
The use of alternative medicine rises with education.................................146
Females are more likely than males to be hospitalized 151
Blacks and non-Hispanic whites account for nearly equal shares of AIDS cases 153
Heart disease and cancer are most likely to kill 155
Life expectancy at birth reached 78.1 years in 2006 157

Chapter 4. Housing Trends

Homeownership rates are highest among older Americans 160
Most immigrants are homeowners 165
The West has the lowest homeownership rate 169
Two bathrooms are a must for most homeowners 176
Most owned homes are air conditioned 182
Most households rate their home and neighborhood highly. 186
Renters are more likely than homeowners to live in a gated community. 192
Many homeowners pay little per month for housing 194
Homeowners paid much less for their home than it is currently worth 197

Chapter 5. Income Trends

More than 20 percent of households have incomes of $100,000 or more 202
The wealthiest households control nearly half the nation's income 204
Married couples are typically found in the higher income quintiles because their
households are likely to include two or more earners. 206
Householders under age 55 saw their median income fall between 2000 and 2007 209
Income varies by household type 211
Asian households have the highest incomes. 213
Incomes vary sharply by age and living arrangement 215
The incomes of married couples are lowest among Hispanics. 217
Household income peaks in middle age 219
Nearly one-third of Asian households have an income of $100,000 or more 221
Women who live alone have the lowest incomes 224
Many married couples have incomes of $100,000 or more 226
Dual-earner couples without children at home have the highest incomes 233
Female-headed families with children have lower incomes 236
The income gap is largest between older men and women 238
Incomes rise with education 240
Men's median income fell 3 percent between 2000 and 2007 242
The incomes of Asian women grew the fastest between 2000 and 2007 245
Even among full-time workers, men's incomes are much higher 248
Income gap between the sexes is narrowing. 251
Young women make almost as much money as young men 253
Earnings are much higher for college graduates 255
In most occupations, women earn less than men 258
Households in the South have the lowest incomes 263
Social Security is the most common source of income 266
Poverty rate is low for married couples 268

Chapter 6. Labor Force Trends

More older men are working 274
Unemployment is highest among young men. 276
Blacks have the highest unemployment rate. 278
Most mothers are in the labor force 283
Dual earners outnumber single earners 286
Non-Hispanic white children are much more likely than others to participate
in after-school activities 288
Part-time work is most common among teens and young adults 291
Nearly half of Asians work in management or professional jobs. 294
Few workers have been with their current employer for 10 or more years 304
Older workers are most likely to choose self-employment 307
Union representation is much greater in some occupations 309

Women dominate the minimum-wage workforce 312
The percentage of workers with alternative work arrangements rises with age 314
More than one-third of college graduates work at home on an average workday 316
For most, the commute is short 318
Most management and professional workers have access to health insurance
coverage through their employer 320
Big gains for workers aged 65 or older 322
The labor force is becoming increasingly diverse 324
Health care and computer jobs are projected to grow the fastest 327
Goods-producing industries will see employment declines 332

Chapter 7. Living Arrangement Trends

Number of married couples has grown more slowly than other household types 336
Number of households headed by the youngest adults is growing 338
Married couples head most households in the 35-to-64 age group 340
Married couples head most Asian, Hispanic, and non-Hispanic white households 342
Two-person households are most common 344
Women are increasingly likely to live alone after middle age 346
Less than half the nation's households are in the Northeast and Midwest 348
Few non-Hispanic white households are in the principal cities of metro areas 350
Children's living arrangements vary greatly by race and Hispanic origin 352
Only 20 percent of married couples have preschoolers 360
One-third of couples with preschoolers have a stay-at-home mom 363
The lifestyles of men and women diverge in old age 365
Most women have married by their late twenties....................................... 368
Only 10 percent of Americans are currently divorced 372
Most husbands and wives share the same educational level 377
More than one in five adults have experienced divorce 380

Chapter 8. Population Trends

Women increasingly outnumber men with age 386
The U.S. population is aging rapidly 389
The non-Hispanic white share of the population is smallest among children 391
Below-average population growth is projected for non-Hispanic whites 396
The Midwest is the least diverse region 398
Louisiana had the biggest population decline.. 402
California is one of the nation's most diverse states 405
New York is the largest metropolitan area 408
Mobility has declined 412
The largest numbers of legal and illegal immigrants to the United States are from Mexico 417
More than 40 percent of the foreign-born are naturalized citizens....................... 421
Spanish is much more likely to be spoken than other non-English languages 425

Chapter 9. Spending Trends

Households are spending less on some items, more on others............................ 428
Spending peaks in middle age 433
High-income households account for a disproportionate share of spending 444
Spending is below average for single parents 464
Spending of Asians and non-Hispanic whites is above average 475
Spending varies by region 486
College graduates spend big on many items 497

Chapter 10. Time Use Trends

Women spend nearly one hour a day doing housework, on average 510
Women have less leisure time than men 519
Time spent at work varies by race and Hispanic origin 523
People spend more time watching TV on weekends 526

Chapter 11. Wealth Trends

Median net worth has fallen since reaching a peak in 2007 534
Homes, businesses, and retirement accounts are the three most important assets 536
Retirement account balances were modest in 2007 and their value has declined since then 538
Stock ownership peaks in the 45-to-64 age group 542
Median housing value peaks in the 45-to-54 age group 545
Home-secured debt accounts for the largest amount owed 549
Highly paid workers are more likely to have access to a retirement plan at work 553
Most workers are not planning on an early retirement 556

Introduction

Times are tough. The United States is in the midst of the most severe economic downturn in at least a generation. Many feel betrayed by the nation's financial institutions and economic policymakers. Although turmoil seems to be everywhere, in fact there is one area of stability: demographics. In contrast to the volatility of economics, demographic change is slow and steady. For those looking for a way out of the wilderness, demographics offer a path. By understanding the demographic trends, businesses and policymakers can rediscover their customers and constituents. But if demographic insight is your goal, where do you start? Billions of statistics are only a mouse click away, creating a confusing cacophony of numbers. To find direction, start here, with the ninth edition of *The American Marketplace: Demographics and Spending Patterns*, a demographic reference tool that cuts through the statistical clutter and offers a roadmap out of the wilderness.

The American Marketplace reveals the latest demographic trends and tells the American story. It examines our changing lifestyles in rich detail, from the number of undocumented immigrants in California to the percentage of babies born out of wedlock, from rising health insurance costs to declining homeownership rates, from what people think about gun control to how much people owe on their mortgages. It also looks into the future, with projections of populations, students, and workers.

The first decade of the 21st century is nearly complete, and the socioeconomic wellbeing of Americans has taken a sharp turn downward. But life goes on, and *The American Marketplace* reveals where it is going—where we stand today and where we will be tomorrow.

Since we published the first edition of *The American Marketplace* in 1992, the Internet has reshaped the reference industry. The government's detailed demographic data, once published in printed reports, are now available almost exclusively online. The government's web sites, which house enormous spreadsheets of data, are of great value to researchers with the time to search for, download, and analyze information themselves. But the shift from printed reports to databases on the Internet has outsourced demographic analysis to the market researcher, student, or library patron sitting at a keyboard. In short, despite the abundance of data available on the Internet, it has become more time-consuming than ever to get no-nonsense answers to questions about the ever-changing demographics of the American population. In *The American Marketplace*, New Strategist has done the work for you, producing indexes and percent change calculations and providing analysis and comparisons.

The American Marketplace has the answers. It has the numbers and the stories behind them. Thumbing through its pages, you can gain more insight into the dynamics of the U.S. population in these hard times than you could by spending all afternoon surfing databases on the Internet. By having *The American Marketplace* on your bookshelf, you can get the answers to your questions faster than you can online—no typing required. Even better, keep *The American Marketplace* on your computer desktop as a pdf download with links to each table as an Excel spreadsheet.

New to this edition of *American Marketplace* is the Attitudes chapter, based on data from the 2008 General Social Survey. Also in this edition of *American Marketplace* you will find the latest data on the changing demographics of homeownership, based on the Census Bureau's 2008 Housing Vacancies and Homeownership Survey. In the Health chapter, you will find the latest data on health insurance coverage, as well as new data on the use of alternative medicine. The Income chapter, with statistics from the 2008 Current Population Survey, reveals the struggle of so many Americans to stay afloat. The latest labor force data show declining participation rates because of the economic downturn. The Labor Force chapter also includes the latest projections of the future workforce and occupations. In the Population chapter, the Census Bureau's latest projections reveal how much the Asian, black, and Hispanic populations will grow between now and 2025. Also in the Population chapter are the fascinating results of the American Time Use Survey, which show how we use our daily allotment of 24 hours. In the Spending chapter, the latest numbers from the Consumer Expenditure Survey reveal how households are adapting to the new economic reality. In the Wealth chapter, you will see a snapshot of American households at the peak of the housing bubble, and the Federal Reserve Board's estimates of how far they have fallen since then.

How to use this book

The American Marketplace is designed for easy use. It is divided into 10 chapters, organized alphabetically: Attitudes, Education, Health, Housing, Income, Labor Force, Living Arrangements, Population, Spending, and Wealth.

Most of the tables in *The American Marketplace* are based on data collected by the federal government, in particular the Census Bureau, the Bureau of Labor Statistics, the National Center for Education Statistics, the National Center for Health Statistics, and the Federal Reserve Board. The federal government continues to be the best, if not the only, source of up-to-date, reliable information on the changing characteristics of Americans. While the government produced most of the data presented here, the tables in *The American Marketplace* are not reproductions of government spreadsheets—as is the case in many other reference books. Instead, each table is individually compiled and created by New Strategist's demographers, with calculations designed to reveal the stories behind the statistics.

Each chapter of *The American Marketplace* includes the demographic and lifestyle data most important to understanding unfolding events in the United States. A page of text accompanies most of the tables, analyzing the data and highlighting the trends. If you want more statistical detail than the tables provide, you can plumb the original source of the data, listed at the bottom of each table. The book contains a comprehensive table list to help you locate the information you need. For a more detailed search, use the index at the back of the book. Also at the back of the book is the glossary, which defines the terms commonly used in the tables and text.

The American Marketplace is a reference tool that will help you cut through the clutter and track the trends. Use it and prosper.

1

Attitude Trends

■ Americans are evenly split on whether life is "exciting" (47 percent) or "pretty routine" (48 percent).

■ Only 27 percent of people aged 18 to 44 say that most people can be trusted. Among people aged 65 or older, a much larger 41 percent trust others.

■ Fewer than one-third of Americans think their income is below average. By demographic segment, the percentage of those who think they earn below average ranges from a low of 14 percent among college graduates to a high of 45 percent among blacks.

■ The largest share of Americans think two children are ideal, but the three-child family is growing in popularity. Between 1998 and 2008, the proportion of those who think three children are ideal climbed from 20 to 27 percent.

■ Americans are almost equally divided between those who believe in evolution (51 percent) and those who do not (49 percent).

■ Thirty-eight percent of the public believes sexual relations between adults of the same sex is "not wrong at all," up from 28 percent in 1998.

■ Nearly half of Americans get most of their news from television. The Internet is in second place, with 22 percent depending on it. Newspapers have fallen to third place, with 20 percent getting most of their news from the newspaper.

Only about One-Third of Americans Are "Very Happy"

Most of the married say they are very happily married, however.

When asked how happy they are, only about one in three Americans say they are "very happy." The 54 percent majority reports feeling only "pretty happy." Older people are happier than middle-aged or younger adults. Forty percent of people aged 65 or older say they are "very happy" compared with 29 to 31 percent of people under age 65.

The 62 percent majority of married Americans say they are very happily married. Married college graduates are much more likely to report being very happily married (72 percent) than married people without a bachelor's degree (57 percent).

Americans are evenly split on whether life is "exciting" (47 percent) or "pretty routine" (48 percent). Again, education makes the biggest difference, and 61 percent of college graduates say life is exciting compared with a smaller 43 percent of those with less education.

Few believe most people can be trusted. Only 32 percent of the public says that most people can be trusted, down from 37 percent who felt that way 10 years earlier. Young adults are far less trusting than older Americans, and only 27 percent of 18-to-44-year-olds believe most people can be trusted compared with 41 percent of people aged 65 or older.

■ Young and middle aged adults are struggling with a deteriorating economy, which reduces their happiness and increases their distrust.

Few young adults trust others

(percent of people aged 18 or older who think most people can be trusted, by age, 2008)

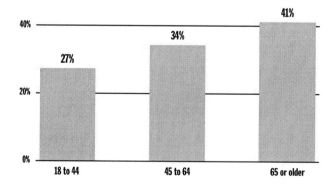

Table 1.1 General Happiness, 1998 and 2008

"Taken all together, how would you say things are these days—would you say
that you are very happy, pretty happy, or not too happy?"

(percent of people aged 18 or older responding, 1998 and 2008; and percent of people aged 18 or older responding by demographic characteristic, 2008)

	very happy	pretty happy	not too happy
TEN-YEAR TREND			
2008	31.7%	54.4%	14.0%
1998	33.3	55.9	10.9
2008 PROFILE			
Total people	**31.7**	**54.4**	**14.0**
Men	30.7	55.6	13.7
Women	32.5	53.3	14.2
Black	22.4	49.1	28.5
Hispanic	26.3	53.0	20.7
White	33.3	55.3	11.4
Aged 18 to 44	29.4	56.6	14.0
Aged 45 to 64	30.6	55.4	14.0
Aged 65 or older	40.4	46.0	13.7
Less than a bachelor's degree	29.7	53.8	16.5
Bachelor's degree or more	37.3	56.0	6.7

Source: Survey Documentation and Analysis, Computer-assisted Survey Methods Program, University of California, Berkeley, General Social Surveys, 1972–2008 Cumulative Data Files, Internet site http://sda.berkeley.edu/cgi-bin32/ hsda?harcsda+gss08; calculations by New Strategist

Table 1.2 Happiness of Marriage, 1998 and 2008

"Taking all things together, how would you describe your marriage?"

(percent of married people responding, 1998 and 2008; and percent responding by demographic characteristic, 2008)

	very happy	pretty happy	not too happy
TEN-YEAR TREND			
2008	62.1%	35.3%	2.6%
1998	63.6	33.7	2.7
2008 PROFILE			
Total people	**62.1**	**35.3**	**2.6**
Men	64.1	34.0	1.9
Women	60.2	36.5	3.3
Black	50.1	42.6	7.3
Hispanic	42.2	54.3	3.6
White	63.4	34.6	2.0
Aged 18 to 44	62.9	34.8	2.3
Aged 45 to 64	60.4	36.4	3.2
Aged 65 or older	64.6	33.4	2.0
Less than a bachelor's degree	57.5	39.7	2.8
Bachelor's degree or more	72.1	25.6	2.3

Source: Survey Documentation and Analysis, Computer-assisted Survey Methods Program, University of California, Berkeley, General Social Surveys, 1972–2008 Cumulative Data Files, Internet site http://sda.berkeley.edu/cgi-bin32/hsda?harcsda+gss08; calculations by New Strategist

Table 1.3 Life Exciting or Dull, 1998 and 2008

"In general, do you find life exciting, pretty routine, or dull?"

(percent of people aged 18 or older responding, 1998 and 2008; and percent of people aged 18 or older responding by demographic characteristic, 2008)

	exciting	pretty routine	dull
TEN-YEAR TREND			
2008	47.2%	48.1%	3.8%
1998	45.2	49.9	4.9
2008 PROFILE			
Total people	**47.2**	**48.1**	**3.8**
Men	48.6	48.2	2.5
Women	46.1	48.1	4.9
Black	39.3	55.0	5.2
Hispanic	45.2	48.7	3.8
White	49.3	46.6	3.6
Aged 18 to 44	47.2	48.5	3.3
Aged 45 to 64	47.1	48.0	4.5
Aged 65 or older	47.4	47.3	3.7
Less than a bachelor's degree	42.6	51.6	4.8
Bachelor's degree or more	60.6	38.2	1.1

Note: Numbers do not add to total because "can't say" is not shown.
Source: Survey Documentation and Analysis, Computer-assisted Survey Methods Program, University of California, Berkeley, General Social Surveys, 1972–2008 Cumulative Data Files, Internet site http://sda.berkeley.edu/cgi-bin32/hsda?harcsda+gss08; calculations by New Strategist

Table 1.4 Trust in Others, 1998 and 2008

"Generally speaking, would you say that most people can be
trusted or that you can't be too careful in life?"

(percent of people aged 18 or older responding, 1998 and 2008; and percent of people aged 18 or older responding by demographic characteristic, 2008)

	can trust	cannot trust	depends
TEN-YEAR TREND			
2008	31.9%	63.9%	4.3%
1998	37.2	57.4	5.4
2008 PROFILE			
Total people	**31.9**	**63.9**	**4.3**
Men	33.2	61.2	5.6
Women	30.7	66.2	3.1
Black	14.4	81.3	4.3
Hispanic	11.9	83.2	4.9
White	35.3	60.5	4.2
Aged 18 to 44	27.2	68.6	4.2
Aged 45 to 64	34.5	61.5	4.1
Aged 65 or older	40.8	54.6	4.6
Less than a bachelor's degree	25.9	70.5	3.6
Bachelor's degree or more	48.6	45.2	6.2

Source: Survey Documentation and Analysis, Computer-assisted Survey Methods Program, University of California, Berkeley, General Social Surveys, 1972–2008 Cumulative Data Files, Internet site http://sda.berkeley.edu/cgi-bin32/ hsda?harcsda+gss08; calculations by New Strategist

One in Eight Americans Is a Business Owner

Whites are twice as likely to own a business as blacks.

Asked whether they currently own and help manage a business, nearly 13 percent of Americans say they do. The proportion of business owners is much larger among men (16 percent) than women (9 percent). Whites and Hispanics are almost equally likely to run their own business (14 and 13 percent, respectively). The likelihood of owning a business rises with education.

How do people get ahead? Two-thirds of Americans say it is by hard work, and another one-fifth cite a combination of hard work and luck. Only 12 percent believe luck alone gets people ahead, up from 10 percent a decade ago. Women believe more strongly in hard work than men do, and Hispanics more than whites or blacks.

By some measures the geographic mobility of Americans has been declining, but respondents to the General Social Survey paint a steady picture over the last 10 years. In both 1998 and 2008, 40 percent of people aged 18 or older still lived in the same place as they did at age 16. Educational attainment is an important predictor of mobility. People with less than a bachelor's degree are twice as likely to stay put as those with more education.

■ Better educated Americans are more geographically mobile because of the jobs they pursue.

Blacks lag in business ownership

(percent of people aged 18 or older who currently own and help manage a business, by race and Hispanic origin, 2008)

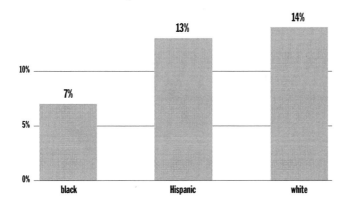

Table 1.5 How People Get Ahead, 1998 and 2008

"Some people say that people get ahead by their own hard work;
others say that lucky breaks or help from other people are more important.
Which do you think is most important?"

(percent of people aged 18 or older responding, 1998 and 2008; and percent of people aged 18 or older responding by demographic characteristic, 2008)

	hard work	both equally	luck
TEN-YEAR TREND			
2008	67.1%	20.8%	12.1%
1998	67.9	21.7	10.4
2008 PROFILE			
Total people	**67.1**	**20.8**	**12.1**
Men	64.6	21.4	14.0
Women	69.2	20.3	10.5
Black	59.4	22.6	18.0
Hispanic	71.2	20.9	7.9
White	67.7	21.1	11.3
Aged 18 to 44	70.5	18.9	10.6
Aged 45 to 64	63.7	24.1	12.2
Aged 65 or older	64.6	19.3	16.1
Less than a bachelor's degree	68.2	18.8	13.0
Bachelor's degree or more	64.2	26.2	9.7

Source: Survey Documentation and Analysis, Computer-assisted Survey Methods Program, University of California, Berkeley, General Social Surveys, 1972–2008 Cumulative Data Files, Internet site http://sda.berkeley.edu/cgi-bin32/hsda?harcsda+gss08; calculations by New Strategist

Table 1.6 Geographic Mobility since Age 16, 1998 and 2008

"When you were 16 years old, were you living in this same (city/town/county)?"

(percent of people aged 18 or older responding, 1998 and 2008; and percent of people aged 18 or older responding by demographic characteristic, 2008)

	same city	same state, different city	different state
TEN-YEAR TREND			
2008	40.0%	23.2%	36.8%
1998	40.1	25.4	34.6
2008 PROFILE			
Total people	**40.0**	**23.2**	**36.8**
Men	39.3	24.8	35.9
Women	40.7	21.7	37.6
Black	57.6	15.8	26.6
Hispanic	33.3	13.1	53.7
White	38.3	25.6	36.1
Aged 18 to 44	44.5	20.3	35.2
Aged 45 to 64	37.6	26.7	35.7
Aged 65 or older	31.9	24.2	43.9
Less than a bachelor's degree	45.9	22.4	31.7
Bachelor's degree or more	23.3	25.5	51.2

Source: Survey Documentation and Analysis, Computer-assisted Survey Methods Program, University of California, Berkeley, General Social Surveys, 1972–2008 Cumulative Data Files, Internet site http://sda.berkeley.edu/cgi-bin32/hsda?harcsda+gss08; calculations by New Strategist

Table 1.7 Business Ownership, 2008

"Are you, alone or with others, currently the owner of a business you help manage,
including self-employment or selling any goods or services to others?"

(percent of people aged 18 or older responding by demographic characteristic, 2008)

	yes	no
Total people	**12.6%**	**87.4%**
Men	16.2	83.8
Women	9.5	90.5
Black	6.8	93.2
Hispanic	12.9	87.1
White	13.7	86.3
Aged 18 to 44	12.9	87.1
Aged 45 to 64	15.0	85.0
Aged 65 or older	6.1	93.9
Less than a bachelor's degree	10.7	89.3
Bachelor's degree or more	18.1	81.9

Source: Survey Documentation and Analysis, Computer-assisted Survey Methods Program, University of California, Berkeley, General Social Surveys, 1972–2008 Cumulative Data Files, Internet site http://sda.berkeley.edu/cgi-bin32/ hsda?harcsda+gss08; calculations by New Strategist

One in Five Think Their Income Is above Average

Fewer than one-third of Americans think their income is below average.

A 47 percent plurality of Americans believes their family income is average, while 32 percent say they earn less than average. Women are more likely than men to say their family income is below average. One in 10 blacks and Hispanics say their family income is far below average, whereas that proportion among whites is just 5 percent.

The share of people who are "satisfied" with their financial situation has declined slightly in the past 10 years—falling from 31 percent in 1998 to 29 percent in 2008. The percentage of those who are "more or less satisfied" has also declined slightly, falling from 44 to 42 percent. Consequently the percentage of Americans "not at all satisfied" with their finances has risen by 4 percentage points to 29 percent in 2008. Discontent is especially high among blacks (46 percent) and Hispanics (34 percent).

Half of blacks say their pay has not kept up with the cost of living, and 46 percent of women agree. Among men the proportion is just 37 percent. Not too surprisingly, Americans with a college education are most likely to say their pay has risen faster than the cost of living, 34 percent saying so. The share of people who think their income is keeping pace with inflation is highest among Hispanics at 44 percent.

Few Americans identify with the "lower class," but even fewer with the "upper class." The highest share of self-identified lower-class people occurs among blacks (12 percent). Hispanics are least likely to believe they are in the upper class, and only 1 percent place themselves there.

■ Financial backsliding was common among working Americans, even before the turmoil in the financial markets that began in 2008.

Dissatisfaction with personal finances has been growing

(percent distribution of people aged 18 or older by response to the question, "How satisfied are you with your present financial situation?" 1998 and 2008)

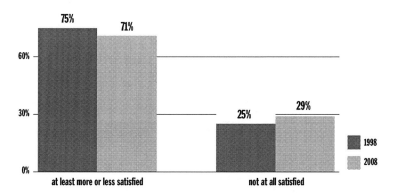

Table 1.8 Social Class Membership, 1998 and 2008

"If you were asked to use one of four names for your social class, which would you say you belong in: the lower class, the working class, the middle class, or the upper class?"

(percent of people aged 18 or older responding, 1998 and 2008; and percent of people aged 18 or older responding by demographic characteristic, 2008)

	lower	working	middle	upper
TEN-YEAR TREND				
2008	7.3%	45.7%	43.4%	3.6%
1998	5.0	45.5	45.7	3.8
2008 PROFILE				
Total people	**7.3**	**45.7**	**43.4**	**3.6**
Men	6.1	47.5	42.6	3.8
Women	8.3	44.1	44.1	3.4
Black	12.5	57.1	28.4	2.0
Hispanic	8.8	58.0	32.5	0.7
White	6.1	43.6	46.1	4.2
Aged 18 to 44	7.3	50.4	38.7	3.6
Aged 45 to 64	7.5	44.9	44.5	3.0
Aged 65 or older	6.3	33.4	55.1	5.2
Less than a bachelor's degree	9.5	53.1	35.7	1.7
Bachelor's degree or more	1.0	24.2	65.8	9.1

Source: Survey Documentation and Analysis, Computer-assisted Survey Methods Program, University of California, Berkeley, General Social Surveys, 1972–2008 Cumulative Data Files, Internet site http://sda.berkeley.edu/cgi-bin32/hsda?harcsda+gss08; calculations by New Strategist

ATTITUDES TRENDS

Table 1.9 Family Income Relative to Others, 1998 and 2008

"Compared with American families in general, would you say your family income is far below average, below average, average, above average, or far above average?"

(percent of people aged 18 or older responding, 1998 and 2008; and percent of people aged 18 or older responding by demographic characteristic, 2008)

	far below average	below average	average	above average	far above average
TEN-YEAR TREND					
2008	6.3%	25.2%	46.7%	19.8%	2.0%
1998	5.5	22.0	48.6	21.6	2.3
2008 PROFILE					
Total people	**6.3**	**25.2**	**46.7**	**19.8**	**2.0**
Men	5.8	24.1	43.9	23.6	2.7
Women	6.7	26.2	49.2	16.5	1.4
Black	10.1	35.2	44.2	9.8	0.8
Hispanic	10.0	31.5	48.7	9.6	0.2
White	4.9	23.0	47.1	22.6	2.4
Aged 18 to 44	7.1	25.6	46.8	19.0	1.5
Aged 45 to 64	5.7	23.3	46.3	21.9	2.9
Aged 65 or older	4.6	28.4	47.6	17.8	1.6
Less than a bachelor's degree	7.9	29.4	48.7	13.4	0.6
Bachelor's degree or more	1.4	13.0	40.9	38.5	6.2

Source: Survey Documentation and Analysis, Computer-assisted Survey Methods Program, University of California, Berkeley, General Social Surveys, 1972–2008 Cumulative Data Files, Internet site http://sda.berkeley.edu/cgi-bin32/hsda?harcsda+gss08; calculations by New Strategist

THE AMERICAN MARKETPLACE   15

Table 1.10 Satisfaction with Financial Situation, 1998 and 2008

"We are interested in how people are getting along financially these days. So far as you and your family are concerned, would you say that you are pretty well satisfied with your present financial situation, more or less satisfied, or not satisfied at all?"

(percent of people aged 18 or older responding, 1998 and 2008; and percent of people aged 18 or older responding by demographic characteristic, 2008)

	satisfied	more or less satisfied	not at all satisfied
TEN-YEAR TREND			
2008	28.9%	41.7%	29.4%
1998	30.6	44.3	25.1
2008 PROFILE			
Total people	**28.9**	**41.7**	**29.4**
Men	29.0	42.6	28.4
Women	28.8	40.9	30.3
Black	19.0	35.3	45.8
Hispanic	14.2	51.4	34.4
White	31.7	42.4	25.9
Aged 18 to 44	23.2	43.4	33.5
Aged 45 to 64	28.1	44.0	27.9
Aged 65 or older	48.2	31.7	20.1
Less than a bachelor's degree	24.5	41.9	33.6
Bachelor's degree or more	41.6	40.9	17.5

Source: Survey Documentation and Analysis, Computer-assisted Survey Methods Program, University of California, Berkeley, General Social Surveys, 1972–2008 Cumulative Data Files, Internet site http://sda.berkeley.edu/cgi-bin32/hsda?harcsda+gss08; calculations by New Strategist

Table 1.11 How Has Pay Changed, 2008

"Thinking about your current employer, how much has your pay changed
on your current job since you began? Would you say . . . "

(percent of people aged 18 to 64 responding by demographic characteristic, 2008)

	my pay has gone up more than the cost of living	my pay has stayed about the same as the cost of living	my pay has not kept up with the cost of living
Total people	**23.5%**	**35.6%**	**40.9%**
Men	29.4	33.7	36.9
Women	15.2	38.3	46.5
Black	17.9	32.6	49.5
Hispanic	15.3	44.2	40.5
White	25.6	35.3	39.1
Aged 18 to 44	24.6	38.7	36.7
Aged 45 to 64	22.3	32.3	45.4
Less than a bachelor's degree	18.8	36.0	45.2
Bachelor's degree or more	34.0	34.9	31.2

Source: Survey Documentation and Analysis, Computer-assisted Survey Methods Program, University of California, Berkeley, General Social Surveys, 1972–2008 Cumulative Data Files, Internet site http://sda.berkeley.edu/cgi-bin32/ hsda?harcsda+gss08; calculations by New Strategist

Many Think Their Standard of Living Is Falling

Fewer Americans believe they are better off than their parents.

When comparing their own standard of living now with that of their parents when they were the same age, 63 percent of respondents say they are better off. The figure was 66 percent 10 years ago. The oldest Americans have the highest propensity to think they are much better situated than their parents were at the same age. Blacks and Hispanics are more likely than whites to say they are doing better.

When asked whether they think they have a good chance to improve their present standard of living, only 59 percent of Americans agree compared with 74 percent who felt that way a decade earlier. Naturally younger people are more hopeful in this regard than older Americans, who may well have seen improvements in their standard of living already. Probably for similar reasons, Hispanics, and to a somewhat lesser extent blacks, are more likely than whites to believe things will get better.

Sixty percent of respondents believe their children will have a better standard of living when they reach the respondent's present age. The share was 63 percent 10 years earlier. Women are more hopeful than men in this regard. Opinions on this question differ sharply by racial and ethnic group. Whereas 78 percent of Hispanic and 72 percent of black respondents think their children will be better off, only 56 percent of whites agree.

■ Those Americans who have the least are most likely to believe that things will be better in the future.

Children will be better off

(percent of people with children who think their children's standard of living will be somewhat better or much better than theirs is today, 2008)

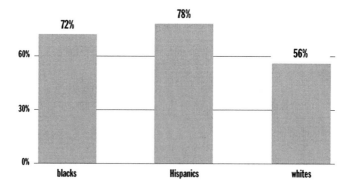

Table 1.12 Parents' Standard of Living, 1998 and 2008

"Compared to your parents when they were the age you are now, do you think your own standard of living now is much better, somewhat better, about the same, somewhat worse, or much worse than theirs was?"

(percent of people aged 18 or older responding, 1998 and 2008; and percent of people aged 18 or older responding by demographic characteristic, 2008)

	much better	somewhat better	about the same	somewhat worse	much worse
TEN-YEAR TREND					
2008	31.7%	31.1%	21.1%	11.5%	4.6%
1998	33.7	32.5	21.6	9.7	2.6
2008 PROFILE					
Total people	**31.7**	**31.1**	**21.1**	**11.5**	**4.6**
Men	30.2	33.7	19.3	12.5	4.2
Women	32.9	28.8	22.7	10.7	4.9
Black	31.3	36.8	13.0	10.3	8.6
Hispanic	39.6	26.1	22.9	6.9	4.6
White	30.5	30.9	22.8	11.9	3.8
Aged 18 to 44	27.7	33.0	21.4	12.9	5.1
Aged 45 to 64	30.0	30.0	22.5	12.5	5.1
Aged 65 or older	47.6	27.7	17.4	5.3	2.0
Less than a bachelor's degree	31.9	30.5	20.2	11.7	5.7
Bachelor's degree or more	30.9	32.8	23.8	11.2	1.4

Source: Survey Documentation and Analysis, Computer-assisted Survey Methods Program, University of California, Berkeley, General Social Surveys, 1972–2008 Cumulative Data Files, Internet site http://sda.berkeley.edu/cgi-bin32/ hsda?harcsda+gss08; calculations by New Strategist

Table 1.13 Standard of Living Will Improve, 1998 and 2008

"The way things are in America, people like me and my family have a good chance of improving our standard of living. Do you agree or disagree?"

(percent of people aged 18 or older responding, 1998 and 2008; and percent of people aged 18 or older responding by demographic characteristic, 2008)

	strongly agree	agree	neither	disagree	strongly disagree
TEN-YEAR TREND					
2008	14.7%	44.7%	13.9%	22.9%	3.8%
1998	18.5	56.0	11.0	11.9	2.5
2008 PROFILE					
Total people	**14.7**	**44.7**	**13.9**	**22.9**	**3.8**
Men	15.8	46.8	13.2	21.0	3.1
Women	13.8	42.8	14.5	24.5	4.3
Black	17.7	45.3	14.0	15.3	7.7
Hispanic	19.5	50.2	9.5	15.3	5.4
White	14.3	42.7	14.6	25.6	2.8
Aged 18 to 44	16.9	49.0	12.0	18.6	3.5
Aged 45 to 64	12.4	44.9	12.2	26.8	3.7
Aged 65 or older	13.3	30.3	24.3	27.1	4.9
Less than a bachelor's degree	13.2	44.4	13.8	24.4	4.2
Bachelor's degree or more	18.9	45.3	14.2	19.0	2.6

Source: Survey Documentation and Analysis, Computer-assisted Survey Methods Program, University of California, Berkeley, General Social Surveys, 1972–2008 Cumulative Data Files, Internet site http://sda.berkeley.edu/cgi-bin32/hsda?harcsda+gss08; calculations by New Strategist

Table 1.14 Children's Standard of Living, 1998 and 2008

"When your children are at the age you are now, do you think their
standard of living will be much better, somewhat better, about the same,
somewhat worse, or much worse than yours is now?"

*(percent of people with children responding, 1998 and 2008; and percent responding by demographic charac-
teristic, 2008)*

	much better	somewhat better	about the same	somewhat worse	much worse
TEN-YEAR TREND					
2008	30.7%	29.2%	20.0%	14.3%	5.8%
1998	24.7	38.4	22.6	10.6	3.6
2008 PROFILE					
Total people	**30.7**	**29.2**	**20.0**	**14.3**	**5.8**
Men	27.0	29.9	19.2	17.4	6.7
Women	33.9	28.6	20.6	11.8	5.0
Black	52.5	19.6	6.3	14.6	7.0
Hispanic	47.8	30.4	11.8	4.3	5.6
White	24.7	31.4	22.9	15.1	5.9
Aged 18 to 44	32.5	31.8	20.9	10.2	4.5
Aged 45 to 64	28.5	28.9	17.9	18.1	6.6
Aged 65 or older	29.3	22.3	22.3	18.6	7.4
Less than a bachelor's degree	33.2	28.8	16.1	15.3	6.6
Bachelor's degree or more	24.0	30.4	31.0	11.5	3.2

*Source: Survey Documentation and Analysis, Computer-assisted Survey Methods Program, University of California,
Berkeley, General Social Surveys, 1972–2008 Cumulative Data Files, Internet site http://sda.berkeley.edu/cgi-bin32/
hsda?harcsda+gss08; calculations by New Strategist*

The Two-Child Family Is Most Popular

But the three-child family is growing in popularity.

In every demographic segment—by sex, race, age, or educational attainment—a plurality of Americans thinks that two is the ideal number of children. A look at the 10-year trend confirms, however, that the two-child ideal has weakened during the past decade, falling from being the preference of 57 percent of the public in 1998 to just 48 percent in 2008. Meanwhile, the percentage of the public that prefers three children grew from 20 to 27 percent during those years.

The great majority of the public believes children should get a "good, hard spanking" when they misbehave. Although the percentage of parents willing to spank has declined to 71 percent from 75 percent in 1998, even among the least-likely-to-spank demographic of college educated parents, three out of five acknowledge an occasional need for such punishment.

Are traditional sex roles making a comeback? The uptick in the percentage of people who believe it is better if the man is the breadwinner and the woman cares for the household is too slight to make that assertion, but it is remarkable that more people agree with this antiquated notion in 2008 than did in 1998. Behind the small increase is the growing Hispanic population, whose traditional values are making inroads into attitudinal data.

Support is growing for the view that government should help people who are sick and in need. In 1998, slightly less than half (49 percent) agreed. Today the share is 54 percent.

■ The more traditional attitudes and values of Hispanics will become increasingly important as the Hispanic share of the U.S. population grows.

Hispanics believe in traditional sex roles

(percent of people aged 18 or older who agree with traditional sex roles, by race and Hispanic origin, 2008)

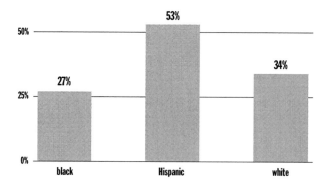

Table 1.15 Ideal Number of Children, 1998 and 2008

"What do you think is the ideal number of children for a family to have?"

(percent of people aged 18 or older responding, 1998 and 2008; and percent of people aged 18 or older responding by demographic characteristic, 2008)

	none	one	two	three	four or more	as many as want
TEN-YEAR TREND						
2008	1.0%	2.5%	47.7%	26.6%	10.1%	12.1%
1998	1.5	2.4	56.8	20.3	10.6	8.6
2008 PROFILE						
Total people	**1.0**	**2.5**	**47.7**	**26.6**	**10.1**	**12.1**
Men	1.4	2.4	50.8	25.1	9.9	10.5
Women	0.6	2.6	44.9	27.9	10.3	13.7
Black	0.3	2.7	39.8	30.0	16.0	11.2
Hispanic	0.0	3.9	40.2	35.7	13.7	6.6
White	1.2	2.2	49.0	25.8	9.3	12.6
Aged 18 to 44	0.4	3.1	41.9	32.2	11.4	11.2
Aged 45 to 64	2.0	2.0	55.9	18.5	8.9	12.8
Aged 65 or older	0.5	1.9	46.1	28.7	9.5	13.4
Less than a bachelor's degree	1.2	2.7	46.0	26.6	12.5	11.0
Bachelor's degree or more	0.5	1.9	53.0	26.4	2.9	15.4

Source: Survey Documentation and Analysis, Computer-assisted Survey Methods Program, University of California, Berkeley, General Social Surveys, 1972–2008 Cumulative Data Files, Internet site http://sda.berkeley.edu/cgi-bin32/ hsda?harcsda+gss08; calculations by New Strategist

Table 1.16 Spanking Children, 1998 and 2008

"Do you strongly agree, agree, disagree, or strongly disagree that it is sometimes necessary to discipline a child with a good, hard spanking?"

(percent of people aged 18 or older responding, 1998 and 2008; and percent of people aged 18 or older responding by demographic characteristic, 2008)

	strongly agree	agree	disagree	strongly disagree
TEN-YEAR TREND				
2008	24.7%	46.2%	23.1%	6.0%
1998	26.7	48.6	17.9	6.8
2008 PROFILE				
Total people	**24.7**	**46.2**	**23.1**	**6.0**
Men	25.8	51.7	18.2	4.3
Women	23.7	41.1	27.7	7.6
Black	41.4	45.3	12.2	1.1
Hispanic	21.0	43.4	28.5	7.1
White	22.3	46.6	24.7	6.4
Aged 18 to 44	25.1	46.0	23.2	5.7
Aged 45 to 64	24.8	46.6	22.1	6.5
Aged 65 or older	22.4	46.0	25.8	5.9
Less than a bachelor's degree	28.0	46.8	20.2	5.1
Bachelor's degree or more	15.2	44.6	31.4	8.8

Source: Survey Documentation and Analysis, Computer-assisted Survey Methods Program, University of California, Berkeley, General Social Surveys, 1972–2008 Cumulative Data Files, Internet site http://sda.berkeley.edu/cgi-bin32/hsda?harcsda+gss08; calculations by New Strategist

Table 1.17 Better for Man to Work, Woman to Tend Home, 1998 and 2008

"It is much better for everyone involved if the man is the achiever outside
the home and the woman takes care of the home and family."

*(percent of people aged 18 or older responding, 1998 and 2008; and percent of people aged 18 or older responding
by demographic characteristic, 2008)*

	strongly agree	agree	disagree	strongly disagree
TEN-YEAR TREND				
2008	8.3%	27.0%	47.2%	17.5%
1998	6.8	27.2	47.2	18.7
2008 PROFILE				
Total people	**8.3**	**27.0**	**47.2**	**17.5**
Men	8.0	30.1	49.4	12.5
Women	8.4	24.2	45.2	22.2
Black	9.5	17.4	54.8	18.4
Hispanic	15.1	38.3	36.6	10.0
White	7.1	27.4	47.9	17.7
Aged 18 to 44	8.3	24.0	46.8	20.9
Aged 45 to 64	6.7	25.1	50.4	17.8
Aged 65 or older	12.3	41.6	40.4	5.6
Less than a bachelor's degree	9.5	30.2	45.2	15.2
Bachelor's degree or more	4.6	18.0	53.2	24.2

*Source: Survey Documentation and Analysis, Computer-assisted Survey Methods Program, University of California,
Berkeley, General Social Surveys, 1972–2008 Cumulative Data Files, Internet site http://sda.berkeley.edu/cgi-bin32/
hsda?harcsda+gss08; calculations by New Strategist*

Table 1.18 Working Mother's Relationship with Children, 1998 and 2008

"Do you strongly agree, agree, disagree, or strongly disagree with the statement:
A working mother can establish just as warm and secure a relationship
with her children as a mother who does not work?"

(percent of people aged 18 or older responding, 1998 and 2008; and percent of people aged 18 or older responding by demographic characteristic, 2008)

	strongly agree	agree	disagree	strongly disagree
TEN-YEAR TREND				
2008	26.3%	46.0%	22.2%	5.4%
1998	22.1	45.8	25.2	7.0
2008 PROFILE				
Total people	**26.3**	**46.0**	**22.2**	**5.4**
Men	16.1	46.3	30.3	7.3
Women	35.8	45.8	14.7	3.8
Black	32.4	45.7	17.9	3.9
Hispanic	15.1	43.7	37.5	3.6
White	26.3	46.6	21.5	5.6
Aged 18 to 44	28.8	45.9	21.2	4.2
Aged 45 to 64	26.0	47.7	20.2	6.1
Aged 65 or older	19.9	42.5	30.0	7.8
Less than a bachelor's degree	24.7	45.0	24.7	5.5
Bachelor's degree or more	30.9	49.0	14.9	5.2

Source: Survey Documentation and Analysis, Computer-assisted Survey Methods Program, University of California, Berkeley, General Social Surveys, 1972–2008 Cumulative Data Files, Internet site http://sda.berkeley.edu/cgi-bin32/hsda?harcsda+gss08; calculations by New Strategist

Table 1.19 Should Government Help the Sick, 1998 and 2008

"Some people think that it is the responsibility of the government in Washington to see to it that people have help in paying for doctors and hospital bills; they are at point 1. Others think that these matters are not the responsibility of the federal government and that people should take care of these things themselves; they are at point 5. Where would you place yourself on this scale?"

(percent of people aged 18 or older responding, 1998 and 2008; and percent of people aged 18 or older responding by demographic characteristic, 2008)

	government should help 1	2	agree with both 3	4	people should help themselves 5
TEN-YEAR TREND					
2008	34.9%	18.7%	30.0%	9.3%	7.2%
1998	25.5	23.4	32.9	10.1	8.3
2008 PROFILE					
Total people	**34.9**	**18.7**	**30.0**	**9.3**	**7.2**
Men	33.6	19.2	27.9	11.0	8.4
Women	36.2	18.2	31.9	7.7	6.0
Black	54.2	18.2	23.8	1.0	2.8
Hispanic	41.6	15.7	32.1	3.5	7.0
White	31.5	18.5	31.3	11.3	7.4
Aged 18 to 44	36.4	21.4	28.9	7.7	5.7
Aged 45 to 64	35.5	17.7	27.5	11.2	8.2
Aged 65 or older	28.9	12.1	39.5	9.8	9.8
Less than a bachelor's degree	37.4	16.5	30.8	7.7	7.6
Bachelor's degree or more	28.0	24.6	27.8	13.6	6.0

Source: Survey Documentation and Analysis, Computer-assisted Survey Methods Program, University of California, Berkeley, General Social Surveys, 1972–2008 Cumulative Data Files, Internet site http://sda.berkeley.edu/cgi-bin32/hsda?harcsda+gss08; calculations by New Strategist

Religion Is Important to Most Americans

Sixty percent of Americans consider themselves at least "moderately religious."

Asked whether science makes our way of life "change too fast," the 52 percent majority of Americans disagrees with the statement. Not surprisingly, people with a college degree are most likely to disagree (63 percent). At the other extreme, 74 percent of Hispanics agree that science makes our way of life change too fast.

Americans are almost equally divided between those who believe in evolution (51 percent) and those who do not (49 percent). More men than women, and more whites than blacks or Hispanics, believe in evolution.

Americans are a religious people, and 60 percent identify themselves as at least moderately religious. In almost every demographic segment, the share of those who call themselves "very religious" surpasses the share of those who say they are "not religious." Religiosity is especially high among women, blacks, and the elderly. The same groups are most likely to see the Bible as the word of God. Half of Americans describe themselves as Protestants, one-quarter as Catholics. All other religions together account for only 8 percent, while the share of those who have no religious preference is 17 percent.

Given this religious fervor, it is no surprise that only a minority of Americans approves of the Supreme Court decision barring local governments from requiring Bible readings in public schools. Support for the decision is greatest among college-educated Americans (57 percent) and smallest among blacks (27 percent).

■ Unique in the developed world, the great majority of Americans makes room for religion in their

Half of Americans are Protestants

(percent distribution of people aged 18 or older by religious preference, 2008)

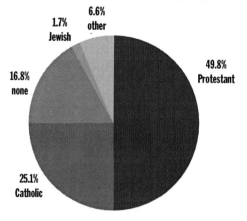

1.7% Jewish
6.6% other
49.8% Protestant
16.8% none
25.1% Catholic

Table 1.20 **Attitude toward Science, 2008**

"Do you strongly agree, agree, disagree, or strongly disagree with the statement:
Science makes our way of life change too fast?"

(percent of people aged 18 or older responding by demographic characteristic, 2008)

	strongly agree	agree	disagree	strongly disagree
Total people	**9.0%**	**38.8%**	**43.9%**	**8.3%**
Men	8.4	38.0	45.0	8.6
Women	9.5	39.6	42.9	8.0
Black	14.6	42.6	37.3	5.5
Hispanic	16.1	57.4	22.1	4.3
White	7.2	36.9	47.1	8.9
Aged 18 to 44	8.7	37.9	45.1	8.3
Aged 45 to 64	9.6	37.6	43.6	9.2
Aged 65 or older	8.2	44.8	40.9	6.2
Less than a bachelor's degree	9.9	41.6	42.3	6.2
Bachelor's degree or more	6.3	31.1	48.4	14.1

Source: Survey Documentation and Analysis, Computer-assisted Survey Methods Program, University of California, Berkeley, General Social Surveys, 1972–2008 Cumulative Data Files, Internet site http://sda.berkeley.edu/cgi-bin32/hsda?harcsda+gss08; calculations by New Strategist

Table 1.21 Attitude toward Evolution, 2008

"True or false: Human beings, as we know them today,
developed from earlier species of animals?"

(percent of people aged 18 or older responding by demographic characteristic, 2008)

	true	false
Total people	**50.9%**	**49.1%**
Men	58.6	41.4
Women	43.6	56.4
Black	40.5	59.5
Hispanic	46.3	53.7
White	52.2	47.8
Aged 18 to 44	56.3	43.7
Aged 45 to 64	47.6	52.4
Aged 65 or older	41.2	58.8
Less than a bachelor's degree	46.2	53.8
Bachelor's degree or more	63.3	36.7

Source: Survey Documentation and Analysis, Computer-assisted Survey Methods Program, University of California, Berkeley, General Social Surveys, 1972–2008 Cumulative Data Files, Internet site http://sda.berkeley.edu/cgi-bin32/hsda?harcsda+gss08; calculations by New Strategist

Table 1.22 Religious Preference, 1998 and 2008

"What is your religious preference?"

(percent of people aged 18 or older responding, 1998 and 2008; and percent of people aged 18 or older responding by demographic characteristic, 2008)

	Protestant	Catholic	Jewish	Buddhism	Hinduism	Moslem/ Islam	other	none
TEN-YEAR TREND								
2008	49.8%	25.1%	1.7%	0.6%	0.4%	0.7%	4.8%	16.8%
1998	53.7	26.2	1.8	0.3	0.3	0.5	3.5	13.7
2008 PROFILE								
Total people	**49.8**	**25.1**	**1.7**	**0.6**	**0.4**	**0.7**	**4.8**	**16.8**
Men	46.1	24.0	1.5	1.1	0.7	0.2	3.7	22.7
Women	53.1	26.1	1.9	0.3	0.2	1.2	5.8	11.6
Black	72.9	5.1	0.3	0.2	0.0	2.4	5.5	13.7
Hispanic	22.0	61.2	0.2	0.0	0.0	0.0	4.1	12.6
White	49.3	26.2	2.1	0.4	0.0	0.0	4.7	17.2
Aged 18 to 44	39.3	27.8	1.9	0.7	0.8	1.2	6.1	22.2
Aged 45 to 64	59.2	20.4	1.1	0.7	0.1	0.5	4.2	13.8
Aged 65 or older	60.0	26.8	2.5	0.4	0.0	0.0	2.6	7.7
Less than a bachelor's degree	51.2	26.0	0.8	0.2	0.1	0.5	4.9	16.4
Bachelor's degree or more	45.9	22.5	4.3	1.8	1.5	1.3	4.7	18.1

Source: Survey Documentation and Analysis, Computer-assisted Survey Methods Program, University of California, Berkeley, General Social Surveys, 1972–2008 Cumulative Data Files, Internet site http://sda.berkeley.edu/cgi-bin32/ hsda?harcsda+gss08; calculations by New Strategist

Table 1.23 Degree of Religiosity, 1998 and 2008

"To what extent do you consider yourself a religious person?"

(percent of people aged 18 or older responding, 1998 and 2008; and percent of people aged 18 or older responding by demographic characteristic, 2008)

	very religious	moderately religious	slightly religious	not religious
TEN-YEAR TREND				
2008	18.2%	42.2%	23.4%	16.2%
1998	18.7	42.9	23.5	14.9
2008 PROFILE				
Total people	**18.2**	**42.2**	**23.4**	**16.2**
Men	13.4	38.9	26.9	20.7
Women	22.5	45.1	20.3	12.1
Black	25.6	48.0	18.5	8.0
Hispanic	16.6	41.0	29.1	13.4
White	17.2	42.0	23.7	17.1
Aged 18 to 44	12.7	37.6	27.0	22.7
Aged 45 to 64	21.0	45.9	21.5	11.7
Aged 65 or older	28.2	47.4	17.4	7.0
Less than a bachelor's degree	18.7	42.3	24.5	14.5
Bachelor's degree or more	16.6	42.0	20.4	21.0

Source: Survey Documentation and Analysis, Computer-assisted Survey Methods Program, University of California, Berkeley, General Social Surveys, 1972–2008 Cumulative Data Files, Internet site http://sda.berkeley.edu/cgi-bin32/hsda?harcsda+gss08; calculations by New Strategist

Table 1.24 Belief in the Bible, 1998 and 2008

"Which of these statements comes closest to describing your feelings about the Bible?
1) The Bible is the actual word of God and is to be taken literally, word for word;
2) The Bible is the inspired word of God but not everything in it should be taken
literally, word for word; 3) The Bible is an ancient book of fables,
legends, history, and moral precepts recorded by men."

(percent of people aged 18 or older responding, 1998 and 2008; and percent of people aged 18 or older responding by demographic characteristic, 2008)

	word of God	inspired word	book of fables	other
TEN-YEAR TREND				
2008	32.0%	47.0%	19.6%	1.4%
1998	32.0	50.9	16.1	1.1
2008 PROFILE				
Total people	**32.0**	**47.0**	**19.6**	**1.4**
Men	28.4	44.6	25.3	1.7
Women	35.2	49.1	14.4	1.2
Black	47.4	40.8	9.9	2.0
Hispanic	43.0	39.8	15.6	1.5
White	29.0	49.0	21.0	1.0
Aged 18 to 44	29.5	47.8	20.7	2.0
Aged 45 to 64	33.0	46.2	20.0	0.7
Aged 65 or older	37.0	46.6	15.3	1.1
Less than a bachelor's degree	37.3	45.7	16.2	0.8
Bachelor's degree or more	16.9	50.8	29.1	3.2

Source: Survey Documentation and Analysis, Computer-assisted Survey Methods Program, University of California, Berkeley, General Social Surveys, 1972–2008 Cumulative Data Files, Internet site http://sda.berkeley.edu/cgi-bin32/hsda?harcsda+gss08; calculations by New Strategist

Table 1.25 Bible in the Public Schools, 1998 and 2008

"The United States Supreme Court has ruled that no state or local government may require the reading of the Lord's Prayer or Bible verses in public schools. What are your views on this? Do you approve or disapprove of the court ruling?"

(percent of people aged 18 or older responding, 1998 and 2008; and percent of people aged 18 or older responding by demographic characteristic, 2008)

	approve	disapprove
TEN-YEAR TREND		
2008	41.8%	58.2%
1998	44.7	55.3
2008 PROFILE		
Total people	**41.8**	**58.2**
Men	43.6	56.4
Women	40.1	59.9
Black	26.6	73.4
Hispanic	42.8	57.3
White	42.9	57.1
Aged 18 to 44	48.9	51.1
Aged 45 to 64	37.8	62.2
Aged 65 or older	29.3	70.7
Less than a bachelor's degree	36.5	63.5
Bachelor's degree or more	57.0	43.0

Source: Survey Documentation and Analysis, Computer-assisted Survey Methods Program, University of California, Berkeley, General Social Surveys, 1972–2008 Cumulative Data Files, Internet site http://sda.berkeley.edu/cgi-bin32/hsda?harcsda+gss08; calculations by New Strategist

Growing Tolerance of Same-Sex Relationships

Most Americans say premarital sex is OK.

The share of Americans who believe that premarital sex is "not wrong at all" grew from 43 percent in 1998 to 55 percent in 2008. Whether sliced by sex, race and ethnicity, age, or educational attainment, the majority of all demographics see nothing wrong with premarital sex—with the sole exception of Americans aged 65 or older. Tolerance of premarital sex is strongest among Hispanics, nearly two-thirds of whom think it is not wrong at all.

When it comes to sexual relations between adults of the same sex, the trend of growing tolerance is there as well, but acceptance is still limited. Overall 38 percent say homosexuality is not wrong at all, up from 28 percent a decade ago. Women are clearly more accepting of same-sex relations than men (42 versus 33 percent), and whites and Hispanics more so than blacks (40 and 37 percent, respectively, versus 22 percent). The younger the adult, the more accepting he or she is of same-sex relationships.

■ As younger, more tolerant adults replace older, less tolerant generations, American attitudes toward sexuality will continue to change.

Most still disapprove of same-sex relationships

(percent distribution of people aged 18 or older by response to the question, "What about sexual relations between two adults of the same sex?" 2008)

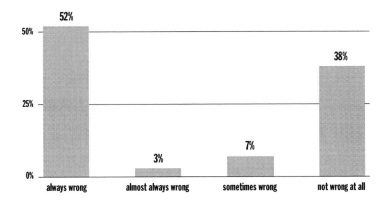

Table 1.26 Premarital Sex, 1998 and 2008

"If a man and woman have sex relations before marriage, do you think it is always wrong, almost always wrong, wrong only sometimes, or not wrong at all?"

(percent of people aged 18 or older responding, 1998 and 2008; and percent of people aged 18 or older responding by demographic characteristic, 2008)

	always wrong	almost always wrong	sometimes wrong	not wrong at all
TEN-YEAR TREND				
2008	22.6%	7.2%	15.4%	54.8%
1998	27.0	8.7	21.1	43.2
2008 PROFILE				
Total people	**22.6**	**7.2**	**15.4**	**54.8**
Men	20.4	5.8	15.8	58.0
Women	24.7	8.4	15.0	51.9
Black	29.2	9.9	9.2	51.7
Hispanic	17.9	9.5	9.3	63.2
White	21.7	6.7	16.4	55.3
Aged 18 to 44	19.3	6.1	16.0	58.6
Aged 45 to 64	23.5	6.7	14.0	55.7
Aged 65 or older	30.8	11.5	17.2	40.5
Less than a bachelor's degree	23.1	7.4	14.9	54.5
Bachelor's degree or more	21.2	6.5	16.7	55.6

Source: Survey Documentation and Analysis, Computer-assisted Survey Methods Program, University of California, Berkeley, General Social Surveys, 1972–2008 Cumulative Data Files, Internet site http://sda.berkeley.edu/cgi-bin32/hsda?harcsda+gss08; calculations by New Strategist

Table 1.27 Homosexual Relations, 1998 and 2008

"What about sexual relations between two adults of the same sex?"

(percent of people aged 18 or older responding, 1998 and 2008; and percent of people aged 18 or older responding by demographic characteristic, 2008)

	always wrong	almost always wrong	sometimes wrong	not wrong at all
TEN-YEAR TREND				
2008	52.4%	3.1%	6.7%	37.8%
1998	58.5	5.9	7.3	28.3
2008 PROFILE				
Total people	**52.4**	**3.1**	**6.7**	**37.8**
Men	56.9	3.4	6.4	33.3
Women	48.4	2.7	7.0	41.8
Black	71.6	2.7	3.2	22.4
Hispanic	51.1	6.7	5.1	37.2
White	49.4	3.1	7.3	40.3
Aged 18 to 44	44.6	2.9	5.1	47.4
Aged 45 to 64	52.8	3.3	9.9	34.0
Aged 65 or older	74.5	3.1	4.4	18.0
Less than a bachelor's degree	59.1	3.0	6.4	31.5
Bachelor's degree or more	33.5	3.3	7.4	55.7

Source: Survey Documentation and Analysis, Computer-assisted Survey Methods Program, University of California, Berkeley, General Social Surveys, 1972–2008 Cumulative Data Files, Internet site http://sda.berkeley.edu/cgi-bin32/hsda?harcsda+gss08; calculations by New Strategist

Television News Is Most Important

The Internet has jumped into the number two position.

Nearly half of Americans get most of their news from television, 22 percent from the Internet, and 20 percent from the newspaper. Together these three news outlets are the main source of news for 90 percent of the public. But there are differences by demographic segment. Men are more likely than women to get news online, and less likely to turn to television for news. Blacks and Hispanics are much more likely than whites to watch news broadcasts on TV. Americans aged 18 to 44 are more than twice as likely as those aged 45 to 64 to get the news from the Internet. More than one-third of people 65 or older rely on the newspaper, while that share is sharply lower among younger age groups. Thirty-four percent of college-educated Americans get most of their news online versus only 18 percent of those with less education.

When asked about their political leanings, the largest share of Americans says they are moderates (39 percent). Thirty-six percent say they are slightly to extremely conservative, and 26 percent say they are slightly to extremely liberal. Liberalism is more prominent among blacks and Hispanics (33 percent), younger Americans (31 percent), and the college-educated (34 percent). Conservative ideas thrive especially among Americans aged 65 or older (45 percent) and whites (39 percent).

■ The political leanings of Americans have changed surprisingly little over the past 10 years, despite the seeming polarization of the public.

Newspapers have fallen into third place as the source for news

(percent distribution of people aged 18 or older by response to the question, "Where do you get most of your information about current events?" 2008)

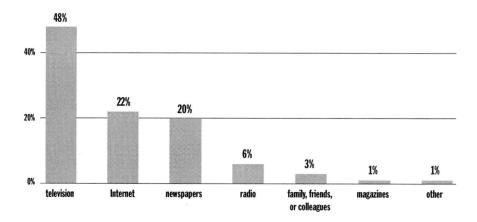

Table 1.28 Main Source of Information about Events in the News, 2008

"We are interested in how people get information about events in the news.
Where do you get most of your information about current news events?"

(percent of people aged 18 or older responding by demographic characteristic, 2008)

	TV	Internet	newspapers	radio	family, friends, or colleagues	magazines	other
Total people	**47.5%**	**22.0%**	**19.6%**	**6.1%**	**2.8%**	**1.1%**	**0.9%**
Men	45.1	25.4	18.6	7.2	1.6	0.7	1.4
Women	49.8	18.8	20.5	5.1	3.9	1.5	0.4
Black	63.7	11.4	17.9	1.2	3.9	0.2	1.7
Hispanic	60.0	16.4	13.8	4.7	1.2	4.0	0.0
White	44.8	22.9	20.3	6.9	2.9	1.2	0.9
Aged 18 to 44	42.0	34.0	12.3	5.9	4.4	0.9	0.6
Aged 45 to 64	52.3	14.0	22.8	7.4	1.5	0.9	1.3
Aged 65 or older	53.2	3.9	34.8	3.8	1.2	2.4	0.8
Less than a bachelor's degree	53.4	17.7	18.3	5.9	3.0	0.7	0.9
Bachelor's degree or more	30.9	34.1	23.1	6.6	2.0	2.2	1.0

Source: Survey Documentation and Analysis, Computer-assisted Survey Methods Program, University of California, Berkeley, General Social Surveys, 1972–2008 Cumulative Data Files, Internet site http://sda.berkeley.edu/cgi-bin32/hsda?harcsda+gss08; calculations by New Strategist

Table 1.29 Political Leanings, 1998 and 2008

"We hear a lot of talk these days about liberals and conservatives. On a seven-point scale from extremely liberal (1) to extremely conservative (7), where would you place yourself?"

(percent of people aged 18 or older responding, 1998 and 2008; and percent of people aged 18 or older responding by demographic characteristic, 2008)

	1 extremely liberal	2 liberal	3 slightly liberal	4 moderate	5 slightly conservative	6 conservative	7 extremely conservative
TEN-YEAR TREND							
2008	2.9%	12.2%	10.6%	38.6%	15.1%	16.7%	3.9%
1998	2.4	12.2	12.7	37.6	15.9	15.7	3.4
2008 PROFILE							
Total people	**2.9**	**12.2**	**10.6**	**38.6**	**15.1**	**16.7**	**3.9**
Men	3.2	11.1	10.3	38.7	15.0	17.4	4.4
Women	2.6	13.3	10.8	38.5	15.2	16.2	3.4
Black	4.6	11.8	16.5	46.3	8.0	7.2	5.7
Hispanic	5.2	16.4	11.5	43.8	11.8	9.6	1.8
White	2.5	11.2	9.5	37.4	16.9	18.8	3.8
Aged 18 to 44	3.3	14.8	13.2	38.7	14.3	12.3	3.5
Aged 45 to 64	2.0	10.5	9.9	38.4	16.3	18.6	4.3
Aged 65 or older	3.6	8.7	4.7	37.8	15.4	25.8	4.1
Less than a bachelor's degree	2.5	10.7	9.5	42.1	14.6	16.5	4.1
Bachelor's degree or more	3.9	16.6	13.5	28.8	16.6	17.4	3.2

Source: Survey Documentation and Analysis, Computer-assisted Survey Methods Program, University of California, Berkeley, General Social Surveys, 1972–2008 Cumulative Data Files, Internet site http://sda.berkeley.edu/cgi-bin32/hsda?harcsda+gss08; calculations by New Strategist

Most Support Right to Die, Gun Permits

Opposition to capital punishment is growing.

Americans have long been in support of the death penalty for convicted murderers. But a growing share of the public opposes capital punishment. In 2008, 32 percent of the public was against the death penalty, up from 27 percent in 1998. Blacks are the only demographic segment in which the majority opposes the death penalty. The strongest support for the death penalty is found among men (71 percent) and whites (72 percent).

The vast majority of Americans favors requiring a permit for gun ownership, but support for gun laws is flagging. In 2008, 79 percent of Americans favored requiring a permit before buying a gun, down from 84 percent in 1998. Men are most opposed to gun laws, and 29 percent are against requiring a police permit before a gun purchase.

Support for legal abortion under certain circumstances is overwhelming. Nine out of 10 Americans approve of abortion if a women's health is in serious danger, and three-quarters do if the pregnancy is the result of rape or there is a chance of serious defect in the baby. Other reasons garner substantially lower approval ratings (40 to 44 percent). Hispanics are least likely to accept abortion for any reason (29 percent).

A solid two-thirds majority of Americans support the terminally ill's right to die with a doctor's assistance, but support has fallen slightly over the past decade from 71 to 66 percent. The biggest differences are by race and Hispanic origin. Sixty-nine percent of whites favor the right to die compared with only 48 percent of Hispanics and 50 percent of blacks.

■ Perhaps alarmed by the number of false convictions coming to light in recent years, Americans increasingly oppose the death penalty.

When abortion should be legal

(percent of people aged 18 or older who responded "yes" to the question, "Should a woman be able to obtain a legal abortion if . . . ?" 2008)

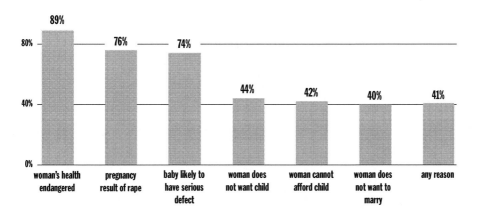

Table 1.30 Favor or Oppose Death Penalty for Murder, 1998 and 2008

"Do you favor or oppose the death penalty for persons convicted of murder?"

(percent of people aged 18 or older responding, 1998 and 2008; and percent of people aged 18 or older responding by demographic characteristic, 2008)

	favor	oppose
TEN-YEAR TREND		
2008	67.6%	32.4%
1998	73.5	26.5
2008 PROFILE		
Total people	**67.6**	**32.4**
Men	71.5	28.5
Women	64.0	36.0
Black	46.0	54.0
Hispanic	56.3	43.7
White	72.5	27.5
Aged 18 to 44	66.8	33.2
Aged 45 to 64	68.3	31.7
Aged 65 or older	68.6	31.4
Less than a bachelor's degree	69.8	30.2
Bachelor's degree or more	61.1	38.9

Source: Survey Documentation and Analysis, Computer-assisted Survey Methods Program, University of California, Berkeley, General Social Surveys, 1972–2008 Cumulative Data Files, Internet site http://sda.berkeley.edu/cgi-bin32/hsda?harcsda+gss08; calculations by New Strategist

Table 1.31 Favor or Oppose Gun Permits, 1998 and 2008

"Would you favor or oppose a law which would require a person to obtain a police permit before he or she could buy a gun?"

(percent of people aged 18 or older responding, 1998 and 2008; and percent of people aged 18 or older responding by demographic characteristic, 2008)

	favor	oppose
TEN-YEAR TREND		
2008	79.1%	20.9%
1998	83.7	16.3
2008 PROFILE		
Total people	**79.1**	**20.9**
Men	71.1	28.9
Women	85.9	14.1
Black	89.7	10.3
Hispanic	86.1	13.9
White	76.7	23.3
Aged 18 to 44	80.2	19.8
Aged 45 to 64	77.5	22.5
Aged 65 or older	78.9	21.1
Less than a bachelor's degree	77.6	22.4
Bachelor's degree or more	83.6	16.4

Source: Survey Documentation and Analysis, Computer-assisted Survey Methods Program, University of California, Berkeley, General Social Surveys, 1972–2008 Cumulative Data Files, Internet site http://sda.berkeley.edu/cgi-bin32/hsda?harcsda+gss08; calculations by New Strategist

Table 1.32 Support for Legal Abortion by Reason, 1998 and 2008

"Please tell me whether or not you think it should be possible for a pregnant woman to obtain a legal abortion if the woman wants it."

(percent of people aged 18 or older responding "yes," 1998 and 2008; and percent of people aged 18 or older responding "yes" by demographic characteristic, 2008)

	her health is seriously endangered	pregnancy is the result of a rape	there is a serious defect in the baby	she cannot afford more children	she does not want more childen	she is single and does not want to marry the man	for any reason
TEN-YEAR TREND							
2008	88.6%	75.6%	73.7%	42.3%	43.7%	40.3%	41.2%
1998	87.6	80.1	77.5	43.0	41.2	41.1	39.9
2008 PROFILE							
Total people	**88.6**	**75.6**	**73.7**	**42.3**	**43.7**	**40.3**	**41.2**
Men	89.3	78.1	74.9	44.2	47.0	43.7	42.4
Women	88.0	73.4	72.7	40.7	40.9	37.4	40.2
Black	91.3	75.0	73.1	42.9	46.1	36.7	38.0
Hispanic	80.1	57.1	60.1	27.3	31.3	24.9	28.8
White	88.8	76.9	74.8	42.7	44.1	41.2	42.8
Aged 18 to 44	87.8	76.2	69.8	42.0	41.8	39.5	41.5
Aged 45 to 64	90.3	74.4	78.3	54.2	50.3	43.0	44.2
Aged 65 or older	87.1	76.1	74.7	34.8	34.1	35.3	33.3
Less than a bachelor's degree	87.3	73.4	70.3	37.4	38.5	33.8	35.8
Bachelor's degree or more	92.4	81.7	83.4	56.6	58.8	58.9	56.8

Source: Survey Documentation and Analysis, Computer-assisted Survey Methods Program, University of California, Berkeley, General Social Surveys, 1972–2008 Cumulative Data Files, Internet site http://sda.berkeley.edu/cgi-bin32/hsda?harcsda+gss08; calculations by New Strategist

Table 1.33 Allow Patients with Incurable Disease to Die, 1998 and 2008

"When a person has a disease that cannot be cured, do you think
doctors should be allowed by law to end the patient's life by
some painless means if the patient and his family request it?"

*(percent of people aged 18 or older responding, 1998 and 2008; and percent of people aged 18 or older responding
by demographic characteristic, 2008)*

	yes	no
TEN-YEAR TREND		
2008	66.2%	33.8%
1998	70.7	29.3
2008 PROFILE		
Total people	**66.2**	**33.8**
Men	68.2	31.8
Women	64.4	35.6
Black	50.1	49.9
Hispanic	48.0	52.0
White	68.7	31.3
Aged 18 to 44	65.0	35.0
Aged 45 to 64	68.6	31.4
Aged 65 or older	63.4	36.6
Less than a bachelor's degree	66.6	33.4
Bachelor's degree or more	64.9	35.1

*Source: Survey Documentation and Analysis, Computer-assisted Survey Methods Program, University of California,
Berkeley, General Social Surveys, 1972–2008 Cumulative Data Files, Internet site http://sda.berkeley.edu/cgi-bin32/
hsda?harcsda+gss08; calculations by New Strategist*

Education Trends

■ **Middle-aged and younger adults are well educated.**

Most of those under age 65 have college experience, and 30 to 33 percent have a college degree.

■ **Asians are much better educated than others.**

The majority of Asian men have a college degree. Among Hispanic men, only 13 percent have graduated from college.

■ **Most parents are satisfied with their child's school.**

A substantial 59 percent of parents with children in kindergarten through 12th grade say they are very satisfied with their child's school.

■ **College enrollment is rising.**

But the number of full-time students attending private, four-year schools fell 12 percent between 2000 and 2007.

■ **College campuses are becoming more diverse.**

Non-Hispanic whites account for 66 percent of the nation's college students, down from 68 percent in 2000.

■ **Women earn most degrees.**

Sixty-two percent of associate's degrees went to women in 2006–07, as did 57 percent of bachelor's degrees and 61 percent of master's degrees.

■ **Many Americans participate in adult education.**

Forty-four percent of adults participated in adult education courses in 2005, including the majority of those under age 35.

Many Americans Are Well Educated

More than half the adult population has some college experience.

The educational attainment of Americans has increased dramatically over the past few decades. Just 30 years ago, more than half of adults had not even graduated from high school. Today, most adults have at least some college education and 29 percent have at least a bachelor's degree.

Among men, the share with a college degree peaks at 34.5 percent among men aged 55 to 64—the age group now filling with the oldest boomers. Boomer men are better educated than younger men because, as young adults during the Vietnam War, many boomers stayed in college to avoid the draft.

Among women aged 65 or older, only 16 percent have a college degree. But among women under age 45, an impressive 35 to 36 percent have a bachelor's degree. Although women overall are slightly less likely than men to have graduated from college (29 versus 30 percent), women under age 45 are better educated than their male counterparts. Among 25-to-34-year-olds, 36 percent of women have a bachelor's degree compared with only 29 percent of men.

■ Because the educational attainment of younger women is higher than that of younger men, women's incomes should continue to gain on men's.

Among Americans under age 55, women are better educated than men

(percent of people with a bachelor's degree, by age and sex, 2008)

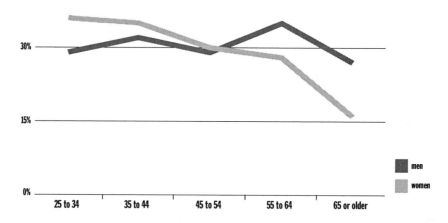

Table 2.1 Educational Attainment by Age, 2008

(number and percent distribution of people aged 25 or older by educational attainment and age, 2008; numbers in thousands)

	total	25 to 34	35 to 44	45 to 54	55 to 64	65 or older
Total people	**196,305**	**40,146**	**42,132**	**43,935**	**33,302**	**36,790**
Not a high school graduate	26,340	4,767	4,792	4,737	3,735	8,308
High school graduate only	61,183	11,297	12,039	14,068	10,221	13,558
Some college, no degree	33,812	7,396	7,200	7,682	6,012	5,523
Associate's degree	17,182	3,717	4,159	4,464	2,966	1,877
Bachelor's degree	37,559	9,421	9,204	8,431	6,096	4,406
Master's degree	14,765	2,792	3,507	3,282	3,055	2,129
Professional degree	2,991	489	693	744	611	453
Doctoral degree	2,472	266	538	527	605	536
High school graduate or more	169,964	35,378	37,340	39,198	29,566	28,482
Some college or more	108,781	24,081	25,301	25,130	19,345	14,924
Associate's degree or more	74,969	16,685	18,101	17,448	13,333	9,401
Bachelor's degree or more	57,787	12,968	13,942	12,984	10,367	7,524
Total people	**100.0%**	**100.0%**	**100.0%**	**100.0%**	**100.0%**	**100.0%**
Not a high school graduate	13.4	11.9	11.4	10.8	11.2	22.6
High school graduate only	31.2	28.1	28.6	32.0	30.7	36.9
Some college, no degree	17.2	18.4	17.1	17.5	18.1	15.0
Associate's degree	8.8	9.3	9.9	10.2	8.9	5.1
Bachelor's degree	19.1	23.5	21.8	19.2	18.3	12.0
Master's degree	7.5	7.0	8.3	7.5	9.2	5.8
Professional degree	1.5	1.2	1.6	1.7	1.8	1.2
Doctoral degree	1.3	0.7	1.3	1.2	1.8	1.5
High school graduate or more	86.6	88.1	88.6	89.2	88.8	77.4
Some college or more	55.4	60.0	60.1	57.2	58.1	40.6
Associate's degree or more	38.2	41.6	43.0	39.7	40.0	25.6
Bachelor's degree or more	29.4	32.3	33.1	29.6	31.1	20.5

Source: Bureau of the Census, 2008 Current Population Survey Annual Social and Economic Supplement, Internet site http:// pubdb3.census.gov/macro/032008/perinc/new03_000.htm; calculations by New Strategist

Table 2.2 Educational Attainment of Men by Age, 2008

(number and percent distribution of men aged 25 or older by educational attainment and age, 2008; numbers in thousands)

	total	25 to 34	35 to 44	45 to 54	55 to 64	65 or older
Total men	**94,470**	**20,210**	**20,880**	**21,539**	**16,079**	**15,762**
Not a high school graduate	13,299	2,760	2,649	2,576	1,829	3,486
High school graduate only	29,491	6,356	6,391	7,234	4,464	5,045
Some college, no degree	15,810	3,597	3,464	3,554	2,869	2,326
Associate's degree	7,436	1,680	1,794	1,899	1,368	695
Bachelor's degree	18,042	4,365	4,251	3,965	3,182	2,279
Master's degree	6,886	1,099	1,609	1,480	1,532	1,165
Professional degree	1,877	219	398	480	429	351
Doctoral degree	1,628	134	324	351	405	414
High school graduate or more	81,170	17,450	18,231	18,963	14,249	12,275
Some college or more	51,679	11,094	11,840	11,729	9,785	7,230
Associate's degree or more	35,869	7,497	8,376	8,175	6,916	4,904
Bachelor's degree or more	28,433	5,817	6,582	6,276	5,548	4,209
Total men	**100.0%**	**100.0%**	**100.0%**	**100.0%**	**100.0%**	**100.0%**
Not a high school graduate	14.1	13.7	12.7	12.0	11.4	22.1
High school graduate only	31.2	31.4	30.6	33.6	27.8	32.0
Some college, no degree	16.7	17.8	16.6	16.5	17.8	14.8
Associate's degree	7.9	8.3	8.6	8.8	8.5	4.4
Bachelor's degree	19.1	21.6	20.4	18.4	19.8	14.5
Master's degree	7.3	5.4	7.7	6.9	9.5	7.4
Professional degree	2.0	1.1	1.9	2.2	2.7	2.2
Doctoral degree	1.7	0.7	1.6	1.6	2.5	2.6
High school graduate or more	85.9	86.3	87.3	88.0	88.6	77.9
Some college or more	54.7	54.9	56.7	54.5	60.9	45.9
Associate's degree or more	38.0	37.1	40.1	38.0	43.0	31.1
Bachelor's degree or more	30.1	28.8	31.5	29.1	34.5	26.7

Source: Bureau of the Census, 2008 Current Population Survey Annual Social and Economic Supplement, Internet site http:// pubdb3.census.gov/macro/032008/perinc/new03_000.htm; calculations by New Strategist

Table 2.3 Educational Attainment of Women by Age, 2008

(number and percent distribution of women aged 25 or older by educational attainment and age, 2008; numbers in thousands)

	total	25 to 34	35 to 44	45 to 54	55 to 64	65 or older
Total women	**101,835**	**19,937**	**21,252**	**22,396**	**17,223**	**21,028**
Not a high school graduate	13,042	2,007	2,144	2,161	1,906	4,822
High school graduate only	31,692	4,941	5,648	6,835	5,756	8,513
Some college, no degree	18,002	3,799	3,735	4,128	3,143	3,197
Associate's degree	9,746	2,038	2,365	2,564	1,598	1,181
Bachelor's degree	19,517	5,056	4,953	4,466	2,915	2,127
Master's degree	7,879	1,694	1,898	1,801	1,523	964
Professional degree	1,114	270	295	265	182	102
Doctoral degree	844	133	214	176	200	121
High school graduate or more	88,794	17,931	19,108	20,235	15,317	16,205
Some college or more	57,102	12,990	13,460	13,400	9,561	7,692
Associate's degree or more	39,100	9,191	9,725	9,272	6,418	4,495
Bachelor's degree or more	29,354	7,153	7,360	6,708	4,820	3,314
Total women	**100.0%**	**100.0%**	**100.0%**	**100.0%**	**100.0%**	**100.0%**
Not a high school graduate	12.8	10.1	10.1	9.6	11.1	22.9
High school graduate only	31.1	24.8	26.6	30.5	33.4	40.5
Some college, no degree	17.7	19.1	17.6	18.4	18.2	15.2
Associate's degree	9.6	10.2	11.1	11.4	9.3	5.6
Bachelor's degree	19.2	25.4	23.3	19.9	16.9	10.1
Master's degree	7.7	8.5	8.9	8.0	8.8	4.6
Professional degree	1.1	1.4	1.4	1.2	1.1	0.5
Doctoral degree	0.8	0.7	1.0	0.8	1.2	0.6
High school graduate or more	87.2	89.9	89.9	90.4	88.9	77.1
Some college or more	56.1	65.2	63.3	59.8	55.5	36.6
Associate's degree or more	38.4	46.1	45.8	41.4	37.3	21.4
Bachelor's degree or more	28.8	35.9	34.6	30.0	28.0	15.8

Source: Bureau of the Census, 2008 Current Population Survey Annual Social and Economic Supplement, Internet site http://pubdb3.census.gov/macro/032008/perinc/new03_000.htm; calculations by New Strategist

Most Asian Men Have a College Degree

Only 13 percent of Hispanic men are college graduates.

Among both men and women, Asians are far better educated than non-Hispanic whites, blacks, or Hispanics. The 55 percent majority of Asian men have a college degree versus a much smaller 34 percent of non-Hispanic white men, 19 percent of black men, and just 13 percent of Hispanic men. The story is similar for Asian women. Nearly 50 percent are college graduates versus 32 percent of non-Hispanic white women, 21 percent of black women, and 14 percent of Hispanic women.

Many Hispanics have not graduated from high school. Among Hispanic men, only 61 percent are high school graduates. The figure is a slightly higher 64 percent among Hispanic women. In contrast, 82 to 84 percent of blacks have a high school diploma. The figure ranges from 87 to 92 percent among Asians and non-Hispanic whites.

■ The educational attainment of Hispanics is well below that of the rest of the population because many are immigrants from countries with little formal schooling.

Blacks are better educated than Hispanics

(percent of people aged 25 or older with a college degree, by sex, race, and Hispanic origin, 2008)

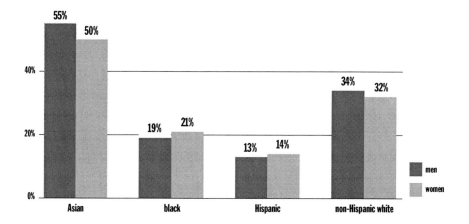

Table 2.4 Educational Attainment of Men by Race and Hispanic Origin, 2008

(number and percent distribution of men aged 25 or older by educational attainment, race, and Hispanic origin, 2008; numbers in thousands)

	total	Asian	black	Hispanic	non-Hispanic white
Total men	**94,470**	**4,445**	**10,137**	**12,994**	**66,082**
Not a high school graduate	13,299	402	1,833	5,080	5,897
High school graduate	29,491	829	3,723	3,954	20,700
Some college, no degree	15,810	490	1,896	1,635	11,599
Associate's degree	7,436	298	776	689	5,572
Bachelor's degree	18,042	1,348	1,325	1,104	14,184
Master's degree	6,886	698	417	371	5,348
Professional degree	1,877	156	89	120	1,499
Doctorate degree	1,628	224	77	42	1,283
High school graduate or more	81,170	4,043	8,303	7,915	60,185
Some college or more	51,679	3,214	4,580	3,961	39,485
Associate's degree or more	35,869	2,724	2,684	2,326	27,886
Bachelor's degree or more	28,433	2,426	1,908	1,637	22,314
Total men	**100.0%**	**100.0%**	**100.0%**	**100.0%**	**100.0%**
Not a high school graduate	14.1	9.0	18.1	39.1	8.9
High school graduate	31.2	18.7	36.7	30.4	31.3
Some college, no degree	16.7	11.0	18.7	12.6	17.6
Associate's degree	7.9	6.7	7.7	5.3	8.4
Bachelor's degree	19.1	30.3	13.1	8.5	21.5
Master's degree	7.3	15.7	4.1	2.9	8.1
Professional degree	2.0	3.5	0.9	0.9	2.3
Doctorate degree	1.7	5.0	0.8	0.3	1.9
High school graduate or more	85.9	91.0	81.9	60.9	91.1
Some college or more	54.7	72.3	45.2	30.5	59.8
Associate's degree or more	38.0	61.3	26.5	17.9	42.2
Bachelor's degree or more	30.1	54.6	18.8	12.6	33.8

Note: Asians and blacks are those who identify themselves as being of the race alone or in combination with other races. Hispanics may be of any race. Non-Hispanic whites are those who identify themselves as being white alone and not Hispanic. Source: Bureau of the Census, 2008 Current Population Survey Annual Social and Economic Supplement, Internet site http://pubdb3.census.gov/macro/032008/perinc/new03_000.htm; calculations by New Strategist

Table 2.5 Educational Attainment of Women by Race and Hispanic Origin, 2008

(number and percent distribution of women aged 25 or older by educational attainment, race, and Hispanic origin, 2008; numbers in thousands)

	total	Asian	black	Hispanic	non-Hispanic white
Total women	**101,835**	**5,047**	**12,709**	**12,280**	**70,997**
Not a high school graduate	13,042	644	2,015	4,458	5,820
High school graduate	31,692	1,035	4,251	3,517	22,635
Some college, no degree	18,002	510	2,608	1,730	12,937
Associate's degree	9,746	347	1,230	845	7,238
Bachelor's degree	19,517	1,668	1,785	1,265	14,707
Master's degree	7,879	624	688	367	6,171
Professional degree	1,114	118	65	69	857
Doctorate degree	844	102	68	30	631
High school graduate or more	88,794	4,404	10,695	7,823	65,176
Some college or more	57,102	3,369	6,444	4,306	42,541
Associate's degree or more	39,100	2,859	3,836	2,576	29,604
Bachelor's degree or more	29,354	2,512	2,606	1,731	22,366
Total women	**100.0%**	**100.0%**	**100.0%**	**100.0%**	**100.0%**
Not a high school graduate	12.8	12.8	15.9	36.3	8.2
High school graduate	31.1	20.5	33.4	28.6	31.9
Some college, no degree	17.7	10.1	20.5	14.1	18.2
Associate's degree	9.6	6.9	9.7	6.9	10.2
Bachelor's degree	19.2	33.0	14.0	10.3	20.7
Master's degree	7.7	12.4	5.4	3.0	8.7
Professional degree	1.1	2.3	0.5	0.6	1.2
Doctorate degree	0.8	2.0	0.5	0.2	0.9
High school graduate or more	87.2	87.3	84.2	63.7	91.8
Some college or more	56.1	66.8	50.7	35.1	59.9
Associate's degree or more	38.4	56.6	30.2	21.0	41.7
Bachelor's degree or more	28.8	49.8	20.5	14.1	31.5

Note: Asians and blacks are those who identify themselves as being of the race alone or in combination with other races. Hispanics may be of any race. Non-Hispanic whites are those who identify themselves as being white alone and not Hispanic.
Source: Bureau of the Census, 2008 Current Population Survey Annual Social and Economic Supplement, Internet site http:// pubdb3.census.gov/macro/032008/perinc/new03_000.htm; calculations by New Strategist

Educational Attainment Varies Widely by State

Massachusetts has the largest share of college graduates.

Among regions, the Northeast has the highest level of education. Thirty-two percent of people aged 25 or older in the Northeast have a bachelor's degree compared with only 25 percent in the South, which is the least educated region. In the Midwest, the figure is 26 percent and in the West 29 percent. Among women aged 25 to 34 in the Northeast, nearly 42 percent have a bachelor's degree—the highest proportion in any region.

The educational attainment of state populations varies even more widely than regional education. The proportion of state populations with a high school diploma ranges from less than 80 percent in Mississippi, Texas, and Louisiana to a high of 91 percent in Minnesota and Wyoming.

The figures vary for college graduates as well. In West Virginia, only 17 percent of people aged 25 or older have a bachelor's degree, the smallest share among the 50 states. In contrast, at least 35 percent of adults are college graduates in Colorado, Maryland, Massachusetts, and the District of Columbia. Since income rises with education, it is no surprise that the states with the least-educated populations are also some of the poorest, while those with the best-educated populations are some of the richest.

■ The educational level of the workforce is one factor behind business location decisions. Better-educated populations attract business investment, which increases economic diversity and employment opportunities.

West Virginia's population is least likely to be college educated

(percent of people aged 25 or older with a bachelor's degree in the states with the largest and the smallest percentage of college-educated residents, 2007)

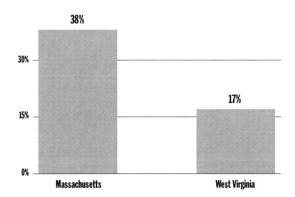

Table 2.6 High School Graduates by Region, Sex, and Age, 2007

(percent of people aged 25 or older who are high school graduates, by region, sex, and age, 2007)

	total	25 to 34	35 to 44	45 to 64	65 or older
Total with a high school diploma or more	**86.3%**	**86.3%**	**87.2%**	**87.2%**	**74.0%**
Northeast	89.7	89.7	90.3	88.7	74.0
Midwest	89.6	89.6	90.7	90.2	75.7
South	84.6	84.6	85.9	85.2	70.6
West	83.6	83.6	83.7	86.3	77.8
Males with a high school diploma or more	**84.2**	**84.2**	**85.6**	**86.6**	**75.0**
Northeast	88.2	88.2	89.1	88.2	74.8
Midwest	88.3	88.3	89.5	89.6	75.7
South	81.8	81.8	83.8	84.0	71.8
West	81.5	81.5	82.3	86.2	79.8
Females with a high school diploma or more	**88.4**	**88.4**	**88.8**	**87.9**	**73.2**
Northeast	91.2	91.2	91.4	89.3	73.5
Midwest	90.9	90.9	92.0	90.9	75.8
South	87.4	87.4	87.9	86.2	69.8
West	85.7	85.7	85.2	86.4	76.3

Source: Bureau of the Census, 2007 American Community Survey, Table B15001, Internet site http://factfinder.census.gov/ servlet/DatasetMainPageServlet?_program=ACS&_submenuId=&_lang=en&_ts=l; calculations by New Strategist

Table 2.7 College Graduates by Region, Sex, and Age, 2007

(percent of people aged 25 or older with at least a bachelor's degree, by region, sex, and age, 2007)

	total	25 to 34	35 to 44	45 to 64	65 or older
Total with bachelor's degree or more	**27.5%**	**29.1%**	**30.4%**	**28.9%**	**19.3%**
Northeast	31.5	37.7	35.5	32.4	19.9
Midwest	26.0	29.7	30.3	26.8	16.2
South	25.4	26.0	27.7	27.1	18.6
West	28.8	27.5	30.7	31.1	23.4
Males with bachelor's degree or more	**28.2**	**25.7**	**29.1**	**30.3**	**25.3**
Northeast	32.4	33.7	33.9	33.7	25.9
Midwest	26.6	26.3	29.1	27.9	21.0
South	26.0	22.5	26.3	28.5	24.5
West	29.8	24.8	29.5	32.9	30.5
Females with bachelor's degree or more	**26.7**	**32.7**	**31.8**	**27.6**	**15.0**
Northeast	30.7	41.6	37.1	31.2	15.8
Midwest	25.5	33.2	31.6	25.7	12.8
South	24.8	29.7	29.2	25.8	14.2
West	27.9	30.5	31.8	29.3	17.9

Source: Bureau of the Census, 2007 American Community Survey, Table B15001, Internet site http://factfinder.census.gov/ servlet/DatasetMainPageServlet?_program=ACS&_submenuId=&_lang=en&_ts=l; calculations by New Strategist

Table 2.8 Educational Attainment by State, 2007

(percent of people aged 25 or older who have at least a high school diploma or bachelor's degree, by state, 2007)

	high school diploma or more	bachelor's degree or more		high school diploma or more	bachelor's degree or more
Total United States	**84.5%**	**27.5%**	Missouri	85.6%	24.5%
Alabama	80.4	21.4	Montana	90.0	27.0
Alaska	90.5	26.0	Nebraska	89.6	27.5
Arizona	83.5	25.3	Nevada	83.7	21.8
Arkansas	81.1	19.3	New Hampshire	90.5	32.5
California	80.2	29.5	New Jersey	87.0	33.9
Colorado	88.9	35.0	New Mexico	82.3	24.8
Connecticut	88.0	34.7	New York	84.1	31.7
Delaware	87.4	26.1	North Carolina	83.0	25.6
District of Columbia	85.7	47.5	North Dakota	89.0	25.7
Florida	84.9	25.8	Ohio	87.1	24.1
Georgia	82.9	27.1	Oklahoma	84.8	22.8
Hawaii	89.4	29.2	Oregon	88.0	28.3
Idaho	88.4	24.5	Pennsylvania	86.8	25.8
Illinois	85.7	29.5	Rhode Island	83.0	29.8
Indiana	85.8	22.1	South Carolina	82.1	23.5
Iowa	89.6	24.3	South Dakota	88.2	25.0
Kansas	89.1	28.8	Tennessee	81.4	21.8
Kentucky	80.1	20.0	Texas	79.1	25.2
Louisiana	79.9	20.4	Utah	90.2	28.7
Maine	89.4	26.7	Vermont	90.3	33.6
Maryland	87.4	35.2	Virginia	85.9	33.6
Massachusetts	88.4	37.9	Washington	89.3	30.3
Michigan	87.4	24.7	West Virginia	81.2	17.3
Minnesota	91.0	31.0	Wisconsin	89.0	25.4
Mississippi	78.5	18.9	Wyoming	91.2	23.4

Source: Bureau of the Census, 2007 American Community Survey, Ranking Tables, Internet site http://factfinder.census.gov/servlet/DatasetMainPageServlet?_program=ACS&_submenuId=&_lang=en&_ts=l; calculations by New Strategist

More than One in Four Americans Are in School

Nearly 76 million people were enrolled in school in 2007.

Americans start school at a younger age than they once did, and many stay in school—or go back to school—well into middle age. In 2007, 27 percent of people aged 3 or older were in school.

Among 3-year-olds, a substantial 41 percent attend school, as are the 68 percent majority of 4-year-olds. Enrollment is above 95 percent for children from ages 6 to 16, and schooling attracts the majority of people through age 20. Even at ages 25 to 29, more than one in eight people are still in school.

The nation's elementary schools enrolled nearly 20 million students in 2007, while middle schools enrolled 12 million and high schools 17 million. Only 56.5 percent of public school students are non-Hispanic white, while a substantial 43.5 percent are American Indian, Asian, black, or Hispanic. In 10 states and the District of Columbia, minorities account for at least half the student body.

■ The economic downturn is driving more of the nation's young adults into college, but the rising cost of higher education may limit this trend.

The number of people in college now surpasses the number in high school

(number of people enrolled in school by level, 2007)

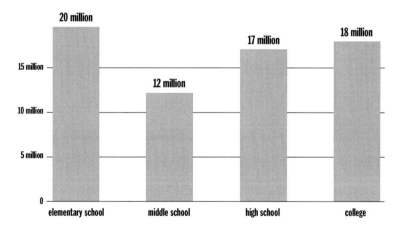

Table 2.9 School Enrollment by Age, 2007

(number of people aged 3 or older, and number and percent enrolled in school by age, fall 2007; numbers in thousands)

	total	enrolled number	enrolled percent
Total people	**285,410**	**75,967**	**26.6%**
Aged 3	4,142	1,717	41.5
Aged 4	4,092	2,774	67.8
Aged 5	4,091	3,780	92.4
Aged 6	4,140	4,012	96.9
Aged 7	3,967	3,875	97.7
Aged 8	3,904	3,830	98.1
Aged 9	3,875	3,815	98.5
Aged 10	4,028	3,953	98.2
Aged 11	3,903	3,866	99.1
Aged 12	4,308	4,234	98.3
Aged 13	4,004	3,958	98.9
Aged 14	4,086	4,020	98.4
Aged 15	4,155	4,116	99.1
Aged 16	4,339	4,169	96.1
Aged 17	4,363	4,035	92.5
Aged 18	4,156	3,049	73.4
Aged 19	4,182	2,517	60.2
Aged 20	4,006	2,078	51.9
Aged 21	4,078	1,837	45.1
Aged 22	4,162	1,350	32.4
Aged 23	4,061	1,079	26.6
Aged 24	4,133	946	22.9
Aged 25 to 29	20,752	2,577	12.4
Aged 30 to 34	19,179	1,379	7.2
Aged 35 to 39	20,740	940	4.5
Aged 40 to 44	21,536	677	3.1
Aged 45 to 49	22,675	602	2.7
Aged 50 to 54	21,036	468	2.2
Aged 55 to 59	18,250	168	0.9
Aged 60 to 64	14,625	83	0.6
Aged 65 or older	36,443	60	0.2

Source: Bureau of the Census, School Enrollment—Social and Economic Characteristics of Students: October 2007, Internet site http://www.census.gov/population/www/socdemo/school/cps2007.html

Table 2.10 School Enrollment by Grade and Year of College, 2007

(number and percent distribution of people attending school by grade and year of college, fall 2007; numbers in thousands)

	number	percent distribution
TOTAL STUDENTS	**75,967**	**100.0%**
Nursery school	**4,628**	**6.1**
Kindergarten	**4,132**	**5.4**
Elementary	**19,933**	**26.2**
First grade	4,174	5.5
Second grade	3,920	5.2
Third grade	3,991	5.3
Fourth grade	4,011	5.3
Fifth grade	3,837	5.1
Middle school	**12,236**	**16.1**
Sixth grade	4,184	5.5
Seventh grade	4,101	5.4
Eighth grade	3,951	5.2
High school	**17,081**	**22.5**
Ninth grade	4,291	5.6
Tenth grade	4,259	5.6
Eleventh grade	4,080	5.4
Twelfth grade	4,451	5.9
College	**17,956**	**23.6**
Undergraduate	14,365	18.9
First year	4,444	5.8
Second year	4,089	5.4
Third year	3,429	4.5
Fourth or higher year	2,403	3.2
Graduate	3,591	4.7
First year	1,303	1.7
Second or higher year	2,288	3.0

Source: Bureau of the Census, School Enrollment—Social and Economic Characteristics of Students: October 2006, Internet site http://www.census.gov/population/www/socdemo/school/cps2007.html

Table 2.11 Enrollment in Public Elementary and Secondary School by State, Race, and Hispanic Origin, 2006

(percent distribution of students enrolled in public elementary and secondary school by state, race, and Hispanic origin, 2006)

| | total | minority students | | | | | non-Hispanic white |
		total	Am. Indian	Asian	black	Hispanic	
Total public school children	**100.0%**	**43.5%**	**1.2%**	**4.7%**	**17.1%**	**20.5%**	**56.5%**
Alabama	100.0	41.0	0.8	1.1	35.9	3.2	59.1
Alaska	100.0	42.6	26.6	7.0	4.6	4.4	57.4
Arizona	100.0	54.6	5.6	2.6	5.4	41.0	45.4
Arkansas	100.0	32.4	0.7	1.5	22.7	7.5	67.6
California	100.0	69.8	0.8	11.7	7.8	49.5	30.2
Colorado	100.0	38.1	1.2	3.3	6.0	27.6	61.9
Connecticut	100.0	34.0	0.4	3.7	13.9	16.0	66.0
Delaware	100.0	46.2	0.4	3.0	33.0	9.8	53.9
District of Columbia	100.0	95.0	0.1	1.6	83.4	9.9	5.0
Florida	100.0	51.6	0.3	2.4	23.9	25.0	48.4
Georgia	100.0	51.7	0.1	2.9	39.2	9.5	48.2
Hawaii	100.0	80.5	0.6	73.0	2.4	4.5	19.6
Idaho	100.0	17.7	1.6	1.6	1.1	13.4	82.3
Illinois	100.0	44.1	0.2	3.9	20.3	19.7	55.9
Indiana	100.0	20.5	0.3	1.3	12.6	6.3	79.5
Iowa	100.0	14.1	0.6	2.0	5.3	6.2	85.9
Kansas	100.0	26.1	1.7	2.5	8.9	13.0	73.9
Kentucky	100.0	14.2	0.1	1.0	10.7	2.4	85.8
Louisiana	100.0	50.0	0.8	1.4	45.4	2.4	50.1
Maine	100.0	5.4	0.7	1.4	2.3	1.0	94.6
Maryland	100.0	52.2	0.4	5.4	38.1	8.3	47.8
Massachusetts	100.0	27.2	0.3	4.9	8.4	13.6	72.9
Michigan	100.0	28.0	0.9	2.4	20.2	4.5	71.8
Minnesota	100.0	22.8	2.1	5.9	9.1	5.7	77.2
Mississippi	100.0	53.5	0.2	0.8	50.8	1.7	46.5
Missouri	100.0	23.6	0.4	1.7	18.1	3.4	76.3
Montana	100.0	16.1	11.4	1.2	1.0	2.5	83.9
Nebraska	100.0	23.5	1.7	1.9	7.7	12.2	76.5
Nevada	100.0	55.7	1.6	7.6	11.1	35.4	44.4
New Hampshire	100.0	7.0	0.3	2.0	1.8	2.9	92.9
New Jersey	100.0	44.3	0.2	7.9	17.4	18.8	55.7
New Mexico	100.0	69.4	10.9	1.3	2.6	54.6	30.6
New York	100.0	48.0	0.5	7.2	19.7	20.6	52.1
North Carolina	100.0	42.6	1.5	2.3	29.2	9.6	57.5
North Dakota	100.0	13.2	8.6	1.0	1.8	1.8	86.8
Ohio	100.0	21.2	0.1	1.4	17.1	2.6	78.8
Oklahoma	100.0	41.4	19.3	1.8	10.8	9.5	58.6
Oregon	100.0	26.8	2.2	4.8	3.1	16.7	73.2
Pennsylvania	100.0	25.5	0.2	2.6	15.9	6.8	74.6

| | total | minority students | | | | | non-Hispanic white |
		total	Am. Indian	Asian	black	Hispanic	
Rhode Island	100.0%	30.6%	0.7%	3.1%	8.8%	18.0%	69.5%
South Carolina	100.0	46.1	0.3	1.4	39.8	4.6	53.9
South Dakota	100.0	15.4	10.6	1.0	1.7	2.1	84.5
Tennessee	100.0	30.9	0.2	1.5	24.8	4.4	69.1
Texas	100.0	64.3	0.3	3.3	14.4	46.3	35.7
Utah	100.0	19.2	1.5	3.1	1.4	13.2	80.8
Vermont	100.0	4.6	0.4	1.6	1.6	1.0	95.3
Virginia	100.0	40.7	0.3	5.4	26.7	8.3	59.3
Washington	100.0	31.0	2.6	8.4	5.7	14.3	68.9
West Virginia	100.0	6.7	0.1	0.7	5.1	0.8	93.3
Wisconsin	100.0	22.8	1.5	3.6	10.5	7.2	77.3
Wyoming	100.0	15.5	3.5	1.1	1.5	9.4	84.5

Source: National Center for Education Statistics, Digest of Education Statistics: 2008, Internet site http://nces.ed.gov/programs/ digest/d07/tables/dt07_040.asp

Parents Are Involved in Their Children's Education

In the past year, most have attended a school meeting, a parent-teacher conference, a school or class event.

Most of today's parents are actively involved in their children's education. The parents of 89 percent of the nation's elementary and secondary school children say they attended a PTA or general school meeting during the past year, according to a survey by the National Center for Education Statistics. Seventy-eight percent attended a parent–teacher conference, 74 percent attended a class event, and 46 percent volunteered.

Participation in a child's education typically rises with the educational attainment of the parent. The percentage of children whose parents attended a class event, for example, climbs from 48 percent among parents who did not graduate from high school to more than 80 percent among parents with at least a bachelor's degree. Surprisingly, however, the most-educated parents are least likely to check their children's homework. Among students with homework, only 81 percent of parents with a graduate degree check to make sure their child has done his homework compared with 94 percent of parents without a high school diploma.

■ Poor parents are more likely than the nonpoor to make sure their child has done his or her homework.

Educated parents are most likely to attend their children's class events

(percent of children whose parents attended a class event in the past year, by educational attainment of parent, 2006–07)

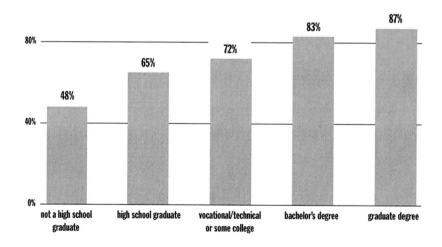

Table 2.12 Parental Involvement in School Activities, 2006–07

(total number and percent of elementary and secondary school children whose parents reported participation in school activities, by selected characteristics of child and parent, 2006–07)

	total		parent attended a PTA or general school meeting	parent attended a parent-teacher conference	parent attended a school or class event	parent volunteered at school	parent participated in school fundraising
	number	percent					
TOTAL CHILDREN	51,600	100%	89%	78%	74%	46%	65%
Race and Hispanic origin of child							
Asian, non-Hispanic	1,566	100	90	80	72	46	62
Black, non-Hispanic	7,837	100	87	77	65	35	58
Hispanic	9,767	100	87	80	65	32	51
White, non-Hispanic	29,832	100	91	78	80	54	72
Educational attainment of parent							
Not a high school graduate	3,504	100	75	70	48	20	34
High school graduate	11,070	100	84	74	65	33	55
Vocational/technical or some college	14,844	100	89	77	72	42	67
Bachelor's degree	11,353	100	94	81	83	56	72
Graduate degree	10,829	100	95	82	87	64	77
School type							
Public, assigned	37,168	100	89	76	72	42	63
Public, chosen	7,951	100	88	81	74	45	62
Private, religious	4,560	100	96	96	86	73	85
Private, nonreligious	1,438	100	97	90	86	68	72
Student's grade level							
Kindergarten through 2nd grade	11,516	100	93	90	78	63	72
3rd through 5th grade	11,519	100	94	92	83	57	71
6th through 8th grade	12,058	100	91	76	72	38	63
9th through 12th grade	16,503	100	83	61	68	34	57
Poverty status							
Poor	10,012	100	81	77	56	26	45
Not poor	41,587	100	91	78	79	51	70

Source: National Center for Education Statistics, Parent and Family Involvement in Education, 2006–07 School Year, from the National Household Education Surveys Program of 2007, August 2008, Internet site http://nces.ed.gov/pubsearch/pubsinfo .asp?pubid=2008050; calculations by New Strategist

Table 2.13 Parental Involvement in Child's Homework, 2006–07

(total number and percent of elementary and secondary school children whose parents reported involvement with child's homework, by selected characteristics of child and parent, 2006–07)

	total		student does homework outside of school		
	number	percent	total	place in home set aside for homework	adult in household checks that homework is done
TOTAL CHILDREN	**51,600**	**100%**	**94%**	**89%**	**85%**
Race and Hispanic origin of child					
Asian, non-Hispanic	1,566	100	96	93	83
Black, non-Hispanic	7,837	100	94	94	94
Hispanic	9,767	100	94	84	91
White, non-Hispanic	29,832	100	95	89	82
Educational attainment of parent					
Not a high school graduate	3,504	100	90	83	94
High school graduate	11,070	100	93	89	89
Vocational/technical or some college	14,844	100	94	90	86
Bachelor's degree	11,353	100	96	87	83
Graduate degree	10,829	100	96	90	81
School type					
Public, assigned	37,168	100	94	89	86
Public, chosen	7,951	100	95	90	88
Private, religious	4,560	100	97	86	79
Private, nonreligious	1,438	100	90	85	84
Student's grade level					
Kindergarten through 2nd grade	11,516	100	93	84	100
3rd through 5th grade	11,519	100	97	89	97
6th through 8th grade	12,058	100	95	91	88
9th through 12th grade	16,503	100	93	91	65
Poverty status					
Poor	10,012	100	93	87	93
Not poor	41,587	100	95	89	84

Source: National Center for Education Statistics, Parent and Family Involvement in Education, 2006–07 School Year, from the National Household Education Surveys Program of 2007, August 2008, Internet site http://nces.ed.gov/pubsearch/pubsinfo .asp?pubid=2008050; calculations by New Strategist

Most Parents Are Satisfied with Their Child's School

Most are also satisfied with their child's teachers and the amount of homework.

Complaints about the nation's schools are commonplace, but in fact the parents of most children in kindergarten through 12th grade are very satisfied with various aspects of their child's school. Fifty-nine percent of school children have parents who claim to be "very satisfied" with their child's school. The percentage of parents very satisfied with the teachers is an even higher 64 percent. Similar proportions are very satisfied with their school's academic standards and discipline. Seventy-five percent say the amount of homework assigned to their child is about right.

The biggest difference in satisfaction levels occurs by type of school and grade level. Typically, private school parents are happier than public school parents, and the parents of younger children are happier than the parents of children in middle or high school. Nevertheless, the majority of parents, regardless of type of school or grade level, say they are very satisfied with their child's school.

■ Although most parents are very satisfied with their child's school, a substantial minority is not. Unhappy parents are driving the push for school reform.

Blacks are least likely to be "very satisfied" with their child's school

(percent of children in kindergarten through 12th grade whose parents are "very satisfied" with their child's school, by race and Hispanic origin, 2006–07)

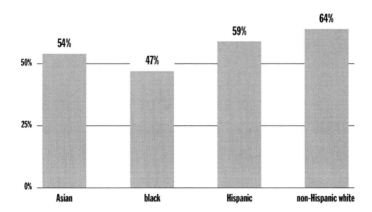

Table 2.14 Parental Satisfaction with School, 2006–07

(total number, percent distribution, and percent of elementary and secondary school children whose parents report satisfaction with school characteristics and amount of homework, by selected characteristics of child and parent, 2006–07)

	total		parent reports being "very satisfied"					
	number	percent	with the school	with teachers student had this year	with academic standards of the school	with order and discipline at the school	with the way school staff interacts with parents	amount of homework assigned is about right
TOTAL CHILDREN	**51,600**	**100%**	**59%**	**64%**	**63%**	**62%**	**55%**	**75%**
Race and Hispanic origin of child								
Asian, non-Hispanic	1,566	100	54	59	56	57	50	67
Black, non-Hispanic	7,837	100	47	57	55	54	49	66
Hispanic	9,767	100	59	65	60	63	59	78
White, non-Hispanic	29,832	100	64	66	66	65	57	77
Educational attainment of parent								
Not a high school graduate	3,504	100	54	62	56	60	55	79
High school graduate	11,070	100	54	59	56	58	51	74
Vocational/technical or some college	14,844	100	55	61	59	57	53	73
Bachelor's degree	11,353	100	64	67	67	65	57	76
Graduate degree	10,829	100	68	70	71	70	62	76
School type								
Public, assigned	37,168	100	55	61	58	58	51	74
Public, chosen	7,951	100	63	68	67	63	59	72
Private, religious	4,560	100	81	79	84	83	77	80
Private, nonreligious	1,438	100	82	78	84	83	76	88
Student's grade level								
Kindergarten through second grade	11,516	100	69	78	69	72	67	80
Third through fifth grade	11,519	100	65	69	67	66	63	79
Sixth through eighth grade	12,058	100	55	58	60	59	51	71
Ninth through twelth grade	16,503	100	52	54	57	54	46	72
Poverty status								
Poor	10,012	100	56	64	59	57	56	73
Not poor	41,587	100	60	64	63	63	55	75

Source: National Center for Education Statistics, Parent and Family Involvement in Education, 2006–07 School Year, from the National Household Education Surveys Program of 2007, August 2008, Internet site http://nces.ed.gov/pubsearch/pubsinfo .asp?pubid=2008050; calculations by New Strategist

School Enrollment Is Projected to Rise

In the Northeast, however, public school enrollment may decline.

Between 2007 and 2017, enrollment in the nation's elementary and secondary schools is projected to rise by a substantial 9 percent, according to projections by the National Center for Education Statistics. Overall, the nation's schools will gain more than 4 million additional students during those years.

High school enrollment is projected to increase by only 3 percent between 2007 and 2017, while enrollment in pre-K through 8th grade is expected to rise by nearly 11 percent. Private school enrollment should increase more slowly than public school enrollment overall, and the number of high school students in private school is projected to decline.

Public school enrollment trends should differ dramatically by region and state between 2007 and 2017. In most Northeastern and some Midwestern states, public elementary and secondary school enrollment is projected to fall. In contrast, public school enrollment is projected to increase by 16 percent in the South and 13 percent in the West.

■ These projections were made before the financial crisis of 2008, the effects of which are likely to lower enrollment growth in states such as Nevada and Florida.

School enrollment is projected to climb the most in the South

(percent change in number of pre-K through 12th grade students in public schools, by region, 2007–17)

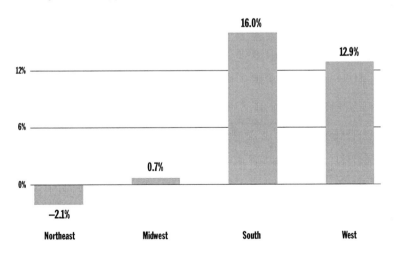

Table 2.15 Projected Enrollment in Prekindergarten through 12th Grade, 2007 and 2017

(number of people enrolled in prekindergarten through 12th grade by control of institution, fall 2007 and 2017; percent change, 2007–17; numbers in thousands)

	2007	2017	percent change 2007–17
TOTAL ENROLLED	**55,710**	**60,443**	**8.5%**
Pre-K through grade 8	39,271	43,465	10.7
Grades 9 through 12	16,439	16,978	3.3
Public enrollment	**49,644**	**54,087**	**9.0**
Pre-K through grade 8	34,589	38,399	11.0
Grades 9 through 12	15,055	15,689	4.2
Private enrollment	**6,066**	**6,356**	**4.8**
Pre-K through grade 8	4,681	5,066	8.2
Grades 9 through 12	1,385	1,290	–6.8

Source: National Center for Education Statistics, Projections of Education Statistics to 2017, Internet site http://nces.ed.gov/ programs/projections/projections2017/tables.asp; calculations by New Strategist

Table 2.16 Projected Enrollment in Prekindergarten through 12th Grade in Public Schools by State, 2007 and 2017

(number of people enrolled in prekindergarten through 12th grade in public schools by state, fall 2007 and 2017; percent change, 2007–17; numbers in thousands)

	2007	2017	percent change 2007–17
TOTAL ENROLLED	**49,644**	**54,087**	**8.9%**
Northeast	**8,123**	**7,953**	**–2.1**
Connecticut	566	539	–4.9
Maine	189	180	–4.9
Massachusetts	960	933	–2.8
New Hampshire	200	198	–1.1
New Jersey	1,393	1,419	1.9
New York	2,765	2,669	–3.5
Pennsylvania	1,810	1,794	–0.9
Rhode Island	148	136	–8.0
Vermont	92	85	–7.3
Midwest	**10,769**	**10,839**	**0.7**
Illinois	2,127	2,179	2.5
Indiana	1,043	1,066	2.2
Iowa	484	485	0.2
Kansas	462	474	2.6
Michigan	1,711	1,634	–4.5
Minnesota	833	874	4.9
Missouri	917	950	3.6
Nebraska	288	300	4.2
North Dakota	95	91	–4.4
Ohio	1,823	1,781	–2.3
South Dakota	121	122	1.2
Wisconsin	865	883	2.0
South	**18,581**	**21,553**	**16.0**
Alabama	749	761	1.6
Arkansas	480	521	8.6
Delaware	124	137	10.6
District of Columbia	76	88	15.2
Florida	2,771	3,448	24.4
Georgia	1,679	2,032	21.0
Kentucky	683	699	2.2
Louisiana	614	573	–6.6
Maryland	854	905	6.0
Mississippi	495	497	0.5
North Carolina	1,472	1,744	18.5
Oklahoma	639	681	6.7
South Carolina	704	756	7.3
Tennessee	968	1,054	8.8
Texas	4,759	6,014	26.4
Virginia	1,234	1,372	11.2
West Virginia	279	271	–2.8

	2007	2017	percent change 2007–17
West	**12,172**	**13,742**	**12.9%**
Alaska	134	150	11.9
Arizona	1,177	1,585	34.6
California	6,471	6,996	8.1
Colorado	803	927	15.4
Hawaii	183	207	12.9
Idaho	272	322	18.5
Montana	143	146	2.2
Nevada	444	590	33.0
New Mexico	329	363	10.3
Oregon	557	614	10.3
Utah	542	648	19.6
Washington	1,033	1,108	7.3
Wyoming	84	86	2.4

Source: National Center for Education Statistics, Projections of Education Statistics to 2017, Internet site http://nces.ed.gov/ programs/projections/projections2017/tables.asp; calculations by New Strategist

Fewer Students Are Dropping Out of High School

The dropout rate is stubbornly high among Hispanics, however.

Among people aged 16 to 24 in 2007, only 8.7 percent were neither high school graduates nor currently enrolled in school, down from 10.9 percent in 2000. Since 2000, dropout rates have fallen for both men and women and for every racial and ethnic group.

Dropout rates remain high for Hispanics. While just 5.3 percent of non-Hispanic whites and 8.4 percent of non-Hispanic blacks aged 16 to 24 have dropped out of high school, a much larger 21.4 percent of Hispanics are high school dropouts. Among Hispanic men, the dropout rate was 24.7 percent in 2007, down from 31.8 in 2000 but still shockingly high. Among Hispanic women aged 16 to 24, a smaller 18.0 percent were high school dropouts in 2007, down from 23.5 percent in 2000.

■ The arrival of millions of poorly educated immigrants to the United States during the past decade explains the high dropout rate among Hispanics. Some did not, in fact, drop out of an American high school, but arrived in the United States without a high school diploma.

Non-Hispanic whites have the lowest dropout rate

(percent of people aged 16 to 24 who were neither enrolled in school nor high school graduates, by race and Hispanic origin, 2007)

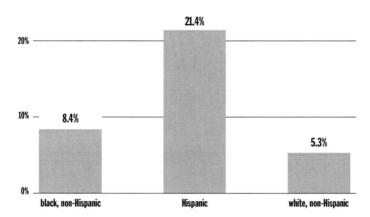

Table 2.17 High School Dropouts by Sex, Race, and Hispanic Origin, 1990 to 2007

(percentage of people aged 16 to 24 who were not enrolled in school and were not high school graduates by sex, race, and Hispanic origin, selected years, 1990 to 2007; percentage point change, 1990–2000 and 2000–07)

	2007	2000	1990	percentage point change 2000–07	percentage point change 1990–2000
TOTAL PEOPLE	**8.7%**	**10.9%**	**12.1%**	**–2.2**	**–1.2**
Black	8.4	13.1	13.2	–4.7	–0.1
Hispanic	21.4	27.8	32.4	–6.4	–4.6
White	5.3	6.9	9.0	–1.6	–2.1
Total men	**9.8**	**12.0**	**12.3**	**–2.2**	**–0.3**
Black	8.0	15.3	11.9	–7.3	3.4
Hispanic	24.7	31.8	34.3	–7.1	–2.5
White	6.0	7.0	9.3	–1.0	–2.3
Total women	**7.7**	**9.9**	**11.8**	**–2.2**	**–1.9**
Black	8.8	11.1	14.4	–2.3	–3.3
Hispanic	18.0	23.5	30.3	–5.5	–6.8
White	4.5	6.9	8.7	–2.4	–1.8

Note: Whites and blacks include Hispanics.
Source: National Center for Education Statistics, Digest of Education Statistics 2008; Internet site http://nces.ed.gov/pubsearch/pubsinfo.asp?pubid=2009020; calculations by New Strategist

Stability in High School Graduates

The number of people graduating from high school will decline slightly between 2007–08 and 2017–18.

As the postmillennial generation moves through the nation's high schools, the number of high school graduates will remain stable at about 3.3 million a year between 2007–08 and 2017–18. The number of public school graduates will barely change during those years, while the number of private school graduates is projected to fall by a substantial 11 percent.

College campuses, which have become accustomed to growing numbers of high school graduates, will have to adjust to the new stability. The changing demographics, coupled with economic uncertainty, suggest that change lies ahead for the nation's institutions of higher education.

■ Ten percent of the nation's high school graduates attended private school, a figure that is projected to decline to 9 percent by 2017–18.

Little change is forecast in the number of high school graduates

(number of high school graduates, 2007–08 and 2017–18)

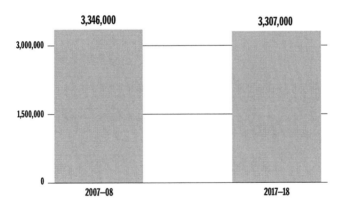

Table 2.18 Projections of High School Graduates, 2007–08 to 2017–18

(projected number of people graduating from high school by control of institution, 2007–08 to 2017–18; percent change 2007–08 to 2017–18; numbers in thousands)

	total	public	private
2007–08	3,346	3,026	320
2008–09	3,328	3,011	317
2009–10	3,327	3,005	321
2010–11	3,286	2,973	313
2011–12	3,234	2,925	309
2012–13	3,235	2,933	302
2013–14	3,197	2,903	295
2014–15	3,199	2,910	288
2015–16	3,231	2,952	279
2016–17	3,250	2,976	273
2017–18	3,307	3,021	286
Percent change			
2007–08 to 2017–18	−1.2%	−0.1%	−10.7%

Source: National Center for Education Statistics, Projections of Education Statistics to 2017, Internet site http://nces.ed.gov/ programs/projections/projections2017/tables.asp; calculations by New Strategist

SAT Scores Vary by Income and Parent's Education

The more educated the parent, the higher the child's score.

It is well known that Scholastic Aptitude Test scores vary by race and Hispanic origin. Asians and whites get higher scores than blacks or Hispanics. It is also no surprise that students with the best grades get the highest scores. Students with an A+ grade point average (97 to 100) averaged a 615 out of 800 on the math section of the SAT in 2007–08, for example. Students with a B grade point average (80 to 89) scored a much lower 484 on the math section of the test.

SAT scores also vary by family income and parental education. Students with family incomes below $20,000 scored a 456 on the math portion of the SAT in 2007–08 compared with a score of 570 among students with family incomes of $200,000 or more. Parental education also has a big impact on test scores. Among students with a parent who did not graduate from high school, the average SAT math score was 441. Among those whose parent had a graduate degree, the average math score was 565.

■ Affluent, educated parents can afford SAT prep courses for their children, which can boost test scores.

Parent's education influences child's test score

(average SAT mathematics score by highest level of parental education, 2007–08)

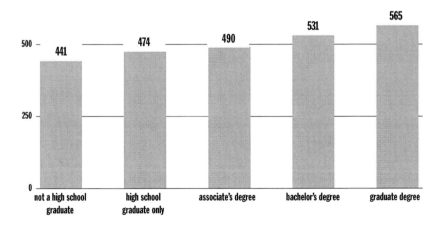

Table 2.19 SAT Scores by Selected Characteristics, 2007–08

(SAT scores by selected characteristics, 2007–08)

	critical reading	mathematics	writing
TOTAL	**502**	**515**	**494**
Sex			
Men	504	533	488
Women	500	500	501
Race and Hispanic origin			
American Indian or Alaska Native	485	491	470
Asian or Pacific Islander	513	581	516
Black	430	426	424
Mexican American	454	463	447
Puerto Rican	456	453	445
Other Hispanic	455	461	448
White	528	537	518
High school grade point average			
A+ (97 to 100)	595	615	592
A (93 to 96)	559	578	555
A– (90 to 92)	529	547	523
B (80 to 89)	474	484	465
C (70 to 79)	421	423	408
D or F (below 70)	402	411	390
Family income			
Less than $20,000	434	456	430
$20,000 to $39,999	462	473	453
$40,000 o $59,999	488	496	477
$60,000 to $79,999	502	510	490
$80,000 to $99,999	514	525	504
$100,000 to $119,999	522	534	512
$120,000 to $139,999	526	537	517
$140,000 to $159,999	533	546	525
$160,000 to $199,999	535	548	529
$200,000 or more	554	570	552
Highest level of parental education			
Not a high school graduate	419	441	417
High school graduate	464	474	455
Associate's degree	482	490	471
Bachelor's degree	518	531	510
Graduate degree	553	565	546

Source: National Center for Education Statistics, Digest of Education Statistics 2008; Internet site http://nces.ed.gov/ pubsearch/pubsinfo.asp?pubid=2009020; calculations by New Strategist

College Enrollment Rates Are at a Peak

The cost of college is taking a toll on enrollment rates.

The rate at which high school graduates enroll in college is higher today than in 1990, but lower than it was a few years ago. Among men and women aged 16 to 24 who graduated from high school in 2007, two out of three had enrolled in college (either two-year or four-year schools) within 12 months. Women's 2007 enrollment rate was 6 percentage points higher than their 62 percent rate of 1990, but down from the rates of 2004 and 2005. Men's college enrollment rate grew by 8 percentage points between 1990 and 2007, but is slightly below the rate of 2005.

The 2007 college enrollment rates of blacks and whites were below the all-time highs reached in 2004 among blacks and 2005 among whites. An examination of enrollment rates by type of institution reveals that the decline in enrollment rates has been limited to four-year schools. In contrast, two-year schools are enjoying record enrollment rates. Among male high school graduates in 2006, 25 percent enrolled in a two-year college and 41 percent enrolled in a four-year school. The figures were almost identical for their female counterparts.

■ The economic downturn is likely to spur an enrollment surge at less-expensive two-year schools and a drop in enrollment rates at four-year institutions.

Enrollment rates were higher in 2007 than in 1990

(percent of people aged 16 to 24 who graduated from high school in the previous 12 months and were enrolled in college as of October of each year, by sex, 1990 and 2007

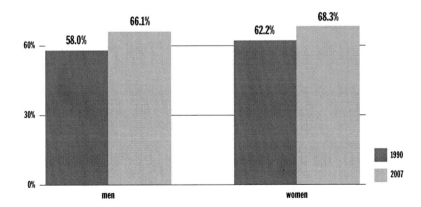

Table 2.20 College Enrollment Rates by Sex, 1990 to 2007

(percentage of people aged 16 to 24 who graduated from high school in the previous 12 months and were enrolled in college as of October, by sex, 1990 to 2007; percentage point change in enrollment rate, 1990–2007)

	total	men	women
2007	67.2%	66.1%	68.3%
2006	66.0	65.8	66.1
2005	68.6	66.5	70.4
2004	66.7	61.4	71.5
2003	63.9	61.2	66.5
2002	65.2	62.1	68.4
2001	61.8	60.1	63.5
2000	63.3	59.9	66.2
1999	62.9	61.4	64.4
1998	65.6	62.4	69.1
1997	67.0	63.6	70.3
1996	65.0	60.1	69.7
1995	61.9	62.6	61.3
1994	61.9	60.6	63.2
1993	62.6	59.9	65.2
1992	61.9	60.0	63.8
1991	62.5	57.9	67.1
1990	60.1	58.0	62.2
Percentage point change			
1990 to 2007	7.1	8.1	6.1

Source: National Center for Education Statistics, Digest of Education Statistics 2008, Internet site http://nces.ed.gov/ pubsearch/pubsinfo.asp?pubid=2009020; calculations by New Strategist

Table 2.21 College Enrollment Rates by Race and Hispanic Origin, 1990 to 2007

(percentage of people aged 16 to 24 who graduated from high school in the previous 12 months and were enrolled in college as of October, by race and Hispanic origin, 1990 to 2007; percentage point change in enrollment rate, 1990–2007)

	total	non-Hispanic black	non-Hispanic white	Hispanic
2007	67.2%	55.7%	69.5%	–
2006	66.0	55.5	68.5	58.6%
2005	68.6	55.7	73.2	57.9
2004	66.7	62.5	68.8	58.1
2003	63.9	57.5	66.2	58.0
2002	65.2	59.4	69.1	54.6
2001	61.8	55.0	64.3	52.7
2000	63.3	54.9	65.7	49.0
1999	62.9	58.9	66.3	47.5
1998	65.6	61.9	68.5	51.8
1997	67.0	58.5	68.2	54.6
1996	65.0	56.0	67.4	56.7
1995	61.9	51.2	64.3	51.2
1994	61.9	50.8	64.5	55.0
1993	62.6	55.6	62.9	55.4
1992	61.9	48.2	64.3	58.1
1991	62.5	46.4	65.4	51.6
1990	60.1	46.8	63.0	51.7
Percentage point change				
1990 to 2007	7.1	8.9	6.5	6.9

Note: "–" means not available; Hispanic enrollment rates are a three-year moving average. Percentage point change in Hispanic enrollment rate is from 1990 to 2006 three-year moving average.
Source: National Center for Education Statistics, Digest of Education Statistics 2008; Internet site http://nces.ed.gov/pubsearch/pubsinfo.asp?pubid=2009020; calculations by New Strategist

Table 2.22 College Enrollment Rate by Sex and Type of Institution, 1990 to 2006

(percentage of people aged 16 to 24 who graduated from high school in the previous 12 months and were enrolled in college as of October, by sex and type of institution, 1990 to 2006; percentage point change, 1990–2006)

	men			women		
	total	two-year	four-year	total	two-year	four-year
2006	65.8%	24.9%	40.9%	66.1%	24.5%	41.7%
2005	66.5	24.7	41.8	70.4	23.4	47.0
2004	61.4	21.8	39.6	71.5	23.1	48.5
2003	61.2	21.9	39.3	66.5	21.0	45.5
2002	62.1	20.5	41.7	68.4	23.0	45.3
2001	60.1	18.6	41.1	63.5	20.7	42.9
2000	59.9	23.1	36.8	66.2	20.0	46.2
1999	61.4	21.0	40.5	64.4	21.1	43.3
1998	62.4	24.4	38.0	69.1	24.3	44.8
1997	63.6	21.4	42.2	70.3	24.1	46.2
1996	60.1	21.5	38.5	69.7	24.6	45.1
1995	62.6	25.3	37.4	61.3	18.1	43.2
1994	60.6	23.0	37.5	63.2	19.1	44.1
1993	59.9	22.9	37.0	65.2	22.8	42.4
1992	60.0	22.1	37.8	63.8	23.9	40.0
1991	57.9	22.9	35.0	67.1	26.8	40.3
1990	58.0	19.6	38.4	62.2	20.6	41.6
Percentage point change						
1990 to 2006	7.8	5.3	2.5	3.9	3.9	0.1

Source: National Center for Education Statistics, The Condition of Education, Internet site http://nces.ed.gov/programs/coe/2008/section3/indicator24.asp;calculations by New Strategist

College Costs Have More than Doubled in Three Decades

The increasing cost of a college education is making it harder for low- and middle-income students to attend.

Between 1977–78 and 2007–08, the average cost of attending a four-year college (including tuition, fees, room, and board) more than doubled, rising from $8,881 to $18,670 after adjusting for inflation. The cost of attending a public college grew by 95 percent during those years (to $12,944), while private college costs rose by a larger 112 percent (to $29,307).

With this kind of increase in the cost of college, it is no surprise that children from families with high incomes are much more likely to attend college than those from low- or middle-income families. In 2006, 81 percent of children from high-income families enrolled in college. This enrollment rate was much higher than the 61 percent of children from middle-income families and the 51 percent of children from low-income families. Similarly, children whose parents have a college degree (who also tend to be more affluent) are far more likely to enroll in college than children whose parents are less educated.

■ College enrollment rates fell between 2005 and 2006 in every income group and most education groups.

College enrollment rate increases with family income

(percent of people aged 16 to 24 who graduated from high school in the previous 12 months and were enrolled in college as of October, by family income, 2006)

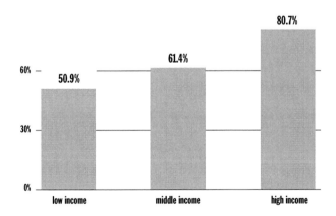

Table 2.23 College Costs, 1977–78 to 2007–08

(average annual tuition, fees, room, and board for undergraduate programs at four-year institutions, by control of school, 1977–78 to 2007–08; in 2007 dollars)

	total institutions	public institutions	private institutions
2007–08	$18,670	$12,944	$29,307
2006–07	18,471	12,797	28,919
2005–06	17,898	12,421	28,023
2004–05	17,581	12,168	27,962
2003–04	17,009	11,709	27,501
2002–03	16,186	10,971	26,665
2001–02	15,625	10,535	26,230
2000–01	15,066	10,089	25,481
1999–00	14,894	9,978	24,968
1998–99	14,749	9,959	24,725
1997–98	14,233	9,685	24,069
1996–97	13,926	9,422	23,691
1995–96	13,649	9,267	23,270
1994–95	13,203	9,053	22,533
1993–94	12,979	8,887	22,204
1992–93	12,543	8,622	21,498
1991–92	12,167	8,409	21,059
1990–91	11,588	7,992	20,178
1989–90	11,594	7,999	19,749
1988–89	11,328	7,880	19,327
1987–88	11,053	7,759	18,784
1986–87	10,945	7,594	18,425
1985–86	10,326	7,238	17,312
1984–85	9,960	7,106	16,310
1983–84	9,521	6,885	15,562
1982–83	9,164	6,647	14,821
1981–82	8,570	6,227	13,731
1980–81	8,247	6,010	13,182
1979–80	8,328	6,120	13,181
1978–79	8,694	6,392	13,737
1977–78	8,881	6,642	13,820
Percent change			
1977–78 to 2007–08	110.2%	94.9%	112.1%

Source: National Center for Education Statistics, Digest of Education Statistics 2008, Internet site http://nces.ed.gov/pubsearch/pubsinfo.asp?pubid=2009020; calculations by New Strategist

Table 2.24 College Enrollment Rate by Family Income, 1990 to 2006

(percentage of people aged 16 to 24 who graduated from high school in the previous 12 months and were enrolled in college as of October, by family income level, 1990 to 2006; percentage point change, 1990–2006)

| | | family income level | | |
	total	low	middle	high
2006	66.0%	50.9%	61.4%	80.7%
2005	68.6	53.5	65.1	81.2
2004	66.7	47.8	63.3	80.1
2003	63.9	52.8	57.6	80.1
2002	65.2	56.4	60.7	78.2
2001	61.8	43.8	56.3	79.9
2000	63.3	49.7	59.5	76.9
1999	62.9	49.4	59.4	76.1
1998	65.6	46.4	64.7	77.5
1997	67.0	57.0	60.7	82.2
1996	65.0	48.6	62.7	78.0
1995	61.9	34.2	56.0	83.5
1994	61.9	43.3	57.8	77.9
1993	62.6	50.4	56.9	79.3
1992	61.9	40.9	57.0	79.0
1991	62.5	39.8	58.4	78.2
1990	60.1	46.7	54.4	76.6
Percentage point change				
1990 to 2006	5.9	4.2	7.0	4.1

Note: Low income refers to the bottom 20 percent of all family incomes, high income refers to the top 20 percent of all family incomes, and middle income refers to the 60 percent in between.
Source: National Center for Education Statistics, The Condition of Education, Internet site http://nces.ed.gov/programs/coe/2008/section3/indicator24.asp;calculations by New Strategist

Table 2.25 College Enrollment Rate by Parents' Education, 1992 to 2006

(percentage of people aged 16 to 24 who graduated from high school in the previous 12 months and were en-rolled in college as of October, by highest level of parental education, 1992 to 2006; percentage point change, 1992–2006)

| | total | parents' highest level of education | | | |
		less than high school	high school graduate	some college	bachelor's degree or more
2006	66.0%	43.0%	56.1%	67.0%	78.2%
2005	68.6	43.0	62.1	65.6	88.8
2004	66.7	40.2	53.8	67.0	85.9
2003	63.9	43.3	53.9	62.9	82.1
2002	65.2	43.3	51.9	65.9	82.6
2001	61.8	39.0	51.9	62.0	81.3
2000	63.3	44.4	51.8	63.8	81.2
1999	62.9	36.3	54.4	60.3	82.2
1998	65.6	49.8	57.2	67.7	82.3
1997	67.0	51.4	61.7	62.6	86.1
1996	65.0	45.0	56.1	66.6	85.2
1995	61.9	27.3	47.0	70.2	87.7
1994	61.9	43.0	49.9	65.0	82.5
1993	62.6	47.1	52.3	62.7	87.9
1992	61.9	33.1	55.5	67.5	81.3
Percentage point change					
1992 to 2006	4.1	9.9	0.6	−0.5	−3.1

Source: National Center for Education Statistics, The Condition of Education, Internet site http://nces.ed.gov/programs/coe/2008/section3/indicator24.asp; calculations by New Strategist

More Americans Attend College

The number of full-time students at four-year private schools has fallen since 2005, however.

Between 2000 and 2007, the number of students enrolled in college—from two-year schools through graduate school—climbed 17 percent to nearly 18 million. Enrollment at two-year schools increased more than enrollment at four-year schools during those years (24 versus 12 percent) and full-time enrollment grew much faster than part-time (25 versus 3 percent). But a closer look at the numbers reveals that enrollment in some institutions of higher education is falling. The number of full-time students attending four-year private colleges peaked in 2005 at 2.1 million and has fallen 12 percent since then, to 1.8 million. In contrast, full-time students at four-year public universities reached a record high of more than 6 million in 2007.

On the nation's college campuses, women outnumber men by a wide margin. Among students attending two-year schools, women account for 57 percent of students. Among undergraduates at four-year schools, women outnumber men by nearly 1 million and account for 55 percent of the student body. At the graduate school level, women are an even larger 60 percent of the total.

■ The number of full-time students at private four-year colleges had begun to decline even before the economic downturn. Expect to see continuing declines in the years ahead.

Among undergraduates at four-year schools, women outnumber men by nearly 1 million

(number of undergraduates who attend four-year institutions, by sex, 2007)

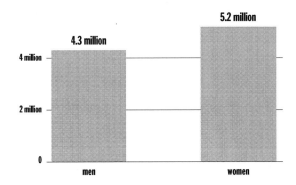

Table 2.26 College Enrollment by Type of College and Attendance Status, 2000 to 2007

(number of students aged 14 or older enrolled in college by type of college and attendance status, 2000 to 2007; percent change in enrollment for selected years; numbers in thousands)

	total	full-time	part-time
TOTAL COLLEGE STUDENTS			
2007	17,956	12,655	5,299
2006	17,232	12,070	5,162
2005	17,473	12,238	5,235
2004	17,382	11,989	5,393
2003	16,638	11,490	5,148
2002	16,498	11,141	5,356
2001	15,873	10,404	5,469
2000	15,314	10,159	5,155
Percent change			
2000 to 2007	17.3%	24.6%	2.8%
TWO-YEAR COLLEGES			
2007	4,813	2,988	1,825
2006	4,294	2,699	1,595
2005	4,327	2,632	1,695
2004	4,340	2,602	1,738
2003	4,384	2,563	1,822
2002	4,378	2,464	1,914
2001	4,159	2,310	1,850
2000	3,881	2,193	1,688
Percent change			
2000 to 2007	24.0%	36.3%	8.1%
FOUR-YEAR COLLEGES			
2007	9,550	7,877	1,673
2006	9,560	7,681	1,879
2005	9,842	8,019	1,823
2004	9,664	7,816	1,848
2003	8,986	7,305	1,680
2002	9,048	7,271	1,776
2001	8,393	6,696	1,696
2000	8,520	6,698	1,822
Percent change			
2000 to 2007	12.1%	17.6%	−8.2%
GRADUATE SCHOOL			
2007	3,591	1,790	1,801
2006	3,378	1,690	1,688
2005	3,304	1,587	1,717
2004	3,378	1,571	1,807
2003	3,268	1,622	1,646
2002	3,072	1,406	1,666
2001	3,321	1,398	1,923
2000	2,913	1,268	1,645
Percent change			
2000 to 2007	23.3%	41.2%	9.5%

Source: Bureau of the Census, School Enrollment, Historical Tables, Internet site http://www.census.gov/population/www/socdemo/school.html; calculations by New Strategist

Table 2.27 **Number of Undergraduates Enrolled Full-Time in Four-Year Colleges by Control of School, 2000 to 2007**

(number of students aged 14 or older enrolled full-time in four-year undergraduate institutions of higher education by control of school, 2000 to 2007; percent change in enrollment, 2000–07 and 2005–07; numbers in thousands)

	total	public	private
2007	7,877	6,058	1,819
2006	7,681	5,883	1,798
2005	8,019	5,941	2,077
2004	7,816	5,938	1,878
2003	7,305	5,693	1,612
2002	7,271	5,497	1,774
2001	6,696	5,046	1,650
2000	6,698	4,971	1,726
Percent change			
2005 to 2007	−1.8%	2.0%	−12.4%
2000 to 2007	17.6	21.9	5.4

Source: Bureau of the Census, School Enrollment, Historical Tables, Internet site http://www.census.gov/population/www/socdemo/school.html; calculations by New Strategist

Table 2.28 College Students by Age and Sex, 2007

(number, percent, and percent distribution of people aged 15 or older enrolled in institutions of higher education, by type of institution, age, and sex, 2007; numbers in thousands)

		men		women	
	total	total	percent of total	total	percent of total
TOTAL COLLEGE STUDENTS					
Total students	**17,956**	**7,826**	**43.6%**	**10,130**	**56.4%**
Aged 15 to 19	4,261	1,980	46.5	2,281	53.5
Aged 20 to 24	7,086	3,253	45.9	3,834	54.1
Aged 25 to 34	3,838	1,625	42.3	2,212	57.6
Aged 35 or older	2,772	968	34.9	1,804	65.1
TWO-YEAR UNDERGRADUATE					
Total students	**4,813**	**2,061**	**42.8**	**2,753**	**57.2**
Aged 15 to 19	1,497	703	47.0	792	52.9
Aged 20 to 24	1,630	728	44.7	902	55.3
Aged 25 to 34	963	394	40.9	569	59.1
Aged 35 or older	725	236	32.6	488	67.3
FOUR-YEAR UNDERGRADUATE					
Total students	**9,550**	**4,345**	**45.5**	**5,207**	**54.5**
Aged 15 to 19	2,741	1,265	46.2	1,476	53.8
Aged 20 to 24	4,614	2,196	47.6	2,419	52.4
Aged 25 to 34	1,314	568	43.2	746	56.8
Aged 35 or older	881	315	35.8	565	64.1
GRADUATE SCHOOL					
Total students	**3,591**	**1,421**	**39.6**	**2,171**	**60.5**
Aged 15 to 19	24	12	50.0	13	54.2
Aged 20 to 24	841	329	39.1	513	61.0
Aged 25 to 34	1,560	663	42.5	898	57.6
Aged 35 or older	1,167	417	35.7	749	64.2

Source: Bureau of the Census, School Enrollment—Social and Economic Characteristics of Students: October 2007, Internet site http://www.census.gov/population/www/socdemo/school/cps2007.html; calculations by New Strategist

Table 2.29 College Students by Age, Type of School, and Attendance Status, 2007

(number, percent, and percent distribution of people aged 15 or older enrolled in institutions of higher education, by age, type of school, and attendance status, 2007; numbers in thousands)

	total	two-year school			four-year school			graduate school		
		number	share of total students in age group	percent distribution	number	share of total students in age group	percent distribution	number	share of total students in age group	percent distribution
TOTAL COLLEGE STUDENTS										
Total students	**17,956**	**4,813**	**26.8%**	**100.0%**	**9,550**	**53.2%**	**100.0%**	**3,591**	**20.0%**	**100.0%**
Aged 15 to 19	4,261	1,497	35.1	31.1	2,741	64.3	28.7	24	0.6	0.7
Aged 20 to 24	7,086	1,630	23.0	33.9	4,614	65.1	48.3	841	11.9	23.4
Aged 25 to 34	3,838	963	25.1	20.0	1,314	34.2	13.8	1,560	40.6	43.4
Aged 35 or older	2,772	725	26.2	15.1	881	31.8	9.2	1,167	42.1	32.5
TOTAL FULL-TIME STUDENTS										
Total students	**12,656**	**2,988**	**23.6**	**100.0**	**7,877**	**62.2**	**100.0**	**1,790**	**14.1**	**100.0**
Aged 15 to 19	3,902	1,276	32.7	42.7	2,603	66.7	33.0	23	0.6	1.3
Aged 20 to 24	5,767	1,051	18.2	35.2	4,087	70.9	51.9	627	10.9	35.0
Aged 25 to 34	2,100	442	21.0	14.8	842	40.1	10.7	815	38.8	45.5
Aged 35 or older	887	219	24.7	7.3	344	38.8	4.4	325	36.6	18.2
TOTAL PART-TIME STUDENTS										
Total students	**5,300**	**1,825**	**34.4**	**100.0**	**1,673**	**31.6**	**100.0**	**1,801**	**34.0**	**100.0**
Aged 15 to 19	359	221	61.6	12.1	138	38.4	8.2	1	0.3	0.1
Aged 20 to 24	1,319	579	43.9	31.7	527	40.0	31.5	214	16.2	11.9
Aged 25 to 34	1,738	521	30.0	28.5	472	27.2	28.2	745	42.9	41.4
Aged 35 or older	1,885	506	26.8	27.7	537	28.5	32.1	842	44.7	46.8

Source: Bureau of the Census, School Enrollment—Social and Economic Characteristics of Students: October 2007, Internet site http://www.census.gov/population/www/socdemo/school/cps2007.html; calculations by New Strategist

More than 30 Percent of College Students Are Minorities

Among the nation's 18 million college students, nearly 6 million are black, Hispanic, Asian, or American Indian.

College campuses are becoming more diverse. Non-Hispanic whites accounted for 64 percent of all college students in 2007, down from 68 percent in 2000. Among students at two-years schools, 38 percent are minorities. At four-year schools, the minority share is a smaller 29 percent.

Non-Hispanic whites received 72 percent of bachelor's degrees awarded in 2006–07. Blacks earned 10 percent, Hispanics and Asians 7 to 8 percent. Non-Hispanic whites earn a much smaller proportion of degrees at the doctoral level (56 percent)—not because minorities are better represented, but because foreign students make up a large share of those earning degrees. Twenty-eight percent of doctoral degrees awarded in 2006–07 went to nonresident aliens.

■ The educational attainment of blacks and Hispanics is inching upward at a painfully slow rate. The current economic downturn may halt their progress.

Blacks, Hispanics, and Asians account for a significant share of college students

(percent distribution of college students by race and Hispanic origin, 2007)

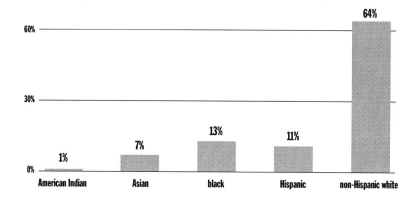

Table 2.30 College Students by Race, Hispanic Origin, and Type of Institution, 2000 and 2007

(number and percent distribution of people enrolled in institutions of higher education by race, Hispanic origin, and type of institution, fall 2000 and fall 2007; percent change in number, 2000–07; numbers in thousands)

	2007		2000		percent change in number, 2000–07
	number	percent distribution	number	percent distribution	
TOTAL ENROLLMENT	**18,248**	**100.0%**	**15,312**	**100.0%**	**19.2%**
White, non-Hispanic	11,756	64.4	10,462	68.3	12.4
Minority, total	5,867	32.2	4,322	28.2	35.8
American Indian	190	1.0	151	1.0	25.7
Asian	1,218	6.7	978	6.4	24.5
Black, non-Hispanic	2,383	13.1	1,730	11.3	37.7
Hispanic	2,076	11.4	1,462	9.5	42.0
Nonresident alien	625	3.4	529	3.5	18.2
Two-year schools	**6,618**	**100.0**	**5,948**	**100.0**	**11.3**
White, non-Hispanic	3,975	60.1	3,804	64.0	4.5
Minority, total	2,547	38.5	2,055	34.6	23.9
American Indian	81	1.2	75	1.3	8.4
Asian	456	6.9	402	6.8	13.5
Black, non-Hispanic	942	14.2	735	12.4	28.2
Hispanic	1,067	16.1	844	14.2	26.4
Nonresident alien	96	1.5	89	1.5	7.9
Four-year schools	**11,630**	**100.0**	**9,364**	**100.0**	**24.2**
White, non-Hispanic	7,781	66.9	6,658	71.1	16.9
Minority, total	3,320	28.5	2,266	24.2	46.5
American Indian	109	0.9	76	0.8	43.4
Asian	761	6.5	576	6.2	32.1
Black, non-Hispanic	1,442	12.4	995	10.6	44.9
Hispanic	1,009	8.7	618	6.6	63.3
Nonresident alien	529	4.5	440	4.7	20.2

Source: National Center for Education Statistics, Digest of Education Statistics 2008, Internet site http://nces.ed.gov/pubsearch/pubsinfo.asp?pubid=2009020; calculations by New Strategist

Table 2.31 Degrees Conferred by Race and Hispanic Origin, 2006–07

(number and percent distribution of degrees conferred by institutions of higher education by level of degree, race, and Hispanic origin of degree holder, 2006–07)

	number	percent distribution
TOTAL DEGREES	**3,007,493**	**100.0%**
American Indian	24,543	0.8
Asian	193,924	6.4
Black	310,957	10.3
Hispanic	241,902	8.0
White, non-Hispanic	2,089,306	69.5
Nonresident alien	146,861	4.9
Associate's degrees	**728,114**	**100.0**
American Indian	8,583	1.2
Asian	37,266	5.1
Black	91,529	12.6
Hispanic	85,410	11.7
White, non-Hispanic	491,572	67.5
Nonresident alien	13,754	1.9
Bachelor's degrees	**1,524,092**	**100.0**
American Indian	11,455	0.8
Asian	105,297	6.9
Black	146,653	9.6
Hispanic	114,936	7.5
White, non-Hispanic	1,099,850	72.2
Nonresident alien	45,901	3.0
Master's degrees	**604,607**	**100.0**
American Indian	3,575	0.6
Asian	36,134	6.0
Black	62,574	10.3
Hispanic	34,822	5.8
White, non-Hispanic	399,267	66.0
Nonresident alien	68,235	11.3
Doctoral degrees	**60,616**	**100.0**
American Indian	249	0.4
Asian	3,541	5.8
Black	3,727	6.1
Hispanic	2,034	3.4
White, non-Hispanic	34,071	56.2
Nonresident alien	16,994	28.0
First-professional degrees	**90,064**	**100.0**
American Indian	681	0.8
Asian	11,686	13.0
Black	6,474	7.2
Hispanic	4,700	5.2
White, non-Hispanic	64,546	71.7
Nonresident alien	1,977	2.2

Source: National Center for Education Statistics, Digest of Education Statistics 2008, Internet site http://nces.ed.gov/pubsearch/pubsinfo.asp?pubid=2009020; calculations by New Strategist

Earning a Bachelor's Degree Often Takes More than Five Years

Earning an associate's degree takes more than four years, on average.

Many students spend more than four years getting their bachelor's degree, according to data from the Census Bureau's Survey of Income and Program Participation. In fact, many students spend more than four years earning an associate's degree. Americans aged 18 or older who have a bachelor's degree report spending an average of 5.6 years working on their degree from start to finish. Those with an associate's degree spent 4.4 years from start to finish.

Among all Americans aged 18 or older with a bachelor's degree, 55 percent finished on time—in four years. A substantial 45 percent spent five or more years working on their degree. Women are more likely than men to graduate in four years (59 versus 51 percent). Non-Hispanic whites are more likely to graduate on time than blacks or Hispanics (56 percent versus 51 and 48 percent, respectively).

■ The high cost of college is one reason why it takes many students extra time to finish their degree. Rather than attending school full-time, they take classes part-time while earning money to pay for school.

Nearly half of college graduates spent at least five years earning their bachelor's degree

(percent distribution of bachelor's degree holders by length of time from start to finish of degree, 2004)

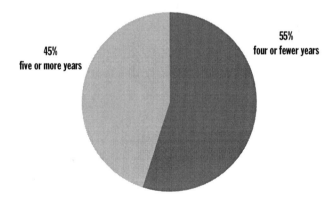

45%
five or more years

55%
four or fewer years

Table 2.32 Average Years to Complete Associate's Degree, 2004

(number and percent distribution of people aged 18 or older whose highest degree is associate's by length of time from high school graduation to start of degree program and time to finish degree, 2004; numbers in thousands)

	total	time from high school to start of degree			time from start to completion of degree			
		same year	within two years	three years or more	under one year	one to three years	four years or more	average years to completion
TOTAL PEOPLE WITH ASSOCIATE'S DEGREE	**16,864**	**8,674**	**3,499**	**4,691**	**415**	**10,661**	**5,788**	**4.4**
Sex								
Men	7,428	3,616	1,637	2,175	157	4,676	2,594	4.4
Women	9,437	5,058	1,863	2,516	258	5,985	3,194	4.3
Race and Hispanic origin								
Black	1,678	699	397	582	63	986	629	4.8
Hispanic	1,376	656	431	289	35	896	445	4.0
Non-Hispanic white	12,847	6,843	2,483	3,521	292	8,167	4,388	4.3
Percent distribution								
TOTAL PEOPLE WITH ASSOCIATE'S DEGREE	**100.0%**	**51.4%**	**20.7%**	**27.8%**	**2.5%**	**63.2%**	**34.3%**	–
Sex								
Men	100.0	48.7	22.0	29.3	2.1	63.0	34.9	–
Women	100.0	53.6	19.7	26.7	2.7	63.4	33.8	–
Race and Hispanic origin								
Black	100.0	41.7	23.7	34.7	3.8	58.8	37.5	–
Hispanic	100.0	47.7	31.3	21.0	2.5	65.1	32.3	–
Non-Hispanic white	100.0	53.3	19.3	27.4	2.3	63.6	34.2	–

Note: "–" means not applicable.
Source: Bureau of the Census, What's It Worth: Field of Training and Economic Status in 2004, Detailed Tables, Internet site http://www.census.gov/population/www/socdemo/education/sipp2004w2.html; calculations by New Strategist

Table 2.33 Average Years to Start and Complete a Bachelor's Degree, 2004

(number and percent distribution of people aged 18 or older whose highest degree is bachelor's by length of time from high school graduation to start of degree program and time to finish degree, 2004; numbers in thousands)

| | total | time from high school to start of degree | | | time from start to completion of degree | | continuous enrollment | | avg. years to completion |
		same year	within two years	three years or more	four years or less	five years or more	continuous	not continuous	
TOTAL PEOPLE WITH BACHELOR'S DEGREE	**33,931**	**25,336**	**4,941**	**3,654**	**18,742**	**15,193**	**26,313**	**7,622**	**5.6**
Sex									
Men	16,401	11,762	2,653	1,986	8,406	7,996	12,425	3,977	5.8
Women	17,530	13,574	2,288	1,668	10,336	7,197	13,888	3,645	5.9
Race and Hispanic origin									
Black	2,444	1,681	446	317	1,242	1,201	1,821	622	6.0
Hispanic	1,635	1,115	325	195	777	857	1,277	357	5.9
Non-Hispanic white	27,137	20,646	3,618	2,873	15,128	12,012	20,980	6,161	5.9
Percent distribution									
TOTAL PEOPLE WITH BACHELOR'S DEGREE	**100.0%**	**74.7%**	**14.6%**	**10.8%**	**55.2%**	**44.8%**	**77.5%**	**22.5%**	**–**
Sex									
Men	100.0	71.7	16.2	12.1	51.3	48.8	75.8	24.2	–
Women	100.0	77.4	13.1	9.5	59.0	41.1	79.2	20.8	–
Race and Hispanic origin									
Black	100.0	68.8	18.2	13.0	50.8	49.1	74.5	25.5	–
Hispanic	100.0	68.2	19.9	11.9	47.5	52.4	78.1	21.8	–
Non-Hispanic white	100.0	76.1	13.3	10.6	55.7	44.3	77.3	22.7	–

Note: "–" means not applicable.
Source: Bureau of the Census, What's It Worth: Field of Training and Economic Status in 2004, Detailed Tables, Internet site http://www.census.gov/population/www/socdemo/education/sipp2004w2.html; calculations by New Strategist

Women Earn Most Degrees

Women earned at least half of degrees granted in 2006–07, from associate's through first-professional.

As women pursue careers, they are eager for credentials that command a premium wage. Women are now a significant presence in most degree programs and fields of study. Sixty-two percent of associate's degrees went to women in 2006–07, as did 57 percent of bachelor's degrees and 61 percent of master's degrees. Women earned only 18 percent of the bachelor's degrees in engineering and just 19 percent of those in computer science in 2006–07. But they accounted for 49 percent of bachelor's degrees awarded in business.

Women earned half of all doctorates and first-professional degrees awarded in 2006–07. They accounted for 49 percent of newly minted physicians, 48 percent of lawyers, 67 percent of pharmacists, and 78 percent of veterinarians.

■ Women's share of the nation's doctors, lawyers, and other professionals will continue to expand in the next few decades as young women now earning degrees replace older men retiring from the professions.

Men earn fewer degrees than women at every level but first-professional

(men's share of degrees awarded, by level of degree, 2006–07)

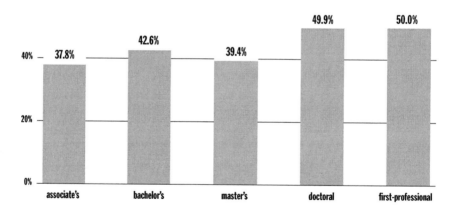

Table 2.34 Associate's Degrees Earned by Field of Study and Sex, 2006–07

(number of associate's degrees conferred by sex, and percent earned by women, by field of study, 2006–07)

	total	men	women number	women percent of total
Total associate's degrees	**728,114**	**275,187**	**452,927**	**62.2%**
Agriculture and natural resources	5,838	3,626	2,212	37.9
Architecture and related services	517	231	286	55.3
Area, ethnic, cultural, and gender studies	164	53	111	67.7
Biological and biomedical sciences	2,060	676	1,384	67.2
Business	116,101	41,413	74,688	64.3
Communications, journalism, and related programs	2,609	1,311	1,298	49.8
Communications technologies	3,095	1,874	1,221	39.5
Computer and information sciences	27,712	20,459	7,253	26.2
Construction trades	3,895	3,696	199	5.1
Education	13,021	1,773	11,248	86.4
Engineering	2,136	1,835	301	14.1
Engineering technologies	29,199	25,155	4,044	13.8
English language and literature/letters	1,249	378	871	69.7
Family and consumer sciences	9,124	333	8,791	96.4
Foreign languages, literatures, and linguistics	1,207	195	1,012	83.8
Health professions and related clinical sciences	145,436	21,214	124,222	85.4
Legal professions and studies	10,391	1,046	9,345	89.9
Liberal arts and sciences, general studies, and humanities	250,030	93,711	156,319	62.5
Library science	84	8	76	90.5
Mathematics and statistics	827	548	279	33.7
Mechanics and repair technologies	15,432	14,720	712	4.6
Military technologies	781	641	140	17.9
Multi/interdisciplinary studies	15,838	6,578	9,260	58.5
Parks, recreation, leisure, and fitness studies	1,251	749	502	40.1
Philosophy and religious studies	375	115	260	69.3
Physical sciences and science technologies	3,404	1,948	1,456	42.8
Precision production	1,973	1,849	124	6.3
Psychology	2,213	517	1,696	76.6
Public administration and social service professions	4,338	596	3,742	86.3
Security and protective services	28,208	15,481	12,727	45.1
Social sciences and history	7,080	2,494	4,586	64.8
Theology and religious vocations	608	313	295	48.5
Transportation and materials moving	1,674	1,442	232	13.9
Visual and performing arts	20,244	8,209	12,035	59.4

Source: National Center for Education Statistics, Digest of Education Statistics 2008, Internet site http://nces.ed.gov/pubsearch/ pubsinfo.asp?pubid=2009020; calculations by New Strategist

Table 2.35 Bachelor's Degrees Earned by Field of Study and Sex, 2006–07

(number of bachelor's degrees conferred by sex, and percent earned by women, by field of study, 2006–07)

	total	men	women number	women percent of total
Total bachelor's degrees	**1,524,092**	**649,570**	**874,522**	**57.4%**
Agriculture and natural resources	23,133	12,309	10,824	46.8
Architecture and related services	9,717	5,393	4,324	44.5
Area, ethnic, cultural, and gender studies	8,194	2,572	5,622	68.6
Biological and biomedical sciences	75,151	29,951	45,200	60.1
Business	327,531	166,350	161,181	49.2
Communications, journalism, and related programs	74,783	26,444	48,339	64.6
Communications technologies	3,637	2,565	1,072	29.5
Computer and information sciences	42,170	34,342	7,828	18.6
Construction trades	129	122	7	5.4
Education	105,641	22,516	83,125	78.7
Engineering	67,092	54,745	12,347	18.4
Engineering technologies	14,588	13,114	1,474	10.1
English language and literature/letters	55,122	17,475	37,647	68.3
Family and consumer sciences	21,400	2,594	18,806	87.9
Foreign languages, literatures, and linguistics	20,275	6,173	14,102	69.6
Health professions and related clinical sciences	101,810	14,325	87,485	85.9
Legal professions and studies	3,596	1,008	2,588	72.0
Liberal arts and sciences, general studies, and humanities	44,255	14,123	30,132	68.1
Library science	82	10	72	87.8
Mathematics and statistics	14,954	8,360	6,594	44.1
Mechanics and repair technologies	263	249	14	5.3
Military technologies	168	152	16	9.5
Multi/interdisciplinary studies	33,792	10,439	23,353	69.1
Parks, recreation, leisure, and fitness studies	27,430	14,190	13,240	48.3
Philosophy and religious studies	11,969	7,430	4,539	37.9
Physical sciences and science technologies	21,073	12,455	8,618	40.9
Precision production	23	12	11	47.8
Psychology	90,039	20,343	69,696	77.4
Public administration and social service professions	23,147	4,354	18,793	81.2
Security and protective services	39,206	19,505	19,701	50.2
Social sciences and history	164,183	82,417	81,766	49.8
Theology and religious vocations	8,696	5,761	2,935	33.8
Transportation and materials moving	5,657	5,043	614	10.9
Visual and performing arts	85,186	32,729	52,457	61.6

Source: National Center for Education Statistics, Digest of Education Statistics 2008, Internet site http://nces.ed.gov/pubsearch/pubsinfo.asp?pubid=2009020; calculations by New Strategist

Table 2.36 Master's Degrees Earned by Field of Study and Sex, 2006–07

(number of master's degrees conferred by sex, and percent earned by women, by field of study, 2006–07)

	total	men	women number	women percent of total
Total master's degrees	**604,607**	**238,189**	**366,418**	**60.6%**
Agriculture and natural resources	4,623	2,174	2,449	53.0
Architecture and related services	5,951	3,304	2,647	44.5
Area, ethnic, cultural, and gender studies	1,699	617	1,082	63.7
Biological and biomedical sciences	8,747	3,568	5,179	59.2
Business	150,211	84,115	66,096	44.0
Communications, journalism, and related programs	6,773	2,153	4,620	68.2
Communications technologies	499	332	167	33.5
Computer and information sciences	16,232	11,985	4,247	26.2
Construction trades	0	0	0	–
Education	176,572	40,164	136,408	77.3
Engineering	29,472	22,872	6,600	22.4
Engineering technologies	2,690	1,993	697	25.9
English language and literature/letters	8,742	2,867	5,875	67.2
Family and consumer sciences	2,080	292	1,788	86.0
Foreign languages, literatures, and linguistics	3,443	1,058	2,385	69.3
Health professions and related clinical sciences	54,531	10,636	43,895	80.5
Legal professions and studies	4,486	2,335	2,151	47.9
Liberal arts and sciences, general studies, and humanities	3,634	1,352	2,282	62.8
Library science	6,767	1,309	5,458	80.7
Mathematics and statistics	4,884	2,859	2,025	41.5
Mechanics and repair technologies	0	0	0	–
Military technologies	202	178	24	11.9
Multi/interdisciplinary studies	4,762	1,703	3,059	64.2
Parks, recreation, leisure, and fitness studies	4,110	2,116	1,994	48.5
Philosophy and religious studies	1,716	1,087	629	36.7
Physical sciences and science technologies	5,839	3,556	2,283	39.1
Precision production	5	2	3	60.0
Psychology	21,037	4,265	16,772	79.7
Public administration and social service professions	31,131	7,758	23,373	75.1
Security and protective services	4,906	2,315	2,591	52.8
Social sciences and history	17,665	8,577	9,088	51.4
Theology and religious vocations	6,446	544	2,537	39.4
Transportation and materials moving	985	44	157	15.9
Visual and performing arts	13,767	2,048	7,857	57.1

Note: "–" means not applicable
Source: National Center for Education Statistics, Digest of Education Statistics 2008, Internet site http://nces.ed.gov/pubsearch/pubsinfo.asp?pubid=2009020; calculations by New Strategist

Table 2.37 Doctoral Degrees Earned by Field of Study and Sex, 2006–07

(number of doctoral degrees conferred by sex, and percent earned by women, by field of study, 2006–07)

			women	
	total	men	number	percent of total
Total doctoral degrees	**60,616**	**30,251**	**30,365**	**50.1%**
Agriculture and natural resources	1,272	768	504	39.6
Architecture and related services	178	104	74	41.6
Area, ethnic, cultural, and gender studies	233	95	138	59.2
Biological and biomedical sciences	6,354	3,221	3,133	49.3
Business	2,029	1,188	841	41.4
Communications, journalism, and related programs	479	188	291	60.8
Communications technologies	1	0	1	100.0
Computer and information sciences	1,595	1,267	328	20.6
Education	8,261	2,681	5,580	67.5
Engineering	8,062	6,377	1,685	20.9
Engineering technologies	61	45	16	26.2
English language and literature/letters	1,178	478	700	59.4
Family and consumer sciences	337	73	264	78.3
Foreign languages, literatures, and linguistics	1,059	437	622	58.7
Health professions and related clinical sciences	8,355	2,242	6,113	73.2
Legal professions and studies	143	78	65	45.5
Liberal arts and sciences, general studies, and humanities	77	38	39	50.6
Library science	52	18	34	65.4
Mathematics and statistics	1,351	949	402	29.8
Multi/interdisciplinary studies	1,093	485	608	55.6
Parks, recreation, leisure, and fitness studies	218	109	109	50.0
Philosophy and religious studies	637	453	184	28.9
Physical sciences and science technologies	4,846	3,317	1,529	31.6
Psychology	5,153	1,382	3,771	73.2
Public administration and social service professions	726	253	473	65.2
Security and protective services	85	43	42	49.4
Social sciences and history	3,844	2,110	1,734	45.1
Theology and religious vocations	1,573	1,227	346	22.0
Visual and performing arts	1,364	625	739	54.2

Source: National Center for Education Statistics, Digest of Education Statistics 2008, Internet site http://nces.ed.gov/pubsearch/ pubsinfo.asp?pubid=2009020; calculations by New Strategist

Table 2.38 First-Professional Degrees Earned by Field of Study and Sex, 2006–07

(number of first-professional degrees conferred by sex, and percent earned by women, by field of study, 2006–07)

	total	men	women number	women percent of total
Total first-professional degrees	**90,064**	**45,057**	**45,007**	**50.0%**
Dentistry (D.D.S. or D.M.D.)	4,596	2,548	2,048	44.6
Medicine (M.D.)	15,730	7,987	7,743	49.2
Optometry (O.D.)	1,311	493	818	62.4
Osteopathic medicine (D.O.)	2,992	1,475	1,517	50.7
Pharmacy (Pharm.D.)	10,439	3,394	7,045	67.5
Podiatry (Pod.D., D.P., or D.P.M.)	331	173	158	47.7
Veterinary medicine (D.V.M.)	2,443	537	1,906	78.0
Chiropractic (D.C. or D.C.M.)	2,525	1,617	908	36.0
Naturopathic medicine	221	56	165	74.7
Law (LL.B. or J.D.)	43,486	22,777	20,709	47.6
Theology (M.Div., M.H.L., B.D., or Ord.)	5,990	4,000	1,990	33.2

Source: National Center for Education Statistics, Digest of Education Statistics 2008, Internet site http://nces.ed.gov/pubsearch/pubsinfo.asp?pubid=2009020; calculations by New Strategist

Many Participate in Adult Education

Work-related courses are most popular as Americans seek to upgrade their skills.

Fully 44 percent of people aged 16 or older took some type of adult education course in 2005. Among people under age 35, the majority participated in adult education. Work-related courses are most popular as workers seek ways to remain competitive in an unforgiving job market. Twenty-seven percent of people aged 16 or older took a work-related course in 2005. This type of course is particularly important for the middle aged, and more than one-third of people aged 35 to 54 took a work-related course. Personal-interest courses rank second in popularity, with 21 percent of the public taking a course for personal interest.

The well educated are most likely to seek further learning by participating in adult education. Sixty-three percent of people with at least a bachelor's degree took an adult education course in 2005 compared with only 33 percent of those who went no further than high school. The likelihood of participating in work-related and personal-interest courses rises with educational attainment.

■ Competition in the labor market has become the dominant force driving the adult education industry.

The middle aged are most likely to participate in work-related adult education

(percent of people aged 16 or older who participated in work-related adult education courses in the past 12 months, by age, 2005)

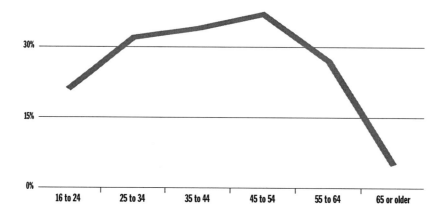

Table 2.39 Participation in Adult Education, 2005

(percent of people aged 16 or older who participated in formal adult education activities, by selected characteristics and type of adult education activity, 2005)

	total	percent participating in any activity	work-related courses	personal-interest courses	part-time degree or diploma programs
TOTAL PEOPLE	**100.0%**	**44.4%**	**26.9%**	**21.4%**	**5.0%**
Sex					
Female	100.0	47.5	29.2	24.3	5.1
Male	100.0	41.1	24.5	18.4	5.0
Age					
Aged 16 to 24	100.0	52.9	21.2	26.6	11.4
Aged 25 to 34	100.0	52.2	31.7	22.1	8.7
Aged 35 to 44	100.0	48.7	33.7	22.1	5.3
Aged 45 to 54	100.0	47.9	36.5	19.7	3.8
Aged 55 to 64	100.0	40.3	27.0	20.7	1.5
Aged 65 or older	100.0	22.9	5.2	18.8	0.3
Race and Hispanic origin					
Asian	100.0	48.3	27.2	26.5	7.9
Black, non-Hispanic	100.0	46.4	27.0	23.7	5.4
Hispanic	100.0	37.6	16.8	15.3	4.9
White, non-Hispanic	100.0	45.6	29.1	22.2	4.9
Education					
Less than high school	100.0	22.1	4.2	11.1	1.0
High school diploma	100.0	32.6	16.5	16.1	2.6
Some college/vocational/technical	100.0	51.4	31.4	24.9	7.7
Bachelor's degree or higher	100.0	62.5	46.2	29.5	7.3
Household income					
$15,000 or less	100.0	29.0	10.9	17.9	2.8
$15,001 to $30,000	100.0	30.7	14.6	15.1	4.9
$30,001 to $50,000	100.0	42.1	22.6	21.8	3.3
$50,001 to $75,000	100.0	47.7	33.0	20.5	5.8
$75,001 or more	100.0	57.6	39.0	27.0	6.7
Employment/occupation					
Employed in past 12 months	100.0	51.7	35.9	22.0	6.4
Professional or managerial	100.0	70.2	56.3	29.2	8.8
Services, sales, or support	100.0	48.3	30.6	22.0	6.3
Trades	100.0	34.0	18.7	12.9	3.3
Not employed in past 12 months	100.0	25.2	4.0	20.0	1.6

Source: National Center for Education Statistics, The Condition of Education, Participation in Adult Education, Indicator 10 (2007), Internet site http://nces.ed.gov/programs/coe/2007/section1/indicator10.asp; calculations by New Strategist

Health Trends

■ **Most Americans say their health is "very good" or "excellent."**

Only among people aged 65 or older does the share fall below 50 percent.

■ **Weight problems are growing in every age group.**

Sixty-one percent of the nation's adults are overweight, and 26 percent are obese.

■ **The babies being born today promise great diversity tomorrow.**

Of the 4.3 million babies born in 2007, only 54 percent were born to non-Hispanic whites. Twenty-five percent were born to Hispanics and 15 percent to blacks.

■ **Fifteen percent of Americans are without health insurance.**

The number of people without health insurance rose 19 percent between 2000 and 2007, to 46 million.

■ **Many children have asthma.**

Thirteen percent of children under age 18 have been diagnosed with asthma. Nearly 8 percent have learning disabilities.

■ **Lower back pain is the most frequently reported health condition.**

More than half of people aged 75 or older have been diagnosed with arthritis. Nearly one in four has had a heart attack.

■ **Heart disease and cancer are the biggest killers.**

Diabetes is the seventh leading cause of death, and Alzheimer's is sixth.

Most Americans Feel "Very Good" or "Excellent"

Just 15 percent say their health is only "fair" or "poor."

Overall, 54 percent of adults say their health is very good or excellent, ranging from a high of 63 percent among people aged 25 to 34 to a low of 39 percent among people aged 65 or older. Among the oldest Americans, those who rate their health as very good or excellent far surpass the 26 percent who say their health is only fair or poor.

The higher their education, the better people feel. Sixty-nine percent of college graduates say their health is very good or excellent compared with just 30 percent of people who did not graduate from high school. One reason for the poorer health of the less educated is that older Americans are disproportionately represented among those with the least education.

■ The proportion of Americans who say their health is very good or excellent has declined over the past decade among all but the oldest Americans.

The majority of people under age 65 say their health is very good or excellent

(percent of people aged 18 or older who say their health is very good or excellent, by age, 2007)

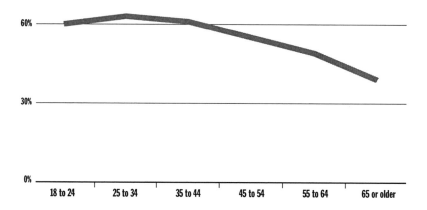

Table 3.1 Health Status, 2007

"How is your general health?"

(percent distribution of people aged 18 or older by health status and selected characteristics, 2007)

	total	excellent	very good	good	fair	poor
Total people	**100.0%**	**20.1%**	**34.1%**	**30.4%**	**10.9%**	**3.9%**
Sex						
Men	100.0	20.4	34.2	31.1	10.6	3.6
Women	100.0	20.2	34.2	30	11.5	4.1
Age						
Aged 18 to 24	100.0	24.0	36.4	30.9	7.3	1.0
Aged 25 to 34	100.0	25.1	38.0	28.4	7.2	1.6
Aged 35 to 44	100.0	23.3	37.5	28.3	8.3	2.3
Aged 45 to 54	100.0	20.1	35.0	29.6	10.4	4.4
Aged 55 to 64	100.0	16.8	32.1	30.2	13.7	6.1
Aged 65 or older	100.0	11.5	27.5	33.9	18.6	7.7
Race and Hispanic origin						
Black	100.0	16.1	25.7	35.0	15.1	5.0
Hispanic	100.0	16.4	21.3	36.5	17.9	4.0
White	100.0	21.4	36.7	28.8	9.5	3.7
Household income						
Under $15,000	100.0	9.6	17.5	31.1	24.8	15.1
$15,000 to $24,999	100.0	11.9	23.2	35.9	20.5	8.1
$25,000 to $34,999	100.0	15.2	30.1	36.1	14.0	4.2
$35,000 to $49,999	100.0	18.9	36.2	32.7	9.7	2.6
$50,000 or more	100.0	27.0	41.5	25.1	5.2	1.3
Education						
Not a high school graduate	100.0	10.9	18.6	34.2	23.5	10.2
High school graduate	100.0	15.6	31.0	34.8	13.9	4.7
Some college	100.0	19.2	35.8	30.9	10.2	3.6
College graduate	100.0	28.4	40.5	23.7	5.2	1.7

Note: Numbers may not add to total because some people did not report their health status.
Source: Centers for Disease Control and Prevention, Behavorial Risk Factor Surveillance System, Prevalence Data, Internet site http://apps.nccd.cdc.gov/brfss/index.asp; calculations by New Strategist

Weight Problems Are the Norm

Sixty-one percent of adults are overweight.

Americans have a weight problem. A government health survey, which measures the height and weight of a representative sample of Americans, found the average man weighing 195 pounds in 2003–06. The average woman weighed 165 pounds. For both men and women, these figures are substantially larger than they were several decades ago. In 1960–62, the average man weighed 166 pounds and the average woman weighed 140 pounds.

Sixty-one percent of people aged 18 or older are overweight, according to another government survey based on self-reported heights and weights. When Americans self-report their weight, however, they often lowball it, so the 61 percent estimate is conservative. Twenty-six percent of adults are obese, according to body mass index calculations based on the self-reported heights and weights. Most men and women are overweight, as are the majority in every age, educational, and income group. By race and Hispanic origin, Asians are the only segment in which the overweight are in the minority. Only 38 percent of Asians are overweight.

■ Most overweight Americans lack the willpower to eat less or exercise more—fueling a diet and weight loss industry that never lacks for customers.

The overweight dominate every age group

(percent of people aged 18 or older who are overweight, by age, 2007)

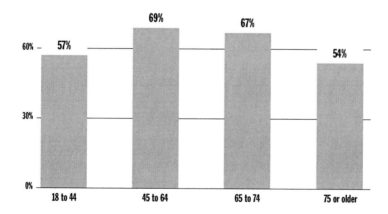

Table 3.2 Average Measured Weight by Age and Sex, 2003–06

(average weight in pounds of people aged 20 or older by age and sex, 2003–06)

	men	women
Total aged 20 or older	**194.7**	**164.7**
Aged 20 to 29	188.3	155.9
Aged 30 to 39	194.1	164.7
Aged 40 to 49	202.3	171.3
Aged 50 to 59	198.8	172.1
Aged 60 to 69	198.3	170.5
Aged 70 to 79	187.4	155.6
Aged 80 or older	168.1	142.2

Note: Data are based on measured weight of a sample of the civilian noninstitutionalized population.
Source: National Center for Health Statistics, Anthropometric Reference Data for Children and Adults: United States, 2003–2006, National Health Statistics Reports, Number 10, 2008, Internet site http://www.cdc.gov/nchs/products/pubs/pubd/nhsr/nhsr.htm; calculations by New Strategist

Table 3.3 Overweight and Obesity by Selected Characteristics, 2007

(percent distribution of people aged 18 or older by weight status, by selected characteristics, 2007; numbers in thousands)

| | total | | | | overweight | |
	number	percent	underweight	healthy weight	total	obese
Total people	223,181	100.0%	1.9%	36.7%	61.5%	26.2%
Sex						
Men	107,750	100.0	1.0	30.3	68.7	26.5
Women	115,431	100.0	2.8	43.9	53.3	25.2
Age						
Aged 18 to 44	110,890	100.0	2.2	41.1	56.7	24.5
Aged 45 to 64	76,136	100.0	1.0	30.3	68.6	30.2
Aged 65 to 74	19,258	100.0	1.4	31.6	67.1	27.2
Aged 75 or older	16,897	100.0	3.7	42.1	54.2	17.7
Race and Hispanic origin						
Asian	10,437	100.0	4.5	57.4	38.1	8.9
Black	26,366	100.0	1.7	28.1	70.2	35.1
Hispanic	29,857	100.0	1.5	30.8	67.8	27.5
Non-Hispanic white	153,359	100.0	1.9	38.8	59.3	24.8
Education						
Not a high school graduate	29,790	100.0	2.0	27.8	70.2	34.4
High school graduate	55,363	100.0	1.5	31.4	67.1	31.1
Some college	50,281	100.0	1.3	32.2	66.5	29.8
College graduate	56,971	100.0	1.6	41.7	56.7	18.9
Household income						
Less than $35,000	69,738	100.0	2.5	36.6	60.9	28.9
$35,000 to $49,999	30,247	100.0	1.8	34.2	64.0	28.7
$50,000 to $74,999	37,717	100.0	1.6	34.7	63.7	27.1
$75,000 to $99,999	24,193	100.0	0.9	35.4	63.6	25.3
$100,000 or more	38,006	100.0	1.5	43.3	55.2	19.8

Note: Overweight is defined as a body mass index of 25 or higher. Obesity is defined as a body mass index of 30 or higher. Body mass index is calculated by dividing weight in kilograms by height in meters squared. Data are based on self-reported height and weight of a sample of the civilian noninstitutionalized population. Numbers may not add to total because not all races are shown and Hispanics may be of any race; because education figures are for people aged 25 or older, and because some respondents did not report income.
Source: National Center for Health Statistics, Summary Health Statistics for U.S. Adults: National Health Interview Survey, 2007, Vital and Health Statistics, Series 10, No. 240, 2008, Internet site http://www.cdc.gov/nchs/nhis.htm; calculations by New Strategist

Fewer than One-Third of Americans Are Physically Active

Forty-one percent do not engage in any physical activity.

Only 30 percent of people aged 18 or older participate in regular physical activity, meaning 30 minutes of light to moderate activity at least five times a week or 20 minutes of vigorous activity at least three times a week. Men are slightly more likely to meet recommended activity levels than women (33 versus 29 percent), and non-Hispanic whites are more active than Asians, blacks, or Hispanics (34 versus 30, 23, and 24 percent, respectively). The affluent and highly educated are the most active, and 44 percent of respondents with a household income of $100,000 or more are getting regular exercise as do 43 percent of those with a college degree.

Exercise walking is the most popular recreational activity. Some 90 million people aged 7 or older (34 percent of the population) participated in exercise walking more than once in 2007, according to a survey by the National Sporting Goods Association. The other recreational activities that rank among the top five in popularity are exercising with equipment (20 percent of people aged 7 or older participated in the past year), swimming (20 percent), camping (18 percent), and bowling (16 percent).

■ With most Americans not getting enough exercise, it is no surprise that the ranks of the overweight are growing.

Physical activity increases with education

(percent of people aged 18 or older who engage in regular physical activity, by educational attainment, 2007)

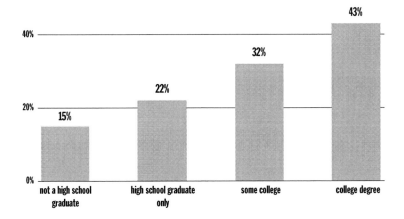

Table 3.4 Participation in Leisure-Time Physical Activity, 2007

(percent distribution of people aged 18 or older by participation in regular leisure-time physical activity, by selected characteristics and level of activity, 2007; numbers in thousands)

	total		inactive	some	regular
	number	percent			
Total people	**223,181**	**100.0%**	**40.6%**	**29.8%**	**29.6%**
Sex					
Men	107,750	100.0	37.0	30.1	32.9
Women	115,431	100.0	41.0	30.1	29.0
Age					
Aged 18 to 44	110,890	100.0	34.4	31.3	34.3
Aged 45 to 64	76,136	100.0	38.9	31.1	30.0
Aged 65 to 74	19,258	100.0	48.1	27.2	24.7
Aged 75 or older	16,897	100.0	60.9	21.2	17.9
Race and Hispanic origin					
Asian	10,437	100.0	38.9	31.0	30.1
Black	26,366	100.0	51.0	26.0	23.0
Hispanic	29,857	100.0	51.3	25.0	23.7
Non-Hispanic white	153,359	100.0	34.7	31.4	33.9
Education					
Less than high school	29,790	100.0	63.8	21.3	14.9
High school graduate	55,363	100.0	49.1	29.2	21.7
Some college	50,281	100.0	35.0	32.9	32.0
College graduate	56,971	100.0	23.1	33.6	43.3
Household income					
Less than $35,000	69,738	100.0	50.4	26.3	23.3
$35,000 to $49,999	30,247	100.0	43.2	28.7	28.1
$50,000 to $74,999	37,717	100.0	34.7	33.6	31.8
$75,000 to $99,999	24,193	100.0	30.2	35.8	34.0
$100,000 or more	38,006	100.0	22.3	33.4	44.3

Note: All questions related to leisure-time physical activity were phrased in terms of current behavior and lack a specific reference period. Adults classified as inactive reported no sessions of light to moderate or vigorous leisure-time activity of at least 10 minutes duration. Adults with some leisure-time activity reported at least one session of light to moderate or vigorous physical activity of at least 10 minutes duration but did not meet the definition for regular leisure-time activity. Adults with regular leisure-time activity reported three or more sessions per week of vigorous activity lasting at least 20 minutes or five or more sessions per week of light to moderate activity lasting at least 30 minutes.
Source: National Center for Health Statistics, Summary Health Statistics for U.S. Adults: National Health Interview Survey, 2007, Vital and Health Statistics, Series 10, No. 240, 2008, Internet site http://www.cdc.gov/nchs/nhis.htm; calculations by New Strategist

Table 3.5 Sports Participation of People Aged 7 or Older, 2007

(total number of people aged 7 or older, and number and percent participating in selected sports more than once during past year, 2007; numbers in millions)

	number	percent
Total people	**265.4**	**100.0%**
Exercise walking	89.8	33.8
Exercising with equipment	52.8	19.9
Swimming	52.3	19.7
Camping (vacation/overnight)	47.5	17.9
Bowling	43.5	16.4
Bicycle riding	37.4	14.1
Fishing	35.3	13.3
Workout at club	33.8	12.7
Boating (motor)	31.9	12.0
Running/jogging	30.4	11.5
Aerobic exercising	30.3	11.4
Billiards/pool	29.5	11.1
Hiking	28.6	10.8
Basketball	24.1	9.1
Golf	22.7	8.6
Target shooting	20.9	7.9
Hunting with firearms	19.5	7.3
Baseball	14.0	5.3
Soccer	13.8	5.2
Backpacking/wilderness camping	13.0	4.9
Tennis	12.3	4.6
Volleyball	12.0	4.5
Skating (in-line)	10.7	4.0
Skateboarding	10.1	3.8
Softball	10.0	3.8
Football (tackle)	9.2	3.5
Mountain biking (off road)	7.4	2.8
Archery (target)	6.6	2.5
Kayaking	5.9	2.2
Hunting with bow and arrow	5.7	2.1
Skiing (alpine)	5.5	2.1
Water skiing	5.3	2.0
Snowboarding	5.1	1.9
Muzzleloading	3.6	1.4
Hockey (ice)	2.1	0.8
Skiing (cross country)	1.7	0.6

Source: National Sporting Goods Association, Internet site http://www.nsga.org

Forty-Six Percent of the Nation's Newborns Are Minorities

The babies being born today promise great diversity tomorrow.

Of the 4.3 million babies born in 2007, nearly 25 percent were born to Hispanic mothers and 15 percent to non-Hispanic black mothers. Only 54 percent were born to non-Hispanic whites. As today's children grow up, they will create an increasingly multicultural society with no single racial or ethnic group claiming the majority of the U.S. population.

In the future, many adults will have little experience with the two-parent family. Forty percent of births in 2007 were to unwed mothers, up from just 11 percent in 1970. Among non-Hispanic blacks, 72 percent of births were out-of-wedlock versus 51 percent among Hispanics, 28 percent among non-Hispanic whites, and 17 percent among Asians.

Among all women giving birth in 2007, the 40 percent plurality was having their first child, and another 32 percent were having their second child. Only 28 percent of women giving birth in 2007 were having a third or higher-order birth, but among women aged 40 or older who gave birth, nearly half were having their third or fourth child.

■ With so many babies born to unmarried mothers, reducing poverty among children is an uphill task.

The nation's newborns are diverse

(percent distribution of births by race and Hispanic origin of mother, 2007)

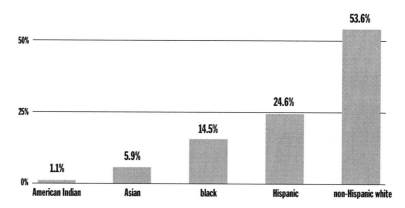

Table 3.6 Births by Age, Race, and Hispanic Origin, 2007

(number and percent distribution of births by age, race, and Hispanic origin, 2007)

	total	American Indian	Asian	black	Hispanic	non-Hispanic white
Total births	**4,317,119**	**49,284**	**254,734**	**627,230**	**1,061,970**	**2,312,473**
Under age 15	6,218	120	92	2,326	2,407	1,269
Aged 15 to 19	445,045	8,925	8,022	106,224	148,453	173,104
Aged 20 to 24	1,082,837	16,759	32,309	200,273	305,107	526,943
Aged 25 to 29	1,208,504	12,420	71,465	157,173	287,730	676,599
Aged 30 to 34	962,179	7,052	86,949	97,332	201,212	566,197
Aged 35 to 39	499,916	3,265	46,379	50,614	95,694	301,666
Aged 40 to 44	105,071	704	8,879	12,428	20,273	62,152
Aged 45 to 54	7,349	38	639	860	1,095	4,544

PERCENT DISTRIBUTION BY RACE AND HISPANIC ORIGIN

	total	American Indian	Asian	black	Hispanic	non-Hispanic white
Total births	**100.0%**	**1.1%**	**5.9%**	**14.5%**	**24.6%**	**53.6%**
Under age 15	100.0	1.9	1.5	37.4	38.7	20.4
Aged 15 to 19	100.0	2.0	1.8	23.9	33.4	38.9
Aged 20 to 24	100.0	1.5	3.0	18.5	28.2	48.7
Aged 25 to 29	100.0	1.0	5.9	13.0	23.8	56.0
Aged 30 to 34	100.0	0.7	9.0	10.1	20.9	58.8
Aged 35 to 39	100.0	0.7	9.3	10.1	19.1	60.3
Aged 40 to 44	100.0	0.7	8.5	11.8	19.3	59.2
Aged 45 to 54	100.0	0.5	8.7	11.7	14.9	61.8

PERCENT DISTRIBUTION BY AGE

	total	American Indian	Asian	black	Hispanic	non-Hispanic white
Total births	**100.0%**	**100.0%**	**100.0%**	**100.0%**	**100.0%**	**100.0%**
Under age 15	0.1	0.2	0.0	0.4	0.2	0.1
Aged 15 to 19	10.3	18.1	3.1	16.9	14.0	7.5
Aged 20 to 24	25.1	34.0	12.7	31.9	28.7	22.8
Aged 25 to 29	28.0	25.2	28.1	25.1	27.1	29.3
Aged 30 to 34	22.3	14.3	34.1	15.5	18.9	24.5
Aged 35 to 39	11.6	6.6	18.2	8.1	9.0	13.0
Aged 40 to 44	2.4	1.4	3.5	2.0	1.9	2.7
Aged 45 to 54	0.2	0.1	0.3	0.1	0.1	0.2

Note: Births by race and Hispanic origin do not add to total because Hispanics may be of any race and "not stated" is not shown.
Source: National Center for Health Statistics, Births: Preliminary Data for 2007, National Vital Statistics Reports, Vol. 57, No. 12, 2009, Internet site http://www.cdc.gov/nchs/products/nvsr.htm#57_12; calculations by New Strategist

Table 3.7 Characteristics of Births by Race and Hispanic Origin, 2007

(total number of births, fertility rate, births in lifetime, and percent of births to unmarried women, by race and Hispanic origin, 2007)

	total	fertility rate	births in lifetime	percent of births to unmarried women
Total births	**4,317,119**	**69.5**	**2.12**	**39.7%**
American Indian	49,284	64.7	1.86	65.2
Asian	254,734	71.4	2.04	16.9
Black, non-Hispanic	627,230	71.6	2.13	71.6
Hispanic	1,061,970	102.1	2.99	51.3
White, non-Hispanic	2,312,473	60.1	1.87	27.8

Note: The fertility rate is the number of births per 1,000 women aged 15 to 44. Births by race and Hispanic origin do not add to total because Hispanics may be of any race and "not stated" is not shown.
Source: National Center for Health Statistics, Births: Preliminary Data for 2007, National Vital Statistics Reports, Vol. 57, No. 12, 2009, Internet site http://www.cdc.gov/nchs/products/nvsr.htm#57_12; calculations by New Strategist

Table 3.8 Births to Unmarried Women by Age, 2007

(total number of births and number and percent of births to unmarried women, by age, 2007)

	total	unmarried women number	percent distribution	percent of total
Total births	**4,317,119**	**1,714,643**	**100.0%**	**39.7%**
Under age 15	6,218	6,142	0.4	98.8
Aged 15 to 19	445,045	380,560	22.2	85.5
Aged 20 to 24	1,082,837	644,591	37.6	59.5
Aged 25 to 29	1,208,504	389,169	22.7	32.2
Aged 30 to 34	962,179	185,425	10.8	19.3
Aged 35 to 39	499,916	86,343	5.0	17.3
Aged 40 to 54	112,420	22,411	1.3	19.9

Source: National Center for Health Statistics, Births: Preliminary Data for 2007, National Vital Statistics Reports, Vol. 57, No. 12, 2009, Internet site http://www.cdc.gov/nchs/products/nvsr.htm#57_12; calculations by New Strategist

Table 3.9 Births by Age of Mother and Birth Order, 2007

(number and percent distribution of births by age of mother and birth order, 2007)

	total	first child	second child	third child	fourth or later child
Total births	**4,317,119**	**1,726,523**	**1,364,048**	**722,883**	**483,766**
Under age 15	6,218	6,088	99	2	1
Aged 15 to 19	445,045	357,092	73,891	10,863	1,472
Aged 20 to 24	1,082,837	524,240	359,732	141,942	52,063
Aged 25 to 29	1,208,504	432,011	400,000	230,640	140,490
Aged 30 to 34	962,179	270,057	334,881	201,033	151,655
Aged 35 to 39	499,916	112,833	163,927	114,878	105,601
Aged 40 to 44	105,071	22,322	29,721	22,220	30,175
Aged 45 to 54	7,349	1,881	1,797	1,307	2,310

PERCENT DISTRIBUTION BY BIRTH ORDER

	total	first child	second child	third child	fourth or later child
Total births	**100.0%**	**40.0%**	**31.6%**	**16.7%**	**11.2%**
Under age 15	100.0	97.9	1.6	0.0	0.0
Aged 15 to 19	100.0	80.2	16.6	2.4	0.3
Aged 20 to 24	100.0	48.4	33.2	13.1	4.8
Aged 25 to 29	100.0	35.7	33.1	19.1	11.6
Aged 30 to 34	100.0	28.1	34.8	20.9	15.8
Aged 35 to 39	100.0	22.6	32.8	23.0	21.1
Aged 40 to 44	100.0	21.2	28.3	21.1	28.7
Aged 45 to 54	100.0	25.6	24.5	17.8	31.4

PERCENT DISTRIBUTION BY AGE

	total	first child	second child	third child	fourth or later child
Total births	**100.0%**	**100.0%**	**100.0%**	**100.0%**	**100.0%**
Under age 15	0.1	0.4	0.0	0.0	0.0
Aged 15 to 19	10.3	20.7	5.4	1.5	0.3
Aged 20 to 24	25.1	30.4	26.4	19.6	10.8
Aged 25 to 29	28.0	25.0	29.3	31.9	29.0
Aged 30 to 34	22.3	15.6	24.6	27.8	31.3
Aged 35 to 39	11.6	6.5	12.0	15.9	21.8
Aged 40 to 44	2.4	1.3	2.2	3.1	6.2
Aged 45 to 54	0.2	0.1	0.1	0.2	0.5

Note: Numbers do not add to total because "not stated" is not shown.
Source: National Center for Health Statistics, Births: Preliminary Data for 2007, National Vital Statistics Reports, Vol. 57, No. 12, 2009, Internet site http://www.cdc.gov/nchs/products/nvsr.htm#57_12; calculations by New Strategist

More Have Hypertension

Cholesterol is down among both men and women, however.

Thirty-two percent of Americans aged 20 or older have high blood pressure or are taking antihypertensive medication. Hypertension increases with age, and women are slightly more likely than men to have high blood pressure. The majority of people aged 55 or older have hypertension. The percentage of men and women with hypertension has grown over the past two decades, especially among women aged 45 to 74.

Thanks to screening programs, dietary changes, and the development of new medications, high cholesterol is less of a health problem for men and women today than in the past. The percentage of adults with high cholesterol fell from 20 to 16 percent between 1988–94 and 2003–06. The biggest declines occurred among men and women aged 55 or older. Among women aged 75 or older, the proportion with high cholesterol fell nearly 20 percentage points between 1988–94 and 2003–06, from 38 to 19 percent.

■ Thanks to medications that control blood pressure and cholesterol levels, life expectancy should continue to climb.

Women are more likely than men to have high blood pressure

(percent of people aged 20 or older with elevated blood pressure, by sex, 2003–06)

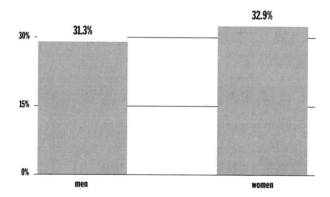

Table 3.10 Hypertension by Sex and Age, 1988–94 and 2003–06

(percent of people aged 20 or older with hypertension or taking antihypertensive medication, by sex and age, 1988–94 and 2003–06; percentage point change, 1988–94 to 2003–06)

	2003–06	1988–94	percentage point change
Total people	**32.1%**	**24.1%**	**8.0**
Total men	**31.3**	**23.8**	**7.5**
Aged 20 to 34	9.2	7.1	2.1
Aged 35 to 44	21.1	17.1	0.0
Aged 45 to 54	36.2	29.2	7.0
Aged 55 to 64	50.2	40.6	9.6
Aged 65 to 74	64.1	54.4	9.7
Aged 75 or older	65.0	60.4	4.6
Total women	**32.9**	**24.4**	**8.5**
Aged 20 to 34	2.2	2.9	–0.7
Aged 35 to 44	12.6	11.2	1.4
Aged 45 to 54	36.2	23.9	12.3
Aged 55 to 64	54.4	42.6	11.8
Aged 65 to 74	70.8	56.2	14.6
Aged 75 or older	80.2	73.6	6.6

Note: A person is defined as having hypertension if he or she has a systolic pressure of at least 140 mmHg, a diastolic pressure of at least 90 mmHg, or takes antihypertensive medication.
Source: National Center for Health Statistics, Health, United States, 2008, Internet site http://www.cdc.gov/nchs/hus.htm; calculations by New Strategist

Table 3.11 High Cholesterol by Sex and Age, 1988–94 and 2003–06

(percent of people aged 20 or older who have high serum cholesterol, by sex and age, 1988–94 and 2003–06; percentage point change, 1988–94 to 2003–06)

	2003–06	1988–94	percentage point change
Total people	**16.4%**	**19.6%**	**–3.2**
Total men	**15.2**	**17.7**	**–2.5**
Aged 20 to 34	9.5	8.2	1.3
Aged 35 to 44	20.5	19.4	1.1
Aged 45 to 54	20.8	26.6	–5.8
Aged 55 to 64	16.0	28.0	–12.0
Aged 65 to 74	10.9	21.9	–11.0
Aged 75 or older	9.6	20.4	–10.8
Total women	**17.5**	**21.3**	**–3.8**
Aged 20 to 34	10.3	7.3	3.0
Aged 35 to 44	12.7	12.3	0.4
Aged 45 to 54	19.7	26.7	–7.0
Aged 55 to 64	30.5	40.9	–10.4
Aged 65 to 74	24.2	41.3	–17.1
Aged 75 or older	18.6	38.2	–19.6

Note: High cholesterol is defined as 240 mg/dL or more.
Source: National Center for Health Statistics, Health, United States, 2008, Internet site http://www.cdc.gov/nchs/hus.htm; calculations by New Strategist

One in Five Americans Smokes Cigarettes

Drinking is more popular than smoking, with the majority having a drink at least occasionally.

Twenty percent of people aged 18 or older currently smoke cigarettes. Fifteen percent smoke every day. Smoking declines with age, from 23 percent of 18-to-44-year-olds to just 4 percent of those aged 75 or older. Only 9 percent of college graduates smoke versus 27 percent of those who went no further than high school.

Drinking is far more common than smoking, with 49 percent of adults reporting current regular drinking. Those most likely to consumer alcohol regularly are people aged 18 to 44 (55 percent), non-Hispanic whites (54 percent), college graduates (60 percent), and people with household incomes of $75,000 or more (65 percent).

Fully 46 percent of people aged 12 or older have used an illicit drug at some point in their lives, but only 8 percent have done so in the past month and 14 percent in the past year. Past-month drug use peaks among people aged 18 to 22, at least one in five of whom has used an illicit drug. The majority of Americans ranging in age from 18 to 59 have used an illicit drug at some point in their life.

■ Despite extensive antismoking campaigns, a significant share of the population still adopts the habit.

Men are more likely than women to drink alcoholic beverages

(percent of people aged 18 or older who are current regular drinkers, by sex, 2007)

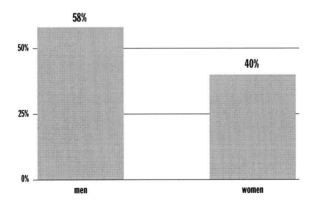

Table 3.12 Percent Distribution of People Aged 18 or Older by Cigarette Smoking Status, 2007

(total number of people aged 18 or older and percent distribution by cigarette smoking status and selected characteristics, 2007; numbers in thousands)

	total		all current smokers			former smokers	nonsmokers
	number	percent	total	every-day smokers	some-day smokers		
Total people	**223,181**	**100.0%**	**19.8%**	**15.4%**	**4.4%**	**21.5%**	**58.7%**
Sex							
Men	107,750	100.0	22.0	16.8	5.2	25.5	52.5
Women	115,431	100.0	17.5	13.8	3.7	17.6	64.9
Age							
Aged 18 to 44	110,890	100.0	22.6	17.0	5.7	12.4	65.0
Aged 45 to 64	76,136	100.0	21.0	17.0	4.0	26.4	52.6
Aged 65 to 74	19,258	100.0	12.2	10.3	1.9	40.1	47.8
Aged 75 or older	16,897	100.0	3.9	3.2	0.7	38.7	57.4
Race and Hispanic origin							
Asian	10,437	100.0	9.2	6.9	2.3	11.5	79.3
Black	26,366	100.0	19.0	14.3	4.7	14.5	66.5
Hispanic	29,857	100.0	12.8	7.7	5.1	16.1	71.0
Non-Hispanic white	153,359	100.0	22.1	17.8	4.4	23.7	54.2
Education							
Less than high school	29,790	100.0	27.0	22.0	5.0	20.3	52.7
High school graduate	55,363	100.0	26.6	22.3	4.3	22.7	50.8
Some college	50,281	100.0	20.1	15.9	4.2	26.8	53.0
College graduate	56,971	100.0	9.1	5.8	3.2	23.5	67.4
Household income							
Less than $35,000	69,738	100.0	26.8	21.3	5.6	19.2	54.0
$35,000 to $49,999	30,247	100.0	23.8	18.4	5.4	21.2	55.0
$50,000 to $74,999	37,717	100.0	19.0	14.9	4.2	23.5	57.5
$75,000 to $99,999	24,193	100.0	14.5	11.1	3.3	24.6	60.9
$100,000 or more	38,006	100.0	12.4	8.5	3.9	23.8	63.8

Note: Current smokers have smoked at least 100 cigarettes in lifetime and still smoke; every-day smokers are current smokers who smoke every day; some-day smokers are current smokers who smoke on some days; former smokers have smoked at least 100 cigarettes in lifetime but currently do not smoke; nonsmokers have smoked fewer than 100 cigarettes in lifetime. Numbers may not add to total because not all races are shown and Hispanics may be of any race; because education figures are for people aged 25 or older, and because some respondents did not report income.
Source: National Center for Health Statistics, Summary Health Statistics for U.S. Adults: National Health Interview Survey, 2007, Vital and Health Statistics, Series 10, No. 240, 2008, Internet site http://www.cdc.gov/nchs/nhis.htm; calculations by New Strategist

Table 3.13 Percent Distribution of People Aged 18 or Older by Alcohol Drinking Status, 2007

(total number of people aged 18 or older and percent distribution by alcohol drinking status and selected characteristics, 2007; numbers in thousands)

	total		current			lifetime
	number	percent	regular	infrequent	former	abstainer
Total people	**223,181**	**100.0%**	**48.5%**	**12.5%**	**14.8%**	**23.8%**
Sex						
Men	107,750	100.0	58.1	9.3	15.1	16.8
Women	115,431	100.0	39.8	15.3	14.2	30.4
Age						
Aged 18 to 44	110,890	100.0	54.5	12.1	8.7	24.0
Aged 45 to 64	76,136	100.0	48.1	13.9	18.0	19.7
Aged 65 to 74	19,258	100.0	35.1	11.3	25.9	27.5
Aged 75 or older	16,897	100.0	26.3	9.9	27.3	36.2
Race and Hispanic origin						
Asian	10,437	100.0	32.5	10.4	9.0	47.6
Black	26,366	100.0	35.8	12.2	16.6	34.8
Hispanic	29,857	100.0	38.0	12.5	13.5	35.5
Non-Hispanic white	153,359	100.0	54.2	12.5	14.6	18.3
Education						
Less than high school	29,790	100.0	33.1	10.7	21.7	34.1
High school graduate	55,363	100.0	43.1	13.5	18.0	25.1
Some college	50,281	100.0	50.1	15.0	16.6	17.9
College graduate	56,971	100.0	60.3	11.6	10.9	16.9
Household income						
Less than $20,000	69,738	100.0	40.2	11.4	18.5	29.3
$20,000 to $34,999	30,247	100.0	45.6	13.3	16.2	24.4
$35,000 to $54,999	37,717	100.0	50.2	14.7	13.6	20.9
$55,000 to $74,999	24,193	100.0	54.7	13.5	12.9	18.6
$75,000 or more	38,006	100.0	65.2	10.6	10.0	13.9

Note: Current drinkers have had 12 or more drinks in lifetime and have had a drink in the past year; regular drinkers have 12 or more drinks a year; infrequent drinkers have fewer than 12 drinks a year; former drinkers have had 12 or more drinks in lifetime, but no drinks in past year; lifetime abstainers have had fewer than 12 drinks in lifetime. Numbers by race and Hispanic origin do not sum to total because not all races are shown, Hispanics may be of any race, education figures are for people aged 25 or older, and some people did not report income.
Source: National Center for Health Statistics, Summary Health Statistics for U.S. Adults: National Health Interview Survey, 2007, Vital and Health Statistics, Series 10, No. 240, 2008, Internet site http://www.cdc.gov/nchs/nhis.htm; calculations by New Strategist

Table 3.14   Illicit Drug Use by People Aged 12 or Older, 2007

(percent of people aged 12 or older who ever used any illicit drug, who used an illicit drug in the past year, and who used an illicit drug in the past month, by age, 2007)

	ever used	used in past year	used in past month
Total people	**46.1%**	**14.4%**	**8.0%**
Aged 12	9.9	5.4	2.7
Aged 13	16.4	10.2	4.0
Aged 14	21.4	14.7	6.7
Aged 15	29.0	21.4	11.0
Aged 16	37.6	28.6	14.8
Aged 17	41.5	30.8	17.4
Aged 18	46.9	34.8	20.7
Aged 19	53.3	36.6	22.3
Aged 20	57.1	36.6	22.0
Aged 21	60.3	37.6	23.1
Aged 22	59.6	32.8	20.0
Aged 23	62.7	31.6	17.5
Aged 24	62.1	28.7	16.1
Aged 25	60.1	25.4	15.4
Aged 26 to 29	57.8	23.0	12.8
Aged 30 to 34	55.5	16.9	9.4
Aged 35 to 39	56.1	13.9	7.3
Aged 40 to 44	58.6	13.1	7.0
Aged 45 to 49	61.0	11.9	7.2
Aged 50 to 54	58.9	10.6	5.7
Aged 55 to 59	51.6	8.0	4.1
Aged 60 to 64	35.0	4.4	1.9
Aged 65 or older	10.7	1.0	0.7

Note: Illicit drugs include marijuana, hashish, cocaine (including crack), heroin, hallucinogens, inhalants, and any prescription-type psychotherapeutic used nonmedically.
Source: SAMHSA, Office of Applied Studies, National Survey on Drug Use and Health, 2007, Table G10, Internet site http://www.oas.samhsa.gov/nsduh/2k7nsduh/2k7Results.pdf

Millions of Americans Lack Health Insurance

The proportion is highest among young adults.

Eighty-five percent of Americans are covered by health insurance, with the 59 percent majority covered by an employer's health plan. Medicare, the federal government's health insurance program for people aged 65 or older, covers 14 percent. Medicaid, the federal health insurance program for the poor, covers another 13 percent.

Fifteen percent of Americans do not have health insurance, or 46 million people in 2007. The number of uninsured has grown by 19 percent since 2000. The percentage of Americans without health insurance is highest among 18-to-24-year-olds, at 28 percent, and Hispanics, at 32 percent. Among all those without health insurance in 2007, the 51 percent majority say cost is the reason. Twenty-five percent say they do not have health insurance because they lost their job or changed jobs. Fifteen percent say their employer did not offer health insurance or the insurance company refused to cover them.

■ The proportion of Americans who lack health insurance will continue to climb as the economic downturn increases unemployment and health insurance costs continue to rise.

One in six Americans lacks health insurance

(percent of people without health insurance coverage, by age, 2007)

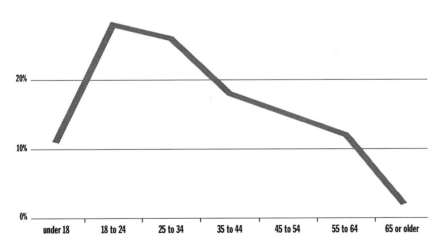

Table 3.15 Health Insurance Coverage by Age, 2007

(number and percent distribution of people by age and health insurance coverage status, 2007; numbers in thousands)

		covered by private or government health insurance									not covered
			private health insurance				government health insurance				
				employment-based		direct					
	total	total	total	total	own	purchase	total	Medicaid	Medicare	military	
Total people	**299,106**	**253,449**	**201,991**	**177,446**	**93,774**	**26,673**	**83,031**	**39,554**	**41,375**	**10,955**	**45,657**
Under age 65	262,316	217,345	180,785	164,888	84,332	17,127	48,567	36,291	7,097	8,351	44,971
Under age 18	74,403	66,254	47,750	44,252	227	3,930	23,041	20,899	518	2,101	8,149
Aged 18 to 24	28,398	20,407	17,074	13,747	5,386	1,635	4,428	3,563	180	823	7,991
Aged 25 to 34	40,146	29,817	26,430	24,505	19,005	2,347	4,539	3,237	501	1,047	10,329
Aged 35 to 44	42,132	34,415	31,067	29,009	20,616	2,687	4,546	3,027	924	1,016	7,717
Aged 45 to 54	43,935	37,161	33,350	30,805	22,486	3,292	5,363	3,103	1,795	1,285	6,774
Aged 55 to 64	33,302	29,291	25,114	22,569	16,612	3,237	6,651	2,462	3,179	2,079	4,011
Aged 65 or older	36,790	36,103	21,206	12,558	9,442	9,546	34,464	3,263	34,278	2,604	686

PERCENT DISTRIBUTION BY COVERAGE STATUS

Total people	**100.0%**	**84.7%**	**67.5%**	**59.3%**	**31.4%**	**8.9%**	**27.8%**	**13.2%**	**13.8%**	**3.7%**	**15.3%**
Under age 65	100.0	82.9	68.9	62.9	32.1	6.5	18.5	13.8	2.7	3.2	17.1
Under age 18	100.0	89.0	64.2	59.5	0.3	5.3	31.0	28.1	0.7	2.8	11.0
Aged 18 to 24	100.0	71.9	60.1	48.4	19.0	5.8	15.6	12.5	0.6	2.9	28.1
Aged 25 to 34	100.0	74.3	65.8	61.0	47.3	5.8	11.3	8.1	1.2	2.6	25.7
Aged 35 to 44	100.0	81.7	73.7	68.9	48.9	6.4	10.8	7.2	2.2	2.4	18.3
Aged 45 to 54	100.0	84.6	75.9	70.1	51.2	7.5	12.2	7.1	4.1	2.9	15.4
Aged 55 to 64	100.0	88.0	75.4	67.8	49.9	9.7	20.0	7.4	9.5	6.2	12.0
Aged 65 or older	100.0	98.1	57.6	34.1	25.7	25.9	93.7	8.9	93.2	7.1	1.9

PERCENT DISTRIBUTION BY AGE

Total people	**100.0%**	**100.0%**	**100.0%**	**100.0%**	**100.0%**	**100.0%**	**100.0%**	**100.0%**	**100.0%**	**100.0%**	**100.0%**
Under age 65	87.7	85.8	89.5	92.9	89.9	64.2	58.5	91.8	17.2	76.2	98.5
Under age 18	24.9	26.1	23.6	24.9	0.2	14.7	27.7	52.8	1.3	19.2	17.8
Aged 18 to 24	9.5	8.1	8.5	7.7	5.7	6.1	5.3	9.0	0.4	7.5	17.5
Aged 25 to 34	13.4	11.8	13.1	13.8	20.3	8.8	5.5	8.2	1.2	9.6	22.6
Aged 35 to 44	14.1	13.6	15.4	16.3	22.0	10.1	5.5	7.7	2.2	9.3	16.9
Aged 45 to 54	14.7	14.7	16.5	17.4	24.0	12.3	6.5	7.8	4.3	11.7	14.8
Aged 55 to 64	11.1	11.6	12.4	12.7	17.7	12.1	8.0	6.2	7.7	19.0	8.8
Aged 65 or older	12.3	14.2	10.5	7.1	10.1	35.8	41.5	8.2	82.8	23.8	1.5

Note: Numbers may not add to total because some people have more than one type of health insurance coverage.
Source: Bureau of the Census, Health Insurance, Table HI01, Internet site http://pubdb3.census.gov/macro/032008/health/toc .htm; calculations by New Strategist

Table 3.16 People without Health Insurance by Age, 2000 to 2007

(number and percent of people without health insurance coverge by age, 2000 to 2007; percent change in number and percentage point change in share, 2000–07; numbers in thousands)

	2007	2000	percent change
Total without coverage	**45,657**	**38,426**	**18.8%**
Under age 18	8,149	8,385	–2.8
Aged 18 to 24	7,991	7,203	10.9
Aged 25 to 34	10,329	8,318	24.2
Aged 35 to 44	7,717	6,746	14.4
Aged 45 to 54	6,774	4,492	50.8
Aged 55 to 64	4,011	3,031	32.3
Aged 65 or older	686	251	173.3

	2007	2000	percentage point change
Total without coverage	**15.3%**	**13.7%**	**1.6**
Under age 18	11.0	11.6	–0.6
Aged 18 to 24	28.1	26.9	1.2
Aged 25 to 34	25.7	21.4	4.3
Aged 35 to 44	18.3	15.1	3.2
Aged 45 to 54	15.4	11.6	3.8
Aged 55 to 64	12.0	12.3	–0.3
Aged 65 or older	1.9	0.7	1.2

Source: Bureau of the Census, Historical Health Insurance Tables, Table HIA-2, Internet site http://www.census.gov/hhes/www/ hlthins/historic/index.html; calculations by New Strategist

Table 3.17 People without Health Insurance by Race and Hispanic Origin, 2002 to 2007

(number and percent of people without health insurance coverge by race and Hispanic Origin, 2002 to 2007; percent change in number and percentage point change in share, 2002–07; numbers in thousands)

	2007	2002	percent change
Total without coverage	**45,657**	**42,019**	**8.7%**
Asian	2,321	2,172	6.9
Black	7,624	7,257	5.1
Hispanic	14,770	12,569	17.5
Non-Hispanic white	20,548	19,674	4.4

	2007	2002	percentage point change
Total without coverage	**15.3%**	**14.7%**	**0.6**
Asian	16.1	17.4	–1.3
Black	19.2	19.4	–0.2
Hispanic	32.1	31.9	0.2
Non-Hispanic white	10.4	10.1	0.3

Note: Asians and blacks are those who identify themselves as being of the race alone and those who identify themselves as being of the race in combination with other races. Hispanics may be of any race. Non-Hispanic whites are those who identify themselves as being white alone and not Hispanic.
Source: Bureau of the Census, Historical Health Insurance Tables, Table HIA-1, Internet site http://www.census.gov/hhes/www/ hlthins/historic/index.html; calculations by New Strategist

Table 3.18 Reason for Lack of Health Insurance Coverage by Selected Characteristics, 2007

(total number and percent distribution of people under age 65 without health insurance by reason for lack of insurance, by selected characteristics, 2007; numbers in thousands)

	total number	total percent	lost job or change in employment	change in marital status or death of parent	ineligible due to age or left school	employer didn't offer or insurance company refused	cost	Medicaid stopped	other reason
Total without health insurance	42,930	100.0%	24.6%	2.5%	8.1%	14.9%	50.8%	10.9%	6.5%
Sex									
Female	19,510	100.0	23.4	3.7	5.8	11.7	48.8	16.9	6.8
Male	23,420	100.0	25.6	1.3	6.6	14.7	52.1	9.0	8.1
Age									
Under age 12	3,882	100.0	21.2	1.5	1.1	6.2	44.0	23.5	14.6
Aged 12 to 17	2,721	100.0	21.0	2.2	1.1	8.3	53.3	17.5	7.4
Aged 18 to 44	26,179	100.0	22.6	2.1	12.5	16.7	48.8	10.7	5.9
Aged 45 to 64	10,149	100.0	32.1	3.8	1.0	14.9	57.8	5.3	5.0
Race and Hispanic origin									
Asian	1,861	100.0	15.6	–	4.7	8.3	60.7	8.8	9.5
Black	5,763	100.0	28.6	2.2	8.1	12.6	42.6	15.0	6.1
Hispanic	13,452	100.0	15.2	0.9	3.3	17.4	57.2	13.9	8.5
Non-Hispanic white	20,771	100.0	29.9	3.3	7.9	11.4	47.3	11.5	7.3
Education									
Less than high school	7,983	100.0	18.5	1.6	1.8	18.8	61.3	9.5	7.1
High school graduate	9,445	100.0	31.9	2.8	3.1	15.7	53.0	7.8	4.6
Some college	6,523	100.0	34.6	5.0	4.7	16.6	50.5	9.5	4.5
College graduate	3,339	100.0	30.5	3.1	6.2	16.0	50.4	4.3	9.3
Household income									
Less than $35,000	20,553	100.0	22.0	2.8	5.7	13.0	49.9	16.5	6.9
$35,000 to $49,999	6,991	100.0	25.9	1.9	5.3	13.7	52.6	13.6	5.8
$50,000 to $74,999	5,825	100.0	29.0	2.8	6.8	12.0	49.6	6.4	10.3
$75,000 to $99,999	2,204	100.0	32.5	–	11.3	16.9	47.4	8.5	5.7
$100,000 or more	1,879	100.0	31.0	1.1	12.2	13.9	39.6	3.9	12.6

Note: Figures do not sum to total because more than one reason may have been cited. "Other reason" includes moved, self-employed, never had coverage, does not want or need coverage. "–" means sample is too small to make a reliable estimate.
Source: National Center for Health Statistics, Summary Health Statistics for the U.S. Population: National Health Interview Survey, 2007, Vital and Health Statistics, Series 10, No. 238, 2008, Internet site http://www.cdc.gov/nchs/nhis.htm; calculations by New Strategist

Asthma and Allergies Affect Many Children

Boys are more likely than girls to have learning disabilities.

Asthma is a growing problem among children. Thirteen percent of the nation's 74 million children under age 18 have been diagnosed with asthma. Boys are more likely to have asthma than girls (15 versus 11 percent), and blacks more than other racial or ethnic groups (20 percent versus 11 to 13 percent for Asians, Hispanics, and non-Hispanic whites). Children in single-parent families headed by women are more likely to have asthma than those from two-parent families (18 versus 12 percent).

Nearly 5 million children (7.5 percent) have been diagnosed with a learning disability, and 4 million have attention deficit hyperactivity disorder. Boys, who are far more likely than girls to have these conditions, account for 66 percent of those with learning disabilities and for 71 percent of those with attention deficit hyperactivity disorder.

Many children use prescription medications. Nine million children have taken prescription medications regularly for at least three months during the past year. That is a substantial 12 percent of the nation's children. Among 12-to-17-year-olds, the figure is an even higher 17 percent.

■ Prescription drug use is becoming common among the nation's children.

Boys are more likely than girls to have attention deficit hyperactivity disorder

(percent of people under age 18 diagnosed with attention deficity hyperactivity disorder, by sex, 2007)

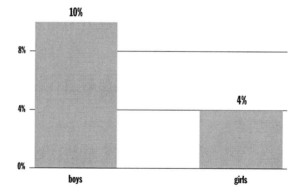

Table 3.19 Health Conditions among Children by Selected Characteristics, 2007

(number of people under age 18 with selected health conditions, by selected characteristics and type of condition, 2007; numbers in thousands)

	total children	diagnosed with asthma	have asthma	hay fever	respiratory allergies	other allergies	learning disability	attention deficit hyperactivity disorder	prescription medication taken regularly at least 3 months
					experienced in past 12 months			ever told had*	
Total children	**73,728**	**9,605**	**6,703**	**7,438**	**7,068**	**8,678**	**4,624**	**4,452**	**9,049**
Sex									
Female	36,042	4,055	3,043	3,476	3,026	4,386	1,590	1,291	4,117
Male	37,686	5,550	3,660	3,962	4,042	4,292	3,034	3,161	4,932
Age									
Aged 0 to 4	20,579	1,636	1,395	915	1,323	2,880	179	170	1,535
Aged 5 to 11	27,932	3,702	2,445	2,888	2,863	3,227	1,867	1,644	3,281
Aged 12 to 17	25,216	4,267	2,862	3,635	2,882	2,571	2,577	2,637	4,234
Race and Hispanic origin									
Asian	2,937	362	217	227	207	299	90	57	236
Black	11,429	2,253	1,769	754	848	1,577	740	718	1,413
Hispanic	15,350	1,937	1,422	1,163	1,020	1,476	817	495	1,273
Non-Hispanic white	41,811	4,591	3,030	5,084	4,675	4,920	2,823	2,948	5,847
Family structure									
Mother and father	52,294	6,029	4,051	5,510	4,905	5,913	2,835	2,597	5,880
Mother, no father	16,935	2,977	2,207	1,499	1,703	2,223	1,430	1,507	2,581
Father, no mother	2,282	280	179	157	203	259	128	122	214
Neither mother nor father	2,216	320	265	272	258	283	231	225	375
Parent's education									
Less than high school diploma	9,038	1,253	894	549	640	637	474	470	750
High school diploma or GED	16,005	1,966	1,401	1,163	1,090	1,668	1,142	1,125	1,659
More than high school	45,877	6,034	4,113	5,430	5,057	6,083	2,732	2,594	6,213
Household income									
Less than $35,000	22,058	3,472	2,529	1,689	1,853	2,541	1,700	1,572	2,924
$35,000 to $49,999	9,732	1,147	723	924	868	1,016	473	563	1,054
$50,000 to $74,999	12,702	1,665	1,231	1,214	1,290	1,668	979	800	1,461
$75,000 to $99,999	9,142	916	559	1,224	989	1,043	565	558	1,114
$100,000 or more	13,641	1,699	1,167	1,756	1,621	1,715	583	682	1,973

* Ever told by a school representative or health professional. Data exclude children under age 3.
Note: "Mother and father" includes biological, adoptive, step, in-law, and foster relationships. Legal guardians are classified as neither mother nor father. Parent's education is the education level of the parent with the higher level of education. Race/Hispanic origin, education, and income categories do not sum to total because not all races are shown and those not reporting education or income are not shown. "Other allergies" include food and digestive allergies, eczema, and other skin allergies.
Source: National Center for Health Statistics, Summary Health Statistics for U.S. Children: National Health Interview Survey, 2007, Series 10, No. 239, 2008, Internet site http://www.cdc.gov/nchs/nhis.htm

Table 3.20 Distribution of Health Conditions by Selected Characteristics of Children, 2007

(percent distribution of people under age 18 with health condition by selected characteristics, 2007)

| | | | | experienced in past 12 months | | | ever told had[*] | | prescription medication |
	total children	diagnosed with asthma	have asthma	hay fever	respiratory allergies	other allergies	learning disability	attention deficit hyperactivity disorder	taken regularly at least 3 months
Total children	100.0%	100.0%	100.0%	100.0%	100.0%	100.0%	100.0%	100.0%	100.0%
Sex									
Female	48.9	42.2	45.4	46.7	42.8	50.5	34.4	29.0	45.5
Male	51.1	57.8	54.6	53.3	57.2	49.5	65.6	71.0	54.5
Age									
Aged 0 to 4	27.9	17.0	20.8	12.3	18.7	33.2	3.9	3.8	17.0
Aged 5 to 11	37.9	38.5	36.5	38.8	40.5	37.2	40.4	36.9	36.3
Aged 12 to 17	34.2	44.4	42.7	48.9	40.8	29.6	55.7	59.2	46.8
Race and Hispanic origin									
Asian	4.0	3.8	3.2	3.1	2.9	3.4	1.9	1.3	2.6
Black	15.5	23.5	26.4	10.1	12.0	18.2	16.0	16.1	15.6
Hispanic	20.8	20.2	21.2	15.6	14.4	17.0	17.7	11.1	14.1
Non-Hispanic white	56.7	47.8	45.2	68.4	66.1	56.7	61.1	66.2	64.6
Family structure									
Mother and father	70.9	62.8	60.4	74.1	69.4	68.1	61.3	58.3	65.0
Mother, no father	23.0	31.0	32.9	20.2	24.1	25.6	30.9	33.8	28.5
Father, no mother	3.1	2.9	2.7	2.1	2.9	3.0	2.8	2.7	2.4
Neither mother nor father	3.0	3.3	4.0	3.7	3.7	3.3	5.0	5.1	4.1
Parent's education									
Less than high school diploma	12.3	13.0	13.3	7.4	9.1	7.3	10.3	10.6	8.3
High school diploma or GED	21.7	20.5	20.9	15.6	15.4	19.2	24.7	25.3	18.3
More than high school	62.2	62.8	61.4	73.0	71.5	70.1	59.1	58.3	68.7
Household income									
Less than $35,000	29.9	36.1	37.7	22.7	26.2	29.3	36.8	35.3	32.3
$35,000 to $49,999	13.2	11.9	10.8	12.4	12.3	11.7	10.2	12.6	11.6
$50,000 to $74,999	17.2	17.3	18.4	16.3	18.3	19.2	21.2	18.0	16.1
$75,000 to $99,999	12.4	9.5	8.3	16.5	14.0	12.0	12.2	12.5	12.3
$100,000 or more	18.5	17.7	17.4	23.6	22.9	19.8	12.6	15.3	21.8

* Ever told by a school representative or health professional. Data exclude children under age 3.
Note: "Mother and father" includes biological, adoptive, step, in-law, and foster relationships. Legal guardians are classified as neither mother nor father. Parent's education is the education level of the parent with the higher level of education. Race/Hispanic origin, education, and income categories do not sum to total because not all races are shown and those not reporting education or income are not shown. "Other allergies" include food and digestive allergies, eczema, and other skin allergies.
Source: National Center for Health Statistics, Summary Health Statistics for U.S. Children: National Health Interview Survey, 2007, Series 10, No. 239, 2008, Internet site http://www.cdc.gov/nchs/nhis.htm; calculations by New Strategist

Table 3.21 Percent of Children with Health Conditions by Selected Characteristics, 2007

(percent of people under age 18 with selected health conditions, by type of condition and selected characteristics, 2007)

| | total children | diagnosed with asthma | have asthma | experienced in past 12 months | | | ever told had* | attention deficit hyperactivity disorder | prescription medication taken regularly at least 3 months |
				hay fever	respiratory allergies	other allergies	learning disability		
Total children	100.0%	13.1%	9.1%	10.1%	9.6%	11.8%	7.5%	7.2%	12.3%
Sex									
Female	100.0	11.3	8.5	9.7	8.4	12.1	5.3	4.3	11.4
Male	100.0	14.8	9.8	10.6	10.8	11.4	9.7	10.0	13.2
Age									
Aged 0 to 4	100.0	8.0	6.8	4.5	6.4	14.0	2.1	2.0	7.5
Aged 5 to 11	100.0	13.3	8.8	10.4	10.3	11.6	6.7	5.9	11.8
Aged 12 to 17	100.0	17.0	11.4	14.4	11.4	10.2	10.2	10.5	16.8
Race and Hispanic origin									
Asian	100.0	12.4	7.5	8.0	7.0	10.0	3.7	2.5	8.2
Black	100.0	19.8	15.6	6.6	7.4	13.9	7.7	7.4	12.4
Hispanic	100.0	12.9	9.4	7.8	6.8	9.6	6.7	4.1	8.6
Non-Hispanic white	100.0	10.8	7.1	12.0	11.1	11.8	7.9	8.2	13.8
Family structure									
Mother and father	100.0	11.7	7.8	10.7	9.5	11.3	6.6	6.0	11.4
Mother, no father	100.0	17.6	13.0	8.8	10.1	13.1	10.0	10.5	15.3
Father, no mother	100.0	11.2	7.5	5.8	7.9	13.5	5.8	5.4	8.9
Neither mother nor father	100.0	14.6	12.2	12.5	12.3	13.7	10.9	10.7	16.7
Parent's education									
Less than high school diploma	100.0	14.4	9.9	6.2	7.0	6.9	6.9	6.5	8.1
High school diploma or GED	100.0	12.3	8.8	7.2	6.9	10.5	8.5	8.3	10.4
More than high school	100.0	13.2	9.0	11.9	11.1	13.2	7.1	6.8	13.6
Household income									
Less than $35,000	100.0	16.2	11.7	8.1	8.6	11.3	10.0	9.2	13.6
$35,000 to $49,999	100.0	12.0	7.6	9.6	9.0	10.5	5.8	7.0	11.0
$50,000 to $74,999	100.0	13.0	9.6	9.6	10.1	13.1	9.1	7.4	11.4
$75,000 to $99,999	100.0	9.7	6.0	13.0	10.7	11.7	7.1	6.9	11.9
$100,000 or more	100.0	11.8	8.2	12.2	11.5	12.8	4.6	5.4	13.8

* Ever told by a school representative or health professional. Data exclude children under age 3.
Note: "Mother and father" includes biological, adoptive, step, in-law, and foster relationships. Legal guardians are classified as neither mother nor father. Parent's education is the education level of the parent with the higher level of education. "Other allergies" include food and digestive allergies, eczema, and other skin allergies.
Source: National Center for Health Statistics, Summary Health Statistics for U.S. Children: National Health Interview Survey, 2007, Series 10, No. 239, 2008, Internet site http://www.cdc.gov/nchs/nhis.htm

Health Problems Are Common among Older Americans

Lower back pain is the most frequently reported health condition.

Twenty-six percent of Americans aged 18 or older have experienced lower back pain for at least one full day in the past three months, making it the most frequently reported health problem. Arthritis has been diagnosed in 21 percent of the adult population, and chronic joints symptoms trouble an even larger 24 percent.

Many ailments are more common among older than younger Americans. Fifty-three percent of people aged 75 or older have been diagnosed with arthritis, for example, compared with only 7 percent of 18-to-44-year-olds. Forty-five percent of the oldest Americans have hearing problems. But only 3.5 percent of people aged 75 or older suffer from migraines or severe headaches compared with a larger 15 percent of people aged 18 to 44.

■ As the baby-boom generation ages into its sixties, the number of people with arthritis and hearing problems will soar.

Most people aged 75 or older have arthritis

(percent of people diagnosed with arthritis, by age, 2007)

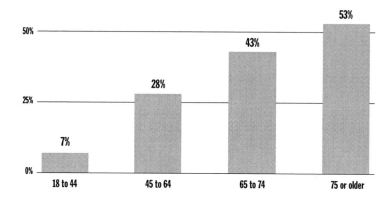

Table 3.22 Number of Adults with Health Conditions by Age, 2007

(number of people aged 18 or older with selected health conditions, by type of condition and age, 2007; numbers in thousands)

	total	18 to 44	45 to 64	aged 65 or older total	65 to 74	75 or older
Total people aged 18 or older	223,181	110,890	76,136	36,155	19,258	16,897
Selected circulatory diseases						
Heart disease, all types	25,095	4,591	9,266	11,239	5,199	6,040
Coronary	13,674	1,041	5,091	7,542	3,571	3,971
Hypertension	52,920	9,094	24,383	19,442	9,763	9,679
Stroke	5,426	285	2,156	2,985	1,205	1,780
Selected respiratory conditions						
Emphysema	3,736	226	1,765	1,745	861	884
Asthma, ever	24,402	12,996	7,895	3,511	2,030	1,481
Asthma, still	16,177	7,996	5,476	2,704	1,591	1,113
Hay fever	16,882	7,420	7,210	2,252	1,302	950
Sinusitis	25,953	10,261	11,154	4,538	2,589	1,949
Chronic bronchitis	7,604	2,515	3,226	1,863	1,050	813
Selected types of cancer						
Any cancer	16,370	2,085	6,305	7,980	3,757	4,223
Breast cancer	2,630	178	1,028	1,424	626	798
Cervical cancer	1,011	437	417	157	92	65
Prostate cancer	2,037	–	543	1,494	651	843
Other selected diseases and conditions						
Diabetes	17,273	2,432	8,093	6,748	3,840	2,908
Ulcers	14,501	4,616	5,641	4,244	2,119	2,125
Kidney disease	3,343	759	1,226	1,359	593	766
Liver disease	2,649	749	1,374	526	368	158
Arthritis	46,429	7,810	21,428	17,192	8,322	8,870
Chronic joint symptoms	53,945	14,776	24,820	14,350	7,140	7,210
Migraines or severe headaches	27,364	16,427	9,277	1,660	1,075	585
Pain in neck	29,019	11,833	12,073	5,113	2,833	2,280
Pain in lower back	57,070	24,555	21,860	10,655	5,650	5,005
Pain in face or jaw	9,062	4,649	3,455	957	607	350
Selected sensory problems						
Hearing	33,318	6,597	13,400	13,320	5,739	7,581
Vision	22,378	7,596	9,297	5,484	2,472	3,012
Absence of all natural teeth	16,997	2,066	5,606	9,325	4,284	5,041

Note: The conditions shown are those that have ever been diagnosed by a doctor, except as noted. Hay fever, sinusitis, and chronic bronchitis have been diagnosed in the past 12 months. Kidney and liver diseases have been diagnosed in the past 12 months and exclude kidney stones, bladder infections, and incontinence. Chronic joint symptoms are shown if respondent had pain, aching, or stiffness in or around a joint (excluding back and neck) and the condition began more than three months ago. Migraines, and pain in neck, lower back, face, or jaw are shown only if pain lasted a whole day or more. "–" means sample is too small to make a reliable estimate.
Source: National Center for Health Statistics, Summary Health Statistics for U.S. Adults: National Health Interview Survey, 2007, Vital and Health Statistics, Series 10, No. 240, 2008, Internet site http://www.cdc.gov/nchs/nhis.htm

Table 3.23 Distribution of Health Conditions among Adults by Age, 2007

(percent distribution of people aged 18 or older with selected health conditions, by type of condition and age, 2007)

	total	18 to 44	45 to 64	aged 65 or older total	65 to 74	75 or older
Total people aged 18 or older	100.0%	49.7%	34.1%	16.2%	8.6%	7.6%
Selected circulatory diseases						
Heart disease, all types	100.0	18.3	36.9	44.8	20.7	24.1
Coronary	100.0	7.6	37.2	55.2	26.1	29.0
Hypertension	100.0	17.2	46.1	36.7	18.4	18.3
Stroke	100.0	5.3	39.7	55.0	22.2	32.8
Selected respiratory conditions						
Emphysema	100.0	6.0	47.2	46.7	23.0	23.7
Asthma, ever	100.0	53.3	32.4	14.4	8.3	6.1
Asthma, still	100.0	49.4	33.9	16.7	9.8	6.9
Hay fever	100.0	44.0	42.7	13.3	7.7	5.6
Sinusitis	100.0	39.5	43.0	17.5	10.0	7.5
Chronic bronchitis	100.0	33.1	42.4	24.5	13.8	10.7
Selected types of cancer						
Any cancer	100.0	12.7	38.5	48.7	23.0	25.8
Breast cancer	100.0	6.8	39.1	54.1	23.8	30.3
Cervical cancer	100.0	43.2	41.2	15.5	9.1	6.4
Prostate cancer	100.0	–	26.7	73.3	32.0	41.4
Other selected diseases and conditions						
Diabetes	100.0	14.1	46.9	39.1	22.2	16.8
Ulcers	100.0	31.8	38.9	29.3	14.6	14.7
Kidney disease	100.0	22.7	36.7	40.7	17.7	22.9
Liver disease	100.0	28.3	51.9	19.9	13.9	6.0
Arthritis	100.0	16.8	46.2	37.0	17.9	19.1
Chronic joint symptoms	100.0	27.4	46.0	26.6	13.2	13.4
Migraines or severe headaches	100.0	60.0	33.9	6.1	3.9	2.1
Pain in neck	100.0	40.8	41.6	17.6	9.8	7.9
Pain in lower back	100.0	43.0	38.3	18.7	9.9	8.8
Pain in face or jaw	100.0	51.3	38.1	10.6	6.7	3.9
Selected sensory problems						
Hearing	100.0	19.8	40.2	40.0	17.2	22.8
Vision	100.0	33.9	41.5	24.5	11.0	13.5
Absence of all natural teeth	100.0	12.2	33.0	54.9	25.2	29.7

Note: The conditions shown are those that have ever been diagnosed by a doctor, except as noted. Hay fever, sinusitis, and chronic bronchitis have been diagnosed in the past 12 months. Kidney and liver diseases have been diagnosed in the past 12 months and exclude kidney stones, bladder infections, and incontinence. Chronic joint symptoms are shown if respondent had pain, aching, or stiffness in or around a joint (excluding back and neck) and the condition began more than three months ago. Migraines, and pain in neck, lower back, face, or jaw are shown only if pain lasted a whole day or more. "–" means sample is too small to make a reliable estimate.
Source: National Center for Health Statistics, Summary Health Statistics for U.S. Adults: National Health Interview Survey, 2007, Vital and Health Statistics, Series 10, No. 240, 2008, Internet site http://www.cdc.gov/nchs/nhis.htm; calculations by New Strategist

Table 3.24 Percent of Adults with Health Conditions by Age, 2007

(percent of people aged 18 or older with selected health conditions, by type of condition and age, 2007)

	total	18 to 44	45 to 64	65 to 74	75 or older
Total people aged 18 or older	100.0%	100.0%	100.0%	100.0%	100.0%
Selected circulatory diseases					
Heart disease, all types	11.3	4.1	12.2	27.1	35.8
Coronary	6.1	0.9	6.7	18.6	23.6
Hypertension	23.7	8.2	32.1	50.9	57.4
Stroke	2.4	0.3	2.8	6.3	10.6
Selected respiratory conditions					
Emphysema	1.7	0.2	2.3	4.5	5.2
Asthma, ever	10.9	11.7	10.4	10.6	8.8
Asthma, still	7.3	7.2	7.2	8.3	6.6
Hay fever	7.6	6.7	9.5	6.8	5.6
Sinusitis	11.6	9.3	14.7	13.5	11.6
Chronic bronchitis	3.4	2.3	4.2	5.5	4.8
Selected types of cancer					
Any cancer	7.3	1.9	8.3	19.6	25.0
Breast cancer	1.2	0.2	1.4	3.3	4.7
Cervical cancer	0.9	0.8	1.1	*0.9	0.6
Prostate cancer	1.9	–	1.5	7.4	12.8
Other selected diseases and conditions					
Diabetes	7.8	2.2	10.7	20.3	17.6
Ulcers	6.5	4.2	7.4	11.0	12.6
Kidney disease	1.5	0.7	1.6	3.1	4.5
Liver disease	1.2	0.7	1.8	1.9	0.9
Arthritis	20.8	7.1	28.2	43.4	52.7
Chronic joint symptoms	24.2	13.3	32.6	37.2	42.9
Migraines or severe headaches	12.3	14.8	12.2	5.6	3.5
Pain in neck	13.0	10.7	15.9	14.7	13.5
Pain in lower back	25.6	22.2	28.7	29.4	29.7
Pain in face or jaw	4.1	4.2	4.5	3.2	2.1
Selected sensory problems					
Hearing	14.9	6.0	17.6	29.8	45.0
Vision	10.0	6.9	12.2	12.9	17.9
Absence of all natural teeth	7.6	1.9	7.4	22.4	30.1

Note: The conditions shown are those that have ever been diagnosed by a doctor, except as noted. Hay fever, sinusitis, and chronic bronchitis have been diagnosed in the past 12 months. Kidney and liver diseases have been diagnosed in the past 12 months and exclude kidney stones, bladder infections, and incontinence. Chronic joint symptoms are shown if respondent had pain, aching, or stiffness in or around a joint (excluding back and neck) and the condition began more than three months ago. Migraines, and pain in neck, lower back, face, or jaw are shown only if pain lasted a whole day or more. "–" means sample is too small to make a reliable estimate.
Source: National Center for Health Statistics, Summary Health Statistics for U.S. Adults: National Health Interview Survey, 2007, Vital and Health Statistics, Series 10, No. 240, 2008, Internet site http://www.cdc.gov/nchs/nhis.htm; calculations by New Strategist

Many People Are Disabled

Fifteen percent of Americans have physical difficulties.

Thirty-three million Americans—or 15 percent of adults— report having physical difficulties performing a variety of tasks, according to the 2007 National Health Interview Survey. Not surprisingly, the percentage of people with physical difficulties rises with age. Among 18-to-44-year-olds, only 5 percent report problems. The figure rises to 46 percent among people aged 75 or older.

Among all adults, two physical difficulties are most common: stooping, bending, and kneeling; and standing for two hours. Nearly 9 percent of people aged 18 or older say either activity would be "very difficult" or they "can't do it at all." Among people aged 75 or older, 29 percent say they would have trouble standing for two hours. Twenty-seven percent of people aged 75 or older have problems stooping, bending, or kneeling. Twenty-eight percent would have difficulty walking a quarter of a mile.

■ As the large baby-boom generation ages, the number of Americans with physical difficulties will grow rapidly.

The percent of people with physical difficulties rises with age

(percent of people with physical difficulties, by age, 2007)

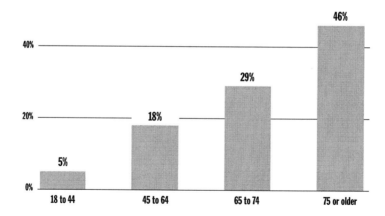

Table 3.25 Difficulties in Physical Functioning among Adults by Age, 2007

(number and percent distribution of people aged 18 or older with difficulties in physical functioning, by type of difficulty and age, 2007; numbers in thousands)

	total	18 to 44	45 to 64	aged 65 or older total	65 to 74	75 or older
Total people aged 18 or older	**223,181**	**110,890**	**76,136**	**36,155**	**19,258**	**16,897**
Total with any physical difficulty	32,977	5,852	13,658	13,467	5,675	7,792
Walk quarter of a mile	16,183	2,000	6,270	7,914	3,142	4,772
Climb 10 steps without resting	12,148	1,469	4,897	5,782	2,128	3,654
Stand for two hours	19,368	2,905	7,971	8,492	3,522	4,970
Sit for two hours	7,220	1,589	3,736	1,895	912	983
Stoop, bend, or kneel	19,943	3,254	8,705	7,983	3,445	4,538
Reach over head	5,543	827	2,517	2,199	861	1,338
Grasp or handle small objects	3,667	482	1,639	1,546	608	938
Lift or carry 10 pounds	8,927	1,237	3,682	4,008	1,574	2,434
Push or pull large objects	14,068	2,333	5,798	5,936	2,465	3,471

PERCENT WITH PHYSICAL DIFFICULTY BY AGE

	total	18 to 44	45 to 64	aged 65 or older total	65 to 74	75 or older
Total people aged 18 or older	**100.0%**	**100.0%**	**100.0%**	**100.0%**	**100.0%**	**100.0%**
Total with any physical difficulty	14.8	5.3	17.9	37.2	29.5	46.1
Walk quarter of a mile	7.3	1.8	8.2	21.9	16.3	28.2
Climb 10 steps without resting	5.4	1.3	6.4	16.0	11.0	21.6
Stand for two hours	8.7	2.6	10.5	23.5	18.3	29.4
Sit for two hours	3.2	1.4	4.9	5.2	4.7	5.8
Stoop, bend, or kneel	8.9	2.9	11.4	22.1	17.9	26.9
Reach over head	2.5	0.7	3.3	6.1	4.5	7.9
Grasp or handle small objects	1.6	0.4	2.2	4.3	3.2	5.6
Lift or carry 10 pounds	4.0	1.1	4.8	11.1	8.2	14.4
Push or pull large objects	6.3	2.1	7.6	16.4	12.8	20.5

PERCENT DISTRIBUTION OF THOSE WITH PHYSICAL DIFFICULTIES BY AGE

	total	18 to 44	45 to 64	aged 65 or older total	65 to 74	75 or older
Total people aged 18 or older	**100.0%**	**49.7%**	**34.1%**	**16.2%**	**8.6%**	**7.6%**
Total with any physical difficulty	100.0	17.7	41.4	40.8	17.2	23.6
Walk quarter of a mile	100.0	12.4	38.7	48.9	19.4	29.5
Climb 10 steps without resting	100.0	12.1	40.3	47.6	17.5	30.1
Stand for two hours	100.0	15.0	41.2	43.8	18.2	25.7
Sit for two hours	100.0	22.0	51.7	26.2	12.6	13.6
Stoop, bend, or kneel	100.0	16.3	43.6	40.0	17.3	22.8
Reach over head	100.0	14.9	45.4	39.7	15.5	24.1
Grasp or handle small objects	100.0	13.1	44.7	42.2	16.6	25.6
Lift or carry 10 pounds	100.0	13.9	41.2	44.9	17.6	27.3
Push or pull large objects	100.0	16.6	41.2	42.2	17.5	24.7

Note: Respondents were classified as having difficulties if they responded "very difficult" or "can't do at all."
Source: National Center for Health Statistics, Summary Health Statistics for U.S. Adults: National Health Interview Survey, 2007, Vital and Health Statistics, Series 10, No. 240, 2008, Internet site http://www.cdc.gov/nchs/nhis.htm; calculations by New Strategist

Women Account for Most Doctor Visits

Americans visited the doctor more than 900 million times in 2006.

Women accounted for 59 percent of the 902 million doctor visits of 2006. They accounted for an even larger 61 percent of hospital outpatient department visits and for a smaller 55 percent of visits to hospital emergency rooms. More than half the people who visited a doctor in 2006 were aged 45 or older, and 23 percent were aged 65 or older.

Among all adults, only 20 percent have not seen a doctor or other health care professional in the past year. The proportion varies considerably by demographic characteristic. More than 30 percent of Hispanics have not been to a doctor in the past year compared with only 17 percent of non-Hispanic whites. Nearly half (46 percent) of adults aged 18 to 64 without health insurance did not see a doctor in the past year compared with only 17 percent of those with private health insurance. People aged 75 or older are most likely to see a doctor frequently. Twenty-two percent have been to the doctor at least 10 times in the past year.

■ As the population ages, health care visits should rise.

Many without health insurance do not go to the doctor

(percent of people aged 18 to 64 who have not visited a doctor or other health care professional in the past year, by health insurance status, 2007)

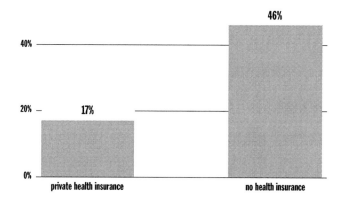

Table 3.26 Health Care Visits by Sex, Age, and Race, 2006

(number and percent distribution of visits to physician's offices, hospital outpatient departments, and emergency rooms, by sex, age, race, and place of care, 2006; numbers in thousands)

	total	physician's offices	hospital outpatient departments	hospital emergency rooms
NUMBER				
Total visits	**1,123,354**	**901,954**	**102,208**	**119,191**
Sex				
Female	660,205	533,292	61,952	64,962
Male	463,148	368,662	40,256	54,230
Age				
Under age 15	199,646	157,906	19,864	21,876
Aged 15 to 24	103,948	72,411	12,012	19,525
Aged 25 to 44	245,443	185,305	25,104	35,034
Aged 45 to 64	310,667	256,494	28,707	25,466
Aged 65 or older	263,649	229,837	16,522	17,290
Race				
Asian	43,742	38,683	2,673	2,386
Black	140,066	87,040	23,468	29,558
Hispanic	151,762	118,695	17,595	15,472
White	923,722	764,636	73,814	85,273
PERCENT DISTRIBUTION BY SEX, AGE, AND RACE				
Total visits	**100.0%**	**100.0%**	**100.0%**	**100.0%**
Sex				
Female	58.8	59.1	60.6	54.5
Male	41.2	40.9	39.4	45.5
Age				
Under age 15	17.8	17.5	19.4	18.4
Aged 15 to 24	9.3	8.0	11.8	16.4
Aged 25 to 44	21.8	20.5	24.6	29.4
Aged 45 to 64	27.7	28.4	28.1	21.4
Aged 65 or older	23.5	25.5	16.2	14.5
Race				
Asian	3.9	4.3	2.6	2.0
Black	12.5	9.7	23.0	24.8
Hispanic	13.5	13.2	17.2	13.0
White	82.2	84.8	72.2	71.5

(continued)

	total	physician's offices	hospital outpatient departments	hospital emergency rooms
PERCENT DISTRIBUTION BY PLACE OF CARE				
Total visits	**100.0%**	**80.3%**	**9.1%**	**10.6%**
Sex				
Female	100.0	80.8	9.4	9.8
Male	100.0	79.6	8.7	11.7
Age				
Under age 15	100.0	79.1	9.9	11.0
Aged 15 to 24	100.0	69.7	11.6	18.8
Aged 25 to 44	100.0	75.5	10.2	14.3
Aged 45 to 64	100.0	82.6	9.2	8.2
Aged 65 or older	100.0	87.2	6.3	6.6
Race				
Asian	100.0	88.4	6.1	5.5
Black	100.0	62.1	16.8	21.1
Hispanic	100.0	78.2	11.6	10.2
White	100.0	82.8	8.0	9.2

Note: Asians, blacks, and whites include only those who are of the race alone. Hispanics may be of any race.
Source: National Center for Health Statistics, Ambulatory Medical Care Utilization Estimates for 2006, National Health Statistics Reports, No. 8, 2008; Internet site http://www.cdc.gov/nchs/about/major/ahcd/adata.htm#CombinedReports; calculations by New Strategist

Table 3.27 Number of Visits to a Doctor or Other Health Care Professional by Selected Characteristics, 2007

(total number and percent distribution of office visits by people aged 18 or older to a doctor or other health care professional in past 12 months, by selected characteristics, 2007; numbers in thousands)

| | total | | | one or more | | | | |
	number	percent	none	total	one	two to three	four to nine	10 more
Total people	**223,181**	**100.0%**	**19.8%**	**80.1%**	**17.5%**	**26.1%**	**23.1%**	**13.4%**
Sex								
Men	107,750	100.0	26.7	73.4	19.8	24.1	19.2	10.3
Women	115,431	100.0	13.6	86.4	15.3	27.9	26.8	16.4
Age								
Aged 18 to 44	110,890	100.0	26.4	73.7	20.0	25.5	17.8	10.4
Aged 45 to 64	76,136	100.0	15.7	84.3	17.6	28.0	24.0	14.7
Aged 65 to 74	19,258	100.0	9.3	90.7	11.0	24.4	36.7	18.6
Aged 75 or older	16,897	100.0	6.4	93.6	8.1	23.9	39.3	22.3
Race and Hispanic origin								
Asian	10,437	100.0	25.8	74.2	21.8	23.4	18.7	10.3
Black	26,366	100.0	20.1	79.8	18.7	24.6	23.6	12.9
Hispanic	29,857	100.0	30.5	69.5	18.0	22.1	18.8	10.6
Non-Hispanic white	153,359	100.0	17.4	82.7	17.0	27.2	24.2	14.3
Education								
Less than high school	29,790	100.0	28.3	71.7	15.3	21.1	21.2	14.1
High school graduate	55,363	100.0	22.1	78.0	17.6	24.5	22.2	13.7
Some college	50,281	100.0	16.4	83.7	16.2	26.5	25.4	15.6
College graduate	56,971	100.0	13.8	86.3	18.3	29.5	25.6	12.9
Household income								
Less than $35,000	69,738	100.0	24.2	75.8	15.3	21.5	22.8	16.2
$35,000 to $49,999	30,247	100.0	24.4	75.5	17.4	22.9	22.1	13.1
$50,000 to $74,999	37,717	100.0	19.0	81.1	18.6	25.7	23.7	13.1
$75,000 to $99,999	24,193	100.0	17.0	83.0	17.4	29.0	23.9	12.7
$100,000 or more	38,006	100.0	13.1	86.8	18.5	33.6	24.5	10.2
Health insurance coverage among people under age 65								
Private	127,870	100.0	16.9	83.1	20.4	29.6	21.7	11.4
Medicaid	14,440	100.0	14.7	85.3	11.7	21.6	24.7	27.3
Other	6,933	100.0	12.8	87.3	17.0	23.2	28.2	18.9
Uninsured	36,974	100.0	45.7	54.3	18.8	17.9	11.1	6.5

Note: Numbers by race and Hispanic origin do not sum to total because not all races are shown, Hispanics may be of any race, education figures are reported only for persons aged 25 or older, and some respondents did not report income.
Source: National Center for Health Statistics, Summary Health Statistics for U.S. Adults: National Health Interview Survey, 2007, Vital and Health Statistics, Series 10, No. 240, 2008, Internet site http://www.cdc.gov/nchs/nhis.htm; calculations by New Strategist

Many Americans Turn to Alternative Medicine

Vitamins are the most popular alternative therapy.

Alternative medicine is a big business. In 2007, fully 38 percent of Americans aged 18 or older used a complementary or alternative medicine or therapy, according to a study by the National Center for Health Statistics. Alternative treatments range from popular regimens such as the South Beach diet to chiropractic care, yoga, and acupuncture.

The adults most likely to use alternative medicines are well-educated, middle-aged, and non-Hispanic white. Fifty-five percent of people with a graduate degree used alternative medicine in 2007, as did 43 percent of non-Hispanic whites and 44 percent of people aged 50 to 59. Not surprisingly, adults with multiple health conditions and frequent doctor visits are more likely to have used alternative medicine than those without health problems.

Twelve percent of children used alternative medicine in 2007. Children whose parents use alternative medicine are twice as likely to be users themselves, at 24 percent. Many are taking vitamins.

■ Among all racial and ethnic groups, American Indians are most likely to use alternative medicine, and 50 percent did in 2007. Many American Indians are visiting traditional healers.

The use of alternative medicine rises with education

(percent of people aged 18 or older who have used alternative medicine in the past 12 months, by education, 2007)

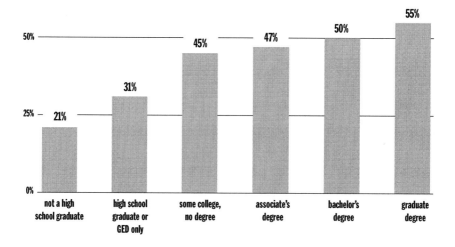

Table 3.28 Use of Alternative and Complementary Medicine by Type, 2007

(number and percent of people who used complementary or alternative medicine in the past 12 months by age, 2007; numbers in thousands)

	children (under age 18)		adults (aged 18 or older)	
	number	percent	number	percent
Any use	**8,720**	**11.8%**	**87,217**	**38.3%**
Alternative medical systems				
Acupuncture	150	0.2	3,141	1.4
Homeopathic treatment	907	1.3	3,909	1.8
Biologically-based therapies				
Nonvitamin, non-mineral natural products	2,850	3.9	38,797	17.7
Diet-based therapies	565	0.8	7,893	3.6
Vegetarian diet	367	0.5	3,351	1.5
Atkins diet	88	0.1	2,673	1.2
South Beach diet	128	0.2	2,334	1.1
Manipulative and body-based therapies				
Chiropractic or osteopathic manipulation	2,020	2.8	18,740	8.6
Massage	743	1.0	18,068	8.3
Movement therapies	299	0.4	3,146	1.5
Pilates	245	0.3	3,015	1.4
Mind-body therapies				
Meditation	725	1.0	20,541	9.4
Guided imagery	293	0.4	4,866	2.2
Progressive relaxation	329	0.5	6,454	2.9
Deep breathing exercises	1,558	2.2	27,794	12.7
Yoga	1,505	2.1	13,172	6.1
Tai chi	113	0.2	2,267	1.0
Energy healing therapy/Reiki	161	0.2	1,216	0.5

Note: Only medicines with at least one million adult users are shown.
Source: National Center for Health Statistics, Complementary and Alternative Medicine Use Among Adults and Children: United States, 2007, National Health Statistics Report, No. 12, 2008; Internet site http://nccam.nih.gov/news/camstats/2007/index.htm

Table 3.29 Characteristics of Adults Who Use Complementary and Alternative Medicine, 2007

(percent of people aged 18 or older who used complementary or alternative medicine in the past 12 months, by selected characteristics, 2007)

	any	biologically based therapies	mind-body therapies	alternative medical systems	manipulative and body-based therapies
Total adults	38.3%	19.9%	19.2%	3.4%	15.2%
Sex					
Female	42.8	21.9	23.8	4.2	18.1
Male	33.5	17.8	14.4	2.7	12.2
Age					
Aged 18 to 29	36.3	15.9	21.3	3.2	15.1
Aged 30 to 39	39.6	19.8	19.9	3.6	17.2
Aged 40 to 49	40.1	20.4	19.7	4.6	17.4
Aged 50 to 59	44.1	24.2	22.9	4.9	17.3
Aged 60 to 69	41.0	25.4	17.3	2.8	13.8
Aged 70 to 84	32.1	19.3	11.9	1.8	9.9
Aged 85 or older	24.2	13.7	9.8	1.9	7.0
Race and Hispanic origin					
American Indian	50.3	23.7	23.3	13.2	13.4
Asian	39.9	19.6	23.4	5.4	11.1
Black	25.5	12.3	14.8	1.4	6.5
Hispanic	23.7	11.8	10.6	3.0	6.7
Non-Hispanic white	43.1	22.7	21.4	3.7	18.7
Education					
Not a high school graduate	20.8	9.8	7.6	2.1	6.4
High school graduate or GED	31.0	16.3	12.1	2.0	11.5
Some college, no degree	45.0	24.4	22.0	4.3	18.0
Associate's degree	47.2	24.9	24.3	3.6	18.2
Bachelor's degree	49.6	27.5	25.5	5.4	20.7
Graduate degree	55.4	30.1	34.2	6.1	23.6
Health insurance status of people under age 65					
Private health insurance	42.7	21.3	22.0	3.9	19.0
Public health insurance	30.6	14.9	18.7	2.6	9.6
No health insurance	31.5	17.0	16.2	4.0	9.8
Number of health conditions					
No conditions	21.3	10.0	9.8	1.4	7.5
One to two conditions	33.3	16.5	16.2	2.2	12.5
Three to five conditions	42.3	22.8	19.5	3.9	18.1
Six or more conditions	53.8	28.4	30.6	5.7	22.1

(continued)

	any	biologically based therapies	mind-body therapies	alternative medical systems	manipulative and body-based therapies
Number of visits to doctor in past 12 months					
No visits	24.5%	13.0%	13.2%	2.0%	6.0%
One visit	32.3	16.8	14.7	2.7	10.7
Two to three visits	39.4	20.9	19.7	3.1	15.0
Four to nine visits	47.2	25.1	23.8	4.2	20.6
10 or more visits	53.4	25.3	28.8	6.7	28.3
Delayed conventional care because of worry about costs					
Yes	48.2	26.3	27.7	5.6	17.6
No	37.0	19.1	18.2	3.2	14.9

Definitions: Biologically based therapies include chelation therapy, nonvitamin, nonmineral, natural products, and diet-based therapies. Mind-body therapies include biofeedback, meditation, guided imagery, progressive relaxation, deep breathing exercises, hypnosis, yoga, tai chi, and qi gong. Alternative medical systems include acupuncture, ayurveda, homeopathic treatment, naturopathy, and traditional healers. Manipulative body-based therapies include chiropractic and osteopathic manipulation, massage, and movement therapies.

Note: Asians and blacks are those who identify themselves as being of the race alone. Non-Hispanic whites are those who identify themselves as being white alone and not Hispanic. American Indians are those who identify themselves as being American Indian or Alaska Native alone.

Source: National Center for Health Statistics, Complementary and Alternative Medicine Use Among Adults and Children: United States, 2007, National Health Statistics Report, No. 12, 2008; Internet site http://nccam.nih.gov/news/camstats/2007/index.htm

Table 3.30 Characteristics of Children Who Use Complementary and Alternative Medicine, 2007

(percent of people under age 18 who used complementary or alternative medicine (CAM) in the past 12 months, by selected characteristics, 2007)

	any	biologically based therapies	mind-body therapies	alternative medical systems	manipulative and body-based therapies
Total children	**11.8%**	**4.7%**	**4.3%**	**2.6%**	**3.7%**
Children whose parent uses CAM	23.9	10.3	9.8	4.2	7.5
Sex					
Female	12.6	4.6	4.9	2.8	4.2
Male	11.0	4.8	3.8	2.4	3.2
Age					
Aged 0 to 4	7.6	3.2	1.9	2.9	2.1
Aged 5 to 11	10.7	4.3	3.9	2.5	2.8
Aged 12 to 17	16.4	6.3	6.8	2.5	5.9
Race and Hispanic origin					
Black	5.9	1.7	3.0	1.4	0.8
Hispanic	7.9	2.8	2.8	2.5	1.9
White	12.8	5.2	4.4	2.8	4.4
Family structure					
Mother and father	12.7	5.2	4.3	2.7	4.2
Mother, no father	9.6	3.3	4.8	2.2	2.5
Parent's education					
Not a high school graduate	4.8	1.7	1.9	1.5	1.3
High school graduate or GED	8.0	2.8	2.3	1.7	2.5
More than high school	14.7	6.1	5.6	3.2	4.6
Number of health conditions					
No conditions	4.0	1.3	1.1	1.9	1.4
One to two conditions	8.5	2.9	3.2	1.5	2.3
Three to five conditions	14.1	6.0	4.8	2.9	4.2
Six or more conditions	23.8	8.8	10.2	5.6	5.4
Number of visits to doctor in past 12 months					
No visits	7.7	4.9	2.5	2.6	1.9
One visit	7.8	3.6	2.1	1.6	1.9
Two to three visits	11.1	3.4	4.5	2.6	3.1
Four to nine visits	15.0	6.0	5.0	2.5	5.6
10 or more visits	28.4	12.0	12.9	6.3	10.0
Delayed conventional care because of worry about costs					
Yes	16.9	7.3	6.6	5.0	6.2
No	11.6	4.6	4.2	2.6	3.6

Definitions: Biologically based therapies include chelation therapy, nonvitamin, nonmineral natural products, and diet-based therapies. Mind-body therapies include biofeedback, meditation, guided imagery, progressive relaxation deep breathing exercises, hypnosis, yoga, tai chi, and qi gong. Alternative medical systems include acupuncture, ayurveda, homeopathic treatment, naturopathy, and traditional healers. Manipulative body-based therapies include chiropractic or osteopathic manipulation, massage, and movement therapies.

Note: Asians and blacks are those who identify themselves as being of the race alone. Non-Hispanic whites are those who identify themselves as being white alone and not Hispanic. American Indians are those who identify themselves as being American Indian or Alaska Native alone.

Source: National Center for Health Statistics, Complementary and Alternative Medicine Use Among Adults and Children: United States, 2007, National Health Statistics Report, No. 12, 2008; Internet site http://nccam.nih.gov/news/camstats/2007/index.htm

One in Twelve Had a Hospital Stay in 2007

Older Americans are most likely to be hospitalized.

As health insurance companies try to cut costs, hospitals have changed their strategy. They are less likely to keep patients overnight and more likely to care for them through outpatient services.

In 2007, only 8 percent of the population was hospitalized overnight. People aged 65 or older are most likely to experience a hospital stay, with 17 percent having been hospitalized overnight in 2007. The least educated and those with the lowest incomes are also most likely to be hospitalized, in large part because older Americans are disproportionately represented in those groups.

■ While greater outpatient care has cut costs for hospitals and insurers, it has increased the caregiving burden on family members.

Females are more likely than males to be hospitalized

(percent of people who experienced an overnight hospital stay, by sex, 2007)

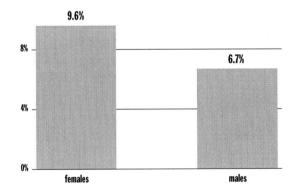

Table 3.31 Number of Overnight Hospital Stays by Selected Characteristics, 2007

(total number of people and percent distribution by experience of an overnight hospital stay in past 12 months, by selected characteristics, 2007; numbers in thousands)

	total		number of stays	
	number	percent	none	one or more
Total people	**296,905**	**100.0%**	**91.8%**	**8.2%**
Sex				
Female	151,471	100.0	90.4	9.6
Male	145,434	100.0	93.3	6.7
Age				
Under age 12	48,526	100.0	92.3	7.7
Aged 12 to 17	25,200	100.0	97.5	2.5
Aged 18 to 44	110,889	100.0	93.3	6.7
Aged 45 to 64	76,110	100.0	91.8	8.2
Aged 65 or older	36,180	100.0	82.7	17.3
Race and Hispanic origin				
Asian	13,449	100.0	94.3	5.7
Black	37,777	100.0	90.8	9.2
Hispanic	45,206	100.0	92.4	7.6
Non-Hispanic white	195,427	100.0	91.8	8.2
Education				
Less than high school	28,052	100.0	89.0	11.0
High school graduate	55,875	100.0	90.9	9.1
Some college	49,166	100.0	89.9	10.1
College graduate	54,896	100.0	91.6	8.4
Household income				
Less than $35,000	84,457	100.0	89.8	10.2
$35,000 to $49,999	37,596	100.0	91.7	8.3
$50,000 to $74,999	47,350	100.0	92.0	8.0
$75,000 to $99,999	31,953	100.0	92.8	7.2
$100,000 or more	50,799	100.0	93.3	6.7
Health insurance coverage among people under age 65				
Private	172,411	100.0	93.8	6.2
Medicaid	34,556	100.0	85.5	14.5
Other	8,329	100.0	88.8	11.2
Uninsured	42,930	100.0	95.6	4.4

Note: Numbers by race and Hispanic origin do not sum to total because not all races are shown and Hispanics may be of any race.

Source: National Center for Health Statistics, Summary Health Statistics for the U.S. Population: National Health Interview Survey, 2007, Vital and Health Statistics, Series 10, No. 238, 2008, Internet site http://www.cdc.gov/nchs/nhis.htm; calculations by New Strategist

Nearly 1 Million Have Been Diagnosed with AIDS

Eight out of 10 people diagnosed with AIDS are males aged 13 or older.

More than 982,000 people had been diagnosed with AIDS through 2006. While new drug therapies have been successful in reducing AIDS mortality, the number of AIDS cases continues to climb.

Males are an overwhelming 80 percent of AIDS victims. The 30-to-44 age group accounts for the 59 percent majority of people diagnosed with AIDS over the years. A substantial 42 percent of AIDS cases have occurred among blacks and another 40 percent among non-Hispanic whites. Hispanics account for just 16 percent of AIDS cases.

■ Only 19 percent of AIDS victims are females aged 13 or older. Children under age 13 account for less than 1 percent.

Blacks and non-Hispanic whites account for nearly equal shares of AIDS cases

(percent distribution of people diagnosed with AIDS by race and Hispanic origin, through December 2006)

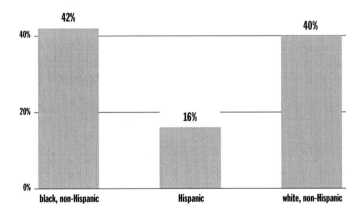

Table 3.32 Cumulative Number of AIDS Cases by Sex and Age, through 2006

(cumulative number and percent distribution of AIDS cases by sex and age at diagnosis, through 2006)

	number	percent distribution
Total cases	982,498	100.0%
Sex		
Males aged 13 or older	783,786	79.8
Females aged 13 or older	189,566	19.3
Age		
Under age 13	9,156	0.9
Aged 13 to 14	1,078	0.1
Aged 15 to 19	5,626	0.6
Aged 20 to 24	36,225	3.7
Aged 25 to 29	117,099	11.9
Aged 30 to 34	197,530	20.1
Aged 35 to 39	213,573	21.7
Aged 40 to 44	170,531	17.4
Aged 45 to 49	107,207	10.9
Aged 50 to 54	59,907	6.1
Aged 55 to 59	32,190	3.3
Aged 60 to 64	17,303	1.8
Aged 65 or older	15,074	1.5

Source: Centers for Disease Control and Prevention, Cases of HIV/AIDS and AIDS, Internet site http://www.cdc.gov/hiv/topics/ surveillance/resources/reports/2006report/table3.htm

Table 3.33 Cumulative Number of AIDS Cases by Race and Hispanic Origin, through 2006

(cumulative number and percent distribution of AIDS cases by race and Hispanic origin, through 2006)

	number	percent distribution
Total cases	982,498	100.0%
American Indian	3,345	0.3
Asian	7,951	0.8
Black, non-Hispanic	409,982	41.7
Hispanic	161,505	16.4
White, non-Hispanic	394,024	40.1

Note: Numbers do not add to total because not all races are shown.
Source: Centers for Disease Control and Prevention, Cases of HIV/AIDS and AIDS, Internet site http://www.cdc.gov/hiv/topics/ surveillance/resources/reports/2006report/table3.htm

Heart Disease and Cancer Are the Biggest Killers

More than half the deaths in 2006 were caused by heart disease or cancer.

Heart disease and cancer each kill more than half a million Americans a year. These illnesses are by far the leading causes of death in the United States, accounting for 26 and 23 percent of deaths in 2006, respectively. The third leading cause of death, cerebrovascular disease, accounts for only 6 percent of the total.

The number of accidental deaths (in fifth place as a cause of death) has declined over the past few years because of the greater use of seat belts and tougher drunk driving laws. Alzheimer's disease is becoming a more important cause of death as the population ages. In 2006, nearly 73,000 people died of Alzheimer's, putting it in sixth place as a cause of death. Parkinson's disease ranks 14th.

■ Although medical science has made considerable progress in combating the problem, heart disease will remain the number-one cause of death for years to come.

Heart disease and cancer are most likely to kill

(percent of deaths caused by the top five causes of death, 2006)

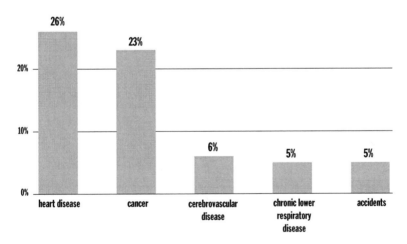

Table 3.34 Leading Causes of Death, 2006

(number and percent distribution of deaths accounted for by the 15 leading causes of death, 2006)

		number	percent distribution
All causes		**2,425,901**	**100.0%**
1.	Diseases of heart	629,191	25.9
2.	Malignant neoplasms	560,102	23.1
3.	Cerebrovascular diseases	137,265	5.7
4.	Chronic lower respiratory diseases	124,614	5.1
5.	Accidents	117,748	4.9
6.	Alzheimer's disease	72,914	3.0
7.	Diabetes mellitus	72,507	3.0
8.	Influenza and pneumonia	56,247	2.3
9.	Nephritis, nephrotic syndrome and nephrosis	44,791	1.8
10.	Septicemia	34,031	1.4
11.	Suicide	32,185	1.3
12.	Chronic liver disease and cirrhosis	27,299	1.1
13.	Essential (primary) hypertension and hypertensive renal disease	23,985	1.0
14.	Parkinson's disease	19,660	0.8
15.	Assault (homicide)	18,029	0.7
All other causes		455,333	18.8

Source: National Center for Health Statistics, Deaths: Preliminary Deaths for 2006, National Vital Statistics Report, Vol. 56, No. 16, 2008, Internet site http://www.cdc.gov/nchs/deaths.htm; calculations by New Strategist

Life Expectancy Is at a Record High

Americans born in 2006 can expect to live 78.1 years.

Since 1950, life expectancy at birth has climbed nearly 10 years, from 68.2 to 78.1 years. Life expectancy at age 65 has grown by five years. Someone who turned age 65 in 2006 could expect to live another 19 years.

Women have longer life expectancies than men at every age. A girl born in 2006 can expect to live to age 80.7. Their male counterparts can expect to live to age 75.4. At age 65, women can expect to live an additional 20.3 years compared with 17.4 years for men. By age 90, however, the difference in life expectancy between men and women is measured in months rather than years.

■ Although life expectancy has increased substantially, the United States ranks well below many other developed nations in expected length of life.

Life expectancy at birth reached 78.1 years in 2006

(years of life remaining at birth for selected years)

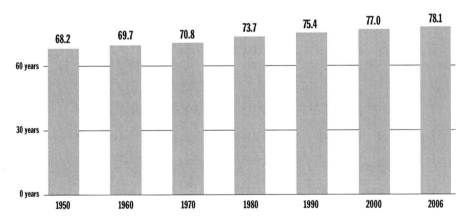

Table 3.35 Life Expectancy by Age, 1950 to 2006

(years of life remaining at birth and age 65, 1950 to 2006; change in years of life remaining for selected years)

	at birth	age 65
2006	78.1	19.0
2000	77.0	17.9
1990	75.4	17.2
1980	73.7	16.4
1970	70.8	15.2
1960	69.7	14.3
1950	68.2	13.9
Change		
2000 to 2006	1.1	1.1
1950 to 2006	9.9	5.1

Source: National Center for Health Statistics, Deaths: Preliminary Deaths for 2006, National Vital Statistics Report, Vol. 56, No. 16, 2008, Internet site http://www.cdc.gov/nchs/deaths.htm; calculations by New Strategist

Table 3.36 Life Expectancy by Age and Sex, 2006

(years of life remaining at selected ages, by sex, 2006)

	total	females	males
At birth	78.1	80.7	75.4
Aged 1	77.7	80.2	75.0
Aged 5	73.7	76.3	71.1
Aged 10	68.8	71.3	66.2
Aged 15	63.8	66.4	61.2
Aged 20	59.0	61.5	56.5
Aged 25	54.3	56.6	51.9
Aged 30	49.6	51.8	47.2
Aged 35	44.8	46.9	42.6
Aged 40	40.2	42.2	37.9
Aged 45	35.6	37.5	33.5
Aged 50	31.2	33.0	29.1
Aged 55	26.9	28.6	25.0
Aged 60	22.8	24.3	21.1
Aged 65	19.0	20.3	17.4
Aged 70	15.4	16.5	14.0
Aged 75	12.2	13.0	10.9
Aged 80	9.3	9.9	8.3
Aged 85	7.0	7.4	6.2
Aged 90	5.1	5.3	4.5
Aged 95	3.7	3.8	3.3
Aged 100	2.7	2.7	2.4

Source: National Center for Health Statistics, Deaths: Preliminary Deaths for 2006, National Vital Statistics Report, Vol. 56, No. 16, 2008, Internet site http://www.cdc.gov/nchs/deaths.htm; calculations by New Strategist

4

Housing Trends

■ **Homeownership is near its record high.**

In 2008, 67.8 percent of households owned their home. This figure was down from 69.0 percent in 2004 but still above the 67.4 percent rate of 2000.

■ **Non-Hispanic whites are most likely to own a home.**

Seventy-five percent of non-Hispanic white households owned their home in 2008. Among blacks the proportion was 47 percent.

■ **The Midwest has the highest homeownership rate.**

Seventy-two percent of households in the Midwest owned their home in 2008, compared with only 63 percent in the West.

■ **American homes have a median of 1,807 square feet of living space.**

Houses have grown larger as homebuyers demanded more bathrooms, bedrooms, and rooms for business.

■ **Most householders are happy with their home.**

When asked how they would rate their housing unit on a scale of 1 (worst) to 10 (best), fully 72 percent of householders rate their home an 8 or higher.

■ **Most homeowners do not have public transportation in their area.**

Seventy percent of renters have public transportation available to them compared with only 46 percent of owners.

■ **The median value of owned homes stood at $191,471 in 2007.**

Home values are lower today because of the ongoing downturn in the housing market.

Homeownership Is Near Its Record High

Rates are down in most age groups, however.

In 2008, 67.8 percent of households owned their home—below the record high of 69.0 percent reached in 2004 but still higher than the homeownership rate of 2000. Homeownership rates fell in all but the youngest age group between 2000 and 2008, with householders aged 45 to 54 experiencing the biggest decline. Their homeownership rate fell by 1.5 percentage points between 2000 and 2008, to 75.0 percent.

Homeownership rates climbed for every household type and every race and Hispanic origin group between 2000 and 2008. Eighty-three percent of couples owned their home in 2008—the highest rate of homeownership among all household types. Seventy-five percent of non-Hispanic whites owned a home in 2008 compared with 47 percent of blacks and 49 percent of Hispanics.

■ Although foreclosures are increasing in number, their impact remains small among the nation's 76 million homeowners.

Homeownership rates are highest among older Americans

(percent of householders who own their home, by age, 2008)

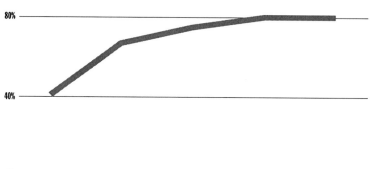

Table 4.1 Homeownership Rates by Age, Household Type, Race, and Hispanic Origin, 2000 and 2008

(percent of households that own their home by age of householder, household type, race, and Hispanic origin of householder, 2000 and 2008; percentage point change, 2000–08)

	2008	2000	percentage point change 2000–08
TOTAL HOUSEHOLDS	**67.8%**	**67.4%**	**0.4**
Age of householder			
Under age 35	41.0	40.8	0.2
Aged 35 to 44	67.0	67.9	–0.9
Aged 45 to 54	75.0	76.5	–1.5
Aged 55 to 64	80.1	80.3	–0.2
Aged 65 or older	80.1	80.4	–0.3
Type of household			
Married couple	83.4	82.4	1.1
Female hh, no spouse present	49.5	49.1	0.4
Male hh, no spouse present	57.6	57.5	0.1
Women living alone	58.6	58.1	0.5
Men living alone	50.6	47.4	3.2
Race and Hispanic origin			
American Indian	56.5	56.2	0.3
Asian	59.5	52.8	6.7
Black	47.4	47.2	0.2
Hispanic	49.1	46.3	2.8
Non-Hispanic white	75.0	73.8	1.2

Note: American Indians, Asians, and blacks are those who identified themselves as being of the race alone.
Source: Bureau of the Census, Housing Vacancy Surveys, Internet site http://www.census.gov/hhes/www/housing/hvs/hvs.html; calculations by New Strategist

Table 4.2 Age of Householder by Homeownership Status, 2008

(number and percent distribution of households by age of householder and homeownership status, 2008; numbers in thousands)

	total	owner	renter
Total households	**111,409**	**75,566**	**35,843**
Under age 35	24,710	10,120	14,589
Aged 35 to 44	21,524	14,425	7,098
Aged 45 to 54	23,382	17,537	5,845
Aged 55 to 64	18,818	15,069	3,748
Aged 65 or older	22,976	18,414	4,562
PERCENT DISTRIBUTION BY HOMEOWNERSHIP STATUS			
Total households	**100.0%**	**67.8%**	**32.2%**
Under age 35	100.0	41.0	59.0
Aged 35 to 44	100.0	67.0	33.0
Aged 45 to 54	100.0	75.0	25.0
Aged 55 to 64	100.0	80.1	19.9
Aged 65 or older	100.0	80.1	19.9
PERCENT DISTRIBUTION BY AGE			
Total households	**100.0%**	**100.0%**	**100.0%**
Under age 35	22.2	13.4	40.7
Aged 35 to 44	19.3	19.1	19.8
Aged 45 to 54	21.0	23.2	16.3
Aged 55 to 64	16.9	19.9	10.5
Aged 65 or older	20.6	24.4	12.7

Source: Bureau of the Census, Housing Vacancy Survey, Internet site http://www.census.gov/hhes/www/housing/hvs/hvs.html; calculations by New Strategist

Table 4.3 Type of Household by Homeownership Status, 2008

(number and percent distribution of households by type and homeownership status, 2008; numbers in thousands)

	total	owner	renter
Total households	**111,409**	**75,566**	**35,843**
Married couple	55,508	46,285	9,223
Female hh, no spouse present	13,602	6,737	6,865
Male hh, no spouse present	5,149	2,965	2,185
Women living alone	17,016	9,970	7,046
Men living alone	13,654	6,902	6,752
PERCENT DISTRIBUTION BY HOMEOWNERSHIP STATUS			
Total households	**100.0%**	**67.8%**	**32.2%**
Married couple	100.0	83.4	16.6
Female hh, no spouse present	100.0	49.5	50.5
Male hh, no spouse present	100.0	57.6	42.4
Women living alone	100.0	58.6	41.4
Men living alone	100.0	50.6	49.4
PERCENT DISTRIBUTION BY HOUSEHOLD TYPE			
Total households	**100.0%**	**100.0%**	**100.0%**
Married couple	49.8	61.3	25.7
Female hh, no spouse present	12.2	8.9	19.2
Male hh, no spouse present	4.6	3.9	6.1
Women living alone	15.3	13.2	19.7
Men living alone	12.3	9.1	18.8

Note: Numbers will not sum to total because not all household types are shown.
Source: Bureau of the Census, Housing Vacancy Survey, Internet site http://www.census.gov/hhes/www/housing/hvs/hvs.html; calculations by New Strategist

Table 4.4 Race and Hispanic Origin of Householders by Homeownership Status, 2007

(number and percent distribution of households by race and Hispanic origin of householder and homeownership status, 2007; numbers in thousands)

	total	owner	renter
Total households	**110,692**	**75,647**	**35,045**
American Indian	891	464	427
Asian	3,869	2,302	1,566
Black	13,856	6,464	7,392
Hispanic	12,609	6,364	6,244
Non-Hispanic white	78,744	59,549	19,195
PERCENT DISTRIBUTION BY HOMEOWNERSHIP STATUS			
Total households	**100.0%**	**68.3%**	**31.7%**
American Indian	100.0	52.1	47.9
Asian	100.0	59.5	40.5
Black	100.0	46.7	53.3
Hispanic	100.0	50.5	49.5
Non-Hispanic white	100.0	75.6	24.4
PERCENT DISTRIBUTION BY RACE AND HISPANIC ORIGIN			
Total households	**100.0%**	**100.0%**	**100.0%**
American Indian	0.8	0.6	1.2
Asian	3.5	3.0	4.5
Black	12.5	8.5	21.1
Hispanic	11.4	8.4	17.8
Non-Hispanic white	71.1	78.7	54.8

Note: Data from 2007 are the latest data available on the number of owners and renters by race and Hispanic origin. American Indians, Asians, and blacks are those who identified themselves as being of the race alone.
Source: Bureau of the Census, American Housing Survey for the United States: 2007, Internet site http://www.census.gov/hhes/ www/housing/ahs/ahs07/ahs07.html; calculations by New Strategist

Homeownership Rises with Income

Because educated householders tend to be the most affluent, homeownership also rises with education.

The majority of households in every income group except the lowest two (with incomes of less than $20,000) own their home. The higher the income the higher the homeownership rate, with the proportion climbing to 92 percent among households with incomes of $120,000 or more.

Homeownership also rises with education, although not as sharply. Among householders without a high school diploma, 57 percent are homeowners. Among those with a graduate degree the figure is 80 percent.

Native-born Americans are more likely to be homeowners than U.S. residents born in another country. Nevertheless, the 54 percent majority of immigrants are homeowners.

■ Among immigrants who came to the U.S. before 1990, from 64 to 73 percent are homeowners.

Most immigrants are homeowners

(percent of householders who own their home, by nativity status, 2007)

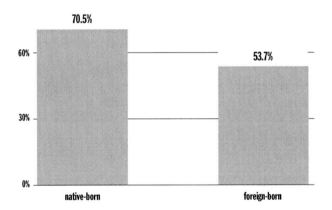

Table 4.5 Household Income by Homeownership Status, 2007

(number and percent distribution of households by household income and homeownership status, 2007; numbers in thousands)

	total	owner	renter
Total households	**110,692**	**75,647**	**35,045**
Less than $10,000	10,105	4,088	6,017
$10,000 to $19,999	11,360	5,613	5,747
$20,000 to $29,999	15,236	8,642	6,594
$30,000 to $39,999	11,247	6,801	4,445
$40,000 to $49,999	9,695	6,444	3,252
$50,000 to $59,999	8,764	6,308	2,456
$60,000 to $79,999	14,275	11,023	3,252
$80,000 to $99,999	9,611	8,169	1,442
$100,000 to $119,999	6,624	5,834	790
$120,000 or more	13,775	12,725	1,050
Median income	$47,632	$59,886	$28,921

PERCENT DISTRIBUTION BY HOMEOWNERSHIP STATUS

Total households	**100.0%**	**68.3%**	**31.7%**
Less than $10,000	100.0	40.5	59.5
$10,000 to $19,999	100.0	49.4	50.6
$20,000 to $29,999	100.0	56.7	43.3
$30,000 to $39,999	100.0	60.5	39.5
$40,000 to $49,999	100.0	66.5	33.5
$50,000 to $59,999	100.0	72.0	28.0
$60,000 to $79,999	100.0	77.2	22.8
$80,000 to $99,999	100.0	85.0	15.0
$100,000 to $119,999	100.0	88.1	11.9
$120,000 or more	100.0	92.4	7.6

PERCENT DISTRIBUTION BY HOUSEHOLD INCOME

Total households	**100.0%**	**100.0%**	**100.0%**
Less than $10,000	9.1	5.4	17.2
$10,000 to $19,999	10.3	7.4	16.4
$20,000 to $29,999	13.8	11.4	18.8
$30,000 to $39,999	10.2	9.0	12.7
$40,000 to $49,999	8.8	8.5	9.3
$50,000 to $59,999	7.9	8.3	7.0
$60,000 to $79,999	12.9	14.6	9.3
$80,000 to $99,999	8.7	10.8	4.1
$100,000 to $119,999	6.0	7.7	2.3
$120,000 or more	12.4	16.8	3.0

Source: Bureau of the Census, American Housing Survey for the United States: 2007, Internet site http://www.census.gov/hhes/www/housing/ahs/ahs07/ahs07.html; calculations by New Strategist

Table 4.6 Educational Attainment of Householders by Homeownership Status, 2007

(number and percent distribution of households by educational attainment of householder and homeownership status, 2007; numbers in thousands)

	total	owner	renter
Total households	**110,692**	**75,647**	**35,045**
Not a high school graduate	16,779	9,581	7,198
High school graduate	33,945	22,744	11,202
Some college, no degree	19,264	12,450	6,814
Associate's degree	8,777	6,265	2,512
Bachelor's degree	20,354	15,307	5,048
Graduate or professional degree	11,572	9,300	2,272
PERCENT DISTRIBUTION BY HOMEOWNERSHIP STATUS			
Total households	**100.0%**	**68.3%**	**31.7%**
Not a high school graduate	100.0	57.1	42.9
High school graduate	100.0	67.0	33.0
Some college, no degree	100.0	64.6	35.4
Associate's degree	100.0	71.4	28.6
Bachelor's degree	100.0	75.2	24.8
Graduate or professional degree	100.0	80.4	19.6
PERCENT DISTRIBUTION BY EDUCATIONAL ATTAINMENT			
Total households	**100.0%**	**100.0%**	**100.0%**
Not a high school graduate	15.2	12.7	20.5
High school graduate	30.7	30.1	32.0
Some college, no degree	17.4	16.5	19.4
Associate's degree	7.9	8.3	7.2
Bachelor's degree	18.4	20.2	14.4
Graduate or professional degree	10.5	12.3	6.5

Source: Bureau of the Census, American Housing Survey for the United States: 2007, Internet site http://www.census.gov/hhes/ www/housing/ahs/ahs07/ahs07.html; calculations by New Strategist

Table 4.7 Nativity of Householder by Homeownership Status, 2007

(number and percent distribution of households headed by native-born and immigrant householders by year of immigration and homeownership status, 2007; numbers in thousands)

	total	owner	renter
Total households	**110,692**	**75,647**	**35,045**
Native-born	96,641	68,105	28,534
Foreign-born	14,051	7,542	6,511
Year of immigration			
Total immigrant householders	14,051	7,542	6,511
2000 to 2007	2,768	597	2,172
1990 to 1999	3,818	1,827	1,991
1980 to 1989	3,495	2,234	1,261
1979 or earlier	3,970	2,884	1,087
PERCENT DISTRIBUTION BY HOMEOWNERSHIP STATUS			
Total households	**100.0%**	**68.3%**	**31.7%**
Native-born	100.0	70.5	29.5
Foreign-born	100.0	53.7	46.3
Year of immigration			
Total immigrant householders	100.0%	53.7%	46.3%
2000 to 2007	100.0	21.6	78.5
1990 to 1999	100.0	47.9	52.1
1980 to 1989	100.0	63.9	36.1
1979 or earlier	100.0	72.6	27.4

Source: Bureau of the Census, American Housing Survey for the United States: 2007, Internet site http://www.census.gov/hhes/ www/housing/ahs/ahs07/ahs07.html; calculations by New Strategist

Homeownership Is Highest in the Midwest

Central city households are least likely to own their home.

The Midwest has the highest homeownership rate in the nation—nearly 72 percent of households in the region owned their home in 2008. Because housing prices were so high in the West, the region has the lowest homeownership rate at 63 percent.

Half of homeowners live in the suburbs. Seventy-three percent of suburban householders are homeowners, as are 76 percent of households in nonmetropolitan areas. In the nation's central cities, a much smaller 53 percent of households own their home.

By state, the highest homeownership rate is found in West Virginia (78 percent). The lowest rate (except for the District of Columbia) is in New York State, where only 55 percent of households own their home. Despite the housing downturn, most states made gains in homeownership between 2000 and 2008. Massachusetts and New Hampshire are the biggest gainers—up nearly 6 percentage points to 66 and 75 percent, respectively.

Among the 75 largest metropolitan areas, homeownership is highest in Grand Rapids–Wyoming, Michigan, where 78 percent of households owned their home in 2008. Homeownership bottoms out at 52 percent in the Los Angeles and Fresno metropolitan areas in California.

■ The homeownership rate is down slightly in many metropolitan areas because of the downturn in the housing market.

The West has the lowest homeownership rate

(percent of households that own their home, by region, 2008)

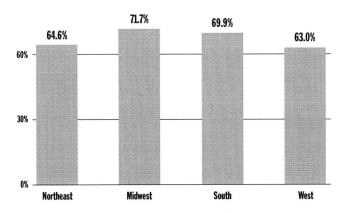

Table 4.8 Region of Residence by Homeownership Status, 2008

(number and percent distribution of households by region of residence and homeownership status, 2008; numbers in thousands)

	total	owner	renter
Total housholds	**111,409**	**75,566**	**35,843**
Northeast	20,421	13,188	7,233
Midwest	25,519	18,307	7,212
South	41,045	28,692	12,353
West	24,424	15,379	9,045
PERCENT DISTRIBUTION BY HOMEOWNERSHIP STATUS			
Total housholds	**100.0%**	**67.8%**	**32.2%**
Northeast	100.0	64.6	35.4
Midwest	100.0	71.7	28.3
South	100.0	69.9	30.1
West	100.0	63.0	37.0
PERCENT DISTRIBUTION BY REGION			
Total housholds	**100.0%**	**100.0%**	**100.0%**
Northeast	18.3	17.5	20.2
Midwest	22.9	24.2	20.1
South	36.8	38.0	34.5
West	21.9	20.4	25.2

Source: Bureau of the Census, Housing Vacancy Survey, Internet site http://www.census.gov/hhes/www/housing/hvs/hvs.html; calculations by New Strategist

Table 4.9 Metropolitan Residence by Homeownership Status, 2007

(number and percent distribution of households by metropolitan residence and homeownership status, 2007; numbers in thousands)

	total	owner	renter
Total households	**110,692**	**75,647**	**35,045**
In metropolitan areas	83,664	55,053	28,612
In central cities	31,602	16,889	14,713
In suburbs	52,062	38,164	13,899
Outside metropolitan areas	27,028	20,594	6,434
PERCENT DISTRIBUTION BY HOMEOWNERSHIP STATUS			
Total households	**100.0%**	**68.3%**	**31.7%**
In metropolitan areas	100.0	65.8	34.2
In central cities	100.0	53.4	46.6
In suburbs	100.0	73.3	26.7
Outside metropolitan areas	100.0	76.2	23.8
PERCENT DISTRIBUTION BY METROPOLITAN RESIDENCE			
Total households	**100.0%**	**100.0%**	**100.0%**
In metropolitan areas	75.6	72.8	81.6
In central cities	28.5	22.3	42.0
In suburbs	47.0	50.5	39.7
Outside metropolitan areas	24.4	27.2	18.4

Source: Bureau of the Census, American Housing Survey for the United States: 2007, Internet site http://www.census.gov/hhes/www/housing/ahs/ahs07/ahs07.html; calculations by New Strategist

Table 4.10 Homeownership Rate by State, 2000 and 2008

(percent of householders who own their home by state, 2000 and 2008; percentage point change, 2000–08)

	2008	2000	percentage point change
Total households	**67.8%**	**67.4%**	**0.4**
Alabama	73.0	73.2	–0.2
Alaska	66.4	66.4	0.0
Arizona	69.1	68.0	1.1
Arkansas	68.9	68.9	0.0
California	57.5	57.1	0.4
Colorado	69.0	68.3	0.7
Connecticut	70.7	70.0	0.7
Delaware	76.2	72.0	4.2
District of Columbia	44.1	41.9	2.2
Florida	71.1	68.4	2.7
Georgia	68.2	69.8	–1.6
Hawaii	59.1	55.2	3.9
Idaho	75.0	70.5	4.5
Illinois	68.9	67.9	1.0
Indiana	74.4	74.9	–0.5
Iowa	74.0	75.2	–1.2
Kansas	68.8	69.3	–0.5
Kentucky	72.8	73.4	–0.6
Louisiana	73.5	68.1	5.4
Maine	73.9	76.5	–2.6
Maryland	70.6	69.9	0.7
Massachusetts	65.7	59.9	5.8
Michigan	75.9	77.2	–1.3
Minnesota	73.1	76.1	–3.0
Mississippi	75.4	75.2	0.2
Missouri	71.4	74.2	–2.8
Montana	70.3	70.2	0.1
Nebraska	69.6	70.2	–0.6
Nevada	63.6	64.0	–0.4
New Hampshire	75.0	69.2	5.8
New Jersey	67.3	66.2	1.1
New Mexico	70.4	73.7	–3.3
New York	55.0	53.4	1.6
North Carolina	69.4	71.1	–1.7
North Dakota	66.6	70.7	–4.1
Ohio	70.8	71.3	–0.5
Oklahoma	70.4	72.7	–2.3
Oregon	66.2	65.3	0.9
Pennsylvania	72.6	74.7	–2.1
Rhode Island	64.5	61.5	3.0

	2008	2000	percentage point change
South Carolina	73.9%	76.5%	−2.6
South Dakota	70.4	71.2	−0.8
Tennessee	71.7	70.9	0.8
Texas	65.5	63.8	1.7
Utah	76.2	72.7	3.5
Vermont	72.8	68.7	4.1
Virginia	70.6	73.9	−3.3
Washington	66.2	63.6	2.6
West Virginia	77.8	75.9	1.9
Wisconsin	70.4	71.8	−1.4
Wyoming	73.3	71.0	2.3

Source: Bureau of the Census, Housing Vacancy Surveys, Internet site http://www.census.gov/hhes/www/housing/hvs/hvs.html; calculations by New Strategist

Table 4.11 Homeownership Rate by Metropolitan Area, 2008

(percent of householders who own their home in the 75 largest metropolitan areas, 2008)

	homeownership rate
Total inside metropolitan areas	**67.8%**
Akron, OH	77.3
Albany–Schenectady–Troy, NY	69.5
Albuquerque, NM	68.2
Allentown–Bethlehem–Easton, PA–NJ	74.0
Atlanta–Sandy Springs–Marietta, GA	67.5
Austin–Round Rock, TX	65.5
Bakersfield, CA	59.4
Baltimore–Towson, MD	69.3
Baton Rouge, LA	74.0
Birmingham–Hoover, AL	73.3
Boston–Cambridge–Quincy, MA–NH	66.2
Bridgeport–Stamford–Norwalk, CT	72.6
Buffalo–Cheektowaga–Tonawanda, NY	63.9
Charlotte–Gastonia–Concord, NC–SC	65.4
Chicago–Naperville–Joliet, IL	68.4
Cincinnati–Middletown, OH–KY–IN	64.7
Cleveland–Elyria–Mentor, OH	73.1
Columbia, SC	71.4
Columbus, OH	61.2
Dallas–Ft. Worth–Arlington, TX	60.9
Dayton, OH	67.4
Denver–Aurora, CO	66.9
Detroit–Warren–Livonia, MI	75.5
El Paso, TX	64.8
Fresno, CA	52.3
Grand Rapids–Wyoming, MI	77.6
Greensboro–High Point, NC	68.0
Hartford–West Hartford–East Hartford, CT	70.5
Honolulu, HI	57.2
Houston–Baytown–Sugar Land, TX	64.8
Indianapolis, IN	75.0
Jacksonville, FL	72.1
Kansas City, MO–KS	70.2
Las Vegas–Paradise, NV	60.3
Los Angeles–Long Beach–Santa Ana, CA	52.1
Louisville, KY–IN	67.9
Memphis, TN–AR–MS	63.9
Miami–Fort Lauderdale–Miami Beach, FL	66.0
Milwaukee–Waukesha–West Allis, WI	60.9
Minneapolis–St. Paul–Bloomington, MN–WI	69.9
Nashville–Davidson–Murfreesboro, TN	71.3
New Haven–Milford, CT	65.5

	homeownership rate
New Orleans–Metairie–Kenner, LA	68.0%
New York–Northern New Jersey–Long Island, NY	52.6
Oklahoma City, OK	69.5
Omaha–Council Bluffs, NE–IA	72.5
Orlando, FL	70.5
Oxnard–Thousand Oaks–Ventura, CA	71.7
Philadelphia–Camden–Wilmington, PA	71.8
Phoenix–Mesa–Scottsdale, AZ	70.2
Pittsburgh, PA	73.2
Portland–Vancouver–Beaverton, OR–WA	62.6
Poughkeepsie–Newburgh–Middletown, NJ	69.9
Providence–New Bedford–Fall River, RI–MA	63.9
Raleigh–Cary, NC	70.7
Richmond, VA	72.4
Riverside–San Bernardino–Ontario, CA	65.8
Rochester, NY	75.0
Sacramento–Arden–Arcade–Roseville, CA	61.1
St. Louis, MO–IL	72.2
Salt Lake City, UT	72.0
San Antonio, TX	66.1
San Diego–Carlsbad–San Marcos, CA	57.1
San Francisco–Oakland–Fremont, CA	56.4
San Jose–Sunnyvale–Santa Clara, CA	54.6
Seattle–Bellevue–Everett, WA	61.3
Springfield, MA	63.7
Syracuse, NY	62.4
Tampa–St. Petersburg–Clearwater, FL	70.5
Toledo, OH	67.2
Tucson, AZ	63.5
Tulsa, OK	66.8
Virginia Beach–Norfolk–Newport News, VA	63.9
Washington–Arlington–Alexandria, DC–VA–MD–WV	68.1
Worcester, MA	68.5

Source: Bureau of the Census, Housing Vacancy Survey, Internet site http://wwwcensusgov/hhes/www/housing/hvs/hvshtml; calculations by New Strategist

Most Americans Live in Single-Family Homes

Thirty-six percent of homes have a room used for business.

Nearly two out of three householders live in a single-family detached home, a reflection of the low population density in the United States compared with many other developed countries. Only 24 percent of householders live in apartments, while 5 percent are in duplexes and another 6 percent in mobile homes. Not surprisingly, renters are far more likely than homeowners to live in apartments—64 versus just 5 percent.

American homes have a median of 1,807 square feet of living space. Sixty-three percent of housing units have three or more bedrooms and half have two or more bathrooms. Thirty-nine percent of homeowners have a room they use for business, as do 29 percent of renters. Nearly one in four of the nation's occupied housing units was built in 1990 or later.

Natural gas is the main heating fuel for the 51 percent majority of households. Another 33 percent depend on electricity as their main heating fuel. Renters are far more likely than homeowners to heat with electricity—43 versus 28 percent.

■ The homes of Americans had been growing larger as families demanded more bathrooms, bedrooms, and rooms for business. The slump in the housing market may reverse that trend.

Two bathrooms are a must for most homeowners

(percent distribution of homeowners by number of bathrooms in home, 2007)

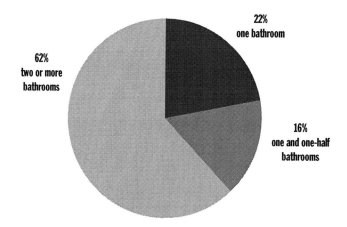

62%
two or more
bathrooms

22%
one bathroom

16%
one and one-half
bathrooms

Table 4.12 Units in Structure by Homeownership Status, 2007

(number and percent distribution of households by number of units in structure and homeownership status, 2007; numbers in thousands)

	total	owner	renter
Total households	**110,692**	**75,647**	**35,045**
One, detached	71,435	62,512	8,923
One, attached	6,083	4,042	2,040
Two to four	8,790	1,414	7,376
Five to nine	5,258	571	4,686
10 to 19	4,697	476	4,221
20 to 49	3,645	489	3,155
50 or more	3,866	723	3,143
Mobile home	6,919	5,419	1,500
PERCENT DISTRIBUTION BY HOMEOWNERSHIP STATUS			
Total households	**100.0%**	**68.3%**	**31.7%**
One, detached	100.0	87.5	12.5
One, attached	100.0	66.4	33.5
Two to four	100.0	16.1	83.9
Five to nine	100.0	10.9	89.1
10 to 19	100.0	10.1	89.9
20 to 49	100.0	13.4	86.6
50 or more	100.0	18.7	81.3
Mobile home	100.0	78.3	21.7
PERCENT DISTRIBUTION BY NUMBER OF UNITS IN STRUCTURE			
Total households	**100.0%**	**100.0%**	**100.0%**
One, detached	64.5	82.6	25.5
One, attached	5.5	5.3	5.8
Two to four	7.9	1.9	21.0
Five to nine	4.8	0.8	13.4
10 to 19	4.2	0.6	12.0
20 to 49	3.3	0.6	9.0
50 or more	3.5	1.0	9.0
Mobile home	6.3	7.2	4.3

Source: Bureau of the Census, American Housing Survey for the United States: 2007, Internet site http://www.census.gov/hhes/ www/housing/ahs/ahs07/ahs07.html; calculations by New Strategist

Table 4.13 Size of Housing Unit by Homeownership Status, 2007

(number and percent distribution of households by size and characteristics of unit and homeownership status, 2007; numbers in thousands)

	number			percent distribution		
	total	owner	renter	total	owner	renter
TOTAL HOUSEHOLDS	**110,692**	**75,647**	**35,045**	**100.0%**	**100.0%**	**100.0%**
Number of bedrooms						
None	852	78	774	0.8	0.1	2.2
One bedroom	11,810	1,674	10,136	10.7	2.2	28.9
Two bedrooms	27,956	13,656	14,299	25.3	18.1	40.8
Three bedrooms	47,521	39,643	7,878	42.9	52.4	22.5
Four or more bedrooms	22,554	20,595	1,958	20.4	27.2	5.6
Number of bathrooms						
None	493	189	304	0.4	0.2	0.9
One bathroom	39,771	16,268	23,503	35.9	21.5	67.1
One-and-one-half bathrooms	15,465	11,964	3,500	14.0	15.8	10.0
Two or more bathrooms	54,963	47,226	7,737	49.7	62.4	22.1
Room(s) used for business						
Total with room(s) used for business	39,979	29,733	10,247	36.1	39.3	29.2
Business only	18,750	13,709	5,042	16.9	18.1	14.4
Business and other use	21,229	16,024	5,205	19.2	21.2	14.9
Median square footage of unit	1,807	1,876	1,344	–	–	–
Median size of lot (acres)	0.36	0.38	0.23	–	–	–

Note: Square footage of unit and size of lot for single-family detached and mobile homes only; "–" means not applicable.
Source: Bureau of the Census, American Housing Survey for the United States: 2007, Internet site http://www.census.gov/hhes/ www/housing/ahs/ahs07/ahs07.html; calculations by New Strategist

Table 4.14 Year Unit Built by Homeownership Status, 2007

(number and percent distribution of households by year structure was built and homeownership status, 2007; numbers in thousands)

	total	owners	renters
Total households	**110,692**	**75,647**	**35,045**
2005 to 2007	3,678	2,964	714
2000 to 2004	8,015	6,344	1,671
1995 to 1999	7,821	6,189	1,631
1990 to 1994	6,159	4,988	1,171
1985 to 1989	7,726	5,267	2,459
1980 to 1984	6,467	4,198	2,269
1975 to 1979	12,411	7,860	4,551
1970 to 1974	9,436	5,759	3,677
1960 to 1969	13,397	8,979	4,418
1950 to 1959	11,501	8,382	3,120
1940 to 1949	6,817	4,423	2,394
1930 to 1939	5,070	3,062	2,007
1920 to 1929	4,582	2,676	1,906
1919 or earlier	7,612	4,555	3,057
Median year built	1973	1975	1971

PERCENT DISTRIBUTION

	total	owners	renters
Total households	**100.0%**	**100.0%**	**100.0%**
2005 to 2007	3.3	3.9	2.0
2000 to 2004	7.2	8.4	4.8
1995 to 1999	7.1	8.2	4.7
1990 to 1994	5.6	6.6	3.3
1985 to 1989	7.0	7.0	7.0
1980 to 1984	5.8	5.5	6.5
1975 to 1979	11.2	10.4	13.0
1970 to 1974	8.5	7.6	10.5
1960 to 1969	12.1	11.9	12.6
1950 to 1959	10.4	11.1	8.9
1940 to 1949	6.2	5.8	6.8
1930 to 1939	4.6	4.0	5.7
1920 to 1929	4.1	3.5	5.4
1919 or earlier	6.9	6.0	8.7

Source: Bureau of the Census, American Housing Survey for the United States: 2007, Internet site http://www.census.gov/hhes/www/housing/ahs/ahs07/ahs07.html; calculations by New Strategist

Table 4.15 Fuels Used by Homeownership Status, 2007

(number and percent of households by fuels used and homeownership status, 2007; numbers in thousands)

	total	owner	renter
Total households	**110,692**	**75,647**	**35,045**
Electricity	110,648	75,608	35,040
Piped gas	67,679	46,487	21,192
Bottled gas	9,720	8,218	1,502
Fuel oil	9,650	6,609	3,041
Kerosene or other liquid fuel	586	423	164
Coal or coke	91	86	5
Wood	1,479	1,273	205
Solar energy	147	128	19
Other	621	403	218
All-electric homes	29,075	17,419	11,656
PERCENT USING FUEL			
Total households	**100.0%**	**100.0%**	**100.0%**
Electricity	100.0	99.9	100.0
Piped gas	61.1	61.5	60.5
Fuel oil	8.8	10.9	4.3
Wood	8.7	8.7	8.7
Bottled gas	0.5	0.6	0.5
Kerosene or other liquid fuel	0.1	0.1	0.0
Coal or coke	1.3	1.7	0.6
Solar energy	0.1	0.2	0.1
Other	0.6	0.5	0.6
All-electric homes	26.3	23.0	33.3

Note: Figures will not add to total because many householders use more than one fuel.
Source: Bureau of the Census, American Housing Survey for the United States: 2007, Internet site http://www.census.gov/hhes/ www/housing/ahs/ahs07/ahs07.html; calculations by New Strategist

Table 4.16 Main Heating Fuel Used by Homeownership Status, 2007

(number and percent distribution of households by main heating fuel used and homeownership status, 2007; numbers in thousands)

	total	owner	renter
Households using heating fuel	**110,215**	**75,403**	**34,811**
Electricity	36,079	21,197	14,882
Piped gas	56,681	40,993	15,688
Bottled gas	6,095	5,101	994
Fuel oil	8,743	6,041	2,702
Kerosene or other liquid fuel	574	416	158
Coal or coke	91	86	5
Wood	1,471	1,266	205
Solar energy	16	11	5
Other	464	292	172
PERCENT DISTRIBUTION BY HOMEOWNERSHIP STATUS			
Households using heating fuel	**100.0%**	**68.4%**	**31.6%**
Electricity	100.0	58.8	41.2
Piped gas	100.0	72.3	27.7
Bottled gas	100.0	83.7	16.3
Fuel oil	100.0	69.1	30.9
Kerosene or other liquid fuel	100.0	72.5	27.5
Coal or coke	100.0	94.5	5.5
Wood	100.0	86.1	13.9
Solar energy	100.0	68.8	31.3
Other	100.0	62.9	37.1
PERCENT DISTRIBUTION BY PRIMARY HEATING FUEL			
Households using heating fuel	**100.0%**	**100.0%**	**100.0%**
Electricity	32.7	28.1	42.8
Piped gas	51.4	54.4	45.1
Bottled gas	5.5	6.8	2.9
Fuel oil	7.9	8.0	7.8
Kerosene or other liquid fuel	0.5	0.6	0.5
Coal or coke	0.1	0.1	0.0
Wood	1.3	1.7	0.6
Solar energy	0.0	0.0	0.0
Other	0.4	0.4	0.5

Source: Bureau of the Census, American Housing Survey for the United States: 2007, Internet site http://www.census.gov/hhes/ www/housing/ahs/ahs07/ahs07.html; calculations by New Strategist

American Households Are Well Equipped

Most have dishwashers, clothes washers, and dryers.

American households are well equipped with appliances and have a variety of other amenities. Eighty-five percent of households have a porch, deck, balcony, or patio. Sixty-five percent have a garage or carport. Thirty-five percent have a useable fireplace.

Not surprisingly, homeowners are more likely than renters to have various amenities. The 58 percent majority of homeowners have a separate dining room, while the figure is just 29 percent for renters. Seventy percent of homeowners have central air conditioning compared with 49 percent of renters. About one in five renters do not have a vehicle compared with just 3 percent of homeowners.

■ Many Americans now think air conditioning is a necessity rather than a luxury.

Most owned homes are air conditioned

(percent of households with central air conditioning, by homeownership status, 2007)

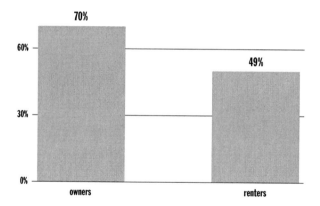

Table 4.17 **Kitchen, Laundry, and Safety Equipment by Homeownership Status, 2007**

(number and percent of total households by presence of kitchen, laundry, and safety equipment and homeownership status, 2007; numbers in thousands)

	total	owner	renter
Total households	**110,692**	**75,647**	**35,045**
With complete kitchen equipment	108,967	75,343	33,624
Dishwasher	70,830	55,681	15,149
Disposal in kitchen sink	55,026	39,619	15,406
Trash compactor	4,018	3,369	648
Washing machine	91,364	72,897	18,467
Clothes dryer	88,506	71,443	17,063
Working smoke detector	102,249	70,431	31,817
Fire extinguisher	48,270	37,215	11,055
Working carbon monoxide detector	36,076	28,325	7,751
Sprinkler system	4,288	1,766	2,523
PERCENT WITH EQUIPMENT			
Total households	**100.0%**	**100.0%**	**100.0%**
With complete kitchen equipment	98.4	99.6	95.9
Dishwasher	64.0	73.6	43.2
Disposal in kitchen sink	49.7	52.4	44.0
Trash compactor	3.6	4.5	1.8
Washing machine	82.5	96.4	52.7
Clothes dryer	80.0	94.4	48.7
Working smoke detector	92.4	93.1	90.8
Fire extinguisher	43.6	49.2	31.5
Working carbon monoxide detector	32.6	37.4	22.1
Sprinkler system	3.9	2.3	7.2

Note: Complete kitchen equipment includes a sink, refrigerator, and oven or burners.
Source: Bureau of the Census, American Housing Survey for the United States: 2007, Internet site http://www.census.gov/hhes/www/housing/ahs/ahs07/ahs07.html; calculations by New Strategist

Table 4.18 Amenities of Home by Homeownership Status, 2007

(number and percent of households with selected amenities by homeownership status, 2007; numbers in thousands)

	total	owners	renters
Total households	**110,692**	**75,647**	**35,045**
Telephone	108,226	74,455	33,771
Car, truck, or van	102,034	73,574	28,461
Porch, deck, balcony, or patio	94,456	69,899	24,557
Garage or carport	72,317	60,059	12,258
Separate dining room	54,083	44,094	9,989
Usable fireplace	38,189	34,070	4,118
Two or more living or recreation rooms	33,156	30,515	2,641
PERCENT WITH AMENITY			
Total households	**100.0%**	**100.0%**	**100.0%**
Telephone	97.8	98.4	96.4
Car, truck, or van	92.2	97.3	81.2
Porch, deck, balcony, or patio	85.3	92.4	70.1
Garage or carport	65.3	79.4	35.0
Separate dining room	48.9	58.3	28.5
Usable fireplace	34.5	45.0	11.8
Two or more living or recreation rooms	30.0	40.3	7.5

Source: Bureau of the Census, American Housing Survey for the United States: 2007, Internet site http://www.census.gov/hhes/ www/housing/ahs/ahs07/ahs07.html; calculations by New Strategist

Table 4.19 Air Conditioning by Homeownership Status, 2007

(number and percent of households with air conditioning by homeownership status, 2007; numbers in thousands)

	total	owner	renter
Total households	**110,692**	**75,647**	**35,045**
With any air conditioning	95,588	67,214	28,374
With central air conditioning	70,397	53,276	17,121
With room units	25,191	13,938	11,253
One room unit	12,416	5,705	6,711
Two room units	7,888	4,668	3,220
Three or more room units	4,887	3,565	1,322
PERCENT DISTRIBUTION			
Total households	**100.0%**	**100.0%**	**100.0%**
With any air conditioning	86.4	88.9	81.0
With central air conditioning	63.6	70.4	48.9
With room units	22.8	18.4	32.1
One room unit	11.2	7.5	19.1
Two room units	7.1	6.2	9.2
Three or more room units	4.4	4.7	3.8

Source: Bureau of the Census, American Housing Survey for the United States: 2007, Internet site http://www.census.gov/hhes/ www/housing/ahs/ahs07/ahs07.html; calculations by New Strategist

Most Are Satisfied with Home and Neighborhood

Homeowners are happier than renters, but few renters are dissatisfied.

When asked to rate their housing unit on a scale of 1 (worst) to 10 (best), 68 percent of householders rate their home an 8 or higher. Homeowners rate their home more highly than renters. While 72 percent of homeowners rate their home an 8 or higher, only 58 percent of renters are that positive. Twenty-seven percent of homeowners, but only 20 percent of renters, give their home a 10. Although few rate their home below 5 on the 10-point scale, those who do are primarily renters.

The patterns are the same when householders rate their neighborhood. Sixty-seven percent of householders rate their neighborhood an 8 or higher, including 71 percent of homeowners and 56 percent of renters. Among the few householders who rate their neighborhood at 4 or below, the majority are renters.

■ Householders are likely to rate their homes and neighborhoods highly because most of those who are unhappy find new places to live.

Most households rate their home and neighborhood highly

(percent of householders who rate their home and neighborhood an 8 or higher on a scale of 1 [worst] to 10 [best], by homeownership status, 2007)

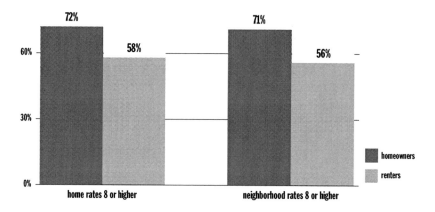

Table 4.20 Opinion of Housing Unit by Homeownership Status, 2007

(number and percent distribution of households by householder's opinion of housing unit and homeownership status, 2007; numbers in thousands)

	total	owner	renter
Total households	**110,692**	**75,647**	**35,045**
1 (worst)	802	299	503
2	651	358	293
3	1,099	470	629
4	1,581	757	824
5	6,386	3,251	3,135
6	6,196	3,642	2,554
7	14,713	9,289	5,424
8	29,183	20,469	8,714
9	18,194	13,512	4,682
10 (best)	27,414	20,484	6,929

PERCENT DISTRIBUTION BY HOMEOWNERSHIP STATUS

	total	owner	renter
Total households	**100.0%**	**68.3%**	**31.7%**
1 (worst)	100.0	37.3	62.7
2	100.0	55.0	45.0
3	100.0	42.8	57.2
4	100.0	47.9	52.1
5	100.0	50.9	49.1
6	100.0	58.8	41.2
7	100.0	63.1	36.9
8	100.0	70.1	29.9
9	100.0	74.3	25.7
10 (best)	100.0	74.7	25.3

PERCENT DISTRIBUTION BY OPINION OF HOUSING UNIT

	total	owner	renter
Total households	**100.0%**	**100.0%**	**100.0%**
1 (worst)	0.7	0.4	1.4
2	0.6	0.5	0.8
3	1.0	0.6	1.8
4	1.4	1.0	2.4
5	5.8	4.3	8.9
6	5.6	4.8	7.3
7	13.3	12.3	15.5
8	26.4	27.1	24.9
9	16.4	17.9	13.4
10 (best)	24.8	27.1	19.8

Note: Numbers do not add to total because "not reported" is not shown.
Source: Bureau of the Census, American Housing Survey for the United States: 2007, Internet site http://www.census.gov/hhes/www/housing/ahs/ahs07/ahs07.html; calculations by New Strategist

Table 4.21 Opinion of Neighborhood by Homeownership Status, 2007

(number and percent distribution of households by householder's opinion of neighborhood and homeownership status, 2007; numbers in thousands)

	total	owner	renter
Total households	**110,692**	**75,647**	**35,045**
1 (worst)	803	314	489
2	674	316	358
3	1,101	469	632
4	1,694	794	900
5	6,499	3,359	3,140
6	5,935	3,567	2,368
7	14,304	9,174	5,131
8	28,505	20,181	8,323
9	17,390	13,109	4,281
10 (best)	27,899	20,761	7,139

PERCENT DISTRIBUTION BY HOMEOWNERSHIP STATUS

	total	owner	renter
Total households	**100.0%**	**68.3%**	**31.7%**
1 (worst)	100.0	39.1	60.9
2	100.0	46.9	53.1
3	100.0	42.6	57.4
4	100.0	46.9	53.1
5	100.0	51.7	48.3
6	100.0	60.1	39.9
7	100.0	64.1	35.9
8	100.0	70.8	29.2
9	100.0	75.4	24.6
10 (best)	100.0	74.4	25.6

PERCENT DISTRIBUTION BY OPINION OF NEIGHBORHOOD

	total	owner	renter
Total households	**100.0%**	**100.0%**	**100.0%**
1 (worst)	0.7	0.4	1.4
2	0.6	0.4	1.0
3	1.0	0.6	1.8
4	1.5	1.0	2.6
5	5.9	4.4	9.0
6	5.4	4.7	6.8
7	12.9	12.1	14.6
8	25.8	26.7	23.7
9	15.7	17.3	12.2
10 (best)	25.2	27.4	20.4

Note: Numbers do not add to total because "not reported" and "no neighborhood" are not shown.
Source: Bureau of the Census, American Housing Survey for the United States: 2007, Internet site http://www.census.gov/hhes/ www/housing/ahs/ahs07/ahs07.html; calculations by New Strategist

Many People Live Near Open Space, Woodlands

Street noise and crime bother renters more than homeowners.

Of the 111 million households in the United States, 85 percent report having single-family detached houses within 300 feet of their home—89 percent of homeowners and 76 percent of renters. Forty-two percent of homeowners and 34 percent of renters report having open space, park, woods, farm, or ranchland close by.

A minority of households report bothersome neighborhood problems. The most common problem is street noise or traffic, reported by 21 percent of homeowners and 30 percent of renters. Crime ranks second and is considered a serious neighborhood problem by 13 percent of homeowners and 21 percent of renters.

Some public services are more readily available to renters than homeowners. Public transportation is available to only 46 percent of homeowners, for example, but to a much larger 70 percent of renters. Both owners and renters are about equally satisfied with police protection in their area.

■ The lack of public transportation in many parts of the United States makes owning a car a necessity.

Most homeowners do not have public transportation available to them

(percent of households with public transportation available in the area, by homeownership status, 2007)

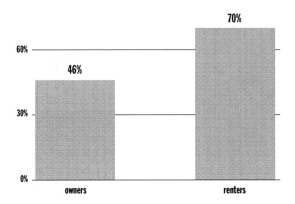

Table 4.22 Characteristics of Neighborhood by Homeownership Status, 2007

(number and percent of households by description of area within 300 feet and homeownership status, 2007; numbers in thousands)

	total	owner	renter
Total households	**110,692**	**75,647**	**35,045**
Single-family detached houses	94,206	67,532	26,674
Single-family attached	21,070	10,617	10,453
Multiunit residential buildings	32,655	10,789	21,868
One-to-three-story multiunit is tallest	24,723	8,523	16,200
Four-to-six-story multiunit is tallest	4,809	1,444	3,366
Seven-or-more-story multiunit is tallest	3,123	822	2,302
Mobile homes	13,041	9,930	3,110
Commerical or institutional establishments	33,988	15,750	18,238
Industrial sites or factories	4,962	2,298	2,665
Open space, park, woods, farm, or ranch	43,415	31,484	11,932
Four-or-more-lane highway, railroad, or airport	17,864	9,361	8,503
Water in area	17,850	13,480	4,370
Waterfront property	3,074	2,479	595
PERCENT WITH NEIGHBORHOOD CHARACTERISTIC			
Total households	**100.0%**	**100.0%**	**100.0%**
Single-family detached houses	85.1	89.3	76.1
Single-family attached	19.0	14.0	29.8
Multiunit residential buildings	29.5	14.3	62.4
One-to-three-story multiunit is tallest	22.3	11.3	46.2
Four-to-six-story multiunit is tallest	4.3	1.9	9.6
Seven-or-more-story multiunit is tallest	2.8	1.1	6.6
Mobile homes	11.8	13.1	8.9
Commerical or institutional establishments	30.7	20.8	52.0
Industrial sites or factories	4.5	3.0	7.6
Open space, park, woods, farm, or ranch	39.2	41.6	34.0
Four-or-more-lane highway, railroad, or airport	16.1	12.4	24.3
Water in area	16.1	17.8	12.5
Waterfront property	2.8	3.3	1.7

Note: Numbers may not add to total because of nonresponse.
Source: Bureau of the Census, American Housing Survey for the United States: 2007, Internet site http://www.census.gov/hhes/www/housing/ahs/ahs07/ahs07.html; calculations by New Strategist

Table 4.23 Neighborhood Problems by Homeownership Status, 2007

(number and percent of households with neighborhood problems, by homeownership status, 2007; numbers in thousands)

	total	owner	renter
Total households	**110,692**	**75,647**	**35,045**
With bothersome street noise or heavy traffic	25,978	15,611	10,367
With serious crime in past 12 months	17,156	9,797	7,360
With bothersome smoke, gas, or bad smells	6,001	3,668	2,333
With noise problem	1,906	1,132	774
With litter or housing deterioration	1,626	1,073	553
With poor city or county services	673	424	249
With undesirable commercial, institutional, industrial establishments	513	318	195
With people problem	5,189	3,239	1,950
PERCENT WITH PROBLEM			
Total households	**100.0%**	**100.0%**	**100.0%**
With bothersome street noise or heavy traffic	23.5	20.6	29.6
With serious crime in past 12 months	15.5	13.0	21.0
With bothersome smoke, gas, or bad smells	5.4	4.8	6.7
With noise problem	1.7	1.5	2.2
With litter or housing deterioration	1.5	1.4	1.6
With poor city or county services	0.6	0.6	0.7
With undesirable commercial, institutional, industrial establishments	0.5	0.4	0.6
With people problem	4.7	4.3	5.6

Source: Bureau of the Census, American Housing Survey for the United States: 2007, Internet site http://www.census.gov/hhes/ www/housing/ahs/ahs07/ahs07.html; calculations by New Strategist

Table 4.24 Public Services in Neighborhood by Homeownership Status, 2007

(number and percent of households by public services in neighborhood and homeownership status, 2007; numbers in thousands)

	total	owner	renter
Total households	**110,692**	**75,647**	**35,045**
With public transportation in area	59,195	34,797	24,398
Grocery or drug stores within 15 minutes of home	104,127	70,626	33,501
Satisfactory police protection in area	99,311	68,254	31,057
PERCENT WITH SERVICES			
Total households	**100.0%**	**100.0%**	**100.0%**
With public transportation	53.5	46.0	69.6
Grocery or drug stores within 15 minutes of home	94.1	93.4	95.6
Satisfactory police protection	89.7	90.2	88.6

Source: Bureau of the Census, American Housing Survey for the United States: 2007, Internet site http://www.census.gov/hhes/ www/housing/ahs/ahs07/ahs07.html; calculations by New Strategist

Few Americans Live in Gated Communities

Among those who do, most are renters.

Overall, 15 percent of the nation's renters and 7 percent of homeowners live in gated communities. About half of those living in gated communities have a special system in place that allows them entry into their community. The rest depend on walls or fences alone to keep intruders out.

Among the 45 million households with people aged 55 or older, only 7 percent are in communities with age restrictions. Again, renters are more likely than homeowners to live in age-restricted communities, many of them in senior-citizen apartment complexes.

Many households are in communities that offer a variety of services and amenities. Twenty-two percent have a community center or clubhouse available to them, 19 percent have trails, 15 percent have a daycare center, and 18 percent have a private park, beach, or shoreline.

■ To attract buyers, home builders added amenities to their developments, which are evident in these statistics.

Renters are more likely than homeowners to live in a gated community

(percent of households living in a community where access is secured by walls or fences, by homeownership status, 2007)

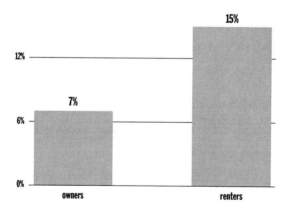

Table 4.25 Characteristics of Community by Homeownership Status, 2007

(number and percent distribution of households by community characteristics and homeownership status, 2007; numbers in thousands)

	number			percent distribution		
	total	owner	renter	total	owner	renter
SECURED COMMUNITIES						
Total households	**110,692**	**75,647**	**35,045**	**100.0%**	**100.0%**	**100.0%**
Community access secured with walls or fences	10,393	5,086	5,308	9.4	6.7	15.1
Special entry system present	5,716	2,513	3,203	5.2	3.3	9.1
Special entry system not present	4,678	2,573	2,105	4.2	3.4	6.0
Community access not secured	99,406	69,960	29,446	89.8	92.5	84.0
SENIOR CITIZEN COMMUNITIES						
Households with persons aged 55 or older	**44,984**	**35,993**	**8,992**	**100.0**	**100.0**	**100.0**
Community age restricted	3,152	1,569	1,584	7.0	4.4	17.6
No age restriction	41,832	34,424	7,408	93.0	95.6	82.4
Community age specific	9,338	8,008	1,330	20.8	22.2	14.8
Community not age specific	29,835	24,225	5,610	66.3	67.3	62.4
COMMUNITY AMENITIES						
Total households	**110,692**	**75,647**	**35,045**	**100.0**	**100.0**	**100.0**
Community center or clubhouse	24,546	14,836	9,710	22.2	19.6	27.7
Golf in community	13,679	10,478	3,202	12.4	13.9	9.1
Trails in community	20,833	14,940	5,893	18.8	19.7	16.8
Shuttle bus available	10,014	5,966	4,048	9.0	7.9	11.6
Daycare center	16,303	10,892	5,411	14.7	14.4	15.4
Private or restricted beach, park, or shoreline	20,252	14,405	5,847	18.3	19.0	16.7

Note: Numbers may not add to total because not reported is not shown.
Source: Bureau of the Census, American Housing Survey for the United States: 2007, Internet site http://www.census.gov/hhes/ www/housing/ahs/ahs07/ahs07.html; calculations by New Strategist

Monthly Housing Costs Are Higher for Homeowners

But renters devote a much larger share of their income to housing.

Homeowners had median monthly housing costs of $927 in 2007, while the median for renters was a smaller $755. Because homeowners have higher incomes than renters, however, housing costs absorb only 20 percent of the monthly income of owners versus a larger 33 percent of renters' income.

Homeowners pay more than renters for utilities, in large part because their homes are bigger. Homeowners pay a median of $107 per month for electricity, for example, versus the $76 paid by renters. The 94 percent of homeowners who have property insurance pay a median of $58 a month for coverage. Just 25 percent of renters have property insurance, which costs them a median of $20 per month.

■ Homeowners who have paid off their mortgages have much lower monthly housing costs than those with mortgages.

Many homeowners pay little per month for housing

(percent distribution of homeowners by total monthly housing costs, 2007)

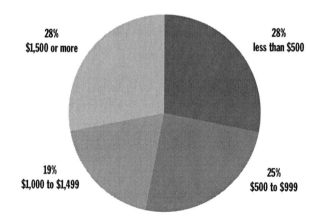

28%
$1,500 or more

28%
less than $500

19%
$1,000 to $1,499

25%
$500 to $999

Table 4.26 Monthly Housing Costs by Homeownership Status, 2007

(number and percent distribution of households by monthly housing costs and housing costs as a percent of current income, by homeownership status, 2007; households in thousands)

	number			percent distribution		
	total	owner	renter	total	owner	renter
MONTHLY HOUSING COSTS						
Total households	**110,692**	**75,647**	**35,045**	**100.0%**	**100.0%**	**100.0%**
Less than $300	12,263	9,613	2,649	11.1	12.7	7.6
$300 to $499	16,011	11,770	4,241	14.5	15.6	12.1
$500 to $799	23,134	12,007	11,129	20.9	15.9	31.8
$800 to $999	12,894	6,992	5,902	11.6	9.2	16.8
$1,000 to $1,249	11,856	7,766	4,090	10.7	10.3	11.7
$1,250 to $1,499	8,595	6,501	2,095	7.8	8.6	6.0
$1,500 to $1,999	10,304	8,686	1,619	9.3	11.5	4.6
$2,000 to $2,499	5,451	4,914	536	4.9	6.5	1.5
$2,500 or more	7,822	7,399	423	7.1	9.8	1.2
No cash rent	2,361	–	2,361	2.1	–	6.7
Median monthly costs	$843	$927	$755	–	–	–
MONTHLY HOUSING COSTS AS A PERCENT OF CURRENT INCOME						
Total households	**110,692**	**75,647**	**35,045**	**100.0%**	**100.0%**	**100.0%**
Less than 5 percent	3,767	3,557	210	3.4	4.7	0.6
5 to 9 percent	11,430	10,483	947	10.3	13.9	2.7
10 to 14 percent	13,684	11,471	2,213	12.4	15.2	6.3
15 to 19 percent	14,357	11,132	3,225	13.0	14.7	9.2
20 to 24 percent	12,787	9,312	3,476	11.6	12.3	9.9
25 to 29 percent	10,455	6,736	3,719	9.4	8.9	10.6
30 to 34 percent	7,918	4,822	3,096	7.2	6.4	8.8
35 to 39 percent	6,116	3,657	2,459	5.5	4.8	7.0
40 to 49 percent	7,535	4,294	3,241	6.8	5.7	9.2
50 to 59 percent	4,291	2,345	1,945	3.9	3.1	5.6
60 to 69 percent	2,813	1,421	1,392	2.5	1.9	4.0
70 to 99 percent	4,316	2,291	2,025	3.9	3.0	5.8
100 percent or more	7,043	3,376	3,668	6.4	4.5	10.5
Median percent of current income	24%	20%	33%	–	–	–

Note: Housing costs include mortgages, rent, utilities, real estate taxes, property insurance, and regime fees; monthly cost as a percent of income excludes no cash rent and zero income; "–" means not applicable.
Source: Bureau of the Census, American Housing Survey for the United States: 2007, Internet site http://www.census.gov/hhes/www/housing/ahs/ahs07/ahs07.html; calculations by New Strategist

Table 4.27 Monthly Utility and Property Insurance Costs by Homeownership Status, 2007

(total number of households, number and percent with utility or insurance expense, and median monthly cost of utility or insurance for households with expense, by homeownership status, 2007; numbers in thousands)

	total	owner	renter
TOTAL HOUSEHOLDS	**110,692**	**75,647**	**35,045**
Electricity			
Number with electricity	110,648	75,608	35,040
Percent with electricity	100.0%	99.9%	100.0%
Median monthly cost of electricity	$97	$107	$76
Piped gas			
Number with piped gas	67,679	46,487	21,192
Percent with piped gas	61.1%	61.5%	60.5%
Median monthly cost of piped gas	$69	$74	$53
Fuel oil			
Number with fuel oil	9,650	6,609	3,041
Percent with fuel oil	8.7%	8.7%	8.7%
Median monthly cost of fuel oil	$130	$134	$97
Water			
Number paying for water separately	61,360	52,558	8,802
Percent paying for water separately	55.4%	69.5%	25.1%
Median monthly cost for water	$38	$39	$27
Trash			
Number paying for trash separately	50,983	44,192	6,791
Percent paying for trash separately	46.1%	58.4%	19.4%
Median monthly cost for trash removal	$22	$22	$19
Property insurance			
Number paying for property insurance	80,287	71,436	8,851
Percent paying for property insurance	72.5%	94.4%	25.3%
Median monthly cost for property insurance	$53	$58	$20

Source: Bureau of the Census, American Housing Survey for the United States: 2007, Internet site http://www.census.gov/hhes/www/housing/ahs/ahs07/ahs07.html; calculations by New Strategist

Median Value of Owned Homes Topped $190,000 in 2007

Most homeowners with mortgages owe much less than their home is worth.

The median value of the homes owned by Americans stood at $191,471 in 2007. Only 25 percent of homeowners report that their home is worth less than $100,000, while a larger share (30 percent) claim a value of $300,000 or more. With home values slipping, some homeowners may be overestimating the value of their home.

Homeowners paid a median of $100,539 for their home. Only 11 percent say they paid $300,000 or more.

Among the nation's 76 million homeowners, 61 percent have a mortgage on their home. Those with a mortgage have a median of 24 years left to pay it off. Median outstanding principal is $100,904. As of 2007, homeowners with a mortgage owed a median of 54 percent of the value of their home.

■ Although homeowners are experiencing a decline in housing values, most still have considerable equity in their home.

Homeowners paid much less for their home than it is currently worth

(median current value and purchase price of owned homes, 2007)

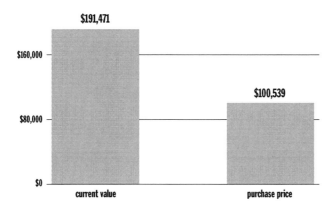

Table 4.28 Homeowners by Housing Value and Purchase Price, 2007

(number and percent distribution of homeowners by value of home, purchase price, first-home status, and major source of down payment, 2007; households in thousands)

	number	percent distribution
VALUE OF HOME		
Total homeowners	**75,647**	**100.%**
Under $100,000	18,779	24.8
$100,000 to $149,999	11,048	14.6
$150,000 to $199,999	9,643	12.7
$200,000 to $299,999	13,132	17.4
$300,000 to $399,999	8,060	10.7
$400,000 to $499,999	4,740	6.3
$500,000 to $749,999	6,234	8.2
$750,000 or more	4,013	5.3
Median value	$191,471	–
PURCHASE PRICE		
Total homes purchased or built	**70,334**	**100.0**
Under $50,000	17,976	25.6
$50,000 to $99,999	14,816	21.1
$100,000 to $149,999	10,536	15.0
$150,000 to $199,999	7,581	10.8
$200,000 to $249,999	4,522	6.4
$250,000 to $299,999	2,820	4.0
$300,000 or more	7,483	10.6
Median purchase price	$100,539	–
FIRST-HOME STATUS		
Total homeowners	**75,647**	**100.0**
First home	30,267	40.0
Not first home	42,823	56.6
MAJOR SOURCE OF DOWN PAYMENT		
Total homes purchased or built	**70,334**	**100.0**
Savings or cash on hand	31,005	44.1
Sale of previous home	22,897	32.6
Borrowing, other than mortgage on this property	2,444	3.5
Inheritance or gift	1,375	2.0
Sale of other investment	737	1.0
Land where building built used for financing	584	0.8
Other	3,060	4.4
No down payment	6,616	9.4

	number	percent distribution
DOWN PAYMENT AS PERCENT OF PURCHASE PRICE		
Total homes purchased or built	**70,334**	**100.0%**
No down payment	6,616	9.4
Less than three percent	4,700	6.7
Three to five percent	5,933	8.4
Six to 10 percent	8,545	12.1
11 to 15 percent	3,355	4.8
16 to 20 percent	6,881	9.8
21 to 40 percent	6,841	9.7
41 to 99 percent	3,904	5.6
Bought outright	5,668	8.1

Note: Numbers may not add to total because "not reported" is not shown; "–" means not applicable.
Source: Bureau of the Census, American Housing Survey for the United States: 2007, Internet site http://www.census.gov/hhes/
www/housing/ahs/ahs07/ahs07.html; calculations by New Strategist

Table 4.29 Homeowners by Mortgage Characteristics, 2007

(number and percent distribution of homeowners with mortgages by mortgage characteristics, 2007; numbers in thousands)

	number	percent
TOTAL HOMEOWNERS	**75,647**	**100.0%**
Homeowners with mortgages	**46,461**	**61.4**
REMAINING YEARS MORTGAGED		
Homeowners with mortgages	**46,461**	**100.0**
Less than 8 years	5,981	12.9
8 to 12 years	5,549	11.9
13 to 17 years	4,602	9.9
18 to 22 years	4,879	10.5
23 to 27 years	12,263	26.4
28 to 32 years	12,791	27.5
33 years or more	241	0.5
Variable	156	0.3
Median years remaining	24 yrs.	–
TOTAL OUTSTANDING PRINCIPAL		
Homeowners with mortgages	**46,461**	**100.0**
Under $10,000	3,122	6.7
$10,000 to $19,999	2,011	4.3
$20,000 to $29,999	2,038	4.4
$30,000 to $39,999	2,188	4.7
$40,000 to $49,999	2,220	4.8
$50,000 to $59,999	2,246	4.8
$60,000 to $69,999	2,373	5.1
$70,000 to $79,999	2,414	5.2
$80,000 to $99,999	4,447	9.6
$100,000 to $119,999	3,790	8.2
$120,000 to $149,999	4,751	10.2
$150,000 to $199,999	5,511	11.9
$200,000 to $249,999	3,081	6.6
$250,000 to $299,999	2,008	4.3
$300,000 or more	4,261	9.2
Median outstanding principal	$100,904	–
CURRENT TOTAL LOAN AS PERCENT OF VALUE		
Homeowners with mortgages	**46,461**	**100.0**
Less than 20 percent	7,204	15.5
20 to 39 percent	9,102	19.6
40 to 59 percent	9,626	20.7
60 to 79 percent	10,365	22.3
80 to 89 percent	4,489	9.7
90 to 99 percent	3,220	6.9
100 percent or more	2,456	5.3
Median percent of value	54.4%	–

Note: "–" means not applicable.
Source: Bureau of the Census, American Housing Survey for the United States: 2007, Internet site http://www.census.gov/hhes/ www/housing/ahs/ahs07/ahs07.html; calculations by New Strategist

Income Trends

■ **One in five households had an income of $100,000 or more in 2007.**

The proportion of households with an income of $100,000 or more reached a record high of 20.2 percent in 2007, a figure that is certain to drop because of the financial turmoil of 2008.

■ **Most households saw their incomes decline between 2000 and 2007.**

But householders of every age had higher incomes in 2007 than they did in 1990, with the greatest gains experienced by householders aged 55 to 64.

■ **The median income of black married couples exceeds $62,000.**

The median income of black couples was 24 percent above the all-household median in 2007. The $48,572 median income of Hispanic couples was 3 percent below average.

■ **College-educated householders had a median income of $84,508 in 2007.**

The median income of households headed by college graduates is 64 percent higher than the national average.

■ **Women are catching up to men.**

Among full-time workers in 2007, women's incomes were 78 percent as high as men's, up from 71 percent in 1990.

■ **Among the nation's 37 million poor, only 43 percent are non-Hispanic white.**

Just 8.2 percent of non-Hispanic whites are poor versus 10.2 percent of Asians, 21.5 percent of Hispanics, and 24.4 percent of blacks.

Peak Affluence in 2007

Before the financial turmoil set in, the percentage of households in the highest income category reached an all-time high.

The proportion of households with incomes of $100,000 or more reached a peak of 20.2 percent in 2007. These statistics, collected by the Census Bureau's Current Population Survey in March 2008, asked respondents about their household income in the preceding year. The survey captured Americans' economic status just as the severe economic downturn began, creating a snapshot of American affluence at its peak. In 1990, only 13.9 percent of households had an income of $100,000 or more, after adjusting for inflation. Behind the increase in high-income households are dual-income baby-boom couples in their peak-earning years.

The share of households with incomes below $25,000 stood at 24.8 percent in 2007, less than the 26.9 percent of 1990, after adjusting for inflation. The proportion of households with incomes in the middle of the distribution also declined between 1990 and 2007, falling from 47.4 to 43.0 percent.

■ The proportion of households with incomes of $100,000 or more is probably on the decline not only because of the recession, but also because boomers are beginning to retire.

More than 20 percent of households have incomes of $100,000 or more

(percent of households with incomes of $100,000 or more, 1990 to 2007; in 2007 dollars)

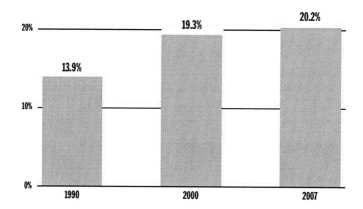

Table 5.1 Distribution of Households by Income, 1990 to 2007

(number of households and percent distribution by income, 1990 to 2007, in 2007 dollars; households in thousands as of the following year)

	total households		under $15,000	$15,000–$24,999	$25,000–$34,999	$35,000–$49,999	$50,000–$74,999	$75,000–$99,999	$100,000 or more
	number	percent							
2007	116,783	100.0%	13.2%	11.6%	10.7%	14.1%	18.2%	11.9%	20.2%
2006	116,011	100.0	13.1	11.6	11.4	14.3	18.1	11.5	19.9
2005	114,384	100.0	13.7	11.8	11.1	14.4	18.3	11.7	19.1
2004	113,343	100.0	13.7	11.9	11.4	14.4	18.1	11.8	18.7
2003	112,000	100.0	13.9	11.9	11.2	14.1	17.9	11.8	19.3
2002	111,278	100.0	13.7	11.6	11.4	14.2	18.1	12.2	18.8
2001	109,297	100.0	13.0	11.7	10.6	15.2	18.0	12.4	19.1
2000	108,209	100.0	12.6	11.4	10.9	14.7	18.5	12.5	19.3
1999	106,434	100.0	12.6	11.7	10.9	14.6	18.4	12.4	19.4
1998	103,874	100.0	13.2	11.7	11.2	14.5	18.8	12.4	18.2
1997	102,528	100.0	13.8	12.2	11.4	14.6	18.9	12.0	17.0
1996	101,018	100.0	14.2	12.5	11.7	14.7	19.0	12.1	15.8
1995	99,627	100.0	14.5	12.6	11.4	15.6	19.1	11.6	15.2
1994	98,990	100.0	15.1	13.0	11.9	15.2	18.4	11.4	14.8
1993	97,107	100.0	15.8	12.7	11.7	15.8	18.6	11.2	14.2
1992	96,426	100.0	15.6	12.9	11.5	15.6	19.3	11.7	13.4
1991	95,669	100.0	15.4	12.4	11.7	15.9	19.6	11.5	13.6
1990	94,312	100.0	14.5	12.4	11.6	15.9	19.9	11.7	13.9

Source: Bureau of the Census, Income, Poverty, and Health Insurance in the United States: 2007, Current Population Reports, P60-235, 2008, Internet site http://www.census.gov/hhes/www/income/histinc/h02AR.html

Income Inequality Is Down Slightly

The share of income controlled by the richest 20 percent of households fell below 50 percent in 2007.

If you add up all the money going to American households, including earnings, interest, dividends, Social Security benefits, and so on, the result is called aggregate household income. Year-to-year changes in how this aggregate is divided among the nation's households can reveal trends in income inequality. The numbers on the next page show how much aggregate income is received by each fifth of households, from poorest to richest. It also shows how much accrues to the 5 percent of households with the highest incomes.

For years, a growing share of income had been accruing to the most affluent households. The percentage of aggregate income received by the richest 20 percent of households (with an income of $100,000 or more in 2007) rose from 46.6 percent in 1990 to 50.5 percent in 2006—an all-time high. During those years, the percentage of aggregate income received by the bottom four-fifths of households fell from 53.3 to 49.4 percent. In 2007, however, the bottom four-fifths made gains, their share of income rising to 50.3 percent. The shift in income away from the most affluent households in 2007 signals the beginning of the economic turmoil to come.

■ A rise or fall in the amount of income accruing to each fifth of households reveals trends in the distribution of income among households, not the economic wellbeing of individual households.

The wealthiest households still control nearly half the nation's income

(percent of aggregate household income accruing to the richest 20 percent of households, 1990 to 2007)

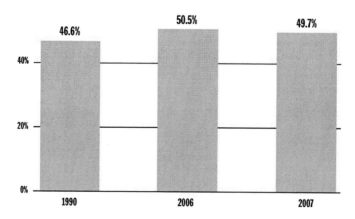

Table 5.2 Distribution of Aggregate Household Income, 1990 to 2007

(total number of households and percent of aggregate household income received by each fifth and top 5 percent of households, 1990 to 2007; households in thousands as of the following year)

	total households		bottom fifth	second fifth	third fifth	fourth fifth	top fifth	top 5 percent
	number	percent						
2007	116,783	100.0%	3.4%	8.7%	14.8%	23.4%	49.7%	21.2%
2006	116,011	100.0	3.4	8.6	14.5	22.9	50.5	22.3
2005	114,384	100.0	3.4	8.6	14.6	23.0	50.4	22.2
2004	113,343	100.0	3.4	8.7	14.7	23.2	50.1	21.8
2003	112,000	100.0	3.4	8.7	14.8	23.4	49.8	21.4
2002	111,278	100.0	3.5	8.8	14.8	23.3	49.7	21.7
2001	109,297	100.0	3.5	8.7	14.6	23.0	50.1	22.4
2000	108,209	100.0	3.6	8.9	14.8	23.0	49.8	22.1
1999	106,434	100.0	3.6	8.9	14.9	23.2	49.4	21.5
1998	103,874	100.0	3.6	9.0	15.0	23.2	49.2	21.4
1997	102,528	100.0	3.6	8.9	15.0	23.2	49.4	21.7
1996	101,018	100.0	3.6	9.0	15.1	23.3	49.0	21.4
1995	99,627	100.0	3.7	9.1	15.2	23.3	48.7	21.0
1994	98,990	100.0	3.6	8.9	15.0	23.4	49.1	21.2
1993	97,107	100.0	3.6	9.0	15.1	23.5	48.9	21.0
1992	96,426	100.0	3.8	9.4	15.8	24.2	46.9	18.6
1991	95,669	100.0	3.8	9.6	15.9	24.2	46.5	18.1
1990	94,312	100.0	3.8	9.6	15.9	24.0	46.6	18.5

Source: Bureau of the Census, Current Population Survey, Historical Income Tables—Households, Internet site http://www .census.gov/hhes/www/income/histinc/h02AR.html

Rich and Poor Have Unique Characteristics

High-income households have more earners than low-income households.

One common way to examine income differences among households is to divide the total number of households into five equally sized groups (called quintiles) based on income and compare household characteristics. Tables 5.2 and 5.3 show, respectively, the distribution of households by income quintile and the characteristics of households within income quintiles.

The demographics of the poorest and the richest households are strikingly different and account in large part for their income differences. Among households with two or more earners, for example, only 2 percent are in the lowest income quintile (with incomes below $20,300) and 36 percent are in the highest income quintile (with incomes of $100,000 or more). To look at the numbers another way, among households in the highest income quintile, more than three out of four have two or more earners. Among households in the lowest income quintile, only 5 percent have two or more earners. The 59 percent majority of households in the lowest income quintile have no earners.

■ Households in the highest income quintile are disproportionately headed by 35-to-54-year-olds, married couples, Asians, and non-Hispanic whites. The elderly, people living alone, blacks, and Hispanics head a disproportionate share of households in the lowest income quintile.

Married couples are typically found in the higher income quintiles because their households are likely to include two or more earners

(percent distribution of married couples by income quintile, 2007)

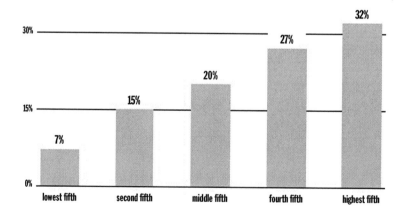

Table 5.3 Distribution of Households by Income Quintile, 2007

(total number of households by income quintile and top 5 percent, lower income limit of quintile and top 5 percent, and percent distribution of households by income quintile and selected characteristics, 2007; households in thousands as of 2008)

	total	lowest fifth	second fifth	middle fifth	fourth fifth	highest fifth	top 5 percent
Number of households	116,783	23,357	23,357	23,357	23,357	23,357	5,839
Lower income limit	–	–	$20,300	$39,100	$62,000	$100,000	$177,000
Age of householder							
Aged 15 to 24	100.0%	31.8%	27.9%	23.5%	11.6%	5.3%	1.0%
Aged 25 to 34	100.0	16.2	21.2	23.5	22.9	16.2	2.9
Aged 35 to 44	100.0	12.8	16.2	21.1	24.1	25.8	6.0
Aged 45 to 54	100.0	13.1	15.0	19.5	24.3	28.1	7.5
Aged 55 to 64	100.0	17.5	16.9	19.5	21.0	25.0	7.1
Aged 65 or older	100.0	35.5	28.1	16.1	11.0	9.2	2.5
Race and Hispanic origin of householder							
Asian	100.0	15.2	14.7	18.0	21.2	30.9	8.3
Black	100.0	32.7	23.0	19.6	14.9	9.8	1.7
Hispanic	100.0	24.9	25.9	21.6	17.4	10.1	1.9
Non-Hispanic white	100.0	17.2	18.8	19.9	21.3	22.8	5.9
Type of household							
Married couples	100.0	6.9	14.9	19.7	26.9	31.6	8.4
Female householder, no spouse present	100.0	30.7	26.7	21.0	14.2	7.3	1.3
Male householder, no spouse present	100.0	15.4	22.9	25.4	20.7	15.6	3.3
Women living alone	100.0	48.1	25.1	16.0	7.1	3.7	0.5
Men living alone	100.0	33.2	27.4	21.0	11.1	7.3	1.5
Number of earners							
No earners	100.0	56.6	25.9	10.0	4.7	2.8	0.6
One earner	100.0	19.2	28.8	25.3	15.3	11.4	2.9
Two or more earners	100.0	2.4	9.3	20.3	31.8	36.2	9.1

Note: Data for Asians and blacks are for those who identify themselves as being of the race alone and those who identify themselves as being of the race in combination with one or more other races. Data for non-Hispanic whites are for those who identify themselves as being white alone and not Hispanic. Hispanics may be of any race. "–" means not applicable.
Source: Bureau of the Census, 2008 Current Population Survey, Internet site http://pubdb3.census.gov/macro/032008/hhinc/new05_000.htm; calculations by New Strategist

Table 5.4 Characteristics of Households within Income Quintiles, 2007

(total number of households by income quintile and top 5 percent, lower income limit of quintile and top 5 percent, and percent distribution of households within income quintiles by selected characteristics, 2007; households in thousands as of 2008)

	total	lowest fifth	second fifth	middle fifth	fourth fifth	highest fifth	top 5 percent
Number of households	116,783	23,357	23,357	23,357	23,357	23,357	5,839
Lower income limit	–	–	$20,300	$39,100	$62,000	$100,000	$177,000
Age of householder							
Total households	100.0%	100.0%	100.0%	100.0%	100.0%	100.0%	100.0%
Aged 15 to 24	5.6	8.9	7.8	6.6	3.2	1.5	1.2
Aged 25 to 34	16.5	13.4	17.4	19.3	18.9	13.3	9.6
Aged 35 to 44	19.2	12.3	15.5	20.3	23.2	24.8	23.0
Aged 45 to 54	21.0	13.8	15.8	20.5	25.5	29.6	31.7
Aged 55 to 64	17.0	14.9	14.4	16.6	17.9	21.3	24.3
Aged 65 or older	20.6	36.7	29.0	16.7	11.3	9.5	10.2
Race and Hispanic origin of householder							
Total households	100.0	100.0	100.0	100.0	100.0	100.0	100.0
Asian	4.0	3.1	3.0	3.6	4.3	6.2	6.7
Black	12.8	21.0	14.7	12.6	9.6	6.3	4.3
Hispanic	11.4	14.2	14.8	12.3	9.9	5.8	4.3
Non-Hispanic white	70.9	60.9	66.6	70.4	75.6	80.9	84.0
Type of household							
Total households	100.0	100.0	100.0	100.0	100.0	100.0	100.0
Married couples	50.0	17.1	37.3	49.3	67.2	78.9	83.5
Female householder, no spouse present	12.3	18.9	16.4	13.0	8.8	4.5	3.3
Male householder, no spouse present	4.4	3.4	5.0	5.5	4.5	3.4	2.9
Women living alone	15.7	37.6	19.7	12.6	5.5	2.9	1.6
Men living alone	11.9	19.7	16.3	12.5	6.6	4.3	3.6
Number of earners							
Total households	100.0	100.0	100.0	100.0	100.0	100.0	100.0
No earners	21.0	59.4	27.2	10.5	4.9	2.9	2.3
One earner	37.1	35.6	53.4	46.9	28.4	21.2	21.4
Two earners or more	41.9	5.0	19.5	42.5	66.7	75.9	76.2

Note: Data for Asians and blacks are for those who identify themselves as being of the race alone and those who identify themselves as being of the race in combination with one or more other races. Data for non-Hispanic whites are for those who identify themselves as being white alone and not Hispanic. Hispanics may be of any race. "–" means not applicable.
Source: Bureau of the Census, 2008 Current Population Survey, Internet site http://pubdb3.census.gov/macro/032008/hhinc/new05_000.htm; calculations by New Strategist

Median Household Income Fell between 2000 and 2007

Only householders aged 55 or older have seen their incomes grow.

Household income growth has varied significantly by age over the past 15 years. Between 1990 and 2007, median household income climbed from $46,049 to $50,233 after adjusting for inflation, a 9 percent increase. Householders aged 55 to 64 experienced the largest boost, a gain of 15 percent. Householders aged 45 to 54 experienced the smallest increase, up less than 2 percent.

Median household income fell among householders under age 55 between 2000 and 2007, after adjusting for inflation. Householders aged 55 to 64 saw their median income rise 6 percent during those years, and the median income of those aged 65 or older grew by 2 percent. Behind these increases was the growing labor force participation of older Americans. Householders under age 55 saw their median income fall by 4 to 6 percent between 2000 and 2007, after adjusting for inflation.

■ In every age group, median household income was higher in 2007 than in 1990, after adjusting for inflation.

Householders under age 55 saw their median income fall between 2000 and 2007

(percent change in median household income by age of householder, 2000 to 2007)

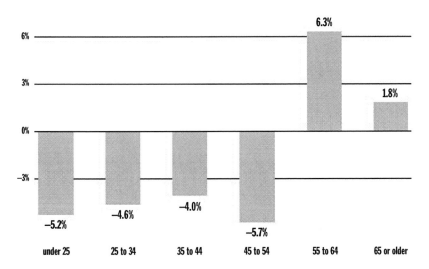

Table 5.5 Median Household Income by Age of Householder, 1990 to 2007

(median household income by age of householder, 1990 to 2007; percent change for selected years; in 2007 dollars)

	total households	under 25	25 to 34	35 to 44	45 to 54	55 to 64	65 or older
2007	$50,233	$31,790	$51,016	$62,124	$65,476	$57,386	$28,305
2006	49,568	31,815	50,559	62,119	66,714	56,141	28,587
2005	49,202	30,556	50,321	61,690	66,300	55,505	27,652
2004	48,665	30,269	49,907	62,219	66,989	55,315	26,911
2003	48,835	30,498	50,482	62,054	67,914	55,483	26,817
2002	48,878	32,073	52,244	61,685	68,024	54,403	26,684
2001	49,455	33,022	52,796	62,446	67,980	53,714	27,075
2000	50,557	33,529	53,476	64,731	69,403	54,005	27,793
1999	50,641	31,294	52,376	63,226	70,807	55,579	28,368
1998	49,397	29,934	50,901	61,549	68,786	54,837	27,603
1997	47,665	29,089	49,171	59,714	66,819	53,269	26,742
1996	46,704	28,210	47,225	58,452	66,416	52,393	25,592
1995	46,034	28,341	46,879	58,718	64,923	51,439	25,797
1994	44,636	26,756	45,863	57,645	65,384	48,742	25,034
1993	44,143	27,317	44,200	57,738	65,290	47,299	25,082
1992	44,359	25,575	45,232	57,704	64,340	49,220	24,810
1991	44,726	27,188	45,789	58,419	64,955	49,445	25,202
1990	46,049	27,685	46,688	59,302	64,471	49,773	25,921
Percent change							
2000 to 2007	–0.6%	–5.2%	–4.6%	–4.0%	–5.7%	6.3%	1.8%
1990 to 2007	9.1	14.8	9.3	4.8	1.6	15.3	9.2

Source: Bureau of the Census, Current Population Surveys, Internet site http://www.census.gov/hhes/www/income/histinc/inchhtoc.html; calculations by New Strategist

Many Household Types Lost Ground between 2000 and 2007

All have higher incomes than they did in 1990, however.

Female-headed families may be one of the poorest household types, but they are not as poor as they once were. Between 1990 and 2007, the median income of female-headed families rose by a substantial 20 percent, after adjusting for inflation—faster than any other household type. The $33,370 median income of female-headed families in 2007 was still far below the $72,785 of married couples, however. It also lagged the $49,839 median of male-headed families. But female-headed families have been catching up to their male counterparts. In 1990, the median income of female-headed families was only 57 percent as high as that of male-headed families. By 2007, the figure had grown to 67 percent.

Between 2000 and 2007, most household types lost ground, after adjusting for inflation. Married couples saw their median household income rise 2 percent during those years, however, making them one of only two household types to make gains. Women who live alone saw their median income rise slightly between 2000 and 2007, while every other household type lost ground.

■ The incomes of married couples will always be above average because most are dual earners.

Income varies by household type

(median household income by household type, 2007)

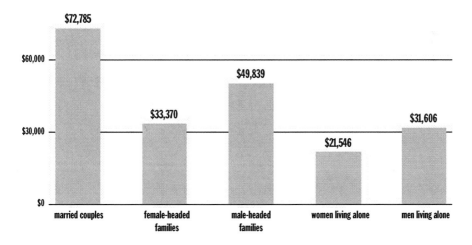

Table 5.6 Median Household Income by Type of Household, 1990 to 2007

(median household income by type of household, 1990 to 2007; percent change for selected years; income in 2007 dollars)

	total households	family households				nonfamily households				
		total	married couples	female hh, no spouse present	male hh, no spouse present	total	female householder		male householder	
							total	living alone	total	living alone
2007	$50,233	$62,359	$72,785	$33,370	$49,839	$30,176	$24,294	$21,546	$36,767	$31,606
2006	49,568	61,593	71,694	32,721	48,414	29,908	24,553	21,952	36,624	32,155
2005	49,202	60,834	70,169	32,553	49,659	29,023	24,097	21,418	36,162	31,884
2004	48,665	60,734	70,046	32,740	49,418	28,816	23,999	21,419	35,139	30,091
2003	48,835	60,867	70,353	33,040	47,303	29,019	24,027	21,055	35,994	30,933
2002	48,878	60,743	70,597	33,425	48,073	29,281	24,103	20,617	36,194	30,897
2001	49,455	61,222	70,821	32,959	47,684	30,018	23,732	20,926	37,842	33,124
2000	50,557	62,263	71,365	34,031	50,756	30,469	24,659	21,464	37,902	32,692
1999	50,641	61,991	70,498	32,595	51,978	30,345	24,604	21,504	38,150	33,317
1998	49,397	60,302	68,949	30,987	50,069	29,778	23,647	20,841	38,636	33,055
1997	47,665	58,410	66,569	29,677	47,187	27,958	22,687	20,004	35,540	30,748
1996	46,704	56,692	65,608	28,376	46,922	27,598	21,578	19,246	35,879	31,647
1995	46,034	55,691	63,668	28,840	45,302	26,923	21,469	19,360	35,155	30,512
1994	44,636	54,495	62,313	27,492	42,157	26,212	20,680	18,581	34,023	29,352
1993	44,143	52,965	60,941	26,204	42,176	26,677	21,030	18,362	34,940	30,198
1992	44,359	53,560	60,764	26,593	43,887	25,672	20,905	18,726	33,463	28,928
1991	44,726	54,045	60,982	26,672	46,039	26,394	21,270	19,054	34,179	30,077
1990	46,049	54,913	61,509	27,788	48,523	27,205	21,683	19,297	34,585	30,702

Percent change

2000 to 2007	−0.6%	0.2%	2.0%	−1.9%	−1.8%	−1.0%	−1.5%	0.4%	−3.0%	−3.3%
1990 to 2007	9.1	13.6	18.3	20.1	2.7	10.9	12.0	11.7	6.3	2.9

Source: Bureau of the Census, Current Population Surveys, Internet site http://www.census.gov/hhes/www/income/histinc/inchhtoc.html; calculations by New Strategist

Asians, Blacks, and Hispanics Have Lost Ground

The median household income of non-Hispanic whites did not change between 2000 and 2007.

Overall, median household income fell 0.6 percent between 2000 and 2007, after adjusting for inflation. Black households saw the biggest loss, experiencing a 5 percent decline in median household income during those years. The median declined 2 percent for Asians and 3 percent for Hispanics.

Despite these declines, median household income was higher in 2007 than in 1990 for every racial and ethnic group. The median income of black households climbed 19 percent between 1990 and 2007, more than double the 9 percent rise in the overall median. The median income of black households in 1990 was only 62 percent as high as the national median. By 2007, it was 68 percent of the national median. Despite the gain, blacks continue to have lower household incomes than any other racial or ethnic group, with a median of just $34,091 in 2007. Asians have the highest median household income, at $65,876—well above the $54,920 median income of households headed by non-Hispanic whites. Hispanic households had a median income of $38,679.

■ Black households have low incomes because many are female-headed families—one of the poorest household types.

Asian households have the highest incomes

(median household income by race and Hispanic origin, 2007)

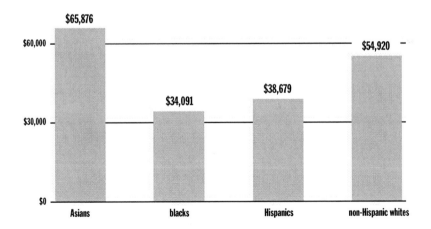

Table 5.7 Median Household Income by Race and Hispanic Origin of Householder, 1990 to 2007

(median household income by race and Hispanic origin of householder, 1990 to 2007; percent change in median for selected years; in 2007 dollars)

	total households	Asian	black	Hispanic	non-Hispanic white
2007	$50,233	$65,876	$34,091	$38,679	$54,920
2006	49,568	65,713	33,044	38,853	53,910
2005	49,202	64,838	32,876	38,200	53,937
2004	48,665	63,061	33,189	37,619	53,688
2003	48,835	62,300	33,470	37,200	53,862
2002	48,878	60,260	33,628	38,152	54,054
2001	49,455	62,815	34,514	39,310	54,230
2000	50,557	67,133	35,720	39,935	54,932
1999	50,641	63,414	34,731	38,260	54,948
1998	49,397	59,245	32,204	35,989	53,912
1997	47,665	58,284	32,266	34,299	52,266
1996	46,704	56,947	30,900	32,774	51,040
1995	46,034	54,867	30,251	30,882	50,225
1994	44,636	56,005	29,090	32,402	48,595
1993	44,143	54,184	27,600	32,338	48,286
1992	44,359	54,733	27,156	32,719	48,202
1991	44,726	54,114	27,922	33,688	47,988
1990	46,049	59,131	28,721	34,341	49,128
Percent change					
2000 to 2007	−0.6%	−1.9%	−4.6%	−3.1%	0.0%
1990 to 2007	9.1	11.4	18.7	12.6	11.8

Note: Asians and blacks in 2002 through 2007 are those who identify themselves as being of the race alone and those who identify themselves as being of the race in combination with other races. Non-Hispanic whites in 2002 through 2007 are those who identify themselves as being white alone and not Hispanic. Hispanics may be of any race.
Source: Bureau of the Census, Current Population Surveys, Internet site http://www.census.gov/hhes/www/income/histinc/inchhtoc.html; calculations by New Strategist

The Median Income of Middle-Aged Married Couples Tops $88,000

The median income of couples aged 45 to 54 is 76 percent above average.

The median income of the average household stood at $50,233 in 2007. Incomes vary considerably by age and household type. The most affluent households are married couples with a householder in the 45-to-54 age group. Their median income stood at $88,257 in 2007. Not only are 45-to-54-year-olds in their peak-earning years, but most couples are dual earners, boosting incomes well above average.

Elderly women who live alone have the lowest incomes. Households headed by women aged 65 or older who live by themselves had a median income of $16,037 in 2007—just 32 percent of the national median. Women under age 25 who live by themselves are not doing much better, with a median income of $19,292. Many of these young women are in college, however, and are likely to have higher incomes in the future.

■ Married-couple householders spanning the ages from 25 to 64 have median incomes that are well above average.

Incomes vary sharply by age and living arrangement

(median income of the richest and the poorest households by household type and age of householder, 2007)

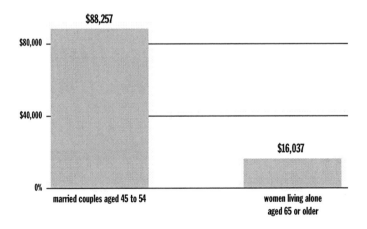

Table 5.8 Median Household Income by Household Type and Age of Householder, 2007

(median household income by type of household and age of householder; and index of age median to national median by household type, 2007)

	total	under 25	25 to 34	35 to 44	45 to 54	55 to 64	65 or older
TOTAL HOUSEHOLDS	$50,233	$31,790	$51,016	$62,124	$65,476	$57,386	$28,305
Family households	62,359	35,524	55,212	70,044	78,344	72,838	41,960
Married couples	72,785	40,706	66,747	82,390	88,257	79,000	43,209
Female householder, no spouse present	33,370	23,008	25,307	33,489	41,741	44,501	35,596
Male householder, no spouse present	49,839	43,188	50,255	52,017	53,038	52,137	39,974
Nonfamily households	30,176	28,811	43,316	42,941	37,292	32,059	17,496
Female householder	24,294	26,665	42,163	40,203	34,423	30,113	16,276
Living alone	21,546	19,292	35,048	35,491	31,791	27,851	16,037
Male householder	36,767	30,989	44,551	45,412	40,576	35,678	23,682
Living alone	31,606	22,507	35,259	40,151	36,672	32,687	22,215

Index

TOTAL HOUSEHOLDS	100	63	102	124	130	114	56
Family households	124	71	110	139	156	145	84
Married couples	145	81	133	164	176	157	86
Female householder, no spouse present	66	46	50	67	83	89	71
Male householder, no spouse present	99	86	100	104	106	104	80
Nonfamily households	60	57	86	85	74	64	35
Female householder	48	53	84	80	69	60	32
Living alone	43	38	70	71	63	55	32
Male householder	73	62	89	90	81	71	47
Living alone	63	45	70	80	73	65	44

Note: The index is calculated by dividing the median income of each age/household type group by the national median and multiplying by 100.
Source: Bureau of the Census, 2008 Current Population Survey, Internet site http://pubdb3.census.gov/macro/032008/hhinc/ new02_000.htm; calculations by New Strategist

The Median Income of Black Married Couples Tops $62,000

The median income of black couples is well above the national household median.

The $34,091 median income of the average black household is 32 percent below the national household median of $50,233 (with an index of 68). But the median income of black married couples is 24 percent above the all-household median (with an index of 124). In 2007, black couples had a median household income of $62,328. Asian couples had the highest median income, at $83,975 in 2007.

Interestingly, while the median income of the average Hispanic household is higher than that of the average black household ($38,679 versus $34,091), the median income of Hispanic couples is well below that of their black counterparts ($48,572 versus $62,328). Behind this pattern are differences in the living arrangements of Hispanics and blacks. The average Hispanic household has a higher income than the average black household because Hispanic households are more likely to be headed by married couples. But black couples have higher incomes than Hispanic couples because black couples are better educated and more likely to be dual earners.

■ Hispanic incomes are low regardless of household type because many Hispanics are recent immigrants with little education or earning power.

The incomes of married couples are lowest among Hispanics

(median income of households headed by married couples, by race and Hispanic origin, 2007)

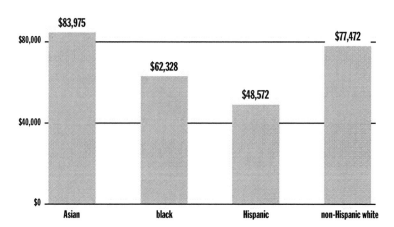

Table 5.9 Median Household Income by Household Type and Race and Hispanic Origin of Householder, 2007

(median household income by type of household and race and Hispanic origin of householder; and index of race/Hispanic origin median to national median by household type, 2007)

	total	Asian	black	Hispanic	non-Hispanic white
TOTAL HOUSEHOLDS	**$50,233**	**$65,876**	**$34,091**	**$38,679**	**$54,920**
Family households	**62,359**	**77,331**	**41,603**	**41,971**	**70,817**
Married couples	72,785	83,975	62,328	48,572	77,472
Female householder, no spouse present	33,370	50,866	25,759	28,459	40,324
Male householder, no spouse present	49,839	62,846	37,613	44,349	52,417
Nonfamily households	**30,176**	**38,204**	**23,567**	**27,076**	**31,322**
Female householder	24,294	35,223	20,614	19,308	25,142
Living alone	21,546	29,162	19,110	15,068	22,231
Male householder	36,767	41,809	26,903	32,686	39,599
Living alone	31,606	34,464	24,080	25,291	34,134
Index					
TOTAL HOUSEHOLDS	**100**	**131**	**68**	**77**	**109**
Family households	**124**	**154**	**83**	**84**	**141**
Married couples	145	167	124	97	154
Female householder, no spouse present	66	101	51	57	80
Male householder, no spouse present	99	125	75	88	104
Nonfamily households	**60**	**76**	**47**	**54**	**62**
Female householder	48	70	41	38	50
Living alone	43	58	38	30	44
Male householder	73	83	54	65	79
Living alone	63	69	48	50	68

Note: The index is calculated by dividing the median income of each race/Hispanic origin/household type group by the national median and multiplying by 100. Non-Hispanic whites are those who identiy themselves as being white alone and not Hispanic. Hispanics may be of any race.

Source: Bureau of the Census, 2008 Current Population Survey, Internet site http://pubdb3.census.gov/macro/032008/hhinc/new01_000.htm; calculations by New Strategist

Householders Aged 45 to 54 Have the Highest Incomes

Median household income peaks at $65,476 in the 45-to-54 age group.

Twenty-eight percent of householders aged 45 to 54 had an income of $100,000 or more in 2007. The age group accounts for 30 percent of the nearly 24 million households with incomes in the highest category. Householders aged 45 to 54 have the highest incomes because workers of that age typically are at the height of their career.

Households headed by people aged 65 or older have the lowest incomes, a median of just $28,305. Despite their low median income, a substantial 2.2 million older householders have incomes of $100,000 or more.

■ With boomers entering their sixties, the household incomes of 55-to-64-year-olds are rising as early retirement becomes less common.

Household income peaks in middle age

(median income of households by age of householder, 2007)

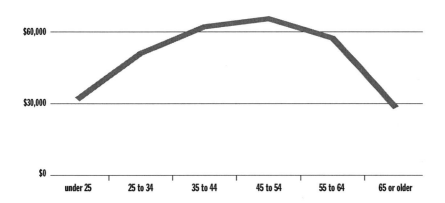

Table 5.10 Household Income by Age of Householder, 2007: Total Households

(number and percent distribution of households by household income and age of householder, 2007; households in thousands as of 2008)

	total	under 25	25 to 34	35 to 44	45 to 54	55 to 64	65 or older
Total households	**116,783**	**6,554**	**19,225**	**22,448**	**24,536**	**19,909**	**24,113**
Under $25,000	29,034	2,506	3,948	3,610	4,053	4,294	10,626
$25,000 to $49,999	29,053	2,201	5,402	5,006	5,107	4,413	6,924
$50,000 to $74,999	21,268	1,079	4,160	4,679	4,730	3,737	2,881
$75,000 to $99,999	13,841	416	2,543	3,296	3,688	2,449	1,451
$100,000 or more	23,586	351	3,172	5,854	6,959	5,016	2,233
Median income	$50,233	$31,790	$51,016	$62,124	$65,476	$57,386	$28,305
Total households	**100.0%**	**100.0%**	**100.0%**	**100.0%**	**100.0%**	**100.0%**	**100.0%**
Under $25,000	24.9	38.2	20.5	16.1	16.5	21.6	44.1
$25,000 to $49,999	24.9	33.6	28.1	22.3	20.8	22.2	28.7
$50,000 to $74,999	18.2	16.5	21.6	20.8	19.3	18.8	11.9
$75,000 to $99,999	11.9	6.3	13.2	14.7	15.0	12.3	6.0
$100,000 or more	20.2	5.4	16.5	26.1	28.4	25.2	9.3

Source: Bureau of the Census, 2008 Current Population Survey, Internet site http://pubdb3.census.gov/macro/032008/hhinc/new02_000.htm; calculations by New Strategist

Income Peaks in Middle Age for Asians, Blacks, Hispanics, and Non-Hispanic Whites

Median household income peaks at ages 45 to 54 for every racial and ethnic group except Asians.

Among non-Hispanic whites, the median income of householders aged 45 to 54 stood at a lofty $73,239 in 2007. Nearly 33 percent of non-Hispanic white householders in the age group had an income of $100,000 or more. Among blacks and Hispanics, incomes peak in the same age group but at a much lower level—$44,703 for blacks and $47,534 for Hispanics. Among Asian households, the income peak occurs at a younger age. Asian householders aged 35 to 44 have the highest incomes of all, a median of $80,337 in 2007.

Householders aged 65 or older have the lowest incomes in every racial and ethnic group. Among the elderly, black householders have the lowest incomes ($19,370) and Asian householders have the highest incomes ($33,759).

■ The incomes of black households are far below those of non-Hispanic whites because black households are much less likely to be headed by married couples—the most affluent household type. Hispanic household incomes are low because many are recent immigrants with little earning power.

Nearly one-third of Asian households have an income of $100,000 or more

(percent of households with incomes of $100,000 or more, by race and Hispanic origin, 2007)

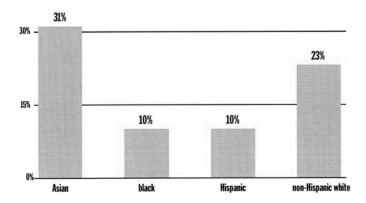

Table 5.11 Household Income by Age of Householder, 2007: Asian Households

(number and percent distribution of Asian households by household income and age of householder, 2007; households in thousands as of 2008)

	total	under 25	25 to 34	35 to 44	45 to 54	55 to 64	65 or older
Total Asian households	**4,715**	**248**	**1,067**	**1,148**	**985**	**663**	**604**
Under $25,000	894	90	185	136	118	124	241
$25,000 to $49,999	899	66	192	184	175	146	141
$50,000 to $74,999	815	45	191	207	185	91	94
$75,000 to $99,999	638	23	186	166	119	95	47
$100,000 or more	1,468	26	311	454	386	207	84
Median income	$65,876	$35,960	$68,289	$80,337	$78,036	$65,565	$33,759
Total Asian households	**100.0%**	**100.0%**	**100.0%**	**100.0%**	**100.0%**	**100.0%**	**100.0%**
Under $25,000	19.0	36.3	17.3	11.8	12.0	18.7	39.9
$25,000 to $49,999	19.1	26.6	18.0	16.0	17.8	22.0	23.3
$50,000 to $74,999	17.3	18.1	17.9	18.0	18.8	13.7	15.6
$75,000 to $99,999	13.5	9.3	17.4	14.5	12.1	14.3	7.8
$100,000 or more	31.1	10.5	29.1	39.5	39.2	31.2	13.9

Note: Asians are those who identify themselves as being of the race alone and those who identify themselves as being of the race in combination with other races.
Source: Bureau of the Census, 2008 Current Population Survey, Internet site http://pubdb3.census.gov/macro/032008/hhinc/new02_000.htm; calculations by New Strategist

Table 5.12 Household Income by Age of Householder, 2007: Black Households

(number and percent distribution of black households by household income and age of householder, 2007; households in thousands as of 2008)

	total	under 25	25 to 34	35 to 44	45 to 54	55 to 64	65 or older
Total black households	**14,976**	**1,182**	**2,758**	**3,202**	**3,255**	**2,308**	**2,272**
Under $25,000	5,716	673	1,068	869	905	863	1,337
$25,000 to $49,999	4,097	316	818	924	904	591	540
$50,000 to $74,999	2,420	119	442	606	669	384	198
$75,000 to $99,999	1,243	37	200	375	351	189	94
$100,000 or more	1,500	35	229	427	425	282	104
Median income	$34,091	$20,753	$32,153	$44,084	$44,703	$35,987	$19,370
Total black households	**100.0%**	**100.0%**	**100.0%**	**100.0%**	**100.0%**	**100.0%**	**100.0%**
Under $25,000	38.2	56.9	38.7	27.1	27.8	37.4	58.8
$25,000 to $49,999	27.4	26.7	29.7	28.9	27.8	25.6	23.8
$50,000 to $74,999	16.2	10.1	16.0	18.9	20.6	16.6	8.7
$75,000 to $99,999	8.3	3.1	7.3	11.7	10.8	8.2	4.1
$100,000 or more	10.0	3.0	8.3	13.3	13.1	12.2	4.6

Note: Blacks are those who identify themselves as being of the race alone and those who identify themselves as being of the race in combination with other races.
Source: Bureau of the Census, 2008 Current Population Survey, Internet site http://pubdb3.census.gov/macro/032008/hhinc/new02_000.htm; calculations by New Strategist

Table 5.13 Household Income by Age of Householder, 2007: Hispanic Households

(number and percent distribution of Hispanic households by household income and age of householder, 2007; households in thousands as of 2008)

	total	under 25	25 to 34	35 to 44	45 to 54	55 to 64	65 or older
Total Hispanic households	**13,339**	**1,182**	**3,401**	**3,385**	**2,480**	**1,497**	**1,394**
Under $25,000	4,106	440	935	825	656	484	769
$25,000 to $49,999	4,114	435	1,223	1,102	628	388	339
$50,000 to $74,999	2,443	180	668	668	512	277	139
$75,000 to $99,999	1,290	77	303	366	325	154	65
$100,000 or more	1,385	49	274	424	360	194	85
Median income	$38,679	$31,628	$38,223	$43,480	$47,534	$40,541	$21,860
Total Hispanic households	**100.0%**	**100.0%**	**100.0%**	**100.0%**	**100.0%**	**100.0%**	**100.0%**
Under $25,000	30.8	37.2	27.5	24.4	26.5	32.3	55.2
$25,000 to $49,999	30.8	36.8	36.0	32.6	25.3	25.9	24.3
$50,000 to $74,999	18.3	15.2	19.6	19.7	20.6	18.5	10.0
$75,000 to $99,999	9.7	6.5	8.9	10.8	13.1	10.3	4.7
$100,000 or more	10.4	4.1	8.1	12.5	14.5	13.0	6.1

Source: Bureau of the Census, 2008 Current Population Survey, Internet site http://pubdb3.census.gov/macro/032008/hhinc/ new02_000.htm; calculations by New Strategist

Table 5.14 Household Income by Age of Householder, 2007: Non-Hispanic White Households

(number and percent distribution of non-Hispanic white households by household income and age of householder, 2007; households in thousands as of 2008)

	total	under 25	25 to 34	35 to 44	45 to 54	55 to 64	65 or older
Total non-Hispanic white households	**82,765**	**3,918**	**11,879**	**14,529**	**17,577**	**15,238**	**19,625**
Under $25,000	18,049	1,300	1,755	1,732	2,320	2,760	8,178
$25,000 to $49,999	19,664	1,370	3,103	2,762	3,330	3,251	5,846
$50,000 to $74,999	15,410	734	2,823	3,163	3,331	2,947	2,412
$75,000 to $99,999	10,576	273	1,849	2,365	2,865	1,992	1,236
$100,000 or more	19,062	240	2,348	4,506	5,729	4,287	1,952
Median income	$54,920	$35,818	$57,638	$71,279	$73,239	$62,449	$21,860
Total non-Hispanic white households	**100.0%**	**100.0%**	**100.0%**	**100.0%**	**100.0%**	**100.0%**	**100.0%**
Under $25,000	21.8	33.2	14.8	11.9	13.2	18.1	41.7
$25,000 to $49,999	23.8	35.0	26.1	19.0	18.9	21.3	29.8
$50,000 to $74,999	18.6	18.7	23.8	21.8	19.0	19.3	12.3
$75,000 to $99,999	12.8	7.0	15.6	16.3	16.3	13.1	6.3
$100,000 or more	23.0	6.1	19.8	31.0	32.6	28.1	9.9

Note: Non-Hispanic whites are those who identify themselves as being white alone and not Hispanic.
Source: Bureau of the Census, 2008 Current Population Survey, Internet site http://pubdb3.census.gov/macro/032008/hhinc/ new02_000.htm; calculations by New Strategist

The Median Income of Married Couples Exceeds $72,000

Married couples are by far the most affluent household type.

Most married couples are dual earners, which accounts for their higher incomes. Nearly one-third of couples had an income of $100,000 or more in 2007, accounting for 79 percent of all households with incomes that high.

Married couples are the only household type whose median income is significantly above the all-household average of $50,233. Female-headed families had a median income of just $33,370, while male-headed families had a median income only slightly below the national median, at $49,839. Sixteen percent of male-headed families had an income of $100,000 or more in 2007 compared with only 7 percent of female-headed families.

Women who live alone have the lowest incomes, a median of $21,546 in 2007. Most women who live alone are older widows, which accounts for their low incomes. Men who live alone have much higher incomes than their female counterparts—a median of $31,606—because most are under age 55 and in the labor force.

■ The incomes of women who live alone are likely to rise in the decades ahead as baby-boom women with their own retirement income become widows.

Women who live alone have the lowest incomes

(median income of people who live alone, by sex, 2007)

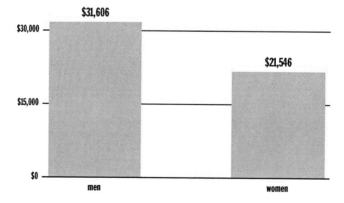

Table 5.15 Household Income by Household Type, 2007: Total Households

(number and percent distribution of households by household income and type of household, 2007; households in thousands as of 2008)

| | | family households | | | | nonfamily households | | | | |
| | | total | married couples | female hh, no spouse present | male hh, no spouse present | total | female householders | | male householders | |
	total	total					total	living alone	total	living alone
Total households	**116,783**	**77,873**	**58,370**	**14,404**	**5,100**	**38,910**	**21,038**	**18,297**	**17,872**	**13,870**
Under $25,000	29,034	12,321	5,911	5,403	1,006	16,714	10,745	10,240	5,968	5,433
$25,000 to $49,999	29,053	18,045	12,037	4,458	1,550	11,006	5,560	4,829	5,448	4,428
$50,000 to $74,999	21,268	15,635	12,106	2,365	1,162	5,632	2,517	1,900	3,117	2,169
$75,000 to $99,999	13,841	11,387	9,698	1,118	571	2,456	1,017	640	1,436	804
$100,000 or more	23,586	20,484	18,615	1,060	809	3,102	1,199	689	1,903	1,037
Median income	$50,233	$62,359	$72,785	$33,370	$49,839	$30,176	$24,294	$21,546	$36,767	$31,606
Total households	**100.0%**	**100.0%**	**100.0%**	**100.0%**	**100.0%**	**100.0%**	**100.0%**	**100.0%**	**100.0%**	**100.0%**
Under $25,000	24.9	15.8	10.1	37.5	19.7	43.0	51.1	56.0	33.4	39.2
$25,000 to $49,999	24.9	23.2	20.6	30.9	30.4	28.3	26.4	26.4	30.5	31.9
$50,000 to $74,999	18.2	20.1	20.7	16.4	22.8	14.5	12.0	10.4	17.4	15.6
$75,000 to $99,999	11.9	14.6	16.6	7.8	11.2	6.3	4.8	3.5	8.0	5.8
$100,000 or more	20.2	26.3	31.9	7.4	15.9	8.0	5.7	3.8	10.6	7.5

Source: Bureau of the Census, 2008 Current Population Survey, Internet site http://pubdb3.census.gov/macro/032008/hhinc/new01_000.htm; calculations by New Strategist

From Young to Old, Incomes Vary by Household Type

In all but the youngest age group, married couples have the highest incomes.

Married couples are the most affluent household type, while the middle aged are the most affluent age group. Combine those characteristics and you have the most affluent households in the country. Married couples in the 45-to-54 age group had a median income of $88,257 in 2007, with 42 percent having an income of $100,000 or more. Among couples aged 35 to 44 and 55 to 64, a substantial 37 to 38 percent have an income of $100,000 or more.

Only 19 percent of households headed by people under age 25 are married couples, which is one reason for the low incomes of the age group. Among householders under age 25, male-headed families have the highest incomes, a median of $43,188 versus $40,706 for married couples.

■ The number of earners in a household is the major determinant of income. Because most married couples are dual earners, their incomes typically are far higher than the incomes of other household types.

Many married couples have incomes of $100,000 or more

(percent of married couples with household incomes of $100,000 or more, by age of householder, 2007)

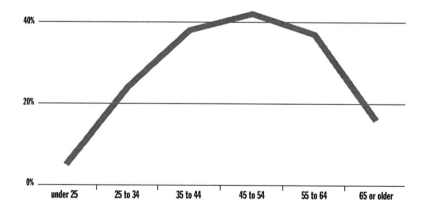

Table 5.16 Household Income by Household Type, 2007: Householders under Age 25

(number and percent distribution of households headed by householders under age 25, by household income and type of household, 2007; households in thousands as of 2008)

		family households				nonfamily households				
							female householders		male householders	
	total	total	married couples	female hh, no spouse present	male hh, no spouse present	total	total	living alone	total	living alone
Total householders under age 25	**6,554**	**3,359**	**1,224**	**1,318**	**817**	**3,195**	**1,527**	**805**	**1,668**	**844**
Under $25,000	2,506	1,156	267	694	195	1,350	704	515	642	481
$25,000 to $49,999	2,201	1,118	515	334	268	1,083	501	238	583	280
$50,000 to $74,999	1,079	597	294	135	168	480	203	50	278	65
$75,000 to $99,999	416	243	90	75	80	173	77	0	96	10
$100,000 or more	351	243	57	80	105	109	41	0	67	9
Median income	$31,790	$35,524	$40,706	$23,008	$43,188	$28,811	$26,665	$19,292	$30,989	$22,507
Total householders under age 25	**100.0%**	**100.0%**	**100.0%**	**100.0%**	**100.0%**	**100.0%**	**100.0%**	**100.0%**	**100.0%**	**100.0%**
Under $25,000	38.2	34.4	21.8	52.7	23.9	42.3	46.1	64.0	38.5	57.0
$25,000 to $49,999	33.6	33.3	42.1	25.3	32.8	33.9	32.8	29.6	35.0	33.2
$50,000 to $74,999	16.5	17.8	24.0	10.2	20.6	15.0	13.3	6.2	16.7	7.7
$75,000 to $99,999	6.3	7.2	7.4	5.7	9.8	5.4	5.0	0.0	5.8	1.2
$100,000 or more	5.4	7.2	4.7	6.1	12.9	3.4	2.7	0.0	4.0	1.1

Source: Bureau of the Census, 2008 Current Population Survey, Internet site http://pubdb3.census.gov/macro/032008/hhinc/new02_000.htm; calculations by New Strategist

Table 5.17 Household Income by Household Type, 2007: Householders Aged 25 to 34

(number and percent distribution of households headed by householders aged 25 to 34, by household income and type of household, 2007; households in thousands as of 2008)

| | | family households | | | | nonfamily households | | | | |
| | | | | female hh, no spouse present | male hh, no spouse present | | female householders | | male householders | |
	total	total	married couples			total	total	living alone	total	living alone
Total householders aged 25 to 34	**19,225**	**13,253**	**8,994**	**3,064**	**1,196**	**5,972**	**2,303**	**1,569**	**3,669**	**2,362**
Under $25,000	3,948	2,568	829	1,514	227	1,378	558	499	822	695
$25,000 to $49,999	5,402	3,354	2,096	892	368	2,048	808	657	1,240	940
$50,000 to $74,999	4,160	2,949	2,303	335	310	1,213	434	240	780	466
$75,000 to $99,999	2,543	1,958	1,642	187	128	586	216	90	368	121
$100,000 or more	3,172	2,424	2,126	134	163	749	287	83	461	137
Median income	$51,016	$55,212	$66,747	$25,307	$50,255	$43,316	$42,163	$35,048	$44,551	$35,259
Total householders aged 25 to 34	**100.0%**	**100.0%**	**100.0%**	**100.0%**	**100.0%**	**100.0%**	**100.0%**	**100.0%**	**100.0%**	**100.0%**
Under $25,000	20.5	19.4	9.2	49.4	19.0	23.1	24.2	31.8	22.4	29.4
$25,000 to $49,999	28.1	25.3	23.3	29.1	30.8	34.3	35.1	41.9	33.8	39.8
$50,000 to $74,999	21.6	22.3	25.6	10.9	25.9	20.3	18.8	15.3	21.3	19.7
$75,000 to $99,999	13.2	14.8	18.3	6.1	10.7	9.8	9.4	5.7	10.0	5.1
$100,000 or more	16.5	18.3	23.6	4.4	13.6	12.5	12.5	5.3	12.6	5.8

Source: Bureau of the Census, 2008 Current Population Survey, Internet site http://pubdb3.census.gov/macro/032008/hhinc/new02_000.htm; calculations by New Strategist

Table 5.18 Household Income by Household Type, 2007: Householders Aged 35 to 44

(number and percent distribution of households headed by householders aged 35 to 44, by household income and type of household, 2007; households in thousands as of 2008)

| | | family households | | | | nonfamily households | | | | |
| | | total | married couples | female hh, no spouse present | male hh, no spouse present | total | female householders | | male householders | |
	total						total	living alone	total	living alone
Total householders aged 35 to 44	**22,448**	**17,601**	**12,989**	**3,551**	**1,061**	**4,847**	**1,838**	**1,479**	**3,009**	**2,321**
Under $25,000	3,610	2,293	842	1,291	163	1,318	540	478	780	708
$25,000 to $49,999	5,006	3,530	1,974	1,234	323	1,476	593	524	885	725
$50,000 to $74,999	4,679	3,640	2,807	569	262	1,042	374	298	666	500
$75,000 to $99,999	3,296	2,825	2,474	223	130	473	162	102	309	175
$100,000 or more	5,854	5,314	4,893	236	184	540	170	77	370	215
Median income	$62,124	$70,044	$82,390	$33,489	$52,017	$42,941	$40,203	$35,491	$45,412	$40,151
Total householders aged 35 to 44	**100.0%**	**100.0%**	**100.0%**	**100.0%**	**100.0%**	**100.0%**	**100.0%**	**100.0%**	**100.0%**	**100.0%**
Under $25,000	16.1	13.0	6.5	36.4	15.4	27.2	29.4	32.3	25.9	30.5
$25,000 to $49,999	22.3	20.1	15.2	34.8	30.4	30.5	32.3	35.4	29.4	31.2
$50,000 to $74,999	20.8	20.7	21.6	16.0	24.7	21.5	20.3	20.1	22.1	21.5
$75,000 to $99,999	14.7	16.1	19.0	6.3	12.3	9.8	8.8	6.9	10.3	7.5
$100,000 or more	26.1	30.2	37.7	6.6	17.3	11.1	9.2	5.2	12.3	9.3

Source: Bureau of the Census, 2008 Current Population Survey, Internet site http://pubdb3.census.gov/macro/032008/hhinc/new02_000.htm; calculations by New Strategist

Table 5.19 Household Income by Household Type, 2007: Householders Aged 45 to 54

(number and percent distribution of households headed by householders aged 45 to 54, by household income and type of household, 2007; households in thousands as of 2008)

| | | family households | | | | nonfamily households | | | | |
| | | | | female hh, | male hh, | | female householders | | male householders | |
	total	total	married couples	no spouse present	no spouse present	total	total	living alone	total	living alone
Total householders aged 45 to 54	**24,536**	**17,949**	**13,842**	**3,043**	**1,065**	**6,587**	**3,125**	**2,713**	**3,462**	**2,866**
Under $25,000	4,053	1,879	810	871	195	2,174	1,151	1,065	1,023	953
$25,000 to $49,999	5,107	3,036	1,829	898	308	2,072	1,018	905	1,055	940
$50,000 to $74,999	4,730	3,578	2,674	676	227	1,154	500	421	653	496
$75,000 to $99,999	3,688	3,189	2,739	315	131	499	205	147	291	220
$100,000 or more	6,959	6,269	5,791	280	198	690	251	175	439	258
Median income	$65,476	$78,344	$88,257	$41,741	$53,038	$37,292	$34,423	$31,791	$40,576	$36,672
Total householders aged 45 to 54	**100.0%**	**100.0%**	**100.0%**	**100.0%**	**100.0%**	**100.0%**	**100.0%**	**100.0%**	**100.0%**	**100.0%**
Under $25,000	16.5	10.5	5.9	28.6	18.3	33.0	36.8	39.3	29.5	33.3
$25,000 to $49,999	20.8	16.9	13.2	29.5	28.9	31.5	32.6	33.4	30.5	32.8
$50,000 to $74,999	19.3	19.9	19.3	22.2	21.3	17.5	16.0	15.5	18.9	17.3
$75,000 to $99,999	15.0	17.8	19.8	10.4	12.3	7.6	6.6	5.4	8.4	7.7
$100,000 or more	28.4	34.9	41.8	9.2	18.6	10.5	8.0	6.5	12.7	9.0

Source: Bureau of the Census, 2008 Current Population Survey, Internet site http://pubdb3.census.gov/macro/032008/hhinc/ new02_000.htm; calculations by New Strategist

Table 5.20   Household Income by Household Type, 2007: Householders Aged 55 to 64

(number and percent distribution of households headed by householders aged 55 to 64, by household income and type of household, 2007; households in thousands as of 2008)

| | | family households | | | | nonfamily households | | | | |
| | | | | | | | female householders | | male householders | |
	total	total	married couples	female hh, no spouse present	male hh, no spouse present	total	total	living alone	total	living alone
Total householders aged 55 to 64	**19,909**	**13,218**	**11,144**	**1,562**	**513**	**6,690**	**3,746**	**3,434**	**2,944**	**2,561**
Under $25,000	4,294	1,568	1,028	434	105	2,725	1,647	1,595	1,079	1,015
$25,000 to $49,999	4,413	2,560	1,991	446	125	1,851	1,068	1,005	781	699
$50,000 to $74,999	3,737	2,694	2,237	333	125	1,042	582	500	462	397
$75,000 to $99,999	2,449	2,014	1,797	160	58	432	201	161	234	169
$100,000 or more	5,016	4,380	4,091	190	98	636	247	174	389	279
Median income	$57,386	$72,838	$79,000	$44,501	$52,137	$32,059	$30,113	$27,851	$35,678	$32,687
Total householders aged 55 to 64	**100.0%**	**100.0%**	**100.0%**	**100.0%**	**100.0%**	**100.0%**	**100.0%**	**100.0%**	**100.0%**	**100.0%**
Under $25,000	21.6	11.9	9.2	27.8	20.5	40.7	44.0	46.4	36.7	39.6
$25,000 to $49,999	22.2	19.4	17.9	28.6	24.4	27.7	28.5	29.3	26.5	27.3
$50,000 to $74,999	18.8	20.4	20.1	21.3	24.4	15.6	15.5	14.6	15.7	15.5
$75,000 to $99,999	12.3	15.2	16.1	10.2	11.3	6.5	5.4	4.7	7.9	6.6
$100,000 or more	25.2	33.1	36.7	12.2	19.1	9.5	6.6	5.1	13.2	10.9

Source: Bureau of the Census, 2008 Current Population Survey, Internet site http://pubdb3.census.gov/macro/032008/hhinc/ new02_000.htm; calculations by New Strategist

Table 5.21 Household Income by Household Type, 2007: Householders Aged 65 or Older

(number and percent distribution of households headed by householders aged 65 or older, by household income and type of household, 2007; households in thousands as of 2008)

| | | family households | | | | nonfamily households | | | | |
| | | | | female hh, | male hh, | | female householders | | male householders | |
	total	total	married couples	no spouse present	no spouse present	total	total	living alone	total	living alone
Total householders aged 65 or older	**24,113**	**12,493**	**10,178**	**1,866**	**449**	**11,620**	**8,500**	**8,297**	**3,120**	**2,917**
Under $25,000	10,626	2,856	2,137	600	120	7,770	6,147	6,089	1,621	1,581
$25,000 to $49,999	6,924	4,450	3,638	656	156	2,476	1,571	1,500	904	841
$50,000 to $74,999	2,881	2,177	1,790	315	70	704	424	390	280	246
$75,000 to $99,999	1,451	1,155	957	157	41	296	158	138	139	108
$100,000 or more	2,233	1,855	1,656	139	60	378	202	179	176	140
Median income	$28,305	$41,960	$43,209	$35,596	$39,974	$17,496	$16,276	$16,037	$23,682	$22,215
Total householders aged 65 or older	**100.0%**	**100.0%**	**100.0%**	**100.0%**	**100.0%**	**100.0%**	**100.0%**	**100.0%**	**100.0%**	**100.0%**
Under $25,000	44.1	22.9	21.0	32.2	26.7	66.9	72.3	73.4	52.0	54.2
$25,000 to $49,999	28.7	35.6	35.7	35.2	34.7	21.3	18.5	18.1	29.0	28.8
$50,000 to $74,999	11.9	17.4	17.6	16.9	15.6	6.1	5.0	4.7	9.0	8.4
$75,000 to $99,999	6.0	9.2	9.4	8.4	9.1	2.5	1.9	1.7	4.5	3.7
$100,000 or more	9.3	14.8	16.3	7.4	13.4	3.3	2.4	2.2	5.6	4.8

Source: Bureau of the Census, 2008 Current Population Survey, Internet site http://pubdb3.census.gov/macro/032008/hhinc/new02_000.htm; calculations by New Strategist

Dual-Earner Couples Have the Highest Incomes

Nearly half have incomes of $100,000 or more.

The median income of all married-couple families stood at $72,589 in 2007. Among dual-income couples, median income was an even higher $99,140. Thirty-two percent of the nation's couples are dual earners with both husband and wife working full-time.

Among all married couples, those with children under age 18 at home have higher incomes than those without children—$76,711 versus $68,957. Those with children at home have higher incomes because they are more likely to be in the labor force, and many are in their peak-earning years. Couples without children at home have lower incomes because many are older and retired.

Among couples in which both husband and wife work full-time, however, those without children at home—many of them empty-nesters—have the highest incomes, a median of more than $100,000 in 2007. The 52 percent majority had an income of $100,000 or more in 2007.

■ The incomes of married couples without children at home may continue to grow in the years ahead, despite the current economic turmoil, as boomers become empty-nesters and postpone retirement.

Dual-earner couples without children at home have the highest incomes

(median income of married couples by work status and presence of children under age 18 at home, 2007)

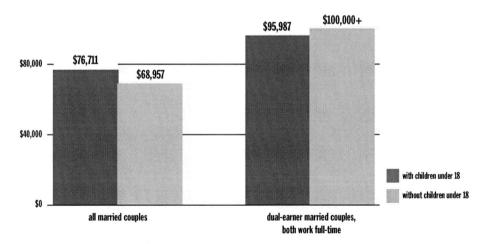

Table 5.22 Income of Married Couples by Presence of Children, 2007

(number and percent distribution of married-couple families by income and presence and age of related children under age 18 at home, 2007; couples in thousands as of 2008)

	total	no children	with one or more children			
			total	all under 6	some under 6, some 6 to 17	all 6 to 17
Total couples	**58,395**	**31,944**	**26,450**	**6,459**	**5,859**	**14,133**
Under $25,000	5,950	3,845	2,101	570	590	943
$25,000 to $49,999	12,083	7,221	4,862	1,309	1,367	2,184
$50,000 to $74,999	12,114	6,332	5,782	1,450	1,330	3,004
$75,000 to $99,999	9,690	4,919	4,770	1,156	942	2,676
$100,000 or more	18,557	9,624	8,933	1,975	1,632	5,326
Median income	$72,589	$68,957	$76,711	$72,710	$66,937	$82,773
Total couples	**100.0%**	**100.0%**	**100.0%**	**100.0%**	**100.0%**	**100.0%**
Under $25,000	10.2	12.0	7.9	8.8	10.1	6.7
$25,000 to $49,999	20.7	22.6	18.4	20.3	23.3	15.5
$50,000 to $74,999	20.7	19.8	21.9	22.4	22.7	21.3
$75,000 to $99,999	16.6	15.4	18.0	17.9	16.1	18.9
$100,000 or more	31.8	30.1	33.8	30.6	27.9	37.7

Note: The median income of married couples in this table is slightly different from the figure shown in the household income tables because this figure includes the incomes of only the family members, not any unrelated members of the household. Source:Bureau of the Census, 2008 Current Population Survey, Internet site http://pubdb3.census.gov/macro/032008/faminc/ new04_001.htm; calculations by New Strategist

Table 5.23 Income of Dual-Earner Married Couples by Presence of Children, 2007

(number and percent distribution of married couples in which both husband and wife work full-time, year-round, by income and presence and age of related children under age 18 at home, 2007; couples in thousands as of 2008)

	total	no children	with one or more children			
			total	all under 6	some under 6, some 6 to 17	all 6 to 17
Total dual-earner couples	**18,920**	**9,512**	**9,408**	**2,089**	**1,644**	**5,675**
Under $25,000	93	39	54	11	8	31
$25,000 to $49,999	1,398	623	773	155	170	447
$50,000 to $74,999	3,751	1,739	2,013	503	363	1,150
$75,000 to $99,999	4,333	2,168	2,164	491	396	1,277
$100,000 or more	9,347	4,942	4,404	928	709	2,768
Median income	$99,140	$100,000+	$95,987	$92,640	$91,280	$98,360
Total dual-earner couples	**100.0%**	**100.0%**	**100.0%**	**100.0%**	**100.0%**	**100.0%**
Under $25,000	0.5	0.4	0.6	0.5	0.5	0.5
$25,000 to $49,999	7.4	6.5	8.2	7.4	10.3	7.9
$50,000 to $74,999	19.8	18.3	21.4	24.1	22.1	20.3
$75,000 to $99,999	22.9	22.8	23.0	23.5	24.1	22.5
$100,000 or more	49.4	52.0	46.8	44.4	43.1	48.8

Source:Bureau of the Census, 2008 Current Population Survey, Internet site http://pubdb3.census.gov/macro/032008/faminc/new04_001.htm; calculations by New Strategist

Single Parents Have Low Incomes

But many male- and female-headed families have incomes close to the average.

Single-parent families are families with children under age 18 headed by a man or a woman without a spouse. Single parents account for 67 percent of female-headed families and 53 percent of families headed by men. The incomes of single-parent families are lower than those of other male- and female-headed families. Female-headed single-parent families had a median income of $24,949 in 2007, while their male counterparts had a median income of $38,083.

Male- and female-headed families without children under age 18 at home have substantially higher incomes. Many of these householders live with other adults such as parents, brothers, or sisters—which adds earners to the household. The median income of male-headed families without children under age 18 at home stood at $51,457, slightly above the national median. A substantial 16 percent had incomes of $100,000 or more. Their female counterparts had a median income of $44,407.

■ Families headed by women may see their incomes grow in the years ahead if women's earnings continue to rise.

Female-headed families with children have lower incomes

(median income of female- and male-headed families by presence of children under age 18 at home, 2007)

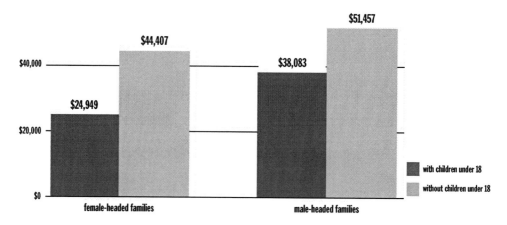

Table 5.24 Income of Female- and Male-Headed Families by Presence of Children, 2007

(number and percent distribution of female- and male-headed families with no spouse present, by family income and presence of children under age 18 at home, 2007; families in thousands as of 2008)

	female-headed families			male-headed families		
	total	no children	one or more children	total	no children	one or more children
Total families	**14,411**	**4,693**	**9,718**	**5,103**	**2,403**	**2,700**
Under $25,000	6,045	1,175	4,869	1,226	445	782
$25,000 to $49,999	4,418	1,468	2,949	1,644	714	932
$50,000 to $74,999	2,125	1,064	1,063	1,042	552	489
$75,000 to $99,999	949	515	432	512	301	212
$100,000 or more	877	472	405	678	393	286
Median income	$30,296	$44,407	$24,949	$44,358	$51,457	$38,083
Total families	**100.0%**	**100.0%**	**100.0%**	**100.0%**	**100.0%**	**100.0%**
Under $25,000	41.9	25.0	50.1	24.0	18.5	29.0
$25,000 to $49,999	30.7	31.3	30.3	32.2	29.7	34.5
$50,000 to $74,999	14.7	22.7	10.9	20.4	23.0	18.1
$75,000 to $99,999	6.6	11.0	4.4	10.0	12.5	7.9
$100,000 or more	6.1	10.1	4.2	13.3	16.4	10.6

Note: Median incomes in this table are slightly different from the figures shown in the household income tables because these figures include the incomes of only the family members, not any unrelated members of the household.
Source: Bureau of the Census, 2008 Current Population Survey, Internet site http://pubdb3.census.gov/macro/032008/faminc/ new03_000.htm; calculations by New Strategist

Older Women Who Live Alone Have Low Incomes

Among the middle aged who live alone, however, women's incomes are almost as high as men's.

Among the nation's 32 million single-person households, women head the 57 percent majority. The median income of women who live alone was just $21,546 in 2007. The median income of men who live alone was a higher $31,606. The gap in median incomes can largely be explained by the age difference between men and women who live alone. The 64 percent majority of women who live alone are aged 55 or older, many of them elderly widows dependent on Social Security. Sixty-one percent of men who live alone are under age 55, many in their peak earning years.

Within age groups, men and women who live alone have much more similar incomes. Among 25-to-34-year-olds who live alone, the median income of women is just $211 less than that of men ($35,048 versus $35,259). The difference in the incomes of men and women who live alone is greatest in the older age groups.

■ The incomes of older men and women who live alone may converge as career-oriented baby-boom women become widows.

The income gap is largest between older men and women

(median income of people who live alone, by age and sex, 2007)

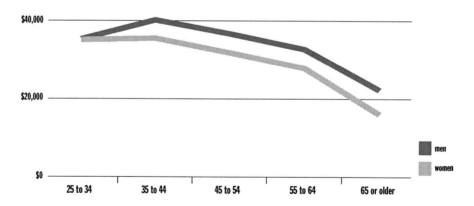

Table 5.25 Household Income of Men Who Live Alone, 2007

(number and percent distribution of male-headed single-person households by household income and age of householder, 2007; households in thousands as of 2008)

	total	15 to 24	25 to 34	35 to 44	45 to 54	55 to 64	65 or older
Total men living alone	**13,870**	**844**	**2,362**	**2,321**	**2,866**	**2,561**	**2,917**
Under $25,000	5,433	481	695	708	953	1,015	1,581
$25,000 to $49,999	4,428	280	940	725	940	699	841
$50,000 to $74,999	2,169	65	466	500	496	397	246
$75,000 to $99,999	804	10	121	175	220	169	108
$100,000 or more	1,037	9	137	215	258	279	140
Median income	$31,606	$22,507	$35,259	$40,151	$36,672	$32,687	$22,215
Total men living alone	**100.0%**	**100.0%**	**100.0%**	**100.0%**	**100.0%**	**100.0%**	**100.0%**
Under $25,000	39.2	57.0	29.4	30.5	33.3	39.6	54.2
$25,000 to $49,999	31.9	33.2	39.8	31.2	32.8	27.3	28.8
$50,000 to $74,999	15.6	7.7	19.7	21.5	17.3	15.5	8.4
$75,000 to $99,999	5.8	1.2	5.1	7.5	7.7	6.6	3.7
$100,000 or more	7.5	1.1	5.8	9.3	9.0	10.9	4.8

Source: Bureau of the Census, 2008 Current Population Survey, Internet site http://pubdb3.census.gov/macro/032008/hhinc/ new02_000.htm; calculations by New Strategist

Table 5.26 Household Income of Women Who Live Alone, 2007

(number and percent distribution of female-headed single-person households by household income and age of householder, 2007; households in thousands as of 2008)

	total	15 to 24	25 to 34	35 to 44	45 to 54	55 to 64	65 or older
Total women living alone	**18,297**	**805**	**1,569**	**1,479**	**2,713**	**3,434**	**8,297**
Under $25,000	10,240	515	499	478	1,065	1,595	6,089
$25,000 to $49,999	4,829	238	657	524	905	1,005	1,500
$50,000 to $74,999	1,900	50	240	298	421	500	390
$75,000 to $99,999	640	0	90	102	147	161	138
$100,000 or more	689	0	83	77	175	174	179
Median income	$21,546	$19,292	$35,048	$35,491	$31,791	$27,851	$16,037
Total women living alone	**100.0%**	**100.0%**	**100.0%**	**100.0%**	**100.0%**	**100.0%**	**100.0%**
Under $25,000	56.0	64.0	31.8	32.3	39.3	46.4	73.4
$25,000 to $49,999	26.4	29.6	41.9	35.4	33.4	29.3	18.1
$50,000 to $74,999	10.4	6.2	15.3	20.1	15.5	14.6	4.7
$75,000 to $99,999	3.5	0.0	5.7	6.9	5.4	4.7	1.7
$100,000 or more	3.8	0.0	5.3	5.2	6.5	5.1	2.2

Source: Bureau of the Census, 2008 Current Population Survey, Internet site http://pubdb3.census.gov/macro/032008/hhinc/ new02_000.htm; calculations by New Strategist

College-Educated Householders Have the Highest Incomes

The median income of households headed by college graduates is 64 percent higher than the national average.

The higher the educational degree, the greater the financial reward. At the top are householders with professional degrees, such as doctors and lawyers. Their median household income was greater than $100,000 in 2007, and 65 percent had household incomes of $100,000 or more.

Thirty percent of householders aged 25 or older have at least a bachelor's degree. Their median income stood at $84,508 in 2007. Those with a master's degree had a median income of $90,660. In contrast, householders who went no further than high school had a median income far below average, just $40,456. Those who did not graduate from high school had a median household income of less than $25,000.

■ Households headed by college graduates account for 59 percent of all households with incomes of $100,000 or more.

Incomes rise with education

(median income of householders aged 25 or older by educational attainment, 2007)

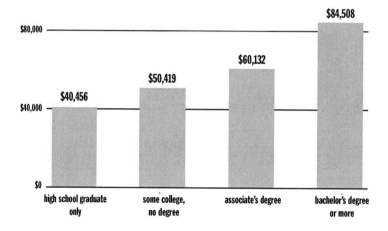

Table 5.27   Household Income by Education of Householder, 2007

(number and percent distribution of householders aged 25 or older by household income and educational attainment of householder, 2007; households in thousands as of 2008)

	total	less than 9th grade	9th to 12th grade, no diploma	high school graduate	some college, no degree	assoc. degree	bachelor's degree or more				
							total	bachelor's degree	master's degree	prof. degree	doctoral degree
Total households	**110,230**	**5,507**	**8,621**	**32,422**	**20,152**	**9,968**	**33,560**	**21,454**	**8,785**	**1,727**	**1,593**
Under $25,000	26,530	3,251	4,386	9,832	4,417	1,606	3,037	2,141	682	102	114
$25,000 to $49,999	26,852	1,363	2,366	9,603	5,559	2,522	5,435	3,896	1,205	156	178
$50,000 to $74,999	20,188	544	1,082	6,196	4,062	2,168	6,137	4,188	1,572	168	208
$75,000 to $99,999	13,425	203	443	3,311	2,746	1,592	5,132	3,343	1,423	184	180
$100,000 or more	23,235	145	344	3,480	3,365	2,081	13,820	7,883	3,906	1,119	912
Median income	$51,427	$20,805	$24,492	$40,456	$50,419	$60,132	$84,508	$77,605	$90,660	$100,000+	$100,000+
Total households	**100.0%**	**100.0%**	**100.0%**	**100.0%**	**100.0%**	**100.0%**	**100.0%**	**100.0%**	**100.0%**	**100.0%**	**100.0%**
Under $25,000	24.1	59.0	50.9	30.3	21.9	16.1	9.0	10.0	7.8	5.9	7.2
$25,000 to $49,999	24.4	24.8	27.4	29.6	27.6	25.3	16.2	18.2	13.7	9.0	11.2
$50,000 to $74,999	18.3	9.9	12.6	19.1	20.2	21.7	18.3	19.5	17.9	9.7	13.1
$75,000 to $99,999	12.2	3.7	5.1	10.2	13.6	16.0	15.3	15.6	16.2	10.7	11.3
$100,000 or more	21.1	2.6	4.0	10.7	16.7	20.9	41.2	36.7	44.5	64.8	57.3

Source: Bureau of the Census, 2008 Current Population Survey, Internet site http://pubdb3.census.gov/macro/032008/hhinc/new01_001.htm; calculations by New Strategist

Women's Incomes Are Growing, Men's Are Shrinking

Between 2000 and 2007, women's median income climbed 8 percent, after adjusting for inflation.

Women's incomes are growing faster than men's as career-oriented baby-boom and younger women replace older just-a-job women in the labor force. Women's median income stood at $20,922 in 2007, still well below the $33,196 median income of men.

Men's incomes are higher than women's in part because men are more likely to work full-time. Incomes peak among men aged 45 to 54 at $45,849. Women's income peak is also in the 45-to-54 age group, at $29,453 (including both full- and part-time workers). Women of all ages saw their incomes grow between 2000 and 2007, but those aged 55 to 64 enjoyed the fastest increase—up 24 percent, after adjusting for inflation. The median income of men under age 55 fell between 2000 and 2007, after adjusting for inflation. Men aged 45 to 54 saw their median income decline by 7 percent during those years. Men aged 25 to 34 experienced an even greater loss of 10 percent.

■ Although women will continue to close the income gap with men, their median income will never equal men's because women are more likely than men to work part-time or not at all when their children are young.

Men's median income fell 3 percent between 2000 and 2007

(median income of people aged 15 or older by sex, 2000 and 2007; in 2007 dollars)

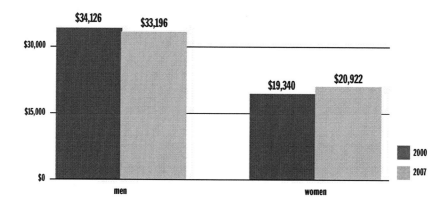

Table 5.28 Median Income of Men by Age, 1990 to 2007

(median income of men aged 15 or older with income by age, 1990 to 2007; percent change in income, 2000–07 and 1990–2007; in 2007 dollars)

	total men	under 25	25 to 34	35 to 44	45 to 54	55 to 64	65 or older
2007	$33,196	$11,209	$32,875	$45,018	$45,849	$42,129	$24,323
2006	33,180	11,275	33,043	43,847	46,989	42,654	24,167
2005	33,217	11,119	33,096	43,507	46,336	43,178	23,136
2004	33,497	11,067	34,020	44,494	45,955	43,126	23,195
2003	33,743	11,230	34,454	44,187	47,438	43,871	22,956
2002	33,698	11,113	35,356	43,672	47,218	41,811	22,401
2001	34,082	10,893	35,732	44,902	48,139	41,736	23,058
2000	34,126	11,494	36,427	45,659	49,412	41,165	23,371
1999	33,963	10,391	36,556	45,292	50,776	41,668	24,017
1998	33,654	10,404	35,718	44,687	49,444	41,637	23,077
1997	32,475	9,619	33,485	42,314	48,462	40,132	22,886
1996	31,363	9,159	33,133	42,329	47,678	38,853	21,955
1995	30,480	9,339	31,894	42,446	48,074	39,150	22,269
1994	30,049	9,751	31,275	42,482	48,328	37,457	21,098
1993	29,817	9,084	30,983	42,873	46,846	35,521	21,171
1992	29,617	9,118	31,126	42,701	46,596	37,089	21,135
1991	30,389	9,325	32,061	43,501	47,180	37,799	21,315
1990	31,208	9,718	32,900	45,787	47,685	38,146	21,812

Percent change

	total men	under 25	25 to 34	35 to 44	45 to 54	55 to 64	65 or older
2000 to 2007	−2.7%	−2.5%	−9.8%	−1.4%	−7.2%	2.3%	4.1%
1990 to 2007	6.4	15.3	−0.1	−1.7	−3.9	10.4	11.5

Source: Bureau of the Census, Current Population Surveys, Internet site http://www.census.gov/hhes/www/income/histinc/incpertoc.html; calculations by New Strategist

Table 5.29 Median Income of Women by Age, 1990 to 2007

(median income of women aged 15 or older with income by age, 1990 to 2007; percent change in income, 2000–07 and 1990–2007; in 2007 dollars)

	total women	under 25	25 to 34	35 to 44	45 to 54	55 to 64	65 or older
2007	$20,922	$8,959	$25,884	$27,702	$29,453	$25,262	$14,021
2006	20,582	8,898	24,865	27,116	28,634	24,872	13,989
2005	19,729	8,730	24,231	27,014	28,120	23,495	13,271
2004	19,393	8,456	24,223	26,786	28,795	22,834	13,261
2003	19,457	8,382	24,793	26,461	29,160	22,962	13,354
2002	19,376	8,739	24,951	25,727	29,004	22,088	13,146
2001	19,458	8,745	25,148	26,317	28,266	20,873	13,249
2000	19,340	8,862	25,344	26,581	28,574	20,372	13,272
1999	19,044	8,310	24,027	25,709	28,083	19,838	13,636
1998	18,331	8,300	23,193	25,769	27,424	18,642	13,344
1997	17,650	8,169	22,731	24,095	26,449	18,517	12,961
1996	16,863	7,739	21,560	24,274	25,063	17,523	12,667
1995	16,387	7,173	21,016	23,502	23,943	16,726	12,638
1994	15,863	7,620	20,591	22,397	23,589	15,034	12,382
1993	15,608	7,561	19,765	22,387	23,066	15,301	12,009
1992	15,513	7,486	19,737	22,323	22,953	14,672	11,848
1991	15,553	7,716	19,247	22,455	21,860	14,701	12,158
1990	15,486	7,539	19,360	22,305	21,884	14,456	12,371

Percent change

	total women	under 25	25 to 34	35 to 44	45 to 54	55 to 64	65 or older
2000 to 2007	8.2%	1.1%	2.1%	4.2%	3.1%	24.0%	5.6%
1990 to 2007	35.1	18.8	33.7	24.2	34.6	74.8	13.3

Source: Bureau of the Census, Current Population Surveys, Internet site http://www.census.gov/hhes/www/income/histinc/incpertoc.html; calculations by New Strategist

Between 2000 and 2007, Asian and Non-Hispanic White Men Lost Ground

Women saw their incomes grow during those years, regardless of race or Hispanic origin.

The median income of Asian men fell 1.1 percent between 2000 and 2007, after adjusting for inflation. Non-Hispanic white men saw their median income fall by a slightly larger 1.5 percent. The median income of black men climbed by just 0.4 percent during those years, while Hispanic men saw their median income rise by 4 percent.

The median incomes of Asian, black, Hispanic, and non-Hispanic white women grew between 2000 and 2007. Asian women experienced the biggest gain, their median income rising by 15 percent, after adjusting for inflation. Hispanics were close behind with a 14 percent increase. The median income of non-Hispanic white women climbed 8 percent, and black women's median income grew by 3 percent.

Among both men and women, Hispanics have the lowest median income—just $16,748 for women and $24,451 for men in 2007. Non-Hispanic whites have the highest incomes among men, a median of $37,373. Among women, Asians have the highest median income, at $24,095 in 2007.

■ Until recently, the incomes of black men and women had been growing faster than the incomes of other racial or ethnic groups.

The incomes of Asian women grew the fastest between 2000 and 2007

(percent change in median income of people aged 15 or older, by sex, race, and Hispanic origin, 2000 to 2007; in 2007 dollars)

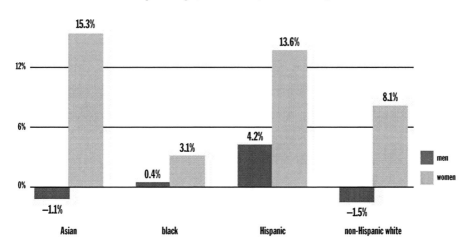

Table 5.30 Median Income of Men by Race and Hispanic Origin, 1990 to 2007

(median income of men aged 15 or older with income by race and Hispanic origin, 1990 to 2007; percent change in income, 2000–07 and 1990–2007; in 2007 dollars)

	total men	Asian	black	Hispanic	non-Hispanic white
2007	$33,196	$36,729	$25,792	$24,451	$37,373
2006	33,180	38,158	25,786	24,117	37,601
2005	33,217	35,087	24,013	23,460	37,539
2004	33,497	35,638	24,932	23,662	36,968
2003	33,743	35,779	24,729	23,734	36,449
2002	33,698	35,543	24,790	23,860	36,920
2001	34,082	36,418	25,140	23,644	37,232
2000	34,126	37,124	25,698	23,476	37,937
1999	33,963	34,691	25,436	22,233	38,413
1998	33,654	31,916	24,544	21,922	37,935
1997	32,475	32,261	23,309	20,887	35,498
1996	31,363	30,758	21,701	20,314	34,595
1995	30,480	29,939	21,623	20,048	34,423
1994	30,049	31,667	20,727	20,060	33,372
1993	29,817	30,579	20,637	19,342	32,740
1992	29,617	28,799	18,916	19,414	32,432
1991	30,389	29,141	19,244	20,515	32,920
1990	31,208	29,826	19,789	20,715	33,769
Percent change					
2000 to 2007	−2.7%	−1.1%	0.4%	4.2%	−1.5%
1990 to 2007	6.4	23.1	30.3	18.0	10.7

Note: Asians and blacks in 2002 through 2007 are those who identify themselves as being of the race alone and those who identify themselves as being of the race in combination with other races. Non-Hispanic whites in 2002 through 2007 are those who identify themselves as being white alone and not Hispanic. Hispanics may be of any race.
Source: Bureau of the Census, Current Population Surveys, Internet site http://www.census.gov/hhes/www/income/histinc/incpertoc.html; calculations by New Strategist

Table 5.31 Median Income of Women by Race and Hispanic Origin, 1990 to 2007

(median income of women aged 15 or older with income by race and Hispanic origin, 1990 to 2007; percent change in income, 2000–07 and 1990–2007; in 2007 dollars)

	total women	Asian	black	Hispanic	non-Hispanic white
2007	$20,922	$24,095	$19,712	$16,748	$21,687
2006	20,582	22,708	19,606	16,205	21,315
2005	19,729	22,965	18,687	15,970	20,659
2004	19,393	22,630	19,042	15,864	20,236
2003	19,457	20,156	18,647	15,379	20,632
2002	19,376	20,628	19,214	15,402	20,041
2001	19,458	21,696	19,069	14,737	20,178
2000	19,340	20,897	19,121	14,747	20,065
1999	19,044	20,902	18,387	14,156	19,799
1998	18,331	19,345	16,688	13,798	19,331
1997	17,650	18,435	16,807	13,216	18,534
1996	16,863	19,257	15,491	12,480	17,783
1995	16,387	17,376	14,808	12,061	17,301
1994	15,863	17,102	14,587	11,916	16,525
1993	15,608	17,472	13,435	11,445	16,389
1992	15,513	17,188	12,868	12,029	16,292
1991	15,553	16,370	13,089	11,896	16,331
1990	15,486	17,049	12,807	11,583	16,272
Percent change					
2000 to 2007	8.2%	15.3%	3.1%	13.6%	8.1%
1990 to 2007	35.1	41.3	53.9	44.6	33.3

Note: Asians and blacks in 2002 through 2007 are those who identify themselves as being of the race alone and those who identify themselves as being of the race in combination with other races. Non-Hispanic whites in 2002 through 2007 are those who identify themselves as being white alone and not Hispanic. Hispanics may be of any race.
Source: Bureau of the Census, Current Population Surveys, Internet site http://www.census.gov/hhes/www/income/histinc/ incpertoc.html; calculations by New Strategist

The Incomes of Men and Women Peak in the 45-to-54 Age Group

Men's income peak is much higher than women's.

Men aged 45 to 54 had a median income of $45,849 in 2007. Their female counterparts had a median income of $29,453—just 64 percent as high as men's. The income gap between men and women is somewhat smaller when comparing only full-time workers. Among full-time workers aged 45 to 54, women's incomes were 76 percent as high as men's ($39,396 versus $52,012).

A substantial 14 percent of men aged 45 to 64 had an income of $100,000 or more in 2007, as did 12 percent of 35-to-44-year-old men. Incomes are lowest for men under age 25, a median of just $11,209, because many are college students working part-time. Even among young men working full-time, median income was just $23,745 in 2007.

Women are much less likely than men to have high incomes. Only 4 to 5 percent of women ranging in age from 35 to 64 had an income of $100,000 or more. But more than one in five women aged 45 to 54 had an income of $50,000 or more in 2007. Older women have much lower incomes than their male counterparts because fewer are covered by pensions. Women aged 65 or older had a median income of just $14,021 versus $24,323 for men.

■ The income gap between older men and women will narrow as working women with pensions replace older women with no work experience.

Even among full-time workers, men's incomes are much higher

(median income of people aged 45 to 54, by work status and sex, 2007)

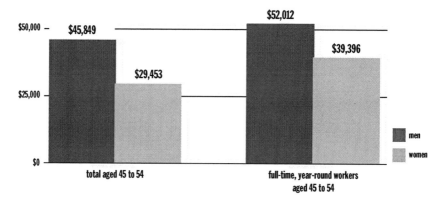

Table 5.32 Income of Men by Age, 2007

(number and percent distribution of men aged 15 or older with income, median income of those with income and of those working full-time year-round, and percent working full-time year-round, by income and age, 2007; men in thousands as of 2008)

	total	15 to 24	25 to 34	35 to 44	45 to 54	55 to 64	65 or older
TOTAL MEN	**115,678**	**21,208**	**20,210**	**20,880**	**21,539**	**16,079**	**15,762**
Without income	**10,889**	**7,066**	**1,193**	**772**	**857**	**557**	**445**
With income	**104,789**	**14,142**	**19,017**	**20,108**	**20,682**	**15,522**	**15,317**
Under $10,000	13,989	6,516	1,727	1,283	1,561	1,251	1,652
$10,000 to $19,999	16,953	3,292	2,881	2,011	1,984	2,088	4,696
$20,000 to $29,999	15,483	2,286	3,507	2,595	2,403	1,862	2,828
$30,000 to $39,999	13,877	1,115	3,300	2,900	2,814	1,972	1,774
$40,000 to $49,999	10,420	460	2,330	2,415	2,432	1,678	1,105
$50,000 to $59,999	8,291	219	1,740	2,081	2,086	1,370	795
$60,000 to $69,999	5,814	81	1,042	1,526	1,526	1,096	541
$70,000 to $79,999	4,677	66	795	1,252	1,338	836	389
$80,000 to $89,999	3,066	36	452	791	898	628	264
$90,000 to $99,999	2,273	5	323	650	625	440	229
$100,000 or more	9,949	67	919	2,604	3,013	2,299	1,046
Median income of men with income	$33,196	$11,209	$32,875	$45,018	$45,849	$42,129	$24,323
Median income of full-time workers	46,224	23,745	39,073	50,524	52,012	56,262	60,589
Percent working full-time	54.5%	22.8%	70.8%	78.3%	74.9%	58.1%	12.7%
TOTAL MEN	**100.0%**	**100.0%**	**100.0%**	**100.0%**	**100.0%**	**100.0%**	**100.0%**
Without income	**9.4**	**33.3**	**5.9**	**3.7**	**4.0**	**3.5**	**2.8**
With income	**90.6**	**66.7**	**94.1**	**96.3**	**96.0**	**96.5**	**97.2**
Under $10,000	12.1	30.7	8.5	6.1	7.2	7.8	10.5
$10,000 to $19,999	14.7	15.5	14.3	9.6	9.2	13.0	29.8
$20,000 to $29,999	13.4	10.8	17.4	12.4	11.2	11.6	17.9
$30,000 to $39,999	12.0	5.3	16.3	13.9	13.1	12.3	11.3
$40,000 to $49,999	9.0	2.2	11.5	11.6	11.3	10.4	7.0
$50,000 to $59,999	7.2	1.0	8.6	10.0	9.7	8.5	5.0
$60,000 to $69,999	5.0	0.4	5.2	7.3	7.1	6.8	3.4
$70,000 to $79,999	4.0	0.3	3.9	6.0	6.2	5.2	2.5
$80,000 to $89,999	2.7	0.2	2.2	3.8	4.2	3.9	1.7
$90,000 to $99,999	2.0	0.0	1.6	3.1	2.9	2.7	1.5
$100,000 or more	8.6	0.3	4.5	12.5	14.0	14.3	6.6

Source: Bureau of the Census, 2008 Current Population Survey, Internet site http://pubdb3.census.gov/macro/032008/perinc/new01_000.htm; calculations by New Strategist

Table 5.33 Income of Women by Age, 2007

(number and percent distribution of women aged 15 or older with income, median income of those with income and of those working full-time year-round, and percent working full-time year-round, by income and age, 2007; women in thousands as of 2008)

	total	15 to 24	25 to 34	35 to 44	45 to 54	55 to 64	65 or older
TOTAL WOMEN	**122,470**	**20,635**	**19,937**	**21,252**	**22,396**	**17,223**	**21,028**
Without income	**17,240**	**7,480**	**2,697**	**2,428**	**2,153**	**1,622**	**861**
With income	**105,230**	**13,155**	**17,240**	**18,824**	**20,243**	**15,601**	**20,167**
Under $10,000	26,931	7,012	3,207	3,564	3,493	3,410	6,246
$10,000 to $19,999	23,616	3,183	3,235	3,284	3,395	3,027	7,491
$20,000 to $29,999	16,710	1,615	3,400	3,071	3,358	2,423	2,842
$30,000 to $39,999	12,457	755	2,790	2,725	2,914	1,893	1,380
$40,000 to $49,999	8,573	339	1,825	1,963	2,190	1,537	719
$50,000 to $59,999	5,461	134	1,010	1,312	1,458	1,050	497
$60,000 to $69,999	3,589	56	721	878	999	665	270
$70,000 to $79,999	2,317	20	390	622	654	454	177
$80,000 to $89,999	1,371	10	195	329	444	275	118
$90,000 to $99,999	958	6	114	250	314	194	82
$100,000 or more	3,246	25	352	826	1,023	676	345
Median income of women with income	$20,922	$8,959	$25,884	$27,702	$29,453	$25,262	$14,021
Median income of full-time workers	36,167	22,652	34,435	37,481	39,396	40,061	41,333
Percent working full-time	37.3%	16.6%	51.0%	53.0%	55.0%	41.9%	6.0%
TOTAL WOMEN	**100.0%**	**100.0%**	**100.0%**	**100.0%**	**100.0%**	**100.0%**	**100.0%**
Without income	**14.1**	**36.2**	**13.5**	**11.4**	**9.6**	**9.4**	**4.1**
With income	**85.9**	**63.8**	**86.5**	**88.6**	**90.4**	**90.6**	**95.9**
Under $10,000	22.0	34.0	16.1	16.8	15.6	19.8	29.7
$10,000 to $19,999	19.3	15.4	16.2	15.5	15.2	17.6	35.6
$20,000 to $29,999	13.6	7.8	17.1	14.5	15.0	14.1	13.5
$30,000 to $39,999	10.2	3.7	14.0	12.8	13.0	11.0	6.6
$40,000 to $49,999	7.0	1.6	9.2	9.2	9.8	8.9	3.4
$50,000 to $59,999	4.5	0.6	5.1	6.2	6.5	6.1	2.4
$60,000 to $69,999	2.9	0.3	3.6	4.1	4.5	3.9	1.3
$70,000 to $79,999	1.9	0.1	2.0	2.9	2.9	2.6	0.8
$80,000 to $89,999	1.1	0.0	1.0	1.5	2.0	1.6	0.6
$90,000 to $99,999	0.8	0.0	0.6	1.2	1.4	1.1	0.4
$100,000 or more	2.7	0.1	1.8	3.9	4.6	3.9	1.6

Source: Bureau of the Census, 2008 Current Population Survey, Internet site http://pubdb3.census.gov/macro/032008/perinc/new01_000.htm; calculations by New Strategist

Women Have Been Gaining on Men

Among full-time workers, women are closing the gap.

Among men working full-time, year-round in 2007, median income stood at $46,224. Among their female counterparts, median income was a smaller $36,167—or 78 percent as high as men's. While a substantial difference remains between the incomes of men and women, the gap is shrinking. In 1990, women made only 71 percent as much as men.

Women are closing the gap with men because their incomes have been growing faster. Among full-time workers, women's median income grew 14 percent between 1990 and 2007, after adjusting for inflation. Men's median income grew only 4 percent during those years. Women continued to gain on men even during the past few years, when the recession reduced the earnings of men. Between 2000 and 2007, the median income of women who work full-time grew 3 percent compared with a loss of 1 percent for men.

■ Women's incomes are growing faster than men's because younger, career-oriented generations are replacing older just-a-job women in the labor force.

Income gap between the sexes is narrowing

(women's median income as a percent of men's median income among full-time, year-round workers, 1990 to 2007)

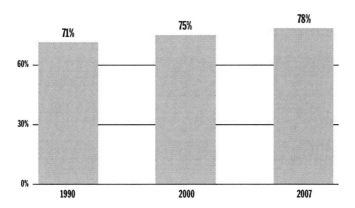

Table 5.34 Median Income of Full-Time Workers by Sex, 1990 to 2007

(median income of people aged 15 or older who work full-time, year-round, by sex, and index of men's income to women's, 1990 to 2007; percent change in income for selected years; in 2007 dollars)

	men	women	index of women's income to men's
2007	$46,224	$36,167	78
2006	46,233	35,982	78
2005	44,807	35,321	79
2004	45,738	35,254	77
2003	46,789	35,684	76
2002	46,686	35,694	76
2001	47,005	35,627	76
2000	46,826	35,065	75
1999	46,602	34,054	73
1998	46,052	34,115	74
1997	45,402	33,527	74
1996	44,133	32,812	74
1995	43,499	32,121	74
1994	43,734	32,186	74
1993	43,912	31,749	72
1992	44,643	31,989	72
1991	45,031	31,541	70
1990	44,566	31,666	71
Percent change			
2000 to 2007	−1.3%	3.1%	–
1990 to 2007	3.7	14.2	–

Note: The index is calculated by dividing the median income of women by the median income of men and multiplying by 100. "–" means not applicable.
Source: Bureau of the Census, Current Population Survey, Historical Income Tables—People, Internet site http://www.census .gov/hhes/www/income/histinc/incpertoc.html; calculations by New Strategist

Income Gap between Men and Women Is Smallest among Young Adults

The gap is largest for older workers and non-Hispanic whites.

Among full-time workers, women's incomes were 78 percent as high as men's in 2007—$36,167 for women versus $46,224 for men. The figure varies by age, race, education, and region, however.

Young women come closest to matching the incomes of men. Among people under age 25 who work full-time, women's incomes are 95 percent as high as men's. The figure drops to 88 percent in the 25-to-34 age group, then falls to 74 percent among 35-to-44-year-olds. Among workers aged 55 to 64, women's incomes are only 71 percent as high as men's. One reason behind the decline is that older men are much better educated and have more job experience than older women. Women's career choices are another reason.

Black and Hispanic women have incomes closer to their male counterparts than non-Hispanic white women (86 and 89 percent, respectively for blacks and Hispanics versus 75 percent for non-Hispanic whites). Onen reason is that black and Hispanic men have much lower incomes than non-Hispanic white men.

The income gap between men and women does not vary much by education. By region, the gap is smallest in the West and largest in the Midwest.

■ Women's incomes will continue to approach men's, but the gap will never close completely because more women than men choose to make economic sacrifices for their family.

Young women make almost as much money as young men

(women's median income as a percent of men's median income among full-time, year-round workers, by age, 2007)

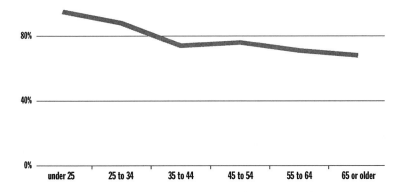

Table 5.35 Median Income of Full-Time Workers by Selected Characteristics and Sex, 2007

(median income of people aged 15 or older working full-time, year-round by selected characteristics and sex, and women's income as a percent of men's, 2007)

	men	women	women's income as a percent of men's
Total people	**$46,224**	**$36,167**	**78.2%**
Age			
Under age 25	23,745	22,652	95.4
Aged 25 to 34	39,073	34,435	88.1
Aged 35 to 44	50,524	37,481	74.2
Aged 45 to 54	52,012	39,396	75.7
Aged 55 to 64	56,262	40,061	71.2
Aged 65 or older	60,589	41,333	68.2
Race and Hispanic origin			
Asian	51,001	41,254	80.9
Black	36,780	31,672	86.1
Hispanic	30,454	27,154	89.2
Non-Hispanic white	51,465	38,678	75.2
Education			
Total, aged 25 or older	49,136	37,282	75.9
Less than 9th grade	23,963	18,932	79.0
9th to 12th grade	29,690	21,064	70.9
High school graduate	39,434	28,734	72.9
Some college, no degree	46,198	35,150	76.1
Associate's degree	50,630	37,370	73.8
Bachelor's degree or more	73,122	51,685	70.7
Bachelor's degree	65,800	47,642	72.4
Master's degree	81,127	58,274	71.8
Professional degree	100,000+	75,662	–
Doctoral degree	100,000+	75,593	–
Region			
Northeast	50,111	39,534	78.9
Midwest	46,440	35,385	76.2
South	43,421	34,057	78.4
West	46,821	38,066	81.3

Note: Asians and blacks are those who identify themselves as being of the race alone and those who identify themselves as being of the race in combination with other races. Non-Hispanic whites are those who identify themselves as being white alone and not Hispanic. Hispanics may be of any race. "–" means data are not available.
Source: Bureau of the Census, 2008 Current Population Survey, Internet site http://pubdb3.census.gov/macro/032008/perinc/new01_000.htm; calculations by New Strategist

Education Boosts Earnings

Although college costs are soaring, the payback is still worth the investment.

Among full-time workers, men with at least a bachelor's degree earned a median of $70,401 in 2007. Those who went no further than high school earned just $37,855. Women with at least a bachelor's degree earned a median of $50,398 versus the $27,240 earned by those who went no further than high school. Women's earnings are much lower than men's in part because the average working woman is younger than the average working man, and job experience increases earnings.

The highest-paid men are those with professional degrees, such as doctors or lawyers. Their median personal earnings exceeded $100,000 in 2007, with 61 percent earning more than that amount. The highest-paid women are also those with professional degrees, with median earnings of $71,098.

■ Because the economy rewards highly educated workers, educational credentials will continue to be important in the years ahead.

Earnings are much higher for college graduates

(median earnings of full-time, year-round workers, by educational attainment and sex, 2007)

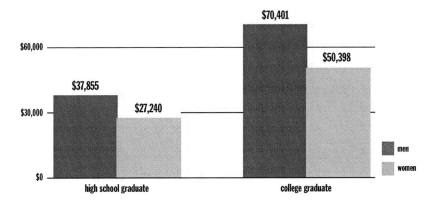

Table 5.36 Earnings of Men Who Work Full-Time by Education, 2007

(number and percent distribution of men aged 25 or older working full-time, year-round by earnings and educational attainment, and median earnings of those with earnings, 2007; men in thousands as of 2008)

	total	less than 9th grade	9th to 12th grade, no diploma	high school graduate	some college, no degree	assoc. degree	bachelor's degree or more				
							total	bachelor's degree	master's degree	prof. degree	doctoral degree
Total men with earnings	**58,161**	**2,142**	**3,455**	**17,229**	**9,867**	**5,248**	**20,220**	**12,963**	**4,800**	**1,332**	**1,125**
Under $10,000	755	59	116	259	141	66	114	88	22	1	2
$10,000 to $19,999	4,312	683	660	1,682	583	219	488	356	96	23	14
$20,000 to $29,999	8,067	684	988	3,384	1,366	578	1,068	830	190	18	28
$30,000 to $39,999	9,375	396	689	3,651	1,968	909	1,761	1,359	313	42	48
$40,000 to $49,999	8,072	131	398	2,945	1,563	899	2,136	1,626	401	61	47
$50,000 to $59,999	6,808	74	269	2,016	1,290	764	2,394	1,658	549	85	100
$60,000 to $69,999	4,877	44	109	1,194	949	566	2,017	1,329	482	95	111
$70,000 to $79,999	3,930	32	96	807	612	452	1,930	1,282	490	77	84
$80,000 to $89,999	2,562	3	37	416	413	294	1,398	902	354	60	80
$90,000 to $99,999	1,756	6	27	229	241	142	1,110	638	314	62	96
$100,000 or more	7,631	31	64	640	740	355	5,802	2,894	1,587	808	513
Median earnings	$47,004	$23,375	$29,317	$37,855	$44,899	$49,042	$70,401	$62,087	$76,284	$100,000+	$92,089
Total men with earnings	**100.0%**	**100.0%**	**100.0%**	**100.0%**	**100.0%**	**100.0%**	**100.0%**	**100.0%**	**100.0%**	**100.0%**	**100.0%**
Under $10,000	1.3	2.8	3.4	1.5	1.4	1.3	0.6	0.7	0.5	0.1	0.2
$10,000 to $19,999	7.4	31.9	19.1	9.8	5.9	4.2	2.4	2.7	2.0	1.7	1.2
$20,000 to $29,999	13.9	31.9	28.6	19.6	13.8	11.0	5.3	6.4	4.0	1.4	2.5
$30,000 to $39,999	16.1	18.5	19.9	21.2	19.9	17.3	8.7	10.5	6.5	3.2	4.3
$40,000 to $49,999	13.9	6.1	11.5	17.1	15.8	17.1	10.6	12.5	8.4	4.6	4.2
$50,000 to $59,999	11.7	3.5	7.8	11.7	13.1	14.6	11.8	12.8	11.4	6.4	8.9
$60,000 to $69,999	8.4	2.1	3.2	6.9	9.6	10.8	10.0	10.3	10.0	7.1	9.9
$70,000 to $79,999	6.8	1.5	2.8	4.7	6.2	8.6	9.5	9.9	10.2	5.8	7.5
$80,000 to $89,999	4.4	0.1	1.1	2.4	4.2	5.6	6.9	7.0	7.4	4.5	7.1
$90,000 to $99,999	3.0	0.3	0.8	1.3	2.4	2.7	5.5	4.9	6.5	4.7	8.5
$100,000 or more	13.1	1.4	1.9	3.7	7.5	6.8	28.7	22.3	33.1	60.7	45.6

Source: Bureau of the Census, 2008 Current Population Survey, Internet site http://pubdb3.census.gov/macro/032008/perinc/new03_000.htm; calculations by New Strategist

Table 5.37 Earnings of Women Who Work Full-Time by Education, 2007

(number and percent distribution of women aged 25 or older working full-time, year-round by earnings and educational attainment, and median earnings of those with earnings, 2007; women in thousands as of 2008)

	total	less than 9th grade	9th to 12th grade, no diploma	high school graduate	some college, no degree	assoc. degree	bachelor's degree or more				
							total	bachelor's degree	master's degree	prof. degree	doctoral degree
Total women with earnings	**42,217**	**824**	**1,653**	**11,451**	**7,918**	**4,893**	**15,478**	**9,938**	**4,390**	**666**	**484**
Under $10,000	799	65	96	313	143	56	123	76	38	7	1
$10,000 to $19,999	5,497	406	697	2,368	973	488	562	437	112	13	3
$20,000 to $29,999	8,910	236	513	3,706	1,969	1,067	1,419	1,193	193	19	13
$30,000 to $39,999	8,557	62	187	2,518	2,022	1,146	2,623	2,029	531	35	29
$40,000 to $49,999	6,310	29	83	1,310	1,231	827	2,832	1,845	825	98	63
$50,000 to $59,999	4,001	14	37	512	693	521	2,226	1,311	788	74	53
$60,000 to $69,999	2,704	6	9	326	382	355	1,627	941	530	72	81
$70,000 to $79,999	1,779	0	14	149	180	187	1,248	688	446	65	49
$80,000 to $89,999	996	0	4	61	112	112	707	358	262	47	41
$90,000 to $99,999	615	0	0	53	42	36	481	255	165	25	34
$100,000 or more	2,027	3	9	130	168	95	1,621	793	496	215	117
Median earnings	$36,086	$18,261	$20,398	$27,240	$32,837	$36,333	$50,398	$45,773	$55,426	$71,098	$68,989
Total women with earnings	**100.0%**	**100.0%**	**100.0%**	**100.0%**	**100.0%**	**100.0%**	**100.0%**	**100.0%**	**100.0%**	**100.0%**	**100.0%**
Under $10,000	1.9	7.9	5.8	2.7	1.8	1.1	0.8	0.8	0.9	1.1	0.2
$10,000 to $19,999	13.0	49.3	42.2	20.7	12.3	10.0	3.6	4.4	2.6	2.0	0.6
$20,000 to $29,999	21.1	28.6	31.0	32.4	24.9	21.8	9.2	12.0	4.4	2.9	2.7
$30,000 to $39,999	20.3	7.5	11.3	22.0	25.5	23.4	16.9	20.4	12.1	5.3	6.0
$40,000 to $49,999	14.9	3.5	5.0	11.4	15.5	16.9	18.3	18.6	18.8	14.7	13.0
$50,000 to $59,999	9.5	1.7	2.2	4.5	8.8	10.6	14.4	13.2	17.9	11.1	11.0
$60,000 to $69,999	6.4	0.7	0.5	2.8	4.8	7.3	10.5	9.5	12.1	10.8	16.7
$70,000 to $79,999	4.2	0.0	0.8	1.3	2.3	3.8	8.1	6.9	10.2	9.8	10.1
$80,000 to $89,999	2.4	0.0	0.2	0.5	1.4	2.3	4.6	3.6	6.0	7.1	8.5
$90,000 to $99,999	1.5	0.0	0.0	0.5	0.5	0.7	3.1	2.6	3.8	3.8	7.0
$100,000 or more	4.8	0.4	0.5	1.1	2.1	1.9	10.5	8.0	11.3	32.3	24.2

Source: Bureau of the Census, 2008 Current Population Survey, Internet site http://pubdb3.census.gov/macro/032008/perinc/new03_000.htm; calculations by New Strategist

Among Wage and Salary Workers, Women Earn 80 Percent as Much as Men

The gap varies greatly by occupation, however.

Men who work full-time as wage or salary workers earned a median of $766 a week in 2007. Women earned a median of $614—or 80 percent of what men earn. Although a substantial gap exists between men's and women's earnings, women have been closing the gap. In many occupations, women now make almost as much or even more than men.

Women in management occupations earn only 72 percent as much as their male counterparts, and for women in professional occupations the figure is 73 percent. But in many individual occupations, the gap is smaller. Among computer software engineers, women earn 87 percent as much as men. Among social workers, the figure is 99 percent.

A big earnings gap exists in some occupations. Among physicians and surgeons, women earn only 59 percent as much as men—largely because the average male doctor is much older and more experienced than the average female doctor. Among human resource managers, women earn only 68 percent as much as their male counterparts. But in a handful of occupations, women earn more than men. These include special education teachers, postal service clerks, and data entry workers.

■ One reason for the earnings gap is that the average male worker has been on the job longer than the average female worker. As women gain job experience, the earnings gap will continue to shrink.

In most occupations, women earn less than men

(women's median weekly earnings as a percent of men's among full-time wage and salary workers, by occupation, 2007)

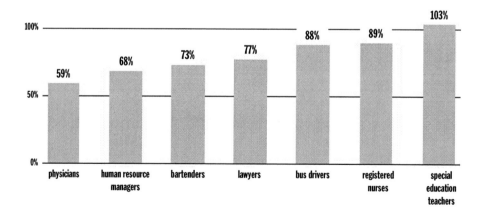

Table 5.38 Median Weekly Earnings of Full-Time Workers by Occupation and Sex, 2007

(median weekly earnings of full-time wage and salary workers aged 16 or older by selected occupation and sex, and index of women's to men's earnings, 2007)

	men	women	index of women's earnings to men's
TOTAL FULL-TIME WORKERS AGED 16 OR OLDER	**$766**	**$614**	**80**
Management, professional, and related occupations	**1,187**	**858**	**72**
Management, business, and financial operations occupations	1,261	908	72
Management occupations	1,337	963	72
Chief executives	1,918	1,536	80
General and operations managers	1,332	987	74
Marketing and sales managers	1,511	1,028	68
Computer and information systems managers	1,596	1,363	85
Financial managers	1,452	909	63
Human resources managers	1,581	1,073	68
Purchasing managers	1,374	1,054	77
Education administrators	1,371	960	70
Food service managers	731	584	80
Medical and health services managers	1,414	1,063	75
Property, real estate, and community association managers	970	732	75
Social and community service managers	1,063	913	86
Managers, all other	1,307	1,006	77
Business and financial operations occupations	1,131	832	74
Wholesale and retail buyers, except farm products	794	737	93
Purchasing agents, except wholesale, retail, farm products	992	753	76
Claims adjusters, appraisers, examiners, investigators	898	743	83
Compliance officers, except agriculture, construction, health and safety, and transportation	1,124	747	66
Human resources, training, labor relations specialists	1,037	811	78
Management analysts	1,388	1,083	78
Other business operations specialists	1,026	772	75
Accountants and auditors	1,186	858	72
Personal financial advisors	1,377	1,047	76
Loan counselors and officers	1,129	844	75
Professional and related occupations	1,148	835	73
Computer and mathematical occupations	1,294	1,047	81
Computer scientists and systems analysts	1,243	1,041	84
Computer programmers	1,268	1,074	85
Computer software engineers	1,509	1,318	87
Computer support specialists	905	764	84
Network systems and data communications analysts	1,181	853	72
Architecture and engineering occupations	1,258	981	78
Engineering technicians, except drafters	958	781	82
Life, physical, and social science occupations	1,151	939	82
Medical scientists	1,374	856	62
Chemists and materials scientists	1,354	980	72
Market and survey researchers	1,160	1,035	89

	men	women	index of women's earnings to men's
Community and social services occupations	$807	$720	89
Counselors	833	724	87
Social workers	764	754	99
Miscellaneous community and social service specialists	788	636	81
Legal occupations	1,579	930	59
Lawyers	1,783	1,381	77
Education, training, and library occupations	1,007	784	78
Postsecondary teachers	1,239	962	78
Elementary and middle school teachers	938	847	90
Secondary school teachers	1,001	900	90
Special education teachers	860	886	103
Other teachers and instructors	987	685	69
Arts, design, entertainment, sports, and media occupations	920	732	80
Designers	894	697	78
Editors	979	804	82
Health care practitioner and technical occupations	1,156	875	76
Pharmacists	1,887	1,603	85
Physicians and surgeons	1,796	1,062	59
Registered nurses	1,098	976	89
Physical therapists	1,247	1,096	88
Clinical laboratory technologists and technicians	1,049	803	77
Diagnostic related technologists and technicians	1,050	845	80
Health diagnosing and treating practitioner support technicians	687	538	78
Service occupations	**515**	**406**	**79**
Health care support occupations	522	447	86
Nursing, psychiatric, and home health aides	500	416	83
Medical assistants and other health care support occupations	575	487	85
Protective service occupations	754	588	78
Bailiffs, correctional officers, and jailers	686	578	84
Police and sheriff's patrol officers	907	791	87
Security guards and gaming surveillance officers	524	465	89
Food preparation and serving related occupations	403	363	90
Chefs and head cooks	535	482	90
First-line supervisors/managers of food preparation and serving workers	586	423	72
Cooks	377	341	90
Food preparation workers	367	335	91
Bartenders	551	404	73
Waiters and waitresses	415	360	87
Dining room and cafeteria attendants and bartender helpers	370	345	93
Building and grounds cleaning and maintenance occupations	472	376	80
First-line supervisors/managers of housekeeping and janitorial work	646	481	74
Janitors and building cleaners	475	388	82
Maids and housekeeping cleaners	439	357	81

	men	women	index of women's earnings to men's
Personal care and service occupations	$578	$402	70
Personal and home care aides	434	373	86
Recreation and fitness workers	626	513	82
Sales and office occupations	**714**	**550**	**77**
Sales and related occupations	791	493	62
First-line supervisors/managers of retail sales workers	746	538	72
First-line supervisors/managers of nonretail sales workers	990	768	78
Cashiers	409	344	84
Retail salespersons	638	409	64
Advertising sales agents	900	683	76
Insurance sales agents	959	644	67
Securities, commodities, and financial services sales agents	1,243	1,031	83
Sales representatives, services, all other	939	713	76
Sales representatives, wholesale and manufacturing	976	784	80
Real estate brokers and sales agents	1,027	701	68
Telemarketers	422	391	93
Sales and related workers, all other	851	682	80
Office and administrative support occupations	619	570	92
First-line supervisors/managers of office and administrative support	803	675	84
Bill and account collectors	586	521	89
Bookkeeping, accounting, and auditing clerks	666	601	90
Customer service representatives	608	521	86
File clerks	574	519	90
Receptionists and information clerks	503	480	95
Reservation and transportation ticket agents and travel clerks	562	565	101
Dispatchers	649	551	85
Postal service clerks	812	850	105
Postal service mail carriers	929	799	86
Production, planning, and expediting clerks	885	658	74
Shipping, receiving, and traffic clerks	514	500	97
Stock clerks and order fillers	448	441	98
Secretaries and administrative assistants	694	597	86
Computer operators	628	562	89
Data entry keyers	511	521	102
Mail clerks and mail machine operators, except postal service	509	523	103
Office clerks, general	584	550	94
Office and administrative support workers, all other	719	634	88
Natural resources, construction, maintenance occupations	**674**	**539**	**80**
Farming, fishing, and forestry occupations	382	348	91
Miscellaneous agricultural workers	357	332	93
Construction and extraction occupations	648	573	88
Installation, maintenance, and repair occupations	750	726	97

	men	women	index of women's earnings to men's
Production, transportation, material-moving occupations	**$616**	**$437**	**71**
Production occupations	641	443	69
First-line supervisors/managers of production and operating workers	864	615	71
Electrical, electronics, and electromechanical assemblers	543	447	82
Miscellaneous assemblers and fabricators	587	460	78
Bakers	498	404	81
Butchers and other meat, poultry, and fish processing workers	558	406	73
Metalworkers and plastic workers, all other	588	482	82
Laundry and dry-cleaning workers	496	340	69
Inspectors, testers, sorters, samplers, and weighers	735	506	69
Packaging and filling machine operators and tenders	493	396	80
Production workers, all other	583	445	76
Transportation and material-moving occupations	596	424	71
Bus drivers	540	476	88
Driver/sales workers and truck drivers	672	499	74
Laborers and freight, stock, and material movers, hand	486	418	86
Packers and packagers, hand	414	362	87
Material-moving workers, all other	662	787	119

Note: The index is calculated by dividing the median earnings of women by the median earnings of men and multiplying by 100.
Source: Bureau of Labor Statistics, Labor Force Statistics from the Current Population Survey, Internet site ftp://ftp.bls.gov/pub/special.requests/lf/aat39.txt; calculations by New Strategist

Incomes Are Highest in the Suburbs

Households in nonmetropolitan areas have the lowest incomes.

Households in the suburbs of the nation's largest metropolitan areas (outside principal cities) have the highest incomes, a median of $57,444 in 2007—14 percent higher than the national median. Many suburban householders are middle-aged married couples in their peak-earning years. Nonmetropolitan households have the lowest incomes, a median of $40,615 in 2007, or just 81 percent of the national average. The elderly head a larger share of households in nonmetro areas.

Households in the Northeast and West have above-average incomes, while those in the Midwest have average incomes and those in the South have incomes well below average. Among the 50 states, New Jersey and Maryland have the highest household incomes, with 2005–07 medians of $65,933 and $65,124, respectively. Mississippi has the lowest median household income, just $35,971 in 2007—28 percent below average. Kentucky, Louisiana, and Arkansas are also at the bottom, with median incomes below $40,000. The gap in the median income of New Jersey and Mississippi households amounted to nearly $30,000 in 2007.

■ The collapse of the financial markets in 2008 has probably reduced the income gap between the richest and poorest states.

Households in the South have the lowest incomes

(median household income by region, 2007)

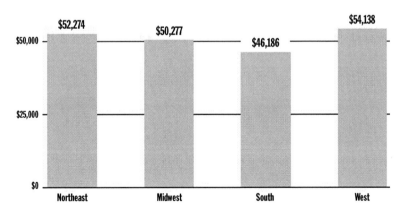

Table 5.39   Median Household Income by Metropolitan Status and Region of Residence, 2007

(number of households, median household income, and index of category median to national median, by metropolitan status, and region and division of residence, 2007; households in thousands as of 2008)

	number of households	median income	index
Total households	**116,783**	**$50,233**	**100**
Metropolitan status			
Inside metropolitan areas	97,591	51,831	103
Inside principal cities	39,072	44,205	88
Outside principal cities	58,520	57,444	114
Outside metropolitan areas	19,192	40,615	81
Region			
Northeast	21,351	52,274	104
New England	5,576	58,568	117
Middle Atlantic	15,774	50,821	101
Midwest	26,266	50,277	100
East North Central	18,130	50,366	100
West North Central	8,136	50,070	100
South	43,062	46,186	92
South Atlantic	23,060	49,021	98
East South Central	7,159	40,246	80
West South Central	12,844	44,833	89
West	26,105	54,138	108
Mountain	8,298	51,604	103
Pacific	17,807	55,653	111

Note: The index is calculated by dividing the median for each metropolitan status and region by the national median and multiplying by 100.
Source: Bureau of the Census, 2008 Current Population Survey, Internet site http://pubdb3.census.gov/macro/032008/hhinc/ new01_001.htm; calculations by New Strategist

Table 5.40 Median Household Income by State, 2005–07

(median income of households by state, and index of state to national median, three-year average, 2005–07; ranked by median income)

	median income	index		median income	index
United States	**$49,668**	**100**	Pennsylvania	$49,155	99
New Jersey	65,933	133	Oregon	48,521	98
Maryland	65,124	131	Wyoming	48,205	97
New Hampshire	63,942	129	Idaho	47,876	96
Hawaii	63,164	127	Arizona	47,750	96
Connecticut	62,893	127	Ohio	47,750	96
Alaska	60,124	121	Maine	47,160	95
Massachusetts	58,286	117	Kansas	46,659	94
Minnesota	57,815	116	Indiana	46,407	93
Virginia	57,679	116	South Dakota	46,321	93
Colorado	57,333	115	Florida	46,142	93
Washington	56,049	113	Missouri	45,834	92
Utah	55,974	113	Texas	44,861	90
California	55,864	112	North Dakota	44,743	90
Delaware	54,310	109	North Carolina	43,035	87
Rhode Island	54,009	109	South Carolina	42,561	86
Nevada	53,008	107	New Mexico	42,295	85
Vermont	51,566	104	Montana	41,852	84
Illinois	51,320	103	Tennessee	41,632	84
Wisconsin	50,619	102	Oklahoma	41,046	83
Nebraska	49,861	100	Alabama	40,232	81
New York	49,546	100	West Virginia	40,103	81
Washington, D.C.	49,474	100	Kentucky	39,678	80
Michigan	49,394	99	Louisiana	39,461	79
Georgia	49,387	99	Arkansas	39,279	79
Iowa	49,262	99	Mississippi	35,971	72

Note: The index is calculated by dividing the median income of each state by the national median and multiplying by 100.
Source: Bureau of the Census, Current Population Surveys, Internet site http://www.census.gov/hhes/www/income/histinc/h08B .html; calculations by New Strategist

Wages and Salaries Rank Number One

Wages and salaries are the most important source of income for the largest share of Americans.

Among the 210 million Americans aged 15 or older with income in 2007, nearly 76 percent received income from earnings—such as wages, salaries, or self-employment income. Among those with earnings, the median amount received was $31,091. Twenty percent of Americans received Social Security income, averaging $11,276 per person.

Forty-six percent of the population received property income in 2007, such as interest, dividends, rent, or royalties. Nearly 91 million people received interest income in 2007, getting a median of $1,536 from this source. Sixteen percent of the population received dividend income (a median of $1,742). Nine percent received retirement income, and 8.5 percent received pensions. Among those with pensions, the median amount received stood at $12,192. Less than 1 percent of the population received public assistance in 2007, and those who did received an average of $2,451.

■ While most people of working age are dependent primarily on wages and salaries, older Americans depend on a wider variety of income sources—from Social Security and pensions to interest and dividends.

Social Security is the third most common source of income

(percent of people aged 15 or older who receive income, by source, for the five most common sources of income, 2007)

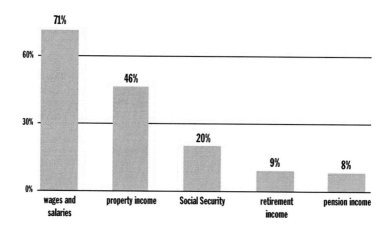

Table 5.41 Sources of Income, 2007

(number and percent of people aged 15 or older with income by source and median income for those with income, 2007; people in thousands as of 2008; ranked by number receiving income)

	number with income	percent with income	median amount received by those with income
Total	**210,019**	**100.0%**	**$26,625**
Earnings	158,777	75.6	31,091
Wages and salary	149,437	71.2	31,185
Nonfarm self-employment	12,499	6.0	17,267
Farm self-employment	2,048	1.0	2,338
Property income	96,484	45.9	1,720
Interest	90,998	43.3	1,536
Dividends	33,480	15.9	1,742
Rents, royalties, estates, or trusts	9,894	4.7	2,210
Social Security	41,897	19.9	11,276
Retirement income	19,583	9.3	11,569
Pension income	15,845	7.5	12,192
Educational assistance	7,270	3.5	3,799
Unemployment compensation	5,200	2.5	2,967
SSI (Supplemental Security Income)	5,039	2.4	6,452
Child support	4,964	2.4	3,663
Survivors' benefits	2,906	1.4	7,466
Veterans' benefits	2,533	1.2	8,003
Financial assistance from other household	2,036	1.0	4,440
Public assistance	1,828	0.9	2,451
Disability benefits	1,615	0.8	8,077
Workers' compensation	1,604	0.8	3,848
Alimony	411	0.2	9,778
Other income	1,054	0.5	1,582

Source: Bureau of the Census, 2008 Current Population Survey, Internet site http://pubdb3.census.gov/macro/032008/perinc/new08_001.htm; calculations by New Strategist

Minorities Account for Most of the Poor

Among the nation's 37 million poor, only 43 percent are non-Hispanic white.

Poverty rates have grown in recent years, after falling during the late 1990s. In 2007, 12.5 percent of Americans were poor, up from a low of 11.3 percent in 2000. Nevertheless, the poverty rate of 2007 was below the 13.5 percent of 1990.

Some segments of society are poorer than others. Only 8.2 percent of non-Hispanic whites and 10.2 percent of Asians are poor versus 24.4 percent of blacks and 21.5 percent of Hispanics. Overall, 18 percent of the nation's children are poor. The figure is 34 percent among black children and 29 percent among Hispanic children.

The poverty rate varies sharply by family type. Regardless of race or Hispanic origin, poverty rates are low among married couples. Overall, only 4.9 percent of married couples are poor compared with 28.3 percent of female-headed families. Among female-headed families with children, the poverty rate is an even higher 37.0 percent.

■ Childhood poverty will remain a chronic problem until single parents become a smaller share of all families.

Poverty rate is low for married couples

(percent of families in poverty by race, Hispanic origin, and family type, 2007)

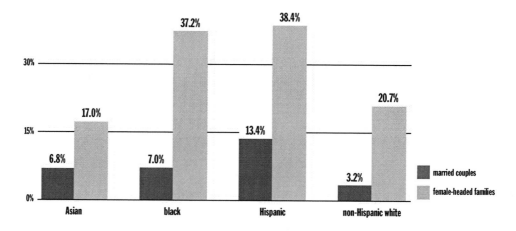

Table 5.42 People in Poverty, 1990 to 2007

(number and percent of people below poverty level, 1990 to 2007; percent and percentage point change for selected years; people in thousands as of the following year)

	number	percent
2007	37,275	12.5%
2006	36,460	12.3
2005	36,950	12.6
2004	37,040	12.7
2003	35,861	12.5
2002	34,570	12.1
2001	32,907	11.7
2000	31,581	11.3
1999	32,791	11.9
1998	34,476	12.7
1997	35,574	13.3
1996	36,529	13.7
1995	36,425	13.8
1994	38,060	14.5
1993	39,265	15.1
1992	38,014	14.8
1991	35,708	14.2
1990	33,584	13.5

	percent change	percentage point change
2000 to 2007	18.0%	1.2
1990 to 2007	11.0	−1.0

Source: Bureau of the Census, Current Population Surveys, Internet site http://www.census.gov/hhes/www/poverty/histpov/perindex.html; calculations by New Strategist

Table 5.43 People in Poverty by Age, Race, and Hispanic Origin, 2007

(number and percent of people in poverty and percent distribution of poor, by age, race, and Hispanic origin, 2007; people in thousands as of 2008)

	total	Asian	black	Hispanic	non-Hispanic white
NUMBER OF POOR					
Total people in poverty	37,276	1,467	9,668	9,890	16,032
Under age 18	13,324	431	4,178	4,482	4,255
Aged 18 to 24	4,901	186	1,185	1,105	2,398
Aged 25 to 34	4,930	243	1,185	1,516	1,955
Aged 35 to 44	3,971	186	919	1,154	1,671
Aged 45 to 54	3,722	149	821	760	1,939
Aged 55 to 59	1,471	58	376	241	779
Aged 60 to 64	1,402	70	256	194	856
Aged 65 or older	3,556	144	748	438	2,179
PERCENT IN POVERTY					
Total people	**12.5%**	**10.2%**	**24.4%**	**21.5%**	**8.2%**
Under age 18	18.0	11.9	33.7	28.6	10.1
Aged 18 to 24	17.3	14.0	27.3	22.0	13.7
Aged 25 to 34	12.3	10.1	21.7	18.6	8.2
Aged 35 to 44	9.4	7.5	17.0	16.7	6.2
Aged 45 to 54	8.5	7.5	15.5	15.6	6.2
Aged 55 to 59	8.0	7.5	18.6	15.0	5.7
Aged 60 to 64	9.4	12.4	18.2	16.4	7.4
Aged 65 tor older	9.7	11.2	23.3	17.1	7.4
PERCENT DISTRIBUTION OF POOR BY RACE AND HISPANIC ORIGIN					
Total people in poverty	**100.0%**	**3.9%**	**25.9%**	**26.5%**	**43.0%**
Under age 18	100.0	3.2	31.4	33.6	31.9
Aged 18 to 24	100.0	3.8	24.2	22.5	48.9
Aged 25 to 34	100.0	4.9	24.0	30.8	39.7
Aged 35 to 44	100.0	4.7	23.1	29.1	42.1
Aged 45 to 54	100.0	4.0	22.1	20.4	52.1
Aged 55 to 59	100.0	3.9	25.6	16.4	53.0
Aged 60 to 64	100.0	5.0	18.3	13.8	61.1
Aged 65 tor older	100.0	4.0	21.0	12.3	61.3

Note: Numbers do not add to total because Asians and blacks are those who identify themselves as being of the race alone and those who identify themselves as being of the race in combination with other races. Non-Hispanic whites are those who identify themselves as being white alone and not Hispanic. Hispanics may be of any race.
Source: Bureau of the Census, 2008 Current Population Survey, Internet site http://pubdb3.census.gov/macro/032008/pov/new01_100.htm; calculations by New Strategist

Table 5.44 Families in Poverty by Family Type, Race, and Hispanic Origin, 2007

(number and percent of families in poverty, and percent distribution of families in poverty, by type of family and race and Hispanic origin of householder, 2007; families in thousands as of 2008)

	total	Asian	black	Hispanic	non-Hispanic white
NUMBER IN POVERTY					
Total families in poverty	**7,623**	**281**	**2,091**	**2,045**	**3,184**
Married couples	2,849	187	313	926	1,338
Female householders, no spouse present	4,078	77	1,570	968	1,489
Male householders, no spouse present	696	17	208	151	308
PERCENT IN POVERTY					
Total families	**9.8%**	**8.1%**	**22.0%**	**19.7%**	**5.9%**
Married couples	4.9	6.8	7.0	13.4	3.2
Female householders, no spouse present	28.3	17.0	37.2	38.4	20.7
Male householders, no spouse present	13.6	7.0	25.1	15.3	10.3
PERCENT DISTRIBUTION OF FAMILIES IN POVERTY BY RACE AND HISPANIC ORIGIN					
Total families in poverty	**100.0%**	**3.7%**	**27.4%**	**26.8%**	**41.8%**
Married couples	100.0	6.6	11.0	32.5	47.0
Female householders, no spouse present	100.0	1.9	38.5	23.7	36.5
Male householders, no spouse present	100.0	2.4	29.9	21.7	44.3
PERCENT DISTRIBUTION OF FAMILIES IN POVERTY BY FAMILY TYPE					
Total families in poverty	**100.0%**	**100.0%**	**100.0%**	**100.0%**	**100.0%**
Married couples	37.4	66.5	15.0	45.3	42.0
Female householders, no spouse present	53.5	27.4	75.1	47.3	46.8
Male householders, no spouse present	9.1	6.0	9.9	7.4	9.7

Note: Numbers do not add to total because Asians and blacks are those who identify themselves as being of the race alone and those who identify themselves as being of the race in combination with other races. Non-Hispanic whites are those who identify themselves as being white alone and not Hispanic. Hispanics may be of any race.
Source: Bureau of the Census, 2008 Current Population Survey, Internet site http://pubdb3.census.gov/macro/032008/pov/new04_100_01.htm

Table 5.45   Families with Children in Poverty by Family Type, Race, and Hispanic Origin, 2007

(number and percent of families with children under age 18 in poverty, and percent distribution of families with children in poverty, by type of family and race and Hispanic origin of householder, 2007; families in thousands as of 2008)

	total	Asian	black	Hispanic	non-Hispanic white
NUMBER IN POVERTY					
Total families with children in poverty	**5,830**	**178**	**1,706**	**1,759**	**2,176**
Married couples	1,765	109	194	766	678
Female householders, no spouse present	3,593	65	1,385	881	1,283
Male householders, no spouse present	471	4	128	112	215
PERCENT IN POVERTY					
Total families with children	**15.0%**	**9.6%**	**29.0%**	**24.9%**	**9.2%**
Married couples	6.7	7.1	8.5	16.4	3.8
Female householders, no spouse present	37.0	27.8	43.7	46.6	29.2
Male householders, no spouse present	17.5	5.1	29.5	22.0	13.2
PERCENT DISTRIBUTION OF FAMILIES IN POVERTY BY RACE AND HISPANIC ORIGIN					
Total families with children in poverty	**100.0%**	**3.1%**	**29.3%**	**30.2%**	**37.3%**
Married couples	100.0	6.2	11.0	43.4	38.4
Female householders, no spouse present	100.0	1.8	38.5	24.5	35.7
Male householders, no spouse present	100.0	0.8	27.2	23.8	45.6
PERCENT DISTRIBUTION OF FAMILIES IN POVERTY BY FAMILY TYPE					
Total families with children in poverty	**100.0%**	**100.0%**	**100.0%**	**100.0%**	**100.0%**
Married couples	30.3	61.2	11.4	43.5	31.2
Female householders, no spouse present	61.6	36.5	81.2	50.1	59.0
Male householders, no spouse present	8.1	2.2	7.5	6.4	9.9

Note: Numbers do not add to total because Asians and blacks are those who identify themselves as being of the race alone and those who identify themselves as being of the race in combination with other races. Non-Hispanic whites are those who identify themselves as being white alone and not Hispanic. Hispanics may be of any race.
Source: Bureau of the Census, 2008 Current Population Survey, Internet site http://pubdb3.census.gov/macro/032008/pov/new04_100_01.htm

6

Labor Force Trends

■ **Older Americans are more likely to work.**

Twenty-one percent of men aged 65 or older are in the labor force, up from 16 percent in 1990.

■ **Working mothers are the norm, even among women with infants.**

Fifty-five percent of mothers with children under age 1 are in the labor force. Among those who work, most have full-time jobs.

■ **Most preschoolers are in day care.**

More than one-third are in center-based programs, such as a day care center, prekindergarten, nursery school, or Head Start.

■ **Long-term employment is less common for middle-aged workers.**

The proportion of men and women who have been with their employer for 10 or more years is falling among workers in their thirties and forties.

■ **Most workers drive to work alone.**

In 2007, 78 percent of workers drove alone. Only 9 percent carpooled and just 5 percent used mass transit.

■ **Big gains for older workers.**

The labor force as a whole will grow 8 percent between 2006 and 2016, but the number of working men aged 65 or older will expand by 78 percent.

Labor Force Participation Has Declined

Older men and women are more likely to work, however.

Men's and women's labor force participation rates fell between 2000 and 2008, with the decline greater for men than for women. One factor behind the decline was the economic downturn, although participation rates include people who are looking for a job. Many Americans are too discouraged by the troubled economy to even look for work, pushing labor force participation rates down.

Labor force participation rates fell for men and women under age 55, the steepest decline occurring among teenagers. One reason for the decline in the labor force participation rate of teenagers is the increase in extracurricular activities among high school students and the rise in college enrollment rates among recent high school graduates.

The labor force participation rate of older men and women increased significantly between 2000 and 2008. Among men aged 65 or older, labor force participation climbed by nearly 4 percentage points. In 2008, a substantial 21 percent of men aged 65 or older were in the labor force. The labor force participation rate of men aged 65 or older has not been that high in more than a generation.

■ As older Americans stay in the labor force, they compete with younger adults for jobs.

More older men are working

(percent of men aged 65 or older in the civilian labor force, by age, 1990 and 2008)

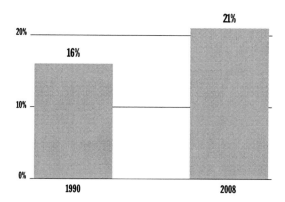

Table 6.1 Labor Force Participation by Sex and Age, 1990 to 2008

(civilian labor force participation rate of people aged 16 or older by sex and age, selected years, 1990 to 2008; percentage point change, 1990–2008 and 2000–08)

	2008	2000	1990	percentage point change 2000–08	percentage point change 1990–2008
Total men	**73.0%**	**74.8%**	**76.1%**	**−1.8**	**−3.1**
Aged 16 to 19	40.1	52.8	55.7	−12.7	−15.6
Aged 20 to 24	78.7	82.6	84.3	−3.9	−5.6
Aged 25 to 34	91.5	93.4	94.2	−1.9	−2.7
Aged 35 to 44	92.2	92.7	94.4	−0.5	−2.2
Aged 45 to 54	88.0	88.6	90.7	−0.6	−2.7
Aged 55 to 64	70.4	67.3	67.7	3.1	2.7
Aged 65 or older	21.5	17.7	16.4	3.8	5.1
Total women	**59.5**	**59.9**	**57.5**	**−0.4**	**2.0**
Aged 16 to 19	40.2	51.2	51.8	−11.0	−11.6
Aged 20 to 24	70.0	73.1	71.6	−3.1	−1.6
Aged 25 to 34	75.2	76.1	73.6	−0.9	1.6
Aged 35 to 44	76.1	77.2	76.5	−1.1	−0.4
Aged 45 to 54	76.1	76.8	71.2	−0.7	4.9
Aged 55 to 64	59.1	51.9	45.3	7.2	13.8
Aged 65 or older	13.3	9.4	8.7	3.9	4.6

Source: Bureau of Labor Statistics, Employment and Earnings, January 1991, and Current Population Survey data for 2000 and 2008, Internet site http://www.bls.gov/cps/tables.htm#empstat; calculations by New Strategist

Sixty-Six Percent of Americans Are in the Labor Force

Among them, nearly 9 million were unemployed in 2008.

Of the nation's 234 million people aged 16 or older, 154 million were in the civilian labor force in 2008. Labor force statistics include both the employed and the unemployed. In 2008, a substantial 8.9 million people were unemployed—5.8 percent of the labor force.

Men's and women's labor force participation rates are similar for 16-to-19-year-olds, 40 percent of whom are in the labor force. Men's participation rises to a peak of 92 percent in the 25-to-44 age group. Women's participation rate peaks at 76 percent in the 35-to-54 age group. Both men's and women's participation falls in the 55-to-64 age group as some workers retire, although most in the age group remain in the labor force. A significant 21 percent of men and 13 percent of women aged 65 or older are in the labor force, however.

Unemployment is highest among the youngest workers. One in five teenage boys aged 16 to 19 was unemployed in 2008.

■ The economic downturn will force many aging boomers to postpone retirement, driving up labor force participation among older workers.

Unemployment is highest among young men

(percent of men who are unemployed, by age, 2008)

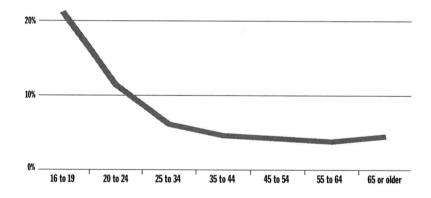

Table 6.2 Employment Status by Sex and Age, 2008

(number and percent of people aged 16 or older in the civilian labor force by sex, age, and employment status, 2008; numbers in thousands)

	civilian noninstitutional population	civilian labor force			unemployed	
		total	percent of population	employed	number	percent of labor force
Total people	**233,788**	**154,287**	**66.0%**	**145,362**	**8,924**	**5.8%**
Aged 16 to 19	17,075	6,858	40.2	5,573	1,285	18.7
Aged 20 to 24	20,409	15,174	74.4	13,629	1,545	10.2
Aged 25 to 34	39,993	33,332	83.3	31,383	1,949	5.8
Aged 35 to 44	41,699	35,061	84.1	33,457	1,604	4.6
Aged 45 to 54	43,960	36,003	81.9	34,529	1,473	4.1
Aged 55 to 64	33,491	21,615	64.5	20,812	803	3.7
Aged 65 or older	37,161	6,243	16.8	5,979	264	4.2
Total men	**113,113**	**82,520**	**73.0**	**77,486**	**5,033**	**6.1**
Aged 16 to 19	8,660	3,472	40.1	2,736	736	21.2
Aged 20 to 24	10,249	8,065	78.7	7,145	920	11.4
Aged 25 to 34	19,999	18,302	91.5	17,183	1,119	6.1
Aged 35 to 44	20,567	18,972	92.2	18,097	875	4.6
Aged 45 to 54	21,512	18,928	88.0	18,124	804	4.2
Aged 55 to 64	16,123	11,345	70.4	10,919	425	3.8
Aged 65 or older	16,002	3,436	21.5	3,282	153	4.5
Total women	**120,675**	**71,767**	**59.5**	**67,876**	**3,891**	**5.4**
Aged 16 to 19	8,415	3,385	40.2	2,837	549	16.2
Aged 20 to 24	10,160	7,109	70.0	6,484	625	8.8
Aged 25 to 34	19,994	15,030	75.2	14,200	830	5.5
Aged 35 to 44	21,132	16,089	76.1	15,360	730	4.5
Aged 45 to 54	22,448	17,075	76.1	16,406	669	3.9
Aged 55 to 64	17,367	10,270	59.1	9,893	377	3.7
Aged 65 or older	21,160	2,808	13.3	2,697	111	3.9

Note: The civilian labor force equals the number of the employed plus the number of the unemployed. The civilian population equals the number in the labor force plus the number not in the labor force.
Source: Bureau of Labor Statistics, Current Population Survey, Internet site http://www.bls.gov/cps/tables.htm#empstat

Labor Force Participation Varies by Race and Hispanic Origin

Among men, Hispanics are most likely to work.

Hispanic men are more likely to work than Asian, black, or white men. In 2008, fully 80 percent of Hispanic men were in the labor force (which includes both the employed and the unemployed). This compares with 75 percent of Asian men, 74 percent of white men, and 67 percent of black men. One reason for the lower labor force participation rate of black men is their difficulty finding a job, discouraging many from even looking for work.

Among women, blacks are most likely to work. In 2008, 61 percent of black women aged 16 or older were in the labor force. Among Asian and white women, the labor force participation rate was 59 percent. Hispanic women are least likely to work, with a participation rate of 56 percent.

■ Unemployment rates increased sharply at the end of 2008—not shown in these statistics—as the stock market fell and corporate layoffs became widespread.

Blacks have the highest unemployment rate

(percent of men aged 16 or older who are unemployed, by race and Hispanic origin, 2008)

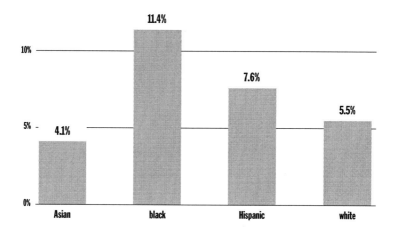

Table 6.3 Employment Status of Asians by Sex and Age, 2008

(number and percent of Asians aged 16 or older in the civilian labor force by sex, age, and employment status, 2008; numbers in thousands)

	civilian noninstitutional population	civilian labor force			unemployed	
		total	percent of population	employed	number	percent of labor force
Total Asians	**10,751**	**7,202**	**67.0%**	**6,917**	**285**	**4.0%**
Aged 16 to 19	630	157	24.9	134	23	14.6
Aged 20 to 24	872	526	60.3	493	33	6.3
Aged 25 to 34	2,278	1,811	79.5	1,737	74	4.1
Aged 35 to 44	2,403	1,989	82.8	1,931	58	2.9
Aged 45 to 54	1,934	1,608	83.2	1,554	54	3.4
Aged 55 to 64	1,343	891	66.4	856	35	3.9
Aged 65 or older	1,291	219	17.0	211	8	3.8
Total Asian men	**5,112**	**3,852**	**75.3**	**3,692**	**160**	**4.1**
Aged 16 to 19	324	85	26.2	71	14	16.6
Aged 20 to 24	429	268	62.5	251	17	6.5
Aged 25 to 34	1,111	996	89.6	953	43	4.3
Aged 35 to 44	1,159	1,089	93.9	1,058	30	2.8
Aged 45 to 54	919	836	91.0	806	29	3.5
Aged 55 to 64	616	457	74.2	438	19	4.3
Aged 65 or older	553	120	21.8	114	6	5.1
Total Asian women	**5,639**	**3,350**	**59.4**	**3,225**	**125**	**3.7**
Aged 16 to 19	306	72	23.6	63	9	12.3
Aged 20 to 24	443	258	58.2	242	16	6.1
Aged 25 to 34	1,167	815	69.8	784	31	3.8
Aged 35 to 44	1,244	900	72.3	873	27	3.0
Aged 45 to 54	1,015	773	76.1	748	25	3.2
Aged 55 to 64	726	434	59.7	418	15	3.5
Aged 65 or older	738	99	13.4	97	2	2.2

Note: The civilian labor force equals the number of the employed plus the number of the unemployed. The civilian population equals the number in the labor force plus the number not in the labor force.
Source: Bureau of Labor Statistics, Current Population Survey, Internet site http://www.bls.gov/cps/tables.htm#empstat

Table 6.4 Employment Status of Blacks by Sex and Age, 2008

(number and percent of blacks aged 16 or older in the civilian labor force by sex, age, and employment status, 2008; numbers in thousands)

	civilian noninstitutional population	civilian labor force			unemployed	
		total	percent of population	employed	number	percent of labor force
Total blacks	**27,843**	**17,740**	**63.7%**	**15,953**	**1,788**	**10.1%**
Aged 16 to 19	2,676	787	29.4	541	246	31.2
Aged 20 to 24	2,914	1,981	68.0	1,625	355	17.9
Aged 25 to 34	5,262	4,328	82.2	3,870	458	10.6
Aged 35 to 44	5,198	4,316	83.0	4,015	301	7.0
Aged 45 to 54	5,183	3,945	76.1	3,670	275	7.0
Aged 55 to 64	3,429	1,908	55.6	1,791	117	6.1
Aged 65 or older	3,182	476	15.0	440	36	7.5
Total black men	**12,516**	**8,347**	**66.7**	**7,398**	**949**	**11.4**
Aged 16 to 19	1,322	385	29.1	247	138	35.9
Aged 20 to 24	1,384	984	71.1	794	190	19.3
Aged 25 to 34	2,398	2,047	85.3	1,805	242	11.8
Aged 35 to 44	2,313	2,008	86.8	1,854	154	7.7
Aged 45 to 54	2,335	1,846	79.1	1,703	143	7.7
Aged 55 to 64	1,519	852	56.1	792	61	7.1
Aged 65 or older	1,245	225	18.1	204	21	9.5
Total black women	**15,328**	**9,393**	**61.3**	**8,554**	**839**	**8.9**
Aged 16 to 19	1,354	402	29.7	294	108	26.8
Aged 20 to 24	1,530	997	65.2	831	166	16.6
Aged 25 to 34	2,864	2,281	79.6	2,065	216	9.5
Aged 35 to 44	2,885	2,308	80.0	2,161	147	6.4
Aged 45 to 54	2,848	2,099	73.7	1,967	132	6.3
Aged 55 to 64	1,910	1,056	55.3	1,000	56	5.3
Aged 65 or older	1,937	251	13.0	236	15	5.8

Note: The civilian labor force equals the number of the employed plus the number of the unemployed. The civilian population equals the number in the labor force plus the number not in the labor force.
Source: Bureau of Labor Statistics, Current Population Survey, Internet site http://www.bls.gov/cps/tables.htm#empstat

Table 6.5 Employment Status of Hispanics by Sex and Age, 2008

(number and percent of Hispanics aged 16 or older in the civilian labor force by sex, age, and employment status, 2008; numbers in thousands)

| | civilian | civilian labor force | | | | |
| | noninstitutional | | | | unemployed | |
	population	total	percent of population	employed	number	percent of labor force
Total Hispanics	**32,141**	**22,024**	**68.5%**	**20,346**	**1,678**	**7.6%**
Aged 16 to 19	3,042	1,121	36.9	870	251	22.4
Aged 20 to 24	3,620	2,668	73.7	2,361	307	11.5
Aged 25 to 34	8,147	6,557	80.5	6,119	437	6.7
Aged 35 to 44	6,946	5,698	82.0	5,371	328	5.8
Aged 45 to 54	4,937	3,862	78.2	3,620	242	6.3
Aged 55 to 64	2,840	1,701	59.9	1,619	81	4.8
Aged 65 or older	2,609	417	16.0	385	32	7.8
Total Hispanic men	**16,524**	**13,255**	**80.2**	**12,248**	**1,007**	**7.6**
Aged 16 to 19	1,553	626	40.3	479	147	23.4
Aged 20 to 24	1,890	1,594	84.3	1,406	188	11.8
Aged 25 to 34	4,438	4,172	94.0	3,897	275	6.6
Aged 35 to 44	3,655	3,425	93.7	3,233	192	5.6
Aged 45 to 54	2,502	2,216	88.6	2,080	136	6.2
Aged 55 to 64	1,365	979	71.7	929	50	5.1
Aged 65 or older	1,121	243	21.7	224	19	7.8
Total Hispanic women	**15,616**	**8,769**	**56.2**	**8,098**	**672**	**7.7**
Aged 16 to 19	1,489	495	33.3	391	104	21.1
Aged 20 to 24	1,730	1,074	62.1	955	119	11.1
Aged 25 to 34	3,710	2,384	64.3	2,222	162	6.8
Aged 35 to 44	3,291	2,274	69.1	2,138	136	6.0
Aged 45 to 54	2,435	1,646	67.6	1,541	105	6.4
Aged 55 to 64	1,475	722	48.9	690	32	4.4
Aged 65 or older	1,488	174	11.7	161	13	7.7

Note: The civilian labor force equals the number of the employed plus the number of the unemployed. The civilian population equals the number in the labor force plus the number not in the labor force.
Source: Bureau of Labor Statistics, Current Population Survey, Internet site http://www.bls.gov/cps/tables.htm#empstat

Table 6.6 Employment Status of Whites by Sex and Age, 2008

(number and percent of whites aged 16 or older in the civilian labor force by sex, age, and employment status, 2008; numbers in thousands)

| | civilian noninstitutional population | civilian labor force | | | unemployed | |
		total	percent of population	employed	number	percent of labor force
Total whites	**189,540**	**125,635**	**66.3%**	**119,126**	**6,509**	**5.2%**
Aged 16 to 19	13,084	5,644	43.1	4,697	947	16.8
Aged 20 to 24	15,914	12,142	76.3	11,055	1,087	9.0
Aged 25 to 34	31,234	26,210	83.9	24,875	1,336	5.1
Aged 35 to 44	33,093	27,932	84.4	26,736	1,196	4.3
Aged 45 to 54	35,941	29,780	82.9	28,686	1,094	3.7
Aged 55 to 64	28,109	18,464	65.7	17,829	634	3.4
Aged 65 or older	32,165	5,463	17.0	5,247	216	4.0
Total white men	**92,725**	**68,351**	**73.7**	**64,624**	**3,727**	**5.5**
Aged 16 to 19	6,669	2,868	43.0	2,320	548	19.1
Aged 20 to 24	8,072	6,526	80.8	5,858	668	10.2
Aged 25 to 34	15,884	14,715	92.6	13,931	784	5.3
Aged 35 to 44	16,599	15,436	93.0	14,775	662	4.3
Aged 45 to 54	17,830	15,905	89.2	15,300	604	3.8
Aged 55 to 64	13,698	9,855	71.9	9,518	337	3.4
Aged 65 or older	13,972	3,046	21.8	2,922	124	4.1
Total white women	**96,814**	**57,284**	**59.2**	**54,501**	**2,782**	**4.9**
Aged 16 to 19	6,414	2,776	43.3	2,377	399	14.4
Aged 20 to 24	7,842	5,616	71.6	5,197	419	7.5
Aged 25 to 34	15,349	11,495	74.9	10,943	552	4.8
Aged 35 to 44	16,493	12,495	75.8	11,961	534	4.3
Aged 45 to 54	18,111	13,875	76.6	13,386	489	3.5
Aged 55 to 64	14,411	8,609	59.7	8,312	298	3.5
Aged 65 or older	18,193	2,417	13.3	2,325	92	3.8

Note: The civilian labor force equals the number of the employed plus the number of the unemployed. The civilian population equals the number in the labor force plus the number not in the labor force.
Source: Bureau of Labor Statistics, Current Population Survey, Internet site http://www.bls.gov/cps/tables.htm#empstat

Working Mothers Are the Norm

Among women with children under age 18 who work, most work full-time.

Working mothers are the norm—even among women with infants. Fifty-five percent of mothers with children under age 1 were in the labor force in 2007. Among the workers, two out of three had full-time jobs.

Labor force participation is higher for mothers with school-aged children than for those with preschoolers. Seventy-seven percent of women with children aged 6 to 17 were in the labor force in 2007 compared with 63 percent of women with children under age 6. The majority of workers in either group has a full-time job.

Sixty-two percent of the nation's married couples with children under age 18 are dual-earners, with both mother and father in the labor force. In just 30 percent of couples, only the father is employed. Even among couples with preschoolers, the 56 percent majority are dual-earners.

■ As unemployment rises, many two-earner families are trying to make ends meet on only one income.

Most mothers are in the labor force

(percent of women in the labor force, by age of children at home, 2007)

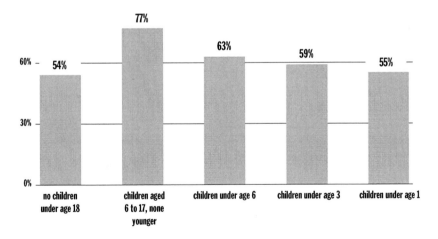

Table 6.7 Labor Force Status of Women by Presence of Children, 2007

(number and percent distribution of women aged 16 or older by labor force status and presence and age of own children under age 18 at home, 2007; numbers in thousands)

	civilian population	civilian labor force total	employed total	full-time	part-time	not in labor force
Total women	**119,694**	**70,988**	**67,792**	**51,056**	**16,736**	**48,706**
No children under age 18	82,577	44,620	42,635	32,003	10,632	37,957
With children under age 18	37,117	26,368	25,157	19,053	6,104	10,749
Children aged 6 to 17, none younger	20,599	15,910	15,310	11,910	3,400	4,689
Children under age 6	16,518	10,458	9,847	7,143	2,704	6,060
Children under age 3	9,659	5,721	5,354	3,783	1,571	3,938
Children under age 1	3,346	1,845	1,721	1,208	513	1,501
Total women	**100.0%**	**59.3%**	**56.6%**	**42.7%**	**14.0%**	**40.7%**
No children under age 18	100.0	54.0	51.6	38.8	12.9	46.0
With children under age 18	100.0	71.0	67.8	51.3	16.4	29.0
Children aged 6 to 17, none younger	100.0	77.2	74.3	57.8	16.5	22.8
Children under age 6	100.0	63.3	59.6	43.2	16.4	36.7
Children under age 3	100.0	59.2	55.4	39.2	16.3	40.8
Children under age 1	100.0	55.1	51.4	36.1	15.3	44.9

Source: Bureau of Labor Statistics, Employment Characteristics of Families, Internet sites http://www.bls.gov/news.release/ famee.t05.htm and http://www.bls.gov/news.release/famee.t06.htm

Table 6.8 Labor Force Status of Families with Children under Age 18, 2007

(number and percent distribution of families by employment status of parent and age of youngest own child under age 18 at home, by family type, 2007; numbers in thousands)

		youngest child	
	total	aged 6 to 17	under age 6
NUMBER			
Married couples with children under 18	**25,125**	**13,823**	**11,302**
One or both parents employed	24,459	13,435	11,024
Mother employed	16,855	10,126	6,729
Both parents employed	15,627	9,341	6,287
Mother employed, not father	1,228	785	442
Father employed, not mother	7,614	3,309	4,295
Neither parent employed	666	388	278
Female-headed families with children under 18	**8,554**	**5,224**	**3,329**
Mother employed	6,224	4,070	2,154
Mother not employed	2,330	1,155	1,175
Male-headed families with children under 18	**2,043**	**1,250**	**793**
Father employed	1,713	1,043	671
Father not employed	330	207	122
PERCENT DISTRIBUTION			
Married couples with children under 18	**100.0%**	**100.0%**	**100.0%**
One or both parents employed	97.3	97.2	97.5
Mother employed	67.1	73.3	59.5
Both parents employed	62.2	67.6	55.6
Mother employed, not father	4.9	5.7	3.9
Father employed, not mother	30.3	23.9	38.0
Neither parent employed	2.7	2.8	2.5
Female-headed families with children under 18	**100.0**	**100.0**	**100.0**
Mother employed	72.8	77.9	64.7
Mother not employed	27.2	22.1	35.3
Male-headed families with chlidren under 18	**100.0**	**100.0**	**100.0**
Father employed	83.8	83.4	84.6
Father not employed	16.2	16.6	15.4

Source: Bureau of Labor Statistics, Employment Characteristics of Families, Internet site http://www.bls.gov/news.release/famee.t04.htm

More than Half of Couples Are Dual Earners

In just 22 percent of married couples is only the husband in the labor force.

Dual incomes are by far the norm among married couples. Both husband and wife are in the labor force in 55 percent of married couples. In another 22 percent, the husband is the only worker. Not far behind are the 16 percent of couples in which neither spouse is in the labor force. The wife is the sole worker among 7 percent of couples.

At least two-thirds of couples aged 30 to 54 are dual earners. This lifestyle accounts for a 49 percent minority among couples aged 55 to 64. The wife is the only spouse employed in a substantial 13 percent of couples aged 55 to 64. In these homes, typically, the older husband is retired while the younger wife is still at work. For 67 percent of couples aged 65 or older, neither husband nor wife is working.

■ As boomers retire, the number of couples in which neither spouse is in the labor force may surpass the number in which only the husband is employed.

Dual earners outnumber single earners

(percent distribution of married couples by labor force status of husband and wife, 2008)

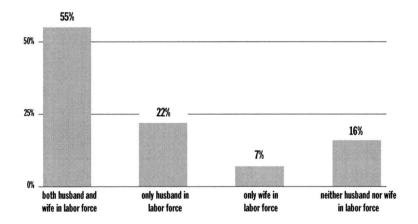

Table 6.9 Labor Force Status of Married-Couple Family Groups, 2008

(number and percent distribution of married-couple family groups aged 20 or older by age of householder and labor force status of husband and wife, 2008; numbers in thousands)

	total	husband and wife	husband only	wife only	neither husband nor wife in labor force
Married couples	**60,129**	**32,988**	**13,141**	**4,118**	**9,882**
Aged 20 to 24	1,417	763	543	60	49
Aged 25 to 29	3,962	2,615	1,136	138	73
Aged 30 to 34	5,408	3,680	1,490	138	99
Aged 35 to 39	6,532	4,456	1,782	197	99
Aged 40 to 44	6,755	4,776	1,588	241	149
Aged 45 to 54	14,210	9,922	3,000	796	491
Aged 55 to 64	11,399	5,613	2,426	1,446	1,915
Aged 65 or older	10,446	1,163	1,176	1,102	7,007
Married couples	**100.0%**	**54.9%**	**21.9%**	**6.8%**	**16.4%**
Aged 20 to 24	100.0	53.8	38.3	4.2	3.5
Aged 25 to 29	100.0	66.0	28.7	3.5	1.8
Aged 30 to 34	100.0	68.0	27.6	2.6	1.8
Aged 35 to 39	100.0	68.2	27.3	3.0	1.5
Aged 40 to 44	100.0	70.7	23.5	3.6	2.2
Aged 45 to 54	100.0	69.8	21.1	5.6	3.5
Aged 55 to 64	100.0	49.2	21.3	12.7	16.8
Aged 65 or older	100.0	11.1	11.3	10.5	67.1

Source: Bureau of the Census, America's Families and Living Arrangements: 2008, Internet site http://www.census.gov/ population/www/socdemo/hh-fam/cps2008.html; calculations by New Strategist

Most Preschoolers Are in Day Care

The children of working mothers are most likely to attend day care centers.

Among the nation's preschoolers, only 39 percent are cared for only by their parents. The 61 percent majority are in nonparental care some of the time. More than one in three is in a center-based program, such as a day care center, prekindergarten, nursery school, or Head Start. The children of mothers with a college degree are most likely to use nonparental care (69.5 percent) and be in a center-based program (45.8 percent).

Among children in kindergarten through 3rd grade, 53 percent are cared for by their parents before and after school and 47 percent are in nonparental care. Among children in 4th through 8th grade, a larger 53 percent are in nonparental care before and after school, but that is because 22 percent take care of themselves. Most 4th through 8th graders participate in after-school activities, with religious activities and sports being most popular. Non-Hispanic white children are far more likely than black or Hispanic children to take part in after-school activities (63 percent versus 40 and 35 percent, respectively).

■ The differences in participation in after-school activities by race and Hispanic origin have long-term effects on school performance and college admissions.

Non-Hispanic white children are much more likely than others to participate in after-school activities

(percent of children in 4th through 8th grades who participate in after-school activities, by race and Hispanic origin, 2005)

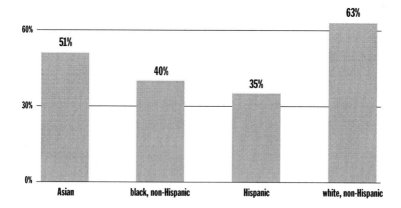

Table 6.10 Day Care Arrangements of Preschoolers, 2005

(percent distribution of children aged 0 to 6 not yet in kindergarten, by type of care, child and family characteristics, 2005)

	total	parental care only	nonparental care	care in a home		center-based program
			total	by a relative	by a nonrelative	
TOTAL CHILDREN	100.0%	39.2%	60.8%	22.3%	13.9%	36.1%
Age						
Aged 0 to 2	100.0	49.3	50.7	22.0	15.6	19.6
Aged 3 to 6	100.0	23.6	73.7	22.7	11.7	57.1
Race and Hispanic origin						
Asian	100.0	43.5	56.5	21.3	9.0	37.0
Black, non-Hispanic	100.0	30.1	69.9	27.7	10.2	43.9
Hispanic	100.0	50.5	49.5	21.2	10.4	25.2
White non-Hispanic	100.0	37.2	62.8	21.0	17.0	37.8
Poverty status						
Below poverty level	100.0	49.2	50.8	23.3	8.0	28.3
100 to 199 percent above poverty level	100.0	47.2	52.8	23.5	9.3	29.4
200 percent or more above poverty level	100.0	31.6	68.4	21.4	18.3	42.2
Family type						
Two parents	100.0	42.9	57.1	18.8	14.1	34.4
Two parents, married	100.0	41.8	58.2	18.6	14.2	35.8
Two parents, unmarried	100.0	53.0	47.0	20.4	13.0	21.7
One parent	100.0	24.9	75.1	36.0	13.4	42.3
No parents	100.0	33.1	66.9	28.3	10.0	43.6
Mother's educational attainment						
Less than high school	100.0	63.7	36.3	16.1	5.5	18.9
High school graduate/GED	100.0	44.4	55.6	24.1	9.9	30.7
Vocational/technical/some college	100.0	36.5	63.5	25.8	14.5	35.2
College graduate	100.0	30.5	69.5	19.1	19.2	45.8
Mother's employment status						
Employed 35 or more hours/week	100.0	14.7	85.3	31.8	23.3	47.6
Employed fewer than 35 hours/week	100.0	30.3	69.7	30.5	18.0	37.8
Looking for work	100.0	53.3	46.7	20.7	7.5	23.3
Not in labor force	100.0	66.1	33.9	7.8	3.6	25.8
Region						
Northeast	100.0	38.3	61.7	21.0	15.1	37.9
Midwest	100.0	38.0	62.0	22.3	11.1	38.8
South	100.0	36.7	63.3	23.8	18.8	33.5
West	100.0	43.9	56.1	21.8	12.6	33.1

Note: Numbers may not sum to total because there may be more than one type of nonparental care arrangement. Center-based care includes day care centers, prekindergartens, nursery schools, Head Start programs, and other early childhood education programs.
Source: Federal Interagency Forum on Child and Family Statistics, America's Children in Brief: Key National Indicators of Well-Being, 2008, Internet site http://childstats.gov/americaschildren/tables.asp

Table 6.11 Before- and After-School Activities of Children, 2005

(percent distribution of children in kindergarten through eighth grade, by type of before- and after-school care, poverty status, race, and Hispanic origin, 2005)

		poverty status			race and Hispanic origin			
	total	below poverty	100%–199% poverty level	200%+ poverty level	Asian	black non-Hispanic	Hispanic	white non-Hispanic
KINDERGARTEN TO 3RD GRADE								
Total children	100.0%	100.0%	100.0%	100.0%	100.0%	100.0%	100.0%	100.0%
Care arrangements								
Parent care only	53.1	52.0	54.5	53.0	49.9	34.6	55.3	58.3
Nonparental care	46.9	48.0	45.5	47.0	50.1	65.4	44.7	41.7
Home-based care	23.6	25.2	24.5	22.6	26.5	32.2	20.4	22.0
Center-based care	24.4	25.0	21.6	25.2	21.4	39.8	23.4	20.5
Activities used for supervision	5.2	3.1	5.3	6.0	13.4	5.8	3.2	4.8
Self-care	2.6	5.1	3.6	1.3	3.6	4.1	4.2	1.6
Activities*								
Any activity	46.2	24.3	34.0	59.5	45.8	30.4	30.4	56.2
Sports	31.8	12.1	19.5	44.3	29.3	16.8	20.8	40.2
Religious activities	19.4	13.5	14.8	23.4	11.5	14.6	11.9	24.0
Arts	17.2	6.0	10.8	24.1	27.1	8.3	8.2	21.8
Scouts	12.9	5.3	8.0	17.8	11.1	4.9	3.8	18.2
Academic activities	4.7	3.8	3.8	5.3	7.4	4.4	3.5	5.1
Community services	4.2	1.9	3.0	5.5	2.6	3.3	1.7	5.3
Clubs	3.2	1.3	2.4	4.3	4.2	1.1	1.8	4.3
4TH TO 8TH GRADE								
Total children	100.0	100.0	100.0	100.0	100.0	100.0	100.0	100.0
Care arrangements								
Parent care only	46.9	46.7	45.2	47.6	44.2	34.5	45.0	51.2
Nonparental care	53.1	53.3	54.8	52.4	55.8	65.5	55.0	48.8
Home-based care	18.1	15.0	20.0	18.4	17.5	24.1	18.6	16.4
Center-based care	19.0	21.3	21.3	17.4	21.9	28.9	25.4	14.2
Activities used for supervision	9.0	7.8	6.9	10.2	11.9	10.5	7.5	8.9
Self-care	22.2	23.5	23.8	21.2	21.0	27.1	19.6	21.1
Activities*								
Any activity	53.7	30.4	40.5	65.9	51.2	39.7	35.4	63.3
Sports	39.3	18.6	26.1	50.8	37.2	24.2	26.7	47.8
Religious activities	24.9	12.5	20.0	30.7	18.3	20.9	14.8	29.7
Arts	21.5	9.7	12.5	28.5	25.5	13.3	13.2	25.8
Community services	12.7	5.0	10.6	15.9	13.1	8.2	7.1	15.6
Scouts	10.1	4.8	6.4	13.2	7.7	5.6	5.4	13.3
Academic activities	9.7	6.6	7.1	11.6	13.0	12.0	5.9	10.0
Clubs	8.7	3.7	4.6	11.8	8.9	4.9	4.1	11.0

Activities are organized programs outside of school hours that are not part of a before- or after-school program.
Note: Numbers may not sum to total because there may be more than one type of arrangement or activity.
Source: Federal Interagency Forum on Child and Family Statistics, America's Children in Brief: Key National Indicators of Well-Being, 2008, Internet site http://childstats.gov/americaschildren/tables.asp

Eighteen Percent of Workers Are Part-Timers

Among women workers, nearly one in four work part-time.

Most of the nation's nonagricultural workers have full-time jobs. Part-timers outnumber those with full-time jobs only in the 16-to-19 age group. Seventy-one percent of workers aged 16 to 19 work part-time. Among 20-to-24-year-olds, a much smaller 31 percent work part-time. The figure drops to 12 percent among 25-to-54-year-olds, then rises again to 22 percent among those aged 55 or older.

Many part-time workers would rather have full-time jobs. Among the 25 million part-time workers, 35 percent of men and 17 percent of women are working part-time for economic reasons—meaning either their hours have been reduced or they cannot find a full-time job. The proportion of part-timers who would rather work full-time peaks at 57 percent among men aged 25 to 54.

■ The economic downturn has forced many Americans into part-time employment to make ends meet.

Part-time work is most common among teens and young adults

(percent of people aged 16 or older in nonagricultural industries who work part-time, by age, 2008)

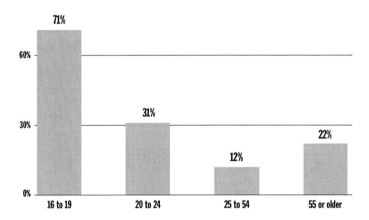

Table 6.12 Full-Time and Part-Time Workers by Age and Sex, 2008

(number and percent distribution of people aged 16 or older at work in nonagricultural industries by age, employment status, and sex, 2008; numbers in thousands)

	total			men			women		
	total	full-time	part-time	total	full-time	part-time	total	full-time	part-time
Total at work	137,739	112,961	24,778	73,471	64,375	9,095	64,268	48,586	15,682
Aged 16 to 19	5,252	1,526	3,727	2,556	875	1,681	2,696	650	2,046
Aged 20 to 24	13,091	9,058	4,033	6,866	5,067	1,798	6,225	3,990	2,235
Aged 25 to 54	94,577	82,960	11,617	50,972	47,468	3,504	43,605	35,492	8,112
Aged 55 or older	24,819	19,418	5,401	13,077	10,964	2,112	11,742	8,454	3,288
PERCENT DISTRIBUTION BY EMPLOYMENT STATUS									
Total at work	100.0%	82.0%	18.0%	100.0%	87.6%	12.4%	100.0%	75.6%	24.4%
Aged 16 to 19	100.0	29.1	71.0	100.0	34.2	65.8	100.0	24.1	75.9
Aged 20 to 24	100.0	69.2	30.8	100.0	73.8	26.2	100.0	64.1	35.9
Aged 25 to 54	100.0	87.7	12.3	100.0	93.1	6.9	100.0	81.4	18.6
Aged 55 or older	100.0	78.2	21.8	100.0	83.8	16.2	100.0	72.0	28.0
PERCENT DISTRIBUTION BY AGE									
Total at work	100.0%	100.0%	100.0%	100.0%	100.0%	100.0%	100.0%	100.0%	100.0%
Aged 16 to 19	3.8	1.4	15.0	3.5	1.4	18.5	4.2	1.3	13.0
Aged 20 to 24	9.5	8.0	16.3	9.3	7.9	19.8	9.7	8.2	14.3
Aged 25 to 54	68.7	73.4	46.9	69.4	73.7	38.5	67.8	73.0	51.7
Aged 55 or older	18.0	17.2	21.8	17.8	17.0	23.2	18.3	17.4	21.0

Note: Part-time work is less than 35 hours per week. Part-time workers exclude those who worked less than 35 hours in the previous week because of vacation, holidays, child care problems, weather issues, and other temporary, noneconomic reasons.
Source: Bureau of Labor Statistics, Current Population Survey, Internet site http://www.bls.gov/cps/tables.htm#empstat; calculations by New Strategist

Table 6.13 Part-Time Workers by Age, Sex, and Reason, 2008

(total number of people aged 16 or older who work in nonagricultural industries part-time, and number and percent working part-time for economic reasons, by sex and age, 2008; numbers in thousands)

		working part-time for economic reasons	
	total	number	share of total
Men working part-time	**9,095**	**3,162**	**34.8%**
Aged 16 to 19	1,681	209	12.4
Aged 20 to 24	1,798	526	29.3
Aged 25 to 54	3,504	2,014	57.5
Aged 55 or older	2,112	412	19.5
Women working part-time	**15,682**	**2,611**	**16.6**
Aged 16 to 19	2,046	173	8.5
Aged 20 to 24	2,235	412	18.4
Aged 25 to 54	8,112	1,637	20.2
Aged 55 or older	3,288	388	11.8

Note: Part-time work is less than 35 hours per week. Part-time workers exclude those who worked less than 35 hours in the previous week because of vacation, holidays, child care problems, weather issues, and other temporary, noneconomic reasons. "Economic reasons" means a worker's hours have been reduced or workers cannot find full-time employment.
Source: Bureau of Labor Statistics, Current Population Survey, Internet site http://www.bls.gov/cps/tables.htm#empstat; calculations by New Strategist

Occupations Differ by Sex

Occupational differences are also considerable by race and Hispanic origin.

Women are more likely than men to work in education or health care occupations. Men are more likely than women to work in computer, construction, and production occupations. Occupational differences are even greater by race and Hispanic origin. While 48 percent of Asians work in management or professional occupations, the proportion is just 18 percent among Hispanics. Thirteen percent of Hispanics work in construction versus less than 2 percent of Asians.

Women account for the majority of workers in many occupations, including human resource managers, registered nurses, librarians, and secretaries. Asians are well represented in many professional occupations. Although they account for fewer than 5 percent of all workers, they are 29 percent of computer software engineers. Blacks are 11 percent of workers, but 25 percent of social workers, 22 percent of LPNs, and 20 percent of dietitians. Hispanics are 14 percent of all workers but 41 percent of grounds maintenance workers and 44 percent of construction laborers.

■ Women account for nearly 31 percent of doctors, but only 10 percent of civil engineers.

Nearly half of Asians work in management or professional jobs

(percent of workers in management or professional occupations, by race and Hispanic origin, 2008)

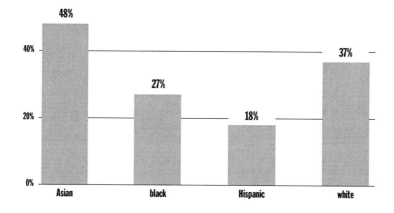

Table 6.14 Workers by Occupation and Sex, 2008

(number and percent distribution of employed people aged 16 or older in the civilian labor force, by occupation and sex, 2008; numbers in thousands)

	number			percent distribution		
	total	men	women	total	men	women
TOTAL EMPLOYED	**145,362**	**77,486**	**67,876**	**100.0%**	**100.0%**	**100.0%**
Management, professional and related occupations	**52,761**	**25,948**	**26,813**	**36.3**	**33.5**	**39.5**
Management, business, and financial operations	22,059	12,647	9,412	15.2	16.3	13.9
Management	15,852	9,925	5,926	10.9	12.8	8.7
Business and financial operations	6,207	2,721	3,486	4.3	3.5	5.1
Professional and related occupations	30,702	13,301	17,401	21.1	17.2	25.6
Computer and mathematical	3,676	2,765	911	2.5	3.6	1.3
Architecture and engineering	2,931	2,536	395	2.0	3.3	0.6
Life, physical, and social science	1,307	704	603	0.9	0.9	0.9
Community and social services	2,293	909	1,383	1.6	1.2	2.0
Legal	1,671	803	867	1.1	1.0	1.3
Education, training, and library	8,605	2,234	6,371	5.9	2.9	9.4
Art, design, entertainment, sports, and media	2,820	1,471	1,349	1.9	1.9	2.0
Health care practitioner and technical	7,399	1,878	5,521	5.1	2.4	8.1
Service occupations	**24,451**	**10,471**	**13,980**	**16.8**	**13.5**	**20.6**
Health care support	3,212	359	2,853	2.2	0.5	4.2
Protective service	3,047	2,352	695	2.1	3.0	1.0
Food preparation and serving related	7,824	3,443	4,381	5.4	4.4	6.5
Building and grounds cleaning and maintenance	5,445	3,254	2,192	3.7	4.2	3.2
Personal care and service	4,923	1,064	3,859	3.4	1.4	5.7
Sales and office occupations	**35,544**	**13,067**	**22,477**	**24.5**	**16.9**	**33.1**
Sales and related	16,295	8,221	8,073	11.2	10.6	11.9
Office and administrative support	19,249	4,845	14,404	13.2	6.3	21.2
Natural resources, construction, and maintenance occupations	**14,806**	**14,181**	**626**	**10.2**	**18.3**	**0.9**
Farming, fishing, and forestry	988	780	208	0.7	1.0	0.3
Construction and extraction	8,667	8,448	219	6.0	10.9	0.3
Installation, maintenance, and repair	5,152	4,953	199	3.5	6.4	0.3
Production, transportation, and material-moving occupations	**17,800**	**13,820**	**3,980**	**12.2**	**17.8**	**5.9**
Production	8,973	6,313	2,661	6.2	8.1	3.9
Transportation and material moving	8,827	7,507	1,319	6.1	9.7	1.9

Source: Bureau of Labor Statistics, Current Population Survey, Internet site http://www.bls.gov/cps/tables.htm#empstat; calculations by New Strategist

Table 6.15 Workers by Occupation, Race, and Hispanic Origin, 2008

(total number and percent distribution of employed people aged 16 or older in the civilian labor force, by occupation, race, and Hispanic origin, 2008; numbers in thousands)

	total	Asian	black	Hispanic	white
TOTAL EMPLOYED, NUMBER	145,362	6,917	15,953	20,346	119,126
TOTAL EMPLOYED, PERCENT	100.0%	100.0%	100.0%	100.0%	100.0%
Management, professional and related occupations	**36.3**	**48.2**	**27.4**	**18.3**	**37.0**
Management, business, and financial operations	15.2	16.5	10.0	8.1	15.9
Professional and related occupations	21.1	31.7	17.4	10.2	21.1
Service occupations	**16.8**	**16.3**	**24.4**	**24.2**	**15.7**
Sales and office occupations	**24.5**	**21.5**	**25.5**	**21.4**	**24.5**
Sales and related	11.2	11.1	9.9	9.3	11.4
Office and administrative support	13.2	10.4	15.7	12.1	13.1
Natural resources, construction, maintenance occupations	**10.2**	**4.1**	**6.4**	**18.2**	**11.0**
Farming, fishing, and forestry	0.7	0.2	0.3	1.9	0.7
Construction and extraction	6.0	1.8	3.4	12.6	6.5
Installation, maintenance, and repair	3.5	2.1	2.7	3.7	3.7
Production, transportation, material-moving occupations	**12.2**	**9.9**	**16.2**	**17.8**	**11.9**
Production	6.2	6.7	6.9	9.3	6.1
Transportation and material moving	6.1	3.2	9.3	8.5	5.8

Source: Bureau of Labor Statistics, Current Population Survey, Internet site http://www.bls.gov/cps/tables.htm#empstat; calculations by New Strategist

Table 6.16 Workers by Detailed Occupation, Sex, Race, and Hispanic Origin, 2008

(percentage of employed civilians aged 16 or older who are women, Asians, blacks, or Hispanics, by selected detailed occupation, 2008)

	women	Asians	blacks	Hispanics
TOTAL EMPLOYED	**46.7%**	**4.8%**	**11.0%**	**14.0%**
Management, professional and related occupations	**50.8**	**6.3**	**8.3**	**7.1**
Management, business, and financial operations occupations	42.7	5.2	7.2	7.5
Management occupations	37.4	4.6	6.4	7.3
Chief executives	23.4	4.0	3.9	4.8
General and operations managers	30.1	4.3	5.4	6.2
Advertising and promotions managers	62.1	5.8	7.6	9.7
Marketing and sales managers	42.0	4.1	4.9	6.2
Public relations managers	60.3	0.0	3.5	5.4
Administrative services managers	32.6	2.3	8.9	5.7
Computer and information systems managers	27.2	10.2	7.7	5.3
Financial managers	54.8	5.7	7.9	8.6
Human resources managers	66.3	4.0	8.2	7.3
Industrial production managers	14.5	3.8	4.9	9.6
Purchasing managers	40.4	2.5	12.9	3.7
Transportation, storage, and distribution managers	17.0	1.7	7.7	12.7
Farm, ranch, and other agricultural managers	23.9	1.7	0.9	4.6
Farmers and ranchers	24.4	0.7	1.0	2.4
Construction managers	8.2	1.4	3.7	9.1
Education administrators	65.1	2.6	12.2	7.6
Engineering managers	6.3	8.0	1.1	4.9
Food service managers	44.8	11.8	7.3	12.9
Lodging managers	46.7	12.2	5.5	9.1
Medical and health services managers	69.4	4.2	10.1	7.3
Property, real estate, and community association managers	49.6	3.1	7.7	8.2
Social and community service managers	68.1	2.2	10.1	7.7
Managers, all other	35.8	5.3	6.8	7.6
Business and financial operations occupations	56.2	6.5	9.4	7.9
Agents and business managers of artists, performers, athletes	36.5	4.8	5.8	6.5
Wholesale and retail buyers, except farm products	47.6	6.1	7.6	12.2
Purchasing agents, except wholesale, retail, farm products	56.5	4.8	6.7	11.2
Claims adjusters, appraisers, examiners, and investigators	65.7	3.6	14.6	7.6
Compliance officers, except agriculture, construction, health and safety, and transportation	52.3	3.1	7.9	6.4
Cost estimators	10.0	1.2	0.7	5.3
Human resources, training, and labor relations specialists	70.7	3.5	14.0	7.9
Logisticians	47.2	5.5	12.3	12.2
Management analysts	43.5	5.8	6.2	4.6
Meeting and convention planners	79.2	4.1	14.0	6.2
Other business operations specialists	66.3	9.2	12.2	10.0
Accountants and auditors	61.1	10.2	8.3	7.6
Appraisers and assessors of real estate	33.4	2.0	5.2	7.2
Budget analysts	57.1	8.3	17.5	5.0
Financial analysts	38.8	12.9	6.0	9.8
Personal financial advisors	34.3	5.9	5.9	6.1
Insurance underwriters	80.3	5.5	13.3	7.1
Loan counselors and officers	58.0	4.4	10.6	11.5
Tax examiners, collectors, and revenue agents	64.2	4.2	19.7	4.4
Tax preparers	66.6	5.7	9.1	12.6
Financial specialists, all other	57.0	5.3	20.6	14.9

	women	Asians	blacks	Hispanics
Professional and related occupations	56.7%	7.1%	9.0%	6.7%
Computer and mathematical occupations	24.8	16.7	7.2	5.1
Computer scientists and systems analysts	27.5	13.7	9.7	5.3
Computer programmers	22.4	14.1	5.7	4.0
Computer software engineers	20.9	29.0	4.7	3.7
Computer support specialists	27.7	8.2	11.1	7.9
Database administrators	29.2	13.5	6.3	3.8
Network and computer systems administrators	21.4	9.8	8.0	7.4
Network systems and data communications analysts	23.7	9.2	7.1	6.4
Operations research analysts	47.6	4.1	8.6	8.3
Architecture and engineering occupations	13.5	9.6	5.1	6.7
Architects, except naval	24.8	6.1	3.3	8.2
Aerospace engineers	10.3	11.1	6.1	5.0
Chemical engineers	13.1	8.6	9.5	0.0
Civil engineers	10.4	11.2	3.2	9.2
Computer hardware engineers	19.4	30.7	3.0	4.1
Electrical and electronics engineers	7.7	13.4	3.0	5.3
Industrial engineers, including health and safety	14.9	7.6	5.9	5.2
Mechanical engineers	6.7	10.6	4.5	4.1
Engineers, all other	11.5	11.7	4.7	4.5
Drafters	23.4	7.2	3.0	9.0
Engineering technicians, except drafters	18.5	5.4	10.9	10.3
Surveying and mapping technicians	4.9	1.2	1.5	8.0
Life, physical, and social science occupations	46.1	12.0	7.1	4.7
Biological scientists	52.9	13.3	4.2	3.9
Medical scientists	52.3	24.8	8.1	2.7
Chemists and materials scientists	33.1	22.3	4.7	6.9
Environmental scientists and geoscientists	29.3	2.7	4.0	4.1
Physical scientists, all other	40.7	27.8	6.1	1.7
Market and survey researchers	57.0	3.3	5.7	5.8
Psychologists	66.9	3.1	7.2	6.6
Chemical technicians	35.2	6.9	18.0	7.0
Other life, physical, and social science technicians	48.3	8.5	12.5	5.7
Community and social services occupations	60.3	2.5	19.0	8.9
Counselors	68.0	2.2	20.5	8.9
Social workers	79.4	2.9	24.5	10.0
Miscellaneous community and social service specialists	61.4	2.6	20.9	14.5
Clergy	14.8	2.7	10.2	3.6
Directors, religious activities and education	63.5	0.8	1.7	4.5
Religious workers, all other	65.6	0.8	10.1	11.0
Legal occupations	51.9	2.8	7.0	6.6
Lawyers	34.4	2.9	4.6	3.8
Judges, magistrates, and other judicial workers	43.6	0.3	6.8	3.2
Paralegals and legal assistants	87.7	2.2	11.6	10.3
Miscellaneous legal support workers	74.5	3.9	10.0	13.3
Education, training, and library occupations	74.0	3.8	9.2	7.5
Postsecondary teachers	46.1	11.9	5.2	4.0
Preschool and kindergarten teachers	97.6	3.5	11.7	9.8
Elementary and middle school teachers	81.2	2.2	9.9	6.8
Secondary school teachers	56.0	1.8	7.2	6.5
Special education teachers	84.9	1.3	8.0	3.7
Other teachers and instructors	66.9	3.8	9.3	8.2
Librarians	83.5	3.5	6.7	3.7
Teacher assistants	91.7	2.8	13.9	15.0
Other education, training, and library workers	76.0	3.6	6.1	5.5

	women	Asians	blacks	Hispanics
Arts, design, entertainment, sports, and media occupations	47.8%	4.1%	6.1%	8.3%
Artists and related workers	48.6	3.7	2.0	5.4
Designers	57.5	6.1	5.6	8.2
Producers and directors	38.5	4.0	8.9	7.3
Athletes, coaches, umpires, and related workers	32.5	2.3	10.3	8.3
Musicians, singers, and related workers	29.3	1.6	9.7	10.8
News analysts, reporters, and correspondents	45.4	3.9	2.1	2.9
Public relations specialists	61.6	1.7	5.1	7.3
Editors	54.8	2.5	3.5	2.2
Writers and authors	57.3	1.1	4.1	3.3
Miscellaneous media and communication workers	72.2	12.1	6.1	27.4
Broadcast and sound engineering technicians, radio operators	16.1	5.9	11.0	12.9
Photographers	44.1	3.9	4.3	10.1
Television, video, motion picture camera operators and editors	15.3	0.1	5.2	12.8
Health care practitioner and technical occupations	74.6	8.0	10.2	5.9
Chiropractors	15.3	0.3	1.8	4.7
Dentists	27.2	12.0	3.3	5.2
Dietitians and nutritionists	90.0	3.7	20.3	7.1
Pharmacists	51.8	12.6	8.7	2.5
Physicians and surgeons	30.5	16.6	6.2	5.8
Physician assistants	66.9	5.2	6.6	9.3
Registered nurses	91.7	7.8	10.0	4.7
Occupational therapists	95.9	6.3	1.2	5.5
Physical therapists	69.0	13.0	3.9	3.5
Respiratory therapists	68.3	4.6	10.4	7.4
Speech-language pathologists	98.1	4.8	2.3	6.2
Therapists, all other	80.8	2.6	14.7	3.7
Veterinarians	56.7	3.7	4.0	4.1
Clinical laboratory technologists and technicians	75.7	8.8	14.6	9.0
Dental hygienists	97.7	2.0	4.1	5.3
Diagnostic related technologists and technicians	72.0	5.3	8.8	5.0
Emergency medical technicians and paramedics	30.2	0.1	4.7	6.6
Health diagnosing and treating practitioner support technicians	76.7	5.2	10.8	10.8
Licensed practical and licensed vocational nurses	93.3	3.6	22.1	7.1
Medical records and health information technicians	95.0	4.0	13.9	9.9
Opticians, dispensing	63.4	0.3	7.5	8.4
Miscellaneous health technologists and technicians	63.0	8.4	23.3	5.5
Other health care practitioners and technical occupations	42.1	6.5	5.6	8.0
Service occupations	**57.2**	**4.6**	**15.9**	**20.2**
Health care support occupations	88.8	4.2	25.8	13.6
Nursing, psychiatric, and home health aides	88.7	4.3	34.5	13.1
Physical therapist assistants and aides	77.0	4.0	8.4	8.0
Massage therapists	84.5	8.0	7.0	7.4
Dental assistants	96.3	2.0	6.9	17.3
Medical assistants and other health care support occupations	88.8	4.2	16.9	15.3
Protective service occupations	22.8	1.8	19.1	10.9
First-line supervisors/managers of police and detectives	14.7	2.9	12.5	6.1
First-line supervisors/mgrs. of fire-fighting, prevention workers	8.7	1.3	5.8	9.5
Supervisors, protective service workers, all other	21.7	2.2	14.5	12.2
Firefighters	4.8	0.3	8.2	9.4
Bailiffs, correctional officers, and jailers	30.0	0.6	22.0	10.4
Detectives and criminal investigators	19.2	2.3	10.6	9.5
Police and sheriff's patrol officers	14.7	1.8	13.6	11.6
Private detectives and investigators	39.4	0.8	13.8	6.5
Security guards and gaming surveillance officers	23.6	3.0	31.0	12.4
Crossing guards	73.5	0.4	29.9	16.4
Lifeguards and other protective service workers	52.3	0.8	5.7	9.6

	women	Asians	blacks	Hispanics
Food preparation and serving related occupations	56.0%	5.4%	12.1%	21.0%
Chefs and head cooks	17.0	14.1	10.3	22.7
First-line supervisors/managers of food prep., serving workers	57.8	3.8	14.4	14.1
Cooks	40.1	5.0	18.1	30.2
Food preparation workers	60.7	6.6	9.8	24.6
Bartenders	58.3	2.3	3.5	9.6
Combined food preparation, serving workers, incl. fast food	68.5	2.0	15.6	17.2
Counter attendants, cafeteria, food concession, coffee shop	64.1	4.5	12.2	15.4
Waiters and waitresses	73.2	6.2	7.3	14.6
Food servers, nonrestaurant	70.5	6.5	20.5	18.0
Dining room and cafeteria attendants and bartender helpers	47.8	5.6	13.1	26.9
Dishwashers	22.7	3.4	12.0	35.7
Hosts and hostesses, restaurant, lounge, and coffee shop	88.7	3.0	6.2	11.6
Building and grounds cleaning and maintenance occupations	40.2	2.8	15.0	33.4
First-line supervisors/mgrs. of housekeeping, janitorial workers	39.9	1.1	18.6	23.7
First-line supervisors/managers of landscaping, lawn service, and groundskeeping workers	7.5	0.6	4.5	16.8
Janitors and building cleaners	32.2	3.4	18.4	28.2
Maids and housekeeping cleaners	89.8	3.7	18.1	40.5
Pest control workers	8.2	2.8	6.1	15.3
Grounds maintenance workers	6.1	1.6	7.7	41.0
Personal care and service occupations	78.4	7.4	14.7	14.2
First-line supervisors/managers of gaming workers	38.6	3.2	7.2	10.3
First-line supervisors/managers of personal service workers	73.2	13.8	11.1	7.5
Nonfarm animal caretakers	73.5	1.9	2.9	12.3
Gaming services workers	51.5	21.8	13.1	3.5
Miscellaneous entertainment attendants and related workers	43.0	2.7	7.1	11.3
Barbers	20.8	4.1	33.3	20.2
Hairdressers, hairstylists, and cosmetologists	90.6	6.5	11.3	11.0
Miscellaneous personal appearance workers	82.3	55.0	4.4	6.3
Baggage porters, bellhops, and concierges	17.3	8.1	23.9	19.9
Transportation attendants	71.0	3.3	16.8	13.1
Child care workers	95.6	2.7	17.4	20.0
Personal and home care aides	85.4	6.7	21.8	17.4
Recreation and fitness workers	68.1	3.3	9.6	9.5
Residential advisors	65.8	0.1	28.1	4.7
Personal care and service workers, all other	54.1	3.7	11.3	12.3
Sales and office occupations	**63.2**	**4.2**	**11.5**	**12.3**
Sales and related occupations	49.5	4.7	9.7	11.7
First-line supervisors/managers of retail sales workers	43.3	5.2	7.3	10.4
First-line supervisors/managers of non–retail sales workers	26.1	4.9	6.9	11.0
Cashiers	75.5	6.4	16.3	16.6
Counter and rental clerks	50.4	7.9	14.8	13.7
Parts salespersons	10.8	1.7	7.5	14.7
Retail salespersons	52.2	4.1	10.7	12.3
Advertising sales agents	54.7	2.2	10.3	8.4
Insurance sales agents	46.9	2.7	7.6	9.4
Securities, commodities, and financial services sales agents	27.9	5.1	7.2	9.2
Travel agents	71.6	10.3	9.8	6.4
Sales representatives, services, all other	34.4	4.5	8.9	8.8
Sales representatives, wholesale and manufacturing	27.3	3.8	3.9	8.6
Models, demonstrators, and product promoters	79.0	6.7	8.0	6.6
Real estate brokers and sales agents	54.4	3.5	7.2	8.6
Telemarketers	66.3	0.7	23.6	16.6
Door-to-door sales workers, news, street vendors, related workers	62.2	3.7	9.5	14.4
Sales and related workers, all other	61.1	1.2	4.8	7.4

	women	Asians	blacks	Hispanics
Office and administrative support occupations	74.8%	3.7%	13.0%	12.8%
First-line supervisors/managers of office and administrative support workers	71.2	3.4	10.4	10.5
Bill and account collectors	68.0	2.2	20.0	18.2
Billing and posting clerks and machine operators	90.9	3.6	13.5	12.6
Bookkeeping, accounting, and auditing clerks	91.5	4.4	6.9	8.0
Payroll and timekeeping clerks	90.1	4.1	11.8	10.8
Tellers	84.8	6.1	12.3	15.8
Court, municipal, and license clerks	75.6	3.7	11.1	10.5
Credit authorizers, checkers, and clerks	71.1	1.4	12.7	12.1
Customer service representatives	68.3	3.7	18.3	14.5
Eligibility interviewers, government programs	83.9	6.5	22.1	23.7
File clerks	83.8	4.4	15.5	12.0
Hotel, motel, and resort desk clerks	71.9	3.9	19.1	9.6
Interviewers, except eligibility and loan	82.2	1.9	18.4	17.7
Library assistants, clerical	83.8	4.5	8.9	5.7
Loan interviewers and clerks	84.7	2.4	7.1	18.3
Order clerks	58.8	1.5	11.8	18.0
Human resources assistants, except payroll and timekeeping	84.8	5.7	15.3	10.0
Receptionists and information clerks	93.6	3.8	9.8	15.2
Reservation and transportation ticket agents and travel clerks	60.9	6.5	14.3	14.8
Information and record clerks, all other	91.1	4.1	15.5	11.7
Couriers and messengers	17.4	1.7	13.9	21.1
Dispatchers	57.4	1.9	15.9	11.8
Postal service clerks	53.7	8.5	27.0	10.5
Postal service mail carriers	33.0	6.4	14.5	9.8
Postal service mail sorters, processors, and processing machine operators	42.7	10.9	34.1	11.4
Production, planning, and expediting clerks	58.2	3.7	8.9	7.3
Shipping, receiving, and traffic clerks	32.8	2.8	11.6	20.2
Stock clerks and order fillers	35.4	3.6	16.8	18.6
Weighers, measurers, checkers, and samplers, recordkeeping	44.7	5.2	13.6	17.8
Secretaries and administrative assistants	96.1	2.3	8.1	9.6
Computer operators	51.4	4.3	19.9	5.1
Data entry keyers	77.3	5.2	17.6	12.9
Word processors and typists	92.9	3.6	17.3	13.1
Insurance claims and policy processing clerks	83.4	2.8	19.4	12.2
Mail clerks and mail machine operators, except postal service	49.0	7.1	20.8	12.9
Office clerks, general	84.4	4.7	15.4	14.1
Office and administrative support workers, all other	77.3	4.8	13.1	9.6
Natural resources, construction, maintenance occupations	**4.2**	**1.9**	**6.9**	**25.0**
Farming, fishing, and forestry occupations	21.1	1.7	4.5	39.3
Graders and sorters, agricultural products	65.3	4.0	13.6	59.3
Miscellaneous agricultural workers	19.3	1.5	3.5	45.1
Logging workers	1.0	0.0	5.9	12.3
Construction and extraction occupations	2.5	1.4	6.3	29.6
First-line supervisors/managers of construction trades and extraction workers	2.7	1.2	3.0	16.1
Brickmasons, blockmasons, and stonemasons	0.4	1.2	7.4	39.9
Carpenters	1.5	1.3	6.0	25.7
Carpet, floor, and tile installers and finishers	2.3	1.0	1.9	42.7
Cement masons, concrete finishers, and terrazzo workers	0.0	0.1	7.4	57.7
Construction laborers	3.1	1.9	7.7	44.1
Operating engineers and other construction equipment operators	1.5	0.5	5.1	17.4
Drywall installers, ceiling tile installers, and tapers	2.1	0.4	3.6	56.9
Electricians	1.0	2.7	5.9	16.2
Painters, construction and maintenance	6.3	2.2	7.3	40.1

	women	Asians	blacks	Hispanics
Pipelayers, plumbers, pipefitters, and steamfitters	1.4%	0.6%	6.4%	19.5%
Roofers	1.3	0.4	8.4	42.9
Sheet metal workers	4.8	1.2	6.2	11.8
Structural iron and steel workers	0.9	0.3	2.2	14.4
Helpers, construction trades	4.1	0.3	18.1	41.3
Construction and building inspectors	9.5	1.6	9.2	5.4
Highway maintenance workers	1.9	0.0	17.2	10.2
Mining machine operators	2.2	5.6	3.3	21.2
Other extraction workers	2.8	1.0	3.5	33.5
Installation, maintenance, and repair occupations	3.9	2.8	8.5	14.5
First-line supervisors/managers of mechanics, installers, repairers	8.0	1.0	6.7	8.7
Computer, automated teller, and office machine repairers	10.5	7.5	10.8	13.0
Radio and telecommunications equipment installers, repairers	11.4	4.4	13.7	11.8
Electronic home entertainment equipment installers, repairers	1.6	8.0	13.5	16.2
Security and fire alarm systems installers	0.0	2.2	8.2	16.8
Aircraft mechanics and service technicians	1.7	6.4	5.5	13.8
Automotive body and related repairers	2.1	0.7	5.2	27.2
Automotive service technicians and mechanics	1.6	2.9	6.5	19.7
Bus and truck mechanics and diesel engine specialists	0.9	1.7	7.5	11.6
Heavy vehicle, mobile equipment service technicians, mechanics	1.1	0.4	5.0	10.5
Small engine mechanics	2.0	0.0	6.0	10.9
Miscellaneous vehicle and mobile equipment mechanics, installers, and repairers	1.9	0.4	7.6	22.0
Heating, air conditioning, refrigeration mechanics and installers	2.0	2.2	8.6	13.2
Home appliance repairers	5.3	5.7	10.2	10.7
Industrial and refractory machinery mechanics	2.6	3.0	8.8	13.0
Maintenance and repair workers, general	3.5	2.4	10.2	13.7
Millwrights	0.9	1.6	4.4	5.9
Electrical power-line installers and repairers	1.4	0.3	8.7	8.9
Telecommunications line installers and repairers	3.3	1.1	16.2	15.0
Precision instrument and equipment repairers	15.4	3.5	4.8	12.4
Other installation, maintenance, and repair workers	7.5	2.4	7.9	18.5
Production, transportation, and material moving occupations	**22.4**	**3.8**	**14.5**	**20.4**
Production occupations	29.7	5.2	12.2	21.1
First-line supervisors/managers of production, operating workers	18.1	5.0	9.5	14.9
Electrical, electronics, and electromechanical assemblers	57.8	17.5	12.2	19.4
Miscellaneous assemblers and fabricators	35.0	5.9	15.3	19.8
Bakers	55.7	5.0	12.1	28.9
Butchers and other meat, poultry, and fish processing workers	26.8	6.7	14.6	38.4
Food batchmakers	53.5	6.2	11.7	29.0
Computer control programmers and operators	8.7	1.6	3.9	6.8
Cutting, punching, and press machine setters, operators, and tenders, metal and plastic	20.2	4.0	9.1	22.0
Grinding, lapping, polishing, and buffing machine tool setters, operators, and tenders, metal and plastic	19.7	5.8	6.6	19.6
Machinists	6.9	4.2	7.0	12.1
Molders and molding machine setters, operators, and tenders, metal and plastic	18.1	1.3	12.2	22.2
Tool and die makers	1.0	1.2	0.9	5.9
Welding, soldering, and brazing workers	4.7	3.7	8.7	21.0
Metalworkers and plastic workers, all other	21.1	5.5	10.0	24.4
Printing machine operators	19.8	2.9	9.1	20.5
Laundry and dry-cleaning workers	60.8	7.7	22.4	29.3
Pressers, textile, garment, and related materials	79.2	10.0	19.7	41.0
Sewing machine operators	78.2	14.1	9.4	36.8
Tailors, dressmakers, and sewers	84.2	12.2	6.1	24.4
Upholsterers	19.7	0.4	27.2	42.1

	women	Asians	blacks	Hispanics
Cabinetmakers and bench carpenters	6.5%	5.7%	2.8%	13.0%
Power plant operators, distributors, and dispatchers	9.2	0.0	2.0	10.5
Stationary engineers and boiler operators	1.7	2.4	13.1	7.2
Water and liquid waste treatment plant and system operators	8.6	0.0	12.3	7.0
Chemical processing machine setters, operators, and tenders	15.4	4.4	16.2	13.2
Crushing, grinding, polishing, mixing, and blending workers	13.3	1.4	14.5	20.6
Cutting workers	26.7	5.1	8.0	27.4
Inspectors, testers, sorters, samplers, and weighers	41.3	5.8	13.4	14.2
Jewelers and precious stone and metal workers	47.0	6.8	1.6	16.7
Medical, dental, and ophthalmic laboratory technicians	56.9	6.9	6.2	13.8
Packaging and filling machine operators and tenders	51.5	5.0	15.0	42.5
Painting workers	13.6	1.1	13.2	26.2
Photographic process workers and processing machine operators	47.8	12.7	8.1	11.8
Production workers, all other	31.0	2.8	16.4	23.9
Transportation and material-moving occupations	14.9	2.5	16.9	19.7
Supervisors, transportation and material-moving workers	20.5	5.5	14.4	12.0
Aircraft pilots and flight engineers	2.6	2.4	1.8	2.5
Bus drivers	49.0	1.8	30.4	12.2
Driver/sales workers and truck drivers	4.9	1.5	14.3	17.8
Taxi drivers and chauffeurs	13.3	10.5	26.3	18.9
Motor vehicle operators, all other	18.0	2.1	24.0	15.2
Locomotive engineers and operators	2.8	0.0	14.5	6.0
Railroad conductors and yardmasters	4.7	2.9	8.8	5.4
Parking lot attendants	12.6	8.7	15.7	27.3
Service station attendants	14.8	4.4	10.3	12.4
Transportation inspectors	11.3	6.5	21.5	9.2
Crane and tower operators	3.7	0.0	13.9	10.6
Dredge, excavating, and loading machine operators	1.2	0.0	4.5	15.7
Industrial truck and tractor operators	8.9	1.5	23.4	26.7
Cleaners of vehicles and equipment	9.5	0.9	17.4	28.8
Laborers and freight, stock, and material movers, hand	17.1	2.4	15.9	21.2
Packers and packagers, hand	58.1	4.6	15.3	43.7
Refuse and recyclable material collectors	14.0	2.4	16.4	31.1

Source: Bureau of Labor Statistics, Current Population Survey, Internet site http://www.bls.gov/cps/tables.htm#empstat

Job Tenure among Middle-Aged Workers Has Decreased

Long-term employment has fallen among men and women aged 30 to 49.

As relationships between employers and employees have eroded, job tenure—the number of years a worker has been with his or her current employer—has been declining. Between 2000 and 2008, median job tenure stabilized for men and women overall, but the decline continued among middle-aged workers.

Median job tenure among men aged 25 or older climbed slightly between 2000 and 2008, creeping up from 4.9 to 5.2 years. But among men aged 35 to 54, job tenure fell. The same pattern occurred among women. While women's median job tenure rose between 2000 and 2008, from 4.4 to 4.9 years, tenure fell among women aged 45 to 64.

Job tenure has declined among the middle aged because long-term employment has become less common. The proportion of men and women who have been with their current employer for 10 or more years fell in most age groups between 2000 and 2008. The percentage of men aged 35 to 49 and of women aged 45 to 49 with long-term jobs fell by at least 4 percentage points. Among men and women aged 65 or older, long-term employment increased as more postponed retirement.

■ The growing number of layoffs is reducing long-term employment.

Few workers have been with their current employer for 10 or more years

(percent of workers aged 25 or older who have worked for their current employer for 10 or more years, by sex, 2008)

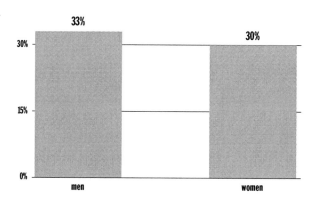

Table 6.17 Job Tenure by Sex and Age, 2000 and 2008

(median number of years workers aged 25 or older have been with their current employer by sex and age, and change in years, 2000 and 2008)

	2008	2000	change 2000–08
Total aged 25 or older	**5.1 yrs.**	**4.7 yrs.**	**0.4 yrs.**
Aged 25 to 34	2.7	2.6	0.1
Aged 35 to 44	4.9	4.8	0.1
Aged 45 to 54	7.6	8.2	−0.6
Aged 55 to 64	9.9	10.0	−0.1
Aged 65 or older	10.2	9.4	0.8
Men aged 25 or older	**5.2**	**4.9**	**0.3**
Aged 25 to 34	2.8	2.7	0.1
Aged 35 to 44	5.2	5.3	−0.1
Aged 45 to 54	8.2	9.5	−1.3
Aged 55 to 64	10.1	10.2	−0.1
Aged 65 or older	10.4	9.0	1.4
Women aged 25 or older	**4.9**	**4.4**	**0.5**
Aged 25 to 34	2.6	2.5	0.1
Aged 35 to 44	4.7	4.3	0.4
Aged 45 to 54	7.0	7.3	−0.3
Aged 55 to 64	9.8	9.9	−0.1
Aged 65 or older	9.9	9.7	0.2

Source: Bureau of Labor Statistics, Employee Tenure, Internet site http://www.bls.gov/news.release/tenure.toc.htm; calculations by New Strategist

Table 6.18 Long-Term Employment by Sex and Age, 2000 and 2008

(percent of employed wage and salary workers aged 25 or older who have been with their current employer for 10 or more years, by sex and age, 2000 and 2008; percentage point change in share, 2000–08)

	2008	2000	percentage point change 2000–08
TOTAL AGED 25 OR OLDER	**31.5%**	**31.5%**	**0.0**
Men aged 25 or older	**32.9**	**33.4**	**–0.5**
Aged 25 to 29	2.4	3.0	–0.6
Aged 30 to 34	11.3	15.1	–3.8
Aged 35 to 39	25.4	29.4	–4.0
Aged 40 to 44	35.8	40.2	–4.4
Aged 45 to 49	43.5	49.0	–5.5
Aged 50 to 54	50.4	51.6	–1.2
Aged 55 to 59	54.9	53.7	1.2
Aged 60 to 64	52.4	52.4	0.0
Aged 65 or older	58.9	48.6	10.3
Women aged 25 or older	**30.0**	**29.5**	**0.5**
Aged 25 to 29	2.1	1.9	0.2
Aged 30 to 34	8.7	12.5	–3.8
Aged 35 to 39	20.3	22.3	–2.0
Aged 40 to 44	29.9	31.2	–1.3
Aged 45 to 49	36.7	41.4	–4.7
Aged 50 to 54	45.0	45.8	–0.8
Aged 55 to 59	50.0	52.5	–2.5
Aged 60 to 64	54.8	53.6	1.2
Aged 65 or older	53.8	51.0	2.8

Source: Bureau of Labor Statistics, Employee Tenure, Internet site http://www.bls.gov/news.release/tenure.toc.htm; calculations by New Strategist

Self-Employment Rises with Age

Older workers are more than twice as likely as the average worker to be self-employed.

Among the 145 million employed wage and salary workers in 2008, only 10 million were self-employed—or just under 7 percent of workers. The figure undoubtedly underestimates the number of people who work for themselves because it excludes those who have a business on the side if it is not their primary source of income. It also excludes sole proprietorships that are incorporated.

Self-employment rises with age, and it peaks at 17 percent among workers aged 65 or older. Older workers are most likely to be self-employed because Medicare, which begins at age 65, frees them from the need to find a job with health insurance coverage.

■ Many more Americans would be self-employed if health insurance were more affordable.

Older workers are most likely to choose self-employment

(percent of workers who are self-employed, by age, 2008)

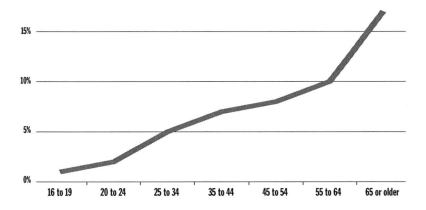

Table 6.19 Self-Employed Workers by Age, 2008

(number of employed workers aged 16 or older, number and percent who are self-employed, and percent distribution of self-employed by age, 2008; numbers in thousands)

	total employed	self-employed number	self-employed percent of total	self-employed percent distribution
Total aged 16 or older	**145,362**	**10,079**	**6.9%**	**100.0%**
Aged 16 to 19	5,573	73	1.3	0.7
Aged 20 to 24	13,629	313	2.3	3.1
Aged 25 to 34	31,383	1,447	4.6	14.4
Aged 35 to 44	33,457	2,286	6.8	22.7
Aged 45 to 54	34,529	2,832	8.2	28.1
Aged 55 to 64	20,812	2,120	10.2	21.0
Aged 65 or older	5,979	1,009	16.9	10.0

Source: Bureau of Labor Statistics, Current Population Survey, Internet site http://www.bls.gov/cps/tables.htm#empstat; calculations by New Strategist

Few Workers Are Represented by Unions

The differences are greatest by occupation.

Union representation has fallen sharply over the past few decades. In 1970, 30 percent of nonagricultural workers were represented by labor unions. In 2008, the figure was just 14 percent.

Unions represent 15 percent of male workers and 13 percent of female workers. Men are more likely than women to be represented by unions because they are more likely to work in jobs that are traditional union strongholds. In fact, the decline of labor unions is partly the result of the shift in jobs from manufacturing to services.

Union representation is higher for blacks than for Asians, Hispanics, or whites. Full-time workers are more likely to be represented than part-time workers. The biggest differences are by occupation. Forty-three percent of workers in education, training, and library occupations are represented by unions, as are 37 percent of protective service workers. In contrast, unions represent only 5 to 6 percent of food preparation workers and farm workers.

■ Union representation has declined in part because the global economy makes it increasingly risky for American workers to make demands on their employers.

Union representation is much greater in some occupations

(percent of employed wage and salary workers aged 16 or older who are represented by unions, by occupation, 2008)

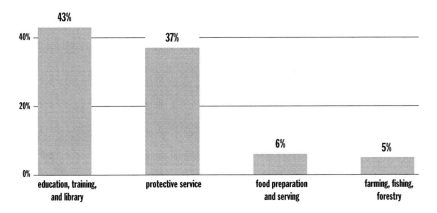

Table 6.20 Workers Represented by Unions by Sex, Race, and Hispanic Origin, 2008

(number of employed wage and salary workers aged 16 or older, and number and percent who are represented by unions, by sex, race, and Hispanic origin, 2008; numbers in thousands)

	total	represented by unions	
		number	percent
Total employed	**129,377**	**17,761**	**13.7%**
Men	66,846	9,724	14.5
Women	62,532	8,036	12.9
Asians	6,157	714	11.6
Blacks	15,030	2,370	15.8
Hispanics	18,572	2,168	11.7
Whites	105,052	14,222	13.5
Full-time workers	106,648	16,029	15.0
Part-time workers	22,497	1,697	7.5

Source: Bureau of Labor Statistics, Current Population Survey, Internet site http://www.bls.gov/cps/tables.htm#empstat

Table 6.21 Workers Represented by Unions by Occupation, 2008

(number of employed wage and salary workers aged 16 or older, and number and percent represented by unions, by occupation, 2008; numbers in thousands)

	total	represented by unions	
		number	percent
TOTAL EMPLOYED	**129,377**	**17,761**	**13.7%**
Management, professional and related occupations	**45,538**	**6,948**	**15.3**
Management, business, and financial operations	17,326	1,039	6.0
Management	11,843	679	5.7
Business and financial operations	5,483	360	6.6
Professional and related occupations	28,212	5,909	20.9
Computer and mathematical	3,488	210	6.0
Architecture and engineering	2,746	233	8.5
Life, physical, and social science	1,209	132	10.9
Community and social services	2,222	406	18.3
Legal	1,318	87	6.6
Education, training, and library	8,424	3,630	43.1
Art, design, entertainment, sports, and media	1,994	167	8.4
Health care practitioner and technical occupations	6,813	1,045	15.3
Service occupations	**22,114**	**2,831**	**12.8**
Health care support	3,028	317	10.5
Protective service	3,023	1,122	37.1
Food preparation and serving related	7,694	444	5.8
Building and grounds cleaning and maintenance	4,648	592	12.7
Personal care and service	3,721	357	9.6
Sales and office occupations	**32,479**	**2,710**	**8.3**
Sales and related	13,708	531	3.9
Office and administrative support	18,770	2,179	11.6
Natural resources, construction, maintenance occupations	**12,444**	**2,303**	**18.5**
Farming, fishing, and forestry	901	46	5.1
Construction and extraction	6,876	1,445	21.0
Installation, maintenance, and repair	4,668	812	17.4
Production, transportation, material-moving occupations	**16,802**	**2,968**	**17.7**
Production	8,601	1,370	15.9
Transportation and material moving	8,202	1,599	19.5

Source: Bureau of Labor Statistics, Current Population Survey, Internet site http://www.bls.gov/cps/tables.htm#empstat; calculations by New Strategist

More than 2 Million Earn Minimum Wage or Less

Most of those who earn minimum wage are food service workers.

Among the nation's 75 million workers who are paid hourly rates, just over 2 million (3.0 percent) earn the minimum wage or less, according to the Bureau of Labor Statistics. Of minimum-wage workers, half are under age 25.

Women are more than twice as likely as men to earn minimum wage or less, and they account for 67 percent of the nation's minimum-wage workers. Part-time workers also dominate the minimum-wage labor force, accounting for the 61 percent majority. Not surprisingly, the least educated also dominate the ranks of the lowest paid. Workers with a high-school diploma or less education account for 58 percent of the total. Interestingly, workers with an associate's degree are slightly less likely to be paid minimum wage or less (1.5 percent) than workers with a bachelor's degree (1.6 percent).

By occupation, 53 percent of minimum-wage workers are in food-service occupations. Eighteen percent of those with food-service jobs are paid minimum wage or less.

■ Minimum wage is most common in the South, where 4 percent of workers earn minimum wage or less.

Women dominate the minimum-wage workforce

(percent distribution of workers who make minimum wage or less, by sex, 2008)

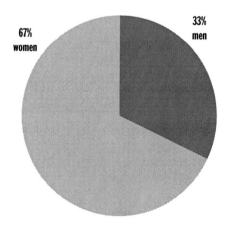

67%
women

33%
men

Table 6.22 Workers Earning Minimum Wage by Selected Characteristics, 2008

(number and percent distribution of employed wage and salary workers paid hourly rates at or below minimum wage, by selected characteristics, 2008; numbers in thousands)

	total paid hourly rates	paid at or below minimum wage		
		number	percent of total	percent distribution
TOTAL AGED 16 OR OLDER	75,305	2,226	3.0%	100.0%
Aged 16 to 24	15,680	1,122	7.2	50.4
Aged 25 or older	59,626	1,104	1.9	49.6
Sex				
Men	37,334	728	1.9	32.7
Women	37,972	1,498	3.9	67.3
Race and Hispanic origin				
Asian	2,844	69	2.4	3.1
Black	9,866	308	3.1	13.8
Hispanic	13,070	324	2.5	14.6
White	60,464	1,783	2.9	80.1
Work status				
Full-time workers	56,837	873	1.5	39.2
Part-time workers	18,334	1,353	7.4	60.8
Region				
Northeast	13,303	318	2.4	14.3
Midwest	18,567	522	2.8	23.5
South	25,942	1,092	4.2	49.1
West	17,764	292	1.6	13.1
Education				
Not a high school graduate	11,253	578	5.1	26.0
High school graduate, no college	27,163	709	2.6	31.9
Some college	17,267	634	3.7	28.5
Associate's degree	8,001	119	1.5	5.3
Bachelor's degree or more	11,622	187	1.6	8.4
Occupation				
Management, business, and financial occupations	4,118	30	0.7	1.3
Professional and related occupations	10,656	84	0.8	3.8
Service occupations	17,261	1,541	8.9	69.2
Health care support	2,564	57	2.2	2.6
Protective service	1,895	46	2.4	2.1
Food preparation and serving related	6,649	1,170	17.6	52.6
Building and grounds cleaning and maintenance	3,627	106	2.9	4.8
Personal care and service	2,526	162	6.4	7.3
Sales and related occupations	7,713	224	2.9	10.1
Office and administrative support occupations	12,850	138	1.1	6.2
Farming, fishing, and forestry occupations	636	13	2.0	0.6
Construction and extraction occupations	5,388	29	0.5	1.3
Installation, maintenance, and repair occupations	3,410	10	0.3	0.4
Production occupations	7,191	44	0.6	2.0
Transportation and material-moving occupations	6,082	113	1.9	5.1

Source: Bureau of Labor Statistics, Characteristics of Minimum Wage Workers, 2008, Internet site http://www.bls.gov/cps/ minwage2008tbls.htm; calculations by New Strategist

Fifteen Million Workers Have Alternative Jobs

Men are more likely than women to choose an alternative work arrangement.

Eleven percent of the nation's workers have nontraditional work arrangements. According to the Bureau of Labor Statistics, nontraditional workers are independent contractors, on-call workers (such as substitute teachers), workers for temporary-help agencies, or workers provided by contract firms (such as lawn service companies). They are considered alternative because they are not employees of the organization for which they perform their services, nor do they necessarily work standard schedules.

Men are more likely than women to choose an alternative work arrangement. Twelve percent of employed men and 9 percent of employed women have an alternative work arrangement. Whites are slightly more likely than Asians, blacks, or Hispanics to be alternative workers. Sixteen percent of part-time workers are in an alternative work arrangement compared with a smaller 9 percent of full-time workers. Most alternative workers are independent contractors—freelancers, consultants, and others who obtain customers on their own for whom they provide a product or service.

■ If health insurance were more affordable, many more workers would opt to be independent contractors.

The percentage of workers with alternative work arrangements rises with age

(percent distribution of workers with alternative work arrangements, by age, 2005)

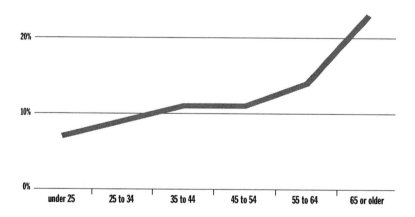

Table 6.23 Workers in Alternative Work Arrangements, 2005

(number and percent distribution of employed workers aged 16 or older by age, sex, race, Hispanic origin, work status, and work arrangement, 2005; numbers in thousands)

	total	alternative workers				
		total	independent contractors	on-call workers	temporary-help agency workers	workers provided by contract firms
Total employed	**138,952**	**14,826**	**10,342**	**2,454**	**1,217**	**813**
Under age 25	18,624	1,262	445	488	235	94
Aged 25 to 34	30,103	2,622	1,520	535	362	205
Aged 35 to 44	34,481	3,774	2,754	571	253	196
Aged 45 to 54	32,947	3,602	2,799	417	200	186
Aged 55 to 64	17,980	2,459	1,943	267	135	114
Aged 65 or older	4,817	1,107	881	175	33	18
Sex						
Men	73,946	9,072	6,696	1,241	574	561
Women	65,006	5,754	3,647	1,212	643	252
Race and Hispanic origin						
Asian	6,083	540	370	64	63	43
Black	14,688	1,192	583	212	276	121
Hispanic	18,062	1,724	951	385	255	133
White	115,043	12,743	9,169	2,097	840	637
Work status						
Full-time worker	113,798	10,776	7,732	1,370	979	695
Part-time worker	25,154	4,052	2,611	1,084	238	119
PERCENT DISTRIBUTION BY WORK ARRANGEMENT						
Total employed	**100.0%**	**10.7%**	**7.4%**	**1.8%**	**0.9%**	**0.6%**
Under age 25	100.0	6.8	2.4	2.6	1.3	0.5
Aged 25 to 34	100.0	8.7	5.0	1.8	1.2	0.7
Aged 35 to 44	100.0	10.9	8.0	1.7	0.7	0.6
Aged 45 to 54	100.0	10.9	8.5	1.3	0.6	0.6
Aged 55 to 64	100.0	13.7	10.8	1.5	0.8	0.6
Aged 65 or older	100.0	23.0	18.3	3.6	0.7	0.4
Sex						
Men	100.0	12.3	9.1	1.7	0.8	0.8
Women	100.0	8.9	5.6	1.9	1.0	0.4
Race and Hispanic origin						
Asian	100.0	8.9	6.1	1.1	1.0	0.7
Black	100.0	8.1	4.0	1.4	1.9	0.8
Hispanic	100.0	9.5	5.3	2.1	1.4	0.7
White	100.0	11.1	8.0	1.8	0.7	0.6
Work status						
Full-time worker	100.0	9.5	6.8	1.2	0.9	0.6
Part-time worker	100.0	16.1	10.4	4.3	0.9	0.5

Note: Numbers may not add to total because the total includes day laborers, an alternative arrangement not shown separately, and a small number of workers who were both on call and provided by contract firms. Independent contractors are self-employed (except incorporated) or wage and salary workers who obtain customers on their own to provide a product or service. On-call workers are in a pool of workers who are only called to work as needed, such as substitute teachers and construction workers supplied by a union hiring hall. Temporary help agency workers are those paid by a temporary help agency. Workers provided by contract firms are those employed by companies providing employees or their services to others under contract, such as security, landscaping, and computer programming.
Source: Bureau of Labor Statistics, Contingent and Alternative Employment Arrangements, Internet site http://www.bls.gov/news.release/conemp.toc.htm; calculations by New Strategist

Millions Work at Home

College graduates are most likely to report working at home.

The Bureau of Labor Statistics' American Time Use Survey reveals just how many Americans work at home. Among the 108 million people who worked on the survey's diary day, 20 percent reported working at least part of their day at home. Those working at home logged an average of 2.82 work hours at home.

Interestingly, there is not much variation in the percentage of workers who work at home by full- or part-time status or by sex. Nineteen percent of full-time workers say they worked at home on diary day, as did 23 percent of part-time workers. Twenty percent of both men and women reported working at home. There are substantial differences by education, however. Just over one-third (34 percent) of college graduates worked at home on diary day versus only 13 percent of those who went no further than high school. Not surprisingly, the self-employed are far more likely to work at home (54 percent) than wage and salary workers (16 percent).

■ The percentage of people who work at home may rise as employers attempt to cut overhead during the economic contraction.

More than one-third of college graduates work at home on an average workday

(percent of workers aged 25 or older who reported working at home on diary day, by educational attainment, 2007)

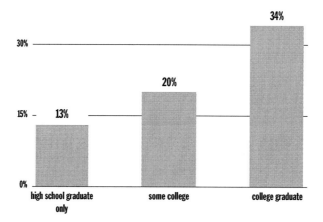

Table 6.24 People Who Work at Home, 2007

(total number of employed workers aged 15 or older, number and percent who worked on diary day and average hours of work, number and percent who worked at home on diary day and average number of hours worked at home, by selected characteristics, 2007)

		total who worked on diary day			total who worked at home on diary day		
	total employed	number	percent of employed	hours of work	number	percent of those working on diary day	hours of work
TOTAL WORKERS	**155,502**	**108,042**	**69.5%**	**7.57**	**21,465**	**19.9%**	**2.82**
Full-time	121,444	89,049	73.3	8.05	17,131	19.2	2.92
Part-time	34,058	18,993	55.8	5.36	4,334	22.8	2.40
Sex of worker							
Men	83,012	59,279	71.4	7.89	11,782	19.9	2.83
Women	72,490	48,763	67.3	7.20	9,683	19.9	2.80
Educational attainment, aged 25 or older							
Not a high school graduate	11,503	8,073	70.2	7.88	500	6.2	–
High school graduate only	38,947	26,457	67.9	7.87	3,398	12.8	2.91
Some college	34,697	23,596	68.0	7.67	4,660	19.7	2.78
Bachelor's degree or more	45,418	33,834	74.5	7.47	11,670	34.5	2.77
Class of worker							
Wage and salary	144,264	99,246	68.8	7.51	15,854	16.0	2.55
Self-employed	11,137	7,347	66.0	6.68	4,003	54.5	3.98

Note: Time spent working excludes travel time related to work. Working at home includes any time the respondent reported doing activities that were identified as part of one's job, and is not restricted to persons whose usual workplace is their home. "–" means sample too small to make a reliable estimate.
Source: Bureau of Labor Statistics, American Time Use Survey, Internet site http://www.bls.gov/news.release/atus.toc.htm; calculations by New Strategist

Most Workers Drive to Work Alone

Few commuters use mass transit to get to work.

Despite the efforts of many to encourage carpooling and the use of public transportation for the commute to work, the great majority of workers drive to work alone. In 2007, fully 78 percent of workers aged 16 or older drove alone. Only 9 percent carpooled, while just 5 percent used mass transit. Three percent of workers walk to work, and 3 percent work exclusively at home.

While horror stories about long commutes abound, in fact, the median commuting time to work was just 22 minutes in 2007. Only 5 percent of workers spend an hour or more getting to work. Most commutes are not overly time consuming because two-thirds of workers live less than 20 miles from their workplace. Only 10 percent live 30 or more miles from the job.

The most popular commuting time is between 6:00 and 7:00 AM, when 17 percent of workers leave for work. The 53 percent majority departs for work between 6:00 and 8:30 in the morning.

■ Although rising gasoline prices might encourage more workers to use mass transit, cars will continue to dominate the commute to work because many Americans do not have public transportation in their area.

For most, the commute is short

(percent distribution of workers by travel time from home to work, 2007)

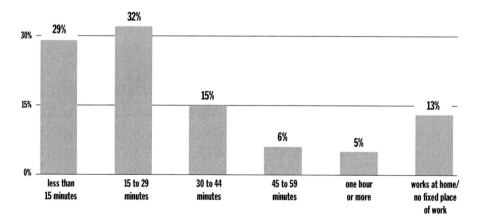

Table 6.25 Journey to Work, 2007

(number and percent distribution of workers aged 16 or older by principal means of transportation to work last week, travel time from home to work, distance from home to work, and departure time to work, 2007; numbers in thousands)

	number	percent distribution
TOTAL WORKERS	125,477	100.0%
Principal means of transportation to work		
Drives self	98,359	78.4
Carpool	11,607	9.3
Mass transportation	5,662	4.5
Taxicab	150	0.1
Bicycle or motorcycle	997	0.8
Walks only	3,300	2.6
Other means	1,058	0.8
Works at home	4,346	3.5
Travel time from home to work		
Less than 15 minutes	36,773	29.3
15 to 29 minutes	40,252	32.1
30 to 44 minutes	18,888	15.1
45 to 59 minutes	7,194	5.7
1 hour or more	6,254	5.0
Works at home	4,346	3.5
No fixed place of work	11,771	9.4
Median travel time (minutes)	22	–
Distance from home to work		
Less than 1 mile	4,229	3.4
1 to 4 miles	22,344	17.8
5 to 9 miles	24,136	19.2
10 to 19 miles	32,030	25.5
20 to 29 miles	14,398	11.5
30 to 49 miles	9,550	7.6
50 miles or more	2,673	2.1
Works at home	4,346	3.5
No fixed place of work	11,771	9.4
Median distance (miles)	11	–
Departure time to work		
Midnight to 2:59 AM	1,604	1.3
3:00 AM TO 5:59 AM	13,064	10.4
6:00 AM TO 6:59 AM	21,594	17.2
7:00 AM TO 7:29 AM	17,229	13.7
7:30 AM TO 7:59 AM	14,635	11.7
8:00 AM TO 8:29 AM	13,369	10.7
8:30 AM TO 8:59 AM	5,992	4.8
9:00 AM TO 9:59 AM	6,886	5.5
10:00 AM to 3:59 PM	11,121	8.9
4:00 PM to midnight	6,875	5.5
Not reported	8,764	7.0

Note: Departure time numbers may not add to total because work at home is not included; "–" means not applicable.
Source: Bureau of the Census, American Housing Survey for the United States: 2007, Internet site http://www.census.gov/hhes/www/ahs.html; calculations by New Strategist

Many Workers Lack Benefits

Service workers are less likely than managers or professionals to have access to most employee benefits.

Some workers are far more likely than others to have access to important health insurance and retirement benefits. Among management and professional workers, fully 87 percent have access to medical care benefits at work compared with only 52 percent of service workers, according to the Bureau of Labor Statistics' Employee Benefits Survey. Among workers with access to medical benefits, most must contribute towards coverage. The average contribution for employees with family coverage is $330 per month.

The 66 percent majority of workers had access to a retirement plan at work in 2008, but the proportion is 81 percent among management and professional workers and just 44 percent among service workers. Less than half of workers, regardless of occupation, have access to a defined benefit retirement plan—which guarantees a certain level of income in retirement.

The percentage of workers with access to a broad array of other benefits is much greater among management and professional workers than among service workers. Only 30 percent of service workers can take paid personal leave, for example, compared with 58 percent of management and professional workers.

■ The lack of access to health insurance at work is one of the barriers to universal health insurance coverage.

Most management and professional workers have access to health insurance coverage through their employer

(percent of civilian workers with access to health insurance coverage through their employer, by occupation, 2008)

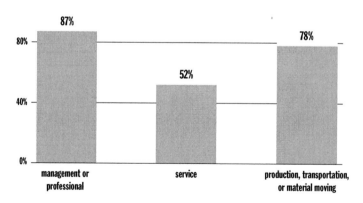

Table 6.26 Employee Benefits by Occupation, 2008

(employed civilian workers with access to selected employee benefits, by selected occupation, 2008; in percent unless otherwise noted)

	total workers	management, professional	service	production, transportation, material moving
Access to retirement benefits	**66%**	**81%**	**44%**	**66%**
Defined benefit	31	46	19	29
Defined contribution	52	59	32	55
Access to medical care benefits	74	87	52	78
Access to dental care benefits	48	60	32	49
Access to vision care benefits	30	38	22	30
Access to prescription drug coverage	71	84	50	75
Employee required to contribute for single coverage medical plan	74	73	76	73
Average flat monthly employee contribution for participants	$85.35	$83.16	$89.27	$80.60
Employee required to contribute for family coverage medical plan	87%	89%	89%	83%
Average flat monthly employee contribution for participants	$330.40	$336.02	$336.64	$289.04
Access to paid holidays	76%	80%	56%	85%
Access to paid vacation days	75	74	63	82
Access to paid personal leave	41	58	30	33
Access to paid funeral leave	71	86	54	70
Access to paid jury duty leave	74	89	60	72
Access to paid military leave	52	69	40	47
Accesss to paid family leave	9	15	7	5
Access to life insurance	62	77	42	67
Access to short-term disability benefits	37	43	23	47
Access to long-term disability benefits	32	51	15	27
Employer provides assistance for child care	16	26	11	10
Employer provides adoption assistance	11	17	4	9
Access to long-term care insurance	15	24	7	10
Employer provides a flexible work schedule	4	9	2	1
Access to subsidized commuting	6	10	3	3
Access to job-related travel accident insurance	21	30	8	18
Access to education assistance				
Work related	52	72	37	46
Non–work related	16	24	9	14
Access to wellness programs	29	46	19	24
Access to fitness centers	15	25	11	10
Access to employee assistance programs	47	64	33	42
Access to pretax benefits				
Health savings account	10	15	5	7
Dependent care reimbursement account	34	53	20	26
Health care reimbursement account	37	57	24	27
Access to any nonproduction bonus	44	47	33	48

Source: Bureau of Labor Statistics, Employee Benefits Survey, Internet site http://www.bls.gov/ncs/ebs/benefits/2008/ ownership_civilian.htm

Number of Older Workers Will Expand Rapidly

Early retirement will become far less common.

As the baby-boom generation enters its late sixties during the next decade, the number of workers aged 65 or older will surge. While the labor force as a whole is projected to increase 8 percent between 2006 and 2016, the number of working men aged 65 or older will grow by 78 percent. The number of working women in the age group will expand by an even larger 91 percent. In contrast, the number of workers aged 35 to 44 will decline.

The Bureau of Labor Statistics projects an increase in the labor force participation rate of men aged 65 or older of nearly 7 percentage points to 27.1 percent. The agency foresees declines in labor force participation among most men under age 55.

Women's labor force participation should also climb in the older age groups between 2006 and 2016. Among women aged 55 or older, labor force participation is projected to rise by at least 5 percentage points.

■ The labor force participation rates of older men and women are likely to rise even more than forecast as baby boomers cope with diminished retirement savings thanks to the economic contraction.

Big gains for workers aged 65 or older

(percent change in number of total workers and workers aged 65 or older, by sex, 2006–16)

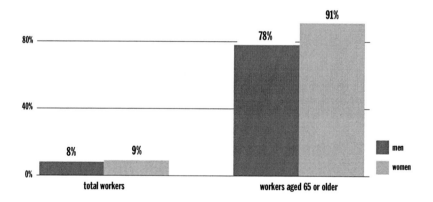

Table 6.27 Projections of the Labor Force by Sex and Age, 2006 and 2016

(number and percent of people aged 16 or older in the civilian labor force by sex and age, 2006 and 2016; percent change in number and percentage point change in participation rate, 2006–16; numbers in thousands)

	number			participation rate		
	2006	2016	percent change 2006–16	2006	2016	percentage point change 2006–16
TOTAL LABOR FORCE	**151,428**	**164,232**	**8.5%**	**66.2%**	**65.5%**	**−0.7**
Total men in labor force	**81,255**	**87,781**	**8.0**	**73.5**	**72.3**	**−1.2**
Aged 16 to 19	3,693	2,923	−20.9	43.7	36.8	−6.9
Aged 20 to 24	8,116	7,992	−1.5	79.6	76.4	−3.2
Aged 25 to 34	17,944	20,913	16.5	91.7	95.7	4.0
Aged 35 to 44	19,407	18,373	−5.3	92.1	91.7	−0.4
Aged 45 to 54	18,489	18,205	−1.5	88.1	86.6	−1.5
Aged 55 to 64	10,509	13,865	31.9	69.6	70.1	0.5
Aged 65 or older	3,096	5,511	78.0	20.3	27.1	6.8
Total women in labor force	**70,173**	**76,450**	**8.9**	**59.4**	**59.2**	**−0.2**
Aged 16 to 19	3,588	2,974	−17.1	43.7	38.3	−5.4
Aged 20 to 24	6,997	6,963	−0.5	69.5	67.2	−2.3
Aged 25 to 34	14,628	16,376	11.9	74.4	75.0	0.6
Aged 35 to 44	16,441	15,281	−7.1	75.9	75.1	−0.8
Aged 45 to 54	16,656	16,877	1.3	76.0	77.8	1.8
Aged 55 to 64	9,475	13,423	41.7	58.2	63.5	5.3
Aged 65 or older	2,388	4,556	90.8	11.7	17.5	5.8

Source: Bureau of Labor Statistics, Labor Force Projections to 2016: More Workers in Their Golden Years, Monthly Labor Review, November 2007, Internet site http://www.bls.gov/opub/mlr/2007/11/contents.htm; calculations by New Strategist

Number of Asian and Hispanic Workers Will Grow the Fastest

Non-Hispanic whites will decline as a share of workers.

Between 2006 and 2016, the labor force will grow by 8 percent—to 164 million, according to projections by the Bureau of Labor Statistics. The number of minority workers will grow much faster than the number of non-Hispanic whites. The number of Asian and Hispanic workers will expand by 30 percent during those years, while the black labor force will grow by 16 percent. The non-Hispanic white labor force is projected to increase by just 1 percent.

The non-Hispanic white share of the labor force will fall from 69 to 65 percent between 2006 and 2016. In contrast, the Hispanic share will climb from 14 to 16 percent during those years. The black share of the labor force will climb from 11 to 12 percent, and the Asian share will increase from 4 to 5 percent.

■ The ability to manage a diverse workforce will become increasingly important as the minority share of American workers grows.

The labor force is becoming increasingly diverse

(percent distribution of the labor force by race and Hispanic origin, 2006 and 2016)

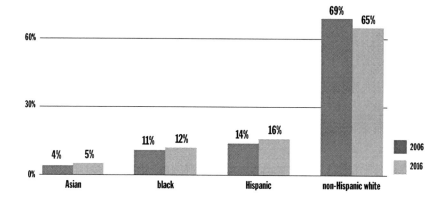

Table 6.28   Labor Force Participation by Race and Hispanic Origin, 2006 and 2016

(number and percent of people aged 16 or older in the civilian labor force by sex, race, and Hispanic origin, 2006 and 2016; percent change in number and percentage point change in rate 2006–16; numbers in thousands)

	number			participation rate		
	2006	2016	percent change 2006–16	2006	2016	percentage point change 2006–16
TOTAL LABOR FORCE	**151,428**	**164,232**	**8.5%**	**66.2%**	**65.5%**	**–0.7**
Asian	6,727	8,741	29.9	65.9	65.9	0.0
Black	17,314	20,121	16.2	63.8	64.9	1.1
Hispanic	20,694	26,889	29.9	68.6	68.6	0.0
Non-Hispanic white	104,629	106,133	1.4	65.9	65.0	–0.9
Men in labor force	**81,255**	**87,781**	**8.0**	**73.5**	**72.3**	**–1.2**
Asian	3,621	4,600	27.0	75.0	74.1	–0.9
Black	8,128	9,420	15.9	66.7	67.1	0.4
Hispanic	12,488	15,802	26.5	80.4	79.0	–1.4
Non-Hispanic white	55,953	56,791	1.5	73.0	71.6	–1.4
Women in labor force	**70,173**	**76,450**	**8.9**	**59.4**	**59.2**	**–0.2**
Asian	3,106	4,141	33.3	57.6	58.7	1.1
Black	9,186	10,701	16.5	61.5	63.1	1.6
Hispanic	8,206	11,087	35.1	56.1	57.8	1.7
Non-Hispanic white	48,676	49,342	1.4	59.3	58.8	–0.5

Source: Bureau of Labor Statistics, Labor Force Projections to 2016: More Workers in Their Golden Years, Monthly Labor Review, November 2007, Internet site http://www.bls.gov/opub/mlr/2007/11/contents.htm; calculations by New Strategist

Table 6.29 Distribution of the Labor Force by Race and Hispanic Origin, 2006 and 2016

(number and percent distribution of people aged 16 or older in the civilian labor force by sex, race, and Hispanic origin, 2006 and 2016; numbers in thousands)

	2006		2016	
	number	percent distribution	number	percent distribution
TOTAL LABOR FORCE	**151,428**	**100.0%**	**164,232**	**100.0%**
Asian	6,727	4.4	8,741	5.3
Black	17,314	11.4	20,121	12.3
Hispanic	20,694	13.7	26,889	16.4
Non-Hispanic white	104,629	69.1	106,133	64.6
Men in labor force	**81,255**	**100.0**	**87,781**	**100.0**
Asian	3,621	4.5	4,600	5.2
Black	8,128	10.0	9,420	10.7
Hispanic	12,488	15.4	15,802	18.0
Non-Hispanic white	55,953	68.9	56,791	64.7
Women in labor force	**70,173**	**100.0**	**76,450**	**100.0**
Asian	3,106	4.4	4,141	5.4
Black	9,186	13.1	10,701	14.0
Hispanic	8,206	11.7	11,087	14.5
Non-Hispanic white	48,676	69.4	49,342	64.5

Source: Bureau of Labor Statistics, Labor Force Projections to 2016: More Workers in Their Golden Years, Monthly Labor Review, November 2007, Internet site http://www.bls.gov/opub/mlr/2007/11/contents.htm; calculations by New Strategist

Biggest Gains Forecast for Registered Nurses

Many health care jobs are projected to be among the fastest growing.

Overall employment in the United States was projected to grow by 10 percent between 2006 and 2016 according to the Bureau of Labor Statistics. The federal government's official projections of employment were released in 2007—just as the housing bubble burst and before the stock market collapse of 2008. Many of the trends forecast at that time have evaporated along with jobs. Nevertheless, a look at the projected winners and losers can shed some light on where growth might resume when the downturn ends.

The Bureau of Labor Statistics projected the number of professional jobs to grow by 17 percent between 2006 and 2016. This gain is much greater than the 6 percent increase forecast for management occupations and contrasts with the decline projected for production jobs. The bureau also forecast a 9 percent gain in construction jobs by 2016, an increase that looks far too optimistic given the downturn in the housing market.

Health care occupations appear repeatedly in the list of occupations projected to grow the fastest between 2006 and 2016. This trend is likely to continue despite the ailing economy. But the recession has likely scuttled the forecast that retail salespersons will rank second only to registered nurses in the number of job openings in the coming decade. Other occupations with dubious growth forecasts are executive secretaries and carpenters.

■ Many occupations involved in processing paper—such as prepress and bindery workers—are projected to be among the biggest losers.

Health care and computer jobs are projected to grow the fastest

(percent change in employment in the five occupations projected to grow the fastest, 2006 to 2016)

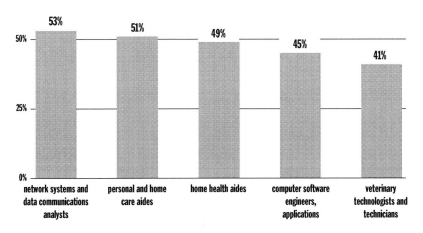

Table 6.30 Employment by Major Occupational Group, 2006 and 2016

(number and percent distribution of people aged 16 or older employed by major occupational group, 2006 and 2016; percent change, 2006–16; numbers in thousands)

	2006 number	2006 percent distribution	2016 number	2016 percent distribution	percent change 2006–16
Total employed	**150,620**	**100.0%**	**166,220**	**100.0%**	**10.4%**
Management occupations	8,789	5.8	9,322	5.6	6.1
Business and financial operations occupations	6,608	4.4	7,671	4.6	16.1
Professional and related occupations	29,819	19.8	34,790	20.9	16.7
Computer and mathematical	3,313	2.2	4,135	2.5	24.8
Architecture and engineering	2,583	1.7	2,852	1.7	10.4
Life, physical, and social science	1,407	0.9	1,610	1.0	14.4
Community and social services	2,386	1.6	2,927	1.8	22.7
Legal	1,222	0.8	1,367	0.8	11.9
Education, training, and library	9,034	6.0	10,298	6.2	14.0
Art, design, entertainment, sports, and media	2,677	1.8	2,982	1.8	11.4
Health care practitioner and technical occupations	7,198	4.8	8,620	5.2	19.8
Service occupations	28,950	19.2	33,780	20.3	16.7
Health care support	3,724	2.5	4,721	2.8	26.8
Protective service	3,163	2.1	3,616	2.2	14.3
Food preparation and serving related	11,352	7.5	12,789	7.7	12.7
Building and grounds cleaning and maintenance	5,745	3.8	6,595	4.0	14.8
Personal care and service	4,966	3.3	6,060	3.6	22.0
Sales and related occupations	15,985	10.6	17,203	10.3	7.6
Office and administrative support occupations	24,344	16.2	26,089	15.7	7.2
Farming, fishing, and forestry occupations	1,039	0.7	1,010	0.6	-2.8
Construction and extraction occupations	8,295	5.5	9,079	5.5	9.5
Installation, maintenance, and repair occupations	5,883	3.9	6,433	3.9	9.3
Production occupations	10,675	7.1	10,147	6.1	-4.9
Transportation and material-moving occupations	10,233	6.8	10,695	6.4	4.5

Source: Bureau of Labor Statistics, Economic and Employment Projections, Internet site http://www.bls.gov/news.release/ ecopro.toc.htm; calculations by New Strategist

Table 6.31 Fastest-Growing Occupations, 2006 to 2016

(number of people aged 16 or older employed in the 30 fastest-growing occupations, 2006 to 2016; numerical and percent change, 2006–16; numbers in thousands)

	2006	2016	change, 2006–16 number	percent
Network systems and data communications analysts	262	402	140	53.4%
Personal and home care aides	767	1,156	389	50.7
Home health aides	787	1,171	384	48.8
Computer software engineers, applications	507	733	226	44.6
Veterinary technologists and technicians	71	100	29	40.8
Personal financial advisors	176	248	72	40.9
Makeup artists, theatrical and performance	2	3	1	50.0
Medical assistants	417	565	148	35.5
Veterinarians	62	84	22	35.5
Substance abuse and behavioral disorder counselors	83	112	29	34.9
Skin care specialists	38	51	13	34.2
Financial analysts	221	295	75	33.9
Social and human service assistants	339	453	114	33.6
Gaming surveillance officers and gaming investigators	9	12	3	33.3
Physical therapist assistants	60	80	20	33.3
Pharmacy assistants	285	376	91	31.9
Forensic science technicians	13	17	4	30.8
Dental hygienists	167	217	50	29.9
Mental health counselors	100	130	30	30.0
Mental health and substance abuse social workers	122	159	37	30.3
Marriage and family therapists	25	32	7	28.0
Dental assistants	280	362	82	29.3
Computer systems analysts	504	650	146	29.0
Database administrators	119	154	34	28.6
Computer software engineers, systems software	350	449	99	28.3
Gaming and sports bookwriters and runners	18	24	5	27.8
Environmental science and protection technicians, including health	36	47	10	27.8
Manicurists and pedicurists	78	100	22	28.2
Physical therapists	173	220	47	27.2
Physician assistants	66	83	18	27.3

Source: Bureau of Labor Statistics, Economic and Employment Projections, Internet site http://www.bls.gov/news.release/ecopro.toc.htm; calculations by New Strategist

Table 6.32 Occupations with the Largest Job Growth, 2006 to 2016

(number of people aged 16 or older employed in the 30 occupations with the largest projected job growth, 2006 to 2016; numerical and percent change, 2006–16; numbers in thousands)

	2006	2016	change, 2006–16 number	change, 2006–16 percent
Registered nurses	2,505	3,092	587	23.4%
Retail salespersons	4,477	5,034	557	12.4
Customer service representatives	2,202	2,747	545	24.8
Food preparation and serving workers, including fast food	2,503	2,955	452	18.1
Office clerks, general	3,200	3,604	404	12.6
Personal and home care aides	767	1,156	389	50.7
Home health aides	787	1,171	384	48.8
Postsecondary teachers	1,672	2,054	382	22.8
Janitors and cleaners (except housekeeping)	2,387	2,732	345	14.5
Nursing aides, orderlies, and attendants	1,447	1,711	264	18.2
Bookkeeping, accounting, and auditing clerks	2,114	2,377	264	12.5
Waiters and waitresses	2,361	2,615	255	10.8
Child care workers	1,388	1,636	248	17.9
Executive secretaries and administrative assistants	1,618	1,857	239	14.8
Computer software engineers, applications	507	733	226	44.6
Accountants and auditors	1,274	1,500	226	17.7
Landscaping and groundskeeping workers	1,220	1,441	221	18.1
Elementary school teachers, except special education	1,540	1,749	209	13.6
Receptionists and information clerks	1,173	1,375	202	17.2
Truck drivers, heavy and tractor-trailer	1,860	2,053	193	10.4
Maids and housekeeping cleaners	1,470	1,656	186	12.7
Security guards	1,040	1,216	175	16.8
Carpenters	1,462	1,612	150	10.3
Management analysts	678	827	149	22.0
Medical assistants	417	565	148	35.5
Computer systems analysts	504	650	146	29.0
Maintenance and repair workers, general	1,391	1,531	140	10.1
Network systems and data communications analysts	262	402	140	53.4
Food preparation workers	902	1,040	138	15.3
Teacher assistants	1,312	1,449	137	10.4

Source: Bureau of Labor Statistics, Economic and Employment Projections, Internet site http://www.bls.gov/news.release/ecopro.toc.htm; calculations by New Strategist

Table 6.33 Occupations with the Largest Job Decline, 2006 to 2016

(number of people aged 16 or older employed in the 30 occupations with the largest projected employment decline, 2006 to 2016; numerical and percent change, 2006–16; numbers in thousands)

	2006	2016	change, 2006–16 number	change, 2006–16 percent
Stock clerks and order fillers	1,705	1,574	–131	–7.7%
Cashiers, except gaming	3,500	3,382	–118	–3.4
Packers and packagers, hand	834	730	–104	–12.5
File clerks	234	137	–97	–41.5
Farmers and ranchers	1,058	969	–90	–8.5
Order clerks	271	205	–66	–24.4
Sewing machine operators	233	170	–63	–27.0
Electrical and electronic equipment assemblers	213	156	–57	–26.8
Cutting, punching, and press machine workers, metal and plastic	272	231	–40	–14.7
Telemarketers	395	356	–39	–9.9
Inspectors, testers, sorters, samplers, and weighers	491	457	–35	–7.1
First-line supervisors of production and operating workers	699	665	–34	–4.9
Computer operators	130	98	–32	–24.6
Photographic processing machine operators	49	25	–25	–51.0
Driver/sales workers	445	421	–24	–5.4
Machine feeders and offbearers	148	125	–22	–14.9
Packaging and filling machine operators and tenders	386	365	–21	–5.4
Word processors and typists	179	158	–21	–11.7
Paper goods machine setters, operators, and tenders	113	93	–21	–18.6
Farmworkers and laborers, crop, nursery, and greenhouse	603	583	–20	–3.3
Molding, coremaking, casting machine workers, metal and plastic	157	137	–20	–12.7
Computer programmers	435	417	–18	–4.1
Mail clerks and mail machine operators, except postal	152	134	–18	–11.8
Postal service mail sorters, processors, and processing machine operators	198	181	–17	–8.6
Lathe and turning machine tool setters, operators, and tenders, metal and plastic	68	52	–16	–23.5
Prepress technicians and workers	71	56	–15	–21.1
Switchboard operators, including answering service	177	163	–15	–8.5
Data entry keyers	313	299	–15	–4.8
Bindery workers	65	51	–14	–21.5

Source: Bureau of Labor Statistics, Economic and Employment Projections, Internet site http://www.bls.gov/news.release/ecopro.toc.htm; calculations by New Strategist

Management, Scientific, and Technical Consulting Services Industry Projected to Grow the Fastest

The employment services industry ranks second in projected growth.

The number of jobs in the management, scientific, and technical consulting services industry will expand by 78 percent between 2006 and 2016, according to Bureau of Labor Statistics projections published in 2007—just as the housing bubble burst and before the collapse of the stock market. The bureau's forecasters were prescient in their prediction that jobs in employment services would grow rapidly. With unemployment rising sharply, the employment services industry should grow despite the downturn.

Overall, jobs in goods-producing industries are projected to decline by 3 percent between 2006 and 2016, while those in service-producing industries are projected to increase by 14 percent. In hindsight, these projections are overly optimistic, particularly the 10 percent increase forecast for employment in construction and the 14 percent increase in employment forecast for the financial services industry.

■ Some industries—such as health care and education—should see continued growth despite the downturn in the economy.

Goods-producing industries will see employment declines

(percent change in employment by industry group, 2006–16)

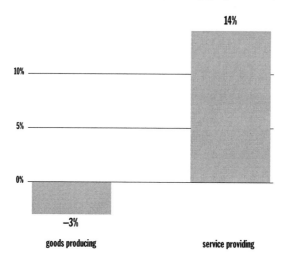

Table 6.34 Employment by Major Industry, 2006 and 2016

(number and percent distribution of people aged 16 or older employed by major industry, 2006 and 2016; percent change in number, 2006–16; numbers in thousands)

	2006		2016		
	number	percent distribution	number	percent distribution	percent change 2006–16
TOTAL EMPLOYED	**150,620**	**100.0%**	**166,220**	**100.0%**	**10.4%**
Nonfarm wage and salary	**136,912**	**90.9**	**151,962**	**91.4**	**11.0**
Goods producing	22,505	14.9	21,773	13.1	–3.3
Mining	619	0.4	608	0.4	–1.8
Construction	7,689	5.1	8,470	5.1	10.2
Manufacturing	14,197	9.4	12,695	7.6	–10.6
Service providing	114,407	76.0	130,190	78.3	13.8
Utilities	549	0.4	518	0.3	–5.6
Wholesale trade	5,898	3.9	6,326	3.8	7.3
Retail trade	15,319	10.2	16,006	9.6	4.5
Transportation and warehousing	4,466	3.0	4,962	3.0	11.1
Information	3,055	2.0	3,267	2.0	6.9
Financial activities	8,363	5.6	9,570	5.8	14.4
Professional and business services	17,552	11.7	21,644	13.0	23.3
Education	2,918	1.9	3,527	2.1	20.9
Health care and social assistance	14,920	9.9	18,954	11.4	27.0
Leisure and hospitality	13,143	8.7	15,017	9.0	14.3
Other services	6,235	4.1	7,077	4.3	13.5
Federal government	2,728	1.8	2,626	1.6	–3.7
State and local government	19,262	12.8	20,696	12.5	7.4
Agriculture	2,139	1.4	1,965	1.2	–8.1
Nonagricultural self-employed and unpaid family workers	9,772	6.5	10,462	6.3	7.1
Secondary wage and salary jobs in agriculture, forestry, fishing, or private households	178	0.1	185	0.1	3.9
Secondary jobs as self-employed or unpaid family workers	1,619	1.1	1,646	1.0	1.7

Source: Bureau of Labor Statistics, Economic and Employment Projections, Internet site http://www.bls.gov/news.release/ ecopro.toc.htm; calculations by New Strategist

Table 6.35 Industries with the Fastest Wage and Salary Employment Growth, 2006 to 2016

(number of people aged 16 or older employed in industries with the fastest wage and salary employment growth, 2006–16; numerical and percent change in employment, 2006–16; ranked by percent change; numbers in thousands)

	2006	2016	change, 2006–16	
			number	percent
Management, scientific, and technical consulting services	921	1,639	718	78.0%
Employment services	3,657	4,348	692	18.9
General medical and surgical hospitals, public and private	4,988	5,679	691	13.9
Elementary and secondary schools, public and private	8,346	8,983	638	7.6
Local government, excluding education and hospitals	5,594	6,206	612	10.9
Offices of physicians	2,154	2,687	534	24.8
Limited-service eating places	4,019	4,548	529	13.2
Colleges, universities, professional schools, public and private	3,434	3,933	499	14.5
Computer systems design and related services	1,278	1,768	489	38.3
Home health care services	867	1,348	481	55.5

Source: Bureau of Labor Statistics, Economic and Employment Projections, Internet site http://www.bls.gov/news.release/ecopro.toc.htm; calculations by New Strategist

Living Arrangement Trends

■ **Married couples are slipping as a share of households.**

Married couples account for only 50 percent of households, and couples with children under age 18 are just 23 percent of the total.

■ **Households headed by older adults are growing rapidly.**

Between 2000 and 2008, the number of households headed by 55-to-64-year-olds grew by 46 percent. In contrast, the number of households headed by 35-to-44-year-olds fell 6 percent.

■ **Sixty-one percent of households are home to only one or two people.**

Overall, only 2.56 people live in the average U.S. household.

■ **Only 60 percent of children live with their married biological parents.**

The figure ranges from a low of 29 percent among black children to a high of 76 percent among Asian children.

■ **Most husbands and wives are close in age and education.**

Seven percent of couples are of mixed race or Hispanic origin.

■ **Men and women in their fifties are most likely to have experienced divorce.**

Divorce is more likely for those who marry young.

Married Couples Account for Half of Households

Their dominance is eroding as other household types grow faster.

Between 2000 and 2008, the number of married couples increased only 5.5 percent, less than the 11.5 percent gain for all households. Consequently, the married couple share of households slipped from 52.8 to 50.0 percent. Married couples with children under age 18 grew even more slowly, up just 0.5 percent during those years. Married couples with children account for only 23 percent of the nation's households, well below the 28 percent share held by people who live alone.

The number of male-headed families is growing the fastest, up 27 percent between 2000 and 2008. The 5 million male-headed families account for a tiny 4 percent of the total, however. They are greatly outnumbered by the 14 million female-headed families.

Nonfamily households grew 19 percent between 2000 and 2008, with male-headed nonfamily households growing slightly faster than their female counterparts. This pattern will reverse as the baby-boom generation enters the older age groups and an increasing number of women become widowed and live alone.

■ Single-person households are already one of the most common household types. Their importance will grow as the population ages.

Number of married couples has grown more slowly than other household types

(percent change in number of households by type, 2000–08)

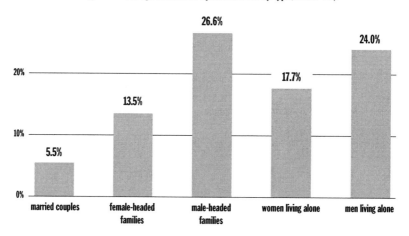

Table 7.1 Households by Type, 2000 and 2008

(number and percent distribution of households by household type, 2000 and 2008; percent change in number, 2000–08; numbers in thousands)

| | 2008 | | 2000 | | percent change |
	number	percent distribution	number	percent distribution	in number 2000–08
TOTAL HOUSEHOLDS	**116,783**	**100.0%**	**104,705**	**100.0%**	**11.5%**
Family households	**77,873**	**66.7**	**72,025**	**68.8**	**8.1**
Married couples	58,370	50.0	55,311	52.8	5.5
With own children under age 18	26,487	22.7	26,359	25.2	0.5
Female householders, no spouse present	14,404	12.3	12,687	12.1	13.5
With own children under age 18	9,725	8.3	8,727	8.3	11.4
Male householders, no spouse present	5,100	4.4	4,028	3.8	26.6
With own children under age 18	2,708	2.3	2,164	2.1	25.1
Nonfamily households	**38,910**	**33.3**	**32,680**	**31.2**	**19.1**
Female householders	21,038	18.0	18,039	17.2	16.6
Living alone	18,297	15.7	15,543	14.8	17.7
Male householders	17,872	15.3	14,641	14.0	22.1
Living alone	13,870	11.9	11,181	10.7	24.0

Source: Bureau of the Census, Current Population Survey Annual Social and Economic Supplement, Internet site http://www .census.gov/hhes/www/income/dinctabs.html; calculations by New Strategist

Number of Households Headed by 55-to-64-Year-Olds Growing Rapidly

The number of households headed by 35-to-44-year-olds fell between 2000 and 2008.

Between 2000 and 2008, the number of households headed by 55-to-64-year-olds grew 46.5 percent, four times as fast as the 11.5 percent gain for all households during those years. Behind the rapid growth was the aging of the baby-boom generation into its late fifties and early sixties.

The 35-to-44 age group was the only one to see its household numbers decline between 2000 and 2008. As the small generation X entered its late thirties and early forties, the number of house-holders aged 35 to 44 fell 6 percent. In contrast, the number of householders under age 25 rose by 12 percent as the large millennial generation entered its twenties.

■ The number of households headed by people aged 55 to 64 will continue to grow during the remainder of this decade.

Number of households headed by the youngest adults is growing

(percent change in number of households by age of householder, 2000–08)

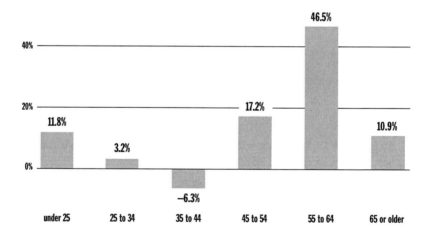

Table 7.2 Households by Age of Householder, 2000 and 2008

(number and percent distribution of households by age of householder, 2000 and 2008; percent change in number, 2000–08; numbers in thousands)

| | 2008 | | 2000 | | percent change |
	number	percent distribution	number	percent distribution	in number 2000–08
Total households	**116,783**	**100.0%**	**104,705**	**100.0%**	**11.5%**
Under age 25	6,554	5.6	5,860	5.6	11.8
Aged 25 to 34	19,225	16.5	18,627	17.8	3.2
Aged 35 to 44	22,448	19.2	23,955	22.9	-6.3
Aged 45 to 54	24,536	21.0	20,927	20.0	17.2
Aged 55 to 64	19,909	17.0	13,592	13.0	46.5
Aged 65 or older	24,113	20.6	21,745	20.8	10.9

Source: Bureau of the Census, Current Population Survey Annual Social and Economic Supplement, Internet site http://www .census.gov/hhes/www/income/dinctabs.html; calculations by New Strategist

Lifestyles Change with Age

The households of young adults are different from those of middle-aged and older Americans.

Married couples are far less common among the youngest and the oldest householders than they are among the middle aged. Only 19 percent of households headed by people under age 25 are comprised of married couples. Among the elderly, married couples head a 42 percent minority of households. In contrast, couples account for the 56 to 58 percent majority of households headed by people aged 35 to 64.

Female-headed families are most commonly found among the youngest householders, at 20 percent. They account for just 8 percent of households headed by people aged 55 or older. Women who live alone are most common among the oldest householders, at 34 percent of households. They are least common among 35-to-44-year-olds, at 7 percent. Men who live alone account for 10 to 13 percent of households regardless of age.

■ With the baby-boom generation now in middle age, household composition has stabilized. More change is in store, however, as boomers age.

Married couples head most households in the 35-to-64 age group

(percent of households headed by married couples, by age of householder, 2008)

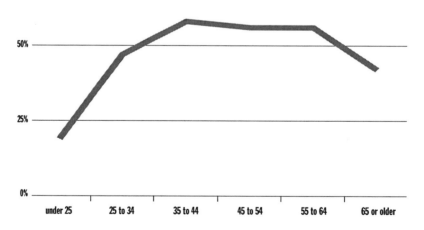

Table 7.3 Households by Household Type and Age of Householder, 2008

(number and percent distribution of households by household type and age of householder, 2008; numbers in thousands)

	total	under 25	25 to 34	35 to 44	45 to 54	55 to 64	65 or older
Total households	**116,783**	**6,554**	**19,225**	**22,448**	**24,536**	**19,909**	**24,113**
Married couples	58,370	1,224	8,994	12,989	13,842	11,144	10,178
Female family householders	14,404	1,318	3,064	3,551	3,043	1,562	1,866
Male family householders	5,100	817	1,196	1,061	1,065	513	449
Women living alone	18,297	805	1,569	1,479	2,713	3,434	8,297
Men living alone	13,870	844	2,362	2,321	2,866	2,561	2,917
Other nonfamily households	6,742	1,546	2,040	1,047	1,007	695	406

PERCENT DISTRIBUTION BY HOUSEHOLD TYPE

Total households	**100.0%**	**100.0%**	**100.0%**	**100.0%**	**100.0%**	**100.0%**	**100.0%**
Married couples	50.0	18.7	46.8	57.9	56.4	56.0	42.2
Female family householders	12.3	20.1	15.9	15.8	12.4	7.8	7.7
Male family householders	4.4	12.5	6.2	4.7	4.3	2.6	1.9
Women living alone	15.7	12.3	8.2	6.6	11.1	17.2	34.4
Men living alone	11.9	12.9	12.3	10.3	11.7	12.9	12.1
Other nonfamily households	5.8	23.6	10.6	4.7	4.1	3.5	1.7

PERCENT DISTRIBUTION BY AGE

Total households	**100.0%**	**5.6%**	**16.5%**	**19.2%**	**21.0%**	**17.0%**	**20.6%**
Married couples	100.0	2.1	15.4	22.3	23.7	19.1	17.4
Female family householders	100.0	9.2	21.3	24.7	21.1	10.8	13.0
Male family householders	100.0	16.0	23.5	20.8	20.9	10.1	8.8
Women living alone	100.0	4.4	8.6	8.1	14.8	18.8	45.3
Men living alone	100.0	6.1	17.0	16.7	20.7	18.5	21.0
Other nonfamily households	100.0	22.9	30.3	15.5	14.9	10.3	6.0

Source: Bureau of the Census, 2008 Current Population Survey Annual Social and Economic Supplement, Internet site http://pubdb3.census.gov/macro/032008/hhinc/new02_000.htm; calculations by New Strategist

Big Differences in Household Type by Race and Hispanic Origin

Married couples head 58 percent of Asian households, but only 30 percent of black households.

Although the Hispanic population is now larger than the black population, black households still outnumber Hispanic ones—15 million versus 13 million in 2008. But Hispanic married couples greatly outnumber black married couples—7 million to 4 million. There are nearly 3 million Asian married couples.

Among blacks, married couples outnumber female-headed families by only 243,000, with married couples accounting for 30 percent of black households and female-headed families for 28 percent. Among Hispanics, married couples account for 52 percent of households and female-headed families for a much smaller 19 percent. Female-headed families account for only 10 percent of Asian and 9 percent of non-Hispanic white households.

Hispanic women are much less likely to live alone than women from other racial and ethnic groups. Only 8 percent of Hispanic households are headed by women who live alone compared with 18 percent of black, 17 percent of non-Hispanic white, and 12 percent of Asian households.

■ Blacks have lower incomes than Asians and non-Hispanic whites in part because a much smaller proportion of their households are headed by married couples.

Married couples head most Asian, Hispanic, and non-Hispanic white households

(percent of households headed by married couples, by race and Hispanic origin, 2008)

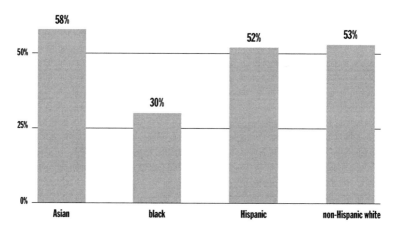

Table 7.4 Households by Household Type, Race, and Hispanic Origin of Householder, 2008

(number and percent distribution of households by household type, race, and Hispanic origin of householder, 2008; numbers in thousands)

	total	Asian	black	Hispanic	non-Hispanic white
Total households	**116,783**	**4,715**	**14,976**	**13,339**	**82,765**
Family households	77,873	3,451	9,503	10,394	53,902
Married couples	58,370	2,757	4,461	6,888	43,739
Female householders, no spouse present	14,404	452	4,218	2,522	7,171
Male householders, no spouse present	5,100	242	824	983	2,991
Nonfamily households	38,910	1,265	5,474	2,945	28,863
Female householders	21,038	662	3,064	1,291	15,844
Living alone	18,297	545	2,748	1,065	13,771
Male householders	17,872	602	2,410	1,654	13,019
Living alone	13,870	420	2,012	1,138	10,151

PERCENT DISTRIBUTION BY HOUSEHOLD TYPE

	total	Asian	black	Hispanic	non-Hispanic white
Total households	**100.0%**	**100.0%**	**100.0%**	**100.0%**	**100.0%**
Family households	66.7	73.2	63.5	77.9	65.1
Married couples	50.0	58.5	29.8	51.6	52.8
Female householders, no spouse present	12.3	9.6	28.2	18.9	8.7
Male householders, no spouse present	4.4	5.1	5.5	7.4	3.6
Nonfamily households	33.3	26.8	36.6	22.1	34.9
Female householders	18.0	14.0	20.5	9.7	19.1
Living alone	15.7	11.6	18.3	8.0	16.6
Male householders	15.3	12.8	16.1	12.4	15.7
Living alone	11.9	8.9	13.4	8.5	12.3

PERCENT DISTRIBUTION BY RACE AND HISPANIC ORIGIN

	total	Asian	black	Hispanic	non-Hispanic white
Total households	**100.0%**	**4.0%**	**12.8%**	**11.4%**	**70.9%**
Family households	100.0	4.4	12.2	13.3	69.2
Married couples	100.0	4.7	7.6	11.8	74.9
Female householders, no spouse present	100.0	3.1	29.3	17.5	49.8
Male householders, no spouse present	100.0	4.7	16.2	19.3	58.6
Nonfamily households	100.0	3.3	14.1	7.6	74.2
Female householders	100.0	3.1	14.6	6.1	75.3
Living alone	100.0	3.0	15.0	5.8	75.3
Male householders	100.0	3.4	13.5	9.3	72.8
Living alone	100.0	3.0	14.5	8.2	73.2

Note: Numbers do not add to total because Hispanics may be of any race, not all races are shown, and some householders may be of more than one race. Asians and blacks are those who identify themselves as being of the race alone and those who identify themselves as being of the race in combination with other races. Non-Hispanic whites are only those who identify themselves as being white alone and not Hispanic.
Source: Bureau of the Census, 2008 Current Population Survey Annual Social and Economic Supplement, Internet site http:// pubdb3.census.gov/macro/032008/hhinc/new01_000.htm; calculations by New Strategist

Most Households Are Small

The number of single-person households is growing the fastest.

Sixty-one percent of the nation's households are home to only one or two people. The number of single-person households climbed 20 percent between 2000 and 2008, significantly faster than the 12 percent growth in households overall. The number of households with two people grew by an average amount, but those with three or more people grew more slowly than average.

Two-person households, the most common, account for 33 percent of the 117 million households in the nation. Single-person households constitute 28 percent of the total. Only 10 percent of households have five or more people. Overall, the average household in the United States was home to 2.56 people in 2008, down from 2.62 in 2000.

■ Household size is shrinking as baby boomers become empty-nesters.

Two-person households are most common

(percent distribution of households by size, 2008)

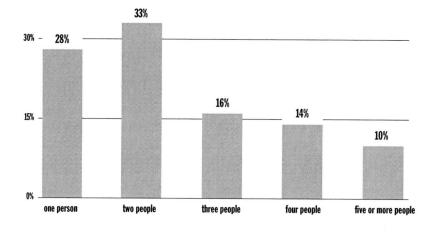

Table 7.5 Households by Size, 2000 and 2008

(number and percent distribution of households by size, 2000 and 2008; percent change in number, 2000–08; number of households in thousands)

	2008		2000		percent change in number 2000–08
	number	percent distribution	number	percent distribution	
Total households	**116,783**	**100.0%**	**104,705**	**100.0%**	**11.5%**
One person	32,167	27.5	26,724	25.5	20.4
Two people	38,737	33.2	34,666	33.1	11.7
Three people	18,522	15.9	17,152	16.4	8.0
Four people	15,865	13.6	15,309	14.6	3.6
Five people	7,332	6.3	6,981	6.7	5.0
Six people	2,694	2.3	2,445	2.3	10.2
Seven or more people	1,467	1.3	1,428	1.4	2.7
Average number of persons per household	2.56	–	2.62	–	–

Note: "–" means not applicable.
Source: Bureau of the Census, Current Population Survey Annual Social and Economic Supplement, Internet site http://www .census.gov/hhes/www/income/dinctabs.html; calculations by New Strategist

More than Eight Million Elderly Women Live Alone

Nearly half of the women who live alone are aged 65 or older.

Among the nation's 32 million single-person households, women head the 57 percent majority. People aged 55 or older head 53 percent of single-person households.

There are sharp differences in the ages of men and women who live alone. Most men who live alone are under age 55, while most women who live alone are aged 55 or older. Among men, those aged 65 or older are most likely to live alone, but the proportion is only 19 percent. In contrast, 39 percent of their female counterparts live by themselves. Most men live alone before marriage or after divorce. Most women live alone following the death of their spouse.

■ The nearly 14 percent of Americans aged 15 or older who live by themselves account for 28 percent of the nation's households.

Women are increasingly likely to live alone after middle age

(percent of women who live alone, by age, 2008)

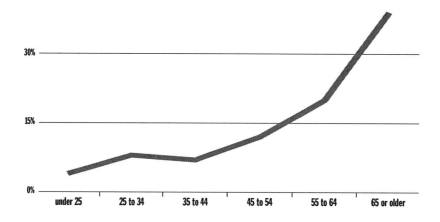

Table 7.6 People Living Alone by Sex and Age, 2008

(total number of people aged 15 or older, number and percent living alone, and percent distribution of people who live alone, by sex and age, 2008; numbers in thousands)

| | | living alone | | |
	total	number	percent of total	percent distribution
Total people	**238,148**	**32,167**	**13.5%**	**100.0%**
Under age 25	41,843	1,649	3.9	5.1
Aged 25 to 34	40,146	3,931	9.8	12.2
Aged 35 to 44	42,132	3,800	9.0	11.8
Aged 45 to 54	43,935	5,579	12.7	17.3
Aged 55 to 64	33,302	5,995	18.0	18.6
Aged 65 or older	36,790	11,214	30.5	34.9
Total men	**115,678**	**13,870**	**12.0**	**100.0**
Under age 25	21,208	844	4.0	6.1
Aged 25 to 34	20,210	2,362	11.7	17.0
Aged 35 to 44	20,880	2,321	11.1	16.7
Aged 45 to 54	21,539	2,866	13.3	20.7
Aged 55 to 64	16,079	2,561	15.9	18.5
Aged 65 or older	15,762	2,917	18.5	21.0
Total women	**122,470**	**18,297**	**14.9**	**100.0**
Under age 25	20,635	805	3.9	4.4
Aged 25 to 34	19,937	1,569	7.9	8.6
Aged 35 to 44	21,252	1,479	7.0	8.1
Aged 45 to 54	22,396	2,713	12.1	14.8
Aged 55 to 64	17,223	3,434	19.9	18.8
Aged 65 or older	21,028	8,297	39.5	45.3

Source: Bureau of the Census, 2008 Current Population Survey Annual Social and Economic Supplement, Internet sites http://pubdb3.census.gov/macro/032008/perinc/new01_000.htm and http://pubdb3.census.gov/macro/032008/hhinc/new02_000.htm; calculations by New Strategist

Household Numbers Are Growing Fastest in the South and West

The South is home to the majority of black households.

A growing proportion of the nation's households are in the South, the share standing at nearly 37 percent in 2008. The number of households in the South rose 15 percent between 2000 and 2008, faster than the 14 percent gain in the West, the 6 percent rise in the Northeast, and the 7 percent increase in the Midwest.

The nation's minority populations are heavily concentrated in some regions. The 54 percent majority of black households are in the South. Forty-six percent of Asian households are in the West. The West is also home to 40 percent of Hispanic households, while the South claims another 37 percent. Blacks are the largest minority in the South, heading 19 percent of households. Hispanics are the largest minority in the West, accounting for 20 percent of households in that region. The Asian presence is also greatest in the West, where they head 8 percent of households.

■ The nation's markets and politics will be shaped increasingly by the concentration of Asians, blacks, and Hispanics in certain regions and states.

Less than half the nation's households are in the Northeast and Midwest

(percent distribution of households by region, 2008)

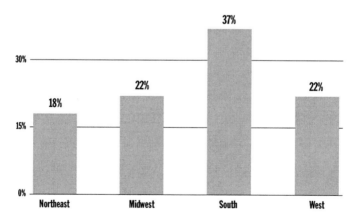

Table 7.7 Households by Region, 2000 and 2008

(number and percent distribution of households by region, 2000 and 2008; percent change in number, 2000–08; numbers in thousands)

	2008		2000		percent change in number 2000–08
	number	percent distribution	number	percent distribution	
Total households	**116,783**	**100.0%**	**104,705**	**100.0%**	**11.5%**
Northeast	21,351	18.3	20,087	19.2	6.3
Midwest	26,266	22.5	24,508	23.4	7.2
South	43,062	36.9	37,303	35.6	15.4
West	26,105	22.4	22,808	21.8	14.5

Source: Bureau of the Census, Current Population Survey Annual Social and Economic Supplement, Internet site http://www .census.gov/hhes/www/income/dinctabs.html; calculations by New Strategist

Table 7.8 Households by Region, Race, and Hispanic Origin, 2008

(number and percent distribution of households by region, race, and Hispanic origin of householder, 2008; numbers in thousands)

	total	Asian	black	Hispanic	non-Hispanic white
Total households	**116,783**	**4,715**	**14,976**	**13,339**	**82,765**
Northeast	21,351	999	2,673	1,954	15,877
Midwest	26,266	561	2,697	1,097	21,671
South	43,062	1,002	8,088	4,944	28,631
West	26,105	2,153	1,519	5,344	16,585
PERCENT DISTRIBUTION BY REGION					
Total households	**100.0%**	**100.0%**	**100.0%**	**100.0%**	**100.0%**
Northeast	18.3	21.2	17.8	14.6	19.2
Midwest	22.5	11.9	18.0	8.2	26.2
South	36.9	21.3	54.0	37.1	34.6
West	22.4	45.7	10.1	40.1	20.0
PERCENT DISTRIBUTION BY RACE AND HISPANIC ORIGIN					
Total households	**100.0%**	**4.0%**	**12.8%**	**11.4%**	**70.9%**
Northeast	100.0	4.7	12.5	9.2	74.4
Midwest	100.0	2.1	10.3	4.2	82.5
South	100.0	2.3	18.8	11.5	66.5
West	100.0	8.2	5.8	20.5	63.5

Note: Numbers do not add to total because Hispanics may be of any race, not all races are shown, and some householders may be of more than one race. Asians and blacks are those who identify themselves as being of the race alone and those who identify themselves as being of the race in combination with other races. Non-Hispanic whites are only those who identify themselves as being white alone and not Hispanic.
Source: Bureau of the Census, 2008 Current Population Survey Annual Social and Economic Supplement, Internet site http:// pubdb3.census.gov/macro/032008/hhinc/new01_000.htm; calculations by New Strategist

More than 80 Percent of Households Are in Metropolitan Areas

Non-Hispanic whites are the ones most likely to live in nonmetropolitan areas.

Of the nation's 117 million households, 84 percent are in metropolitan areas, defined as counties with a city of 50,000 or more population plus any adjacent counties with economic ties to the core county. Only 16 percent of households are in nonmetropolitan areas. Asians are more likely than blacks, Hispanics, or non-Hispanic whites to be metropolitan residents.

The 52 percent majority of the nation's Asian and black households are in the principal cities of metropolitan areas. Among Hispanics, nearly half are in the principal cities. The figure is a much smaller 27 percent among non-Hispanic whites. Conversely, the 54 percent majority of non-Hispanic white households are in the suburbs of metropolitan areas (outside principal cities) compared with 38 to 45 percent of Asian, black, and Hispanic households. Nineteen percent of non-Hispanic white households are in nonmetropolitan areas versus only 3 percent of Asian households.

■ The nation's central cities are much more diverse than the suburbs or nonmetropolitan areas.

Few non-Hispanic white households are in the principal cities of metro areas

(percent of households in the principal cities of metropolitan areas, by race and Hispanic origin, 2008)

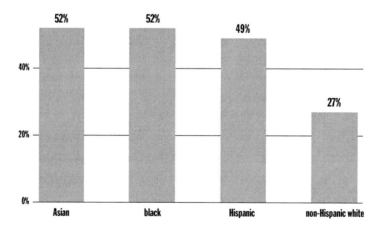

Table 7.9 Households by Metropolitan Status, Race, and Hispanic Origin, 2008

(number and percent distribution of households by metropolitan status, race, and Hispanic origin, 2008; numbers in thousands)

	total	Asian	black	Hispanic	non-Hispanic white
Total households	**116,783**	**4,715**	**14,976**	**13,339**	**82,765**
Inside metropolitan areas	97,591	4,580	13,434	12,377	66,712
Inside principal cities	39,072	2,452	7,818	6,537	22,208
Outside principal cities	58,520	2,127	5,616	5,840	44,504
Outside metropolitan areas	19,192	135	1,543	961	16,052
PERCENT DISTRIBUTION BY METROPOLITAN STATUS					
Total households	**100.0%**	**100.0%**	**100.0%**	**100.0%**	**100.0%**
Inside metropolitan areas	83.6	97.1	89.7	92.8	80.6
Inside principal cities	33.5	52.0	52.2	49.0	26.8
Outside principal cities	50.1	45.1	37.5	43.8	53.8
Outside metropolitan areas	16.4	2.9	10.3	7.2	19.4
PERCENT DISTRIBUTION BY RACE AND HISPANIC ORIGIN					
Total households	**100.0%**	**4.0%**	**12.8%**	**11.4%**	**70.9%**
Inside metropolitan areas	100.0	4.7	13.8	12.7	68.4
Inside principal cities	100.0	6.3	20.0	16.7	56.8
Outside principal cities	100.0	3.6	9.6	10.0	76.0
Outside metropolitan areas	100.0	0.7	8.0	5.0	83.6

Note: Numbers do not add to total because Hispanics may be of any race, not all races are shown, and some householders may be of more than one race. Asians and blacks are those who identify themselves as being of the race alone and those who identify themselves as being of the race in combination with other races. Non-Hispanic whites are only those who identify themselves as being white alone and not Hispanic.
Source: Bureau of the Census, 2008 Current Population Survey Annual Social and Economic Supplement, Internet site http:// pubdb3.census.gov/macro/032008/hhinc/new01_000.htm; calculations by New Strategist

Nearly One in Four Children Lives with Mother Only

Fewer than 4 percent live with their father only.

Among the nation's 74 million children under age 18, only 70 percent lived with two parents in 2008—down from 85 percent in 1970. The proportion of children who live with two parents (married or unmarried) ranges from a low of 38 percent among black children to a high of 85 percent among Asian children. A smaller share of children lives with two biological parents, ranging from 29 percent of blacks to 76 percent of Asians.

The proportion of children who live with their mother only ranges from a low of 11 percent among Asians to a high of 50 percent among blacks. Only 3.5 percent of children live with their father only, and another 4 percent live with neither parent.

Among men aged 15 to 44 whho have children under age 19, a substantial 27 percent do not live with all or some of their children. The figure is much higher for blacks (53 percent) than for non-Hispanic whites (19 percent). Men who did not graduate from high school are much more likely to live apart from some or all of their children (35 percent) than college graduates (14 percent).

■ The poverty rate among children is unlikely to decline significantly until fewer children live in single-parent families.

Children's living arrangements vary greatly by race and Hispanic origin

(percent of children living with their married biological parents, by race and Hispanic origin, 2008)

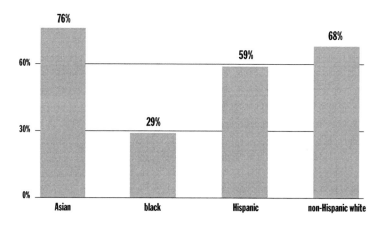

Table 7.10 Living Arrangements of Children, 1970 to 2008

(number and percent distribution of children under age 18 by living arrangement, 1970 to 2008; numbers in thousands)

	total		children living with			
	number	percent	both parents	mother only	father only	neither parent
Total children						
2008*	74,104	100.0%	69.9%	22.8%	3.5%	3.8%
2007*	73,746	100.0	70.7	22.6	3.2	3.5
2007	73,746	100.0	67.8	24.2	4.5	3.5
2006	73,664	100.0	67.4	23.3	4.7	4.6
2005	73,523	100.0	67.4	23.4	4.7	4.5
2000	72,012	100.0	69.1	22.4	4.2	4.2
1995	70,254	100.0	68.7	23.5	3.5	4.3
1990	64,137	100.0	72.5	21.6	3.1	2.8
1985	62,475	100.0	73.9	20.9	2.5	2.7
1980	63,427	100.0	76.7	18.0	1.7	3.7
1975	66,087	100.0	80.3	15.5	1.5	2.7
1970	69,162	100.0	85.2	10.8	1.1	2.9

* Before 2007, the Current Population Survey classified children as living with two parents only if the parents were married. Beginning in 2007, children were counted as living with two parents if there were two parents in the home regardless of marital status. Results for both the original and new methodology in 2007 are shown here for comparative purposes.
Source: Bureau of the Census, Families and Living Arrangements, Historical Time Series, Internet site http://www.census .gov/population/www/socdemo/hh-fam.html; calculations by New Strategist

Table 7.11 Living Arrangements of Children, 2008: Total Children

(number and percent distribution of total children under age 18 by living arrangement, 2008; numbers in thousands)

	number	percent distribution
TOTAL CHILDREN	**74,104**	**100.0%**
Living with two parents	**51,785**	**69.9**
Married parents	49,426	66.7
Unmarried parents	2,360	3.2
Biological mother and father	46,427	62.7
Married parents	44,376	59.9
Biological mother and stepfather	3,183	4.3
Biological father and stepmother	930	1.3
Biological mother and adoptive father	195	0.3
Biological father and adoptive mother	42	0.1
Adoptive mother and father	795	1.1
Other	213	0.3
Living with one parent	**19,501**	**26.3**
Mother only	16,888	22.8
Father only	2,613	3.5
Living with no parents	**2,818**	**3.8**
Grandparents	1,510	2.0
Other	1,308	1.8

Source: Bureau of the Census, Current Population Survey Annual Social and Economic Supplement, America's Families and Living Arrangements: 2008, detailed tables, Internet site http://www.census.gov/population/www/socdemo/hh-fam/cps2008 .html; calculations by New Strategist

Table 7.12 Living Arrangements of Children, 2008: Asian Children

(number and percent distribution of Asian children under age 18 by living arrangement, 2008; numbers in thousands)

	number	percent distribution
ASIAN CHILDREN	**3,608**	**100.0%**
Living with two parents	**3,058**	**84.8**
Married parents	2,979	82.6
Unmarried parents	79	2.2
Biological mother and father	2,826	78.3
Married parents	2,758	76.4
Biological mother and stepfather	88	2.4
Biological father and stepmother	36	1.0
Biological mother and adoptive father	7	0.2
Biological father and adoptive mother	4	0.1
Adoptive mother and father	94	2.6
Other	2	0.1
Living with one parent	**469**	**13.0**
Mother only	384	10.6
Father only	85	2.4
Living with no parents	**81**	**2.2**
Grandparents	18	0.5
Other	63	1.7

Note: Asians are those who identify themselves as being of the race alone and those who identify themselves as being of the race in combination with other races.
Source: Bureau of the Census, Current Population Survey Annual Social and Economic Supplement, America's Families and Living Arrangements: 2008, detailed tables, Internet site http://www.census.gov/population/www/socdemo/hh-fam/cps2008 .html; calculations by New Strategist

Table 7.13 Living Arrangements of Children, 2008: Black Children

(number and percent distribution of black children under age 18 by living arrangement, 2008; numbers in thousands)

	number	percent distribution
BLACK CHILDREN	**12,424**	**100.0%**
Living with two parents	**4,781**	**38.5**
Married parents	4,360	35.1
Unmarried parents	421	3.4
Biological mother and father	3,981	32.0
Married parents	3,611	29.1
Biological mother and stepfather	459	3.7
Biological father and stepmother	107	0.9
Biological mother and adoptive father	25	0.2
Biological father and adoptive mother	0	0.0
Adoptive mother and father	167	1.3
Other	42	0.3
Living with one parent	**6,652**	**53.5**
Mother only	6,247	50.3
Father only	405	3.3
Living with no parents	**991**	**8.0**
Grandparents	616	5.0
Other	375	3.0

Note: Blacks are those who identify themselves as being of the race alone and those who identify themselves as being of the race in combination with other races.
Source: Bureau of the Census, Current Population Survey Annual Social and Economic Supplement, America's Families and Living Arrangements: 2008, detailed tables, Internet site http://www.census.gov/population/www/socdemo/hh-fam/cps2008 .html; calculations by New Strategist

Table 7.14 Living Arrangements of Children, 2008: Hispanic Children

(number and percent distribution of Hispanic children under age 18 by living arrangement, 2008; numbers in thousands)

	number	percent distribution
HISPANIC CHILDREN	**15,644**	**100.0%**
Living with two parents	**10,902**	**69.7**
Married parents	10,046	64.2
Unmarried parents	855	5.5
Biological mother and father	9,982	63.8
Married parents	9,195	58.8
Biological mother and stepfather	635	4.1
Biological father and stepmother	139	0.9
Biological mother and adoptive father	28	0.2
Biological father and adoptive mother	8	0.1
Adoptive mother and father	81	0.5
Other	28	0.2
Living with one parent	**4,132**	**26.4**
Mother only	3,764	24.1
Father only	368	2.4
Living with no parents	**610**	**3.9**
Grandparents	235	1.5
Other	375	2.4

Source: Bureau of the Census, Current Population Survey Annual Social and Economic Supplement, America's Families and Living Arrangements: 2008, detailed tables, Internet site http://www.census.gov/population/www/socdemo/hh-fam/cps2008 .html; calculations by New Strategist

Table 7.15 Living Arrangements of Children, 2008: Non-Hispanic White Children

(number and percent distribution of non-Hispanic white children under age 18 by living arrangement, 2008; numbers in thousands)

	number	percent distribution
NON-HISPANIC WHITE CHILDREN	**42,051**	**100.0%**
Living with two parents	**32,712**	**77.8**
Married parents	31,700	75.4
Unmarried parents	1,012	2.4
Biological mother and father	29,365	69.8
Married parents	28,534	67.9
Biological mother and stepfather	1,969	4.7
Biological father and stepmother	641	1.5
Biological mother and adoptive father	133	0.3
Biological father and adoptive mother	31	0.1
Adoptive mother and father	436	1.0
Other	137	0.3
Living with one parent	**8,239**	**19.6**
Mother only	6,522	15.5
Father only	1,717	4.1
Living with no parents	**1,101**	**2.6**
Grandparents	618	1.5
Other	483	1.1

Note: Non-Hispanic whites are only those who identify themselves as being white alone and not Hispanic.
Source: Bureau of the Census, Current Population Survey Annual Social and Economic Supplement, America's Families and Living Arrangements: 2008, detailed tables, Internet site http://www.census.gov/population/www/socdemo/hh-fam/cps2008 .html; calculations by New Strategist

Table 7.16   Fathers' Living Arrangements with Children, 2002

(number of men aged 15 to 44 who have biological or adopted children under age 19, and percent distribution by living arrangement with children, by selected characteristics, 2002; numbers in thousands)

	total		living with all children	not living with any children	living with some but not others
	number	percent			
Total men aged 15 to 44 with children	**27,821**	**100.0%**	**73.4%**	**14.3%**	**12.4%**
Aged 15 to 24	1,832	100.0	65.8	23.2	11.1
Aged 25 to 29	4,107	100.0	77.4	13.9	8.7
Aged 30 to 44	21,882	100.0	73.3	13.6	13.2
Marital status					
Currently married	20,133	100.0	83.7	6.0	10.3
First marriage	16,400	100.0	90.2	4.8	5.0
Second or later marriage	3,733	100.0	55.2	11.5	33.3
Currently cohabiting	3,046	100.0	60.0	13.5	26.5
Never married, not cohabiting	1,592	100.0	34.8	54.1	11.2
Formerly married, not cohabiting	3,049	100.0	38.9	48.5	12.6
Race and Hispanic origin					
Black, non-Hispanic	3,292	100.0	47.0	25.5	27.5
Hispanic	5,542	100.0	65.8	18.4	15.8
White, non-Hispanic	16,596	100.0	80.8	11.0	8.2
Education					
Not a high school graduate	4,480	100.0	64.8	16.9	18.3
High school graduate or GED	10,456	100.0	71.4	14.8	13.9
Some college, no degree	6,650	100.0	73.8	13.6	12.7
Bachelor's degree or more	5,600	100.0	85.7	10.4	4.0

Note: Education categories include only people aged 22 to 44.
Source: National Center for Health Statistics, Fertility, Contraception, and Fatherhood: Data on Men and Women from Cycle 6 of the 2002 National Survey of Family Growth, Vital and Health Statistics, Series 23, No. 26, 2006, Internet site http://www.cdc .gov/nchs/nsfg.htm

Most Married Couples Do Not Have Children under Age 18 at Home

Among those who do, few have more than one or two.

Among the nation's 78 million families, only 46 percent include children under age 18. When children aged 18 or older are also considered, the 60 percent majority of families include children. Among married couples, only 43 percent have children under age 18 at home and 54 percent have children of any age living with them. Female-headed families are more likely to have children at home—58 percent include children under age 18 and 85 percent include children of any age. A much smaller 42 percent of male-headed families include children under age 18.

Among married couples with children under age 18 in their home, 39 percent have only one and another 39 percent have two. Female-headed families are more likely to have only one child under age 18 at home (49 percent), and male-headed families are most likely to have only one (61 percent).

■ The traditional nuclear family—husband, wife, and children under age 18—accounts for a shrinking share of households as a growing proportion of baby boomers become empty-nesters.

Only 20 percent of married couples have preschoolers

(percent of married-couple households with children of selected ages in the home, 2008)

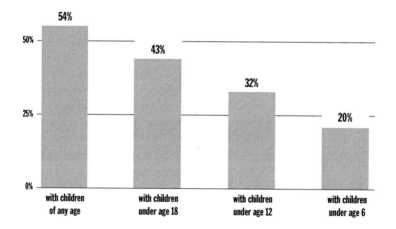

Table 7.17 Total Families by Presence and Age of Children, 2008

(number and percent distribution of family households by presence and age of own children under age 18 and type of family, 2008; numbers in thousands)

	total	married couples	female householder, no spouse present	male householder, no spouse present
Total family households	**77,873**	**58,370**	**14,404**	**5,100**
With children of any age	46,995	31,696	12,206	3,093
With children under age 18	35,709	25,173	8,374	2,162
With children under age 12	26,125	18,722	5,933	1,470
With children under age 6	15,733	11,510	3,312	912
PERCENT DISTRIBUTION BY PRESENCE AND AGE OF CHILDREN				
Total family households	**100.0%**	**100.0%**	**100.0%**	**100.0%**
With children of any age	60.3	54.3	84.7	60.6
With children under age 18	45.9	43.1	58.1	42.4
With children under age 12	33.5	32.1	41.2	28.8
With children under age 6	20.2	19.7	23.0	17.9
PERCENT DISTRIBUTION BY FAMILY TYPE				
Total family households	**100.0%**	**75.0%**	**18.5%**	**6.5%**
With children of any age	100.0	67.4	26.0	6.6
With children under age 18	100.0	70.5	23.5	6.1
With children under age 12	100.0	71.7	22.7	5.6
With children under age 6	100.0	73.2	21.1	5.8

Source: Bureau of the Census, America's Families and Living Arrangements: 2008, Current Population Survey Annual Social and Economic Supplement, Internet site http://www.census.gov/population/www/socdemo/hh-fam/cps2008.html; calculations by New Strategist

Table 7.18 Families by Number of Children under Age 18, 2008

(number and percent distribution of family households with own children under age 18 by number of children and type of family, 2008; numbers in thousands)

	total	married couples	female householder, no spouse present	male householder, no spouse present
Total families with children under age 18	**35,709**	**25,173**	**8,374**	**2,162**
One child	15,160	9,733	4,104	1,323
Two children	13,158	9,886	2,675	597
Three children	5,234	3,953	1,107	174
Four or more children	2,157	1,602	487	68
PERCENT DISTRIBUTION BY NUMBER OF CHILDREN				
Total families with children under age 18	**100.0%**	**100.0%**	**100.0%**	**100.0%**
One child	42.5	38.7	49.0	61.2
Two children	36.8	39.3	31.9	27.6
Three children	14.7	15.7	13.2	8.0
Four or more children	6.0	6.4	5.8	3.1
PERCENT DISTRIBUTION BY FAMILY TYPE				
Total families with children under age 18	**100.0%**	**70.5%**	**23.5%**	**6.1%**
One child	100.0	64.2	27.1	8.7
Two children	100.0	75.1	20.3	4.5
Three children	100.0	75.5	21.2	3.3
Four or more children	100.0	74.3	22.6	3.2

Source: Bureau of the Census, America's Families and Living Arrangements: 2008, Current Population Survey Annual Social and Economic Supplement, Internet site http://www.census.gov/population/www/socdemo/hh-fam/cps2008.html; calculations by New Strategist

Most Moms Are in the Labor Force

Stay-at-home mothers are not the norm, even among couples with preschoolers.

Among married couples with children under age 15, the 70 percent majority has a mom in the labor force. Only 26 percent have a mom who stays home to care for her family. Stay-at-home dads are even less common. Fewer than 1 percent of married couples with children under age 15 have a dad who is not in the labor force because he is caring for the family.

Couples with preschoolers are only slightly more likely than average to have a stay-at-home mother, at 32 percent. They are about equally as likely to have a stay-at-home father, at 1 percent.

■ Perhaps no characteristic distinguishes today's children from those in the past more than working parents. With both mother and father in the labor force, family life has become much more complicated.

One-third of couples with preschoolers have a stay-at-home mom

(percent distribution of married-couple family groups with children under age 6, by labor force status of mother during past year, 2008)

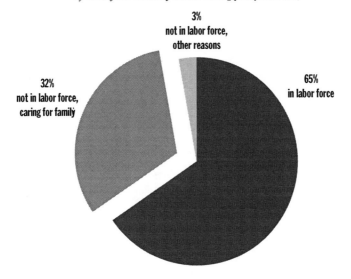

3%
not in labor force,
other reasons

32%
not in labor force,
caring for family

65%
in labor force

Table 7.19 Stay-at-Home Parents among Married Couples, 2008

(number and percent distribution of married-couple family groups with children under age 15 by stay-at-home status of mother and father and age of child, 2008; numbers in thousands)

	with children under age 15		with children under age 6	
	number	percent distribution	number	percent distribution
Total married couple family groups	**22,445**	**100.0%**	**11,848**	**100.0%**
Mother's labor force status in past year				
In labor force one or more weeks	15,770	70.3	7,715	65.1
Not in labor force, caring for family	5,907	26.3	3,786	32.0
Not in labor force, other reason	767	3.4	347	2.9
Father's labor force status in past year				
In labor force one or more weeks	21,409	95.4	11,416	96.4
Not in labor force, caring for family	197	0.9	116	1.0
Not in labor force, other reason	838	3.7	315	2.7

Note: Married-couple family groups include married-couple householders and married couples living in households headed by others.
Source: Bureau of the Census, America's Families and Living Arrangements: 2008, Current Population Survey Annual Social and Economic Supplement, Internet site http://www.census.gov/population/www/socdemo/hh-fam/cps2008.html; calculations by New Strategist

Most Americans Live in Family Households

Women aged 65 or older are most likely to live in a nonfamily household.

The 78 percent majority of the nation's 238 million people aged 15 or older live in a family household. Nearly half are married-couple householders or their spouses. Another 15 percent are children of the householder. Twenty-two percent of Americans aged 15 or older live in nonfamily households—meaning they live alone or with nonrelatives.

Women aged 65 or older are much more likely to live in a nonfamily household than the average American, with a large proportion of older women living by themselves. Only 59 percent of women aged 65 or older live in a family household, and 41 percent live in a nonfamily household. Thirty-nine percent of women aged 65 or older live alone.

■ As the baby-boom generation ages, the proportion of people who live alone will rise.

The lifestyles of men and women diverge in old age

(percent distribution of people aged 65 or older by living arrangement and sex, 2007)

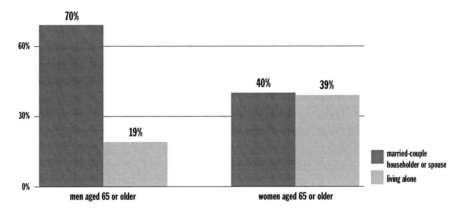

Table 7.20 Living Arrangements by Sex, 2008

(number and percent distribution of noninstitutionalized people aged 15 or older by living arrangement and sex, 2008; numbers in thousands)

	total		female		male	
	number	percent distribution	number	percent distribution	number	percent distribution
Total people	**237,993**	**100.0%**	**122,394**	**100.0%**	**115,599**	**100.0%**
Living in family household	185,492	77.9	95,529	78.1	89,963	77.8
Living in nonfamily household	52,500	22.1	26,864	21.9	25,636	22.2
Householder	**116,783**	**49.1**	**57,499**	**47.0**	**59,284**	**51.3**
Family householder	77,873	32.7	36,461	29.8	41,412	35.8
Married-couple householder	58,370	24.5	22,058	18.0	36,312	31.4
Other family householder	19,503	8.2	14,403	11.8	5,100	4.4
Nonfamily householder	38,910	16.3	21,038	17.2	17,872	15.5
Living alone	32,167	13.5	18,297	14.9	13,870	12.0
Living with nonrelatives	6,743	2.8	2,742	2.2	4,002	3.5
Not a householder	**121,209**	**50.9**	**64,894**	**53.0**	**56,315**	**48.7**
In family household	107,619	45.2	59,068	48.3	48,551	42.0
Spouse of householder	58,370	24.5	36,312	29.7	22,058	19.1
Child of householder	35,982	15.1	15,953	13.0	20,029	17.3
Other relative of householder	13,267	5.6	6,803	5.6	6,464	5.6
In nonfamily household	13,590	5.7	5,826	4.8	7,764	6.7

Source: Bureau of the Census, America's Families and Living Arrangements: 2008, Current Population Survey Annual Social and Economic Supplement, Internet site http://www.census.gov/population/www/socdemo/hh-fam/cps2008.html; calculations by New Strategist

Table 7.21 Living Arrangements of People Aged 65 or Older by Sex, 2008

(number and percent distribution of noninstitutionalized people aged 65 or older by living arrangement and sex, 2008; numbers in thousands)

	total aged 65 or older		female		male	
	number	percent distribution	number	percent distribution	number	percent distribution
Total people aged 65 or older	**36,767**	**100.0%**	**21,013**	**100.0%**	**15,754**	**100.0%**
Living in family household	24,686	67.1	12,303	58.5	12,382	78.6
Living in nonfamily household	12,082	32.9	8,709	41.4	3,372	21.4
Householder	**24,113**	**65.6**	**13,276**	**63.2**	**10,835**	**68.8**
Family householder	12,493	34.0	4,776	22.7	7,716	49.0
Married-couple householder	10,177	27.7	2,911	13.9	7,267	46.1
Other family householder	2,316	6.3	1,865	8.9	449	2.9
Nonfamily householder	11,620	31.6	8,500	40.5	3,119	19.8
Living alone	11,213	30.5	8,296	39.5	2,916	18.5
Living with nonrelatives	406	1.1	203	1.0	203	1.3
Not a householder	**12,655**	**34.4**	**7,736**	**36.8**	**4,919**	**31.2**
In family household	12,193	33.2	7,527	35.8	4,666	29.6
Spouse of householder	9,274	25.2	5,563	26.5	3,712	23.6
Child of householder	36	0.1	17	0.1	19	0.1
Other relative of householder	2,883	7.8	1,947	9.3	935	5.9
In nonfamily household	462	1.3	209	1.0	253	1.6

Source: Bureau of the Census, America's Families and Living Arrangements: 2008, Current Population Survey Annual Social and Economic Supplement, Internet site http://www.census.gov/population/www/socdemo/hh-fam/cps2008.html; calculations by New Strategist

More than Three Out of Four Women Aged 20 to 24 Are Single

Many young adults live with a romantic partner before marrying.

Men and women are remaining single longer than they once did as more attend college and embark on a career before tying the knot. Among women aged 20 to 24, nearly 79 percent have not yet married. The figure is 87 percent for their male counterparts. The proportion of women who are still single falls below 50 percent in the 25-to-29 age group. Among men, it falls below the 50 percent threshold in the 30-to-34 age group.

Just because young adults are unmarried does not mean they are living the single life. Many live together outside of marriage—called cohabiting. Among women aged 15 to 44, half have lived with a romantic partner outside of marriage. Nine percent of women aged 15 to 44 are currently cohabiting, including 16 percent of women aged 20 to 24. The figures for men are about the same, with the percentage currently cohabiting peaking at 18 percent among men aged 25 to 29.

■ The percentage of 15-to-44-year-olds who have ever cohabited exceeds 60 percent among women aged 25 to 39 and men aged 30 to 44.

Most women have married by their late twenties

(percent of women who have never married, by age, 2008)

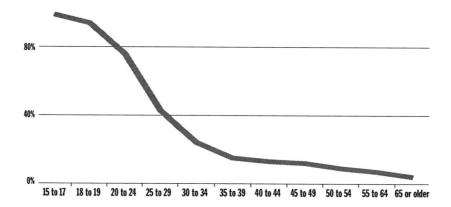

Table 7.22 Never-Married People by Age and Sex, 2008

(percent of people aged 15 or older who have never married, by age and sex, 2008)

	total	men	women
Total never married	**30.0%**	**33.5%**	**26.8%**
Aged 15 to 17	98.3	98.5	98.0
Aged 18 to 19	96.3	97.7	94.9
Aged 20 to 24	83.2	87.3	78.9
Aged 25 to 29	52.3	58.8	45.5
Aged 30 to 34	30.3	34.5	26.1
Aged 35 to 39	19.6	23.2	16.0
Aged 40 to 44	16.6	19.7	13.5
Aged 45 to 49	13.7	16.3	11.2
Aged 50 to 54	10.7	12.2	9.3
Aged 55 to 64	7.2	7.5	6.9
Aged 65 or older	4.1	4.1	4.0

Source: Bureau of the Census, America's Families and Living Arrangements: 2008, Current Population Survey Annual Social and Economic Supplement, Internet site http://www.census.gov/population/www/socdemo/hh-fam/cps2008.html; calculations by New Strategist

Table 7.23 Cohabitation Experience of Women, 2002

(total number of women aged 15 to 44, and percent who have ever cohabited or are currently cohabiting, by selected characteristics, 2002; numbers in thousands)

	total		ever cohabited	currently cohabiting
	number	percent		
Total women aged 15 to 44	**61,561**	**100.0%**	**50.0%**	**9.1%**
Aged 15 to 19	9,834	100.0	11.7	5.6
Aged 20 to 24	9,840	100.0	43.1	15.7
Aged 25 to 29	9,249	100.0	60.9	12.9
Aged 30 to 34	10,272	100.0	63.2	7.9
Aged 35 to 39	10,853	100.0	61.3	6.7
Aged 40 to 44	11,512	100.0	57.4	6.6
Number of children ever borne				
None	25,622	100.0	31.8	8.9
One	11,193	100.0	63.1	10.7
Two	13,402	100.0	61.4	6.1
Three or more	11,343	100.0	64.9	11.2
Race and Hispanic origin				
Black, non-Hispanic	8,250	100.0	51.1	9.6
Hispanic	9,107	100.0	48.8	13.4
White, non-Hispanic	39,498	100.0	50.5	7.9
Education				
Not a high school graduate	5,627	100.0	69.4	17.2
High school graduate or GED	14,264	100.0	68.5	11.3
Some college, no degree	14,279	100.0	58.3	7.6
Bachelor's degree or more	13,551	100.0	46.3	5.4
Family structure at age 14				
Living with both parents	43,921	100.0	45.5	7.4
Other	17,640	100.0	61.3	13.2

Note: Education categories include only people aged 22 to 44.
Source: National Center for Health Statistics, Fertility, Family Planning, and Reproductive Health of U.S. Women: Data from the 2002 National Survey of Family Growth, Vital and Health Statistics, Series 23, No. 25, 2005, Internet site http://www.cdc.gov/nchs/nsfg.htm

Table 7.24 Cohabitation Experience of Men, 2002

(total number of men aged 15 to 44, and percent who have ever cohabited or are currently cohabiting, by selected characteristics, 2002; numbers in thousands)

	total		ever cohabited	currently cohabiting
	number	percent		
Total men aged 15 to 44	**61,147**	**100.0%**	**48.8%**	**9.2%**
Aged 15 to 19	10,208	100.0	5.5	1.9
Aged 20 to 24	9,883	100.0	33.9	13.4
Aged 25 to 29	9,226	100.0	58.5	17.8
Aged 30 to 34	10,138	100.0	62.3	9.6
Aged 35 to 39	10,557	100.0	64.7	8.2
Aged 40 to 44	11,135	100.0	66.5	6.0
Number of biological children				
None	32,593	100.0	32.6	7.9
One	10,457	100.0	68.4	13.7
Two	9,829	100.0	63.0	7.9
Three or more	8,269	100.0	71.2	10.7
Race and Hispanic origin				
Black, non-Hispanic	6,940	100.0	52.6	10.0
Hispanic	10,188	100.0	47.3	14.0
White, non-Hispanic	38,738	100.0	49.4	7.9
Education				
Not a high school graduate	6,355	100.0	67.2	16.6
High school graduate or GED	15,659	100.0	66.6	12.3
Some college, no degree	13,104	100.0	55.0	9.8
Bachelor's degree or more	11,901	100.0	54.0	7.0
Family structure at age 14				
Living with both parents	45,166	100.0	46.5	8.4
Other	15,981	100.0	55.5	11.7

Note: Education categories include only people aged 22 to 44.
Source: National Center for Health Statistics, Fertility, Contraception, and Fatherhood: Data on Men and Women from Cycle 6 of the 2002 National Survey of Family Growth, Vital and Health Statistics, Series 23, No. 26, 2006, Internet site http://www.cdc .gov/nchs/nsfg.htm

Most Men and Women Are Currently Married

Some of the married have gone to the altar more than once, however.

Over the past few decades, Americans have increasingly postponed marriage to pursue a college degree and start a career. The median age at first marriage stood at 27.4 years for men and 25.6 years for women in 2008—five years later than the median age of marriage in 1950. Overall, 51 percent of Americans aged 15 or older are currently married, 10 percent are currently divorced, and 6 percent are widowed.

Many men and women have been married more than once. Among 15-to-44-year-olds, 8.5 percent of women and 7.2 percent of men are now in their second or higher marriage. Among women aged 40 to 44, nearly half—46 percent—are currently in their first marriage and 21 percent are in a second or higher marriage. The figures are similar for men in the age group, 43 percent being in their first marriage and 20 percent in their second or higher marriage.

■ Divorce and multiple marriages are much more common among baby boomers and younger adults than among older generations of Americans.

Only 10 percent of Americans are currently divorced

(percent distribution of people aged 15 or older by current marital status, 2008)

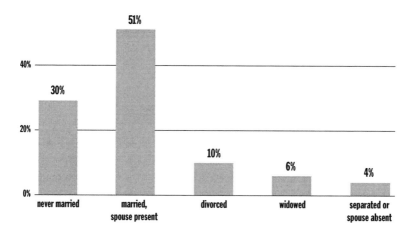

Table 7.25   Median Age at First Marriage by Sex, 1890 to 2008

(median age at first marriage by sex, selected years, 1890 to 2008; change in years, 1890–1950 and 1950–2008)

	men	women
2007	27.5	25.6
2000	26.8	25.1
1990	26.1	23.9
1980	24.7	22.0
1970	23.2	20.8
1960	22.8	20.3
1950	22.8	20.3
1940	24.3	21.5
1930	24.3	21.3
1920	24.6	21.2
1910	25.1	21.6
1900	25.9	21.9
1890	26.1	22.0
Change in years		
1950 to 2007	4.7	5.3
1890 to 1950	–3.3	–1.7

Source: Bureau of the Census, Families and Living Arrangements, Historical Time Series, Internet site, http://www.census .gov/population/www/socdemo/hh-fam.html; calculations by New Strategist

Table 7.26 Marital Status by Sex, 2008

(number and percent distribution of people aged 15 or older by marital status and sex, 2008; numbers in thousands)

	total	men	women
Total people	**237,993**	**115,599**	**122,394**
Never married	71,479	38,685	32,794
Married, spouse present	120,258	60,129	60,129
Married, spouse absent	3,413	1,944	1,470
Separated	5,183	2,144	3,039
Divorced	23,346	9,782	13,564
Widowed	14,314	2,916	11,398
PERCENT DISTRIBUTION BY MARITAL STATUS			
Total people	**100.0%**	**100.0%**	**100.0%**
Never married	30.0	33.5	26.8
Married, spouse present	50.5	52.0	49.1
Married, spouse absent	1.4	1.7	1.2
Separated	2.2	1.9	2.5
Divorced	9.8	8.5	11.1
Widowed	6.0	2.5	9.3
PERCENT DISTRIBUTION BY SEX			
Total people	**100.0%**	**48.6%**	**51.4%**
Never married	100.0	54.1	45.9
Married, spouse present	100.0	50.0	50.0
Married, spouse absent	100.0	57.0	43.1
Separated	100.0	41.4	58.6
Divorced	100.0	41.9	58.1
Widowed	100.0	20.4	79.6

Source: Bureau of the Census, America's Families and Living Arrangements: 2008, Current Population Survey Annual Social and Economic Supplement, Internet site http://www.census.gov/population/www/socdemo/hh-fam/cps2008.html; calculations by New Strategist

Table 7.27 Current Marital Status of Women, 2002

(total number of women aged 15 to 44, and percent distribution by current marital status, by selected characteristics, 2002; numbers in thousands)

	total		never married	currently married			formerly married		
	number	percent		total	first marriage	second or higher marriage	separated	divorced	widowed
Total women aged 15 to 44	**61,561**	**100.0%**	**41.8%**	**46.0%**	**37.5%**	**8.5%**	**3.0%**	**8.7%**	**0.4%**
Aged 15 to 19	9,834	100.0	97.6	2.0	2.0	0.0	0.3	0.1	0.0
Aged 20 to 24	9,840	100.0	72.7	23.1	22.6	0.5	2.1	2.0	0.1
Aged 25 to 29	9,249	100.0	39.8	51.6	47.7	4.0	3.0	5.3	0.3
Aged 30 to 34	10,272	100.0	22.4	61.8	54.1	7.8	5.6	9.9	0.2
Aged 35 to 39	10,853	100.0	16.7	64.4	49.5	14.9	3.3	14.7	0.9
Aged 40 to 44	11,512	100.0	10.1	67.2	46.3	20.9	3.6	18.0	1.0
Number of children ever borne									
None	25,622	100.0	75.2	20.1	18.1	2.0	0.9	3.7	0.1
One	11,193	100.0	28.9	56.8	47.9	9.0	3.2	10.4	0.6
Two	13,402	100.0	11.9	70.2	57.4	12.8	4.8	12.5	0.7
Three or more	11,343	100.0	14.2	65.4	47.6	17.8	5.7	14.0	0.7
Race and Hispanic origin									
Black, non-Hispanic	8,250	100.0	60.7	25.8	22.0	3.8	4.6	8.5	0.4
Hispanic	9,107	100.0	42.1	45.4	39.5	5.9	5.5	6.1	0.8
White, non-Hispanic	39,498	100.0	37.2	50.8	40.3	10.5	2.1	9.6	0.3
Education									
Not a high school graduate	5,627	100.0	32.2	49.1	39.0	10.2	8.1	9.4	1.2
High school graduate or GED	14,264	100.0	25.1	56.7	39.8	17.0	3.8	13.6	0.8
Some college, no degree	14,279	100.0	24.9	57.4	47.2	10.2	3.8	13.4	0.5
Bachelor's degree or more	13,551	100.0	28.2	62.9	57.0	5.9	1.7	7.0	0.2
Family structure at age 14									
Living with both parents	43,921	100.0	39.0	49.3	41.2	8.1	2.9	8.5	0.5
Other	17,640	100.0	48.9	38.0	28.3	9.7	3.3	9.4	0.3

Note: Education categories include only people aged 22 to 44.
Source: National Center for Health Statistics, Fertility, Family Planning, and Reproductive Health of U.S. Women: Data from the 2002 National Survey of Family Growth, Vital and Health Statistics, Series 23, No. 25, 2005, Internet site http://www.cdc
.gov/nchs/nsfg.htm

Table 7.28 Current Marital Status of Men, 2002

(total number of men aged 15 to 44, and percent distribution by current marital status, by selected characteristics, 2002; numbers in thousands)

	total		never married	currently married			formerly married		
				total	first marriage	second or higher marriage	separated	divorced	widowed
	number	percent							
Total men aged 15 to 44	**61,147**	**100.0%**	**49.4%**	**42.2%**	**35.0%**	**7.2%**	**1.7%**	**6.6%**	**0.1%**
Aged 15 to 19	10,208	100.0	99.3	0.4	0.4	0.0	–	0.0	0.0
Aged 20 to 24	9,883	100.0	83.2	15.4	15.4	0.0	1.2	–	0.0
Aged 25 to 29	9,226	100.0	50.3	45.3	44.4	0.9	1.3	3.2	0.0
Aged 30 to 34	10,138	100.0	29.9	60.6	52.0	8.6	2.4	6.9	–
Aged 35 to 39	10,557	100.0	21.8	65.5	53.8	11.7	2.2	10.3	–
Aged 40 to 44	11,135	100.0	16.6	62.9	43.1	19.8	2.8	17.7	–
Number of biological children									
None	32,593	100.0	79.7	16.8	15.0	1.8	0.6	2.8	–
One	10,457	100.0	23.7	61.5	50.5	11.0	3.4	11.4	–
Two	9,829	100.0	9.4	76.3	67.6	8.7	3.2	11.0	–
Three or more	8,269	100.0	9.7	77.3	55.5	21.8	2.4	10.5	–
Race and Hispanic origin									
Black, non-Hispanic	6,940	100.0	58.3	31.5	24.9	6.6	2.8	7.1	–
Hispanic	10,188	100.0	50.3	42.7	38.6	4.1	2.5	4.5	0.0
White, non-Hispanic	38,738	100.0	46.8	44.4	36.2	8.2	1.5	7.3	–
Education									
Not a high school graduate	6,355	100.0	36.5	53.2	41.6	11.6	3.6	6.7	–
High school graduate or GED	15,659	100.0	31.1	53.9	41.1	12.8	2.8	12.0	–
Some college, no degree	13,104	100.0	41.3	48.7	40.7	8.0	1.6	8.3	–
Bachelor's degree or more	11,901	100.0	31.7	61.7	56.6	5.1	1.0	5.6	–
Family structure at age 14									
Living with both parents	45,166	100.0	48.5	43.8	36.5	7.3	1.7	6.0	0.1
Other	15,981	100.0	51.8	37.8	30.9	6.9	1.9	8.4	–

Note: Education categories include only people aged 22 to 44. "–" means sample is too small to make a reliable estimate.
Source: National Center for Health Statistics, Fertility, Contraception, and Fatherhood: Data on Men and Women from Cycle 6 of the 2002 National Survey of Family Growth, Vital and Health Statistics, Series 23, No. 26, 2006, Internet site http://www .cdc.gov/nchs/nsfg.htm

Husbands and Wives Are Alike in Many Ways

Most couples are close in age and education.

Women usually marry slightly older men, but most husbands and wives are close in age. Thirty-two percent are within one year of each other in age, and in another 20 percent the husband is only two to three years older than the wife. In less than 1 percent of couples is the husband 20 or more years older than the wife.

In the 57 percent majority of married couples, neither spouse has a bachelor's degree. In another 22 percent, both husband and wife have a bachelor's degree. Only 21 percent of couples are educationally dissimilar, with one spouse having a bachelor's degree and the other having less education.

There are bigger differences between spouses by earnings. Only 24 percent of couples are within $4,999 of one another's earnings. For 58 percent of couples, the husband earns at least $5,000 more than his wife. For only 18 percent of couples does the wife earn at least $5,000 more than her husband.

Changing racial and ethnic categories make analysis of interracial marriage a complex task. The Census Bureau estimates that 7 percent of married couples are of mixed race or Hispanic origin, numbering 4.3 million. No single type of mixed marriage accounts for more than 2 percent of all marriages.

■ The similarities between husbands and wives mean that well-educated high earners tend to marry one another, boosting incomes.

Most husbands and wives share the same educational level

(percent distribution of married couples by education of husband and wife, 2008)

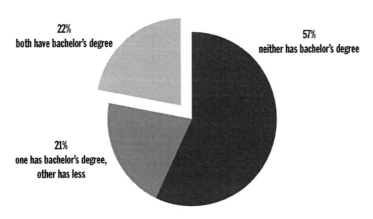

22%
both have bachelor's degree

57%
neither has bachelor's degree

21%
one has bachelor's degree,
other has less

Table 7.29 Age Difference between Husbands and Wives, 2008

(number and percent distribution of married-couple family groups by age difference between husband and wife, 2008; numbers in thousands)

	number	percent distribution
AGE DIFFERENCE		
Total married couples	**60,129**	**100.0%**
Husband 20 or more years older than wife	564	0.8
Husband 15 to 19 years older than wife	916	1.5
Husband 10 to 14 years older than wife	3,115	5.2
Husband 6 to 9 years older than wife	6,995	12.3
Husband 4 to 5 years older than wife	8,244	13.4
Husband 2 to 3 years older than wife	12,245	20.4
Husband and wife within 1 year	19,176	32.1
Wife 2 to 3 years older than husband	4,290	7.0
Wife 4 to 5 years older than husband	2,092	3.4
Wife 6 to 9 years older than husband	1,551	2.6
Wife 10 to 14 years older than husband	610	0.9
Wife 15 to 19 years older than husband	176	0.3
Wife 20 or more years older than husband	156	0.2

Note: Married-couple family groups include married-couple householders and married couples living in households headed by others.
Source: Bureau of the Census, America's Families and Living Arrangements, 2008 Current Population Survey, Internet site http://www.census.gov/population/www/socdemo/hh-fam/cps2008.html; calculations by New Strategist

Table 7.30 Earnings Difference between Husbands and Wives, 2008

(number and percent distribution of married-couple family groups by earnings difference between husbands and wives and presence of children under age 18, 2008; numbers in thousands)

	number	percent distribution
Total married couples	**60,129**	**100.0%**
Husband earns at least $50,000 more than wife	12,706	21.1
Husband earns $30,000 to $49,999 more than wife	8,077	13.4
Husband earns $10,000 to $29,999 more than wife	11,171	18.6
Husband earns $5,000 to $9,999 more than wife	2,689	4.5
Husband earns within $4,999 of wife	14,447	24.0
Wife earns $5,000 to $9,999 more than husband	1,828	3.0
Wife earns $10,000 to $29,999 more than husband	5,041	8.4
Wife earns $30,000 to $49,999 more than husband	2,334	3.9
Wife earns at least $50,000 more than husband	1,837	3.1

Note: Married-couple family groups include married-couple householders and married couples living in households headed by others.
Source: Bureau of the Census, America's Families and Living Arrangements: 2008, Internet site http://www.census.gov/population/www/socdemo/hh-fam/cps2008.html; calculations by New Strategist

Table 7.31 Educational Difference between Husbands and Wives, 2008

(number and percent distribution of married-couple family groups by educational difference between husband and wife, 2008; numbers in thousands)

	number	percent distribution
EDUCATIONAL DIFFERENCE		
Total married couples	**60,129**	**100.0%**
Neither has bachelor's degree	34,049	56.6
One has bachelor's degree, other has less	12,771	21.2
Both have bachelor's degree	13,309	22.1

Note: Married-couple family groups include married-couple householders and married couples living in households headed by others.
Source: Bureau of the Census, America's Families and Living Arrangements, 2008 Current Population Survey, Internet site http://www.census.gov/population/www/socdemo/hh-fam/cps2008.html; calculations by New Strategist

Table 7.32 Race and Hispanic Origin Differences between Husbands and Wives, 2008

(number and percent distribution of married-couple family groups by race and Hispanic origin differences between husband and wife, 2008; numbers in thousands)

	number	percent distribution
Total married-couple family groups	**60,129**	**100.0%**
Both non-Hispanic white	42,448	70.6
Both Hispanic	6,390	10.6
Both non-Hispanic black	3,917	6.5
Both non-Hispanic other	3,049	5.1
Mixed race/Hispanic origin couples, total	**4,325**	**7.2**
Husband non-Hispanic white, wife non-Hispanic black	135	0.2
Husband non-Hispanic white, wife Hispanic	993	1.7
Husband non-Hispanic white, wife non-Hispanic other	994	1.7
Husband non-Hispanic black, wife non-Hispanic white	275	0.5
Husband non-Hispanic black, wife Hispanic	108	0.2
Husband non-Hispanic black, wife non-Hispanic other	76	0.1
Husband Hispanic, wife non-Hispanic white	935	1.6
Husband Hispanic, wife non-Hispanic black	45	0.1
Husband Hispanic, wife non-Hispanic other	74	0.1
Husband non-Hispanic other, wife non-Hispanic white	587	1.0
Husband non-Hispanic other, wife non-Hispanic black	37	0.1
Husband non-Hispanic other, wife Hispanic	66	0.1

Note: "Other" category includes Asians and American Indians. Hispanics may be of any race. Married-couple family groups include married-couple householders and married couples living in households headed by others.
Source: Bureau of the Census, America's Families and Living Arrangements, 2008 Current Population Survey, Internet site http://www.census.gov/population/www/socdemo/hh-fam/cps2008.html; calculations by New Strategist

Divorce Is Highest among Men and Women in Their Fifties

The oldest boomers are most likely to have gone through a divorce.

The experience of divorce is most common among men and women aged 50 to 59. Among men in the age group in 2004, 37.5 percent had ever divorced, according to a Census Bureau study of marriage and divorce. Among women in the age group, the percentage who had ever divorce was an even higher 40.7 percent. Among all Americans aged 15 or older, 41 percent of women and 44 percent of men had married once and were still married. The figure topped 50 percent for men aged 30 or older and for women aged 30 to 39.

Among ever-married women aged 15 to 44, a substantial 35 percent have seen their first marriage dissolve, according to a survey by the National Center for Health Statistics. For men the figure is 31 percent. Marital problems are much more likely for those who marry at a young age. Among women who married for the first time before age 18, the 63 percent majority has seen the marriage dissolve. For men who married for the first time before age 20, fully 59 percent have seen the marriage end.

■ Government studies have suggested that the Vietnam War and women's changing roles are factors in the higher divorce rates of boomers.

More than one in five adults have experienced divorce

(percent of people aged 15 or older by selected marital history and sex, 2004)

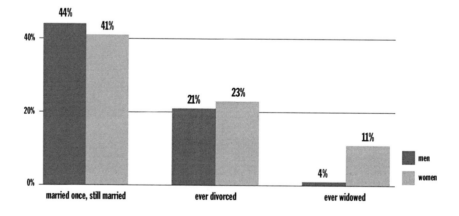

Table 7.33 Marital History of Women by Age, 2004

(number of women aged 15 or older and percent distribution by marital history and age, 2004; numbers in thousands)

	total	15–19	20–24	25–29	30–34	35–39	40–49	50–59	60–69	70+
Total women, number	117,677	10,082	10,027	9,484	10,097	10,319	22,818	18,412	11,852	14,586
Total women, percent	100.0%	100.0%	100.0%	100.0%	100.0%	100.0%	100.0%	100.0%	100.0%	100.0%
Never married	25.8	97.3	73.3	41.3	22.3	16.2	11.9	7.6	4.3	4.9
Ever married	74.2	2.7	26.7	58.7	77.7	83.8	88.1	92.4	95.7	95.1
Married once	57.9	2.7	25.8	55.5	68.4	67.5	65.3	62.8	71.1	77.4
Still married	40.6	2.4	23.0	48.6	57.6	54.6	49.7	44.4	46.2	29.0
Married twice	13.2	0.1	0.8	3.1	8.2	14.1	18.9	22.6	18.7	14.9
Still married	8.8	0.0	0.7	2.8	6.6	11.3	14.0	15.5	11.3	5.3
Married three or more times	3.1	0.0	0.0	0.1	1.2	2.2	3.9	7.0	5.9	2.8
Still married	1.9	0.0	0.0	0.1	0.8	1.6	2.8	4.4	3.6	1.0
Ever divorced	22.9	0.2	2.5	7.0	17.1	25.6	33.9	40.7	32.3	17.8
Currently divorced	10.9	0.1	1.7	4.1	9.1	11.7	16.4	19.4	15.0	7.2
Ever widowed	10.8	0.1	0.1	0.3	0.7	1.1	2.5	7.8	21.2	54.5
Currently widowed	9.6	0.1	0.1	0.2	0.5	0.9	1.6	5.7	18.0	51.6

Source: Bureau of the Census, Number, Timing, and Duration of Marriages and Divorces: 2004, Detailed Tables, Internet site http://www.census.gov/population/www/socdemo/marr-div/2004detailed_tables.html

Table 7.34 Marital History of Men by Age, 2004

(number of men aged 15 or older and percent distribution by marital history and age, 2004; numbers in thousands)

	total	15–19	20–24	25–29	30–34	35–39	40–49	50–59	60–69	70+
Total men, number	109,830	10,473	10,022	9,511	9,848	10,121	21,857	17,352	10,571	10,075
Total men, percent	100.0%	100.0%	100.0%	100.0%	100.0%	100.0%	100.0%	100.0%	100.0%	100.0%
Never married	31.2	98.1	84.0	53.6	30.3	20.2	14.1	8.7	4.8	3.2
Ever married	68.8	1.9	16.0	46.4	69.7	79.8	85.9	91.3	95.2	96.8
Married once	54.0	1.9	15.9	44.3	62.4	68.1	66.8	63.4	66.8	74.9
Still married	43.8	1.5	14.4	39.7	54.4	56.6	52.8	50.3	54.7	55.1
Married twice	11.8	0.0	0.1	2.0	6.7	10.3	15.7	21.3	20.6	17.0
Still married	9.2	0.0	0.1	1.9	6.0	8.5	12.5	16.1	16.1	12.6
Married three or more times	3.1	0.0	0.0	0.1	0.6	1.4	3.3	6.6	7.7	4.9
Still married	2.3	0.0	0.0	0.0	0.4	1.2	2.7	5.1	5.6	3.1
Ever divorced	20.7	0.1	0.8	5.1	13.1	20.7	30.3	37.5	34.1	20.6
Currently divorced	9.3	0.1	0.7	3.2	6.6	10.9	14.7	16.2	13.0	6.2
Ever widowed	3.6	0.2	0.0	0.1	0.1	0.6	1.1	2.8	7.1	23.8
Currently widowed	2.5	0.2	0.0	0.0	0.1	0.4	0.6	1.4	4.2	18.9

Source: Bureau of the Census, Number, Timing, and Duration of Marriages and Divorces: 2004, Detailed Tables, Internet site http://www.census.gov/population/www/socdemo/marr-div/2004detailed_tables.html

Table 7.35 Cumulative Percentage of Women Whose First Marriage Has Dissolved, 2002

(number of ever-married women aged 15 to 44 and cumulative percentage of women whose first marriage dissolved through separation, annulment, or divorce, by selected characteristics and years since first marriage, 2002; numbers in thousands)

	total		years since first marriage			all marital durations
	number	percent	one year	five years	ten years	
Total ever-married women aged 15 to 44	**35,849**	**100.0%**	**5.5%**	**19.9%**	**29.1%**	**34.7%**
Age at first marriage						
Under age 18	2,983	100.0	6.7	34.2	48.1	62.6
Aged 18 to 19	6,155	100.0	10.4	28.3	39.1	50.1
Aged 20 to 22	10,094	100.0	5.6	21.5	31.9	37.8
Aged 23 or older	16,617	100.0	3.5	13.3	20.2	22.0
First cohabitation relative to first marriage						
Did not cohabit before first marriage	18,572	100.0	5.0	18.4	28.6	35.3
Cohabited with first husband	13,385	100.0	6.1	22.2	30.9	35.9
Cohabited with someone else	3,892	100.0	6.3	19.2	25.2	27.1
Race and Hispanic origin						
Black, non-Hispanic	3,242	100.0	7.7	23.9	37.1	42.8
Hispanic	5,269	100.0	4.7	17.4	25.6	30.0
White, non-Hispanic	24,817	100.0	5.1	19.6	28.9	35.1
Education						
Not a high school graduate	3,816	100.0	7.6	23.5	31.7	40.6
High school graduate or GED	10,691	100.0	7.0	25.0	38.2	45.4
Some college, no degree	10,728	100.0	5.5	21.3	31.3	36.4
Bachelor's degree or more	9,728	100.0	2.9	11.8	17.0	20.3
Family structure at age 14						
Living with both parents	26,839	100.0	5.1	18.0	25.8	31.6
Other	9,009	100.0	6.9	25.6	38.8	43.8

Note: Education categories include only people aged 22 to 44.
Source: National Center for Health Statistics, Fertility, Family Planning, and Reproductive Health of U.S. Women: Data from the 2002 National Survey of Family Growth, Vital and Health Statistics, Series 23, No. 25, 2005, Internet site http://www.cdc .gov/nchs/nsfg.htm

Table 7.36 Cumulative Percentage of Men Whose First Marriage Has Dissolved, 2002

(number of ever-married men aged 15 to 44 and cumulative percentage of men whose first marriage dissolved through separation, annulment, or divorce, by selected characteristics and years since first marriage, 2002; numbers in thousands)

	total		years since first marriage			all marital durations
	number	percent	one year	five years	ten years	
Total ever-married men aged 15 to 44	**30,972**	**100.0%**	**5.8%**	**19.3%**	**26.7%**	**30.6%**
Age at first marriage						
Under age 20	3,854	100.0	15.8	42.6	50.2	58.6
Aged 20 to 22	7,249	100.0	6.3	20.8	30.1	35.5
Aged 23 to 25	8,101	100.0	5.0	19.3	27.2	29.8
Aged 25 or older	11,767	100.0	2.7	10.8	16.7	18.9
First cohabitation relative to first marriage						
Did not cohabit before first marriage	13,649	100.0	5.9	18.8	25.5	29.8
Cohabited with first wife	12,734	100.0	5.4	20.7	28.0	31.8
Cohabited with someone else	4,566	100.0	5.8	16.8	26.5	29.2
Race and Hispanic origin						
Black, non-Hispanic	2,894	100.0	5.6	22.8	34.8	39.2
Hispanic	5,064	100.0	5.2	15.3	19.7	22.3
White, non-Hispanic	20,611	100.0	5.5	19.8	27.7	31.8
Education						
Not a high school graduate	4,037	100.0	9.7	26.2	32.0	34.4
High school graduate or GED	10,793	100.0	6.1	23.0	33.9	39.9
Some college, no degree	7,695	100.0	5.6	19.7	27.6	30.5
Bachelor's degree or more	8,131	100.0	3.3	10.8	14.2	17.0
Family structure at age 14						
Living with both parents	23,270	100.0	5.5	17.9	24.5	29.0
Other	7,702	100.0	6.5	23.7	33.5	35.5

Note: Education categories include only people aged 22 to 44.
Source: National Center for Health Statistics, Fertility, Contraception, and Fatherhood: Data on Men and Women from Cycle 6 of the 2002 National Survey of Family Growth, Vital and Health Statistics, Series 23, No. 26, 2006; Internet site http://www.cdc .gov/nchs/nsfg.htm

CHAPTER
8

Population Trends

■ The number of people in their sixties is growing rapidly.

The 60-to-64 age group grew the fastest between 2000 and 2008—up 39 percent as the oldest boomers aged into their sixties. Between 2008 and 2025, the fastest-growing age group is projected to be 65 or older, with a 64 percent increase as the entire baby-boom generation ages beyond 60.

■ The non-Hispanic white population is growing slowly.

Overall, 67 percent of Americans are non-Hispanic white, a figure that is falling as younger generations replace older ones. The non-Hispanic white share of the population will fall to 58 percent by 2025, according to Census Bureau projections.

■ In four states, minorities are the majority.

In California, the nation's most-populous state, only 42 percent of residents are non-Hispanic white. In the nation's second-most-populous state, Texas, non-Hispanic whites account for 47 percent of the population.

■ Raleigh is the fastest-growing major metropolitan area.

Las Vegas is now number two, up 34 percent between 2000 and 2008—just below Raleigh's 35 percent gain.

■ Most immigrants settle in only five states.

California, New York, Florida, Texas, and New Jersey receive most of the nation's immigrants.

More Women than Men

Females outnumber males by more than 4 million.

Although there are more females than males in the population, females do not begin to outnumber males until the 45-to-49 age group. Among people aged 85 or older, there are only 48 men for every 100 women. Males slightly outnumber females at younger ages because boys outnumber girls at birth. Women outnumber men at older ages because, throughout life, males have a higher death rate than females. Research has shown that the higher male death rate is due primarily to biological factors rather than lifestyle differences.

Between 2000 and 2008, the U.S. population grew by 8 percent, to more than 304 million. The most-populous five-year age group is 45 to 49, numbering nearly 23 million in 2008. This age group is larger than any other because it is filled with the youngest members of the baby-boom generation. The 60-to-64 age group grew the fastest between 2000 and 2008—up 39 percent as the oldest boomers aged into their sixties. Another relatively large generation is now entering adulthood. Millennials, spanning the ages from 14 to 31 in 2008, are behind the 10 to 11 percent increase in the number of 20-to-29-year-olds since 2000.

■ Because death rates are higher for males than for females, women will always greatly outnumber men in old age.

Women increasingly outnumber men with age

(number of males per 100 females at selected aged, 2008)

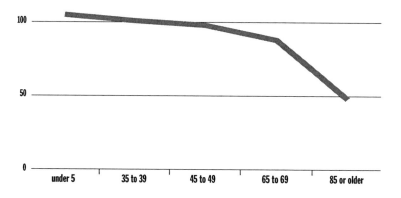

Table 8.1 Population by Age and Sex, 2008

(number of people by age and sex, and sex ratio by age, 2008; numbers in thousands)

	total	female	male	sex ratio
Total people	**304,060**	**154,135**	**149,925**	**97**
Under age 5	21,006	10,258	10,748	105
Aged 5 to 9	20,065	9,806	10,259	105
Aged 10 to 14	20,055	9,792	10,262	105
Aged 15 to 19	21,514	10,487	11,027	105
Aged 20 to 24	21,059	10,214	10,845	106
Aged 25 to 29	21,334	10,393	10,941	105
Aged 30 to 34	19,598	9,639	9,959	103
Aged 35 to 39	20,994	10,425	10,569	101
Aged 40 to 44	21,507	10,762	10,746	100
Aged 45 to 49	22,880	11,566	11,314	98
Aged 50 to 54	21,492	10,954	10,539	96
Aged 55 to 59	18,583	9,569	9,015	94
Aged 60 to 64	15,103	7,867	7,236	92
Aged 65 to 69	11,349	6,042	5,306	88
Aged 70 to 74	8,774	4,816	3,959	82
Aged 75 to 79	7,275	4,178	3,097	74
Aged 80 to 84	5,750	3,510	2,239	64
Aged 85 or older	5,722	3,858	1,864	48
Aged 18 to 24	29,757	14,449	15,309	106
Aged 18 or older	230,118	118,027	112,091	95
Aged 65 or older	38,870	22,405	16,465	73
Median age (years)	36.8	38.1	35.5	–

Note: The sex ratio is the number of men per 100 women; "–" means not applicable.
Source: Bureau of the Census, National Population Estimates, Internet site http://www.census.gov/popest/national/asrh/
NC-EST2008-sa.html; calculations by New Strategist

Table 8.2 Population by Age, 2000 and 2008

(number of people by age, 2000 and 2008, and percent change, 2000–08; numbers in thousands)

	2008	2000	percent change
Total people	**304,060**	**282,172**	**7.8%**
Under age 5	21,006	19,186	9.5
Aged 5 to 9	20,065	20,475	−2.0
Aged 10 to 14	20,055	20,619	−2.7
Aged 15 to 19	21,514	20,259	6.2
Aged 20 to 24	21,059	19,124	10.1
Aged 25 to 29	21,334	19,302	10.5
Aged 30 to 34	19,598	20,538	−4.6
Aged 35 to 39	20,994	22,658	−7.3
Aged 40 to 44	21,507	22,523	−4.5
Aged 45 to 49	22,880	20,221	13.1
Aged 50 to 54	21,492	17,774	20.9
Aged 55 to 59	18,583	13,559	37.1
Aged 60 to 64	15,103	10,856	39.1
Aged 65 to 69	11,349	9,517	19.2
Aged 70 to 74	8,774	8,852	−0.9
Aged 75 to 79	7,275	7,436	−2.2
Aged 80 to 84	5,750	4,986	15.3
Aged 85 or older	5,722	4,286	33.5
Aged 18 to 24	29,757	27,308	9.0
Aged 18 or older	230,118	209,816	9.7
Aged 65 or older	38,870	35,077	10.8

Note: Numbers are for July 1 of each year.
Source: Bureau of the Census, National Population Estimates, Internet site http://www.census.gov/popest/national/asrh/ NC-EST2008-sa.html; calculations by New Strategist

The Number of Older Americans Will Soar

The number of people aged 65 or older will grow by 64 percent between 2008 and 2025.

The U.S. population is projected to grow 18 percent between 2008 and 2025, from 304 million to 357 million people, according to projections by the Census Bureau. But growth will vary by age group.

Between 2008 and 2025, the fastest-growing age group is projected to be 65 or older, with a 64 percent increase as the entire baby-boom generation ages beyond 60. In contrast, the number of people aged 45 to 64 will grow by only 7 percent during those years as the small generation X enters late middle age. The number of people under age 18 is projected to grow by 15 percent—slightly below the average growth rate.

■ Rapid growth in the number of retirees will shift the focus of the nation's attention toward health care and retirement security.

The U.S. population is aging rapidly

(percent change in size of selected age groups, 2008–25)

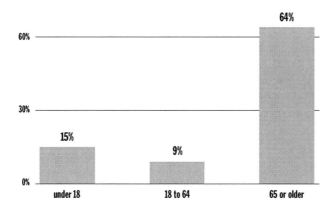

Table 8.3 Population by Age, 2008 to 2025

(projected number of people by age, 2008 to 2025, and percent change for selected years; numbers in thousands)

	2008	2010	2015	2025	percent change 2008–10	percent change 2008–15	percent change 2008–25
Total people	**304,060**	**310,233**	**325,540**	**357,452**	**2.0%**	**7.1%**	**17.6%**
Under age 18	73,942	75,217	78,106	84,866	1.7	5.6	14.8
Under age 5	21,006	21,100	22,076	23,484	0.4	5.1	11.8
Aged 5 to 13	36,005	37,123	39,011	42,490	3.1	8.3	18.0
Aged 14 to 17	16,931	16,994	17,019	18,892	0.4	0.5	11.6
Aged 18 to 64	191,248	194,787	200,597	208,678	1.9	4.9	9.1
Aged 18 to 24	29,757	30,713	30,885	32,555	3.2	3.8	9.4
Aged 25 to 44	83,433	83,095	85,801	92,612	−0.4	2.8	11.0
Aged 45 to 64	78,058	80,980	83,911	83,510	3.7	7.5	7.0
Aged 65 or older	38,870	40,229	46,837	63,907	3.5	20.5	64.4

Source: Bureau of the Census, 2008 National Population Projections, Internet site http://www.census.gov/population/www/ projections/2008projections.html; calculations by New Strategist

The Non-Hispanic White Population Is Growing Slowly

Children and young adults are far more diverse than older generations.

The United States is steadily becoming more diverse, with slow growth of the majority non-Hispanic white population and rapid growth of most minority groups. Between 2000 and 2008, the non-Hispanic white population grew by just 2 percent, according to Census Bureau estimates. In contrast, the Hispanic population grew 32 percent and Asians (alone or in combination) added 28 percent. Overall, 67 percent of Americans are non-Hispanic white, a figure that is falling as younger generations replace older ones. The non-Hispanic white share of the population ranges from a low of 53 percent among children under age 5 to a high of 80 percent among people aged 65 or older.

The nation's racial and ethnic composition is also becoming more complex because of the rapid growth of the Hispanic population and the fact that Hispanics may be of any race. Of the nation's 47 million Hispanics, more than 2 million are black.

■ Because younger generations are more diverse than older Americans, a multicultural generation gap is emerging.

The non-Hispanic white share of the population is smallest among children

(percent distribution of children under age 5 and people aged 65 or older, by race and Hispanic origin, 2008)

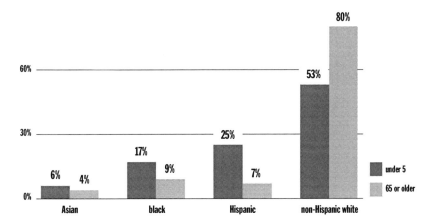

Table 8.4 Total Population by Race, 2000 and 2008

(number of people by race and Hispanic origin, 2000 and 2008; numerical and percent change, 2000–08; numbers in thousands)

	2008	2000	change numerical	change percent
TOTAL POPULATION	**304,060**	**282,172**	**21,888**	**7.8%**
Race alone				
American Indian	3,083	2,676	408	15.2
Asian	13,549	10,687	2,862	26.8
Black	39,059	35,807	3,252	9.1
Native Hawaiian	562	466	97	20.8
White	242,639	228,604	14,035	6.1
Race alone or in combination				
American Indian	4,862	4,243	619	14.6
Asian	15,480	12,119	3,361	27.7
Black	41,127	37,225	3,902	10.5
Native Hawaiian	1,112	913	200	21.9
White	247,113	231,965	5,931	6.5
Hispanic	**46,944**	**35,644**	**11,300**	**31.7**
Non-Hispanic white	**199,491**	**195,763**	**1,569**	**1.9**

Note: Numbers by race alone do not add to total because they do not include those who identify themselves as being of more than one race. Numbers by race in combination do not add to total because they include those who identify themselves as being of the race alone and those who identify themselves as being of the race in combination with other races. Hispanics may be of any race. Non-Hispanic whites are those who identify themselves as being white alone and not Hispanic. Numbers are for July 1 of each year.
Source: Bureau of the Census, National Population Estimates, Internet site http://www.census.gov/popest/national/asrh/ NC-EST2008-sa.html; calculations by New Strategist

Table 8.5 Hispanics and Non-Hispanics by Race, 2008

(number and percent distribution of Hispanics and non-Hispanics by race, 2008; numbers in thousands)

	Hispanics		non-Hispanics	
	number	percent distribution	number	percent of distribution
TOTAL POPULATION	**46,944**	**100.0%**	**257,116**	**100.0%**
Race alone				
American Indian	754	1.6	2,329	0.9
Asian	311	0.7	13,238	5.1
Black	1,887	4.0	37,172	14.5
Native Hawaiian	128	0.3	435	0.2
White	43,148	91.9	199,491	77.6
Race alone or in combination				
American Indian	1,034	2.2	3,828	1.5
Asian	523	1.1	14,957	5.8
Black	2,211	4.7	38,916	15.1
Native Hawaiian	213	0.5	899	0.3
White	43,777	93.3	203,336	79.1

Note: Numbers by race alone do not add to total because they do not include those who identify themselves as being of more than one race. Numbers by race in combination do not add to total because they include those who identify themselves as being of the race alone and those who identify themselves as being of the race in combination with other races. Hispanics may be of any race.
Source: Bureau of the Census, National Population Estimates, Internet site http://www.census.gov/popest/national/asrh/ NC-EST2008-sa.html; calculations by New Strategist

Table 8.6 Population by Age, Race, and Hispanic Origin, 2008

(number and percent distribution of people by age, race, and Hispanic origin, 2008; numbers in thousands)

	total	Asian	black	Hispanic	non-Hispanic white
Total people	**304,060**	**15,480**	**41,127**	**46,944**	**199,491**
Under age 5	21,006	1,242	3,573	5,288	11,065
Aged 5 to 9	20,065	1,107	3,298	4,464	11,222
Aged 10 to 14	20,055	1,033	3,363	3,989	11,660
Aged 15 to 19	21,514	1,018	3,667	3,850	12,903
Aged 20 to 24	21,059	1,027	3,307	3,663	12,949
Aged 25 to 29	21,334	1,206	3,166	4,141	12,740
Aged 30 to 34	19,598	1,334	2,724	4,041	11,456
Aged 35 to 39	20,994	1,404	2,823	3,730	12,981
Aged 40 to 44	21,507	1,210	2,847	3,279	14,085
Aged 45 to 49	22,880	1,107	2,882	2,795	15,964
Aged 50 to 54	21,492	986	2,563	2,187	15,615
Aged 55 to 59	18,583	829	2,068	1,650	13,907
Aged 60 to 64	15,103	612	1,471	1,204	11,706
Aged 65 or older	38,870	1,367	3,375	2,661	31,238

PERCENT DISTRIBUTION BY RACE AND HISPANIC ORIGIN

Total people	**100.0%**	**5.1%**	**13.5%**	**15.4%**	**65.6%**
Under age 5	100.0	5.9	17.0	25.2	52.7
Aged 5 to 9	100.0	5.5	16.4	22.2	55.9
Aged 10 to 14	100.0	5.1	16.8	19.9	58.1
Aged 15 to 19	100.0	4.7	17.0	17.9	60.0
Aged 20 to 24	100.0	4.9	15.7	17.4	61.5
Aged 25 to 29	100.0	5.7	14.8	19.4	59.7
Aged 30 to 34	100.0	6.8	13.9	20.6	58.5
Aged 35 to 39	100.0	6.7	13.4	17.8	61.8
Aged 40 to 44	100.0	5.6	13.2	15.2	65.5
Aged 45 to 49	100.0	4.8	12.6	12.2	69.8
Aged 50 to 54	100.0	4.6	11.9	10.2	72.7
Aged 55 to 59	100.0	4.5	11.1	8.9	74.8
Aged 60 to 64	100.0	4.1	9.7	8.0	77.5
Aged 65 or older	100.0	3.5	8.7	6.8	80.4

	total	Asian	black	Hispanic	non-Hispanic white
PERCENT DISTRIBUTION BY AGE					
Total people	**100.0%**	**100.0%**	**100.0%**	**100.0%**	**100.0%**
Under age 5	6.9	8.0	8.7	11.3	5.5
Aged 5 to 9	6.6	7.1	8.0	9.5	5.6
Aged 10 to 14	6.6	6.7	8.2	8.5	5.8
Aged 15 to 19	7.1	6.6	8.9	8.2	6.5
Aged 20 to 24	6.9	6.6	8.0	7.8	6.5
Aged 25 to 29	7.0	7.8	7.7	8.8	6.4
Aged 30 to 34	6.4	8.6	6.6	8.6	5.7
Aged 35 to 39	6.9	9.1	6.9	7.9	6.5
Aged 40 to 44	7.1	7.8	6.9	7.0	7.1
Aged 45 to 49	7.5	7.1	7.0	6.0	8.0
Aged 50 to 54	7.1	6.4	6.2	4.7	7.8
Aged 55 to 59	6.1	5.4	5.0	3.5	7.0
Aged 60 to 64	5.0	4.0	3.6	2.6	5.9
Aged 65 or older	12.8	8.8	8.2	5.7	15.7

Note: Numbers by race and Hispanic origin do not add to total because they include those who identify themselves as being of the race alone and those who identify themselves as being of the race in combination with other races. Hispanics may be of any race. Non-Hispanic whites are those who identify themselves as being white alone and not Hispanic.
Source: Bureau of the Census, National Population Estimates, Internet site http://www.census.gov/popest/national/asrh/ NC-EST2008-sa.html; calculations by New Strategist

Number of Asians and Hispanics Will Grow the Fastest

Slow growth is projected for non-Hispanic whites.

Among the nation's racial and ethnic groups, the Census Bureau projects that Asians and Hispanics will grow the fastest, far outpacing growth of the black ans non-Hispanic white populations. The number of Asians is projected to increase 58 percent between 2008 and 2025 for an overall gain of 9 million during those years. The Hispanic population is projected to grow by an even larger 61 percent between 2008 and 2025 for an overall gain of 29 million.

The non-Hispanic white population will grow by only 4 percent during the 2008-to-2025 time period. The non-Hispanic white share of the population will fall to 58 percent by 2025. The black population will grow faster than the non-Hispanic white population, but slower than the Asian and Hispanic populations. In 2008, Hispanics outnumbered blacks by 6 million. By 2025, Hispanics will outnumber blacks by 25 million.

■ The growing diversity of the population will affect domestic policy and international affairs as well as consumer markets.

Below-average growth is projected for non-Hispanic whites

(percent change in population by race and Hispanic origin, 2008 to 2025)

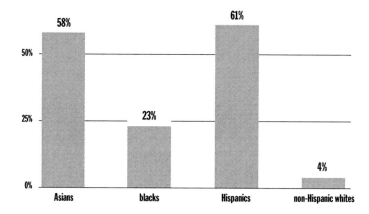

Table 8.7 Population by Race and Hispanic Origin, 2008 to 2025

(projected number and percent distribution of people by race and Hispanic origin, 2008 to 2025, percent change in number and percentage point change in share for selected years; numbers in thousands)

	2008	2010	2015	2025	percent change 2008–10	2008–15	2008–25
Total population	**304,060**	**310,233**	**325,540**	**357,452**	**2.0%**	**7.1%**	**17.6%**
Asian	15,480	16,472	18,952	24,385	6.4	22.4	57.5
Black	41,127	42,163	44,906	50,626	2.5	9.2	23.1
Hispanic	46,944	49,726	57,711	75,772	5.9	22.9	61.4
Non-Hispanic white	199,491	200,853	203,208	206,662	0.7	1.9	3.6

	2008	2010	2015	2025	percentage point change 2008–10	2008–15	2008–25
PERCENT DISTRIBUTION							
Total population	**100.0%**	**100.0%**	**100.0%**	**100.0%**	–	–	–
Asian	5.1	5.3	5.8	6.8	0.2	0.7	1.7
Black	13.5	13.6	13.8	14.2	0.1	0.3	0.6
Hispanic	15.4	16.0	17.7	21.2	0.6	2.3	5.8
Non-Hispanic white	65.6	64.7	62.4	57.8	–0.9	–3.2	–7.8

Note: Numbers by race and Hispanic origin do not add to total because they include those who identify themselves as being of the race alone and those who identify themselves as being of the race in combination with other races. Hispanics may be of any race. Non-Hispanic whites are those who identify themselves as being white alone and not Hispanic. "–" means not applicable. Source: Bureau of the Census, 2008 National Population Projections, Internet site http://www.census.gov/population/www/projections/2008projections.html; calculations by New Strategist

The South Is the Most Populous Region

The West is the most diverse.

The South is by far the most populous region. Nearly 37 percent of Americans live in the South, according to 2008 estimates by the Census Bureau. The Northeast is the least populous region, home to 18 percent of the total population. Between 2000 and 2008, the Mountain states of the West were the fastest growing part of the country, their population expanding by 20 percent. The Middle Atlantic states experienced the smallest population gain during those years, up just 2 percent.

Only 55 percent of the population of the West is non-Hispanic white. In the Pacific states of the West, the proportion is below 50 percent. In contrast, 85 percent of the residents of the West North Central states (Iowa, Kansas, Minnesota, Missouri, Nebraska, North Dakota, and South Dakota) are non-Hispanic white.

The South is home to the 54 percent majority of the nation's blacks. Within the region, blacks account for one-fifth of the population. Forty-two percent of Hispanics live in the West, where they account for 28 percent of the population. Forty-seven percent of Asians live in the West, and they account for one in 10 Western residents.

■ Asians, blacks, and Hispanics will soon account for the majority of the population in the Western states.

The Midwest is the least diverse region

(non-Hispanic white share of the population, by region, 2008)

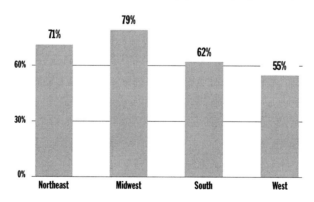

Table 8.8 Population by Region, 2000 and 2008

(number and percent distribution of population by region and division, 2000 and 2008; percent change in number 2000–08; numbers in thousands)

	2008		2000		
	number	percent distribution	number	percent distribution	percent change 2000–08
TOTAL POPULATION	**304,060**	**100.0%**	**281,422**	**100.0%**	**8.0%**
Northeast	**54,925**	**18.1**	**53,594**	**19.0**	**2.5**
New England	14,304	4.7	13,923	4.9	2.7
Middle Atlantic	40,621	13.4	39,672	14.1	2.4
Midwest	**66,561**	**21.9**	**64,393**	**22.9**	**3.4**
East North Central	46,396	15.3	45,155	16.0	2.7
West North Central	20,166	6.6	19,238	6.8	4.8
South	**111,719**	**36.7**	**100,237**	**35.6**	**11.5**
South Atlantic	58,398	19.2	51,769	18.4	12.8
East South Central	18,085	5.9	17,023	6.0	6.2
West South Central	35,236	11.6	31,445	11.2	12.1
West	**70,855**	**23.3**	**63,198**	**22.5**	**12.1**
Mountain	21,785	7.2	18,172	6.5	19.9
Pacific	49,070	16.1	45,026	16.0	9.0

Note: Numbers in 2000 are from the April 1, 2000 census.
Source: Bureau of the Census, State Population Estimates, Internet site http://www.census.gov/popest/states/asrh/; calculations by New Strategist

Table 8.9 Population by Region, Division, Race, and Hispanic Origin, 2008

(number and percent distribution of people by region, division, race, and Hispanic origin, 2008; numbers in thousands)

	total	Asian	black	Hispanic	non-Hispanic white
TOTAL POPULATION	**304,060**	**15,480**	**41,127**	**46,944**	**199,491**
Northeast	**54,925**	**3,108**	**7,317**	**6,421**	**38,816**
New England	14,304	574	1,020	1,159	11,630
Middle Atlantic	40,621	2,534	6,297	5,263	27,186
Midwest	**66,561**	**1,837**	**7,354**	**4,264**	**52,707**
East North Central	46,396	1,341	5,957	3,301	35,665
West North Central	20,166	496	1,397	963	17,042
South	**111,719**	**3,312**	**22,293**	**16,520**	**69,219**
South Atlantic	58,398	1,923	13,275	6,529	36,749
East South Central	18,085	239	3,780	534	13,453
West South Central	35,236	1,149	5,239	9,457	19,017
West	**70,855**	**7,224**	**4,163**	**19,738**	**38,749**
Mountain	21,785	715	944	5,067	14,463
Pacific	49,070	6,509	3,218	14,671	24,287

Percent distribution by race and Hispanic origin

TOTAL POPULATION	**100.0%**	**5.1%**	**13.5%**	**15.4%**	**65.6%**
Northeast	**100.0**	**5.7**	**13.3**	**11.7**	**70.7**
New England	100.0	4.0	7.1	8.1	81.3
Middle Atlantic	100.0	6.2	15.5	13.0	66.9
Midwest	**100.0**	**2.8**	**11.0**	**6.4**	**79.2**
East North Central	100.0	2.9	12.8	7.1	76.9
West North Central	100.0	2.5	6.9	4.8	84.5
South	**100.0**	**3.0**	**20.0**	**14.8**	**62.0**
South Atlantic	100.0	3.3	22.7	11.2	62.9
East South Central	100.0	1.3	20.9	3.0	74.4
West South Central	100.0	3.3	14.9	26.8	54.0
West	**100.0**	**10.2**	**5.9**	**27.9**	**54.7**
Mountain	100.0	3.3	4.3	23.3	66.4
Pacific	100.0	13.3	6.6	29.9	49.5

	total	Asian	black	Hispanic	non-Hispanic white
Percent distribution by region and division					
TOTAL POPULATION	**100.0%**	**100.0%**	**100.0%**	**100.0%**	**100.0%**
Northeast	**18.1**	**20.1**	**17.8**	**13.7**	**19.5**
New England	4.7	3.7	2.5	2.5	5.8
Middle Atlantic	13.4	16.4	15.3	11.2	13.6
Midwest	**21.9**	**11.9**	**17.9**	**9.1**	**26.4**
East North Central	15.3	8.7	14.5	7.0	17.9
West North Central	6.6	3.2	3.4	2.1	8.5
South	**36.7**	**21.4**	**54.2**	**35.2**	**34.7**
South Atlantic	19.2	12.4	32.3	13.9	18.4
East South Central	5.9	1.5	9.2	1.1	6.7
West South Central	11.6	7.4	12.7	20.1	9.5
West	**23.3**	**46.7**	**10.1**	**42.0**	**19.4**
Mountain	7.2	4.6	2.3	10.8	7.2
Pacific	16.1	42.0	7.8	31.3	12.2

Note: Numbers by race and Hispanic origin do not add to total because they include those who identify themselves as being of the race alone and those who identify themselves as being of the race in combination with other races. Hispanics may be of any race. Non-Hispanic whites are those who identify themselves as being white alone and not Hispanic.
Source: Bureau of the Census, State Population Estimates, Internet site http://www.census.gov/popest/states/asrh/; calculations by New Strategist

Nevada Was Growing the Fastest

Between 2000 and 2008, Nevada grew by 30 percent.

Nevada had the fastest-growing population between 2000 and 2008, with a 30 percent gain according to estimates by the Census Bureau. Arizona ranked second in growth with a 27 percent increase. Texas, California, and Florida gained the most people, however, each up by 2 to 3 million between 2000 and 2008.

Louisiana and North Dakota were the only states to lose population between 2000 and 2008. Louisiana lost 1.3 percent of its population—or 58,000 people—primarily because of Hurricane Katrina. North Dakota lost an estimated 1,000 people, a miniscule 0.1 percent. Rhode Island, West Virginia, and Michigan all grew by less than 1 percent between 2000 and 2008.

■ The population growth rates in Nevada and Arizona have slowed considerably in the past few years because of the economic downturn.

Louisiana had the biggest population decline

(percent change in population in the three fastest and slowest growing states, 2000 to 2008)

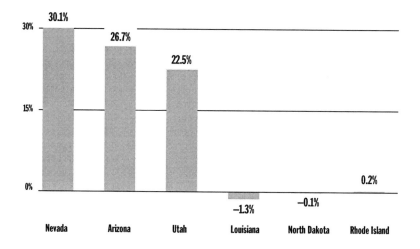

Table 8.10 Population by State, 2000 and 2008

(number of people by state, 2000 and 2008; numerical and percent change, 2000–08; numbers in thousands)

	2008	2000	change, 2000–08 numerical	change, 2000–08 percent
United States	**304,060**	**281,422**	**22,638**	**8.0%**
Alabama	4,662	4,447	215	4.8
Alaska	686	627	59	9.5
Arizona	6,500	5,131	1,370	26.7
Arkansas	2,855	2,673	182	6.8
California	36,757	33,872	2,885	8.5
Colorado	4,939	4,301	638	14.8
Connecticut	3,501	3,406	96	2.8
Delaware	873	784	89	11.4
District of Columbia	592	572	20	3.5
Florida	18,328	15,982	2,346	14.7
Georgia	9,686	8,186	1,499	18.3
Hawaii	1,288	1,212	77	6.3
Idaho	1,524	1,294	230	17.8
Illinois	12,902	12,419	482	3.9
Indiana	6,377	6,080	296	4.9
Iowa	3,003	2,926	76	2.6
Kansas	2,802	2,688	114	4.2
Kentucky	4,269	4,042	227	5.6
Louisiana	4,411	4,469	-58	-1.3
Maine	1,316	1,275	42	3.3
Maryland	5,634	5,296	337	6.4
Massachusetts	6,498	6,349	149	2.3
Michigan	10,003	9,938	65	0.7
Minnesota	5,220	4,919	301	6.1
Mississippi	2,939	2,845	94	3.3
Missouri	5,912	5,595	316	5.7
Montana	967	902	65	7.2
Nebraska	1,783	1,711	72	4.2
Nevada	2,600	1,998	602	30.1
New Hampshire	1,316	1,236	80	6.5
New Jersey	8,683	8,414	268	3.2
New Mexico	1,984	1,819	165	9.1
New York	19,490	18,976	514	2.7
North Carolina	9,222	8,049	1,173	14.6
North Dakota	641	642	-1	-0.1
Ohio	11,486	11,353	133	1.2
Oklahoma	3,642	3,451	192	5.6
Oregon	3,790	3,421	369	10.8
Pennsylvania	12,448	12,281	167	1.4
Rhode Island	1,051	1,048	2	0.2

	2008	2000	change, 2000–08	
			numerical	percent
South Carolina	4,480	4,012	468	11.7%
South Dakota	804	755	49	6.5
Tennessee	6,215	5,689	526	9.2
Texas	24,327	20,852	3,475	16.7
Utah	2,736	2,233	503	22.5
Vermont	621	609	12	2.0
Virginia	7,769	7,079	691	9.8
Washington	6,549	5,894	655	11.1
West Virginia	1,814	1,808	6	0.3
Wisconsin	5,628	5,364	264	4.9
Wyoming	533	494	39	7.9

Note: Numbers in 2000 are from the April 1, 2000 census.
Source: Bureau of the Census, State Population Estimates, Internet site http://www.census.gov/popest/states/asrh/; calculations by New Strategist

Four States Have Minority Majorities

Maine and Vermont are more than 95 percent non-Hispanic white.

Among the 50 states, Hawaii has the smallest share of non-Hispanic whites—only 25 percent of its population is non-Hispanic white and 54 percent is Asian. In New Mexico, non-Hispanic whites account for just 42 percent of the population and Hispanics for a larger 45 percent. In California, the nation's most populous state, 37 percent of residents are Hispanic, 14 percent are Asian, and 42 percent are non-Hispanic white. In the nation's second most-populous state, Texas, non-Hispanic whites account for 47 percent of the population. Thirty-six percent of Texas residents are Hispanic.

At the other extreme, non-Hispanic whites account for more than 95 percent of the populations of Maine and Vermont. In quite a few states of the West and Midwest, minorities account for less than 15 percent of the population.

■ Although Hispanics and Asians are growing in number, their political power is muted by low voter participation rates.

California is one of the nation's most diverse states

(percent distribution of population in California, by race and Hispanic origin, 2008)

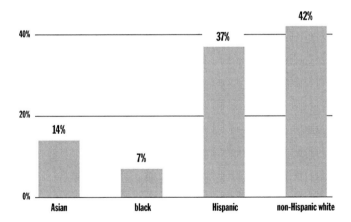

Table 8.11 Population by State, Race, and Hispanic Origin, 2008

(number and percent distribution of people by state, race, and Hispanic origin, 2008; numbers in thousands)

| | number | | | | | percent distribution | | | | |
	total	Asian	black	Hispanic	non-Hispanic white	total	Asian	black	Hispanic	non-Hispanic white
United States	**304,060**	**15,480**	**41,127**	**46,944**	**199,491**	**100.0%**	**5.1%**	**13.5%**	**15.4%**	**65.6%**
Alabama	4,662	56	1,249	135	3,191	100.0	1.2	26.8	2.9	68.4
Alaska	686	40	36	42	451	100.0	5.9	5.3	6.1	65.7
Arizona	6,500	203	312	1,956	3,796	100.0	3.1	4.8	30.1	58.4
Arkansas	2,855	38	464	160	2,160	100.0	1.3	16.2	5.6	75.6
California	36,757	5,073	2,726	13,457	15,538	100.0	13.8	7.4	36.6	42.3
Colorado	4,939	165	245	997	3,507	100.0	3.3	5.0	20.2	71.0
Connecticut	3,501	135	392	419	2,584	100.0	3.9	11.2	12.0	73.8
Delaware	873	28	191	59	597	100.0	3.3	21.8	6.8	68.3
District of Columbia	592	23	329	51	196	100.0	3.9	55.5	8.6	33.1
Florida	18,328	508	3,037	3,845	11,059	100.0	2.8	16.6	21.0	60.3
Georgia	9,686	317	2,972	777	5,629	100.0	3.3	30.7	8.0	58.1
Hawaii	1,288	696	51	112	321	100.0	54.0	3.9	8.7	24.9
Idaho	1,524	27	19	156	1,297	100.0	1.7	1.3	10.2	85.1
Illinois	12,902	617	1,996	1,967	8,348	100.0	4.8	15.5	15.2	64.7
Indiana	6,377	105	618	332	5,305	100.0	1.6	9.7	5.2	83.2
Iowa	3,003	56	97	126	2,711	100.0	1.9	3.2	4.2	90.3
Kansas	2,802	74	194	255	2,250	100.0	2.6	6.9	9.1	80.3
Kentucky	4,269	52	352	102	3,748	100.0	1.2	8.2	2.4	87.8
Louisiana	4,411	77	1,432	148	2,731	100.0	1.7	32.5	3.4	61.9
Maine	1,316	15	18	17	1,254	100.0	1.2	1.4	1.3	95.3
Maryland	5,634	320	1,711	376	3,252	100.0	5.7	30.4	6.7	57.7
Massachusetts	6,498	351	506	557	5,147	100.0	5.4	7.8	8.6	79.2
Michigan	10,003	273	1,499	414	7,751	100.0	2.7	15.0	4.1	77.5
Minnesota	5,220	209	277	217	4,458	100.0	4.0	5.3	4.1	85.4
Mississippi	2,939	31	1,105	66	1,724	100.0	1.1	37.6	2.2	58.7
Missouri	5,912	106	715	190	4,856	100.0	1.8	12.1	3.2	82.1
Montana	967	10	9	29	851	100.0	1.0	1.0	3.0	87.9
Nebraska	1,783	37	91	140	1,500	100.0	2.1	5.1	7.9	84.1
Nevada	2,600	195	233	669	1,486	100.0	7.5	9.0	25.7	57.1
New Hampshire	1,316	30	21	35	1,225	100.0	2.3	1.6	2.6	93.1
New Jersey	8,683	711	1,324	1,419	5,354	100.0	8.2	15.2	16.3	61.7
New Mexico	1,984	38	69	891	828	100.0	1.9	3.5	44.9	41.7
New York	19,490	1,484	3,549	3,250	11,697	100.0	7.6	18.2	16.7	60.0
North Carolina	9,222	210	2,051	685	6,198	100.0	2.3	22.2	7.4	67.2
North Dakota	641	7	9	13	575	100.0	1.0	1.4	2.1	89.6
Ohio	11,486	214	1,470	302	9,474	100.0	1.9	12.8	2.6	82.5
Oklahoma	3,642	78	321	279	2,600	100.0	2.1	8.8	7.6	71.4
Oregon	3,790	171	99	416	3,033	100.0	4.5	2.6	11.0	80.0
Pennsylvania	12,448	339	1,424	594	10,134	100.0	2.7	11.4	4.8	81.4
Rhode Island	1,051	33	77	122	828	100.0	3.2	7.3	11.6	78.8
South Carolina	4,480	68	1,301	184	2,921	100.0	1.5	29.0	4.1	65.2
South Dakota	804	8	13	21	692	100.0	1.1	1.6	2.6	86.1
Tennessee	6,215	100	1,074	231	4,791	100.0	1.6	17.3	3.7	77.1
Texas	24,327	956	3,022	8,870	11,526	100.0	3.9	12.4	36.5	47.4

	number					percent distribution				
	total	Asian	black	Hispanic	non-Hispanic white	total	Asian	black	Hispanic	non-Hispanic white
Utah	2,736	73	47	329	2,236	100.0%	2.7%	1.7%	12.0%	81.7%
Vermont	621	9	7	9	591	100.0	1.4	1.2	1.4	95.2
Virginia	7,769	434	1,611	531	5,201	100.0	5.6	20.7	6.8	67.0
Washington	6,549	528	307	644	4,944	100.0	8.1	4.7	9.8	75.5
West Virginia	1,814	15	73	21	1,696	100.0	0.8	4.0	1.1	93.5
Wisconsin	5,628	132	374	286	4,787	100.0	2.3	6.7	5.1	85.1
Wyoming	533	6	9	41	463	100.0	1.1	1.6	7.7	86.8

Note: Numbers by race and Hispanic origin do not add to total because they include those who identify themselves as being of the race alone and those who identify themselves as being of the race in combination with other races. Hispanics may be of any race. Non-Hispanic whites are those who identify themselves as being white alone and not Hispanic.
Source: Bureau of the Census, State Population Estimates, Internet site http://www.census.gov/popest/states/asrh/; calculations by New Strategist

Most People Live in Metropolitan Areas

Raleigh is the fastest-growing large metropolitan area.

Eighty percent of Americans live in a metropolitan area, according to the 2000 census. Fifty years earlier, only 56 percent of Americans were metropolitan residents. Within metropolitan areas, the population distribution has changed dramatically as well. The suburbs were home to half of Americans in 2000, up from just 23 percent in 1950.

Among the nation's 50 most-populous metropolitan areas, Raleigh is the fastest-growing—up 35 percent between 2000 and 2008. Las Vegas fell to second place, with 34 percent growth during those years. In all, 10 metropolitan areas grew by more than 20 percent between 2000 and 2008. In North Carolina, both Raleigh and Charlotte are among the fastest growing large metropolitan areas. In Texas, Houston, Dallas, and Austin all grew rapidly. Other fast-growing large metropolitan areas are Orlando, Phoenix, Atlanta, and Riverside–San Bernardino. Six large metropolitan areas lost population between 2000 and 2008, with New Orleans losing the most—down 14 percent. Other cities with shrinking populations are Buffalo, Pittsburgh, Cleveland, Rochester, and Detroit.

■ Although the New York metropolitan area is growing more slowly than many others, it is still the largest by far with more than 19 million people.

New York is the largest metropolitan area

(population of the five most populous metropolitan areas, 2008)

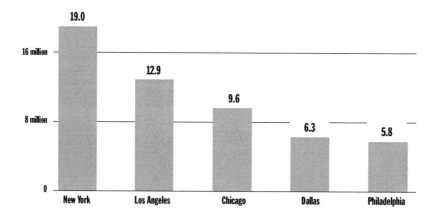

Table 8.12 Population by Metropolitan Status, 1950 to 2000

(number and percent distribution of people by metropolitan status, 1950 to 2000; numbers in thousands; metropolitan areas as defined at the respective time periods)

| | number | | percent distribution by metropolitan status | | | | |
| | | | | metropolitan | | | |
	total	metropolitan	total	total	central cities	suburbs	nonmetro areas
2000	281,422	225,968	100.0%	80.3%	30.3%	50.0%	19.7%
1990	249,464	198,249	100.0	77.5	31.3	46.2	22.5
1980	227,225	177,361	100.0	74.8	30.0	44.8	25.2
1970	203,212	139,480	100.0	69.0	31.4	37.6	31.0
1960	179,323	112,885	100.0	63.3	32.3	30.9	36.7
1950	150,697	84,501	100.0	56.1	32.8	23.3	43.9

Note: The suburbs are the portion of a metropolitan area outside the central city.
Source: Bureau of the Census, 2000 Census, Table DP-1: Profile of General Demographic Characteristics: 2000; and Metropolitan Areas and Cities, 1990 Census Profile, No. 3, 1991; and Historical Statistics of the United States, Colonial Times to 1970, Part 1, 1975; calculations by New Strategist

Table 8.13 Population of Metropolitan Areas, 2000 and 2008

(number of people in metropolitan areas with at least 1 million residents, 2000 and 2008; percent change, 2000–08; numbers in thousands)

	2008	2000	percent change 2000–08
Atlanta–Sandy Springs–Marietta, GA	5,376,285	4,281,896	25.6%
Austin–Round Rock, TX	1,652,602	1,265,665	30.6
Baltimore–Towson, MD	2,667,117	2,557,238	4.3
Birmingham–Hoover, AL	1,117,608	1,053,365	6.1
Boston–Cambridge–Quincy, MA–NH	4,522,858	4,402,149	2.7
Buffalo–Niagara Falls, NY	1,124,309	1,169,112	–3.8
Charlotte–Gastonia–Concord, NC–SC	1,701,799	1,340,283	27.0
Chicago–Naperville–Joliet, IL–IN–WI	9,569,624	9,117,995	5.0
Cincinnati–Middletown, OH–KY–IN	2,155,137	2,014,615	7.0
Cleveland–Elyria–Mentor, OH	2,088,291	2,147,944	–2.8
Columbus, OH	1,773,120	1,619,505	9.5
Dallas–Fort Worth–Arlington, TX	6,300,006	5,196,259	21.2
Denver–Aurora, CO	2,506,626	2,193,882	14.3
Detroit–Warren–Livonia, MI	4,425,110	4,457,507	–0.7
Hartford–West Hartford–East Hartford, CT	1,190,512	1,150,906	3.4
Houston–Sugar Land–Baytown, TX	5,728,143	4,739,625	20.9
Indianapolis–Carmel, IN	1,715,459	1,531,079	12.0
Jacksonville, FL	1,313,228	1,126,182	16.6
Kansas City, MO–KS	2,002,047	1,842,814	8.6
Las Vegas–Paradise, NV	1,865,746	1,393,240	33.9
Los Angeles–Long Beach–Santa Ana, CA	12,872,808	12,401,030	3.8
Louisville/Jefferson County, KY–IN	1,244,696	1,165,060	6.8
Memphis, TN–MS–AR	1,285,732	1,208,246	6.4
Miami–Fort Lauderdale–Pompano Beach, FL	5,414,772	5,026,518	7.7
Milwaukee–Waukesha–West Allis, WI	1,549,308	1,502,261	3.1
Minneapolis–St. Paul–Bloomington, MN–WI	3,229,878	2,981,508	8.3
Nashville–Davidson–Murfreesboro–Franklin, TN	1,550,733	1,317,514	17.7
New Orleans–Metairie–Kenner, LA	1,134,029	1,315,540	–13.8
New York–Northern New Jersey–Long Island, NY–NJ–PA	19,006,798	18,353,354	3.6
Oklahoma City, OK	1,206,142	1,097,834	9.9
Orlando–Kissimmee, FL	2,054,574	1,656,741	24.0
Philadelphia–Camden–Wilmington, PA–NJ–DE–MD	5,838,471	5,692,916	2.6
Phoenix–Mesa–Scottsdale, AZ	4,281,899	3,278,776	30.6
Pittsburgh, PA	2,351,192	2,429,014	–3.2
Portland–Vancouver–Beaverton, OR–WA	2,207,462	1,936,110	14.0
Providence–New Bedford–Fall River, RI–MA	1,596,611	1,586,794	0.6
Raleigh–Cary, NC	1,088,765	804,363	35.4
Richmond, VA	1,225,626	1,100,126	11.4
Riverside–San Bernardino–Ontario, CA	4,115,871	3,277,952	25.6
Rochester, NY	1,034,090	1,041,805	–0.7
Sacramento–Arden–Arcade—Roseville, CA	2,109,832	1,808,500	16.7

	2008	2000	percent change 2000–08
Salt Lake City, UT	1,115,692	972,606	14.7%
San Antonio, TX	2,031,445	1,719,270	18.2
San Diego–Carlsbad–San Marcos, CA	3,001,072	2,825,395	6.2
San Francisco–Oakland–Fremont, CA	4,274,531	4,137,271	3.3
San Jose–Sunnyvale–Santa Clara, CA	1,819,198	1,739,977	4.6
Seattle–Tacoma–Bellevue, WA	3,344,813	3,052,495	9.6
St. Louis, MO–IL	2,816,710	2,701,537	4.3
Tampa–St. Petersburg–Clearwater, FL	2,733,761	2,404,281	13.7
Tucson, AZ	1,012,018	848,549	19.3
Virginia Beach–Norfolk–Newport News, VA–NC	1,658,292	1,580,294	4.9
Washington–Arlington–Alexandria, DC–VA–MD–WV	5,358,130	4,821,195	11.1

Source: Bureau of the Census, Metropolitan and Micropolitan Statistical Area Estimates, Internet site http://www.census .gov/popest/metro/CBSA-est2008-annual.html; calculations by New Strategist

Americans Are Moving Less

The mobility rate is the lowest ever recorded.

Only 12 percent of Americans moved between March 2007 and March 2008, down from the 14 percent rate of 2000–01 and the 21 percent of 1950–51. The 2007–08 rate was the lowest ever recorded by the Census Bureau because the collapse of the housing market made it difficult to buy and sell houses. The number of people who moved between 2007 and 2008 (35 million) was the fewest since 1959–60.

Most moves are local, motivated by housing needs rather than job relocations. Among movers between 2007 and 2008, the 65 percent majority remained in the same county. Only 13 percent moved to a different state. In 2000–01, 56 percent of movers stayed in the same county and 20 percent moved to a different state.

Young adults are most likely to move, many of them seeking jobs. Twenty-seven percent of 20-to-24-year-olds moved between 2007 and 2008. Some moved to take a job after graduating from college. Others moved out of their parents' home and into a home of their own. Mobility rates fall with age to less than 5 percent among people aged 60 or older.

Although mobility rates are lower than they once were, they add up to big changes over the years. Only 59 percent of Americans were born in their state of residence, according to the Census Bureau's 2007 American Community Survey.

■ With so many Americans unable to sell their homes, millions are stuck in place until the housing market stabilizes.

Mobility has declined

(percent of people aged 1 or older who moved in a 12-month period, selected years, 1950–51 to 2007–08)

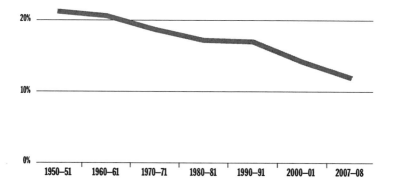

Table 8.14 Geographical Mobility, 1950 to 2008

(number and percent distribution of people aged 1 or older by mobility status, 1950–51 to 2007–08; numbers in thousands)

| | total people aged 1+ | same house (nonmovers) | total movers | different house in U.S. | | different county | | | movers from abroad |
				total	same county	total	same state	different state	
2007–08	294,851	259,685	35,166	34,022	23,013	11,009	6,282	4,727	1,145
2000–01	275,611	236,605	39,006	37,251	21,918	15,333	7,550	7,783	1,756
1990–91	244,884	203,345	41,539	40,154	25,151	15,003	7,881	7,122	1,385
1980–81	221,641	183,442	38,199	36,887	23,097	13,789	7,614	6,175	1,313
1970–71	201,506	163,800	37,706	36,161	23,018	13,143	6,197	6,946	1,544
1960–61	177,354	140,821	36,533	35,535	24,289	11,246	5,493	5,753	998
1950–51	148,400	116,936	31,464	31,158	20,694	10,464	5,276	5,188	306

PERCENT DISTRIBUTION OF POPULATION BY MOBILITY STATUS

2007–08	100.0%	88.1%	11.9%	11.5%	7.8%	3.7%	2.1%	1.6%	0.4%
2000–01	100.0	85.8	14.2	13.5	8.0	5.6	2.7	2.8	0.6
1990–91	100.0	83.0	17.0	16.4	10.3	6.1	3.2	2.9	0.6
1980–81	100.0	82.8	17.2	16.6	10.4	6.2	3.4	2.8	0.6
1970–71	100.0	81.3	18.7	17.9	11.4	6.5	3.1	3.4	0.8
1960–61	100.0	79.4	20.6	20.0	13.7	6.3	3.1	3.2	0.6
1950–51	100.0	78.8	21.2	21.0	13.9	7.1	3.6	3.5	0.2

PERCENT DISTRIBUTION OF MOVERS BY TYPE OF MOVE

2007–08	–	–	100.0%	96.7%	65.4%	31.3%	17.9%	13.4%	3.3%
2000–01	–	–	100.0	95.5	56.2	39.3	19.4	20.0	4.5
1990–91	–	–	100.0	96.7	60.5	36.1	19.0	17.1	3.3
1980–81	–	–	100.0	96.6	60.5	36.1	19.9	16.2	3.4
1970–71	–	–	100.0	95.9	61.0	34.9	16.4	18.4	4.1
1960–61	–	–	100.0	97.3	66.5	30.8	15.0	15.7	2.7
1950–51	–	–	100.0	99.0	65.8	33.3	16.8	16.5	1.0

Note: "–" means not applicable.
Source: Bureau of the Census, Geographical Mobility/Migration, Internet site http://www.census.gov/population/www/socdemo/ migrate.html; calculations by New Strategist

Table 8.15 Geographic Mobility by Age and Type of Move, 2007–08

(total number of people aged 1 or older, and number and percent who moved between March 2007 and March 2008, by age and type of move; numbers in thousands)

	total	same house (nonmovers)	total movers	same county	different county, same state	different state total	same region	different region	movers from abroad
Total, 1 or older	294,851	259,685	35,166	23,013	6,282	4,727	2,248	2,479	1,145
Aged 1 to 4	16,648	13,740	2,908	2,055	429	342	176	166	82
Aged 5 to 9	20,018	17,367	2,651	1,863	404	318	147	171	65
Aged 10 to 14	20,038	17,984	2,054	1,427	290	283	133	150	52
Aged 15 to 17	13,445	12,249	1,196	840	158	148	88	60	48
Aged 18 to 19	7,869	6,708	1,161	743	232	133	80	53	54
Aged 20 to 24	20,529	14,886	5,643	3,691	1,060	703	328	375	188
Aged 25 to 29	21,057	15,772	5,285	3,354	1,005	721	328	393	205
Aged 30 to 34	19,089	15,768	3,321	2,066	597	504	229	275	154
Aged 35 to 39	20,733	18,113	2,620	1,718	438	381	179	202	83
Aged 40 to 44	21,399	19,316	2,083	1,387	376	270	132	138	50
Aged 45 to 49	22,701	20,978	1,723	1,169	287	215	119	96	52
Aged 50 to 54	21,234	19,772	1,462	942	275	223	93	130	22
Aged 55 to 59	18,371	17,365	1,006	605	219	166	84	82	16
Aged 60 to 61	6,941	6,613	328	184	98	36	10	26	9
Aged 62 to 64	7,990	7,623	367	203	90	61	20	41	13
Aged 65 to 69	11,165	10,702	463	234	104	94	44	50	32
Aged 70 to 74	8,423	8,122	301	165	93	36	11	25	7
Aged 75 to 79	7,353	7,128	225	139	58	25	5	20	4
Aged 80 to 84	5,559	5,339	220	127	43	44	27	17	5
Aged 85 or older	4,289	4,138	151	102	23	24	17	7	2

PERCENT DISTRIBUTION BY MOBILITY STATUS

	total	same house (nonmovers)	total movers	same county	different county, same state	different state total	same region	different region	movers from abroad
Total, 1 or older	100.0%	88.1%	11.9%	7.8%	2.1%	1.6%	0.8%	0.8%	0.4%
Aged 1 to 4	100.0	82.5	17.5	12.3	2.6	2.1	1.1	1.0	0.5
Aged 5 to 9	100.0	86.8	13.2	9.3	2.0	1.6	0.7	0.9	0.3
Aged 10 to 14	100.0	89.7	10.3	7.1	1.4	1.4	0.7	0.7	0.3
Aged 15 to 17	100.0	91.1	8.9	6.2	1.2	1.1	0.7	0.4	0.4
Aged 18 to 19	100.0	85.2	14.8	9.4	2.9	1.7	1.0	0.7	0.7
Aged 20 to 24	100.0	72.5	27.5	18.0	5.2	3.4	1.6	1.8	0.9
Aged 25 to 29	100.0	74.9	25.1	15.9	4.8	3.4	1.6	1.9	1.0
Aged 30 to 34	100.0	82.6	17.4	10.8	3.1	2.6	1.2	1.4	0.8
Aged 35 to 39	100.0	87.4	12.6	8.3	2.1	1.8	0.9	1.0	0.4
Aged 40 to 44	100.0	90.3	9.7	6.5	1.8	1.3	0.6	0.6	0.2
Aged 45 to 49	100.0	92.4	7.6	5.1	1.3	0.9	0.5	0.4	0.2
Aged 50 to 54	100.0	93.1	6.9	4.4	1.3	1.1	0.4	0.6	0.1
Aged 55 to 59	100.0	94.5	5.5	3.3	1.2	0.9	0.5	0.4	0.1
Aged 60 to 61	100.0	95.3	4.7	2.7	1.4	0.5	0.1	0.4	0.1
Aged 62 to 64	100.0	95.4	4.6	2.5	1.1	0.8	0.3	0.5	0.2
Aged 65 to 69	100.0	95.9	4.1	2.1	0.9	0.8	0.4	0.4	0.3
Aged 70 to 74	100.0	96.4	3.6	2.0	1.1	0.4	0.1	0.3	0.1
Aged 75 to 79	100.0	96.9	3.1	1.9	0.8	0.3	0.1	0.3	0.1
Aged 80 to 84	100.0	96.0	4.0	2.3	0.8	0.8	0.5	0.3	0.1
Aged 85 or older	100.0	96.5	3.5	2.4	0.5	0.6	0.4	0.2	0.0

Source: Bureau of the Census, Geographic Mobility: 2007 to 2008, Detailed Tables, Internet site http://www.census.gov/population/www/socdemo/migrate/cps2008.html; calculations by New Strategist

Table 8.16 Movers by Age and Type of Move, 2007–08

(number and percent distribution of people aged 1 or older who moved between March 2007 and March 2008, by age and type of move; numbers in thousands)

	total movers	same county	different county, same state	different state total	different state same region	different state different region	movers from abroad
Total, aged 1 or older	**35,166**	**23,013**	**6,282**	**4,727**	**2,248**	**2,479**	**1,145**
Aged 1 to 4	2,908	2,055	429	342	176	166	82
Aged 5 to 9	2,651	1,863	404	318	147	171	65
Aged 10 to 14	2,054	1,427	290	283	133	150	52
Aged 15 to 17	1,196	840	158	148	88	60	48
Aged 18 to 19	1,161	743	232	133	80	53	54
Aged 20 to 24	5,643	3,691	1,060	703	328	375	188
Aged 25 to 29	5,285	3,354	1,005	721	328	393	205
Aged 30 to 34	3,321	2,066	597	504	229	275	154
Aged 35 to 39	2,620	1,718	438	381	179	202	83
Aged 40 to 44	2,083	1,387	376	270	132	138	50
Aged 45 to 49	1,723	1,169	287	215	119	96	52
Aged 50 to 54	1,462	942	275	223	93	130	22
Aged 55 to 59	1,006	605	219	166	84	82	16
Aged 60 to 61	328	184	98	36	10	26	9
Aged 62 to 64	367	203	90	61	20	41	13
Aged 65 to 69	463	234	104	94	44	50	32
Aged 70 to 74	301	165	93	36	11	25	7
Aged 75 to 79	225	139	58	25	5	20	4
Aged 80 to 84	220	127	43	44	27	17	5
Aged 85 or older	151	102	23	24	17	7	2

PERCENT DISTRIBUTION BY TYPE OF MOVE

	total movers	same county	different county, same state	different state total	different state same region	different state different region	movers from abroad
Total, aged 1 or older	**100.0%**	**65.4%**	**17.9%**	**13.4%**	**6.4%**	**7.0%**	**3.3%**
Aged 1 to 4	100.0	70.7	14.8	11.8	6.1	5.7	2.8
Aged 5 to 9	100.0	70.3	15.2	12.0	5.5	6.5	2.5
Aged 10 to 14	100.0	69.5	14.1	13.8	6.5	7.3	2.5
Aged 15 to 17	100.0	70.2	13.2	12.4	7.4	5.0	4.0
Aged 18 to 19	100.0	64.0	20.0	11.5	6.9	4.6	4.7
Aged 20 to 24	100.0	65.4	18.8	12.5	5.8	6.6	3.3
Aged 25 to 29	100.0	63.5	19.0	13.6	6.2	7.4	3.9
Aged 30 to 34	100.0	62.2	18.0	15.2	6.9	8.3	4.6
Aged 35 to 39	100.0	65.6	16.7	14.5	6.8	7.7	3.2
Aged 40 to 44	100.0	66.6	18.1	13.0	6.3	6.6	2.4
Aged 45 to 49	100.0	67.8	16.7	12.5	6.9	5.6	3.0
Aged 50 to 54	100.0	64.4	18.8	15.3	6.4	8.9	1.5
Aged 55 to 59	100.0	60.1	21.8	16.5	8.3	8.2	1.6
Aged 60 to 61	100.0	56.1	29.9	11.0	3.0	7.9	2.7
Aged 62 to 64	100.0	55.3	24.5	16.6	5.4	11.2	3.5
Aged 65 to 69	100.0	50.5	22.5	20.3	9.5	10.8	6.9
Aged 70 to 74	100.0	54.8	30.9	12.0	3.7	8.3	2.3
Aged 75 to 79	100.0	61.8	25.8	11.1	2.2	8.9	1.8
Aged 80 to 84	100.0	57.7	19.5	20.0	12.3	7.7	2.3
Aged 85 or older	100.0	67.5	15.2	15.9	11.3	4.6	1.3

Source: Bureau of the Census, Geographic Mobility: 2007 to 2008, Detailed Tables, Internet site http://www.census.gov/ population/www/socdemo/migrate/cps2008.html; calculations by New Strategist

Table 8.17 Place of Birth, 2007

(number and percent distribution of people by place of birth, 2007; numbers in thousands)

	number	percent
TOTAL POPULATION	**301,621**	**100.0%**
Native-born	**263,561**	**87.4**
Born in United States	259,763	86.1
Born in state of residence	177,509	58.9
Born in other state in the U.S.	82,253	27.3
Born outside United States*	3,799	1.3
Foreign-born	**38,060**	**12.6**

* Born in Puerto Rico, U.S. island areas, or abroad to American parents.
Source: Bureau of the Census, 2007 American Community Survey, Data Profiles, Internet site http://factfinder.census.gov/
servlet/DatasetMainPageServlet?_program=ACS&_submenuId=&_lang=en&_ts=

Legal Immigration Adds Millions to the Population

Illegal immigration adds even more, especially in California.

Between 2001 and 2008, more than 8 million immigrants were granted permanent legal residence in the United States, a figure that by the end of the decade is likely to exceed the record high of 9 million who came here during the 1991 to 2000 decade. Another 11.6 million unauthorized immigrants were in the U.S. as of 2008, according to government estimates—37 percent more than in 2000.

The impact of immigration varies dramatically by state. The 60 percent majority of legal immigrants who came to the U.S. in 2008 planned to live in one of just five states: California, New York, Florida, Texas, and New Jersey. California is the number-one state for immigrants, both legal and illegal. Twenty-two percent of legal immigrants coming to the U.S. in 2008 said they planned to live in California. Twenty-five percent of unauthorized immigrants in the U.S. in 2008 lived in California.

Mexico sends the largest number of legal immigrants to the U.S., and Mexicans account for 17 percent of the total in 2008. Mexico has also sent the largest number of illegals to the U.S. Unauthorized immigrants from Mexico account for 61 percent of all illegals in the U.S. as of 2008, according to government estimates.

The largest numbers of legal and illegal immigrants to the United States are from Mexico

(Mexicans' share of total legal immigrants to the U.S. in 2008 and share of unauthorized immigrants living in the U.S. as of 2008)

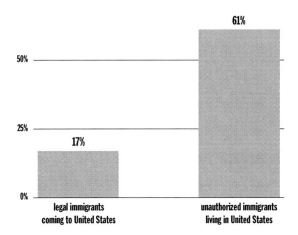

Table 8.18 Legal Immigration to the United States, 1901 to 2008

(number of legal immigrants granted permanent residence in the U.S. by single year, 2001 to 2008, and by decade, 1901 to 2008)

Single year	
2008	1,107,126
2007	1,052,415
2006	1,266,129
2005	1,122,373
2004	957,883
2003	703,542
2002	1,059,356
2001	1,058,902
Decade	
2001–08	8,327,726
1991-00	9,080,528
1981–90	7,255,956
1971–80	4,399,172
1961–70	3,321,677
1951–60	2,515,479
1941–50	1,035,039
1931–40	528,431
1921–30	4,107,209
1911–20	5,735,811
1901–10	8,795,386

Note: Immigrants are those granted legal permanent residence in the United States. They either arrive in the U.S. with immigrant visas issued abroad or adjust their status in the United States from temporary to permanent residence.
Source: Department of Homeland Security, 2008 Yearbook of Immigration Statistics, Internet site http://www.uscis.gov/graphics/shared/statistics/yearbook/index.htm

Table 8.19 Legal Immigrants by Country of Birth and State of Intended Residence, 2008

(number and percent distribution of legal immigrants admitted to the U.S. from the 10 leading countries of birth and percent distribution by intended state of residence, 2008, for the five states receiving the largest total number of legal immigrants in 2008)

	total	total in top five states	California	New York	Florida	Texas	New Jersey
Total legal immigrants	**1,107,126**	**659,376**	**238,444**	**143,679**	**133,445**	**89,811**	**53,997**
Mexico	189,989	122,732	73,648	2,337	4,632	41,060	1,055
China, People's Republic	80,271	53,358	21,925	23,981	1,690	3,131	2,631
India	63,352	34,352	14,112	5,561	1,785	4,811	8,083
Philippines	54,030	32,096	22,423	2,570	2,189	2,567	2,347
Cuba	49,500	44,248	576	602	40,946	1,120	1,004
Dominican Republic	31,879	22,799	112	15,563	2,779	186	4,159
Vietnam	31,497	16,825	11,086	537	1,197	3,534	471
Colombia	30,213	22,644	1,442	3,546	13,481	1,423	2,752
Korea (North and South)	26,666	15,567	9,315	2,290	509	1,267	2,186
Haiti	26,007	21,317	97	4,608	14,682	69	1,861

PERCENT DISTRIBUTION BY STATE OF INTENDED RESIDENCE

Total legal immigrants	**100.0%**	**59.6%**	**21.5%**	**13.0%**	**12.1%**	**8.1%**	**4.9%**
Mexico	100.0	64.6	38.8	1.2	2.4	21.6	0.6
China, People's Republic	100.0	66.5	27.3	29.9	2.1	3.9	3.3
India	100.0	54.2	22.3	8.8	2.8	7.6	12.8
Philippines	100.0	59.4	41.5	4.8	4.1	4.8	4.3
Cuba	100.0	89.4	1.2	1.2	82.7	2.3	2.0
Dominican Republic	100.0	71.5	0.4	48.8	8.7	0.6	13.0
Vietnam	100.0	53.4	35.2	1.7	3.8	11.2	1.5
Colombia	100.0	74.9	4.8	11.7	44.6	4.7	9.1
Korea (North and South)	100.0	58.4	34.9	8.6	1.9	4.8	8.2
Haiti	100.0	82.0	0.4	17.7	56.5	0.3	7.2

PERCENT DISTRIBUTION BY COUNTRY OF BIRTH

Total legal immigrants	**100.0%**	**100.0%**	**100.0%**	**100.0%**	**100.0%**	**100.0%**	**100.0%**
Mexico	17.2	18.6	30.9	1.6	3.5	45.7	2.0
China, People's Republic	7.3	8.1	9.2	16.7	1.3	3.5	4.9
India	5.7	5.2	5.9	3.9	1.3	5.4	15.0
Philippines	4.9	4.9	9.4	1.8	1.6	2.9	4.3
Cuba	4.5	6.7	0.2	0.4	30.7	1.2	1.9
Dominican Republic	2.9	3.5	0.0	10.8	2.1	0.2	7.7
Vietnam	2.8	2.6	4.6	0.4	0.9	3.9	0.9
Colombia	2.7	3.4	0.6	2.5	10.1	1.6	5.1
Korea (North and South)	2.4	2.4	3.9	1.6	0.4	1.4	4.0
Haiti	2.3	3.2	0.0	3.2	11.0	0.1	3.4

Note: Total includes immigrants from other countries not shown separately. Immigrants are people granted legal permanent residence in the United States. They either arrive in the U.S. with immigrant visas issued abroad or adjust their status in the United States from temporary to permanent residence.
Source: Department of Homeland Security, 2008 Yearbook of Immigration Statistics, Internet site http://www.uscis.gov/graphics/shared/statistics/yearbook/index.htm

Table 8.20 Unauthorized Immigrant Population, 2000 and 2008

(number and percent distribution of unauthorized persons living in the U.S. by country of birth and state of residence, 2000 and 2008; percent change in number, 2000–08; numbers in thousands)

	2008		2000		percent change 2000–08
	number	percent distribution	number	percent distribution	
COUNTRY OF BIRTH					
Total unauthorized immigrants	**11,600**	**100.0%**	**8,460**	**100.0%**	**37%**
Mexico	7,030	60.6	4,680	55.3	50
El Salvador	570	4.9	430	5.1	35
Guatemala	430	3.7	290	3.4	48
Philippines	300	2.6	200	2.4	51
Honduras	300	2.6	160	1.9	81
Korea	240	2.1	180	2.1	37
China	220	1.9	190	2.2	14
Brazil	180	1.6	100	1.2	72
Ecuador	170	1.5	110	1.3	50
India	160	1.4	120	1.4	29
Other countries	2,000	17.2	2,000	23.6	0
STATE OF RESIDENCE					
Total unauthorized immigrants	**11,600**	**100.0**	**8,460**	**100.0**	**37**
California	2,850	24.6	2,510	29.7	14
Texas	1,680	14.5	1,090	12.9	55
Florida	840	7.2	800	9.5	6
New York	640	5.5	540	6.4	19
Arizona	560	4.8	330	3.9	70
Illinois	550	4.7	440	5.2	26
Georgia	460	4.0	220	2.6	105
New Jersey	400	3.4	350	4.1	12
North Carolina	380	3.3	260	3.1	46
Nevada	280	2.4	170	2.0	70
Other states	2,950	25.4	1,760	20.8	68

Note: Percent change calculations are based on unrounded figures.
Source: Department of Homeland Security, Estimates of the Unauthorized Immigrant Population Residing in the United States: January 2008, Internet site http://www.uscis.gov/graphics/shared/statistics/yearbook/index.htm

Many U.S. Residents Are Foreign-Born

One in eight was born in another country.

Thirty-eight million U.S. residents were born in a foreign country, according to the Census Bureau's 2007 American Community Survey. More than one-fourth of the foreign-born came to the U.S. since 2000. The 54 percent majority of the foreign-born are from Latin America. Twenty-seven percent are from Asia, and only 13 percent are from Europe.

The foreign-born share of the population varies by age and sex, peaking at 17 percent among men aged 18 to 34. A smaller 12 percent of people aged 65 or older and an even smaller 4 percent of children were born outside the United States.

Thanks to immigration, the population of the United States is a diverse mixture of ancestries. German is the most common ancestry, reported by 17 percent of Americans, or 51 million people. The second most common ancestry is Irish, specified by 12 percent. Nineteen million people say their ancestry is American.

■ The number of foreign-born in the U.S. will continue to expand as long as immigration remains high, creating a dynamic multicultural market.

More than 40 percent of the foreign-born are naturalized citizens

(percent distribution of the foreign-born by citizenship status, 2008)

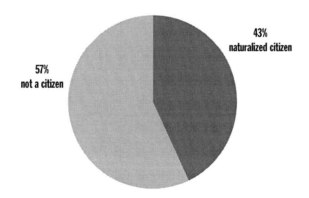

43%
naturalized citizen

57%
not a citizen

Table 8.21 Foreign-Born by Citizenship Status, Year of Entry, and World Region of Birth, 2007

(number and percent distribution of the foreign-born by citizenship status, year of entry, and world region of birth, 2007; numbers in thousands)

	number	percent
Total population	**301,621**	**100.0%**
Total foreign-born	**38,060**	**12.6**
CITIZENSHIP STATUS		
Total foreign-born	**38,060**	**100.0**
Naturalized citizen	16,176	42.5
Not a citizen	21,885	57.5
YEAR OF ENTRY		
Total foreign-born	**38,060**	**100.0**
Entered U.S. 2000 or later	10,543	27.7
Entered U.S. before 2000	27,517	72.3
WORLD REGION OF BIRTH		
Total foreign-born	**38,060**	**100.0**
Africa	1,408	3.7
Asia	10,200	26.8
Europe	4,986	13.1
Latin America	20,400	53.6
North America	837	2.2
Oceania	228	0.6

Source: Bureau of the Census, 2007 American Community Survey, Internet site http://factfinder.census.gov/home/saff/main .html?_lang=en; calculations by New Strategist

Table 8.22 Foreign-Born Population by Age, 2007

(total number of people, and number and percent who are foreign-born, by age, 2007; numbers in thousands)

	total	foreign-born	
		number	percent
Total people	**301,621**	**38,060**	**12.6%**
Under age 18	73,908	2,973	4.0
Aged 18 to 34	69,808	11,439	16.4
Aged 35 to 64	120,065	19,171	16.0
Aged 65 or older	37,841	4,478	11.8
Total females	**152,922**	**18,916**	**12.4**
Under age 18	36,067	1,454	4.0
Aged 18 to 34	34,136	5,239	15.3
Aged 35 to 64	60,873	9,547	15.7
Aged 65 or older	21,910	2,660	12.1
Total males	**148,699**	**19,144**	**12.9**
Under age 18	37,841	1,519	4.0
Aged 18 to 34	35,672	6,200	17.4
Aged 35 to 64	59,192	9,624	16.3
Aged 65 or older	15,931	1,818	11.4

Source: Bureau of the Census, 2007 American Community Survey, Internet site http://factfinder.census.gov/home/saff/main .html?_lang=en; calculations by New Strategist

Table 8.23 Ancestry of the U.S. Population, 2007

(number and percent distribution of U.S. residents by ancestry group, 2007; numbers in thousands)

	number	percent
Total people	**301,621**	**100.0%**
American	19,381	6.4
Arab	1,546	0.5
Czech	1,625	0.5
Danish	1,449	0.5
Dutch	5,071	1.7
English	28,177	9.3
French (except Basque)	9,616	3.2
French Canadian	2,184	0.7
German	50,754	16.8
Greek	1,380	0.5
Hungarian	1,565	0.5
Irish	36,496	12.1
Italian	17,844	5.9
Lithuanian	746	0.2
Norwegian	4,656	1.5
Polish	9,976	3.3
Portuguese	1,472	0.5
Russian	3,153	1.0
Scotch-Irish	5,314	1.8
Scottish	6,019	2.0
Slovak	814	0.3
Sub-Saharan African	2,702	0.9
Swedish	4,340	1.4
Swiss	1,019	0.3
Ukrainian	971	0.3
Welsh	1,921	0.6
West Indian (excluding Hispanic origin groups)	2,479	0.8

Note: Ancestries sum to more than the total population because more than one ancestry could be reported.
Source: Bureau of the Census, 2007 American Community Survey, Data Profiles, Internet site http://factfinder.census.gov/servlet/DatasetMainPageServlet?_program=ACS&_submenuId=&_lang=en&_ts=;

Millions of U.S. Residents Speak Spanish at Home

Most Spanish speakers also speak English very well.

More than 55 million U.S. residents speak a language other than English at home, or 18 percent of the population aged 5 or older according to the Census Bureau's 2007 American Community Survey. Spanish is by far the most common non-English language spoken at home, with 35 million speaking Spanish—or 62 percent of all those speaking a language other than English at home.

Overall, 24 million U.S. residents aged 5 or older do not speak English very well (9 percent of the population). But among people who do not speak English at home, a larger 44 percent do not speak English very well. Forty-seven percent of those who speak Spanish at home say they do not speak English very well, and neither do 49 percent of those who speak an Asian language at home.

■ The number of Spanish speakers in the U.S. will continue to grow rapidly because of immigration from Mexico and other Latin American countries.

Spanish is much more likely to be spoken than other non-English languages

(number of people aged 5 or older who speak a language other than English at home, by language group, 2008)

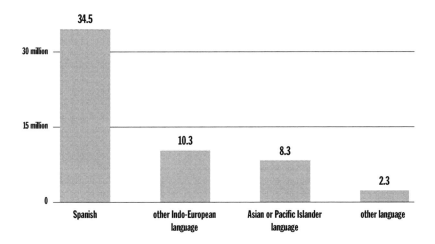

Table 8.24 Language Spoken at Home, 2007

(number and percent distribution of people aged 5 or older by language spoken at home, and percent who speak English less than very well, 2007; numbers in thousands)

	number	percent distribution
Total population aged 5 or older	**280,950**	**100.0%**
Speak only English at home	225,506	82.1
Speak a language other than English at home	55,444	17.9
Total who speak a language other than English at home	**55,444**	**100.0**
Speak Spanish	34,547	62.3
Speak other Indo-European language	10,321	18.6
Speak Asian or Pacific Islander language	8,316	15.0
Speak other language	2,260	4.1

	number	percent who speak English less than very well
Total who speak English less than very well	**24,469**	**44.1%**
Spanish speakers	16,368	47.4
Other Indo-European language speakers	3,384	32.8
Asian/Pacific Islander language speakers	4,042	48.6
Other language speakers	676	29.9

Source: Bureau of the Census, 2007 American Community Survey, Internet site http://factfinder.census.gov/servlet/ DatasetMainPageServlet?_program=ACS&_submenuId=&_lang=en&_ts=; calculations by New Strategist

Spending Trends

■ **Average household spending rose 8 percent between 2000 and 2007, after adjusting for inflation.**

Spending surged primarily because households had to spend more on mortgage interest, property taxes, utilities, gasoline, health insurance, and education.

■ **Households headed by people aged 35 to 44 spent the most in 2007—$58,934.**

The youngest householders, under age 25, spent the least—only $29,457.

■ **Households with incomes of $100,000 or more spend more than twice as much as the average household.**

While the affluent represent only 17 percent of households, they control 35 percent of spending.

■ **Married couples with children spend much more than average.**

In 2007, couples with kids spent an average of $69,101 versus the $49,638 spent by the average household.

■ **Asians spend more than non-Hispanic whites, blacks, or Hispanics.**

Hispanics and blacks spend more than average on children's clothes and rent.

■ **Spending is higher in the West than in the other regions.**

Households in the West spent $56,291 in 2007, or 13 percent more than average.

■ **College graduates earn more and spend more than the average household.**

In 2007, households headed by college graduates spent $70,605—42 percent more than average.

Average Household Spending Increased between 2000 and 2007

The average household spent less in 2007 than in 2000 on many items, however.

Between 2000 and 2007, spending by the average household rose by a substantial 8 percent, after adjusting for inflation. In 2007, the average household spent $49,638, according to the Bureau of Labor Statistics' Consumer Expenditure Survey, about $3,800 more than it spent in 2000. Much of the spending increase was devoted to nondiscretionary items however, three of four additional dollars spent went to mortgage interest, property tax, utilities, health care, gasoline, and education.

Spending surged on a number of items between 2000 and 2007. Not surprisingly, one of the biggest gainers was gasoline. The average household spent 53 percent more on gasoline in 2007 than in 2000, after adjusting for inflation. The average household spent $1,545 on out-of-pocket health insurance costs, 31 percent more than in 2000. Spending on property taxes increased 25 percent and spending on natural gas, 30 percent. As college costs soared, average household spending on education rose by a substantial 24 percent.

Households boosted their spending on a handful of discretionary categories. Spending on entertainment grew 20 percent, driven in part by a 32 percent increase in spending on audio and visual

Households are spending less on some items, more on others

(percent change in spending by the average household on selected products and services, 2000 to 2007; in 2007 dollars)

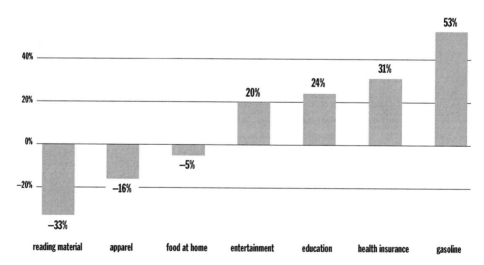

equipment. Behind the gain was the growing popularity of high-priced high-definition television sets. Spending on food away from home (primarily restaurant meals) climbed a modest 4 percent between 2000 and 2007.

Spending on food at home (primarily groceries) fell nearly 5 percent between 2000 and 2007, after adjusting for inflation. Apparel spending fell by a substantial 16 percent. Spending on gifts for people living in other households declined 8 percent during those years. Spending on new cars and trucks shrank by 19 percent.

■ Household spending climbed between 2000 and 2007 primarily because of the rising cost of living. The economic turmoil of 2008 is likely to reduce average household spending for the next few years.

Table 9.1 Household Spending Trends, 2000 to 2007

(average annual spending of total consumer units, 2000 and 2007; percent change, 2000–07; in 2007 dollars)

	2007	2000	percent change 2000–07
Number of consumer units (in 000s)	120,171	109,367	9.9%
Average before-tax income	$63,091	$53,761	17.4
Average annual spending	49,638	45,809	8.4
FOOD	6,133	6,211	−1.2
Food at home	3,465	3,638	−4.7
Cereals and bakery products	460	545	−15.7
Cereals and cereal products	143	188	−23.9
Bakery products	317	358	−11.4
Meats, poultry, fish, and eggs	777	957	−18.8
Beef	216	287	−24.6
Pork	150	201	−25.4
Other meats	104	122	−14.5
Poultry	142	175	−18.7
Fish and seafood	122	132	−7.9
Eggs	43	41	5.0
Dairy products	387	391	−1.1
Fresh milk and cream	154	158	−2.4
Other dairy products	234	232	0.7
Fruits and vegetables	600	627	−4.4
Fresh fruits	202	196	2.9
Fresh vegetables	190	191	−0.8
Processed fruits	112	138	−19.1
Processed vegetables	96	101	−5.1
Other food at home	1,241	1,116	11.2
Sugar and other sweets	124	141	−12.0
Fats and oils	91	100	−8.9
Miscellaneous foods	650	526	23.5
Nonalcoholic beverages	333	301	10.6
Food prepared by consumer unit on trips	43	48	−10.7
Food away from home	2,668	2,573	3.7
ALCOHOLIC BEVERAGES	457	448	2.0
HOUSING	16,920	14,833	14.1
Shelter	10,023	8,566	17.0
Owned dwellings	6,730	5,541	21.5
Mortgage interest and charges	3,890	3,178	22.4
Property taxes	1,709	1,371	24.6
Maintenance, repair, insurance, other expenses	1,131	993	13.9
Rented dwellings	2,602	2,449	6.2
Other lodging	691	576	20.1

	2007	2000	percent change 2000–07
Utilities, fuels, and public services	**$3,477**	**$2,997**	**16.0%**
Natural gas	480	370	29.9
Electricity	1,303	1,097	18.8
Fuel oil and other fuels	151	117	29.3
Telephone services	1,110	1,056	5.1
Water and other public services	434	356	21.8
Household services	**984**	**824**	**19.5**
Personal services	415	393	5.7
Other household services	569	431	32.0
Housekeeping supplies	**639**	**580**	**10.1**
Laundry and cleaning supplies	140	158	−11.2
Other household products	347	272	27.5
Postage and stationery	152	152	0.2
Household furnishings and equipment	**1,797**	**1,865**	**−3.7**
Household textiles	133	128	4.2
Furniture	446	471	−5.3
Floor coverings	46	53	−13.2
Major appliances	231	228	1.5
Small appliances, miscellaneous housewares	101	105	−3.6
Miscellaneous household equipment	840	880	−4.6
APPAREL AND RELATED SERVICES	**1,881**	**2,235**	**−15.8**
Men and boys	**435**	**530**	**−17.9**
Men, aged 16 or older	351	414	−15.3
Boys, aged 2 to 15	84	116	−27.3
Women and girls	**749**	**873**	**−14.2**
Women, aged 16 or older	627	731	−14.2
Girls, aged 2 to 15	122	142	−14.1
Children under age 2	**93**	**99**	**−5.8**
Footwear	**327**	**413**	**−20.8**
Other apparel products and services	**276**	**320**	**−13.8**
TRANSPORTATION	**8,758**	**8,931**	**−1.9**
Vehicle purchases	**3,244**	**4,116**	**−21.2**
Cars and trucks, new	1,572	1,933	−18.7
Cars and trucks, used	1,567	2,131	−26.5
Gasoline and motor oil	**2,384**	**1,554**	**53.4**
Other vehicle expenses	**2,592**	**2,746**	**−5.6**
Vehicle finance charges	305	395	−22.8
Maintenance and repairs	738	751	−1.8
Vehicle insurance	1,071	937	14.3
Vehicle rentals, leases, licenses, other charges	478	663	−28.0
Public transportation	**538**	**514**	**4.6**
HEALTH CARE	**2,853**	**2,488**	**14.7**
Health insurance	1,545	1,184	30.5
Medical services	709	684	3.7
Drugs	481	501	−4.0
Medical supplies	118	119	−1.0

	2007	2000	percent change 2000–07
ENTERTAINMENT	**$2,698**	**$2,243**	**20.3%**
Fees and admissions	658	620	6.1
Audio and visual equipment and services	987	749	31.8
Pets, toys, hobbies, and playground equipment	560	402	39.2
Other entertainment products and services	493	473	4.2
PERSONAL CARE PRODUCTS AND SERVICES	**588**	**679**	**–13.4**
READING	**118**	**176**	**–32.9**
EDUCATION	**945**	**761**	**24.2**
TOBACCO PRODUCTS, SMOKING SUPPLIES	**323**	**384**	**–15.9**
MISCELLANEOUS	**808**	**934**	**–13.5**
CASH CONTRIBUTIONS	**1,821**	**1,435**	**26.9**
PERSONAL INSURANCE AND PENSIONS	**5,336**	**4,052**	**31.7**
Life and other personal insurance	309	480	–35.7
Pensions and Social Security	5,027	3,571	*
PERSONAL TAXES	**2,233**	**3,753**	**–40.5**
Federal income taxes	1,569	2,901	–45.9
State and local income taxes	468	677	–30.8
Other taxes	196	176	11.5
GIFTS FOR PEOPLE IN **OTHER HOUSEHOLDS**	**1,198**	**1,304**	**–8.1**

* Pension and Social Security spending in 2007 is not comparable with spending in 2000 because of changes in methodology.
Note: Average spending is rounded to the nearest dollar. The percent change calculation is based on unrounded figures. The Bureau of Labor Statistics uses consumer unit rather than household as the sampling unit in the Consumer Expenditure Survey. For the definition of consumer unit, see the glossary. Spending on gifts is also included in the preceding product and service categories.
Source: Bureau of Labor Statistics, 2000 and 2007 Consumer Expenditure Surveys, Internet site http://www.bls.gov/cex/; calculations by New Strategist

Householders Aged 35 to 54 Spend the Most

The youngest and the oldest householders spend the least.

Households headed by people aged 35 to 44 spent an average of $58,934 in 2007—19 percent more than the average household. Close behind are householders aged 45 to 54, who spent an average of $58,331, according to the Bureau of Labor Statistics' Consumer Expenditure Survey. Middle-aged householders spend more than younger and older householders not only because they have higher incomes, but also because their households typically are larger than average because they include children.

Households headed by people under age 25 spend less than any other age group, just $29,457 in 2007. This figure is slightly below the spending of householders aged 75 or older, which stood at $30,414 in 2007.

The Indexed Spending table shows spending by age of householder in comparison with average household spending. An index of 100 means households in the age group spend an average amount on the item. An index above 100 indicates that households in the age group spend more than average on the item, while an index below 100 reveals below-average spending.

A look at Table 9.3 shows that spending is below average on most items for households headed by the youngest and the oldest householders—those under age 25 and those aged 75 or

Spending peaks in middle age

(average annual spending of consumer units by age of consumer unit reference person, 2007)

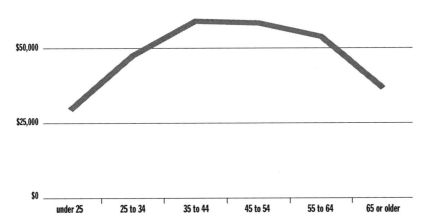

older. Spending is close to the average on most items for households headed by 25-to-34-year-olds and 65-to-74-year-olds. Spending is above average in most categories for householders spanning the ages from 35 to 64. There are some exceptions, however. Householders under age 25 spend 79 percent more than average on rent (with an index of 179). They spend 56 percent more than average on baby clothes and 89 percent more than average on education because many are in college. The oldest householders spend 54 percent more than the average household on fuel oil and 50 percent more on health care. Householders aged 65 to 74 spend 51 percent less than average on rent since most are homeowners.

The Market Share table (9.4) shows how much of total spending by category is accounted for by the various age groups. Householders aged 35 to 54 accounted for 48 percent of total household spending in 2007, down from their 51 percent share a few years ago as boomers exit the age group. Nevertheless, the 35-to-54 age group still accounts for more than half of spending on many products and services such as children's clothes (63 percent), mortgage interest (59 percent), personal insurance and pensions (55 percent), and education (54 percent). Householders under age 35 control only 20 percent of spending, while a larger 32 percent is accounted for by householders aged 55 or older.

■ The share of spending controlled by householders aged 55 to 64 is growing as boomers fill the age group and early retirement becomes less common.

Table 9.2 Average Spending by Age of Householder, 2007

(average annual spending of consumer units by product and service category and age of consumer unit reference person, 2007)

	total consumer units	under 25	25 to 34	35 to 44	45 to 54	55 to 64	aged 65 or older total	65 to 74	75 or older
Number of consumer units (in 000s)	120,171	8,150	20,499	23,416	25,245	19,462	23,400	12,011	11,390
Average number of persons per CU	2.5	2.0	2.8	3.2	2.7	2.1	1.7	1.8	1.5
Average income before taxes	$63,091	$31,443	$57,256	$76,540	$80,560	$71,048	$40,305	$47,708	$32,499
Average annual spending	49,638	29,457	47,510	58,934	58,331	53,786	36,530	42,262	30,414
FOOD	6,133	4,141	6,000	7,393	7,181	6,241	4,515	5,226	3,738
Food at home	3,465	2,265	3,210	4,125	4,003	3,457	2,905	3,348	2,419
Cereals and bakery products	460	274	427	548	522	456	405	459	346
Cereals and cereal products	143	93	144	177	161	129	116	137	94
Bakery products	317	180	282	371	361	327	289	322	252
Meats, poultry, fish, and eggs	777	491	692	976	907	758	634	738	520
Beef	216	155	197	284	243	200	174	190	156
Pork	150	84	127	185	173	147	135	166	102
Other meats	104	71	89	127	125	107	83	93	72
Poultry	142	90	138	179	173	134	101	125	73
Fish and seafood	122	64	99	152	146	127	103	122	81
Eggs	43	27	41	49	47	44	39	42	36
Dairy products	387	238	368	459	442	384	332	376	284
Fresh milk and cream	154	103	157	187	172	142	126	136	115
Other dairy products	234	136	211	271	271	242	206	240	169
Fruits and vegetables	600	340	529	677	684	640	557	628	479
Fresh fruits	202	112	168	227	232	219	193	212	172
Fresh vegetables	190	103	163	220	217	207	175	205	142
Processed fruits	112	66	111	125	123	113	106	113	99
Processed vegetables	96	58	87	105	112	102	84	99	67
Other food at home	1,241	922	1,194	1,465	1,447	1,219	976	1,147	789
Sugar and other sweets	124	69	100	151	150	119	118	136	99
Fats and oils	91	53	76	101	107	95	89	97	80
Miscellaneous foods	650	528	683	781	729	599	489	569	403
Nonalcoholic beverages	333	255	305	382	411	343	247	297	192
Food prepared by consumer unit on trips	43	17	30	50	50	63	33	49	16
Food away from home	2,668	1,876	2,790	3,268	3,178	2,784	1,610	1,878	1,319
ALCOHOLIC BEVERAGES	457	461	514	469	498	533	285	346	218
HOUSING	16,920	9,598	17,329	20,952	19,195	17,223	12,396	13,547	11,173
Shelter	10,023	6,220	10,536	12,758	11,617	9,763	6,656	7,271	6,009
Owned dwellings	6,730	1,398	5,985	9,232	8,626	7,063	4,414	5,329	3,448
Mortgage interest and charges	3,890	919	4,286	6,239	5,093	3,421	1,320	2,049	550
Property taxes	1,709	325	1,076	1,950	2,178	2,127	1,651	1,767	1,529
Maintenance, repair, insurance, other expenses	1,131	154	623	1,043	1,356	1,515	1,443	1,513	1,369
Rented dwellings	2,602	4,649	4,288	2,849	2,055	1,539	1,639	1,277	2,020
Other lodging	691	173	263	677	936	1,161	604	664	540

	total consumer units	under 25	25 to 34	35 to 44	45 to 54	55 to 64	aged 65 or older		
							total	65 to 74	75 or older
Utilities, fuels, and public services	**$3,477**	**$1,813**	**$3,063**	**$3,928**	**$4,053**	**$3,754**	**$3,117**	**$3,392**	**$2,828**
Natural gas	480	169	379	534	539	557	497	522	470
Electricity	1,303	706	1,148	1,479	1,499	1,403	1,175	1,289	1,055
Fuel oil and other fuels	151	28	85	132	192	171	208	185	232
Telephone services	1,110	744	1,094	1,295	1,330	1,135	806	946	659
Water and other public services	434	166	357	487	493	488	431	451	411
Household services	**984**	**363**	**1,175**	**1,422**	**867**	**860**	**825**	**715**	**941**
Personal services	415	174	780	844	193	159	205	83	334
Other household services	569	189	394	579	674	701	620	632	607
Housekeeping supplies	**639**	**278**	**522**	**646**	**724**	**902**	**562**	**661**	**453**
Laundry and cleaning supplies	140	84	129	178	161	134	115	138	90
Other household products	347	134	265	343	365	572	296	348	240
Postage and stationery	152	60	127	125	198	197	150	175	123
Household furnishings and equipment	**1,797**	**925**	**2,034**	**2,198**	**1,933**	**1,944**	**1,235**	**1,508**	**943**
Household textiles	133	65	120	169	120	170	117	145	86
Furniture	446	281	537	625	461	437	235	308	159
Floor coverings	46	4	48	50	54	48	48	58	37
Major appliances	231	122	213	251	285	266	180	205	152
Small appliances, misc. housewares	101	59	103	110	115	92	98	115	79
Miscellaneous household equipment	840	394	1,013	993	898	931	558	678	429
APPAREL, RELATED SERVICES	**1,881**	**1,477**	**2,106**	**2,335**	**2,191**	**1,888**	**1,040**	**1,323**	**732**
Men and boys	**435**	**323**	**508**	**582**	**514**	**402**	**209**	**255**	**160**
Men, aged 16 or older	351	290	396	403	428	367	187	220	152
Boys, aged 2 to 15	84	33	112	178	87	35	22	36	8
Women and girls	**749**	**535**	**729**	**855**	**952**	**793**	**487**	**636**	**325**
Women, aged 16 or older	627	510	570	604	822	723	460	590	316
Girls, aged 2 to 15	122	25	158	251	130	70	28	46	8
Children under age 2	**93**	**145**	**206**	**119**	**54**	**55**	**23**	**32**	**14**
Footwear	**327**	**237**	**383**	**399**	**383**	**351**	**160**	**209**	**106**
Other apparel products and services	**276**	**237**	**281**	**381**	**287**	**286**	**160**	**190**	**128**
TRANSPORTATION	**8,758**	**5,708**	**9,065**	**10,558**	**9,943**	**9,608**	**5,785**	**7,669**	**3,784**
Vehicle purchases	**3,244**	**2,273**	**3,930**	**4,183**	**3,223**	**3,348**	**1,977**	**2,701**	**1,213**
Cars and trucks, new	1,572	1,058	1,541	1,955	1,645	1,700	1,209	1,721	668
Cars and trucks, used	1,567	1,126	2,256	2,106	1,404	1,582	740	925	545
Gasoline and motor oil	**2,384**	**1,760**	**2,446**	**2,870**	**2,846**	**2,504**	**1,461**	**1,862**	**1,039**
Other vehicle expenses	**2,592**	**1,365**	**2,293**	**2,966**	**3,213**	**2,993**	**1,928**	**2,536**	**1,270**
Vehicle finance charges	305	221	384	400	335	325	122	197	43
Maintenance and repairs	738	437	609	809	941	885	543	693	384
Vehicle insurance	1,071	492	802	1,173	1,382	1,214	975	1,321	597
Vehicle rentals, leases, licenses, other charges	478	216	498	584	555	569	287	325	247
Public transportation	**538**	**310**	**396**	**540**	**661**	**763**	**420**	**569**	**262**
HEALTH CARE	**2,853**	**800**	**1,740**	**2,315**	**2,792**	**3,476**	**4,631**	**4,967**	**4,275**
Health insurance	1,545	397	918	1,269	1,386	1,751	2,770	2,821	2,716
Medical services	709	267	556	651	772	883	844	1,027	651
Drugs	481	103	203	303	498	674	859	935	777
Medical supplies	118	34	64	93	135	168	159	184	132

	total consumer units	under 25	25 to 34	35 to 44	45 to 54	55 to 64	aged 65 or older		
							total	65 to 74	75 or older
ENTERTAINMENT	**$2,698**	**$1,448**	**$2,462**	**$3,551**	**$3,163**	**$2,730**	**$1,966**	**$2,636**	**$1,255**
Fees and admissions	658	290	500	967	823	645	450	575	318
Audio and visual equipment and services	987	726	1,034	1,196	1,126	965	694	812	570
Pets, toys, hobbies, playground equipment	560	243	480	730	711	653	338	429	239
Other entertainment products and services	493	189	448	658	504	468	484	821	128
PERSONAL CARE PRODUCTS AND SERVICES	**588**	**337**	**512**	**662**	**686**	**632**	**528**	**599**	**451**
READING	**118**	**51**	**72**	**107**	**137**	**151**	**143**	**151**	**136**
EDUCATION	**945**	**1,787**	**604**	**819**	**1,687**	**929**	**292**	**245**	**341**
TOBACCO PRODUCTS AND SMOKING SUPPLIES	**323**	**290**	**331**	**379**	**388**	**353**	**176**	**243**	**106**
MISCELLANEOUS	**808**	**368**	**589**	**845**	**1,008**	**1,084**	**672**	**787**	**548**
CASH CONTRIBUTIONS	**1,821**	**549**	**1,027**	**1,569**	**1,972**	**2,746**	**2,282**	**1,923**	**2,661**
PERSONAL INSURANCE AND PENSIONS	**5,336**	**2,440**	**5,159**	**6,980**	**7,489**	**6,193**	**1,819**	**2,600**	**996**
Life and other personal insurance	309	39	164	286	402	461	329	375	279
Pensions and Social Security	5,027	2,401	4,995	6,694	7,087	5,732	1,491	2,225	716
PERSONAL TAXES	**2,233**	**641**	**1,491**	**2,489**	**3,485**	**3,083**	**1,126**	**1,374**	**864**
Federal income taxes	1,569	433	982	1,741	2,490	2,234	760	1,003	505
State and local income taxes	468	191	413	561	754	551	143	139	147
Other taxes	196	17	96	188	241	298	223	232	212
GIFTS FOR PEOPLE IN OTHER HOUSEHOLDS	**1,198**	**427**	**582**	**806**	**1,847**	**1,948**	**1,085**	**1,265**	**889**

Note: Spending by category does not add to total spending because gift spending is also included in the preceding product and service categories and personal taxes are not included in the total "CU" is short for consumer unit.
Source: Bureau of Labor Statistics, 2007 Consumer Expenditure Survey, Internet site http://www.bls.gov/cex/

Table 9.3 Indexed Spending by Age of Householder, 2007

(indexed average annual spending of consumer units by product and service category and age of consumer unit reference person, 2007; index definition: an index of 100 is the average for all consumer units; an index of 125 means that spending by consumer units in that group is 25 percent above the average for all consumer units; an index of 75 indicates spending that is 25 percent below the average for all consumer units)

	total consumer units	under 25	25 to 34	35 to 44	45 to 54	55 to 64	aged 65 or older total	65 to 74	75 or older
Average spending of consumer units	$49,638	$29,457	$47,510	$58,934	$58,331	$53,786	$36,530	$42,262	$30,414
Indexed spending of consumer units	100	59	96	119	118	108	74	85	61
FOOD	100	68	98	121	117	102	74	85	61
Food at home	100	65	93	119	116	100	84	97	70
Cereals and bakery products	100	60	93	119	113	99	88	100	75
Cereals and cereal products	100	65	101	124	113	90	81	96	66
Bakery products	100	57	89	117	114	103	91	102	79
Meats, poultry, fish, and eggs	100	63	89	126	117	98	82	95	67
Beef	100	72	91	131	113	93	81	88	72
Pork	100	56	85	123	115	98	90	111	68
Other meats	100	68	86	122	120	103	80	89	69
Poultry	100	63	97	126	122	94	71	88	51
Fish and seafood	100	52	81	125	120	104	84	100	66
Eggs	100	63	95	114	109	102	91	98	84
Dairy products	100	61	95	119	114	99	86	97	73
Fresh milk and cream	100	67	102	121	112	92	82	88	75
Other dairy products	100	58	90	116	116	103	88	103	72
Fruits and vegetables	100	57	88	113	114	107	93	105	80
Fresh fruits	100	55	83	112	115	108	96	105	85
Fresh vegetables	100	54	86	116	114	109	92	108	75
Processed fruits	100	59	99	112	110	101	95	101	88
Processed vegetables	100	60	91	109	117	106	88	103	70
Other food at home	100	74	96	118	117	98	79	92	64
Sugar and other sweets	100	56	81	122	121	96	95	110	80
Fats and oils	100	58	84	111	118	104	98	107	88
Miscellaneous foods	100	81	105	120	112	92	75	88	62
Nonalcoholic beverages	100	77	92	115	123	103	74	89	58
Food prepared by consumer unit on trips	100	40	70	116	116	147	77	114	37
Food away from home	100	70	105	122	119	104	60	70	49
ALCOHOLIC BEVERAGES	100	101	112	103	109	117	62	76	48
HOUSING	100	57	102	124	113	102	73	80	66
Shelter	100	62	105	127	116	97	66	73	60
Owned dwellings	100	21	89	137	128	105	66	79	51
Mortgage interest and charges	100	24	110	160	131	88	34	53	14
Property taxes	100	19	63	114	127	124	97	103	89
Maintenance, repair, insurance, other expenses	100	14	55	92	120	134	128	134	121
Rented dwellings	100	179	165	109	79	59	63	49	78
Other lodging	100	25	38	98	135	168	87	96	78

	total consumer units	under 25	25 to 34	35 to 44	45 to 54	55 to 64	aged 65 or older total	65 to 74	75 or older
Utilities, fuels, and public services	**100**	**52**	**88**	**113**	**117**	**108**	**90**	**98**	**81**
Natural gas	100	35	79	111	112	116	104	109	98
Electricity	100	54	88	114	115	108	90	99	81
Fuel oil and other fuels	100	19	56	87	127	113	138	123	154
Telephone services	100	67	99	117	120	102	73	85	59
Water and other public services	100	38	82	112	114	112	99	104	95
Household services	**100**	**37**	**119**	**145**	**88**	**87**	**84**	**73**	**96**
Personal services	100	42	188	203	47	38	49	20	80
Other household services	100	33	69	102	118	123	109	111	107
Housekeeping supplies	**100**	**44**	**82**	**101**	**113**	**141**	**88**	**103**	**71**
Laundry and cleaning supplies	100	60	92	127	115	96	82	99	64
Other household products	100	39	76	99	105	165	85	100	69
Postage and stationery	100	39	84	82	130	130	99	115	81
Household furnishings and equipment	**100**	**51**	**113**	**122**	**108**	**108**	**69**	**84**	**52**
Household textiles	100	49	90	127	90	128	88	109	65
Furniture	100	63	120	140	103	98	53	69	36
Floor coverings	100	9	104	109	117	104	104	126	80
Major appliances	100	53	92	109	123	115	78	89	66
Small appliances, misc. housewares	100	58	102	109	114	91	97	114	78
Miscellaneous household equipment	100	47	121	118	107	111	66	81	51
APPAREL AND RELATED SERVICES	**100**	**79**	**112**	**124**	**116**	**100**	**55**	**70**	**39**
Men and boys	**100**	**74**	**117**	**134**	**118**	**92**	**48**	**59**	**37**
Men, aged 16 or older	100	83	113	115	122	105	53	63	43
Boys, aged 2 to 15	100	39	133	212	104	42	26	43	10
Women and girls	**100**	**71**	**97**	**114**	**127**	**106**	**65**	**85**	**43**
Women, aged 16 or older	100	81	91	96	131	115	73	94	50
Girls, aged 2 to 15	100	20	130	206	107	57	23	38	7
Children under age 2	**100**	**156**	**222**	**128**	**58**	**59**	**25**	**34**	**15**
Footwear	**100**	**72**	**117**	**122**	**117**	**107**	**49**	**64**	**32**
Other apparel products and services	**100**	**86**	**102**	**138**	**104**	**104**	**58**	**69**	**46**
TRANSPORTATION	**100**	**65**	**104**	**121**	**114**	**110**	**66**	**88**	**43**
Vehicle purchases	**100**	**70**	**121**	**129**	**99**	**103**	**61**	**83**	**37**
Cars and trucks, new	100	67	98	124	105	108	77	109	42
Cars and trucks, used	100	72	144	134	90	101	47	59	35
Gasoline and motor oil	**100**	**74**	**103**	**120**	**119**	**105**	**61**	**78**	**44**
Other vehicle expenses	**100**	**53**	**88**	**114**	**124**	**115**	**74**	**98**	**49**
Vehicle finance charges	100	72	126	131	110	107	40	65	14
Maintenance and repairs	100	59	83	110	128	120	74	94	52
Vehicle insurance	100	46	75	110	129	113	91	123	56
Vehicle rentals, leases, licenses, other charges	100	45	104	122	116	119	60	68	52
Public transportation	**100**	**58**	**74**	**100**	**123**	**142**	**78**	**106**	**49**
HEALTH CARE	**100**	**28**	**61**	**81**	**98**	**122**	**162**	**174**	**150**
Health insurance	100	26	59	82	90	113	179	183	176
Medical services	100	38	78	92	109	125	119	145	92
Drugs	100	21	42	63	104	140	179	194	162
Medical supplies	100	29	54	79	114	142	135	156	112

	total consumer units	under 25	25 to 34	35 to 44	45 to 54	55 to 64	aged 65 or older total	65 to 74	75 or older
ENTERTAINMENT	**100**	**54**	**91**	**132**	**117**	**101**	**73**	**98**	**47**
Fees and admissions	100	44	76	147	125	98	68	87	48
Audio and visual equipment and services	100	74	105	121	114	98	70	82	58
Pets, toys, hobbies, playground equipment	100	43	86	130	127	117	60	77	43
Other entertainment products and services	100	38	91	133	102	95	98	167	26
PERSONAL CARE PRODUCTS AND SERVICES	**100**	**57**	**87**	**113**	**117**	**107**	**90**	**102**	**77**
READING	**100**	**43**	**61**	**91**	**116**	**128**	**121**	**128**	**115**
EDUCATION	**100**	**189**	**64**	**87**	**179**	**98**	**31**	**26**	**36**
TOBACCO PRODUCTS AND SMOKING SUPPLIES	**100**	**90**	**102**	**117**	**120**	**109**	**54**	**75**	**33**
MISCELLANEOUS	**100**	**46**	**73**	**105**	**125**	**134**	**83**	**97**	**68**
CASH CONTRIBUTIONS	**100**	**30**	**56**	**86**	**108**	**151**	**125**	**106**	**146**
PERSONAL INSURANCE AND PENSIONS	**100**	**46**	**97**	**131**	**140**	**116**	**34**	**49**	**19**
Life and other personal insurance	100	13	53	93	130	149	106	121	90
Pensions and Social Security	100	48	99	133	141	114	30	44	14
PERSONAL TAXES	**100**	**29**	**67**	**111**	**156**	**138**	**50**	**62**	**39**
Federal income taxes	100	28	63	111	159	142	48	64	32
State and local income taxes	100	41	88	120	161	118	31	30	31
Other taxes	100	9	49	96	123	152	114	118	108
GIFTS FOR PEOPLE IN OTHER HOUSEHOLDS	**100**	**36**	**49**	**67**	**154**	**163**	**91**	**106**	**74**

Source: Calculations by New Strategist based on the Bureau of Labor Statistics 2007 Consumer Expenditure Survey, Internet site http://www.bls.gov/cex/home.htm

Table 9.4 Market Shares by Age of Householder, 2007

(share of total household spending accounted for by age group, 2007)

	total consumer units	under 25	25 to 34	35 to 44	45 to 54	55 to 64	aged 65 or older		
							total	65 to 74	75 or older
Share of total consumer units	100.0%	6.8%	17.1%	19.5%	21.0%	16.2%	19.5%	10.0%	9.5%
Share of total spending	100.0	4.0	16.3	23.1	24.7	17.5	14.3	8.5	5.8
FOOD	100.0	4.6	16.7	23.5	24.6	16.5	14.3	8.5	5.8
Food at home	100.0	4.4	15.8	23.2	24.3	16.2	16.3	9.7	6.6
Cereals and bakery products	100.0	4.0	15.8	23.2	23.8	16.1	17.1	10.0	7.1
Cereals and cereal products	100.0	4.4	17.2	24.1	23.7	14.6	15.8	9.6	6.2
Bakery products	100.0	3.9	15.2	22.8	23.9	16.7	17.8	10.2	7.5
Meats, poultry, fish, and eggs	100.0	4.3	15.2	24.5	24.5	15.8	15.9	9.5	6.3
Beef	100.0	4.9	15.6	25.6	23.6	15.0	15.7	8.8	6.8
Pork	100.0	3.8	14.4	24.0	24.2	15.9	17.5	11.1	6.4
Other meats	100.0	4.6	14.6	23.8	25.2	16.7	15.5	8.9	6.6
Poultry	100.0	4.3	16.6	24.6	25.6	15.3	13.8	8.8	4.9
Fish and seafood	100.0	3.6	13.8	24.3	25.1	16.9	16.4	10.0	6.3
Eggs	100.0	4.3	16.3	22.2	23.0	16.6	17.7	9.8	7.9
Dairy products	100.0	4.2	16.2	23.1	24.0	16.1	16.7	9.7	7.0
Fresh milk and cream	100.0	4.5	17.4	23.7	23.5	14.9	15.9	8.8	7.1
Other dairy products	100.0	3.9	15.4	22.6	24.3	16.7	17.1	10.3	6.8
Fruits and vegetables	100.0	3.8	15.0	22.0	23.9	17.3	18.1	10.5	7.6
Fresh fruits	100.0	3.8	14.2	21.9	24.1	17.6	18.6	10.5	8.1
Fresh vegetables	100.0	3.7	14.6	22.6	24.0	17.6	17.9	10.8	7.1
Processed fruits	100.0	4.0	16.9	21.7	23.1	16.3	18.4	10.1	8.4
Processed vegetables	100.0	4.1	15.5	21.3	24.5	17.2	17.0	10.3	6.6
Other food at home	100.0	5.0	16.4	23.0	24.5	15.9	15.3	9.2	6.0
Sugar and other sweets	100.0	3.8	13.8	23.7	25.4	15.5	18.5	11.0	7.6
Fats and oils	100.0	3.9	14.2	21.6	24.7	16.9	19.0	10.7	8.3
Miscellaneous foods	100.0	5.5	17.9	23.4	23.6	14.9	14.6	8.7	5.9
Nonalcoholic beverages	100.0	5.2	15.6	22.4	25.9	16.7	14.4	8.9	5.5
Food prepared by CU on trips	100.0	2.7	11.9	22.7	24.4	23.7	14.9	11.4	3.5
Food away from home	100.0	4.8	17.8	23.9	25.0	16.9	11.8	7.0	4.7
ALCOHOLIC BEVERAGES	100.0	6.8	19.2	20.0	22.9	18.9	12.1	7.6	4.5
HOUSING	100.0	3.8	17.5	24.1	23.8	16.5	14.3	8.0	6.3
Shelter	100.0	4.2	17.9	24.8	24.3	15.8	12.9	7.3	5.7
Owned dwellings	100.0	1.4	15.2	26.7	26.9	17.0	12.8	7.9	4.9
Mortgage interest and charges	100.0	1.6	18.8	31.3	27.5	14.2	6.6	5.3	1.3
Property taxes	100.0	1.3	10.7	22.2	26.8	20.2	18.8	10.3	8.5
Maintenance, repair, insurance, other expenses	100.0	0.9	9.4	18.0	25.2	21.7	24.8	13.4	11.5
Rented dwellings	100.0	12.1	28.1	21.3	16.6	9.6	12.3	4.9	7.4
Other lodging	100.0	1.7	6.5	19.1	28.5	27.2	17.0	9.6	7.4

	total consumer units	under 25	25 to 34	35 to 44	45 to 54	55 to 64	aged 65 or older total	65 to 74	75 or older
Utilities, fuels, and public services	**100.0%**	**3.5%**	**15.0%**	**22.0%**	**24.5%**	**17.5%**	**17.5%**	**9.8%**	**7.7%**
Natural gas	100.0	2.4	13.5	21.7	23.6	18.8	20.2	10.9	9.3
Electricity	100.0	3.7	15.0	22.1	24.2	17.4	17.6	9.9	7.7
Fuel oil and other fuels	100.0	1.3	9.6	17.0	26.7	18.3	26.8	12.2	14.6
Telephone services	100.0	4.5	16.8	22.7	25.2	16.6	14.1	8.5	5.6
Water and other public services	**100.0**	**2.6**	**14.0**	**21.9**	**23.9**	**18.2**	**19.3**	**10.4**	**9.0**
Household services	100.0	2.5	20.4	28.2	18.5	14.2	16.3	7.3	9.1
Personal services	100.0	2.8	32.1	39.6	9.8	6.2	9.6	2.0	7.6
Other household services	100.0	2.3	11.8	19.8	24.9	20.0	21.2	11.1	10.1
Housekeeping supplies	**100.0**	**3.0**	**13.9**	**19.7**	**23.8**	**22.9**	**17.1**	**10.3**	**6.7**
Laundry and cleaning supplies	100.0	4.1	15.7	24.8	24.2	15.5	16.0	9.9	6.1
Other household products	100.0	2.6	13.0	19.3	22.1	26.7	16.6	10.0	6.6
Postage and stationery	100.0	2.7	14.3	16.0	27.4	21.0	19.2	11.5	7.7
Household furnishings and equipment	**100.0**	**3.5**	**19.3**	**23.8**	**22.6**	**17.5**	**13.4**	**8.4**	**5.0**
Household textiles	100.0	3.3	15.4	24.8	19.0	20.7	17.1	10.9	6.1
Furniture	100.0	4.3	20.5	27.3	21.7	15.9	10.3	6.9	3.4
Floor coverings	100.0	0.6	17.8	21.2	24.7	16.9	20.3	12.6	7.6
Major appliances	100.0	3.6	15.7	21.2	25.9	18.6	15.2	8.9	6.2
Small appliances, misc. housewares	100.0	4.0	17.4	21.2	23.9	14.8	18.9	11.4	7.4
Miscellaneous household equipment	100.0	3.2	20.6	23.0	22.5	17.9	12.9	8.1	4.8
APPAREL, RELATED SERVICES	**100.0**	**5.3**	**19.1**	**24.2**	**24.5**	**16.3**	**10.8**	**7.0**	**3.7**
Men and boys	**100.0**	**5.0**	**19.9**	**26.1**	**24.8**	**15.0**	**9.4**	**5.9**	**3.5**
Men, aged 16 or older	100.0	5.6	19.2	22.4	25.6	16.9	10.4	6.3	4.1
Boys, aged 2 to 15	100.0	2.7	22.7	41.3	21.8	6.7	5.1	4.3	0.9
Women and girls	**100.0**	**4.8**	**16.6**	**22.2**	**26.7**	**17.1**	**12.7**	**8.5**	**4.1**
Women, aged 16 or older	100.0	5.5	15.5	18.8	27.5	18.7	14.3	9.4	4.8
Girls, aged 2 to 15	100.0	1.4	22.1	40.1	22.4	9.3	4.5	3.8	0.6
Children under age 2	**100.0**	**10.6**	**37.8**	**24.9**	**12.2**	**9.6**	**4.8**	**3.4**	**1.4**
Footwear	**100.0**	**4.9**	**20.0**	**23.8**	**24.6**	**17.4**	**9.5**	**6.4**	**3.1**
Other apparel products and services	**100.0**	**5.8**	**17.4**	**26.9**	**21.8**	**16.8**	**11.3**	**6.9**	**4.4**
TRANSPORTATION	**100.0**	**4.4**	**17.7**	**23.5**	**23.8**	**17.8**	**12.9**	**8.8**	**4.1**
Vehicle purchases	**100.0**	**4.8**	**20.7**	**25.1**	**20.9**	**16.7**	**11.9**	**8.3**	**3.5**
Cars and trucks, new	100.0	4.6	16.7	24.2	22.0	17.5	15.0	10.9	4.0
Cars and trucks, used	100.0	4.9	24.6	26.2	18.8	16.4	9.2	5.9	3.3
Gasoline and motor oil	**100.0**	**5.0**	**17.5**	**23.5**	**25.1**	**17.0**	**11.9**	**7.8**	**4.1**
Other vehicle expenses	**100.0**	**3.6**	**15.1**	**22.3**	**26.0**	**18.7**	**14.5**	**9.8**	**4.6**
Vehicle finance charges	100.0	4.9	21.5	25.6	23.1	17.3	7.8	6.5	1.3
Maintenance and repairs	100.0	4.0	14.1	21.4	26.8	19.4	14.3	9.4	4.9
Vehicle insurance	100.0	3.1	12.8	21.3	27.1	18.4	17.7	12.3	5.3
Vehicle rentals, leases, licenses, other charges	100.0	3.1	17.8	23.8	24.4	19.3	11.7	6.8	4.9
Public transportation	**100.0**	**3.9**	**12.6**	**19.6**	**25.8**	**23.0**	**15.2**	**10.6**	**4.6**
HEALTH CARE	**100.0**	**1.9**	**10.4**	**15.8**	**20.6**	**19.7**	**31.6**	**17.4**	**14.2**
Health insurance	100.0	1.7	10.1	16.0	18.8	18.4	34.9	18.2	16.7
Medical services	100.0	2.6	13.4	17.9	22.9	20.2	23.2	14.5	8.7
Drugs	100.0	1.5	7.2	12.3	21.8	22.7	34.8	19.4	15.3
Medical supplies	100.0	2.0	9.3	15.4	24.0	23.1	26.2	15.6	10.6

	total consumer units	under 25	25 to 34	35 to 44	45 to 54	55 to 64	aged 65 or older		
							total	65 to 74	75 or older
ENTERTAINMENT	**100.0%**	**3.6%**	**15.6%**	**25.6%**	**24.6%**	**16.4%**	**14.2%**	**9.8%**	**4.4%**
Fees and admissions	100.0	3.0	13.0	28.6	26.3	15.9	13.3	8.7	4.6
Audio and visual equipment and services	100.0	5.0	17.9	23.6	24.0	15.8	13.7	8.2	5.5
Pets, toys, hobbies, playground equipment	100.0	2.9	14.6	25.4	26.7	18.9	11.8	7.7	4.0
Other entertainment products and services	100.0	2.6	15.5	26.0	21.5	15.4	19.1	16.6	2.5
PERSONAL CARE PRODUCTS AND SERVICES	**100.0**	**3.9**	**14.9**	**21.9**	**24.5**	**17.4**	**17.5**	**10.2**	**7.3**
READING	**100.0**	**2.9**	**10.4**	**17.7**	**24.4**	**20.7**	**23.6**	**12.8**	**10.9**
EDUCATION	**100.0**	**12.8**	**10.9**	**16.9**	**37.5**	**15.9**	**6.0**	**2.6**	**3.4**
TOBACCO PRODUCTS AND SMOKING SUPPLIES	**100.0**	**6.1**	**17.5**	**22.9**	**25.2**	**17.7**	**10.6**	**7.5**	**3.1**
MISCELLANEOUS	**100.0**	**3.1**	**12.4**	**20.4**	**26.2**	**21.7**	**16.2**	**9.7**	**6.4**
CASH CONTRIBUTIONS	**100.0**	**2.0**	**9.6**	**16.8**	**22.7**	**24.4**	**24.4**	**10.6**	**13.9**
PERSONAL INSURANCE AND PENSIONS	**100.0**	**3.1**	**16.5**	**25.5**	**29.5**	**18.8**	**6.6**	**4.9**	**1.8**
Life and other personal insurance	100.0	0.9	9.1	18.0	27.3	24.2	20.7	12.1	8.6
Pensions and Social Security	100.0	3.2	16.9	25.9	29.6	18.5	5.8	4.4	1.3
PERSONAL TAXES	**100.0**	**1.9**	**11.4**	**21.7**	**32.8**	**22.4**	**9.8**	**6.2**	**3.7**
Federal income taxes	100.0	1.9	10.7	21.6	33.3	23.1	9.4	6.4	3.1
State and local income taxes	100.0	2.8	15.1	23.4	33.8	19.1	5.9	3.0	3.0
Other taxes	100.0	0.6	8.4	18.7	25.8	24.6	22.2	11.8	10.3
GIFTS FOR PEOPLE IN OTHER HOUSEHOLDS	**100.0**	**2.4**	**8.3**	**13.1**	**32.4**	**26.3**	**17.6**	**10.6**	**7.0**

Note: "CU" is short for consumer unit.
Source: Calculations by New Strategist based on the Bureau of Labor Statistics 2007 Consumer Expenditure Survey, Internet site http://www.bls.gov/cex/home.htm

Spending Rises with Income

Households with incomes of $100,000 or more spend more than twice as much as the average household.

Households with incomes of $100,000 or more spent an average of $101,041 in 2007—more than twice the $49,638 of the average household. The most affluent households are also the largest, with an average of 3.2 people according to the Bureau of Labor Statistics' Consumer Expenditure Survey, compared with 2.5 for the average household. Households with incomes of $150,000 or more (shown in the high-income tables) spent $126,443 in 2007. They are the only income group to spend more on restaurant meals than groceries.

The Indexed Spending tables show spending by household income in comparison with average household spending. An index of 100 means households in the income group spend an average amount on the item. An index above 100 indicates that households in the income group spend more than average on the item, while an index below 100 reveals below-average spending.

A look at tables 9.6 and 9.9 shows that spending is at or below average on most items for households with incomes below $50,000 and above average for households with incomes higher than that. There are some exceptions, however. Households with incomes below $50,000 spend more than average on rent. Households with incomes of $100,000 or more spend less than average on tobacco.

High-income households account for a disproportionate share of spending

(share of spending accounted for by consumer unit income groups, 2007)

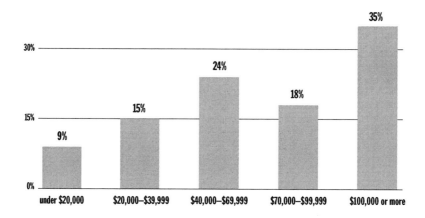

The most affluent households—those with incomes of $150,000 or more—spend at least three times the average on items such as property and personal taxes, other lodging (which includes college dorm rooms as well as hotels and motels), personal and other household services, furniture, floor coverings, apparel, vehicle rental and leases, public transportation (which is dominated by airfares), fees and admission to entertainment events, education, and cash contributions. On some of these items the spending of the most affluent households is more than five times the average.

The Market Share tables show how much of total spending by category is accounted for by the various income groups. Table 9.10 shows how much high-income households dominate spending. While 17 percent of households have annual incomes of $100,000 or more, they control 35 percent of household spending. Households with incomes of $150,000 or more account for only 7 percent of households but control 17 percent of total household spending. These most affluent households control at least one-fourth of spending on other lodging, public transportation, fees and admissions to entertainment events, education, and furniture.

■ With the cost of necessities spiraling upward, high-income households are often the only ones able to devote a substantial sum to discretionary products and services.

Table 9.5 Average Spending by Household Income, 2007

(average annual spending of consumer units by product and service category and before-tax income of consumer unit, 2007)

	total consumer units	under $10,000	$10,000–$19,999	$20,000–$29,999	$30,000–$39,999	$40,000–$49,999	$50,000–$69,999	$70,000 or more
Number of consumer units (in 000s)	120,171	9,590	15,114	14,720	13,211	11,824	18,390	37,322
Average number of persons per consumer unit	2.5	1.5	1.8	2.2	2.3	2.4	2.7	3.1
Average income before taxes	$63,091	$4,095	$14,993	$24,893	$34,751	$44,555	$59,527	$130,455
Average annual spending	49,638	17,964	22,360	29,704	34,739	41,083	50,428	84,072
FOOD	6,133	2,708	3,201	4,071	4,645	5,689	6,371	9,464
Food at home	3,465	1,765	2,128	2,648	2,913	3,368	3,630	4,853
Cereals and bakery products	460	234	289	347	384	440	495	638
Cereals and cereal products	143	80	95	119	121	137	149	192
Bakery products	317	154	194	229	263	303	346	446
Meats, poultry, fish, and eggs	777	409	502	647	664	777	822	1,038
Beef	216	101	147	177	189	217	233	287
Pork	150	83	99	138	131	156	171	183
Other meats	104	58	68	79	93	98	113	141
Poultry	142	77	87	118	126	136	138	197
Fish and seafood	122	62	67	96	85	127	124	178
Eggs	43	28	34	39	41	42	43	52
Dairy products	387	185	237	288	326	370	412	548
Fresh milk and cream	154	85	104	124	140	151	159	204
Other dairy products	234	100	133	164	186	219	253	344
Fruits and vegetables	600	316	362	454	504	580	615	850
Fresh fruits	202	103	121	146	155	204	198	296
Fresh vegetables	190	101	115	144	156	180	198	270
Processed fruits	112	59	67	90	99	103	117	157
Processed vegetables	96	53	58	74	94	93	102	127
Other food at home	1,241	621	737	911	1,035	1,200	1,286	1,779
Sugar and other sweets	124	60	75	90	101	119	133	178
Fats and oils	91	48	63	77	83	93	96	119
Miscellaneous foods	650	310	379	473	534	631	674	939
Nonalcoholic beverages	333	192	208	256	290	329	339	459
Food prepared by consumer unit on trips	43	11	14	15	28	29	43	84
Food away from home	2,668	942	1,073	1,423	1,731	2,321	2,741	4,611
ALCOHOLIC BEVERAGES	457	149	174	257	305	423	489	768
HOUSING	16,920	7,346	8,925	10,994	12,389	13,997	17,014	27,408
Shelter	10,023	4,424	5,296	6,456	7,365	8,180	9,908	16,363
Owned dwellings	6,730	1,383	1,964	3,016	3,701	4,655	6,698	13,245
Mortgage interest and charges	3,890	623	716	1,273	1,935	2,555	4,004	8,106
Property taxes	1,709	510	672	891	1,058	1,209	1,547	3,228
Maintenance, repair, insurance, other expenses	1,131	250	576	852	708	891	1,147	1,911
Rented dwellings	2,602	2,933	3,221	3,286	3,389	3,195	2,659	1,501
Other lodging	691	107	111	154	275	331	551	1,617

	total consumer units	under $10,000	$10,000– $19,999	$20,000– $29,999	$30,000– $39,999	$40,000– $49,999	$50,000– $69,999	$70,000 or more
Utilities, fuels, and public services	$3,477	$1,750	$2,326	$2,748	$3,072	$3,282	$3,697	$4,772
Natural gas	480	215	317	352	405	427	481	709
Electricity	1,303	725	937	1,079	1,193	1,256	1,363	1,712
Fuel oil and other fuels	151	58	100	125	130	122	159	217
Telephone services	1,110	551	705	868	984	1,071	1,231	1,510
Water and other public services	434	201	268	324	361	407	464	623
Household services	984	218	390	437	496	640	890	1,966
Personal services	415	53	124	130	181	227	400	890
Other household services	569	166	266	306	314	414	490	1,076
Housekeeping supplies	639	252	301	427	482	544	632	1,035
Laundry and cleaning supplies	140	62	93	111	128	150	150	184
Other household products	347	119	138	209	205	292	342	606
Postage and stationery	152	71	69	107	149	102	140	245
Household furnishings and equipment	1,797	703	613	926	974	1,350	1,887	3,272
Household textiles	133	31	55	76	83	108	146	231
Furniture	446	142	147	194	202	294	424	889
Floor coverings	46	15	14	14	43	20	37	95
Major appliances	231	103	97	147	138	140	222	418
Small appliances, miscellaneous housewares	101	36	49	55	77	93	104	164
Miscellaneous household equipment	840	378	249	440	430	695	954	1,475
APPAREL AND RELATED SERVICES	1,881	807	755	1,016	1,274	1,517	1,856	3,275
Men and boys	435	199	156	244	263	323	435	777
Men, aged 16 or older	351	167	114	199	193	252	349	638
Boys, aged 2 to 15	84	32	42	45	70	71	86	139
Women and girls	749	268	310	386	514	585	781	1,301
Women, aged 16 or older	627	235	269	317	415	494	670	1,083
Girls, aged 2 to 15	122	33	41	69	99	91	111	218
Children under age 2	93	81	40	62	80	84	90	140
Footwear	327	155	147	194	277	297	317	525
Other apparel products and services	276	106	101	131	140	228	232	532
TRANSPORTATION	8,758	2,632	3,764	5,434	6,503	7,346	9,828	14,362
Vehicle purchases	3,244	678	1,404	1,887	2,233	2,149	3,840	5,595
Cars and trucks, new	1,572	213	632	619	788	901	1,508	3,199
Cars and trucks, used	1,567	450	741	1,220	1,359	1,226	2,216	2,187
Gasoline and motor oil	2,384	907	1,152	1,695	1,999	2,335	2,788	3,486
Other vehicle expenses	2,592	916	1,008	1,644	1,971	2,514	2,788	4,167
Vehicle finance charges	305	53	84	139	217	267	400	522
Maintenance and repairs	738	231	304	464	564	688	769	1,212
Vehicle insurance	1,071	498	482	840	936	1,213	1,179	1,480
Vehicle rentals, leases, licenses, other charges	478	134	137	200	255	346	439	953
Public transportation	538	133	202	208	300	348	412	1,115
HEALTH CARE	2,853	1,003	1,825	2,481	2,493	2,800	3,066	3,928
Health insurance	1,545	574	1,126	1,418	1,439	1,502	1,643	2,017
Medical services	709	160	289	532	514	664	809	1,125
Drugs	481	206	370	451	445	515	488	604
Medical supplies	118	62	40	81	95	119	126	182

	total consumer units	under $10,000	$10,000– $19,999	$20,000– $29,999	$30,000– $39,999	$40,000– $49,999	$50,000– $69,999	$70,000 or more
ENTERTAINMENT	**$2,698**	**$862**	**$996**	**$1,375**	**$1,766**	**$2,029**	**$2,660**	**$4,927**
Fees and admissions	658	124	124	177	321	378	539	1,466
Audio and visual equipment and services	987	462	533	688	764	886	1,062	1,497
Pets, toys, hobbies, and playground equipment	560	138	191	300	412	427	584	995
Other entertainment products and services	493	138	148	211	269	338	475	969
PERSONAL CARE PRODUCTS AND SERVICES	**588**	**202**	**270**	**350**	**414**	**505**	**573**	**998**
READING	**118**	**42**	**64**	**71**	**70**	**96**	**110**	**205**
EDUCATION	**945**	**1,017**	**344**	**382**	**285**	**501**	**632**	**1,921**
TOBACCO PRODUCTS AND SMOKING SUPPLIES	**323**	**253**	**267**	**319**	**380**	**361**	**405**	**293**
MISCELLANEOUS	**808**	**209**	**415**	**410**	**685**	**648**	**836**	**1,354**
CASH CONTRIBUTIONS	**1,821**	**368**	**684**	**794**	**1,052**	**1,737**	**1,468**	**3,534**
PERSONAL INSURANCE AND PENSIONS	**5,336**	**367**	**676**	**1,749**	**2,478**	**3,435**	**5,120**	**11,635**
Life and other personal insurance	309	61	118	216	166	184	254	606
Pensions and Social Security	5,027	306	558	1,534	2,312	3,251	4,866	11,030
PERSONAL TAXES	**2,233**	**78**	**−53**	**184**	**427**	**927**	**1,691**	**5,842**
Federal income taxes	1,569	40	−130	17	188	500	1,093	4,325
State and local income taxes	468	−1	19	81	121	257	397	1,148
Other taxes	196	39	59	87	117	170	201	369
GIFTS FOR PEOPLE IN OTHER HOUSEHOLDS	**1,198**	**422**	**302**	**466**	**634**	**676**	**1,132**	**2,443**

Note: Spending by category does not add to total spending because gift spending is also included in the preceding product and service categories and personal taxes are not included in the total.
Source: Bureau of Labor Statistics, 2007 Consumer Expenditure Survey, Internet site http://www.bls.gov/cex/; calculations by New Strategist

Table 9.6 Indexed Spending by Household Income, 2007

(indexed average annual spending of consumer units by product and service category and before-tax income of consumer unit reference person, 2007; index definition: an index of 100 is the average for all consumer units; an index of 125 means that spending by consumer units in that group is 25 percent above the average for all consumer units; an index of 75 indicates spending that is 25 percent below the average for all consumer units)

	total consumer units	under $10,000	$10,000– $19,999	$20,000– $29,999	$30,000– $39,999	$40,000– $49,999	$50,000– $69,999	$70,000 or more
Average spending of consumer units	$49,638	$17,964	$22,360	$29,704	$34,739	$41,083	$50,428	$84,072
Indexed spending of consumer units	100	36	45	60	70	83	102	169
FOOD	100	44	52	66	76	93	104	154
Food at home	100	51	61	76	84	97	105	140
Cereals and bakery products	100	51	63	75	83	96	108	139
Cereals and cereal products	100	56	66	83	85	96	104	134
Bakery products	100	49	61	72	83	96	109	141
Meats, poultry, fish, and eggs	100	53	65	83	85	100	106	134
Beef	100	47	68	82	88	100	108	133
Pork	100	55	66	92	87	104	114	122
Other meats	100	56	65	76	89	94	109	136
Poultry	100	54	61	83	89	96	97	139
Fish and seafood	100	51	55	79	70	104	102	146
Eggs	100	66	79	91	95	98	100	121
Dairy products	100	48	61	74	84	96	106	142
Fresh milk and cream	100	55	68	81	91	98	103	132
Other dairy products	100	43	57	70	79	94	108	147
Fruits and vegetables	100	53	60	76	84	97	103	142
Fresh fruits	100	51	60	72	77	101	98	147
Fresh vegetables	100	53	61	76	82	95	104	142
Processed fruits	100	53	60	80	88	92	104	140
Processed vegetables	100	55	61	77	98	97	106	132
Other food at home	100	50	59	73	83	97	104	143
Sugar and other sweets	100	48	60	73	81	96	107	144
Fats and oils	100	53	69	85	91	102	105	131
Miscellaneous foods	100	48	58	73	82	97	104	144
Nonalcoholic beverages	100	58	62	77	87	99	102	138
Food prepared by consumer unit on trips	100	25	31	35	65	67	100	195
Food away from home	100	35	40	53	65	87	103	173
ALCOHOLIC BEVERAGES	100	33	38	56	67	93	107	168
HOUSING	100	43	53	65	73	83	101	162
Shelter	100	44	53	64	73	82	99	163
Owned dwellings	100	21	29	45	55	69	100	197
Mortgage interest and charges	100	16	18	33	50	66	103	208
Property taxes	100	30	39	52	62	71	91	189
Maintenance, repair, insurance, other expenses	100	22	51	75	63	79	101	169
Rented dwellings	100	113	124	126	130	123	102	58
Other lodging	100	15	16	22	40	48	80	234

	total consumer units	under $10,000	$10,000–$19,999	$20,000–$29,999	$30,000–$39,999	$40,000–$49,999	$50,000–$69,999	$70,000 or more
Utilities, fuels, and public services	**100**	**50**	**67**	**79**	**88**	**94**	**106**	**137**
Natural gas	100	45	66	73	84	89	100	148
Electricity	100	56	72	83	92	96	105	131
Fuel oil and other fuels	100	38	66	83	86	81	105	144
Telephone services	100	50	64	78	89	96	111	136
Water and other public services	100	46	62	75	83	94	107	144
Household services	**100**	**22**	**40**	**44**	**50**	**65**	**90**	**200**
Personal services	100	13	30	31	44	55	96	214
Other household services	100	29	47	54	55	73	86	189
Housekeeping supplies	**100**	**40**	**47**	**67**	**75**	**85**	**99**	**162**
Laundry and cleaning supplies	100	44	67	79	91	107	107	131
Other household products	100	34	40	60	59	84	99	175
Postage and stationery	100	47	45	70	98	67	92	161
Household furnishings and equipment	**100**	**39**	**34**	**52**	**54**	**75**	**105**	**182**
Household textiles	100	23	41	57	62	81	110	174
Furniture	100	32	33	43	45	66	95	199
Floor coverings	100	32	30	30	93	43	80	207
Major appliances	100	45	42	64	60	61	96	181
Small appliances, miscellaneous housewares	100	35	49	54	76	92	103	162
Miscellaneous household equipment	100	45	30	52	51	83	114	176
APPAREL AND RELATED SERVICES	**100**	**43**	**40**	**54**	**68**	**81**	**99**	**174**
Men and boys	**100**	**46**	**36**	**56**	**60**	**74**	**100**	**179**
Men, aged 16 or older	100	48	33	57	55	72	99	182
Boys, aged 2 to 15	100	38	50	54	83	85	102	165
Women and girls	**100**	**36**	**41**	**52**	**69**	**78**	**104**	**174**
Women, aged 16 or older	100	37	43	51	66	79	107	173
Girls, aged 2 to 15	100	27	34	57	81	75	91	179
Children under age 2	**100**	**87**	**43**	**67**	**86**	**90**	**97**	**151**
Footwear	**100**	**47**	**45**	**59**	**85**	**91**	**97**	**161**
Other apparel products and services	**100**	**38**	**37**	**47**	**51**	**83**	**84**	**193**
TRANSPORTATION	**100**	**30**	**43**	**62**	**74**	**84**	**112**	**164**
Vehicle purchases	**100**	**21**	**43**	**58**	**69**	**66**	**118**	**172**
Cars and trucks, new	100	14	40	39	50	57	96	203
Cars and trucks, used	100	29	47	78	87	78	141	140
Gasoline and motor oil	**100**	**38**	**48**	**71**	**84**	**98**	**117**	**146**
Other vehicle expenses	**100**	**35**	**39**	**63**	**76**	**97**	**108**	**161**
Vehicle finance charges	100	17	28	46	71	88	131	171
Maintenance and repairs	100	31	41	63	76	93	104	164
Vehicle insurance	100	46	45	78	87	113	110	138
Vehicle rentals, leases, licenses, other charges	100	28	29	42	53	72	92	199
Public transportation	**100**	**25**	**37**	**39**	**56**	**65**	**77**	**207**
HEALTH CARE	**100**	**35**	**64**	**87**	**87**	**98**	**107**	**138**
Health insurance	100	37	73	92	93	97	106	131
Medical services	100	23	41	75	72	94	114	159
Drugs	100	43	77	94	93	107	101	126
Medical supplies	100	53	34	69	81	101	107	154

	total consumer units	under $10,000	$10,000–$19,999	$20,000–$29,999	$30,000–$39,999	$40,000–$49,999	$50,000–$69,999	$70,000 or more
ENTERTAINMENT	**100**	**32**	**37**	**51**	**65**	**75**	**99**	**183**
Fees and admissions	100	19	19	27	49	57	82	223
Audio and visual equipment and services	100	47	54	70	77	90	108	152
Pets, toys, hobbies, and playground equipment	100	25	34	54	74	76	104	178
Other entertainment products and services	100	28	30	43	55	69	96	197
PERSONAL CARE PRODUCTS AND SERVICES	**100**	**34**	**46**	**60**	**70**	**86**	**97**	**170**
READING	**100**	**36**	**54**	**60**	**59**	**81**	**93**	**174**
EDUCATION	**100**	**108**	**36**	**40**	**30**	**53**	**67**	**203**
TOBACCO PRODUCTS AND SMOKING SUPPLIES	**100**	**78**	**83**	**99**	**118**	**112**	**125**	**91**
MISCELLANEOUS	**100**	**26**	**51**	**51**	**85**	**80**	**103**	**168**
CASH CONTRIBUTIONS	**100**	**20**	**38**	**44**	**58**	**95**	**81**	**194**
PERSONAL INSURANCE AND PENSIONS	**100**	**7**	**13**	**33**	**46**	**64**	**96**	**218**
Life and other personal insurance	100	20	38	70	54	60	82	196
Pensions and Social Security	100	6	11	31	46	65	97	219
PERSONAL TAXES	**100**	**3**	**–2**	**8**	**19**	**42**	**76**	**262**
Federal income taxes	100	3	–8	1	12	32	70	276
State and local income taxes	100	0	4	17	26	55	85	245
Other taxes	100	20	30	44	60	87	103	188
GIFTS FOR PEOPLE IN OTHER HOUSEHOLDS	**100**	**35**	**25**	**39**	**53**	**56**	**94**	**204**

Source: Calculations by New Strategist based on the Bureau of Labor Statistics 2007 Consumer Expenditure Survey, Internet site http://www.bls.gov/cex/home.htm

Table 9.7 Market Shares by Household Income, 2007

(share of total household spending accounted for by household income group, 2007)

	total consumer units	under $10,000	$10,000– $19,999	$20,000– $29,999	$30,000– $39,999	$40,000– $49,999	$50,000– $69,999	$70,000 or more
Share of total consumer units	100.0%	8.0%	12.6%	12.2%	11.0%	9.8%	15.3%	31.1%
Share of total spending	100.0	2.9	5.7	7.3	7.7	8.1	15.5	52.6
FOOD	100.0	3.5	6.6	8.1	8.3	9.1	15.9	47.9
Food at home	100.0	4.1	7.7	9.4	9.2	9.6	16.0	43.5
Cereals and bakery products	100.0	4.1	7.9	9.2	9.2	9.4	16.5	43.1
Cereals and cereal products	100.0	4.5	8.4	10.2	9.3	9.4	15.9	41.7
Bakery products	100.0	3.9	7.7	8.8	9.1	9.4	16.7	43.7
Meats, poultry, fish, and eggs	100.0	4.2	8.1	10.2	9.4	9.8	16.2	41.5
Beef	100.0	3.7	8.6	10.0	9.6	9.9	16.5	41.3
Pork	100.0	4.4	8.3	11.3	9.6	10.2	17.4	37.9
Other meats	100.0	4.5	8.2	9.3	9.8	9.3	16.6	42.1
Poultry	100.0	4.3	7.7	10.2	9.8	9.4	14.9	43.1
Fish and seafood	100.0	4.0	7.0	9.6	7.7	10.2	15.6	45.3
Eggs	100.0	5.3	9.9	11.1	10.5	9.6	15.3	37.6
Dairy products	100.0	3.8	7.7	9.1	9.3	9.4	16.3	44.0
Fresh milk and cream	100.0	4.4	8.5	9.9	10.0	9.6	15.8	41.1
Other dairy products	100.0	3.4	7.1	8.6	8.7	9.2	16.5	45.7
Fruits and vegetables	100.0	4.2	7.6	9.3	9.2	9.5	15.7	44.0
Fresh fruits	100.0	4.1	7.5	8.9	8.4	9.9	15.0	45.5
Fresh vegetables	100.0	4.2	7.6	9.3	9.0	9.3	15.9	44.1
Processed fruits	100.0	4.2	7.5	9.8	9.7	9.0	16.0	43.5
Processed vegetables	100.0	4.4	7.7	9.4	10.8	9.5	16.3	41.1
Other food at home	100.0	4.0	7.5	9.0	9.2	9.5	15.9	44.5
Sugar and other sweets	100.0	3.9	7.6	8.9	9.0	9.4	16.4	44.6
Fats and oils	100.0	4.2	8.7	10.4	10.0	10.1	16.1	40.6
Miscellaneous foods	100.0	3.8	7.3	8.9	9.0	9.6	15.9	44.9
Nonalcoholic beverages	100.0	4.6	7.9	9.4	9.6	9.7	15.6	42.8
Food prepared by consumer unit on trips	100.0	2.0	3.9	4.3	7.2	6.6	15.3	60.7
Food away from home	100.0	2.8	5.1	6.5	7.1	8.6	15.7	53.7
ALCOHOLIC BEVERAGES	100.0	2.6	4.8	6.9	7.3	9.1	16.4	52.2
HOUSING	100.0	3.5	6.6	8.0	8.0	8.1	15.4	50.3
Shelter	100.0	3.5	6.6	7.9	8.1	8.0	15.1	50.7
Owned dwellings	100.0	1.6	3.7	5.5	6.0	6.8	15.2	61.1
Mortgage interest and charges	100.0	1.3	2.3	4.0	5.5	6.5	15.8	64.7
Property taxes	100.0	2.4	4.9	6.4	6.8	7.0	13.9	58.7
Maintenance, repair, insurance, other expenses	100.0	1.8	6.4	9.2	6.9	7.8	15.5	52.5
Rented dwellings	100.0	9.0	15.6	15.5	14.3	12.1	15.6	17.9
Other lodging	100.0	1.2	2.0	2.7	4.4	4.7	12.2	72.7

	total consumer units	under $10,000	$10,000–$19,999	$20,000–$29,999	$30,000–$39,999	$40,000–$49,999	$50,000–$69,999	$70,000 or more
Utilities, fuels, and public services	**100.0%**	**4.0%**	**8.4%**	**9.7%**	**9.7%**	**9.3%**	**16.3%**	**42.6%**
Natural gas	100.0	3.6	8.3	9.0	9.3	8.8	15.3	45.9
Electricity	100.0	4.4	9.0	10.1	10.1	9.5	16.0	40.8
Fuel oil and other fuels	100.0	3.0	8.3	10.1	9.5	7.9	16.1	44.6
Telephone services	100.0	4.0	8.0	9.6	9.7	9.5	17.0	42.2
Water and other public services	100.0	3.7	7.8	9.1	9.1	9.2	16.4	44.6
Household services	**100.0**	**1.8**	**5.0**	**5.4**	**5.5**	**6.4**	**13.8**	**62.1**
Personal services	100.0	1.0	3.7	3.8	4.8	5.4	14.8	66.6
Other household services	100.0	2.3	5.9	6.6	6.1	7.2	13.2	58.7
Housekeeping supplies	**100.0**	**3.2**	**5.9**	**8.2**	**8.3**	**8.4**	**15.1**	**50.3**
Laundry and cleaning supplies	100.0	3.5	8.4	9.7	10.1	10.5	16.4	40.8
Other household products	100.0	2.7	5.0	7.4	6.5	8.3	15.1	54.2
Postage and stationery	100.0	3.8	5.7	8.6	10.8	6.6	14.1	50.1
Household furnishings and equipment	**100.0**	**3.1**	**4.3**	**6.3**	**6.0**	**7.4**	**16.1**	**56.5**
Household textiles	100.0	1.8	5.2	7.0	6.9	8.0	16.8	53.9
Furniture	100.0	2.5	4.1	5.3	5.0	6.5	14.5	61.9
Floor coverings	100.0	2.6	3.8	3.7	10.3	4.3	12.3	64.1
Major appliances	100.0	3.6	5.3	7.8	6.6	6.0	14.7	56.2
Small appliances, miscellaneous housewares	100.0	2.8	6.2	6.7	8.4	9.1	15.8	50.4
Miscellaneous household equipment	100.0	3.6	3.7	6.4	5.6	8.1	17.4	54.5
APPAREL AND RELATED SERVICES	**100.0**	**3.4**	**5.0**	**6.6**	**7.4**	**7.9**	**15.1**	**54.1**
Men and boys	**100.0**	**3.7**	**4.5**	**6.9**	**6.6**	**7.3**	**15.3**	**55.5**
Men, aged 16 or older	100.0	3.8	4.1	6.9	6.0	7.1	15.2	56.5
Boys, aged 2 to 15	100.0	3.1	6.3	6.6	9.2	8.3	15.7	51.4
Women and girls	**100.0**	**2.9**	**5.2**	**6.3**	**7.5**	**7.7**	**16.0**	**53.9**
Women, aged 16 or older	100.0	3.0	5.4	6.2	7.3	7.8	16.4	53.6
Girls, aged 2 to 15	100.0	2.2	4.3	6.9	8.9	7.3	13.9	55.5
Children under age 2	**100.0**	**6.9**	**5.4**	**8.2**	**9.5**	**8.9**	**14.8**	**46.8**
Footwear	**100.0**	**3.8**	**5.7**	**7.3**	**9.3**	**8.9**	**14.8**	**49.9**
Other apparel products and services	**100.0**	**3.1**	**4.6**	**5.8**	**5.6**	**8.1**	**12.9**	**59.9**
TRANSPORTATION	**100.0**	**2.4**	**5.4**	**7.6**	**8.2**	**8.3**	**17.2**	**50.9**
Vehicle purchases	**100.0**	**1.7**	**5.4**	**7.1**	**7.6**	**6.5**	**18.1**	**53.6**
Cars and trucks, new	100.0	1.1	5.1	4.8	5.5	5.6	14.7	63.2
Cars and trucks, used	100.0	2.3	5.9	9.5	9.5	7.7	21.6	43.3
Gasoline and motor oil	**100.0**	**3.0**	**6.1**	**8.7**	**9.2**	**9.6**	**17.9**	**45.4**
Other vehicle expenses	**100.0**	**2.8**	**4.9**	**7.8**	**8.4**	**9.5**	**16.5**	**49.9**
Vehicle finance charges	100.0	1.4	3.5	5.6	7.8	8.6	20.1	53.2
Maintenance and repairs	100.0	2.5	5.2	7.7	8.4	9.2	15.9	51.0
Vehicle insurance	100.0	3.7	5.7	9.6	9.6	11.1	16.8	42.9
Vehicle rentals, leases, licenses, other charges	100.0	2.2	3.6	5.1	5.9	7.1	14.1	61.9
Public transportation	**100.0**	**2.0**	**4.7**	**4.7**	**6.1**	**6.4**	**11.7**	**64.4**
HEALTH CARE	**100.0**	**2.8**	**8.0**	**10.7**	**9.6**	**9.7**	**16.4**	**42.8**
Health insurance	100.0	3.0	9.2	11.2	10.2	9.6	16.3	40.5
Medical services	100.0	1.8	5.1	9.2	8.0	9.2	17.5	49.3
Drugs	100.0	3.4	9.7	11.5	10.2	10.5	15.5	39.0
Medical supplies	100.0	4.2	4.3	8.4	8.9	9.9	16.3	47.9

	total consumer units	under $10,000	$10,000– $19,999	$20,000– $29,999	$30,000– $39,999	$40,000– $49,999	$50,000– $69,999	$70,000 or more
ENTERTAINMENT	**100.0%**	**2.5%**	**4.6%**	**6.2%**	**7.2%**	**7.4%**	**15.1%**	**56.7%**
Fees and admissions	100.0	1.5	2.4	3.3	5.4	5.7	12.5	69.2
Audio and visual equipment and services	100.0	3.7	6.8	8.5	8.5	8.8	16.5	47.1
Pets, toys, hobbies, and playground equipment	100.0	2.0	4.3	6.6	8.1	7.5	16.0	55.2
Other entertainment products and services	100.0	2.2	3.8	5.2	6.0	6.7	14.7	61.0
PERSONAL CARE PRODUCTS AND SERVICES	**100.0**	**2.7**	**5.8**	**7.3**	**7.7**	**8.5**	**14.9**	**52.7**
READING	**100.0**	**2.8**	**6.8**	**7.4**	**6.5**	**8.0**	**14.3**	**54.0**
EDUCATION	**100.0**	**8.6**	**4.6**	**5.0**	**3.3**	**5.2**	**10.2**	**63.1**
TOBACCO PRODUCTS AND SMOKING SUPPLIES	**100.0**	**6.2**	**10.4**	**12.1**	**12.9**	**11.0**	**19.2**	**28.2**
MISCELLANEOUS	**100.0**	**2.1**	**6.5**	**6.2**	**9.3**	**7.9**	**15.8**	**52.0**
CASH CONTRIBUTIONS	**100.0**	**1.6**	**4.7**	**5.3**	**6.4**	**9.4**	**12.3**	**60.3**
PERSONAL INSURANCE AND PENSIONS	**100.0**	**0.5**	**1.6**	**4.0**	**5.1**	**6.3**	**14.7**	**67.7**
Life and other personal insurance	100.0	1.6	4.8	8.6	5.9	5.9	12.6	60.9
Pensions and Social Security	100.0	0.5	1.4	3.7	5.1	6.4	14.8	68.1
PERSONAL TAXES	**100.0**	**0.3**	**−0.3**	**1.0**	**2.1**	**4.1**	**11.6**	**81.3**
Federal income taxes	100.0	0.2	−1.0	0.1	1.3	3.1	10.7	85.6
State and local income taxes	100.0	0.0	0.5	2.1	2.8	5.4	13.0	76.2
Other taxes	100.0	1.6	3.8	5.4	6.6	8.5	15.7	58.5
GIFTS FOR PEOPLE IN OTHER HOUSEHOLDS	**100.0**	**2.8**	**3.2**	**4.8**	**5.8**	**5.6**	**14.5**	**63.3**

Source: Calculations by New Strategist based on the Bureau of Labor Statistics 2007 Consumer Expenditure Survey, Internet site http://www.bls.gov/cex/home.htm

Table 9.8 Average Spending by High-Income Households, 2007

(average annual spending of consumer units by product and service category and before-tax income of consumer unit, 2007)

	total consumer units	less than $70,000	$70,000– $79,999	$80,000– $99,999	$100,000 or more total	$100,000– $119,999	$120,000– $149,999	$150,000 or more
Number of consumer units (in 000s)	120,171	82,849	6,957	9,777	20,588	6,651	5,708	8,229
Average number of persons per consumer unit	2.5	2.2	2.9	3.0	3.2	3.1	3.2	3.2
Average income before taxes	$63,091	$32,745	$74,679	$88,830	$169,072	$108,502	$132,523	$243,376
Average annual spending	49,638	34,109	58,005	67,640	101,041	77,838	91,864	126,443
FOOD	6,133	4,625	7,541	8,128	10,890	8,856	10,567	12,849
Food at home	3,465	2,836	4,080	4,335	5,428	4,550	5,433	6,178
Cereals and bakery products	460	379	536	598	699	571	733	784
Cereals and cereal products	143	120	167	179	208	176	223	226
Bakery products	317	258	369	419	490	395	510	558
Meats, poultry, fish, and eggs	777	658	874	922	1,165	1,007	1,168	1,300
Beef	216	184	258	281	300	253	300	339
Pork	150	134	168	166	199	197	188	209
Other meats	104	88	121	120	162	139	152	188
Poultry	142	117	145	170	232	220	243	234
Fish and seafood	122	97	133	139	216	147	227	268
Eggs	43	39	49	46	56	50	56	61
Dairy products	387	315	469	496	606	513	628	671
Fresh milk and cream	154	131	185	194	217	194	229	227
Other dairy products	234	184	284	302	390	319	399	444
Fruits and vegetables	600	487	682	710	990	791	985	1,166
Fresh fruits	202	159	234	232	355	279	326	443
Fresh vegetables	190	154	207	227	318	243	338	367
Processed fruits	112	92	131	138	177	138	174	213
Processed vegetables	96	81	110	113	140	132	147	142
Other food at home	1,241	998	1,520	1,609	1,967	1,669	1,920	2,257
Sugar and other sweets	124	100	142	167	197	161	206	222
Fats and oils	91	79	95	107	134	119	138	143
Miscellaneous foods	650	518	815	867	1,026	871	1,012	1,170
Nonalcoholic beverages	333	276	411	411	505	442	478	578
Food prepared by consumer unit on trips	43	25	58	57	106	75	87	144
Food away from home	2,668	1,789	3,461	3,793	5,462	4,307	5,134	6,671
ALCOHOLIC BEVERAGES	457	316	463	586	979	628	871	1,357
HOUSING	16,920	12,193	19,178	21,703	32,965	24,952	30,391	41,294
Shelter	10,023	7,166	11,396	12,850	19,710	15,064	18,543	24,274
Owned dwellings	6,730	3,795	8,793	10,313	16,141	12,230	15,542	19,718
Mortgage interest and charges	3,890	1,991	5,375	6,557	9,765	7,770	9,554	11,523
Property taxes	1,709	1,025	2,052	2,327	4,053	2,891	3,632	5,285
Maintenance, repair, insurance, other expenses	1,131	780	1,367	1,430	2,323	1,570	2,357	2,910
Rented dwellings	2,602	3,098	1,971	1,771	1,214	1,413	1,342	965
Other lodging	691	273	631	765	2,354	1,420	1,658	3,592

	total consumer units	less than $70,000	$70,000–$79,999	$80,000–$99,999	$100,000 or more			
					total	$100,000–$119,999	$120,000–$149,999	$150,000 or more
Utilities, fuels, and public services	**$3,477**	**$2,894**	**$4,129**	**$4,256**	**$5,234**	**$4,657**	**$5,077**	**$5,809**
Natural gas	480	377	590	610	796	668	772	917
Electricity	1,303	1,118	1,468	1,523	1,885	1,643	1,846	2,107
Fuel oil and other fuels	151	121	176	157	260	231	224	309
Telephone services	1,110	929	1,374	1,406	1,605	1,494	1,579	1,712
Water and other public services	434	348	521	559	688	621	654	765
Household services	**984**	**542**	**1,120**	**1,440**	**2,501**	**1,527**	**2,143**	**3,537**
Personal services	415	202	525	704	1,101	714	1,088	1,423
Other household services	569	340	596	736	1,400	813	1,055	2,115
Housekeeping supplies	**639**	**459**	**747**	**836**	**1,254**	**875**	**1,094**	**1,700**
Laundry and cleaning supplies	140	120	152	167	205	196	209	210
Other household products	347	229	403	441	775	451	638	1,154
Postage and stationery	152	110	193	228	275	227	247	336
Household furnishings and equipment	**1,797**	**1,131**	**1,785**	**2,321**	**4,266**	**2,830**	**3,535**	**5,973**
Household textiles	133	89	132	216	272	181	264	354
Furniture	446	246	401	500	1,242	746	931	1,859
Floor coverings	46	25	42	44	137	43	79	252
Major appliances	231	147	284	324	508	404	433	645
Small appliances, miscellaneous housewares	101	72	148	141	182	155	221	176
Miscellaneous household equipment	840	552	778	1,096	1,924	1,301	1,606	2,686
APPAREL AND RELATED SERVICES	**1,881**	**1,250**	**2,189**	**2,470**	**4,096**	**2,819**	**3,373**	**5,698**
Men and boys	**435**	**281**	**497**	**580**	**985**	**747**	**736**	**1,368**
Men, aged 16 or older	351	221	394	455	826	614	577	1,188
Boys, aged 2 to 15	84	60	103	124	159	133	159	180
Women and girls	**749**	**499**	**946**	**992**	**1,601**	**1,059**	**1,462**	**2,167**
Women, aged 16 or older	627	421	804	785	1,352	897	1,191	1,859
Girls, aged 2 to 15	122	78	142	208	250	163	271	308
Children under age 2	**93**	**72**	**154**	**141**	**135**	**126**	**103**	**167**
Footwear	**327**	**238**	**349**	**413**	**653**	**480**	**551**	**877**
Other apparel products and services	**276**	**160**	**243**	**344**	**722**	**406**	**521**	**1,119**
TRANSPORTATION	**8,758**	**6,232**	**10,886**	**13,039**	**16,163**	**13,892**	**16,050**	**18,074**
Vehicle purchases	**3,244**	**2,185**	**4,046**	**5,386**	**6,217**	**5,626**	**6,198**	**6,708**
Cars and trucks, new	1,572	839	1,856	3,138	3,681	3,042	3,465	4,347
Cars and trucks, used	1,567	1,288	1,907	2,051	2,346	2,378	2,549	2,178
Gasoline and motor oil	**2,384**	**1,887**	**3,041**	**3,243**	**3,751**	**3,600**	**3,772**	**3,859**
Other vehicle expenses	**2,592**	**1,882**	**3,329**	**3,705**	**4,666**	**3,837**	**4,857**	**5,201**
Vehicle finance charges	305	208	457	503	553	524	534	588
Maintenance and repairs	738	524	1,040	1,061	1,337	1,275	1,233	1,460
Vehicle insurance	1,071	886	1,234	1,515	1,548	1,201	2,053	1,473
Vehicle rentals, leases, licenses, other charges	478	264	598	626	1,229	837	1,037	1,680
Public transportation	**538**	**278**	**470**	**704**	**1,528**	**829**	**1,223**	**2,307**
HEALTH CARE	**2,853**	**2,368**	**3,136**	**3,619**	**4,348**	**3,794**	**4,297**	**4,836**
Health insurance	1,545	1,332	1,720	1,971	2,139	1,872	2,183	2,324
Medical services	709	522	773	930	1,337	1,168	1,287	1,509
Drugs	481	425	500	558	667	563	636	776
Medical supplies	118	89	144	161	205	191	191	226

	total consumer units	less than $70,000	$70,000–$79,999	$80,000–$99,999	$100,000 or more			
					total	$100,000–$119,999	$120,000–$149,999	$150,000 or more
ENTERTAINMENT	**$2,698**	**$1,692**	**$2,913**	**$3,722**	**$6,225**	**$5,382**	**$5,220**	**$7,632**
Fees and admissions	658	294	654	956	1,994	1,244	1,625	2,870
Audio and visual equipment and services	987	757	1,043	1,345	1,721	1,382	1,650	2,049
Pets, toys, hobbies, and playground equipment	560	363	763	847	1,157	1,174	1,079	1,196
Other entertainment products and services	493	278	453	575	1,353	1,582	867	1,518
PERSONAL CARE PRODUCTS AND SERVICES	**588**	**402**	**701**	**860**	**1,172**	**888**	**1,239**	**1,358**
READING	**118**	**78**	**141**	**168**	**244**	**195**	**226**	**296**
EDUCATION	**945**	**506**	**841**	**997**	**2,725**	**1,580**	**2,227**	**3,996**
TOBACCO PRODUCTS AND SMOKING SUPPLIES	**323**	**336**	**356**	**350**	**245**	**280**	**275**	**196**
MISCELLANEOUS	**808**	**561**	**958**	**1,110**	**1,601**	**1,217**	**1,179**	**2,206**
CASH CONTRIBUTIONS	**1,821**	**1,050**	**2,047**	**2,481**	**4,537**	**2,640**	**3,106**	**7,064**
PERSONAL INSURANCE AND PENSIONS	**5,336**	**2,499**	**6,655**	**8,406**	**14,852**	**10,715**	**12,843**	**19,588**
Life and other personal insurance	309	176	333	482	756	542	676	984
Pensions and Social Security	5,027	2,322	6,321	7,924	14,096	10,173	12,168	18,604
PERSONAL TAXES	**2,233**	**608**	**2,550**	**3,192**	**8,213**	**5,005**	**5,731**	**12,527**
Federal income taxes	1,569	328	1,665	2,294	6,189	3,587	4,179	9,685
State and local income taxes	468	162	648	667	1,545	1,060	1,192	2,182
Other taxes	196	118	237	231	480	358	360	661
GIFTS FOR PEOPLE IN OTHER HOUSEHOLDS	**1,198**	**636**	**1,500**	**1,498**	**3,226**	**1,929**	**2,587**	**4,743**

Note: Spending by category does not add to total spending because gift spending is also included in the preceding product and service categories and personal taxes are not included in the total.
Source: Bureau of Labor Statistics, 2007 Consumer Expenditure Survey, Internet site http://www.bls.gov/cex/

Table 9.9 Indexed Spending by High-Income Households, 2007

(indexed average annual spending of consumer units by product and service category and before-tax income of consumer unit reference person, 2007; index definition: an index of 100 is the average for all consumer units; an index of 125 means that spending by consumer units in that group is 25 percent above the average for all consumer units; an index of 75 indicates spending that is 25 percent below the average for all consumer units)

	total consumer units	less than $70,000	$70,000–$79,999	$80,000–$99,999	$100,000 or more total	$100,000–$119,999	$120,000–$149,999	$150,000 or more
Average spending of consumer units	$49,638	$34,109	$58,005	$67,640	$101,041	$77,838	$91,864	$126,443
Indexed spending of consumer units	100	69	117	136	204	157	185	255
FOOD	100	75	123	133	178	144	172	210
Food at home	100	82	118	125	157	131	157	178
Cereals and bakery products	100	82	117	130	152	124	159	170
Cereals and cereal products	100	84	117	125	145	123	156	158
Bakery products	100	81	116	132	155	125	161	176
Meats, poultry, fish, and eggs	100	85	112	119	150	130	150	167
Beef	100	85	119	130	139	117	139	157
Pork	100	89	112	111	133	131	125	139
Other meats	100	85	116	115	156	134	146	181
Poultry	100	82	102	120	163	155	171	165
Fish and seafood	100	80	109	114	177	120	186	220
Eggs	100	91	114	107	130	116	130	142
Dairy products	100	81	121	128	157	133	162	173
Fresh milk and cream	100	85	120	126	141	126	149	147
Other dairy products	100	79	121	129	167	136	171	190
Fruits and vegetables	100	81	114	118	165	132	164	194
Fresh fruits	100	79	116	115	176	138	161	219
Fresh vegetables	100	81	109	119	167	128	178	193
Processed fruits	100	82	117	123	158	123	155	190
Processed vegetables	100	84	115	118	146	138	153	148
Other food at home	100	80	122	130	159	134	155	182
Sugar and other sweets	100	81	115	135	159	130	166	179
Fats and oils	100	87	104	118	147	131	152	157
Miscellaneous foods	100	80	125	133	158	134	156	180
Nonalcoholic beverages	100	83	123	123	152	133	144	174
Food prepared by consumer unit on trips	100	58	135	133	247	174	202	335
Food away from home	100	67	130	142	205	161	192	250
ALCOHOLIC BEVERAGES	100	69	101	128	214	137	191	297
HOUSING	100	72	113	128	195	147	180	244
Shelter	100	71	114	128	197	150	185	242
Owned dwellings	100	56	131	153	240	182	231	293
Mortgage interest and charges	100	51	138	169	251	200	246	296
Property taxes	100	60	120	136	237	169	213	309
Maintenance, repair, insurance, other expenses	100	69	121	126	205	139	208	257
Rented dwellings	100	119	76	68	47	54	52	37
Other lodging	100	40	91	111	341	205	240	520

	total consumer units	less than $70,000	$70,000–$79,999	$80,000–$99,999	$100,000 or more total	$100,000–$119,999	$120,000–$149,999	$150,000 or more
Utilities, fuels, and public services	100	83	119	122	151	134	146	167
Natural gas	100	79	123	127	166	139	161	191
Electricity	100	86	113	117	145	126	142	162
Fuel oil and other fuels	100	80	117	104	172	153	148	205
Telephone services	100	84	124	127	145	135	142	154
Water and other public services	100	80	120	129	159	143	151	176
Household services	100	55	114	146	254	155	218	359
Personal services	100	49	127	170	265	172	262	343
Other household services	100	60	105	129	246	143	185	372
Housekeeping supplies	100	72	117	131	196	137	171	266
Laundry and cleaning supplies	100	86	109	119	146	140	149	150
Other household products	100	66	116	127	223	130	184	333
Postage and stationery	100	72	127	150	181	149	163	221
Household furnishings and equipment	100	63	99	129	237	157	197	332
Household textiles	100	67	99	162	205	136	198	266
Furniture	100	55	90	112	278	167	209	417
Floor coverings	100	54	91	96	298	93	172	548
Major appliances	100	64	123	140	220	175	187	279
Small appliances, miscellaneous housewares	100	71	147	140	180	153	219	174
Miscellaneous household equipment	100	66	93	130	229	155	191	320
APPAREL AND RELATED SERVICES	100	66	116	131	218	150	179	303
Men and boys	100	65	114	133	226	172	169	314
Men, aged 16 or older	100	63	112	130	235	175	164	338
Boys, aged 2 to 15	100	71	123	148	189	158	189	214
Women and girls	100	67	126	132	214	141	195	289
Women, aged 16 or older	100	67	128	125	216	143	190	296
Girls, aged 2 to 15	100	64	116	170	205	134	222	252
Children under age 2	100	77	166	152	145	135	111	180
Footwear	100	73	107	126	200	147	169	268
Other apparel products and services	100	58	88	125	262	147	189	405
TRANSPORTATION	100	71	124	149	185	159	183	206
Vehicle purchases	100	67	125	166	192	173	191	207
Cars and trucks, new	100	53	118	200	234	194	220	277
Cars and trucks, used	100	82	122	131	150	152	163	139
Gasoline and motor oil	100	79	128	136	157	151	158	162
Other vehicle expenses	100	73	128	143	180	148	187	201
Vehicle finance charges	100	68	150	165	181	172	175	193
Maintenance and repairs	100	71	141	144	181	173	167	198
Vehicle insurance	100	83	115	141	145	112	192	138
Vehicle rentals, leases, licenses, other charges	100	55	125	131	257	175	217	351
Public transportation	100	52	87	131	284	154	227	429
HEALTH CARE	100	83	110	127	152	133	151	170
Health insurance	100	86	111	128	138	121	141	150
Medical services	100	74	109	131	189	165	182	213
Drugs	100	88	104	116	139	117	132	161
Medical supplies	100	75	122	136	174	162	162	192

	total consumer units	less than $70,000	$70,000–$79,999	$80,000–$99,999	$100,000 or more			
					total	$100,000–$119,999	$120,000–$149,999	$150,000 or more
ENTERTAINMENT	100	63	108	138	231	199	193	283
Fees and admissions	100	45	99	145	303	189	247	436
Audio and visual equipment and services	100	77	106	136	174	140	167	208
Pets, toys, hobbies, and playground equipment	100	65	136	151	207	210	193	214
Other entertainment products and services	100	56	92	117	274	321	176	308
PERSONAL CARE PRODUCTS AND SERVICES	100	68	119	146	199	151	211	231
READING	100	66	119	142	207	165	192	251
EDUCATION	100	54	89	106	288	167	236	423
TOBACCO PRODUCTS AND SMOKING SUPPLIES	100	104	110	108	76	87	85	61
MISCELLANEOUS	100	69	119	137	198	151	146	273
CASH CONTRIBUTIONS	100	58	112	136	249	145	171	388
PERSONAL INSURANCE AND PENSIONS	100	47	125	158	278	201	241	367
Life and other personal insurance	100	57	108	156	245	175	219	318
Pensions and Social Security	100	46	126	158	280	202	242	370
PERSONAL TAXES	100	27	114	143	368	224	257	561
Federal income taxes	100	21	106	146	394	229	266	617
State and local income taxes	100	35	138	143	330	226	255	466
Other taxes	100	60	121	118	245	183	184	337
GIFTS FOR PEOPLE IN OTHER HOUSEHOLDS	100	53	125	125	269	161	216	396

Source: Calculations by New Strategist based on the Bureau of Labor Statistics 2007 Consumer Expenditure Survey, Internet site http://www.bls.gov/cex/home.htm

Table 9.10 Market Shares of High-Income Households, 2007

(share of total household spending accounted for by income groups, 2007)

	total consumer units	less than $70,000	$70,000– $79,999	$80,000– $99,999	$100,000 or more total	$100,000– $119,999	$120,000– $149,999	$150,000 or more
Share of total consumer units	100.0%	68.9%	5.8%	8.1%	17.1%	5.5%	4.7%	6.8%
Share of total spending	100.0	47.4	6.8	11.1	34.9	8.7	8.8	17.4
FOOD	100.0	52.0	7.1	10.8	30.4	8.0	8.2	14.3
Food at home	100.0	56.4	6.8	10.2	26.8	7.3	7.4	12.2
Cereals and bakery products	100.0	56.8	6.7	10.6	26.0	6.9	7.6	11.7
Cereals and cereal products	100.0	57.9	6.8	10.2	24.9	6.8	7.4	10.8
Bakery products	100.0	56.1	6.7	10.8	26.5	6.9	7.6	12.1
Meats, poultry, fish, and eggs	100.0	58.4	6.5	9.7	25.7	7.2	7.1	11.5
Beef	100.0	58.7	6.9	10.6	23.8	6.5	6.6	10.7
Pork	100.0	61.6	6.5	9.0	22.7	7.3	6.0	9.5
Other meats	100.0	58.3	6.7	9.4	26.7	7.4	6.9	12.4
Poultry	100.0	56.8	5.9	9.7	28.0	8.6	8.1	11.3
Fish and seafood	100.0	54.8	6.3	9.3	30.3	6.7	8.8	15.0
Eggs	100.0	62.5	6.6	8.7	22.3	6.4	6.2	9.7
Dairy products	100.0	56.1	7.0	10.4	26.8	7.3	7.7	11.9
Fresh milk and cream	100.0	58.6	7.0	10.2	24.1	7.0	7.1	10.1
Other dairy products	100.0	54.2	7.0	10.5	28.6	7.5	8.1	13.0
Fruits and vegetables	100.0	56.0	6.6	9.6	28.3	7.3	7.8	13.3
Fresh fruits	100.0	54.3	6.7	9.3	30.1	7.6	7.7	15.0
Fresh vegetables	100.0	55.9	6.3	9.7	28.7	7.1	8.4	13.2
Processed fruits	100.0	56.6	6.8	10.0	27.1	6.8	7.4	13.0
Processed vegetables	100.0	58.2	6.6	9.6	25.0	7.6	7.3	10.1
Other food at home	100.0	55.4	7.1	10.5	27.2	7.4	7.3	12.5
Sugar and other sweets	100.0	55.6	6.6	11.0	27.2	7.2	7.9	12.3
Fats and oils	100.0	59.9	6.0	9.6	25.2	7.2	7.2	10.8
Miscellaneous foods	100.0	54.9	7.3	10.9	27.0	7.4	7.4	12.3
Nonalcoholic beverages	100.0	57.1	7.1	10.0	26.0	7.3	6.8	11.9
Food prepared by consumer unit on trips	100.0	40.1	7.8	10.8	42.2	9.7	9.6	22.9
Food away from home	100.0	46.2	7.5	11.6	35.1	8.9	9.1	17.1
ALCOHOLIC BEVERAGES	100.0	47.7	5.9	10.4	36.7	7.6	9.1	20.3
HOUSING	100.0	49.7	6.6	10.4	33.4	8.2	8.5	16.7
Shelter	100.0	49.3	6.6	10.4	33.7	8.3	8.8	16.6
Owned dwellings	100.0	38.9	7.6	12.5	41.1	10.1	11.0	20.1
Mortgage interest and charges	100.0	35.3	8.0	13.7	43.0	11.1	11.7	20.3
Property taxes	100.0	41.3	7.0	11.1	40.6	9.4	10.1	21.2
Maintenance, repair, insurance, other expenses	100.0	47.5	7.0	10.3	35.2	7.7	9.9	17.6
Rented dwellings	100.0	82.1	4.4	5.5	8.0	3.0	2.4	2.5
Other lodging	100.0	27.2	5.3	9.0	58.4	11.4	11.4	35.6

	total consumer units	less than $70,000	$70,000– $79,999	$80,000– $99,999	$100,000 or more total	$100,000– $119,999	$120,000– $149,999	$150,000 or more
Utilities, fuels, and public services	**100.0%**	**57.4%**	**6.9%**	**10.0%**	**25.8%**	**7.4%**	**6.9%**	**11.4%**
Natural gas	100.0	54.1	7.1	10.3	28.4	7.7	7.6	13.1
Electricity	100.0	59.2	6.5	9.5	24.8	7.0	6.7	11.1
Fuel oil and other fuels	100.0	55.2	6.7	8.5	29.5	8.5	7.0	14.0
Telephone services	100.0	57.7	7.2	10.3	24.8	7.4	6.8	10.6
Water and other public services	100.0	55.3	6.9	10.5	27.2	7.9	7.2	12.1
Household services	**100.0**	**38.0**	**6.6**	**11.9**	**43.5**	**8.6**	**10.3**	**24.6**
Personal services	100.0	33.6	7.3	13.8	45.5	9.5	12.5	23.5
Other household services	100.0	41.2	6.1	10.5	42.2	7.9	8.8	25.5
Housekeeping supplies	**100.0**	**49.5**	**6.8**	**10.6**	**33.6**	**7.6**	**8.1**	**18.2**
Laundry and cleaning supplies	100.0	59.1	6.3	9.7	25.1	7.7	7.1	10.3
Other household products	100.0	45.5	6.7	10.3	38.3	7.2	8.7	22.8
Postage and stationery	100.0	49.9	7.4	12.2	31.0	8.3	7.7	15.1
Household furnishings and equipment	**100.0**	**43.4**	**5.8**	**10.5**	**40.7**	**8.7**	**9.3**	**22.8**
Household textiles	100.0	46.1	5.7	13.2	35.0	7.5	9.4	18.2
Furniture	100.0	38.0	5.2	9.1	47.7	9.3	9.9	28.5
Floor coverings	100.0	37.5	5.3	7.8	51.0	5.2	8.2	37.5
Major appliances	100.0	43.9	7.1	11.4	37.7	9.7	8.9	19.1
Small appliances, miscellaneous housewares	100.0	49.1	8.5	11.4	30.9	8.5	10.4	11.9
Miscellaneous household equipment	100.0	45.3	5.4	10.6	39.2	8.6	9.1	21.9
APPAREL AND RELATED SERVICES	**100.0**	**45.8**	**6.7**	**10.7**	**37.3**	**8.3**	**8.5**	**20.7**
Men and boys	**100.0**	**44.5**	**6.6**	**10.8**	**38.8**	**9.5**	**8.0**	**21.5**
Men, aged 16 or older	100.0	43.4	6.5	10.5	40.3	9.7	7.8	23.2
Boys, aged 2 to 15	100.0	49.2	7.1	12.0	32.4	8.8	9.0	14.7
Women and girls	**100.0**	**45.9**	**7.3**	**10.8**	**36.6**	**7.8**	**9.3**	**19.8**
Women, aged 16 or older	100.0	46.3	7.4	10.2	36.9	7.9	9.0	20.3
Girls, aged 2 to 15	100.0	44.1	6.7	13.9	35.1	7.4	10.6	17.3
Children under age 2	**100.0**	**53.4**	**9.6**	**12.3**	**24.9**	**7.5**	**5.3**	**12.3**
Footwear	**100.0**	**50.2**	**6.2**	**10.3**	**34.2**	**8.1**	**8.0**	**18.4**
Other apparel products and services	**100.0**	**40.0**	**5.1**	**10.1**	**44.8**	**8.1**	**9.0**	**27.8**
TRANSPORTATION	**100.0**	**49.1**	**7.2**	**12.1**	**31.6**	**8.8**	**8.7**	**14.1**
Vehicle purchases	**100.0**	**46.4**	**7.2**	**13.5**	**32.8**	**9.6**	**9.1**	**14.2**
Cars and trucks, new	100.0	36.8	6.8	16.2	40.1	10.7	10.5	18.9
Cars and trucks, used	100.0	56.7	7.0	10.6	25.6	8.4	7.7	9.5
Gasoline and motor oil	**100.0**	**54.6**	**7.4**	**11.1**	**27.0**	**8.4**	**7.5**	**11.1**
Other vehicle expenses	**100.0**	**50.1**	**7.4**	**11.6**	**30.8**	**8.2**	**8.9**	**13.7**
Vehicle finance charges	100.0	47.0	8.7	13.4	31.1	9.5	8.3	13.2
Maintenance and repairs	100.0	49.0	8.2	11.7	31.0	9.6	7.9	13.5
Vehicle insurance	100.0	57.0	6.7	11.5	24.8	6.2	9.1	9.4
Vehicle rentals, leases, licenses, other charges	100.0	38.1	7.2	10.7	44.0	9.7	10.3	24.1
Public transportation	**100.0**	**35.6**	**5.1**	**10.6**	**48.7**	**8.5**	**10.8**	**29.4**
HEALTH CARE	**100.0**	**57.2**	**6.4**	**10.3**	**26.1**	**7.4**	**7.2**	**11.6**
Health insurance	100.0	59.4	6.4	10.4	23.7	6.7	6.7	10.3
Medical services	100.0	50.8	6.3	10.7	32.3	9.1	8.6	14.6
Drugs	100.0	60.9	6.0	9.4	23.8	6.5	6.3	11.0
Medical supplies	100.0	52.0	7.1	11.1	29.8	9.0	7.7	13.1

	total consumer units	less than $70,000	$70,000–$79,999	$80,000–$99,999	$100,000 or more			
					total	$100,000–$119,999	$120,000–$149,999	$150,000 or more
ENTERTAINMENT	**100.0%**	**43.2%**	**6.3%**	**11.2%**	**39.5%**	**11.0%**	**9.2%**	**19.4%**
Fees and admissions	100.0	30.8	5.8	11.8	51.9	10.5	11.7	29.9
Audio and visual equipment and services	100.0	52.9	6.1	11.1	29.9	7.7	7.9	14.2
Pets, toys, hobbies, and playground equipment	100.0	44.7	7.9	12.3	35.4	11.6	9.2	14.6
Other entertainment products and services	100.0	38.9	5.3	9.5	47.0	17.8	8.4	21.1
PERSONAL CARE PRODUCTS AND SERVICES	**100.0**	**47.1**	**6.9**	**11.9**	**34.1**	**8.4**	**10.0**	**15.8**
READING	**100.0**	**45.6**	**6.9**	**11.6**	**35.4**	**9.1**	**9.1**	**17.2**
EDUCATION	**100.0**	**36.9**	**5.2**	**8.6**	**49.4**	**9.3**	**11.2**	**29.0**
TOBACCO PRODUCTS AND SMOKING SUPPLIES	**100.0**	**71.7**	**6.4**	**8.8**	**13.0**	**4.8**	**4.0**	**4.2**
MISCELLANEOUS	**100.0**	**47.9**	**6.9**	**11.2**	**33.9**	**8.3**	**6.9**	**18.7**
CASH CONTRIBUTIONS	**100.0**	**39.8**	**6.5**	**11.1**	**42.7**	**8.0**	**8.1**	**26.6**
PERSONAL INSURANCE AND PENSIONS	**100.0**	**32.3**	**7.2**	**12.8**	**47.7**	**11.1**	**11.4**	**25.1**
Life and other personal insurance	100.0	39.3	6.2	12.7	41.9	9.7	10.4	21.8
Pensions and Social Security	100.0	31.8	7.3	12.8	48.0	11.2	11.5	25.3
PERSONAL TAXES	**100.0**	**18.8**	**6.6**	**11.6**	**63.0**	**12.4**	**12.2**	**38.4**
Federal income taxes	100.0	14.4	6.1	11.9	67.6	12.7	12.7	42.3
State and local income taxes	100.0	23.9	8.0	11.6	56.6	12.5	12.1	31.9
Other taxes	100.0	41.5	7.0	9.6	42.0	10.1	8.7	23.1
GIFTS FOR PEOPLE IN OTHER HOUSEHOLDS	**100.0**	**36.6**	**7.2**	**10.2**	**46.1**	**8.9**	**10.3**	**27.1**

Source: Calculations by New Strategist based on the Bureau of Labor Statistics 2007 Consumer Expenditure Survey, Internet site http://www.bls.gov/cex/home.htm

Couples with Children Spend the Most

Married couples with children spend 39 percent more than the average household.

Married couples with children spend much more than average because they have the highest incomes and the largest households. In 2007, couples with kids spent an average of $69,101 versus the $49,638 spent by the average household, according to the Bureau of Labor Statistics' Consumer Expenditure Survey.

Married couples without children at home spend 18 percent more than average. Most are empty-nesters whose grown children live elsewhere or young couples who have not yet had children. Single-parent households spent $38,239 in 2007, and single-person households spent the least—just $29,285.

The Indexed Spending table shows spending by household type in comparison with average household spending. An index of 100 means the household type spends an average amount on the item. An index above 100 indicates that the household type spends more than average on the item, while an index below 100 reveals below-average spending.

A look at Table 9.12 shows that spending is well below average for single-parent and single-person households, although single-parent households spend close to the average on most foods.

Spending is below average for single parents

(average annual spending of consumer units by type, 2007)

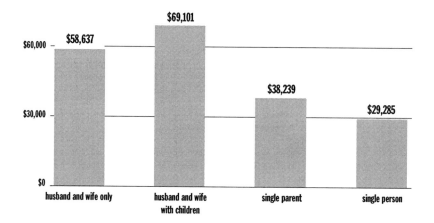

Single-parent households spend 60 percent more than the average (with an index of 160) on household personal services, most of which is day care expenses. Married couples without children at home spend more than average on many items. But they spend less than average on household personal services, children's clothing, and education.

The Market Share table shows how much of total spending by category is accounted for by each household type. Married couples with children account for 25 percent of households and 35 percent of household spending. Single-person households account for 30 percent of households but only 18 percent of spending.

Married couples with children account for more than half of all household spending on some items such as household personal services (day care) and children's clothing. Married couples without children at home, who represent 22 percent of households, account for at least 35 percent of spending on other lodging (hotels and motels), public transportation (mostly airline fares), drugs, and gifts for people in other households. Single parents, who represent 6 percent of households, account for less than 10 percent of spending on all but boys' and girls' clothing. Single-person households account for a larger-than-average share of spending on rent.

■ The spending of married couples without children at home may grow faster than average in the years ahead as two-income baby-boom couples enter the empty-nest years.

Table 9.11 Average Spending by Household Type, 2007

(average annual spending of consumer units by product and service category and type of consumer unit, 2007)

	total consumer units	total married couples	married couples, no children	married couples with children — total	oldest child under 6	oldest child 6 to 17	oldest child 18 or older	single parent, at least one child <18	single person
Number of consumer units (in 000s)	120,171	60,747	25,923	29,984	5,865	15,265	8,854	7,139	35,740
Average number of persons per CU	2.5	3.2	2.0	3.9	3.5	4.2	3.9	2.9	1.0
Average income before taxes	$63,091	$85,803	$78,434	$92,655	$83,372	$92,569	$98,952	$35,490	$31,962
Average annual spending	49,638	64,104	58,637	69,101	62,403	70,766	70,822	38,239	29,285
FOOD	6,133	7,900	6,690	8,876	7,137	9,151	9,623	5,614	3,328
Food at home	3,465	4,460	3,617	5,080	4,243	5,115	5,626	3,295	1,814
Cereals and bakery products	460	596	472	693	516	730	750	456	238
Cereals and cereal products	143	183	134	221	163	242	221	149	72
Bakery products	317	414	337	472	353	488	529	307	166
Meats, poultry, fish, and eggs	777	986	790	1,113	784	1,122	1,337	793	390
Beef	216	277	214	319	254	325	353	191	104
Pork	150	190	162	208	151	209	249	168	69
Other meats	104	131	101	154	103	153	193	113	54
Poultry	142	182	134	213	138	213	269	146	70
Fish and seafood	122	152	135	159	93	159	207	132	67
Eggs	43	53	44	60	45	63	66	42	24
Dairy products	387	511	424	581	514	605	582	356	201
Fresh milk and cream	154	199	150	239	229	254	216	153	80
Other dairy products	234	312	274	342	285	351	366	203	121
Fruits and vegetables	600	780	676	848	735	856	914	492	322
Fresh fruits	202	265	233	287	264	290	297	148	111
Fresh vegetables	190	253	224	269	222	271	299	131	100
Processed fruits	112	142	118	159	141	157	177	110	62
Processed vegetables	96	120	101	133	107	138	142	104	49
Other food at home	1,241	1,586	1,255	1,845	1,694	1,802	2,043	1,198	662
Sugar and other sweets	124	160	135	181	121	192	201	115	66
Fats and oils	91	120	106	128	92	127	155	82	47
Miscellaneous foods	650	827	618	995	1,069	945	1,041	663	346
Nonalcoholic beverages	333	418	329	480	367	465	595	317	180
Food prepared by consumer unit on trips	43	62	67	61	45	73	51	21	23
Food away from home	2,668	3,440	3,073	3,796	2,894	4,036	3,997	2,319	1,514
ALCOHOLIC BEVERAGES	457	506	559	470	513	405	566	212	428
HOUSING	16,920	20,922	18,420	23,078	24,354	24,032	20,596	14,354	11,269
Shelter	10,023	12,036	10,358	13,458	13,815	14,343	11,696	8,512	7,212
Owned dwellings	6,730	9,350	7,707	10,819	10,757	11,627	9,466	3,931	3,628
Mortgage interest and charges	3,890	5,491	3,757	6,961	7,568	7,621	5,422	2,584	1,818
Property taxes	1,709	2,348	2,273	2,470	2,037	2,619	2,500	902	1,030
Maintenance, repair, insurance, other expenses	1,131	1,511	1,677	1,387	1,152	1,387	1,544	445	780
Rented dwellings	2,602	1,657	1,370	1,774	2,637	1,779	1,195	4,323	3,228
Other lodging	691	1,029	1,280	865	421	937	1,035	258	356

	total consumer units	total married couples	married couples, no children	married couples with children				single parent, at least one child <18	single person
				total	oldest child under 6	oldest child 6 to 17	oldest child 18 or older		
Utilities, fuels, and public services	**$3,477**	**$4,233**	**$3,785**	**$4,518**	**$3,828**	**$4,567**	**$4,891**	**$3,214**	**$2,206**
Natural gas	480	588	537	631	526	632	697	369	325
Electricity	1,303	1,597	1,431	1,688	1,431	1,722	1,800	1,265	804
Fuel oil and other fuels	151	184	190	177	169	188	165	80	107
Telephone services	1,110	1,318	1,126	1,449	1,204	1,442	1,622	1,121	706
Water and other public services	434	546	500	573	497	583	606	380	264
Household services	**984**	**1,351**	**879**	**1,786**	**3,431**	**1,644**	**943**	**1,056**	**486**
Personal services	415	614	89	1,074	2,811	886	249	662	92
Other household services	569	737	790	712	620	758	694	395	394
Housekeeping supplies	**639**	**869**	**963**	**789**	**750**	**767**	**861**	**500**	**316**
Laundry and cleaning supplies	140	177	149	191	154	197	207	174	69
Other household products	347	501	601	418	449	379	472	237	156
Postage and stationery	152	192	213	180	147	191	181	90	91
Household furnishings and equipment	**1,797**	**2,433**	**2,436**	**2,527**	**2,531**	**2,711**	**2,206**	**1,071**	**1,049**
Household textiles	133	178	170	186	238	181	160	77	88
Furniture	446	622	619	657	657	763	477	359	228
Floor coverings	46	65	56	75	87	88	44	26	24
Major appliances	231	319	345	300	296	299	305	153	112
Small appliances, misc. housewares	101	128	127	132	141	121	148	62	72
Miscellaneous household equipment	840	1,121	1,119	1,177	1,112	1,259	1,072	394	525
APPAREL AND RELATED SERVICES	**1,881**	**2,369**	**1,956**	**2,723**	**2,400**	**2,766**	**2,876**	**2,077**	**971**
Men and boys	**435**	**542**	**408**	**644**	**470**	**663**	**743**	**361**	**267**
Men, aged 16 or older	351	424	385	451	348	379	667	149	253
Boys, aged 2 to 15	84	118	23	193	122	284	76	212	14
Women and girls	**749**	**944**	**842**	**1,045**	**696**	**1,169**	**1,062**	**977**	**352**
Women, aged 16 or older	627	776	798	756	531	736	959	679	334
Girls, aged 2 to 15	122	168	44	289	165	433	104	299	18
Children under age 2	**93**	**130**	**54**	**189**	**545**	**121**	**66**	**118**	**20**
Footwear	**327**	**414**	**321**	**494**	**380**	**524**	**519**	**435**	**158**
Other apparel products and services	**276**	**339**	**332**	**350**	**309**	**289**	**485**	**186**	**175**
TRANSPORTATION	**8,758**	**11,600**	**10,347**	**12,609**	**10,876**	**12,688**	**13,651**	**6,359**	**4,539**
Vehicle purchases	**3,244**	**4,435**	**3,828**	**4,919**	**4,529**	**4,912**	**5,190**	**2,139**	**1,478**
Cars and trucks, new	1,572	2,255	2,352	2,185	1,935	2,218	2,293	635	743
Cars and trucks, used	1,567	2,022	1,307	2,575	2,565	2,475	2,753	1,498	683
Gasoline and motor oil	**2,384**	**3,109**	**2,649**	**3,421**	**2,717**	**3,474**	**3,797**	**1,771**	**1,276**
Other vehicle expenses	**2,592**	**3,332**	**2,994**	**3,639**	**3,112**	**3,605**	**4,076**	**2,085**	**1,461**
Vehicle finance charges	305	424	349	476	476	478	472	217	122
Maintenance and repairs	738	939	875	1,010	760	998	1,202	504	471
Vehicle insurance	1,071	1,311	1,214	1,391	1,075	1,393	1,620	1,069	621
Vehicle rentals, leases, licenses, other charges	478	658	556	762	801	736	782	295	247
Public transportation	**538**	**725**	**875**	**630**	**517**	**697**	**588**	**364**	**324**
HEALTH CARE	**2,853**	**3,870**	**4,542**	**3,328**	**2,826**	**3,286**	**3,737**	**1,282**	**1,790**
Health insurance	1,545	2,074	2,459	1,765	1,480	1,742	1,993	640	994
Medical services	709	992	1,065	940	919	957	925	383	403
Drugs	481	639	829	472	340	434	628	202	325
Medical supplies	118	165	189	151	88	153	190	57	69

	total consumer units	total married couples	married couples, no children	married couples with children				single parent, at least one child <18	single person
				total	oldest child under 6	oldest child 6 to 17	oldest child 18 or older		
ENTERTAINMENT	$2,698	$3,578	$3,324	$3,915	$3,102	$4,366	$3,682	$2,062	$1,413
Fees and admissions	658	958	857	1,100	704	1,386	863	468	323
Audio and visual equipment and services	987	1,207	1,072	1,334	1,118	1,398	1,376	831	642
Pets, toys, hobbies, playground equipment	560	731	713	756	703	767	775	487	291
Other entertainment products and services	493	681	683	725	576	816	669	275	157
PERSONAL CARE PRODUCTS AND SERVICES	588	741	716	768	637	758	881	522	364
READING	118	147	166	137	105	143	149	61	97
EDUCATION	945	1,250	860	1,643	431	1,560	2,587	768	621
TOBACCO PRODUCTS AND SMOKING SUPPLIES	323	324	293	316	257	321	346	256	223
MISCELLANEOUS	808	979	1,069	892	749	883	1,011	746	533
CASH CONTRIBUTIONS	1,821	2,466	3,232	1,937	1,407	1,991	2,194	729	1,219
PERSONAL INSURANCE AND PENSIONS	5,336	7,452	6,462	8,408	7,607	8,416	8,923	3,197	2,491
Life and other personal insurance	309	465	441	489	306	504	585	145	146
Pensions and Social Security	5,027	6,988	6,021	7,918	7,301	7,912	8,339	3,052	2,345
PERSONAL TAXES	2,233	3,079	3,629	2,826	2,665	2,730	3,100	445	1,423
Federal income taxes	1,569	2,161	2,656	1,906	1,806	1,812	2,135	143	1,033
State and local income taxes	468	642	676	658	667	654	657	179	269
Other taxes	196	276	297	263	193	264	307	122	121
GIFTS FOR PEOPLE IN OTHER HOUSEHOLDS	1,198	1,587	2,261	1,103	618	1,104	1,426	695	837

Note: Spending by category does not add to total spending because gift spending is also included in the preceding product and service categories and personal taxes are not included in the total. "CU" is short for consumer unit.
Source: Bureau of Labor Statistics, 2007 Consumer Expenditure Survey, Internet site http://www.bls.gov/cex/; calculations by New Strategist

Table 9.12 Indexed Spending by Household Type, 2007

(indexed average annual spending of consumer units by product and service category and type of consumer unit, 2007; index definition: an index of 100 is the average for all consumer units; an index of 125 means that spending by consumer units in that group is 25 percent above the average for all consumer units; an index of 75 indicates spending that is 25 percent below the average for all consumer units)

	total consumer units	total married couples	married couples, no children	married couples with children				single parent,	single person
				total	oldest child under 6	oldest child 6 to 17	oldest child 18 or older	at least one child <18	
Average spending of consumer units	$49,638	$64,104	$58,637	$69,101	$62,403	$70,766	$70,822	$38,239	$29,285
Indexed spending of consumer units	100	129	118	139	126	143	143	77	59
FOOD	100	129	109	145	116	149	157	92	54
Food at home	100	129	104	147	122	148	162	95	52
Cereals and bakery products	100	130	103	151	112	159	163	99	52
Cereals and cereal products	100	128	94	155	114	169	155	104	50
Bakery products	100	131	106	149	111	154	167	97	52
Meats, poultry, fish, and eggs	100	127	102	143	101	144	172	102	50
Beef	100	128	99	148	118	150	163	88	48
Pork	100	127	108	139	101	139	166	112	46
Other meats	100	126	97	148	99	147	186	109	52
Poultry	100	128	94	150	97	150	189	103	49
Fish and seafood	100	125	111	130	76	130	170	108	55
Eggs	100	123	102	140	105	147	153	98	56
Dairy products	100	132	110	150	133	156	150	92	52
Fresh milk and cream	100	129	97	155	149	165	140	99	52
Other dairy products	100	133	117	146	122	150	156	87	52
Fruits and vegetables	100	130	113	141	123	143	152	82	54
Fresh fruits	100	131	115	142	131	144	147	73	55
Fresh vegetables	100	133	118	142	117	143	157	69	53
Processed fruits	100	127	105	142	126	140	158	98	55
Processed vegetables	100	125	105	139	111	144	148	108	51
Other food at home	100	128	101	149	137	145	165	97	53
Sugar and other sweets	100	129	109	146	98	155	162	93	53
Fats and oils	100	132	116	141	101	140	170	90	52
Miscellaneous foods	100	127	95	153	164	145	160	102	53
Nonalcoholic beverages	100	126	99	144	110	140	179	95	54
Food prepared by consumer unit on trips	100	144	156	142	105	170	119	49	53
Food away from home	100	129	115	142	108	151	150	87	57
ALCOHOLIC BEVERAGES	100	111	122	103	112	89	124	46	94
HOUSING	100	124	109	136	144	142	122	85	67
Shelter	100	120	103	134	138	143	117	85	72
Owned dwellings	100	139	115	161	160	173	141	58	54
Mortgage interest and charges	100	141	97	179	195	196	139	66	47
Property taxes	100	137	133	145	119	153	146	53	60
Maintenance, repair, insurance, other expenses	100	134	148	123	102	123	137	39	69
Rented dwellings	100	64	53	68	101	68	46	166	124
Other lodging	100	149	185	125	61	136	150	37	52

	total consumer units	total married couples	married couples, no children	married couples with children				single parent, at least one child <18	single person
				total	oldest child under 6	oldest child 6 to 17	oldest child 18 or older		
Utilities, fuels, and public services	100	122	109	130	110	131	141	92	63
Natural gas	100	123	112	131	110	132	145	77	68
Electricity	100	123	110	130	110	132	138	97	62
Fuel oil and other fuels	100	122	126	117	112	125	109	53	71
Telephone services	100	119	101	131	108	130	146	101	64
Water and other public services	100	126	115	132	115	134	140	88	61
Household services	100	137	89	182	349	167	96	107	49
Personal services	100	148	21	259	677	213	60	160	22
Other household services	100	130	139	125	109	133	122	69	69
Housekeeping supplies	100	136	151	123	117	120	135	78	49
Laundry and cleaning supplies	100	126	106	136	110	141	148	124	49
Other household products	100	144	173	120	129	109	136	68	45
Postage and stationery	100	126	140	118	97	126	119	59	60
Household furnishings and equipment	100	135	136	141	141	151	123	60	58
Household textiles	100	134	128	140	179	136	120	58	66
Furniture	100	139	139	147	147	171	107	80	51
Floor coverings	100	141	122	163	189	191	96	57	52
Major appliances	100	138	149	130	128	129	132	66	48
Small appliances, misc. housewares	100	127	126	131	140	120	147	61	71
Miscellaneous household equipment	100	133	133	140	132	150	128	47	63
APPAREL AND RELATED SERVICES	100	126	104	145	128	147	153	110	52
Men and boys	100	125	94	148	108	152	171	83	61
Men, aged 16 or older	100	121	110	128	99	108	190	42	72
Boys, aged 2 to 15	100	140	27	230	145	338	90	252	17
Women and girls	100	126	112	140	93	156	142	130	47
Women, aged 16 or older	100	124	127	121	85	117	153	108	53
Girls, aged 2 to 15	100	138	36	237	135	355	85	245	15
Children under age 2	100	140	58	203	586	130	71	127	22
Footwear	100	127	98	151	116	160	159	133	48
Other apparel products and services	100	123	120	127	112	105	176	67	63
TRANSPORTATION	100	132	118	144	124	145	156	73	52
Vehicle purchases	100	137	118	152	140	151	160	66	46
Cars and trucks, new	100	143	150	139	123	141	146	40	47
Cars and trucks, used	100	129	83	164	164	158	176	96	44
Gasoline and motor oil	100	130	111	143	114	146	159	74	54
Other vehicle expenses	100	129	116	140	120	139	157	80	56
Vehicle finance charges	100	139	114	156	156	157	155	71	40
Maintenance and repairs	100	127	119	137	103	135	163	68	64
Vehicle insurance	100	122	113	130	100	130	151	100	58
Vehicle rentals, leases, licenses, other charges	100	138	116	159	168	154	164	62	52
Public transportation	100	135	163	117	96	130	109	68	60
HEALTH CARE	100	136	159	117	99	115	131	45	63
Health insurance	100	134	159	114	96	113	129	41	64
Medical services	100	140	150	133	130	135	130	54	57
Drugs	100	133	172	98	71	90	131	42	68
Medical supplies	100	140	160	128	75	130	161	48	58

	total consumer units	total married couples	married couples, no children	married couples with children				single parent, at least one child <18	single person
				total	oldest child under 6	oldest child 6 to 17	oldest child 18 or older		
ENTERTAINMENT	100	133	123	145	115	162	136	76	52
Fees and admissions	100	146	130	167	107	211	131	71	49
Audio and visual equipment and services	100	122	109	135	113	142	139	84	65
Pets, toys, hobbies, playground equipment	100	131	127	135	126	137	138	87	52
Other entertainment products and services	100	138	139	147	117	166	136	56	32
PERSONAL CARE PRODUCTS AND SERVICES	100	126	122	131	108	129	150	89	62
READING	100	125	141	116	89	121	126	52	82
EDUCATION	100	132	91	174	46	165	274	81	66
TOBACCO PRODUCTS AND SMOKING SUPPLIES	100	100	91	98	80	99	107	79	69
MISCELLANEOUS	100	121	132	110	93	109	125	92	66
CASH CONTRIBUTIONS	100	135	177	106	77	109	120	40	67
PERSONAL INSURANCE AND PENSIONS	100	140	121	158	143	158	167	60	47
Life and other personal insurance	100	150	143	158	99	163	189	47	47
Pensions and Social Security	100	139	120	158	145	157	166	61	47
PERSONAL TAXES	100	138	163	127	119	122	139	20	64
Federal income taxes	100	138	169	121	115	115	136	9	66
State and local income taxes	100	137	144	141	143	140	140	38	57
Other taxes	100	141	152	134	98	135	157	62	62
GIFTS FOR PEOPLE IN OTHER HOUSEHOLDS	100	132	189	92	52	92	119	58	70

Source: Calculations by New Strategist based on the Bureau of Labor Statistics 2007 Consumer Expenditure Survey, Internet site http://www.bls.gov/cex/home.htm

Table 9.13 Market Shares by Household Type, 2007

(share of total household spending accounted for by household type, 2007)

	total consumer units	total married couples	married couples, no children	married couples with children				single parent, at least one child <18	single person
				total	oldest child under 6	oldest child 6 to 17	oldest child 18 or older		
Share of total consumer units	100.0%	50.6%	21.6%	25.0%	4.9%	12.7%	7.4%	5.9%	29.7%
Share of total spending	100.0	65.3	25.5	34.7	6.1	18.1	10.5	4.6	17.5
FOOD	100.0	65.1	23.5	36.1	5.7	19.0	11.6	5.4	16.1
Food at home	100.0	65.1	22.5	36.6	6.0	18.8	12.0	5.6	15.6
Cereals and bakery products	100.0	65.5	22.1	37.6	5.5	20.2	12.0	5.9	15.4
Cereals and cereal products	100.0	64.7	20.2	38.6	5.6	21.5	11.4	6.2	15.0
Bakery products	100.0	66.0	22.9	37.2	5.4	19.6	12.3	5.8	15.6
Meats, poultry, fish, and eggs	100.0	64.1	21.9	35.7	4.9	18.3	12.7	6.1	14.9
Beef	100.0	64.8	21.4	36.8	5.7	19.1	12.0	5.3	14.3
Pork	100.0	64.0	23.3	34.6	4.9	17.7	12.2	6.7	13.7
Other meats	100.0	63.7	20.9	36.9	4.8	18.7	13.7	6.5	15.4
Poultry	100.0	64.8	20.4	37.4	4.7	19.1	14.0	6.1	14.7
Fish and seafood	100.0	63.0	23.9	32.5	3.7	16.6	12.5	6.4	16.3
Eggs	100.0	62.3	22.1	34.8	5.1	18.6	11.3	5.8	16.6
Dairy products	100.0	66.7	23.6	37.5	6.5	19.9	11.1	5.5	15.4
Fresh milk and cream	100.0	65.3	21.0	38.7	7.3	21.0	10.3	5.9	15.4
Other dairy products	100.0	67.4	25.3	36.5	5.9	19.1	11.5	5.2	15.4
Fruits and vegetables	100.0	65.7	24.3	35.3	6.0	18.1	11.2	4.9	16.0
Fresh fruits	100.0	66.3	24.9	35.5	6.4	18.2	10.8	4.4	16.3
Fresh vegetables	100.0	67.3	25.4	35.3	5.7	18.1	11.6	4.1	15.7
Processed fruits	100.0	64.1	22.7	35.4	6.1	17.8	11.6	5.8	16.5
Processed vegetables	100.0	63.2	22.7	34.6	5.4	18.3	10.9	6.4	15.2
Other food at home	100.0	64.6	21.8	37.1	6.7	18.4	12.1	5.7	15.9
Sugar and other sweets	100.0	65.2	23.5	36.4	4.8	19.7	11.9	5.5	15.8
Fats and oils	100.0	66.7	25.1	35.1	4.9	17.7	12.5	5.4	15.4
Miscellaneous foods	100.0	64.3	20.5	38.2	8.0	18.5	11.8	6.1	15.8
Nonalcoholic beverages	100.0	63.5	21.3	36.0	5.4	17.7	13.2	5.7	16.1
Food prepared by CU on trips	100.0	72.9	33.6	35.4	5.1	21.6	8.7	2.9	15.9
Food away from home	100.0	65.2	24.8	35.5	5.3	19.2	11.0	5.2	16.9
ALCOHOLIC BEVERAGES	100.0	56.0	26.4	25.7	5.5	11.3	9.1	2.8	27.9
HOUSING	100.0	62.5	23.5	34.0	7.0	18.0	9.0	5.0	19.8
Shelter	100.0	60.7	22.3	33.5	6.7	18.2	8.6	5.0	21.4
Owned dwellings	100.0	70.2	24.7	40.1	7.8	21.9	10.4	3.5	16.0
Mortgage interest and charges	100.0	71.4	20.8	44.6	9.5	24.9	10.3	3.9	13.9
Property taxes	100.0	69.5	28.7	36.1	5.8	19.5	10.8	3.1	17.9
Maintenance, repair, insurance, other expenses	100.0	67.5	32.0	30.6	5.0	15.6	10.1	2.3	20.5
Rented dwellings	100.0	32.2	11.4	17.0	4.9	8.7	3.4	9.9	36.9
Other lodging	100.0	75.3	40.0	31.2	3.0	17.2	11.0	2.2	15.3

	total consumer units	total married couples	married couples, no children	married couples with children				single parent, at least one child <18	single person
				total	oldest child under 6	oldest child 6 to 17	oldest child 18 or older		
Utilities, fuels, and public services	**100.0%**	**61.5%**	**23.5%**	**32.4%**	**5.4%**	**16.7%**	**10.4%**	**5.5%**	**18.9%**
Natural gas	100.0	61.9	24.1	32.8	5.3	16.7	10.7	4.6	20.1
Electricity	100.0	62.0	23.7	32.3	5.4	16.8	10.2	5.8	18.4
Fuel oil and other fuels	100.0	61.6	27.1	29.2	5.5	15.8	8.1	3.1	21.1
Telephone services	100.0	60.0	21.9	32.6	5.3	16.5	10.8	6.0	18.9
Water and other public services	100.0	63.6	24.9	32.9	5.6	17.1	10.3	5.2	18.1
Household services	**100.0**	**69.4**	**19.3**	**45.3**	**17.0**	**21.2**	**7.1**	**6.4**	**14.7**
Personal services	100.0	74.8	4.6	64.6	33.1	27.1	4.4	9.5	6.6
Other household services	100.0	65.5	30.0	31.2	5.3	16.9	9.0	4.1	20.6
Housekeeping supplies	**100.0**	**68.7**	**32.5**	**30.8**	**5.7**	**15.2**	**9.9**	**4.6**	**14.7**
Laundry and cleaning supplies	100.0	63.9	23.0	34.0	5.4	17.9	10.9	7.4	14.7
Other household products	100.0	73.0	37.4	30.1	6.3	13.9	10.0	4.1	13.4
Postage and stationery	100.0	63.9	30.2	29.5	4.7	16.0	8.8	3.5	17.8
Household furnishings and equipment	**100.0**	**68.4**	**29.2**	**35.1**	**6.9**	**19.2**	**9.0**	**3.5**	**17.4**
Household textiles	100.0	67.7	27.6	34.9	8.7	17.3	8.9	3.4	19.7
Furniture	100.0	70.5	29.9	36.8	7.2	21.7	7.9	4.8	15.2
Floor coverings	100.0	71.4	26.3	40.7	9.2	24.3	7.0	3.4	15.5
Major appliances	100.0	69.8	32.2	32.4	6.3	16.4	9.7	3.9	14.4
Small appliances, misc. housewares	100.0	64.1	27.1	32.6	6.8	15.2	10.8	3.6	21.2
Miscellaneous household equipment	100.0	67.5	28.7	35.0	6.5	19.0	9.4	2.8	18.6
APPAREL, RELATED SERVICES	**100.0**	**63.7**	**22.4**	**36.1**	**6.2**	**18.7**	**11.3**	**6.6**	**15.4**
Men and boys	**100.0**	**63.0**	**20.2**	**36.9**	**5.3**	**19.4**	**12.6**	**4.9**	**18.3**
Men, aged 16 or older	100.0	61.1	23.7	32.1	4.8	13.7	14.0	2.5	21.4
Boys, aged 2 to 15	100.0	71.0	5.9	57.3	7.1	42.9	6.7	15.0	5.0
Women and girls	**100.0**	**63.7**	**24.3**	**34.8**	**4.5**	**19.8**	**10.4**	**7.7**	**14.0**
Women, aged 16 or older	100.0	62.6	27.5	30.1	4.1	14.9	11.3	6.4	15.8
Girls, aged 2 to 15	100.0	69.6	7.8	59.1	6.6	45.1	6.3	14.6	4.4
Children under age 2	**100.0**	**70.7**	**12.5**	**50.7**	**28.6**	**16.5**	**5.2**	**7.5**	**6.4**
Footwear	**100.0**	**64.0**	**21.2**	**37.7**	**5.7**	**20.4**	**11.7**	**7.9**	**14.4**
Other apparel products and services	**100.0**	**62.1**	**25.9**	**31.6**	**5.5**	**13.3**	**12.9**	**4.0**	**18.9**
TRANSPORTATION	**100.0**	**67.0**	**25.5**	**35.9**	**6.1**	**18.4**	**11.5**	**4.3**	**15.4**
Vehicle purchases	**100.0**	**69.1**	**25.5**	**37.8**	**6.8**	**19.2**	**11.8**	**3.9**	**13.6**
Cars and trucks, new	100.0	72.5	32.3	34.7	6.0	17.9	10.7	2.4	14.1
Cars and trucks, used	100.0	65.2	18.0	41.0	8.0	20.1	12.9	5.7	13.0
Gasoline and motor oil	**100.0**	**65.9**	**24.0**	**35.8**	**5.6**	**18.5**	**11.7**	**4.4**	**15.9**
Other vehicle expenses	**100.0**	**65.0**	**24.9**	**35.0**	**5.9**	**17.7**	**11.6**	**4.8**	**16.8**
Vehicle finance charges	100.0	70.3	24.7	38.9	7.6	19.9	11.4	4.2	11.9
Maintenance and repairs	100.0	64.3	25.6	34.1	5.0	17.2	12.0	4.1	19.0
Vehicle insurance	100.0	61.9	24.5	32.4	4.9	16.5	11.1	5.9	17.2
Vehicle rentals, leases, licenses, other charges	100.0	69.6	25.1	39.8	8.2	19.6	12.1	3.7	15.4
Public transportation	**100.0**	**68.1**	**35.1**	**29.2**	**4.7**	**16.5**	**8.1**	**4.0**	**17.9**
HEALTH CARE	**100.0**	**68.6**	**34.3**	**29.1**	**4.8**	**14.6**	**9.7**	**2.7**	**18.7**
Health insurance	100.0	67.9	34.3	28.5	4.7	14.3	9.5	2.5	19.1
Medical services	100.0	70.7	32.4	33.1	6.3	17.1	9.6	3.2	16.9
Drugs	100.0	67.2	37.2	24.5	3.4	11.5	9.6	2.5	20.1
Medical supplies	100.0	70.7	34.6	31.9	3.6	16.5	11.9	2.9	17.4

	total consumer units	total married couples	married couples, no children	married couples with children				single parent, at least one child <18	single person
				total	oldest child under 6	oldest child 6 to 17	oldest child 18 or older		
ENTERTAINMENT	**100.0%**	**67.0%**	**26.6%**	**36.2%**	**5.6%**	**20.6%**	**10.1%**	**4.5%**	**15.6%**
Fees and admissions	100.0	73.6	28.1	41.7	5.2	26.8	9.7	4.2	14.6
Audio and visual equipment and services	100.0	61.8	23.4	33.7	5.5	18.0	10.3	5.0	19.3
Pets, toys, hobbies, playground equipment	100.0	66.0	27.5	33.7	6.1	17.4	10.2	5.2	15.5
Other entertainment products and services	100.0	69.8	29.9	36.7	5.7	21.0	10.0	3.3	9.5
PERSONAL CARE PRODUCTS AND SERVICES	**100.0**	**63.7**	**26.3**	**32.6**	**5.3**	**16.4**	**11.0**	**5.3**	**18.4**
READING	**100.0**	**63.0**	**30.3**	**29.0**	**4.3**	**15.4**	**9.3**	**3.1**	**24.4**
EDUCATION	**100.0**	**66.9**	**19.6**	**43.4**	**2.2**	**21.0**	**20.2**	**4.8**	**19.5**
TOBACCO PRODUCTS AND SMOKING SUPPLIES	**100.0**	**50.7**	**19.6**	**24.4**	**3.9**	**12.6**	**7.9**	**4.7**	**20.5**
MISCELLANEOUS	**100.0**	**61.2**	**28.5**	**27.5**	**4.5**	**13.9**	**9.2**	**5.5**	**19.6**
CASH CONTRIBUTIONS	**100.0**	**68.5**	**38.3**	**26.5**	**3.8**	**13.9**	**8.9**	**2.4**	**19.9**
PERSONAL INSURANCE AND PENSIONS	**100.0**	**70.6**	**26.1**	**39.3**	**7.0**	**20.0**	**12.3**	**3.6**	**13.9**
Life and other personal insurance	100.0	76.1	30.8	39.5	4.8	20.7	13.9	2.8	14.1
Pensions and Social Security	100.0	70.3	25.8	39.3	7.1	20.0	12.2	3.6	13.9
PERSONAL TAXES	**100.0**	**69.7**	**35.1**	**31.6**	**5.8**	**15.5**	**10.2**	**1.2**	**19.0**
Federal income taxes	100.0	69.6	36.5	30.3	5.6	14.7	10.0	0.5	19.6
State and local income taxes	100.0	69.3	31.2	35.1	7.0	17.8	10.3	2.3	17.1
Other taxes	100.0	71.2	32.7	33.5	4.8	17.1	11.5	3.7	18.4
GIFTS FOR PEOPLE IN OTHER HOUSEHOLDS	**100.0**	**67.0**	**40.7**	**23.0**	**2.5**	**11.7**	**8.8**	**3.4**	**20.8**

Note: "CU" is short for consumer unit.
Source: Calculations by New Strategist based on the Bureau of Labor Statistics 2007 Consumer Expenditure Survey, Internet site http://www.bls.gov/cex/home.htm

Asians Spend the Most

Blacks and Hispanics spend far less than the average household.

Asian households have the highest incomes and they spend the most—an average of $60,402 in 2007, or 22 percent more than the average household. Non-Hispanic whites and others (a category that also includes Asians and American Indians) spent 7 percent more than average. Hispanic households spent 16 percent less than average, and black households spent 27 percent less. There is great variation in spending by category, however.

The Indexed Spending table shows household spending for each racial and Hispanic origin group relative to average household spending. An index of 100 means households in the racial/Hispanic origin group spend an average amount on the item. An index above 100 indicates that households in the racial/Hispanic origin group spend more than average on the item, while an index below 100 reveals below-average spending.

A look at Table 9.15 shows below-average spending on most items by black and Hispanic households, close-to-average spending by non-Hispanic white households, and above-average spending by Asian households. There are some important exceptions, however. Black households spend more than average on pork, poultry, and fish. They spend 29 percent more on boys' clothes and 18 percent more more on shoes.

Spending of Asians and non-Hispanic whites is above average

(average annual spending of consumer units by race and Hispanic origin of householder, 2007)

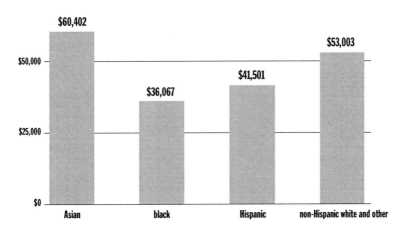

Hispanic households spend more than the average household on many foods, probably because their households are above average in size—3.2 people compared with 2.5 in the average household. Hispanic households also spend 21 percent more than average on laundry and cleaning products, 51 percent more on infants' clothes, and 25 percent more on shoes.

Asian households spend 22 percent more than the average household on food away from home. They spend almost three times the average amount on public transportation—a category that includes airfares. They spend nearly twice the average on education.

Because Asian, black, and Hispanic households account for a small share of total households, they account for a small share of overall spending on most products and services. Blacks and Hispanics together, however, account for 29 percent of the footwear market. Asians account for a single-digit share of the market in every product and service category except public transportation.

■ The spending of black households is likely to remain below average because few are headed by married couples—the most affluent household type. The spending of Hispanics will remain below average because many are recent immigrants with low incomes.

Table 9.14 Average Spending by Race and Hispanic Origin of Householder, 2007

(average annual spending of consumer units by product and service category and by race and Hispanic origin of consumer unit reference person, 2007)

	total consumer units	Asian	black	Hispanic	non-Hispanic white and other
Number of consumer units (in 000s)	120,171	4,240	14,422	14,185	91,734
Average number of persons per consumer unit	2.5	2.8	2.6	3.2	2.3
Average income before taxes	$63,091	$80,487	$44,381	$48,330	$68,285
Average annual spending	49,638	60,402	36,067	41,501	53,003
FOOD	**6,133**	**7,139**	**4,601**	**5,933**	**6,399**
Food at home	**3,465**	**3,890**	**2,831**	**3,424**	**3,568**
Cereals and bakery products	460	469	365	410	481
Cereals and cereal products	143	195	127	154	143
Bakery products	317	275	237	255	338
Meats, poultry, fish, and eggs	777	1,026	834	890	752
Beef	216	221	185	255	215
Pork	150	160	185	162	142
Other meats	104	106	95	101	107
Poultry	142	158	189	193	127
Fish and seafood	122	321	138	119	120
Eggs	43	60	41	60	40
Dairy products	387	349	259	368	410
Fresh milk and cream	154	154	111	168	158
Other dairy products	234	196	147	200	252
Fruits and vegetables	600	887	455	652	615
Fresh fruits	202	309	131	227	209
Fresh vegetables	190	369	133	229	194
Processed fruits	112	116	107	106	114
Processed vegetables	96	93	83	91	98
Other food at home	1,241	1,159	919	1,104	1,310
Sugar and other sweets	124	133	88	97	134
Fats and oils	91	93	81	90	93
Miscellaneous foods	650	549	456	546	694
Nonalcoholic beverages	333	343	279	345	340
Food prepared by consumer unit on trips	43	40	15	27	50
Food away from home	**2,668**	**3,249**	**1,771**	**2,508**	**2,831**
ALCOHOLIC BEVERAGES	**457**	**290**	**198**	**262**	**525**
HOUSING	**16,920**	**22,554**	**13,494**	**15,573**	**17,662**
Shelter	**10,023**	**15,383**	**8,084**	**9,794**	**10,367**
Owned dwellings	6,730	10,387	4,110	5,419	7,346
Mortgage interest and charges	3,890	6,383	2,723	3,609	4,118
Property taxes	1,709	2,754	893	1,218	1,912
Maintenance, repair, insurance, other expenses	1,131	1,249	494	592	1,317
Rented dwellings	2,602	4,073	3,669	4,135	2,200
Other lodging	691	923	305	239	820

	total consumer units	Asian	black	Hispanic	non-Hispanic white and other
Utilities, fuels, and public services	**$3,477**	**$3,436**	**$3,500**	**$3,274**	**$3,505**
Natural gas	480	577	475	378	497
Electricity	1,303	1,169	1,355	1,258	1,301
Fuel oil and other fuels	151	44	56	62	179
Telephone services	1,110	1,172	1,196	1,167	1,088
Water and other public services	434	475	418	409	440
Household services	**984**	**1,157**	**616**	**681**	**1,088**
Personal services	415	529	297	348	444
Other household services	569	627	319	333	644
Housekeeping supplies	**639**	**496**	**383**	**571**	**688**
Laundry and cleaning supplies	140	103	142	170	136
Other household products	347	238	184	245	386
Postage and stationery	152	155	58	157	166
Household furnishings and equipment	**1,797**	**2,081**	**910**	**1,253**	**2,014**
Household textiles	133	125	51	112	149
Furniture	446	858	313	364	478
Floor coverings	46	35	32	15	54
Major appliances	231	196	119	136	263
Small appliances, miscellaneous housewares	101	103	58	98	108
Miscellaneous household equipment	840	765	336	528	962
APPAREL AND RELATED SERVICES	**1,881**	**2,709**	**1,743**	**1,994**	**1,886**
Men and boys	**435**	**602**	**344**	**539**	**435**
Men, aged 16 or older	351	512	236	425	358
Boys, aged 2 to 15	84	91	108	113	77
Women and girls	**749**	**1,234**	**671**	**636**	**777**
Women, aged 16 or older	627	1,080	513	505	663
Girls, aged 2 to 15	122	155	158	131	115
Children under age 2	**93**	**107**	**103**	**140**	**85**
Footwear	**327**	**514**	**387**	**408**	**306**
Other apparel products and services	**276**	**252**	**238**	**272**	**283**
TRANSPORTATION	**8,758**	**10,921**	**6,458**	**8,035**	**9,234**
Vehicle purchases	**3,244**	**4,007**	**2,223**	**2,876**	**3,463**
Cars and trucks, new	1,572	2,797	729	1,271	1,752
Cars and trucks, used	1,567	1,210	1,460	1,541	1,588
Gasoline and motor oil	**2,384**	**2,391**	**1,935**	**2,304**	**2,466**
Other vehicle expenses	**2,592**	**2,978**	**2,001**	**2,525**	**2,697**
Vehicle finance charges	305	236	252	314	312
Maintenance and repairs	738	729	505	557	802
Vehicle insurance	1,071	1,550	872	1,280	1,073
Vehicle rentals, leases, licenses, other charges	478	463	371	375	510
Public transportation	**538**	**1,545**	**299**	**330**	**608**
HEALTH CARE	**2,853**	**2,170**	**1,689**	**1,486**	**3,244**
Health insurance	1,545	1,378	1,001	744	1,752
Medical services	709	487	370	468	799
Drugs	481	220	262	213	556
Medical supplies	118	86	57	62	136

	total consumer units	Asian	black	Hispanic	non-Hispanic white and other
ENTERTAINMENT	**$2,698**	**$2,454**	**$1,288**	**$1,674**	**$3,072**
Fees and admissions	658	895	212	316	779
Audio and visual equipment and services	987	973	753	815	1,050
Pets, toys, hobbies, and playground equipment	560	316	173	315	657
Other entertainment products and services	493	270	149	229	586
PERSONAL CARE PRODUCTS AND SERVICES	**588**	**564**	**485**	**526**	**614**
READING	**118**	**98**	**46**	**38**	**141**
EDUCATION	**945**	**1,627**	**700**	**415**	**1,065**
TOBACCO PRODUCTS AND SMOKING SUPPLIES	**323**	**135**	**219**	**165**	**363**
MISCELLANEOUS	**808**	**719**	**453**	**478**	**913**
CASH CONTRIBUTIONS	**1,821**	**2,153**	**1,178**	**1,083**	**2,035**
PERSONAL INSURANCE AND PENSIONS	**5,336**	**6,868**	**3,515**	**3,837**	**5,851**
Life and other personal insurance	309	353	245	109	350
Pensions and Social Security	5,027	6,515	3,271	3,729	5,501
PERSONAL TAXES	**2,233**	**2,295**	**771**	**703**	**2,697**
Federal income taxes	1,569	1,489	511	463	1,905
State and local income taxes	468	628	175	172	559
Other taxes	196	179	85	68	233
GIFTS FOR PEOPLE IN OTHER HOUSEHOLDS	**1,198**	**1,455**	**698**	**679**	**1,355**

Note: "Asian" and "black" include Hispanics and non-Hispanics who identify themselves as being of the respective race alone. "Hispanic" includes people of any race who identify themselves as being Hispanic. "Other" includes people who identify themselves as being non-Hispanic and as Alaska Native, American Indian, Asian (who are also included in the Asian column), Native Hawaiian or other Pacific Islander, as well as non-Hispanics reporting more than one race. Spending by category does not add to total spending because gift spending is also included in the preceding product and service categories and personal taxes are not included in the total.
Source: Bureau of Labor Statistics, 2007 Consumer Expenditure Survey, Internet site http://www.bls.gov/cex/

Table 9.15 Indexed Spending by Race and Hispanic Origin of Householder, 2007

(indexed average annual spending of consumer units by product and service category and by race and Hispanic origin of consumer unit reference person, 2007; index definition: an index of 100 is the average for all consumer units; an index of 125 means that spending by consumer units in that group is 25 percent above the average for all consumer units; an index of 75 indicates spending that is 25 percent below the average for all consumer units)

	total consumer units	Asian	black	Hispanic	non-Hispanic white and other
Average spending of consumer units	$49,638	$60,402	$36,067	$41,501	$53,003
Indexed spending of consumer units	100	122	73	84	107
FOOD	100	116	75	97	104
Food at home	100	112	82	99	103
Cereals and bakery products	100	102	79	89	105
Cereals and cereal products	100	136	89	108	100
Bakery products	100	87	75	80	107
Meats, poultry, fish, and eggs	100	132	107	115	97
Beef	100	102	86	118	100
Pork	100	107	123	108	95
Other meats	100	102	91	97	103
Poultry	100	111	133	136	89
Fish and seafood	100	263	113	98	98
Eggs	100	140	95	140	93
Dairy products	100	90	67	95	106
Fresh milk and cream	100	100	72	109	103
Other dairy products	100	84	63	85	108
Fruits and vegetables	100	148	76	109	103
Fresh fruits	100	153	65	112	103
Fresh vegetables	100	194	70	121	102
Processed fruits	100	104	96	95	102
Processed vegetables	100	97	86	95	102
Other food at home	100	93	74	89	106
Sugar and other sweets	100	107	71	78	108
Fats and oils	100	102	89	99	102
Miscellaneous foods	100	84	70	84	107
Nonalcoholic beverages	100	103	84	104	102
Food prepared by consumer unit on trips	100	93	35	63	116
Food away from home	100	122	66	94	106
ALCOHOLIC BEVERAGES	100	63	43	57	115
HOUSING	100	133	80	92	104
Shelter	100	153	81	98	103
Owned dwellings	100	154	61	81	109
Mortgage interest and charges	100	164	70	93	106
Property taxes	100	161	52	71	112
Maintenance, repair, insurance, other expenses	100	110	44	52	116
Rented dwellings	100	157	141	159	85
Other lodging	100	134	44	35	119

	total consumer units	Asian	black	Hispanic	non-Hispanic white and other
Utilities, fuels, and public services	**100**	**99**	**101**	**94**	**101**
Natural gas	100	120	99	79	104
Electricity	100	90	104	97	100
Fuel oil and other fuels	100	29	37	41	119
Telephone services	100	106	108	105	98
Water and other public services	100	109	96	94	101
Household services	**100**	**118**	**63**	**69**	**111**
Personal services	100	127	72	84	107
Other household services	100	110	56	59	113
Housekeeping supplies	**100**	**78**	**60**	**89**	**108**
Laundry and cleaning supplies	100	74	101	121	97
Other household products	100	69	53	71	111
Postage and stationery	100	102	38	103	109
Household furnishings and equipment	**100**	**116**	**51**	**70**	**112**
Household textiles	100	94	38	84	112
Furniture	100	192	70	82	107
Floor coverings	100	76	70	33	117
Major appliances	100	85	52	59	114
Small appliances, miscellaneous housewares	100	102	57	97	107
Miscellaneous household equipment	100	91	40	63	115
APPAREL AND RELATED SERVICES	**100**	**144**	**93**	**106**	**100**
Men and boys	**100**	**138**	**79**	**124**	**100**
Men, aged 16 or older	100	146	67	121	102
Boys, aged 2 to 15	100	108	129	135	92
Women and girls	**100**	**165**	**90**	**85**	**104**
Women, aged 16 or older	100	172	82	81	106
Girls, aged 2 to 15	100	127	130	107	94
Children under age 2	**100**	**115**	**111**	**151**	**91**
Footwear	**100**	**157**	**118**	**125**	**94**
Other apparel products and services	**100**	**91**	**86**	**99**	**103**
TRANSPORTATION	**100**	**125**	**74**	**92**	**105**
Vehicle purchases	**100**	**124**	**69**	**89**	**107**
Cars and trucks, new	100	178	46	81	111
Cars and trucks, used	100	77	93	98	101
Gasoline and motor oil	**100**	**100**	**81**	**97**	**103**
Other vehicle expenses	**100**	**115**	**77**	**97**	**104**
Vehicle finance charges	100	77	83	103	102
Maintenance and repairs	100	99	68	75	109
Vehicle insurance	100	145	81	120	100
Vehicle rentals, leases, licenses, other charges	100	97	78	78	107
Public transportation	**100**	**287**	**56**	**61**	**113**
HEALTH CARE	**100**	**76**	**59**	**52**	**114**
Health insurance	100	89	65	48	113
Medical services	100	69	52	66	113
Drugs	100	46	54	44	116
Medical supplies	100	73	48	53	115

	total consumer units	Asian	black	Hispanic	non-Hispanic white and other
ENTERTAINMENT	100	91	48	62	114
Fees and admissions	100	136	32	48	118
Audio and visual equipment and services	100	99	76	83	106
Pets, toys, hobbies, and playground equipment	100	56	31	56	117
Other entertainment products and services	100	55	30	46	119
PERSONAL CARE PRODUCTS AND SERVICES	100	96	82	89	104
READING	100	83	39	32	119
EDUCATION	100	172	74	44	113
TOBACCO PRODUCTS AND SMOKING SUPPLIES	100	42	68	51	112
MISCELLANEOUS	100	89	56	59	113
CASH CONTRIBUTIONS	100	118	65	59	112
PERSONAL INSURANCE AND PENSIONS	100	129	66	72	110
Life and other personal insurance	100	114	79	35	113
Pensions and Social Security	100	130	65	74	109
PERSONAL TAXES	100	103	35	31	121
Federal income taxes	100	95	33	30	121
State and local income taxes	100	134	37	37	119
Other taxes	100	91	43	35	119
GIFTS FOR PEOPLE IN OTHER HOUSEHOLDS	100	121	58	57	113

Note: "Asian" and "black" include Hispanics and non-Hispanics who identify themselves as being of the respective race alone. "Hispanic" includes people of any race who identify themselves as being Hispanic. "Other" includes people who identify themselves as being non-Hispanic and as Alaska Native, American Indian, Asian (who are also included in the Asian column), Native Hawaiian or other Pacific Islander, as well as non-Hispanics reporting more than one race. Spending by category does not add to total spending because gift spending is also included in the preceding product and service categories and personal taxes are not included in the total.

Source: Bureau of Labor Statistics, 2007 Consumer Expenditure Survey, Internet site http://www.bls.gov/cex/

Table 9.16 Market Shares by Race and Hispanic Origin of Householder, 2007

(share of total household spending accounted for by race and Hispanic origin group, 2007)

	total consumer units	Asian	black	Hispanic	non-Hispanic white and other
Share of total consumer units	100.0%	3.5%	12.0%	11.8%	76.3%
Share of total spending	100.0	4.3	8.7	9.9	81.5
FOOD	100.0	4.1	9.0	11.4	79.6
Food at home	100.0	4.0	9.8	11.7	78.6
Cereals and bakery products	100.0	3.6	9.5	10.5	79.8
Cereals and cereal products	100.0	4.8	10.7	12.7	76.3
Bakery products	100.0	3.1	9.0	9.5	81.4
Meats, poultry, fish, and eggs	100.0	4.7	12.9	13.5	73.9
Beef	100.0	3.6	10.3	13.9	76.0
Pork	100.0	3.8	14.8	12.7	72.3
Other meats	100.0	3.6	11.0	11.5	78.5
Poultry	100.0	3.9	16.0	16.0	68.3
Fish and seafood	100.0	9.3	13.6	11.5	75.1
Eggs	100.0	4.9	11.4	16.5	71.0
Dairy products	100.0	3.2	8.0	11.2	80.9
Fresh milk and cream	100.0	3.5	8.7	12.9	78.3
Other dairy products	100.0	3.0	7.5	10.1	82.2
Fruits and vegetables	100.0	5.2	9.1	12.8	78.2
Fresh fruits	100.0	5.4	7.8	13.3	79.0
Fresh vegetables	100.0	6.9	8.4	14.2	77.9
Processed fruits	100.0	3.7	11.5	11.2	77.7
Processed vegetables	100.0	3.4	10.4	11.2	77.9
Other food at home	100.0	3.3	8.9	10.5	80.6
Sugar and other sweets	100.0	3.8	8.5	9.2	82.5
Fats and oils	100.0	3.6	10.7	11.7	78.0
Miscellaneous foods	100.0	3.0	8.4	9.9	81.5
Nonalcoholic beverages	100.0	3.6	10.1	12.2	77.9
Food prepared by consumer unit on trips	100.0	3.3	4.2	7.4	88.8
Food away from home	100.0	4.3	8.0	11.1	81.0
ALCOHOLIC BEVERAGES	100.0	2.2	5.2	6.8	87.7
HOUSING	100.0	4.7	9.6	10.9	79.7
Shelter	100.0	5.4	9.7	11.5	79.0
Owned dwellings	100.0	5.4	7.3	9.5	83.3
Mortgage interest and charges	100.0	5.8	8.4	11.0	80.8
Property taxes	100.0	5.7	6.3	8.4	85.4
Maintenance, repair, insurance, other expenses	100.0	3.9	5.2	6.2	88.9
Rented dwellings	100.0	5.5	16.9	18.8	64.5
Other lodging	100.0	4.7	5.3	4.1	90.6

	total consumer units	Asian	black	Hispanic	non-Hispanic white and other
Utilities, fuels, and public services	**100.0%**	**3.5%**	**12.1%**	**11.1%**	**77.0%**
Natural gas	100.0	4.2	11.9	9.3	79.0
Electricity	100.0	3.2	12.5	11.4	76.2
Fuel oil and other fuels	100.0	1.0	4.5	4.8	90.5
Telephone services	100.0	3.7	12.9	12.4	74.8
Water and other public services	100.0	3.9	11.6	11.1	77.4
Household services	**100.0**	**4.1**	**7.5**	**8.2**	**84.4**
Personal services	100.0	4.5	8.6	9.9	81.7
Other household services	100.0	3.9	6.7	6.9	86.4
Housekeeping supplies	**100.0**	**2.7**	**7.2**	**10.5**	**82.2**
Laundry and cleaning supplies	100.0	2.6	12.2	14.3	74.2
Other household products	100.0	2.4	6.4	8.3	84.9
Postage and stationery	100.0	3.6	4.6	12.2	83.4
Household furnishings and equipment	**100.0**	**4.1**	**6.1**	**8.2**	**85.6**
Household textiles	100.0	3.3	4.6	9.9	85.5
Furniture	100.0	6.8	8.4	9.6	81.8
Floor coverings	100.0	2.7	8.3	3.8	89.6
Major appliances	100.0	3.0	6.2	6.9	86.9
Small appliances, miscellaneous housewares	100.0	3.6	6.9	11.5	81.6
Miscellaneous household equipment	100.0	3.2	4.8	7.4	87.4
APPAREL AND RELATED SERVICES	**100.0**	**5.1**	**11.1**	**12.5**	**76.5**
Men and boys	**100.0**	**4.9**	**9.5**	**14.6**	**76.3**
Men, aged 16 or older	100.0	5.1	8.1	14.3	77.9
Boys, aged 2 to 15	100.0	3.8	15.4	15.9	70.0
Women and girls	**100.0**	**5.8**	**10.8**	**10.0**	**79.2**
Women, aged 16 or older	100.0	6.1	9.8	9.5	80.7
Girls, aged 2 to 15	100.0	4.5	15.5	12.7	72.0
Children under age 2	**100.0**	**4.1**	**13.3**	**17.8**	**69.8**
Footwear	**100.0**	**5.5**	**14.2**	**14.7**	**71.4**
Other apparel products and services	**100.0**	**3.2**	**10.3**	**11.6**	**78.3**
TRANSPORTATION	**100.0**	**4.4**	**8.8**	**10.8**	**80.5**
Vehicle purchases	**100.0**	**4.4**	**8.2**	**10.5**	**81.5**
Cars and trucks, new	100.0	6.3	5.6	9.5	85.1
Cars and trucks, used	100.0	2.7	11.2	11.6	77.4
Gasoline and motor oil	**100.0**	**3.5**	**9.7**	**11.4**	**79.0**
Other vehicle expenses	**100.0**	**4.1**	**9.3**	**11.5**	**79.4**
Vehicle finance charges	100.0	2.7	9.9	12.2	78.1
Maintenance and repairs	100.0	3.5	8.2	8.9	83.0
Vehicle insurance	100.0	5.1	9.8	14.1	76.5
Vehicle rentals, leases, licenses, other charges	100.0	3.4	9.3	9.3	81.4
Public transportation	**100.0**	**10.1**	**6.7**	**7.2**	**86.3**
HEALTH CARE	**100.0**	**2.7**	**7.1**	**6.1**	**86.8**
Health insurance	100.0	3.1	7.8	5.7	86.6
Medical services	100.0	2.4	6.3	7.8	86.0
Drugs	100.0	1.6	6.5	5.2	88.2
Medical supplies	100.0	2.6	5.8	6.2	88.0

	total consumer units	Asian	black	Hispanic	non-Hispanic white and other
ENTERTAINMENT	**100.0%**	**3.2%**	**5.7%**	**7.3%**	**86.9%**
Fees and admissions	100.0	4.8	3.9	5.7	90.4
Audio and visual equipment and services	100.0	3.5	9.2	9.7	81.2
Pets, toys, hobbies, and playground equipment	100.0	2.0	3.7	6.6	89.6
Other entertainment products and services	100.0	1.9	3.6	5.5	90.7
PERSONAL CARE PRODUCTS AND SERVICES	**100.0**	**3.4**	**9.9**	**10.6**	**79.7**
READING	**100.0**	**2.9**	**4.7**	**3.8**	**91.2**
EDUCATION	**100.0**	**6.1**	**8.9**	**5.2**	**86.0**
TOBACCO PRODUCTS AND SMOKING SUPPLIES	**100.0**	**1.5**	**8.1**	**6.0**	**85.8**
MISCELLANEOUS	**100.0**	**3.1**	**6.7**	**7.0**	**86.3**
CASH CONTRIBUTIONS	**100.0**	**4.2**	**7.8**	**7.0**	**85.3**
PERSONAL INSURANCE AND PENSIONS	**100.0**	**4.5**	**7.9**	**8.5**	**83.7**
Life and other personal insurance	100.0	4.0	9.5	4.2	86.5
Pensions and Social Security	100.0	4.6	7.8	8.8	83.5
PERSONAL TAXES	**100.0**	**3.6**	**4.1**	**3.7**	**92.2**
Federal income taxes	100.0	3.3	3.9	3.5	92.7
State and local income taxes	100.0	4.7	4.5	4.3	91.2
Other taxes	100.0	3.2	5.2	4.1	90.7
GIFTS FOR PEOPLE IN OTHER HOUSEHOLDS	**100.0**	**4.3**	**7.0**	**6.7**	**86.3**

Note: "Asian" and "black" include Hispanics and non-Hispanics who identify themselves as being of the respective race alone. "Hispanic" includes people of any race who identify themselves as being Hispanic. "Other" includes people who identify themselves as being non-Hispanic and as Alaska Native, American Indian, Asian (who are also included in the Asian column), Native Hawaiian or other Pacific Islander, as well as non-Hispanics reporting more than one race. Spending by category does not add to total spending because gift spending is also included in the preceding product and service categories and personal taxes are not included in the total.
Source: Bureau of Labor Statistics, 2007 Consumer Expenditure Survey, Internet site http://www.bls.gov/cex/

Spending Is Highest in the West

Households in the South spend the least.

The average household in the West spent $56,291 in 2007, or 13 percent more than the average household. Households in the Northeast spent only 4 percent more than average—or $51,624 in 2007. In the Midwest, households spent slightly less than the all-household average of $49,638. In the South, the average household spent 8 percent less than average. By product and service category, however, spending varies by region.

The Indexed Spending table shows spending by the average household in each region relative to average household spending. An index of 100 means households in the region spend an average amount on the item. An index above 100 indicates that households in the region spend more than average on the item, while an index below 100 reveals below-average spending.

Households in the West and Northeast spend more than the average household on most foods. Spending on housing is also above average in the West and Northeast. Households in the Northeast spend 55 percent more than the average household on property taxes and 39 percent more on public transportation. Households in the Midwest spend 13 percent more on tobacco, those in the West 18 percent less than average. Households in the South spend less than the average household on most items with some exceptions—such as electricity, vehicle finance charges, and drugs.

Spending varies by region

(average annual spending of consumer units by region, 2007)

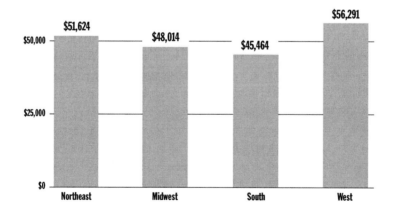

The Market Share table shows how much of total spending by category is accounted for by households in each region. In most categories, spending closely matches each region's share of total households. The South, which is home to 36 percent of households, accounts for 33 percent of household spending. With 23 percent of households, the West accounts for 26 percent of household spending. There are some exceptions, however. Households in the South, for example, account for a disproportionate share of spending on electricity (43 percent), while those in the West account for only 19 percent of spending on this item.

■ Because regional spending patterns are partly determined by climate, spending by region is not likely to change much in the years ahead.

Table 9.17 Average Spending by Region, 2007

(average annual spending of consumer units by product and service category and region of residence, 2007)

	total consumer units	Northeast	Midwest	South	West
Number of consumer units (in 000s)	120,171	22,382	27,462	43,152	27,176
Average number of persons per consumer unit	2.5	2.4	2.4	2.5	2.6
Average income before taxes	$63,091	$69,937	$59,389	$58,224	$68,923
Average annual spending	**49,638**	**51,624**	**48,014**	**45,464**	**56,291**
FOOD	**6,133**	**6,419**	**5,793**	**5,780**	**6,811**
Food at home	**3,465**	**3,595**	**3,252**	**3,311**	**3,822**
Cereals and bakery products	460	495	444	438	480
Cereals and cereal products	143	157	131	134	157
Bakery products	317	339	313	304	323
Meats, poultry, fish, and eggs	777	832	691	770	830
Beef	216	207	201	219	235
Pork	150	149	140	160	144
Other meats	104	121	109	97	98
Poultry	142	151	112	148	154
Fish and seafood	122	159	96	103	148
Eggs	43	45	33	42	51
Dairy products	387	400	375	366	422
Fresh milk and cream	154	151	145	156	161
Other dairy products	234	249	230	211	261
Fruits and vegetables	600	647	546	552	693
Fresh fruits	202	216	191	177	241
Fresh vegetables	190	205	161	175	233
Processed fruits	112	133	105	102	119
Processed vegetables	96	93	89	98	100
Other food at home	1,241	1,221	1,196	1,185	1,396
Sugar and other sweets	124	125	125	117	136
Fats and oils	91	93	87	90	97
Miscellaneous foods	650	626	630	622	734
Nonalcoholic beverages	333	333	313	325	366
Food prepared by consumer unit on trips	43	44	42	31	63
Food away from home	**2,668**	**2,824**	**2,541**	**2,470**	**2,988**
ALCOHOLIC BEVERAGES	**457**	**508**	**501**	**382**	**488**
HOUSING	**16,920**	**19,085**	**15,380**	**14,911**	**19,885**
Shelter	**10,023**	**11,640**	**8,839**	**8,233**	**12,729**
Owned dwellings	6,730	7,616	6,238	5,723	8,097
Mortgage interest and charges	3,890	3,715	3,310	3,420	5,366
Property taxes	1,709	2,649	1,801	1,259	1,555
Maintenance, repair, insurance, other expenses	1,131	1,252	1,126	1,044	1,176
Rented dwellings	2,602	3,036	1,883	2,072	3,811
Other lodging	691	988	717	437	821

	total consumer units	Northeast	Midwest	South	West
Utilities, fuels, and public services	**$3,477**	**$3,832**	**$3,323**	**$3,547**	**$3,229**
Natural gas	480	653	689	285	437
Electricity	1,303	1,276	1,116	1,568	1,093
Fuel oil and other fuels	151	455	116	71	62
Telephone services	1,110	1,120	1,025	1,167	1,095
Water and other public services	434	330	377	456	541
Household services	**984**	**1,011**	**855**	**933**	**1,174**
Personal services	415	434	394	400	447
Other household services	569	577	462	533	727
Housekeeping supplies	**639**	**576**	**620**	**595**	**782**
Laundry and cleaning supplies	140	121	145	152	132
Other household products	347	303	320	309	471
Postage and stationery	152	152	155	134	179
Household furnishings and equipment	**1,797**	**2,026**	**1,742**	**1,604**	**1,970**
Household textiles	133	148	107	129	155
Furniture	446	589	401	382	472
Floor coverings	46	69	44	36	47
Major appliances	231	240	233	222	237
Small appliances, miscellaneous housewares	101	104	91	92	123
Miscellaneous household equipment	840	877	866	741	936
APPAREL AND RELATED SERVICES	**1,881**	**2,068**	**1,866**	**1,692**	**2,042**
Men and boys	**435**	**450**	**379**	**425**	**498**
Men, aged 16 or older	351	354	292	346	417
Boys, aged 2 to 15	84	97	87	79	81
Women and girls	**749**	**812**	**821**	**638**	**800**
Women, aged 16 or older	627	690	703	515	677
Girls, aged 2 to 15	122	121	117	124	123
Children under age 2	**93**	**83**	**89**	**86**	**119**
Footwear	**327**	**350**	**334**	**297**	**350**
Other apparel products and services	**276**	**374**	**244**	**246**	**275**
TRANSPORTATION	**8,758**	**8,014**	**8,684**	**8,485**	**9,882**
Vehicle purchases	**3,244**	**2,508**	**3,407**	**3,216**	**3,729**
Cars and trucks, new	1,572	1,373	1,532	1,524	1,852
Cars and trucks, used	1,567	1,095	1,698	1,597	1,776
Gasoline and motor oil	**2,384**	**2,080**	**2,408**	**2,522**	**2,389**
Other vehicle expenses	**2,592**	**2,678**	**2,418**	**2,378**	**3,042**
Vehicle finance charges	305	250	281	342	318
Maintenance and repairs	738	716	694	689	876
Vehicle insurance	1,071	1,069	908	1,041	1,290
Vehicle rentals, leases, licenses, other charges	478	642	536	306	558
Public transportation	**538**	**749**	**451**	**368**	**721**
HEALTH CARE	**2,853**	**2,645**	**3,097**	**2,800**	**2,860**
Health insurance	1,545	1,535	1,632	1,539	1,475
Medical services	709	576	811	639	829
Drugs	481	421	514	526	425
Medical supplies	118	114	141	96	131

	total consumer units	Northeast	Midwest	South	West
ENTERTAINMENT	**$2,698**	**$2,811**	**$2,585**	**$2,320**	**$3,319**
Fees and admissions	658	803	630	476	857
Audio and visual equipment and services	987	1,010	913	971	1,068
Pets, toys, hobbies, and playground equipment	560	581	523	517	650
Other entertainment products and services	493	417	519	357	744
PERSONAL CARE PRODUCTS AND SERVICES	**588**	**609**	**544**	**565**	**650**
READING	**118**	**135**	**126**	**89**	**140**
EDUCATION	**945**	**1,163**	**1,187**	**744**	**842**
TOBACCO PRODUCTS AND SMOKING SUPPLIES	**323**	**361**	**365**	**332**	**234**
MISCELLANEOUS	**808**	**826**	**778**	**652**	**1,071**
CASH CONTRIBUTIONS	**1,821**	**1,421**	**1,792**	**1,762**	**2,275**
PERSONAL INSURANCE AND PENSIONS	**5,336**	**5,558**	**5,315**	**4,948**	**5,791**
Life and other personal insurance	309	342	347	298	262
Pensions and Social Security	5,027	5,216	4,968	4,650	5,529
PERSONAL TAXES	**2,233**	**2,497**	**1,875**	**2,048**	**2,674**
Federal income taxes	1,569	1,596	1,164	1,582	1,935
State and local income taxes	468	599	467	325	589
Other taxes	196	301	245	140	150
GIFTS FOR PEOPLE IN OTHER HOUSEHOLDS	**1,198**	**1,284**	**1,310**	**1,073**	**1,213**

Note: Spending by category does not add to total spending because gift spending is also included in the preceding product and service categories and personal taxes are not included in the total.
Source: Bureau of Labor Statistics, 2007 Consumer Expenditure Survey, Internet site http://www.bls.gov/cex/

Table 9.18 Indexed Spending by Region, 2007

(indexed average annual spending of consumer units by product and service category and region of residence, 2007; index definition: an index of 100 is the average for all consumer units; an index of 125 means that spending by consumer units in that group is 25 percent above the average for all consumer units; an index of 75 indicates spending that is 25 percent below the average for all consumer units)

	total consumer units	Northeast	Midwest	South	West
Average spending of consumer units	$49,638	$51,624	$48,014	$45,464	$56,291
Indexed spending of consumer units	100	104	97	92	113
FOOD	100	105	94	94	111
Food at home	100	104	94	96	110
Cereals and bakery products	100	108	97	95	104
Cereals and cereal products	100	110	92	94	110
Bakery products	100	107	99	96	102
Meats, poultry, fish, and eggs	100	107	89	99	107
Beef	100	96	93	101	109
Pork	100	99	93	107	96
Other meats	100	116	105	93	94
Poultry	100	106	79	104	108
Fish and seafood	100	130	79	84	121
Eggs	100	105	77	98	119
Dairy products	100	103	97	95	109
Fresh milk and cream	100	98	94	101	105
Other dairy products	100	106	98	90	112
Fruits and vegetables	100	108	91	92	116
Fresh fruits	100	107	95	88	119
Fresh vegetables	100	108	85	92	123
Processed fruits	100	119	94	91	106
Processed vegetables	100	97	93	102	104
Other food at home	100	98	96	95	112
Sugar and other sweets	100	101	101	94	110
Fats and oils	100	102	96	99	107
Miscellaneous foods	100	96	97	96	113
Nonalcoholic beverages	100	100	94	98	110
Food prepared by consumer unit on trips	100	102	98	72	147
Food away from home	100	106	95	93	112
ALCOHOLIC BEVERAGES	100	111	110	84	107
HOUSING	100	113	91	88	118
Shelter	100	116	88	82	127
Owned dwellings	100	113	93	85	120
Mortgage interest and charges	100	96	85	88	138
Property taxes	100	155	105	74	91
Maintenance, repair, insurance, other expenses	100	111	100	92	104
Rented dwellings	100	117	72	80	146
Other lodging	100	143	104	63	119

	total consumer units	Northeast	Midwest	South	West
Utilities, fuels, and public services	100	110	96	102	93
Natural gas	100	136	144	59	91
Electricity	100	98	86	120	84
Fuel oil and other fuels	100	301	77	47	41
Telephone services	100	101	92	105	99
Water and other public services	100	76	87	105	125
Household services	100	103	87	95	119
Personal services	100	105	95	96	108
Other household services	100	101	81	94	128
Housekeeping supplies	100	90	97	93	122
Laundry and cleaning supplies	100	86	104	109	94
Other household products	100	87	92	89	136
Postage and stationery	100	100	102	88	118
Household furnishings and equipment	100	113	97	89	110
Household textiles	100	111	80	97	117
Furniture	100	132	90	86	106
Floor coverings	100	150	96	78	102
Major appliances	100	104	101	96	103
Small appliances, miscellaneous housewares	100	103	90	91	122
Miscellaneous household equipment	100	104	103	88	111
APPAREL AND RELATED SERVICES	100	110	99	90	109
Men and boys	100	103	87	98	114
Men, aged 16 or older	100	101	83	99	119
Boys, aged 2 to 15	100	115	104	94	96
Women and girls	100	108	110	85	107
Women, aged 16 or older	100	110	112	82	108
Girls, aged 2 to 15	100	99	96	102	101
Children under age 2	100	89	96	92	128
Footwear	100	107	102	91	107
Other apparel products and services	100	136	88	89	100
TRANSPORTATION	100	92	99	97	113
Vehicle purchases	100	77	105	99	115
Cars and trucks, new	100	87	97	97	118
Cars and trucks, used	100	70	108	102	113
Gasoline and motor oil	100	87	101	106	100
Other vehicle expenses	100	103	93	92	117
Vehicle finance charges	100	82	92	112	104
Maintenance and repairs	100	97	94	93	119
Vehicle insurance	100	100	85	97	120
Vehicle rentals, leases, licenses, other charges	100	134	112	64	117
Public transportation	100	139	84	68	134
HEALTH CARE	100	93	109	98	100
Health insurance	100	99	106	100	95
Medical services	100	81	114	90	117
Drugs	100	88	107	109	88
Medical supplies	100	97	119	81	111

	total consumer units	Northeast	Midwest	South	West
ENTERTAINMENT	**100**	**104**	**96**	**86**	**123**
Fees and admissions	100	122	96	72	130
Audio and visual equipment and services	100	102	93	98	108
Pets, toys, hobbies, and playground equipment	100	104	93	92	116
Other entertainment products and services	100	85	105	72	151
PERSONAL CARE PRODUCTS AND SERVICES	**100**	**104**	**93**	**96**	**111**
READING	**100**	**114**	**107**	**75**	**119**
EDUCATION	**100**	**123**	**126**	**79**	**89**
TOBACCO PRODUCTS AND SMOKING SUPPLIES	**100**	**112**	**113**	**103**	**72**
MISCELLANEOUS	**100**	**102**	**96**	**81**	**133**
CASH CONTRIBUTIONS	**100**	**78**	**98**	**97**	**125**
PERSONAL INSURANCE AND PENSIONS	**100**	**104**	**100**	**93**	**109**
Life and other personal insurance	100	111	112	96	85
Pensions and Social Security	100	104	99	93	110
PERSONAL TAXES	**100**	**112**	**84**	**92**	**120**
Federal income taxes	100	102	74	101	123
State and local income taxes	100	128	100	69	126
Other taxes	100	154	125	71	77
GIFTS FOR PEOPLE IN OTHER HOUSEHOLDS	**100**	**107**	**109**	**90**	**101**

Source: Calculations by New Strategist based on the Bureau of Labor Statistics 2007 Consumer Expenditure Survey, Internet site http://www.bls.gov/cex/home.htm

Table 9.19 Market Shares by Region, 2007

(share of total household spending accounted for by region of residence, 2007)

	total consumer units	Northeast	Midwest	South	West
Share of total consumer units	100.0%	18.6%	22.9%	35.9%	22.6%
Share of total spending	100.0	19.4	22.1	32.9	25.6
FOOD	100.0	19.5	21.6	33.8	25.1
Food at home	100.0	19.3	21.4	34.3	24.9
Cereals and bakery products	100.0	20.0	22.1	34.2	23.6
Cereals and cereal products	100.0	20.4	20.9	33.6	24.8
Bakery products	100.0	19.9	22.6	34.4	23.0
Meats, poultry, fish, and eggs	100.0	19.9	20.3	35.6	24.2
Beef	100.0	17.8	21.3	36.4	24.6
Pork	100.0	18.5	21.3	38.3	21.7
Other meats	100.0	21.7	24.0	33.5	21.3
Poultry	100.0	19.8	18.0	37.4	24.5
Fish and seafood	100.0	24.3	18.0	30.3	27.4
Eggs	100.0	19.5	17.5	35.1	26.8
Dairy products	100.0	19.3	22.1	34.0	24.7
Fresh milk and cream	100.0	18.3	21.5	36.4	23.6
Other dairy products	100.0	19.8	22.5	32.4	25.2
Fruits and vegetables	100.0	20.1	20.8	33.0	26.1
Fresh fruits	100.0	19.9	21.6	31.5	27.0
Fresh vegetables	100.0	20.1	19.4	33.1	27.7
Processed fruits	100.0	22.1	21.4	32.7	24.0
Processed vegetables	100.0	18.0	21.2	36.7	23.6
Other food at home	100.0	18.3	22.0	34.3	25.4
Sugar and other sweets	100.0	18.8	23.0	33.9	24.8
Fats and oils	100.0	19.0	21.8	35.5	24.1
Miscellaneous foods	100.0	17.9	22.1	34.4	25.5
Nonalcoholic beverages	100.0	18.6	21.5	35.0	24.9
Food prepared by consumer unit on trips	100.0	19.1	22.3	25.9	33.1
Food away from home	100.0	19.7	21.8	33.2	25.3
ALCOHOLIC BEVERAGES	100.0	20.7	25.1	30.0	24.1
HOUSING	100.0	21.0	20.8	31.6	26.6
Shelter	100.0	21.6	20.2	29.5	28.7
Owned dwellings	100.0	21.1	21.2	30.5	27.2
Mortgage interest and charges	100.0	17.8	19.4	31.6	31.2
Property taxes	100.0	28.9	24.1	26.5	20.6
Maintenance, repair, insurance, other expenses	100.0	20.6	22.8	33.1	23.5
Rented dwellings	100.0	21.7	16.5	28.6	33.1
Other lodging	100.0	26.6	23.7	22.7	26.9

	total consumer units	Northeast	Midwest	South	West
Utilities, fuels, and public services	**100.0%**	**20.5%**	**21.8%**	**36.6%**	**21.0%**
Natural gas	100.0	25.3	32.8	21.3	20.6
Electricity	100.0	18.2	19.6	43.2	19.0
Fuel oil and other fuels	100.0	56.1	17.6	16.9	9.3
Telephone services	100.0	18.8	21.1	37.8	22.3
Water and other public services	100.0	14.2	19.9	37.7	28.2
Household services	**100.0**	**19.1**	**19.9**	**34.0**	**27.0**
Personal services	100.0	19.5	21.7	34.6	24.4
Other household services	100.0	18.9	18.6	33.6	28.9
Housekeeping supplies	**100.0**	**16.8**	**22.2**	**33.4**	**27.7**
Laundry and cleaning supplies	100.0	16.1	23.7	39.0	21.3
Other household products	100.0	16.3	21.1	32.0	30.7
Postage and stationery	100.0	18.6	23.3	31.7	26.6
Household furnishings and equipment	**100.0**	**21.0**	**22.2**	**32.1**	**24.8**
Household textiles	100.0	20.7	18.4	34.8	26.4
Furniture	100.0	24.6	20.5	30.8	23.9
Floor coverings	100.0	27.9	21.9	28.1	23.1
Major appliances	100.0	19.4	23.1	34.5	23.2
Small appliances, miscellaneous housewares	100.0	19.2	20.6	32.7	27.5
Miscellaneous household equipment	100.0	19.4	23.6	31.7	25.2
APPAREL AND RELATED SERVICES	**100.0**	**20.5**	**22.7**	**32.3**	**24.6**
Men and boys	**100.0**	**19.3**	**19.9**	**35.1**	**25.9**
Men, aged 16 or older	100.0	18.8	19.0	35.4	26.9
Boys, aged 2 to 15	100.0	21.5	23.7	33.8	21.8
Women and girls	**100.0**	**20.2**	**25.0**	**30.6**	**24.2**
Women, aged 16 or older	100.0	20.5	25.6	29.5	24.4
Girls, aged 2 to 15	100.0	18.5	21.9	36.5	22.8
Children under age 2	**100.0**	**16.6**	**21.9**	**33.2**	**28.9**
Footwear	**100.0**	**19.9**	**23.3**	**32.6**	**24.2**
Other apparel products and services	**100.0**	**25.2**	**20.2**	**32.0**	**22.5**
TRANSPORTATION	**100.0**	**17.0**	**22.7**	**34.8**	**25.5**
Vehicle purchases	**100.0**	**14.4**	**24.0**	**35.6**	**26.0**
Cars and trucks, new	100.0	16.3	22.3	34.8	26.6
Cars and trucks, used	100.0	13.0	24.8	36.6	25.6
Gasoline and motor oil	**100.0**	**16.3**	**23.1**	**38.0**	**22.7**
Other vehicle expenses	**100.0**	**19.2**	**21.3**	**32.9**	**26.5**
Vehicle finance charges	100.0	15.3	21.1	40.3	23.6
Maintenance and repairs	100.0	18.1	21.5	33.5	26.8
Vehicle insurance	100.0	18.6	19.4	34.9	27.2
Vehicle rentals, leases, licenses, other charges	100.0	25.0	25.6	23.0	26.4
Public transportation	**100.0**	**25.9**	**19.2**	**24.6**	**30.3**
HEALTH CARE	**100.0**	**17.3**	**24.8**	**35.2**	**22.7**
Health insurance	100.0	18.5	24.1	35.8	21.6
Medical services	100.0	15.1	26.1	32.4	26.4
Drugs	100.0	16.3	24.4	39.3	20.0
Medical supplies	100.0	18.0	27.3	29.2	25.1

	total consumer units	Northeast	Midwest	South	West
ENTERTAINMENT	**100.0%**	**19.4%**	**21.9%**	**30.9%**	**27.8%**
Fees and admissions	100.0	22.7	21.9	26.0	29.5
Audio and visual equipment and services	100.0	19.1	21.1	35.3	24.5
Pets, toys, hobbies, and playground equipment	100.0	19.3	21.3	33.2	26.2
Other entertainment products and services	100.0	15.8	24.1	26.0	34.1
PERSONAL CARE PRODUCTS AND SERVICES	**100.0**	**19.3**	**21.1**	**34.5**	**25.0**
READING	**100.0**	**21.3**	**24.4**	**27.1**	**26.8**
EDUCATION	**100.0**	**22.9**	**28.7**	**28.3**	**20.1**
TOBACCO PRODUCTS AND SMOKING SUPPLIES	**100.0**	**20.8**	**25.8**	**36.9**	**16.4**
MISCELLANEOUS	**100.0**	**19.0**	**22.0**	**29.0**	**30.0**
CASH CONTRIBUTIONS	**100.0**	**14.5**	**22.5**	**34.7**	**28.3**
PERSONAL INSURANCE AND PENSIONS	**100.0**	**19.4**	**22.8**	**33.3**	**24.5**
Life and other personal insurance	100.0	20.6	25.7	34.6	19.2
Pensions and Social Security	100.0	19.3	22.6	33.2	24.9
PERSONAL TAXES	**100.0**	**20.8**	**19.2**	**32.9**	**27.1**
Federal income taxes	100.0	18.9	17.0	36.2	27.9
State and local income taxes	100.0	23.8	22.8	24.9	28.5
Other taxes	100.0	28.6	28.6	25.6	17.3
GIFTS FOR PEOPLE IN OTHER HOUSEHOLDS	**100.0**	**20.0**	**25.0**	**32.2**	**22.9**

Source: Calculations by New Strategist based on the Bureau of Labor Statistics 2007 Consumer Expenditure Survey, Internet site http://www.bls.gov/cex/home.htm

College Graduates Spend More

The incomes of college graduates are much higher than average, and they spend more on most items.

College graduates have much higher incomes than those with less education. Consequently, they spend more. In 2007, households headed by college graduates spent $70,605—42 percent more than the average household. Householders who went no further than high school spent just $39,164, or 21 percent less than the average household.

The Indexed Spending table compares the spending of households by level of education with average household spending. An index of 100 means households in the educational group spend an average amount on the item. An index above 100 indicates that households in the educational group spend more than average on the item, while an index below 100 signifies below-average spending.

Households headed by college graduates spend like the more sophisticated consumers they are. They spend well above average on fish and seafood, fresh fruits and vegetables, restaurant meals (food away from home), and alcoholic beverages. They spend only slightly more than average on laundry and cleaning supplies, but much more than average on household textiles (bedroom and bathroom linens, for example) and floor coverings. They spend twice the average on fees and admissions to entertainment events, but less than half the average on tobacco.

College graduates spend big on many items

(indexed average annual spending of consumer units headed by college graduates on selected items, 2007)

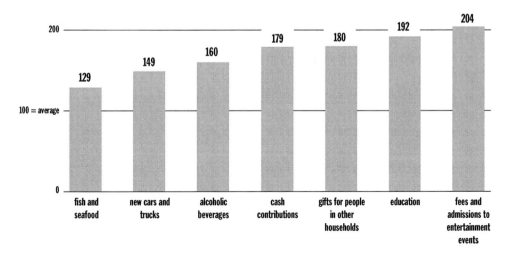

The Market Share table shows how much of total household spending by category is accounted for by households in each educational group. College graduates spend disproportionately more than their share of households, while those who did not graduate from college spend less.

College graduates head 29 percent of households, but account for 41 percent of household spending. On some items their spending is even higher. They account for 63 percent of spending on other lodging, which includes dorm rooms, hotels, and motels. They account for 36 percent of spending on public transportation, which includes airline fares, for 59 percent of spending on fees and admission to entertainment events, and for 56 percent of education spending.

■ As the educational level of the population rises, college graduates will increasingly dominate spending on a growing number of products and services.

Table 9.20 Average Spending by Education of Householder, 2007

(average annual spending of consumer units by product and service category and educational attainment of consumer unit reference person, 2007)

	total consumer units	not a high school graduate	high school graduate	some college	associate's degree	college degree or more
Number of consumer units (in 000s)	120,171	18,227	30,313	26,169	10,680	34,783
Average number of persons per consumer unit	2.5	2.6	2.5	2.4	2.6	2.4
Average income before taxes	$63,091	$33,913	$46,938	$54,881	$64,537	$98,193
Average annual spending	49,638	30,201	39,164	45,876	52,721	70,605
FOOD	**6,133**	**4,491**	**5,231**	**5,729**	**6,524**	**7,878**
Food at home	**3,465**	**3,027**	**3,196**	**3,173**	**3,669**	**4,055**
Cereals and bakery products	460	396	427	428	477	535
Cereals and cereal products	143	135	128	129	157	165
Bakery products	317	261	299	299	321	370
Meats, poultry, fish, and eggs	777	772	779	714	813	812
Beef	216	224	226	206	206	215
Pork	150	162	168	135	158	136
Other meats	104	90	108	98	115	109
Poultry	142	144	135	127	170	150
Fish and seafood	122	107	101	107	125	157
Eggs	43	45	42	42	40	44
Dairy products	387	311	348	367	403	467
Fresh milk and cream	154	146	147	150	157	164
Other dairy products	234	165	201	217	246	303
Fruits and vegetables	600	515	504	520	597	781
Fresh fruits	202	168	158	168	194	282
Fresh vegetables	190	170	158	163	181	250
Processed fruits	112	92	98	97	123	142
Processed vegetables	96	85	89	92	100	107
Other food at home	1,241	1,033	1,138	1,144	1,379	1,460
Sugar and other sweets	124	99	114	113	137	150
Fats and oils	91	81	85	90	97	101
Miscellaneous foods	650	530	584	589	757	774
Nonalcoholic beverages	333	308	327	313	343	362
Food prepared by consumer unit on trips	43	15	28	38	45	74
Food away from home	**2,668**	**1,464**	**2,035**	**2,555**	**2,855**	**3,823**
ALCOHOLIC BEVERAGES	**457**	**174**	**329**	**421**	**448**	**729**
HOUSING	**16,920**	**10,947**	**13,026**	**15,424**	**17,959**	**24,214**
Shelter	**10,023**	**6,311**	**7,532**	**9,111**	**10,380**	**14,715**
Owned dwellings	6,730	3,195	4,747	5,741	7,516	10,813
Mortgage interest and charges	3,890	1,827	2,621	3,435	4,311	6,290
Property taxes	1,709	783	1,246	1,394	1,794	2,808
Maintenance, repair, insurance, other expenses	1,131	586	879	913	1,411	1,716
Rented dwellings	2,602	2,995	2,463	2,884	2,320	2,391
Other lodging	691	120	321	485	544	1,511

	total consumer units	not a high school graduate	high school graduate	some college	associate's degree	college degree or more
Utilities, fuels, and public services	**$3,477**	**$2,930**	**$3,312**	**$3,272**	**$3,686**	**$3,998**
Natural gas	480	374	439	408	484	625
Electricity	1,303	1,184	1,285	1,250	1,353	1,405
Fuel oil and other fuels	151	125	157	116	204	169
Telephone services	1,110	909	1,043	1,088	1,209	1,258
Water and other public services	434	337	388	410	436	541
Household services	**984**	**340**	**581**	**842**	**1,062**	**1,756**
Personal services	415	137	230	349	489	750
Other household services	569	203	351	493	574	1,005
Housekeeping supplies	**639**	**420**	**500**	**566**	**601**	**924**
Laundry and cleaning supplies	140	128	128	149	142	149
Other household products	347	183	267	282	309	549
Postage and stationery	152	110	104	135	150	227
Household furnishings and equipment	**1,797**	**947**	**1,101**	**1,633**	**2,230**	**2,821**
Household textiles	133	51	83	123	183	208
Furniture	446	202	275	405	492	737
Floor coverings	46	21	28	35	52	83
Major appliances	231	135	177	234	278	312
Small appliances, miscellaneous housewares	101	66	54	116	109	146
Miscellaneous household equipment	840	471	484	719	1,115	1,335
APPAREL AND RELATED SERVICES	**1,881**	**1,207**	**1,328**	**1,622**	**1,865**	**2,878**
Men and boys	**435**	**295**	**302**	**374**	**412**	**670**
Men, aged 16 or older	351	228	238	292	299	566
Boys, aged 2 to 15	84	67	63	83	113	104
Women and girls	**749**	**379**	**519**	**668**	**819**	**1,161**
Women, aged 16 or older	627	314	422	553	662	996
Girls, aged 2 to 15	122	65	97	115	156	165
Children under age 2	**93**	**94**	**81**	**93**	**106**	**101**
Footwear	**327**	**276**	**269**	**276**	**275**	**453**
Other apparel products and services	**276**	**163**	**157**	**211**	**253**	**493**
TRANSPORTATION	**8,758**	**5,655**	**7,614**	**8,658**	**10,092**	**11,031**
Vehicle purchases	**3,244**	**2,112**	**2,761**	**3,231**	**3,924**	**4,060**
Cars and trucks, new	1,572	847	1,088	1,310	2,326	2,338
Cars and trucks, used	1,567	1,246	1,568	1,726	1,439	1,654
Gasoline and motor oil	**2,384**	**1,785**	**2,269**	**2,429**	**2,740**	**2,654**
Other vehicle expenses	**2,592**	**1,550**	**2,368**	**2,613**	**3,024**	**3,171**
Vehicle finance charges	305	154	289	358	395	331
Maintenance and repairs	738	425	615	757	755	987
Vehicle insurance	1,071	766	1,123	1,091	1,386	1,062
Vehicle rentals, leases, licenses, other charges	478	204	340	407	487	792
Public transportation	**538**	**209**	**216**	**386**	**404**	**1,146**
HEALTH CARE	**2,853**	**2,003**	**2,594**	**2,654**	**2,998**	**3,625**
Health insurance	1,545	1,136	1,502	1,381	1,643	1,889
Medical services	709	391	533	735	706	1,011
Drugs	481	411	466	431	532	550
Medical supplies	118	65	92	106	116	175

	total consumer units	not a high school graduate	high school graduate	some college	associate's degree	college degree or more
ENTERTAINMENT	**$2,698**	**$1,295**	**$1,966**	**$2,481**	**$2,957**	**$4,130**
Fees and admissions	658	131	288	551	622	1,342
Audio and visual equipment and services	987	638	854	975	1,091	1,261
Pets, toys, hobbies, and playground equipment	560	274	485	538	686	742
Other entertainment products and services	493	252	338	417	559	786
PERSONAL CARE PRODUCTS AND SERVICES	**588**	**312**	**462**	**534**	**639**	**858**
READING	**118**	**40**	**80**	**100**	**110**	**207**
EDUCATION	**945**	**145**	**405**	**1,063**	**725**	**1,813**
TOBACCO PRODUCTS AND SMOKING SUPPLIES	**323**	**374**	**457**	**367**	**297**	**154**
MISCELLANEOUS	**808**	**386**	**591**	**790**	**940**	**1,192**
CASH CONTRIBUTIONS	**1,821**	**757**	**1,333**	**1,384**	**1,404**	**3,263**
PERSONAL INSURANCE AND PENSIONS	**5,336**	**2,415**	**3,749**	**4,650**	**5,763**	**8,635**
Life and other personal insurance	309	136	257	269	328	471
Pensions and Social Security	5,027	2,278	3,492	4,381	5,436	8,164
PERSONAL TAXES	**2,233**	**526**	**1,041**	**1,778**	**2,130**	**4,542**
Federal income taxes	1,569	274	650	1,199	1,432	3,369
State and local income taxes	468	166	265	410	482	843
Other taxes	196	86	127	169	216	329
GIFTS FOR PEOPLE IN OTHER HOUSEHOLDS	**1,198**	**391**	**705**	**1,011**	**1,262**	**2,157**

Note: Spending by category does not add to total spending because gift spending is also included in the preceding product and service categories and personal taxes are not included in the total.
Source: Bureau of Labor Statistics, 2007 Consumer Expenditure Survey, Internet site http://www.bls.gov/cex/

Table 9.21 Indexed Spending by Education of Householder, 2007

(indexed average annual spending of consumer units by product and service category and educational attainment of consumer unit reference person, 2007; index definition: an index of 100 is the average for all consumer units; an index of 125 means that spending by consumer units in that group is 25 percent above the average for all consumer units; an index of 75 indicates spending that is 25 percent below the average for all consumer units)

	total consumer units	not a high school graduate	high school graduate	some college	associate's degree	college degree or more
Average spending of consumer units	$49,638	$30,201	$39,164	$45,876	$52,721	$70,605
Indexed spending of consumer units	100	61	79	92	106	142
FOOD	100	73	85	93	106	128
Food at home	100	87	92	92	106	117
Cereals and bakery products	100	86	93	93	104	116
Cereals and cereal products	100	94	90	90	110	115
Bakery products	100	82	94	94	101	117
Meats, poultry, fish, and eggs	100	99	100	92	105	105
Beef	100	104	105	95	95	100
Pork	100	108	112	90	105	91
Other meats	100	87	104	94	111	105
Poultry	100	101	95	89	120	106
Fish and seafood	100	88	83	88	102	129
Eggs	100	105	98	98	93	102
Dairy products	100	80	90	95	104	121
Fresh milk and cream	100	95	95	97	102	106
Other dairy products	100	71	86	93	105	129
Fruits and vegetables	100	86	84	87	100	130
Fresh fruits	100	83	78	83	96	140
Fresh vegetables	100	89	83	86	95	132
Processed fruits	100	82	88	87	110	127
Processed vegetables	100	89	93	96	104	111
Other food at home	100	83	92	92	111	118
Sugar and other sweets	100	80	92	91	110	121
Fats and oils	100	89	93	99	107	111
Miscellaneous foods	100	82	90	91	116	119
Nonalcoholic beverages	100	92	98	94	103	109
Food prepared by consumer unit on trips	100	35	65	88	105	172
Food away from home	100	55	76	96	107	143
ALCOHOLIC BEVERAGES	100	38	72	92	98	160
HOUSING	100	65	77	91	106	143
Shelter	100	63	75	91	104	147
Owned dwellings	100	47	71	85	112	161
Mortgage interest and charges	100	47	67	88	111	162
Property taxes	100	46	73	82	105	164
Maintenance, repair, insurance, other expenses	100	52	78	81	125	152
Rented dwellings	100	115	95	111	89	92
Other lodging	100	17	46	70	79	219

	total consumer units	not a high school graduate	high school graduate	some college	associate's degree	college degree or more
Utilities, fuels, and public services	**100**	**84**	**95**	**94**	**106**	**115**
Natural gas	100	78	91	85	101	130
Electricity	100	91	99	96	104	108
Fuel oil and other fuels	100	83	104	77	135	112
Telephone services	100	82	94	98	109	113
Water and other public services	100	78	89	94	100	125
Household services	**100**	**35**	**59**	**86**	**108**	**178**
Personal services	100	33	55	84	118	181
Other household services	100	36	62	87	101	177
Housekeeping supplies	**100**	**66**	**78**	**89**	**94**	**145**
Laundry and cleaning supplies	100	91	91	106	101	106
Other household products	100	53	77	81	89	158
Postage and stationery	100	72	68	89	99	149
Household furnishings and equipment	**100**	**53**	**61**	**91**	**124**	**157**
Household textiles	100	38	62	92	138	156
Furniture	100	45	62	91	110	165
Floor coverings	100	46	61	76	113	180
Major appliances	100	58	77	101	120	135
Small appliances, miscellaneous housewares	100	65	53	115	108	145
Miscellaneous household equipment	100	56	58	86	133	159
APPAREL AND RELATED SERVICES	**100**	**64**	**71**	**86**	**99**	**153**
Men and boys	**100**	**68**	**69**	**86**	**95**	**154**
Men, aged 16 or older	100	65	68	83	85	161
Boys, aged 2 to 15	100	80	75	99	135	124
Women and girls	**100**	**51**	**69**	**89**	**109**	**155**
Women, aged 16 or older	100	50	67	88	106	159
Girls, aged 2 to 15	100	53	80	94	128	135
Children under age 2	**100**	**101**	**87**	**100**	**114**	**109**
Footwear	**100**	**84**	**82**	**84**	**84**	**139**
Other apparel products and services	**100**	**59**	**57**	**76**	**92**	**179**
TRANSPORTATION	**100**	**65**	**87**	**99**	**115**	**126**
Vehicle purchases	**100**	**65**	**85**	**100**	**121**	**125**
Cars and trucks, new	100	54	69	83	148	149
Cars and trucks, used	100	80	100	110	92	106
Gasoline and motor oil	**100**	**75**	**95**	**102**	**115**	**111**
Other vehicle expenses	**100**	**60**	**91**	**101**	**117**	**122**
Vehicle finance charges	100	50	95	117	130	109
Maintenance and repairs	100	58	83	103	102	134
Vehicle insurance	100	72	105	102	129	99
Vehicle rentals, leases, licenses, other charges	100	43	71	85	102	166
Public transportation	**100**	**39**	**40**	**72**	**75**	**213**
HEALTH CARE	**100**	**70**	**91**	**93**	**105**	**127**
Health insurance	100	74	97	89	106	122
Medical services	100	55	75	104	100	143
Drugs	100	85	97	90	111	114
Medical supplies	100	55	78	90	98	148

	total consumer units	not a high school graduate	high school graduate	some college	associate's degree	college degree or more
ENTERTAINMENT	**100**	**48**	**73**	**92**	**110**	**153**
Fees and admissions	100	20	44	84	95	204
Audio and visual equipment and services	100	65	87	99	111	128
Pets, toys, hobbies, and playground equipment	100	49	87	96	123	133
Other entertainment products and services	100	51	69	85	113	159
PERSONAL CARE PRODUCTS AND SERVICES	**100**	**53**	**79**	**91**	**109**	**146**
READING	**100**	**34**	**68**	**85**	**93**	**175**
EDUCATION	**100**	**15**	**43**	**112**	**77**	**192**
TOBACCO PRODUCTS AND SMOKING SUPPLIES	**100**	**116**	**141**	**114**	**92**	**48**
MISCELLANEOUS	**100**	**48**	**73**	**98**	**116**	**148**
CASH CONTRIBUTIONS	**100**	**42**	**73**	**76**	**77**	**179**
PERSONAL INSURANCE AND PENSIONS	**100**	**45**	**70**	**87**	**108**	**162**
Life and other personal insurance	100	44	83	87	106	152
Pensions and Social Security	100	45	69	87	108	162
PERSONAL TAXES	**100**	**24**	**47**	**80**	**95**	**203**
Federal income taxes	100	17	41	76	91	215
State and local income taxes	100	35	57	88	103	180
Other taxes	100	44	65	86	110	168
GIFTS FOR PEOPLE IN OTHER HOUSEHOLDS	**100**	**33**	**59**	**84**	**105**	**180**

Source: Calculations by New Strategist based on the Bureau of Labor Statistics 2007 Consumer Expenditure Survey, Internet site http://www.bls.gov/cex/home.htm

Table 9.22 Market Shares by Education of Householder, 2007

(share of total household spending accounted for by educational group, 2007)

	total consumer units	not a high school graduate	high school graduate	some college	associate's degree	college degree or more
Share of total consumer units	100.0%	15.2%	25.2%	21.8%	8.9%	28.9%
Share of total spending	100.0	9.2	19.9	20.1	9.4	41.2
FOOD	100.0	11.1	21.5	20.3	9.5	37.2
Food at home	100.0	13.3	23.3	19.9	9.4	33.9
Cereals and bakery products	100.0	13.1	23.4	20.3	9.2	33.7
Cereals and cereal products	100.0	14.3	22.6	19.6	9.8	33.4
Bakery products	100.0	12.5	23.8	20.5	9.0	33.8
Meats, poultry, fish, and eggs	100.0	15.1	25.3	20.0	9.3	30.2
Beef	100.0	15.7	26.4	20.8	8.5	28.8
Pork	100.0	16.4	28.3	19.6	9.4	26.2
Other meats	100.0	13.1	26.2	20.5	9.8	30.3
Poultry	100.0	15.4	24.0	19.5	10.6	30.6
Fish and seafood	100.0	13.3	20.9	19.1	9.1	37.2
Eggs	100.0	15.9	24.6	21.3	8.3	29.6
Dairy products	100.0	12.2	22.7	20.7	9.3	34.9
Fresh milk and cream	100.0	14.4	24.1	21.2	9.1	30.8
Other dairy products	100.0	10.7	21.7	20.2	9.3	37.5
Fruits and vegetables	100.0	13.0	21.2	18.9	8.8	37.7
Fresh fruits	100.0	12.6	19.7	18.1	8.5	40.4
Fresh vegetables	100.0	13.6	21.0	18.7	8.5	38.1
Processed fruits	100.0	12.5	22.1	18.9	9.8	36.7
Processed vegetables	100.0	13.4	23.4	20.9	9.3	32.3
Other food at home	100.0	12.6	23.1	20.1	9.9	34.1
Sugar and other sweets	100.0	12.1	23.2	19.8	9.8	35.0
Fats and oils	100.0	13.5	23.6	21.5	9.5	32.1
Miscellaneous foods	100.0	12.4	22.7	19.7	10.4	34.5
Nonalcoholic beverages	100.0	14.0	24.8	20.5	9.2	31.5
Food prepared by consumer unit on trips	100.0	5.3	16.4	19.2	9.3	49.8
Food away from home	100.0	8.3	19.2	20.9	9.5	41.5
ALCOHOLIC BEVERAGES	100.0	5.8	18.2	20.1	8.7	46.2
HOUSING	100.0	9.8	19.4	19.9	9.4	41.4
Shelter	100.0	9.6	19.0	19.8	9.2	42.5
Owned dwellings	100.0	7.2	17.8	18.6	9.9	46.5
Mortgage interest and charges	100.0	7.1	17.0	19.2	9.8	46.8
Property taxes	100.0	6.9	18.4	17.8	9.3	47.6
Maintenance, repair, insurance, other expenses	100.0	7.9	19.6	17.6	11.1	43.9
Rented dwellings	100.0	17.5	23.9	24.1	7.9	26.6
Other lodging	100.0	2.6	11.7	15.3	7.0	63.3

	total consumer units	not a high school graduate	high school graduate	some college	associate's degree	college degree or more
Utilities, fuels, and public services	100.0%	12.8%	24.0%	20.5%	9.4%	33.3%
Natural gas	100.0	11.8	23.1	18.5	9.0	37.7
Electricity	100.0	13.8	24.9	20.9	9.2	31.2
Fuel oil and other fuels	100.0	12.6	26.2	16.7	12.0	32.4
Telephone services	100.0	12.4	23.7	21.3	9.7	32.8
Water and other public services	100.0	11.8	22.6	20.6	8.9	36.1
Household services	100.0	5.2	14.9	18.6	9.6	51.7
Personal services	100.0	5.0	14.0	18.3	10.5	52.3
Other household services	100.0	5.4	15.6	18.9	9.0	51.1
Housekeeping supplies	100.0	10.0	19.7	19.3	8.4	41.9
Laundry and cleaning supplies	100.0	13.9	23.1	23.2	9.0	30.8
Other household products	100.0	8.0	19.4	17.7	7.9	45.8
Postage and stationery	100.0	11.0	17.3	19.3	8.8	43.2
Household furnishings and equipment	100.0	8.0	15.5	19.8	11.0	45.4
Household textiles	100.0	5.8	15.7	20.1	12.2	45.3
Furniture	100.0	6.9	15.6	19.8	9.8	47.8
Floor coverings	100.0	6.9	15.4	16.6	10.0	52.2
Major appliances	100.0	8.9	19.3	22.1	10.7	39.1
Small appliances, miscellaneous housewares	100.0	9.9	13.5	25.0	9.6	41.8
Miscellaneous household equipment	100.0	8.5	14.5	18.6	11.8	46.0
APPAREL AND RELATED SERVICES	100.0	9.7	17.8	18.8	8.8	44.3
Men and boys	100.0	10.3	17.5	18.7	8.4	44.6
Men, aged 16 or older	100.0	9.9	17.1	18.1	7.6	46.7
Boys, aged 2 to 15	100.0	12.1	18.9	21.5	12.0	35.8
Women and girls	100.0	7.7	17.5	19.4	9.7	44.9
Women, aged 16 or older	100.0	7.6	17.0	19.2	9.4	46.0
Girls, aged 2 to 15	100.0	8.1	20.1	20.5	11.4	39.1
Children under age 2	100.0	15.3	22.0	21.8	10.1	31.4
Footwear	100.0	12.8	20.8	18.4	7.5	40.1
Other apparel products and services	100.0	9.0	14.3	16.6	8.1	51.7
TRANSPORTATION	100.0	9.8	21.9	21.5	10.2	36.5
Vehicle purchases	100.0	9.9	21.5	21.7	10.8	36.2
Cars and trucks, new	100.0	8.2	17.5	18.1	13.2	43.0
Cars and trucks, used	100.0	12.1	25.2	24.0	8.2	30.6
Gasoline and motor oil	100.0	11.4	24.0	22.2	10.2	32.2
Other vehicle expenses	100.0	9.1	23.0	22.0	10.4	35.4
Vehicle finance charges	100.0	7.7	23.9	25.6	11.5	31.4
Maintenance and repairs	100.0	8.7	21.0	22.3	9.1	38.7
Vehicle insurance	100.0	10.8	26.4	22.2	11.5	28.7
Vehicle rentals, leases, licenses, other charges	100.0	6.5	17.9	18.5	9.1	48.0
Public transportation	100.0	5.9	10.1	15.6	6.7	61.7
HEALTH CARE	100.0	10.6	22.9	20.3	9.3	36.8
Health insurance	100.0	11.2	24.5	19.5	9.5	35.4
Medical services	100.0	8.4	19.0	22.6	8.8	41.3
Drugs	100.0	13.0	24.4	19.5	9.8	33.1
Medical supplies	100.0	8.4	19.7	19.6	8.7	42.9

	total consumer units	not a high school graduate	high school graduate	some college	associate's degree	college degree or more
ENTERTAINMENT	**100.0%**	**7.3%**	**18.4%**	**20.0%**	**9.7%**	**44.3%**
Fees and admissions	100.0	3.0	11.0	18.2	8.4	59.0
Audio and visual equipment and services	100.0	9.8	21.8	21.5	9.8	37.0
Pets, toys, hobbies, and playground equipment	100.0	7.4	21.8	20.9	10.9	38.4
Other entertainment products and services	100.0	7.8	17.3	18.4	10.1	46.1
PERSONAL CARE PRODUCTS AND SERVICES	**100.0**	**8.0**	**19.8**	**19.8**	**9.7**	**42.2**
READING	**100.0**	**5.1**	**17.1**	**18.5**	**8.3**	**50.8**
EDUCATION	**100.0**	**2.3**	**10.8**	**24.5**	**6.8**	**55.5**
TOBACCO PRODUCTS AND SMOKING SUPPLIES	**100.0**	**17.6**	**35.7**	**24.7**	**8.2**	**13.8**
MISCELLANEOUS	**100.0**	**7.2**	**18.5**	**21.3**	**10.3**	**42.7**
CASH CONTRIBUTIONS	**100.0**	**6.3**	**18.5**	**16.6**	**6.9**	**51.9**
PERSONAL INSURANCE AND PENSIONS	**100.0**	**6.9**	**17.7**	**19.0**	**9.6**	**46.8**
Life and other personal insurance	100.0	6.7	21.0	19.0	9.4	44.1
Pensions and Social Security	100.0	6.9	17.5	19.0	9.6	47.0
PERSONAL TAXES	**100.0**	**3.6**	**11.8**	**17.3**	**8.5**	**58.9**
Federal income taxes	100.0	2.6	10.5	16.6	8.1	62.2
State and local income taxes	100.0	5.4	14.3	19.1	9.2	52.1
Other taxes	100.0	6.7	16.3	18.8	9.8	48.6
GIFTS FOR PEOPLE IN OTHER HOUSEHOLDS	**100.0**	**5.0**	**14.8**	**18.4**	**9.4**	**52.1**

Source: Calculations by New Strategist based on the Bureau of Labor Statistics 2007 Consumer Expenditure Survey; Internet site http://www.bls.gov/cex/home.htm

10

Time Use Trends

■ Time use statistics show that traditional sex roles are still alive and well. On an average day, women spend much more time than men doing housework. Men spend more time than women on home maintenance and repair.

■ Time use varies by age, with teenagers and older Americans having the most leisure time and the middle aged having the least. Women aged 25 to 44 have less leisure time than anyone else.

■ Hispanic men spend more time at work than either white or black men. On an average day, Hispanic men work for 5.18 hours—15 percent more than the average man.

■ Hispanic women spend 17 percent more time than the average woman in household activities (housework, food preparation, etc.) and 24 percent more time caring for household members.

■ Time use changes on weekends. People sleep longer, work less, and watch more television. The average amount of time devoted to watching television rises from 2.43 hours on the average weekday to 3.07 hours on the average weekend day.

Americans Spend More than One Hour a Day Eating and Drinking

They spend more than two hours a day watching television.

For the past few years, the Bureau of Labor Statistics has been asking Americans how they spend their time through the American Time Use Survey. This annual survey collects time use data by asking a representative sample of the population about their activities during the past 24 hours. The diary data are combined and analyzed by type of activity and demographic characteristic.

Not surprisingly, sleep takes up the most time. The average person reported sleeping 8.57 hours per day in 2007. People work an average of 3.81 hours a day, a figure that includes both those who worked on diary day and those who had the day off. Among the 48 percent of people who worked on diary day, work consumed an average of 7.98 hours.

Traditional sex roles are still abundantly evident in these statistics. On an average day, women spend much more time than men doing housework and caring for household children. Men spend more time than women on home maintenance and repair, caring for vehicles, and tending the lawn.

■ The results of the time use survey are used by researchers and public policymakers to determine how people balance work and family issues.

Women spend nearly one hour a day doing housework, on average

(average number of hours per day people spend on selected primary activities, by sex, 2007)

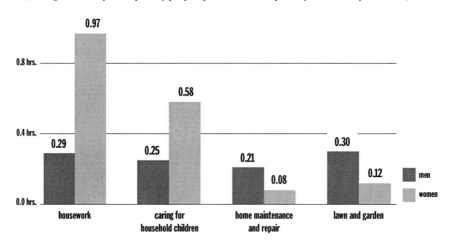

Table 10.1 Total Time Use and Percent Reporting Activity, 2007

(hours per day spent in primary activities by people aged 15 or older, percent reporting activity on diary day, and hours per day spent on activity by those reporting activity on diary day, 2007)

	hours per day for total people	percent reporting activity on diary day	hours per day for those reporting activity on diary day
TOTAL, ALL ACTIVITIES	**24.00**	**100.0%**	–
Personal care activities	**9.33**	**100.0**	**9.33**
Sleeping	8.57	99.9	8.58
Grooming	0.67	79.1	0.84
Health-related self-care	0.07	5.1	1.29
Personal activities	0.01	0.5	1.25
Travel related to personal care	0.02	2.4	0.69
Eating and drinking	**1.24**	**95.4**	**1.30**
Eating and drinking	1.11	95.4	1.16
Travel related to eating and drinking	0.12	25.7	0.48
Household activities	**1.84**	**74.4**	**2.47**
Housework	0.64	36.2	1.76
Food preparation and cleanup	0.52	50.8	1.02
Lawn and garden care	0.21	10.3	2.00
Household management	0.14	18.2	0.78
Interior maintenance, repair, and decoration	0.08	3.6	2.33
Exterior maintenance, repair, and decoration	0.06	2.8	2.12
Animals and pets	0.09	14.2	0.67
Vehicles	0.04	2.6	1.34
Appliances, tools, and toys	0.02	1.6	1.13
Travel related to household activities	0.05	9.6	0.49
Purchasing goods and services	**0.78**	**44.3**	**1.77**
Consumer goods purchases	0.39	40.6	0.97
Grocery shopping	0.10	12.9	0.74
Professional and personal care services	0.09	8.4	1.04
Financial services and banking	0.01	3.4	0.27
Medical and care services	0.05	3.2	1.57
Personal care services	0.02	1.6	1.31
Household services	0.01	2.0	0.74
Household maintenance, repair, decoration, and construction (not done by self)	0.01	0.4	–
Vehicle maintenance and repair services (not done by self)	0.01	1.0	0.61
Government services	0.00	0.4	–
Travel related to purchasing goods and services	0.28	42.6	0.66
Caring for and helping household members	**0.53**	**25.5**	**2.08**
Caring for and helping household children	0.42	21.8	1.92
Caring for and helping household children (except activities related to education and health)	0.38	21.5	1.75
Activities related to household children's education	0.03	3.5	0.93
Activities related to household children's health	0.01	0.8	1.30
Caring for and helping household adults	0.03	4.9	0.71
Caring for household adults	0.03	1.8	1.42
Helping household adults	0.01	3.3	0.28
Travel related to caring for and helping household members	0.08	13.1	0.59

	hours per day for total people	percent reporting activity on diary day	hours per day for those reporting activity on diary day
Caring for and helping people in other households	**0.20**	**12.8%**	**1.56**
Caring for and helping children in other households	0.07	5.5	1.23
Caring for and helping adults in other households	0.07	8.0	0.87
Caring for adults in other households	0.01	0.6	2.08
Helping adults in other households	0.06	7.7	0.74
Travel related to caring for, helping people in other households	0.06	10.4	0.61
Working and work-related activities	**3.81**	**47.8**	**7.98**
Working	3.47	45.9	7.56
Work-related activities	0.01	0.4	–
Other income-generating activities	0.03	1.0	2.73
Job search and interviewing	0.02	1.1	2.06
Travel related to work	0.28	39.7	0.71
Educational activities	**0.43**	**7.9**	**5.42**
Attending class	0.26	5.0	5.15
Homework and research	0.14	5.4	2.53
Travel related to education	0.03	4.8	0.55
Organizational, civic, and religious activities	**0.35**	**14.5**	**2.42**
Religious and spiritual activities	0.15	8.9	1.66
Volunteering	0.16	7.1	2.22
Volunteer activities	0.16	7.0	2.24
Administrative and support activities	0.03	2.4	1.26
Social service and care activities (except medical)	0.04	1.8	2.22
Indoor and outdoor maintenance, building, cleanup activities	0.01	0.6	1.51
Participating in performance and cultural activities	0.01	0.5	–
Attending meetings, conferences, and training	0.02	1.0	2.07
Civic obligations and participation	0.00	0.1	
Travel related to organizational, civic, and religious activities	0.04	9.4	0.48
Leisure and sports	**5.11**	**95.8**	**5.33**
Socializing, relaxing, and leisure	4.52	95.1	4.76
Socializing and communicating	0.73	38.4	1.89
Socializing and communicating (except social events)	0.64	36.7	1.73
Attending or hosting social events	0.09	2.9	3.12
Relaxing and leisure	3.70	91.1	4.06
Watching television	2.62	79.5	3.30
Arts and entertainment (other than sports)	0.09	3.5	2.63
Sports, exercise, and recreation	0.35	19.2	1.80
Participating in sports, exercise, and recreation	0.32	18.5	1.71
Attending sporting or recreational events	0.03	1.1	2.86
Travel related to leisure and sports	0.24	35.6	0.67
Telephone calls, mail, and e-mail	**0.19**	**24.4**	**0.76**
Telephone calls (to or from)	0.11	14.4	0.75
Household and personal messages	0.08	13.5	0.56
Household and personal mail and messages	0.02	6.6	0.37
Household and personal e-mail and messages	0.05	8.1	0.63
Travel related to telephone calls	0.00	0.6	0.36
Other activities, not elsewhere classified	**0.20**	**14.1**	**1.40**

Note: Primary activities are those respondents identified as their main activity. Other activities done simultaneously are not included. All major activities include related travel time. "–" means not applicable or sample is too small to make a reliable estimate.
Source: Bureau of Labor Statistics, 2007 American Time Use Survey, Internet site http://www.bls.gov/tus/home.htm

Table 10.2 Men's Time Use and Percent Reporting Activity, 2007

(hours per day spent in primary activities by men aged 15 or older, percent of men reporting activity on diary day, and hours per day spent on activity by men reporting activity on diary day, 2007)

	hours per day for total men	percent reporting activity on diary day	hours per day for those reporting activity on diary day
TOTAL, ALL ACTIVITIES	**24.00**	**100.0%**	–
Personal care activities	**9.14**	**100.0**	**9.14**
Sleeping	8.52	99.9	8.53
Grooming	0.54	75.9	0.71
Health-related self-care	0.05	4.3	1.23
Personal activities	0.01	0.4	–
Travel related to personal care	0.02	2.7	0.65
Eating and drinking	**1.27**	**95.7**	**1.33**
Eating and drinking	1.13	95.7	1.18
Travel related to eating and drinking	0.13	27.3	0.49
Household activities	**1.43**	**65.6**	**2.18**
Housework	0.29	19.7	1.46
Food preparation and cleanup	0.28	37.3	0.75
Lawn and garden care	0.30	12.9	2.32
Household management	0.12	15.2	0.82
Interior maintenance, repair, and decoration	0.12	4.7	2.53
Exterior maintenance, repair, and decoration	0.09	3.7	2.42
Animals and pets	0.09	13.0	0.69
Vehicles	0.07	4.4	1.49
Appliances, tools, and toys	0.03	2.1	1.30
Travel related to household activities	0.05	9.2	0.53
Purchasing goods and services	**0.63**	**40.1**	**1.58**
Consumer goods purchases	0.31	37.2	0.83
Grocery shopping	0.07	10.3	0.69
Professional and personal care services	0.06	6.3	0.88
Financial services and banking	0.01	3.1	0.27
Medical and care services	0.04	2.2	1.63
Personal care services	–	0.6	–
Household services	0.02	2.2	0.85
Household maintenance, repair, decoration, and construction (not done by self)	0.01	0.3	–
Vehicle maintenance and repair services (not done by self)	0.01	1.2	–
Government services	–	0.4	–
Travel related to purchasing goods and services	0.25	38.4	0.65
Caring for and helping household members	**0.33**	**20.3**	**1.62**
Caring for and helping household children	0.25	16.4	1.49
Caring for and helping household children (except activities related to education and health)	0.22	16.1	1.38
Activities related to household children's education	0.02	2.0	0.90
Activities related to household children's health	0.01	0.3	–
Caring for and helping household adults	0.03	4.8	0.60
Caring for household adults	0.02	1.5	–
Helping household adults	0.01	3.5	0.29
Travel related to caring for and helping household members	0.06	9.5	0.58

	hours per day for total men	percent reporting activity on diary day	hours per day for those reporting activity on diary day
Caring for and helping people in other households	**0.17**	**10.7%**	**1.56**
Caring for and helping children in other households	0.04	3.8	1.09
Caring for and helping adults in other households	0.07	7.2	0.95
Caring for adults in other households	0.01	0.3	–
Helping adults in other households	0.06	7.1	0.89
Travel related to caring for, helping people in other households	0.06	8.9	0.64
Working and work-related activities	**4.52**	**54.2**	**8.34**
Working	4.09	51.9	7.87
Work-related activities	0.01	0.5	–
Other income-generating activities	0.03	1.1	–
Job search and interviewing	0.03	1.3	–
Travel related to work	0.36	45.4	0.79
Educational activities	**0.41**	**7.6**	**5.39**
Attending class	0.26	4.9	5.20
Homework and research	0.12	4.6	2.52
Travel related to education	0.02	4.7	0.52
Organizational, civic, and religious activities	**0.28**	**11.8**	**2.42**
Religious and spiritual activities	0.11	6.9	1.64
Volunteering	0.13	6.0	2.21
Volunteer activities	0.13	5.9	2.24
Administrative and support activities	0.02	1.8	1.19
Social service and care activities (except medical)	0.04	1.4	2.61
Indoor and outdoor maintenance, building, cleanup activities	0.01	0.7	–
Participating in performance and cultural activities	0.01	0.3	–
Attending meetings, conferences, and training	0.02	1.1	–
Civic obligations and participation	0.00	0.1	–
Travel related to organizational, civic, and religious activities	0.04	8.1	0.48
Leisure and sports	**5.48**	**96.0**	**5.71**
Socializing, relaxing, and leisure	4.77	95.2	5.01
Socializing and communicating	0.67	35.3	1.89
Socializing and communicating (except social events)	0.59	33.8	1.73
Attending or hosting social events	0.08	2.4	3.33
Relaxing and leisure	4.02	92.0	4.37
Watching television	2.88	81.4	3.54
Arts and entertainment (other than sports)	0.09	3.5	2.57
Sports, exercise, and recreation	0.45	22.2	2.04
Participating in sports, exercise, and recreation	0.42	21.4	1.96
Attending sporting or recreational events	0.03	1.0	3.19
Travel related to leisure and sports	0.26	36.9	0.70
Telephone calls, mail, and e-mail	**0.13**	**19.1**	**0.66**
Telephone calls (to or from)	0.06	9.4	0.65
Household and personal messages	0.06	11.8	0.53
Household and personal mail and messages	0.02	5.4	0.28
Household and personal e-mail and messages	0.05	7.4	0.64
Travel related to telephone calls	0.00	0.5	–
Other activities, not elsewhere classified	**0.20**	**13.0**	**1.57**

Note: Primary activities are those respondents identified as their main activity. Other activities done simultaneously are not included. All major activities include related travel time. "–" means not applicable or sample is too small to make a reliable estimate.
Source: Bureau of Labor Statistics, 2007 American Time Use Survey, Internet site http://www.bls.gov/tus/home.htm

Table 10.3 Women's Time Use and Percent Reporting Activity, 2007

(hours per day spent in primary activities by women aged 15 or older, percent of women reporting activity on diary day, and hours per day spent on activity by women reporting activity on diary day, 2007)

	hours per day for total women	percent reporting activity on diary day	hours per day for those reporting activity on diary day
TOTAL, ALL ACTIVITIES	**24.00**	**100.0%**	–
Personal care activities	**9.51**	**100.0**	**9.51**
Sleeping	8.63	99.9	8.63
Grooming	0.79	82.1	0.96
Health-related self-care	0.08	5.8	1.34
Personal activities	0.01	0.5	–
Travel related to personal care	0.02	2.1	0.74
Eating and drinking	**1.20**	**95.1**	**1.26**
Eating and drinking	1.09	95.1	1.14
Travel related to eating and drinking	0.11	24.2	0.46
Household activities	**2.22**	**82.7**	**2.69**
Housework	0.97	51.7	1.87
Food preparation and cleanup	0.74	63.5	1.17
Lawn and garden care	0.12	7.9	1.51
Household management	0.16	21.0	0.75
Interior maintenance, repair, and decoration	0.05	2.6	1.98
Exterior maintenance, repair, and decoration	0.03	1.8	1.56
Animals and pets	0.10	15.3	0.64
Vehicles	0.01	1.0	0.73
Appliances, tools, and toys	0.01	1.0	0.81
Travel related to household activities	0.05	10.0	0.46
Purchasing goods and services	**0.92**	**48.2**	**1.92**
Consumer goods purchases	0.48	43.8	1.09
Grocery shopping	0.12	15.3	0.77
Professional and personal care services	0.12	10.4	1.13
Financial services and banking	0.01	3.6	0.26
Medical and care services	0.06	4.0	1.54
Personal care services	0.04	2.6	1.45
Household services	0.01	1.8	0.61
Household maintenance, repair, decoration, and construction (not done by self)	0.01	0.4	–
Vehicle maintenance and repair services (not done by self)	–	0.8	–
Government services	0.01	0.5	–
Travel related to purchasing goods and services	0.31	46.5	0.67
Caring for and helping household members	**0.72**	**30.4**	**2.38**
Caring for and helping household children	0.58	26.9	2.17
Caring for and helping household children (except education and health)	0.52	26.6	1.96
Activities related to household children's education	0.04	4.8	0.93
Activities related to household children's health	0.02	1.4	1.20
Caring for and helping household adults	0.04	4.9	0.82
Caring for household adults	0.03	2.1	1.52
Helping household adults	0.01	3.1	0.27
Travel related to caring for and helping household members	0.10	16.5	0.59

	hours per day for total women	percent reporting activity on diary day	hours per day for those reporting activity on diary day
Caring for and helping people in other households	**0.23**	**14.8%**	**1.56**
Caring for and helping children in other households	0.09	7.0	1.30
Caring for and helping adults in other households	0.07	8.8	0.81
Caring for adults in other households	0.02	0.9	2.21
Helping adults in other households	0.05	8.3	0.62
Travel related to caring for and helping people in other households	0.07	11.8	0.58
Working and work-related activities	**3.14**	**41.7**	**7.53**
Working	2.89	40.2	7.18
Work-related activities	–	0.2	–
Other income-generating activities	0.02	0.9	2.64
Job search and interviewing	0.02	0.9	–
Travel related to work	0.21	34.3	0.61
Educational activities	**0.44**	**8.2**	**5.44**
Attending class	0.25	5.0	5.10
Homework and research	0.15	6.0	2.54
Travel related to education	0.03	4.9	0.59
Organizational, civic, and religious activities	**0.41**	**17.1**	**2.42**
Religious and spiritual activities	0.18	10.8	1.67
Volunteering	0.18	8.2	2.23
Volunteer activities	0.18	8.1	2.24
Administrative and support activities	0.04	3.0	1.30
Social service and care activities (except medical)	0.04	2.2	1.98
Indoor and outdoor maintenance, building, and cleanup activities	0.01	0.5	–
Participating in performance and cultural activities	0.01	0.6	–
Attending meetings, conferences, and training	0.02	0.9	2.27
Civic obligations and participation	0.00	0.1	–
Travel related to organizational, civic, and religious activities	0.05	10.7	0.47
Leisure and sports	**4.76**	**95.6**	**4.98**
Socializing, relaxing, and leisure	4.29	94.9	4.52
Socializing and communicating	0.78	41.4	1.89
Socializing and communicating (except social events)	0.69	39.5	1.73
Attending or hosting social events	0.10	3.3	2.97
Relaxing and leisure	3.40	90.2	3.77
Watching television	2.38	77.7	3.07
Arts and entertainment (other than sports)	0.10	3.6	2.68
Sports, exercise, and recreation	0.25	16.4	1.50
Participating in sports, exercise, and recreation	0.22	15.7	1.39
Attending sporting or recreational events	0.03	1.1	2.58
Travel related to leisure and sports	0.22	34.4	0.65
Telephone calls, mail, and e-mail	**0.24**	**29.3**	**0.82**
Telephone calls (to or from)	0.15	19.1	0.80
Household and personal messages	0.09	15.1	0.58
Household and personal mail and messages	0.03	7.8	0.43
Household and personal e-mail and messages	0.05	8.7	0.62
Travel related to telephone calls	0.00	0.7	–
Other activities, not elsewhere classified	**0.19**	**15.1**	**1.26**

Note: Primary activities are those respondents identified as their main activity. Other activities done simultaneously are not included. All major activities include related travel time. "–" means not applicable or sample is too small to make a reliable estimate.
Source: Bureau of Labor Statistics, 2007 American Time Use Survey, Internet site http://www.bls.gov/tus/home.htm

Table 10.4 Time Use by Sex, 2007

(hours per day spent in primary activities by people aged 15 or older by sex, and index of women's time to men's, 2007)

	hours per day		index, women's time to men's
	men	women	
TOTAL, ALL ACTIVITIES	**24.00**	**24.00**	**100**
Personal care activities	**9.14**	**9.51**	**104**
Sleeping	8.52	8.63	101
Grooming	0.54	0.79	146
Health-related self-care	0.05	0.08	160
Personal activities	0.01	0.01	100
Travel related to personal care	0.02	0.02	100
Eating and drinking	**1.27**	**1.20**	**94**
Eating and drinking	1.13	1.09	96
Travel related to eating and drinking	0.13	0.11	85
Household activities	**1.43**	**2.22**	**155**
Housework	0.29	0.97	334
Food preparation and cleanup	0.28	0.74	264
Lawn and garden care	0.30	0.12	40
Household management	0.12	0.16	133
Interior maintenance, repair, and decoration	0.12	0.05	42
Exterior maintenance, repair, and decoration	0.09	0.03	33
Animals and pets	0.09	0.10	111
Vehicles	0.07	0.01	14
Appliances, tools, and toys	0.03	0.01	33
Travel related to household activities	0.05	0.05	100
Purchasing goods and services	**0.63**	**0.92**	**146**
Consumer goods purchases	0.31	0.48	155
Grocery shopping	0.07	0.12	171
Professional and personal care services	0.06	0.12	200
Financial services and banking	0.01	0.01	100
Medical and care services	0.04	0.06	150
Personal care services	–	0.04	–
Household services	0.02	0.01	50
Household maintenance, repair, decoration, and construction (not done by self)	0.01	0.01	100
Vehicle maintenance and repair services (not done by self)	0.01	–	–
Government services	–	0.01	–
Travel related to purchasing goods and services	0.25	0.31	124
Caring for and helping household members	**0.33**	**0.72**	**218**
Caring for and helping household children	0.25	0.58	232
Caring for and helping household children (except activities related to education and health)	0.22	0.52	236
Activities related to household children's education	0.02	0.04	200
Activities related to household children's health	0.01	0.02	200
Caring for and helping household adults	0.03	0.04	133
Caring for household adults	0.02	0.03	150
Helping household adults	0.01	0.01	100
Travel related to caring for and helping household members	0.06	0.10	167

	hours per day		index, women's time to men's
	men	women	
Caring for and helping people in other households	**0.17**	**0.23**	**135**
Caring for and helping children in other households	0.04	0.09	225
Caring for and helping adults in other households	0.07	0.07	100
Caring for adults in other households	0.01	0.02	200
Helping adults in other households	0.06	0.05	83
Travel related to caring for and helping people in other households	0.06	0.07	117
Working and work-related activities	**4.52**	**3.14**	**69**
Working	4.09	2.89	71
Work-related activities	0.01	–	–
Other income-generating activities	0.03	0.02	67
Job search and interviewing	0.03	0.02	67
Travel related to work	0.36	0.21	58
Educational activities	**0.41**	**0.44**	**107**
Attending class	0.26	0.25	96
Homework and research	0.12	0.15	125
Travel related to education	0.02	0.03	150
Organizational, civic, and religious activities	**0.28**	**0.41**	**146**
Religious and spiritual activities	0.11	0.18	164
Volunteering (organizational and civic activities)	0.13	0.18	138
Volunteer activities	0.13	0.18	138
Administrative and support activities	0.02	0.04	200
Social service and care activities (except medical)	0.04	0.04	100
Indoor and outdoor maintenance, building, and cleanup activities	0.01	0.01	100
Participating in performance and cultural activities	0.01	0.01	100
Attending meetings, conferences, and training	0.02	0.02	100
Civic obligations and participation	0.00	0.00	–
Travel related to organizational, civic, and religious activities	0.04	0.05	125
Leisure and sports	**5.48**	**4.76**	**87**
Socializing, relaxing, and leisure	4.77	4.29	90
Socializing and communicating	0.67	0.78	116
Socializing and communicating (except social events)	0.59	0.69	117
Attending or hosting social events	0.08	0.10	125
Relaxing and leisure	4.02	3.40	85
Watching television	2.88	2.38	83
Arts and entertainment (other than sports)	0.09	0.10	111
Sports, exercise, and recreation	0.45	0.25	56
Participating in sports, exercise, and recreation	0.42	0.22	52
Attending sporting or recreational events	0.03	0.03	100
Travel related to leisure and sports	0.26	0.22	85
Telephone calls, mail, and e-mail	**0.13**	**0.24**	**185**
Telephone calls (to or from)	0.06	0.15	250
Household and personal messages	0.06	0.09	150
Household and personal mail and messages	0.02	0.03	150
Household and personal e-mail and messages	0.05	0.05	100
Travel related to telephone calls	0.00	0.00	–
Other activities, not elsewhere classified	**0.20**	**0.19**	**95**

Note: Primary activities are those respondents identified as their main activity. Other activities done simultaneously are not included. All major activities include related travel time. "–" means sample is too small to make a reliable estimate. The index is calculated by dividing women's time by men's time and multiplying by 100.
Source: Bureau of Labor Statistics, 2007 American Time Use Survey, Internet site http://www.bls.gov/tus/home.htm

Women Aged 25 to 44 Have the Least Amount of Leisure Time

Men aged 25 to 44 spend the most time working.

Time use varies sharply by age, with teenagers and older Americans having the most leisure time and the middle aged having the least. People aged 25 to 44 spend much more time than the average person caring for household members and working.

Among men, leisure time is greatest for those aged 75 or older, with 8.28 hours of leisure a day—51 percent more than the average man. Teenage boys aged 15 to 19 have 13 percent more leisure time than average. Men aged 25 to 44 spend 31 to 33 percent more time than the average man at work. Because many men in this age group are raising children, they spend twice as much time as the average man caring for household members. Teenage boys spend the most time on telephone calls, mail, and e-mail.

Women aged 25 to 44 spend more than twice as much time as the average woman caring for household children. They also spend 26 to 28 percent more time than the average woman at work. That explains why women aged 25 to 44 have 20 percent less leisure time than the average woman. Women aged 55 to 64 spend the most time shopping, and teenage girls aged 15 to 19 spend the most time on telephone calls, mail, and e-mail.

■ Women aged 25 to 44 have far less leisure time than their male counterparts—3.83 hours per day versus more than 4.60 hours per day for men in the age group.

Women have less leisure time than men

(average number of hours per day people spend participating in leisure and sports as a primary activity, by sex and selected age group, 2007)

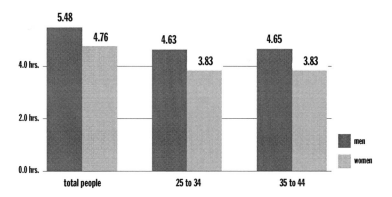

Table 10.5 Time Use by Age, 2007

(average hours per day spent in primary activities by people aged 15 or older by age; index of time use by age to average for total people, by type of activity, 2007)

	total people	15–19	20–24	25–34	35–44	45–54	55–64	65–74	75+
HOURS									
Personal care activities	9.33	10.27	9.54	9.28	9.06	9.03	9.04	9.47	9.85
Eating and drinking	1.24	0.98	1.18	1.19	1.17	1.21	1.30	1.50	1.53
Household activities	1.84	0.68	1.09	1.58	1.89	2.07	2.38	2.42	2.39
Purchasing goods and services	0.78	0.53	0.76	0.74	0.75	0.81	0.96	0.89	0.78
Caring for, helping household members	0.53	0.11	0.39	1.12	1.07	0.37	0.16	0.13	0.08
Caring for and helping people in other households	0.20	0.19	0.19	0.14	0.16	0.18	0.32	0.28	0.19
Working and work-related activities	3.81	1.65	4.50	4.98	4.95	4.97	3.63	1.34	0.26
Educational activities	0.43	3.05	0.88	0.19	0.12	0.08	0.03	0.05	0.00
Organizational, civic, religious activities	0.35	0.30	0.23	0.25	0.29	0.35	0.45	0.52	0.58
Leisure and sports	5.11	5.71	4.90	4.23	4.23	4.59	5.34	6.83	7.79
Telephone calls, mail, and e-mail	0.19	0.36	0.12	0.14	0.12	0.15	0.20	0.27	0.29
Other activities, not elsewhere classified	0.20	0.17	0.22	0.16	0.18	0.18	0.18	0.31	0.26
INDEX OF TIME TO AVERAGE FOR TOTAL PEOPLE									
Personal care activities	100	110	102	99	97	97	97	102	106
Eating and drinking	100	79	95	96	94	98	105	121	123
Household activities	100	37	59	86	103	113	129	132	130
Purchasing goods and services	100	68	97	95	96	104	123	114	100
Caring for, helping household members	100	21	74	211	202	70	30	25	15
Caring for and helping people in other households	100	95	95	70	80	90	160	140	95
Working and work-related activities	100	43	118	131	130	130	95	35	7
Educational activities	100	709	205	44	28	19	7	12	0
Organizational, civic, religious activities	100	86	66	71	83	100	129	149	166
Leisure and sports	100	112	96	83	83	90	105	134	152
Telephone calls, mail, and e-mail	100	189	63	74	63	79	105	142	153
Other activities, not elsewhere classified	100	85	110	80	90	90	90	155	130

Note: Primary activities are those respondents identified as their main activity. Other activities done simultaneously are not included. All major activities include related travel time. The index is calculated by dividing time use of people in each age group by time use of the average person and multiplying by 100.
Source: Bureau of Labor Statistics, American Time Use Survey, Internet site http://www.bls.gov/tus/home.htm; calculations by New Strategist

Table 10.6 Men's Time Use by Age, 2007

(average hours per day spent in primary activities by men aged 15 or older by age; index of time use by age to average for total men, by type of activity, 2007)

	total men	15–19	20–24	25–34	35–44	45–54	55–64	65–74	75+
HOURS									
Personal care activities	9.14	10.00	9.34	9.04	8.85	8.83	8.99	9.16	9.89
Eating and drinking	1.27	0.97	1.15	1.22	1.20	1.29	1.34	1.57	1.68
Household activities	1.43	0.55	1.01	1.25	1.33	1.60	2.01	1.94	1.83
Purchasing goods and services	0.63	0.42	0.66	0.58	0.61	0.67	0.68	0.80	0.73
Caring for, helping household members	0.33	0.06	0.16	0.57	0.67	0.31	0.14	0.08	0.08
Caring for and helping people in other households	0.17	0.18	0.22	0.13	0.18	0.17	0.20	0.15	0.13
Working and work-related activities	4.52	1.79	4.79	6.00	5.93	5.66	4.13	1.93	0.47
Educational activities	0.41	3.09	0.65	0.12	0.08	0.08	0.04	0.03	0.00
Organizational, civic, religious activities	0.28	0.24	0.16	0.22	0.26	0.29	0.39	0.39	0.42
Leisure and sports	5.48	6.20	5.51	4.63	4.65	4.85	5.76	7.41	8.28
Telephone calls, mail, and e-mail	0.13	0.31	0.08	0.09	0.08	0.08	0.14	0.18	0.21
Other activities, not elsewhere classified	0.20	0.18	0.28	0.16	0.17	0.17	0.18	0.37	0.29
INDEX OF TIME TO AVERAGE FOR TOTAL MEN									
Personal care activities	100	109	102	99	97	97	98	100	108
Eating and drinking	100	76	91	96	94	102	106	124	132
Household activities	100	38	71	87	93	112	141	136	128
Purchasing goods and services	100	67	105	92	97	106	108	127	116
Caring for, helping household members	100	18	48	173	203	94	42	24	24
Caring for and helping people in other households	100	106	129	76	106	100	118	88	76
Working and work-related activities	100	40	106	133	131	125	91	43	10
Educational activities	100	754	159	29	20	20	10	7	0
Organizational, civic, religious activities	100	86	57	79	93	104	139	139	150
Leisure and sports	100	113	101	84	85	89	105	135	151
Telephone calls, mail, and e-mail	100	238	62	69	62	62	108	138	162
Other activities, not elsewhere classified	100	90	140	80	85	85	90	185	145

Note: Primary activities are those respondents identified as their main activity. Other activities done simultaneously are not included. All major activities include related travel time. The index is calculated by dividing time use of men in each age group by time use of the average man and multiplying by 100.
Source: Bureau of Labor Statistics, American Time Use Survey, Internet site http://www.bls.gov/tus/home.htm; calculations by New Strategist

Table 10.7 Women's Time Use by Age, 2007

(average hours per day spent in primary activities by women aged 15 or older by age; index of time use by age to average for total women, by type of activity, 2007)

	total women	15–19	20–24	25–34	35–44	45–54	55–64	65–74	75+
HOURS									
Personal care activities	9.51	10.55	9.75	9.52	9.26	9.23	9.09	9.73	9.83
Eating and drinking	1.20	1.00	1.20	1.16	1.14	1.13	1.26	1.45	1.43
Household activities	2.22	0.81	1.19	1.92	2.43	2.52	2.74	2.82	2.76
Purchasing goods and services	0.92	0.64	0.86	0.90	0.89	0.95	1.21	0.97	0.81
Caring for, helping household members	0.72	0.15	0.62	1.68	1.46	0.43	0.18	0.17	0.08
Caring for and helping people in other households	0.23	0.20	0.16	0.16	0.14	0.19	0.44	0.38	0.23
Working and work-related activities	3.14	1.50	4.21	3.95	4.01	4.30	3.17	0.84	0.13
Educational activities	0.44	3.01	1.10	0.27	0.15	0.08	0.02	0.06	0.00
Organizational, civic, religious activities	0.41	0.36	0.29	0.27	0.33	0.41	0.50	0.63	0.68
Leisure and sports	4.76	5.20	4.28	3.83	3.83	4.34	4.94	6.34	7.48
Telephone calls, mail, and e-mail	0.24	0.41	0.17	0.18	0.16	0.22	0.26	0.34	0.34
Other activities, not elsewhere classified	0.19	0.17	0.16	0.15	0.19	0.20	0.18	0.25	0.25
INDEX OF TIME TO AVERAGE FOR TOTAL WOMEN									
Personal care activities	100	111	103	100	97	97	96	102	103
Eating and drinking	100	83	100	97	95	94	105	121	119
Household activities	100	36	54	86	109	114	123	127	124
Purchasing goods and services	100	70	93	98	97	103	132	105	88
Caring for, helping household members	100	21	86	233	203	60	25	24	11
Caring for and helping people in other households	100	87	70	70	61	83	191	165	100
Working and work-related activities	100	48	134	126	128	137	101	27	4
Educational activities	100	684	250	61	34	18	5	14	0
Organizational, civic, religious activities	100	88	71	66	80	100	122	154	166
Leisure and sports	100	109	90	80	80	91	104	133	157
Telephone calls, mail, and e-mail	100	171	71	75	67	92	108	142	142
Other activities, not elsewhere classified	100	89	84	79	100	105	95	132	132

Note: Primary activities are those respondents identified as their main activity. Other activities done simultaneously are not included. All major activities include related travel time. The index is calculated by dividing time use of women in each age group by time use of the average woman and multiplying by 100.
Source: Bureau of Labor Statistics, American Time Use Survey, Internet site http://www.bls.gov/tus/home.htm; calculations by New Strategist

Hispanic Men Spend the Most Time Working

Hispanic women spend the most time caring for household members.

Time use varies by race and Hispanic origin, although not as much as it does by age. Hispanic men spend more time at work than either white or black men. On an average day, Hispanic men work for 5.18 hours—15 percent more than the average man. Black men spend more time than the average man on organizational, civic, and religious activities. They also spend more time caring for people in other households. On an average day, white men spend considerably more time than either blacks or Hispanics eating and drinking.

Among women, blacks spend more time at work than Hispanic or white women. They also spend more time participating in organizational, civic, and religious activities. Hispanic women spend 17 percent more time than the average woman in household activities (housework, food preparation, etc.) and 24 percent more time caring for household members. As is true among men, white women spend more time than black or Hispanic women eating and drinking.

■ The Hispanic population is considerably younger than the white population and therefore is more likely to be raising children. This explains why Hispanic women spend more time than white women caring for household members.

Time spent at work varies by race and Hispanic origin

(average number of hours per day people spend working as a primary activity, by sex, race, and Hispanic origin, 2007)

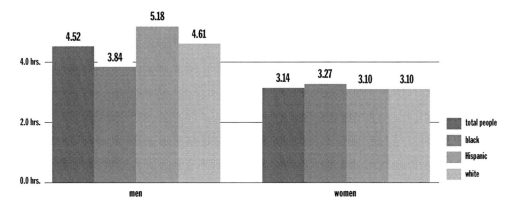

Table 10.8 Time Use of Men by Race and Hispanic Origin, 2007

(average hours per day spent in primary activities by men aged 15 or older by race and Hispanic origin; index of time use by race/Hispanic origin to average for total men, by type of activity, 2007)

	total men	black	Hispanic	white
HOURS				
Personal care activities	9.14	9.34	9.46	9.07
Eating and drinking	1.27	0.84	1.13	1.33
Household activities	1.43	1.07	1.21	1.50
Purchasing goods and services	0.63	0.59	0.57	0.65
Caring for and helping household members	0.33	0.25	0.30	0.33
Caring for and helping people in other households	0.17	0.22	0.10	0.17
Working and work-related activities	4.52	3.84	5.18	4.61
Educational activities	0.41	0.37	0.58	0.38
Organizational, civic, and religious activities	0.28	0.45	0.20	0.26
Leisure and sports	5.48	6.57	5.04	5.37
Telephone calls, mail, and e-mail	0.13	0.22	0.10	0.11
Other activities, not elsewhere classified	0.20	0.22	0.12	0.20
INDEX OF TIME TO AVERAGE FOR TOTAL MEN				
Personal care activities	100	102	104	99
Eating and drinking	100	66	89	105
Household activities	100	75	85	105
Purchasing goods and services	100	94	90	103
Caring for and helping household members	100	76	91	100
Caring for and helping people in other households	100	129	59	100
Working and work-related activities	100	85	115	102
Educational activities	100	90	141	93
Organizational, civic, and religious activities	100	161	71	93
Leisure and sports	100	120	92	98
Telephone calls, mail, and e-mail	100	169	77	85
Other activities, not elsewhere classified	100	110	60	100

Note: Primary activities are those respondents identified as their main activity. Other activities done simultaneously are not included. All major activities include related travel time. The index is calculated by dividing time use of men in each race/Hispanic origin group by time use of the average man and multiplying by 100.
Source: Bureau of Labor Statistics, American Time Use Survey, Internet site http://www.bls.gov/tus/home.htm; calculations by New Strategist

Table 10.9 Time Use of Women by Race and Hispanic Origin, 2007

(average hours per day spent in primary activities by women aged 15 or older by race and Hispanic origin; index of time use by race/Hispanic origin to average for total women, by type of activity, 2007)

	total women	black	Hispanic	white
HOURS				
Personal care activities	9.51	10.04	9.85	9.42
Eating and drinking	1.20	0.90	1.14	1.24
Household activities	2.22	1.54	2.59	2.34
Purchasing goods and services	0.92	0.94	0.84	0.92
Caring for and helping household members	0.72	0.67	0.89	0.71
Caring for and helping people in other households	0.23	0.22	0.12	0.23
Working and work-related activities	3.14	3.27	3.10	3.10
Educational activities	0.44	0.46	0.47	0.42
Organizational, civic, and religious activities	0.41	0.48	0.43	0.40
Leisure and sports	4.76	5.05	4.25	4.77
Telephone calls, mail, and e-mail	0.24	0.27	0.13	0.24
Other activities, not elsewhere classified	0.19	0.17	0.18	0.19
INDEX OF TIME TO AVERAGE FOR TOTAL WOMEN				
Personal care activities	100	106	104	99
Eating and drinking	100	75	95	103
Household activities	100	69	117	105
Purchasing goods and services	100	102	91	100
Caring for and helping household members	100	93	124	99
Caring for and helping people in other households	100	96	52	100
Working and work-related activities	100	104	99	99
Educational activities	100	105	107	95
Organizational, civic, and religious activities	100	117	105	98
Leisure and sports	100	106	89	100
Telephone calls, mail, and e-mail	100	113	54	100
Other activities, not elsewhere classified	100	89	95	100

Note: Primary activities are those respondents identified as their main activity. Other activities done simultaneously are not included. All major activities include related travel time. The index is calculated by dividing time use of women in each race/Hispanic origin group by time use of the average woman and multiplying by 100.
Source: Bureau of Labor Statistics, American Time Use Survey, Internet site http://www.bls.gov/tus/home.htm; calculations by New Strategist

Time Use Differs on Weekends and Weekdays

Not surprisingly, leisure time is much greater on weekends.

Let's start with sleep. The average person gets much more sleep on weekends than on weekdays. On a weekday night, the average person gets 8.29 hours of sleep. On a weekend night, the average person gets nearly a full hour of sleep more—9.24 hours.

Many activities expand on weekends. The time people spend watching television increases from 2.43 hours on the average weekday to 3.07 hours on the average weekend day. The average person devotes five times as much time to attending or hosting social events on weekends versus weekdays. On an average weekday, only 6 percent of adults participate in religious activities. This proportion rises to 16 percent on the average weekend day. Even among participants, the time spent on certain activities on the weekend exceeds the time they spend doing the same activity on weekdays. Those attending or hosting a social event on a weekday, for example, spend an average of 2.32 hours at the activity. Those involved with a social event on a weekend spend a larger 3.71 hours participating in the activity.

■ Not surprisingly, time spent at work is much less on weekends than on weekdays. The average person spends 4.81 hours at work on the average weekday and only 1.47 hours at work on the average weekend day.

People spend more time watching TV on weekends

(number of hours per day spent watching television as a primary activity, by day of the week, 2007)

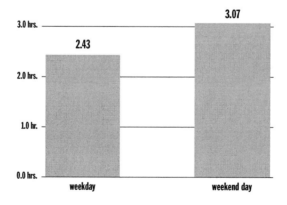

Table 10.10 Average Time Use on Weekdays and Weekends, 2007

(average hours per day spent in primary activities by people aged 15 or older by day of week, and index of weekends to weekdays, 2007

	time spent by average person		index of weekends to weekdays
	weekdays	weekends and holidays	
TOTAL, ALL ACTIVITIES	**24.00**	**24.00**	**100**
Personal care activities	**9.06**	**9.97**	**110**
Sleeping	8.29	9.24	111
Grooming	0.69	0.63	91
Health-related self-care	0.06	0.07	117
Personal activities	0.01	0.01	100
Travel related to personal care	0.01	0.02	200
Eating and drinking	**1.19**	**1.33**	**112**
Eating and drinking	1.09	1.16	106
Travel related to eating and drinking	0.10	0.17	170
Household activities	**1.69**	**2.19**	**130**
Housework	0.59	0.76	129
Food preparation and cleanup	0.49	0.57	116
Lawn and garden care	0.18	0.28	156
Household management	0.13	0.16	123
Interior maintenance, repair, and decoration	0.07	0.11	157
Exterior maintenance, repair, and decoration	0.05	0.08	160
Animals and pets	0.09	0.10	111
Vehicles	0.03	0.04	133
Appliances, tools, and toys	0.01	0.03	300
Travel related to household activities	0.04	0.06	150
Purchasing goods and services	**0.74**	**0.88**	**119**
Consumer goods purchases	0.34	0.52	153
Grocery shopping	0.08	0.13	163
Professional and personal care services	0.11	0.04	36
Financial services and banking	0.01	0.00	0
Medical and care services	0.07	0.01	14
Personal care services	0.02	0.02	100
Household services	0.02	0.01	50
Household maintenance, repair, decoration, and construction (not done by self)	0.01	0.00	0
Vehicle maintenance and repair services (not done by self)	0.01	0.00	0
Government services	0.01	0.00	0
Travel related to purchasing goods and services	0.27	0.31	115
Caring for and helping household members	**0.57**	**0.45**	**79**
Caring for and helping household children	0.43	0.39	91
Caring for and helping household children (except activities related to education and health)	0.38	0.37	97
Activities related to household children's education	0.04	0.01	25
Activities related to household children's health	0.01	0.01	100
Caring for and helping household adults	0.04	0.02	50
Caring for household adults	0.03	0.01	33
Helping household adults	0.01	0.01	100
Travel related to caring for and helping household members	0.09	0.04	44

	time spent by average person		index of weekends to weekdays
	weekdays	weekends and holidays	
Caring for and helping people in other households	**0.18**	**0.24**	**133**
Caring for and helping children in other households	0.07	0.07	100
Caring for and helping adults in other households	0.06	0.10	167
Caring for adults in other households	0.01	0.01	100
Helping adults in other households	0.04	0.08	200
Travel related to caring for, helping people in other households	0.06	0.07	117
Working and work-related activities	**4.81**	**1.47**	**31**
Working	4.39	1.31	30
Work-related activities	0.01	0.00	0
Other income-generating activities	0.02	0.05	250
Job search and interviewing	0.03	0.01	33
Travel related to work	0.36	0.10	28
Educational activities	**0.53**	**0.18**	**34**
Attending class	0.36	0.02	6
Homework and research	0.13	0.15	115
Travel related to education	0.04	0.01	25
Organizational, civic, and religious activities	**0.26**	**0.55**	**212**
Religious and spiritual activities	0.07	0.32	457
Volunteering	0.16	0.16	100
Volunteer activities	0.15	0.16	107
Administrative and support activities	0.03	0.03	100
Social service and care activities (except medical)	0.04	0.04	100
Indoor and outdoor maintenance, building, cleanup activities	0.01	0.01	100
Participating in performance and cultural activities	0.01	0.01	100
Attending meetings, conferences, and training	0.02	0.02	100
Civic obligations and participation	0.00	0.00	100
Travel related to organizational, civic, and religious activities	0.03	0.07	233
Leisure and sports	**4.57**	**6.37**	**139**
Socializing, relaxing, and leisure	4.08	5.56	136
Socializing and communicating	0.55	1.13	205
Socializing and communicating (except social events)	0.51	0.92	180
Attending or hosting social events	0.04	0.20	500
Relaxing and leisure	3.47	4.25	122
Watching television	2.43	3.07	126
Arts and entertainment (other than sports)	0.06	0.18	300
Sports, exercise, and recreation	0.30	0.47	157
Participating in sports, exercise, and recreation	0.28	0.41	146
Attending sporting or recreational events	0.02	0.05	250
Travel related to leisure and sports	0.20	0.34	170
Telephone calls, mail, and e-mail	**0.19**	**0.16**	**84**
Telephone calls (to or from)	0.11	0.10	91
Household and personal messages	0.08	0.06	75
Household and personal mail and messages	0.03	0.02	67
Household and personal e-mail and messages	0.05	0.04	80
Travel related to telephone calls	0.00	0.00	100
Other activities, not elsewhere classified	**0.19**	**0.20**	**105**

Note: Primary activities are those respondents identified as their main activity. Other activities done simultaneously are not included. All major activities include related travel time. The index is calculated by dividing time use on weekends by time use on weekdays and multiplying by 100.
Source: Bureau of Labor Statistics, 2007 American Time Use Survey, Internet site http://www.bls.gov/tus/home.htm

Table 10.11 Percent Participating in Activity on Weekdays and Weekends, 2007

(percent of people aged 15 or older participating in primary activity by day of week, and index of weekends to weekdays, 2007)

	percent participating		index of
	weekdays	**weekends and holidays**	**weekends to weekdays**
TOTAL, ALL ACTIVITIES	100.0%	100.0%	100
Personal care activities	100.0	100.0	100
Sleeping	99.9	100.0	100
Grooming	82.4	71.3	87
Health-related self-care	5.3	4.6	87
Personal activities	0.5	0.5	100
Travel related to personal care	2.3	2.5	109
Eating and drinking	**95.6**	**94.9**	**99**
Eating and drinking	95.6	94.9	99
Travel related to eating and drinking	24.7	28.1	114
Household activities	**74.1**	**75.0**	**101**
Housework	35.1	38.8	111
Food preparation and cleanup	52.0	47.9	92
Lawn and garden care	9.5	12.4	131
Household management	18.0	18.6	103
Interior maintenance, repair, and decoration	3.3	4.3	130
Exterior maintenance, repair, and decoration	2.4	3.6	150
Animals and pets	14.5	13.4	92
Vehicles	2.5	2.9	116
Appliances, tools, and toys	1.5	1.8	120
Travel related to household activities	9.4	10.2	109
Purchasing goods and services	**43.7**	**45.7**	**105**
Consumer goods purchases	39.1	44.1	113
Grocery shopping	12.1	14.8	122
Professional and personal care services	10.1	4.4	44
Financial services and banking	4.1	1.8	44
Medical and care services	4.2	0.6	14
Personal care services	1.8	1.3	72
Household services	2.2	1.4	64
Household maintenance, repair, decoration, and construction (not done by self)	0.4	0.3	75
Vehicle maintenance and repair services (not done by self)	1.1	0.6	55
Government services	0.6	0.1	17
Travel related to purchasing goods and services	41.8	44.5	106
Caring for and helping household members	**27.0**	**22.0**	**81**
Caring for and helping household children	23.0	19.0	83
Caring for and helping household children (except activities related to education and health)	22.7	18.7	82
Activities related to household children's education	4.5	1.0	22
Activities related to household children's health	1.0	0.5	50
Caring for and helping household adults	5.3	4.0	75
Caring for household adults	2.0	1.4	70
Helping household adults	3.6	2.6	72
Travel related to caring for and helping household members	15.6	7.4	47

	percent participating		index of weekends to weekdays
	weekdays	weekends and holidays	
Caring for and helping people in other households	**12.2%**	**14.1%**	**116**
Caring for and helping children in other households	5.6	5.1	91
Caring for and helping adults in other households	7.3	9.7	133
Caring for adults in other households	0.6	0.8	133
Helping adults in other households	7.1	9.1	128
Travel related to caring for, helping people in other households	10.0	11.3	113
Working and work-related activities	**57.4**	**25.1**	**44**
Working	55.5	23.3	42
Work-related activities	0.4	0.2	50
Other income-generating activities	0.8	1.5	188
Job search and interviewing	1.4	0.5	36
Travel related to work	49.8	16.1	32
Educational activities	**8.8**	**5.6**	**64**
Attending class	6.9	0.5	7
Homework and research	5.5	5.1	93
Travel related to education	6.4	0.9	14
Organizational, civic, and religious activities	**12.1**	**20.1**	**166**
Religious and spiritual activities	5.9	15.9	269
Volunteering	7.2	6.9	96
Volunteer activities	7.1	6.9	97
Administrative and support activities	2.6	2.0	77
Social service and care activities (except medical)	1.7	1.9	112
Indoor and outdoor maintenance, building, cleanup activities	0.6	0.6	100
Participating in performance and cultural activities	0.4	0.5	125
Attending meetings, conferences, and training	1.1	0.9	82
Civic obligations and participation	0.2	0.0	100
Travel related to organizational, civic, and religious activities	6.6	16.1	244
Leisure and sports	**95.4**	**96.8**	**101**
Socializing, relaxing, and leisure	94.6	96.0	101
Socializing and communicating	35.9	44.3	123
Socializing and communicating (except social events)	34.9	41.0	117
Attending or hosting social events	1.8	5.5	306
Relaxing and leisure	91.2	90.7	99
Watching television	79.3	79.7	101
Arts and entertainment (other than sports)	2.4	6.2	258
Sports, exercise, and recreation	19.0	19.8	104
Participating in sports, exercise, and recreation	18.4	18.7	102
Attending sporting or recreational events	0.8	1.7	213
Travel related to leisure and sports	32.5	42.9	132
Telephone calls, mail, and e-mail	**26.1**	**20.3**	**78**
Telephone calls (to or from)	15.0	12.9	86
Household and personal messages	15.1	9.9	66
Household and personal mail and messages	7.8	3.9	50
Household and personal e-mail and messages	8.8	6.5	74
Travel related to telephone calls	0.6	0.6	100
Other activities, not elsewhere classified	**14.3**	**13.7**	**96**

Note: Primary activities are those respondents identified as their main activity. Other activities done simultaneously are not included. All major activities include related travel time. The index is calculated by dividing percent participating on weekends by percent participating on weekdays and multiplying by 100.
Source: Bureau of Labor Statistics, 2007 American Time Use Survey, Internet site http://www.bls.gov/tus/home.htm

Table 10.12 Average Time Spent by Participants in Activity on Weekdays and Weekends, 2007

(hours per day spent in primary activities by participants aged 15 or older by day of week, and index of weekends to weekdays, 2007

	time spent by participants		index of
	weekdays	weekends and holidays	weekends to weekdays
TOTAL, ALL ACTIVITIES	**24.00**	**24.00**	**100**
Personal care activities	**9.06**	**9.97**	**110**
Sleeping	8.29	9.25	112
Grooming	0.83	0.88	106
Health-related self-care	1.22	1.48	121
Personal activities	–	–	–
Travel related to personal care	0.56	0.96	171
Eating and drinking	**1.25**	**1.40**	**112**
Eating and drinking	1.14	1.22	107
Travel related to eating and drinking	0.41	0.61	149
Household activities	**2.28**	**2.92**	**128**
Housework	1.67	1.96	117
Food preparation and cleanup	0.95	1.20	126
Lawn and garden care	1.85	2.26	122
Household management	0.73	0.88	121
Interior maintenance, repair, and decoration	2.23	2.50	112
Exterior maintenance, repair, and decoration	2.07	2.19	106
Animals and pets	0.62	0.78	126
Vehicles	1.35	1.33	99
Appliances, tools, and toys	0.96	1.47	153
Travel related to household activities	0.44	0.61	139
Purchasing goods and services	**1.70**	**1.92**	**113**
Consumer goods purchases	0.87	1.18	136
Grocery shopping	0.67	0.87	130
Professional and personal care services	1.05	0.97	92
Financial services and banking	0.27	0.23	85
Medical and care services	1.55	–	–
Personal care services	1.34	1.22	91
Household services	0.76	0.64	84
Household maintenance, repair, decoration, and construction (not done by self)	–	–	–
Vehicle maintenance and repair services (not done by self)	–	–	–
Government services	–	–	–
Travel related to purchasing goods and services	0.65	0.69	106
Caring for and helping household members	**2.09**	**2.06**	**99**
Caring for and helping household children	1.88	2.05	109
Caring for and helping household children (except activities related to education and health)	1.67	1.97	118
Activities related to household children's education	0.92	1.02	111
Activities related to household children's health	1.18	–	–
Caring for and helping household adults	0.77	0.54	70
Caring for household adults	1.55	0.99	64
Helping household adults	0.28	0.29	104
Travel related to caring for and helping household members	0.59	0.59	100

	time spent by participants		index of weekends to weekdays
	weekdays	weekends and holidays	
Caring for and helping people in other households	**1.50**	**1.69**	**113**
Caring for and helping children in other households	1.19	1.32	111
Caring for and helping adults in other households	0.78	1.02	131
Caring for adults in other households	–	–	–
Helping adults in other households	0.63	0.93	148
Travel related to caring for, helping people in other households	0.59	0.63	107
Working and work-related activities	**8.38**	**5.84**	**70**
Working	7.91	5.60	71
Work-related activities	–	–	–
Other income-generating activities	–	3.06	–
Job search and interviewing	2.05	–	–
Travel related to work	0.72	0.63	88
Educational activities	**6.01**	**3.23**	**54**
Attending class	5.18	–	–
Homework and research	2.35	3.01	128
Travel related to education	0.55	–	–
Organizational, civic, and religious activities	**2.18**	**2.76**	**127**
Religious and spiritual activities	1.25	2.01	161
Volunteering	2.16	2.38	110
Volunteer activities	2.18	2.38	109
Administrative and support activities	1.26	1.25	99
Social service and care activities (except medical)	2.27	2.12	93
Indoor and outdoor maintenance, building, cleanup activities	–	–	–
Participating in performance and cultural activities	–	–	–
Attending meetings, conferences, and training	2.09	–	–
Civic obligations and participation	–	–	–
Travel related to organizational, civic, and religious activities	0.51	0.44	86
Leisure and sports	**4.79**	**6.58**	**137**
Socializing, relaxing, and leisure	4.31	5.79	134
Socializing and communicating	1.54	2.55	166
Socializing and communicating (except social events)	1.47	2.26	154
Attending or hosting social events	2.32	3.71	160
Relaxing and leisure	3.80	4.69	123
Watching television	3.07	3.85	125
Arts and entertainment (other than sports)	2.38	2.86	120
Sports, exercise, and recreation	1.56	2.36	151
Participating in sports, exercise, and recreation	1.50	2.20	147
Attending sporting or recreational events	–	3.22	–
Travel related to leisure and sports	0.60	0.80	133
Telephone calls, mail, and e-mail	**0.74**	**0.81**	**109**
Telephone calls (to or from)	0.73	0.79	108
Household and personal messages	0.55	0.60	109
Household and personal mail and messages	0.36	0.39	108
Household and personal e-mail and messages	0.62	0.68	110
Travel related to telephone calls	–	–	100
Other activities, not elsewhere classified	**1.36**	**1.49**	**110**

Note: Primary activities are those respondents identified as their main activity. Other activities done simultaneously are not included. All major activities include related travel time. The index is calculated by dividing time use on weekends by time use on weekdays and multiplying by 100. "–" means sample is too small to make a reliable estimate.
Source: Bureau of Labor Statistics, 2007 American Time Use Survey, Internet site http://www.bls.gov/tus/home.htm

11

Wealth Trends

■ Net worth has declined

Median net worth peaked in 2007 at $120,300, but fell in 2008. The Federal Reserve Board estimates that median household net worth was just $99,000 in October 2008.

■ Financial assets climbed, then fell.

The median value of the financial assets owned by the average household increased by a substantial 14 percent between 2004 and 2007, after adjusting for inflation. The stock market plunge of 2008 greatly reduced their value, however.

■ Home values have declined.

The median value of the average owned home stood at $200,000 in 2007. The Federal Reserve Board estimates that this figure had fallen to $181,600 by October 2008.

■ Most households are in debt.

Seventy-seven percent of households were in debt in 2007, owing a median of $67,300—most of it in the form of mortgages.

■ Most workers have access to a retirement plan at work.

Nearly two out of three employees consider a defined-contribution plan (such as a 401k) to be their primary way of saving for retirement. These plans were hurt by the stock market decline of 2008.

■ The expected age of retirement is climbing.

Only 13 percent of workers are "very confident" in their ability to afford a comfortable retirement—a record low, according to the 2009 Retirement Confidence Survey.

Net Worth Climbed Sharply during the Housing Bubble

Net worth is what remains when a household's debts are subtracted from its assets. During this decade's housing bubble, housing values rose faster than mortgage debt. Consequently, net worth grew substantially—up 18 percent between 2004 and 2007 after adjusting for inflation.

Not surprisingly, net worth rose the most in the South and West, where housing prices grew the fastest. Median net worth climbed 37 percent in the South and 50 percent in the West between 2004 and 2007. The gains did not last, however. The Federal Reserve Board estimates that by October 2008, median household net worth had fallen to $99,000—3 percent less than in 2004.

Net worth typically rises with age as people pay off their debts. In 2007, median net worth peaked in the 55-to-64 age group at $253,700. Although this age group had the highest net worth, it experienced a 7 percent decline in net worth between 2004 and 2007 as debt climbed more than assets.

Median net worth has fallen since reaching a peak in 2007

(median household net worth, 2004 to 2008; in 2007 dollars)

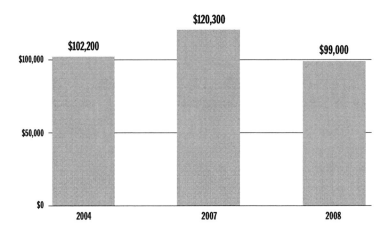

Table 11.1 Net Worth of Households, 2004 and 2007

(median net worth of households by selected characteristics, 2004 and 2007; percent change, 2004–07; in 2007 dollars)

	2007	2004	percent change
TOTAL HOUSEHOLDS	$120,300	$102,200	17.7%
Household income percentile			
Below 20 percent	8,100	8,200	−1.2
20 to 39.9 percent	37,900	37,100	2.2
40 to 59.9 percent	88,100	79,000	11.5
60 to 79.9 percent	204,900	175,700	16.6
80 to 89.9 percent	356,200	344,100	3.5
90 percent or higher	1,119,000	1,015,000	10.2
Age of householder			
Under age 35	11,800	15,600	−24.4
Aged 35 to 44	86,600	76,200	13.6
Aged 45 to 54	182,500	158,900	14.9
Aged 55 to 64	253,700	273,100	−7.1
Aged 65 to 74	239,400	208,800	14.7
Aged 75 or older	213,500	179,100	19.2
Education of householder			
No high school diploma	33,200	22,600	46.9
High school diploma	80,300	75,500	6.4
Some college	84,700	76,100	11.3
College degree	280,800	248,400	13.0
Race and Hispanic origin of householder			
Non-Hispanic white	170,400	154,500	10.3
Nonwhite or Hispanic	27,800	27,200	2.2
Region			
Northeast	159,400	177,600	−10.2
Midwest	107,500	126,300	−14.9
South	96,000	70,100	36.9
West	156,200	104,100	50.0
Housing status			
Owner	234,200	202,600	15.6
Renter or other	5,100	4,400	15.9

Source: Federal Reserve Board, Changes in U.S. Family Finances from 2004 to 2007: Evidence from the Survey of Consumer Finances, Federal Reserve Bulletin, February 2009, Internet site http://www.federalreserve.gov/pubs/oss/oss2/2007/ scf2007home.html; calculations by New Strategist

Two-Thirds of Household Assets Are Nonfinancial

The primary residence accounts for the largest share of household assets by far.

For most households, their home is their biggest asset. The primary residence accounted for 31.8 percent of the average household's assets in 2007, down slightly from the 32.3 percent of 2004. Business equity ranks second (19.6 percent) and retirement accounts are third (11.7 percent). Seventy-five percent of the debt owed by the average household is for the mortgage on their primary residence.

The effects of the housing bubble can be seen in the statistics. Among types of debt, money owed on other residential property—which includes investment real estate, rental units, and vacation homes—increased more than any other category. Between 2004 and 2007, this type of debt climbed from 8.5 to 10.1 percent of all debt, reflecting the rush of money into real estate speculation.

■ Some households that took on real estate debt during the housing bubble now owe more than the property is worth.

Homes, businesses, and retirement accounts are the three most important assets

(top five assets as a percentage of total household assets, 2007)

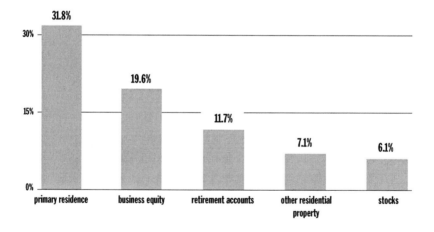

Table 11.2 Distribution of Household Assets and Debts by Type, 2004 and 2007

(percent distribution of household assets and debts by type, 2004 and 2007; percentage point change, 2004–07; ranked by relative importance of asset or debt)

	2007	2004	percentage point change
TOTAL ASSETS	100.0%	100.0%	–
Financial assets, total	**33.9**	**35.7**	**−1.8**
Retirement accounts	11.7	11.4	0.3
Stocks	6.1	6.3	−0.2
Pooled investment funds	5.4	5.2	0.2
Transaction accounts	3.7	4.7	−1.0
Other managed assets	2.2	2.9	−0.7
Bonds	1.4	1.9	−0.5
Certificates of deposit	1.4	1.3	0.1
Cash value of life insurance	1.1	1.1	0.0
Savings bonds	0.1	0.2	−0.1
Other	0.7	0.7	0.0
Nonfinancial assets, total	**66.1**	**64.3**	**1.8**
Primary residence	31.8	32.3	−0.5
Business equity	19.6	16.7	2.9
Other residential real estate	7.1	6.4	0.7
Equity in nonresidential property	3.8	4.7	−0.9
Vehicles	2.9	3.3	−0.4
Other	0.9	1.0	−0.1
TOTAL DEBT	**100.0**	**100.0**	–
Home-secured debt	74.7	75.2	−0.5
Installment loans	10.2	11.0	−0.8
Other residential property	10.1	8.5	1.6
Credit card balances	3.5	3.0	0.5
Other lines of credit	0.4	0.7	−0.3
Other	1.1	1.6	−0.5

Note: "–" means not applicable.
Source: Federal Reserve Board, Changes in U.S. Family Finances from 2004 to 2007: Evidence from the Survey of Consumer Finances, Federal Reserve Bulletin, February 2009, Internet site http://www.federalreserve.gov/pubs/oss/oss2/2007/scf2007home.html; calculations by New Strategist

Financial Asset Values Rose between 2004 and 2007

For most households, the gains made between 2004 and 2007 were erased by the decline in the stock market in 2008.

Most households own financial assets, which range from transaction accounts (checking and saving) to stocks, mutual funds, retirement accounts, and life insurance. The median value of the financial assets owned by the average household stood at $28,800 in 2007, up 14 percent since 2004 after adjusting for inflation. The stock market plunge of 2008 greatly reduced the value of the financial assets owned by the average household, however.

Transaction accounts, the most commonly owned financial asset, are held by 92 percent of households. Their median value was just $4,000 in 2007. Retirement accounts are the second most commonly owned financial asset, with 53 percent of households having one. Most retirement accounts are not large, however, with an overall median value of just $45,000 in 2007. This figure has most certainly fallen since the survey was taken.

Eighteen percent of households owned stock directly in 2007 (outside of a retirement account), and 11 percent owned pooled investment funds or mutual funds directly. Among the stockholders, the median value of their stock was just $17,000. For those with pooled investment funds, the median value was a larger $56,000.

■ Financial assets peaked in the 55-to-64 age group in 2007, at $72,400.

Retirement account balances were modest in 2007 and their value has declined since then

(median value of retirement accounts owned by households, by age of householder, 2007)

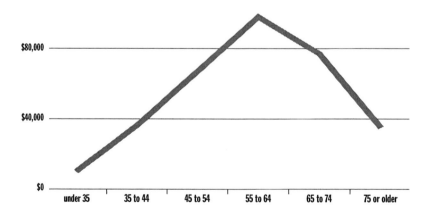

Table 11.3 Ownership and Value of Financial Assets, 2004 and 2007

(percentage of households owning any financial asset and median value of financial assets for owners, by selected characteristics, 2004 and 2007; percentage point change in ownership and percent change in value, 2004–07; in 2007 dollars)

	percent owning any financial asset			median value of financial assets		
	2007	2004	percentage point change	2007	2004	percent change
TOTAL HOUSEHOLDS	**93.9%**	**93.8%**	**0.1**	**$28,800**	**$25,300**	**13.8%**
Household income percentile						
Below 20 percent	79.1	80.1	−1.0	1,700	1,500	13.3
20 to 39.9 percent	93.2	91.5	1.7	7,000	5,300	32.1
40 to 59.9 percent	97.2	98.5	−1.3	18,600	17,000	9.4
60 to 79.9 percent	99.7	99.1	0.6	58,300	53,200	9.6
80 to 89.9 percent	100.0	99.8	0.2	129,900	119,100	9.1
90 percent or higher	100.0	100.0	0.0	404,500	401,200	0.8
Age of householder						
Under age 35	89.2	90.1	−0.9	6,800	5,700	19.3
Aged 35 to 44	93.1	93.6	−0.5	25,800	20,900	23.4
Aged 45 to 54	93.3	93.6	−0.3	54,000	42,400	27.4
Aged 55 to 64	97.8	95.2	2.6	72,400	85,700	−15.5
Aged 65 to 74	96.1	96.5	−0.4	68,100	39,600	72.0
Aged 75 or older	97.4	97.6	−0.2	41,500	42,600	−2.6
Education of householder						
No high school diploma	79.7	77.4	2.3	3,000	2,400	25.0
High school diploma	93.3	92.9	0.4	14,200	13,200	7.6
Some college	95.5	96.6	−1.1	20,000	17,600	13.6
College degree	98.9	99.6	−0.7	95,700	85,900	11.4
Race and Hispanic origin of householder						
Non-Hispanic white	96.8	97.2	−0.4	44,300	39,500	12.2
Nonwhite or Hispanic	86.7	85.0	1.7	9,000	5,500	63.6
Region						
Northeast	92.5	96.4	−3.9	43,800	47,400	−7.6
Midwest	95.4	96.5	−1.1	31,000	33,900	−8.6
South	93.5	90.7	2.8	20,800	13,400	55.2
West	93.9	94.0	−0.1	29,100	25,300	15.0
Housing status						
Owner	98.4	97.5	0.9	54,300	52,600	3.2
Renter or other	84.0	85.5	−1.5	3,800	3,300	15.2

Source: Federal Reserve Board, Changes in U.S. Family Finances from 2004 to 2007: Evidence from the Survey of Consumer Finances, Federal Reserve Bulletin, February 2009, Internet site http://www.federalreserve.gov/pubs/oss/oss2/2007/ scf2007home.html; calculations by New Strategist

Table 11.4 Percent of Households Owning Financial Assets by Type of Asset, 2007

(percent of households owning financial assets by selected characteristics of households and type of asset, 2007)

	any financial asset	transaction accounts	certificates of deposit	savings bonds	bonds	stocks	pooled investment funds	retirement accounts	cash value life insurance	other managed	other financial
TOTAL HOUSEHOLDS	**93.9%**	**92.1%**	**16.1%**	**14.9%**	**1.6%**	**17.9%**	**11.4%**	**52.6%**	**23.0%**	**5.8%**	**9.3%**
Household income percentile											
Below 20 percent	79.1	74.9	9.4	3.6	–	5.5	3.4	10.7	12.8	2.7	6.6
20 to 39.9 percent	93.2	90.1	12.7	8.5	–	7.8	4.6	35.6	16.4	4.7	8.8
40 to 59.9 percent	97.2	96.4	15.4	15.2	–	14.0	7.1	55.2	21.6	5.3	10.2
60 to 79.9 percent	99.7	99.3	19.3	20.9	1.4	23.2	14.6	73.3	29.4	5.7	8.4
80 to 89.9 percent	100.0	100.0	19.9	26.2	1.8	30.5	18.9	86.7	30.6	7.6	9.8
90 percent or higher	100.0	100.0	27.7	26.1	8.9	47.5	35.5	89.6	38.9	13.6	15.3
Age of householder											
Under age 35	89.2	87.3	6.7	13.7	–	13.7	5.3	41.6	11.4	–	10.0
Aged 35 to 44	93.1	91.2	9.0	16.8	0.7	17.0	11.6	57.5	17.5	2.2	9.6
Aged 45 to 54	93.3	91.7	14.3	19.0	1.1	18.6	12.6	64.7	22.3	5.1	10.5
Aged 55 to 64	97.8	96.4	20.5	16.2	2.1	21.3	14.3	60.9	35.2	7.7	9.2
Aged 65 to 74	96.1	94.6	24.2	10.3	4.2	19.1	14.6	51.7	34.4	13.2	9.4
Aged 75 or older	97.4	95.3	37.0	7.9	3.5	20.2	13.2	30.0	27.6	14.0	5.3
Education of householder											
No high school diploma	79.7	75.7	9.5	3.4	–	3.9	2.2	21.6	12.6	1.7	7.1
High school diploma	93.3	90.9	14.1	11.5	0.6	9.3	5.8	43.2	22.6	4.2	8.2
Some college	95.5	93.9	14.1	16.4	1.2	17.4	8.9	52.5	23.4	6.6	9.8
College degree	98.9	98.7	21.6	21.6	3.3	31.5	21.4	73.3	27.1	8.5	10.9
Race and Hispanic origin of householder											
Non-Hispanic white	96.8	95.5	19.4	17.8	2.1	21.4	13.7	58.2	25.3	7.3	9.7
Nonwhite or Hispanic	86.7	83.9	8.2	7.8	0.4	9.4	5.8	39.1	17.6	2.3	8.3
Region											
Northeast	92.5	91.3	18.1	18.9	2.0	21.4	15.5	53.3	23.5	6.4	5.4
Midwest	95.4	93.6	16.8	16.0	1.2	17.9	10.6	57.8	26.6	6.7	9.2
South	93.5	91.3	15.1	12.0	1.7	15.4	9.7	48.8	23.3	5.2	8.6
West	93.9	92.7	15.5	15.0	1.6	19.2	11.5	52.9	18.3	5.5	13.9
Housing status											
Owner	98.4	97.3	20.0	18.2	2.2	22.4	15.0	63.3	28.9	7.5	9.4
Renter or other	84.0	80.8	7.7	7.5	0.4	8.1	3.5	29.2	10.1	2.1	9.1

Note: "–" means sample is too small to make a reliable estimate.
Source: Federal Reserve Board, Changes in U.S. Family Finances from 2004 to 2007: Evidence from the Survey of Consumer Finances, Federal Reserve Bulletin, February 2009, Internet site http://www.federalreserve.gov/pubs/oss/oss2/2007/scf2007home.html; calculations by New Strategist

Table 11.5 Median Value of Financial Assets by Type of Asset, 2007

(median value of financial assets for households owning asset, by selected characteristics of households and type of asset, 2007)

	any financial asset	transaction accounts	certificates of deposit	savings bonds	bonds	stocks	pooled investment funds	retirement accounts	cash value life insurance	other managed	other financial
TOTAL HOUSEHOLDS	$28,800	$4,000	$20,000	$1,000	$80,000	$17,000	$56,000	$45,000	$8,000	$70,000	$6,000
Household income percentile											
Below 20 percent	1,700	800	18,000	500	–	3,800	30,000	6,500	2,500	100,000	1,500
20 to 39.9 percent	7,000	1,600	18,000	1,000	–	10,000	30,000	12,000	5,000	86,000	3,000
40 to 59.9 percent	18,600	2,700	17,000	700	–	5,500	37,500	23,900	5,200	59,000	4,000
60 to 79.9 percent	58,300	6,000	11,000	1,000	19,000	14,000	35,000	48,000	10,000	52,000	10,000
80 to 89.9 percent	129,900	12,900	20,000	2,000	81,000	15,000	46,000	85,000	9,000	30,000	10,000
90 percent or higher	404,500	36,700	42,000	2,500	250,000	75,000	180,000	200,000	28,100	90,000	45,000
Age of householder											
Under age 35	6,800	2,400	5,000	700	–	3,000	18,000	10,000	2,800	–	1,500
Aged 35 to 44	25,800	3,400	5,000	1,000	9,700	15,000	22,500	36,000	8,300	24,000	8,000
Aged 45 to 54	54,000	5,000	15,000	1,000	20,000	18,500	50,000	67,000	10,000	45,000	6,000
Aged 55 to 64	72,400	5,200	23,000	1,900	90,800	24,000	112,000	98,000	10,000	59,000	20,000
Aged 65 to 74	68,100	7,700	23,200	1,000	50,000	38,000	86,000	77,000	10,000	70,000	10,000
Aged 75 or older	41,500	6,100	30,000	20,000	100,000	40,000	75,000	35,000	5,000	100,000	15,000
Education of householder											
No high school diploma	3,000	1,200	14,000	1,000	–	2,700	64,000	15,000	2,500	30,000	1,500
High school diploma	14,200	2,500	16,000	1,000	46,500	10,000	30,000	28,500	5,200	80,000	5,000
Some college	20,000	2,800	18,000	1,000	50,000	6,000	25,000	32,000	8,000	52,000	4000.0
College degree	95,700	10,000	25,000	1,100	100,000	25,000	75,000	75,000	13,000	75,000	10000.0
Race and Hispanic origin of householder											
Non-Hispanic white	44,300	5,100	20,000	1,000	95,900	19,000	64,000	52,700	9,000	70,000	10,000
Nonwhite or Hispanic	9,000	2,000	10,000	1,000	23,100	8,000	30,000	25,400	5,000	30,000	3,000
Region											
Northeast	43,800	5,100	20,000	1,000	114,700	17,900	50,000	57,500	9,000	73,000	10,000
Midwest	31,000	3,800	12,000	1,000	49,300	14,000	37,500	36,000	7,000	67,000	6,000
South	20,800	3,500	20,000	1,200	100,000	17,900	70,000	40,000	8,000	80,000	4,000
West	29,100	4,300	23,000	1,000	60,000	18,000	58,800	45,600	10,000	60,000	6,000
Housing status											
Owner	54,300	6,200	20,000	1,000	100,000	20,000	60,000	57,000	10,000	70,000	10,000
Renter or other	3,800	1,200	10,000	700	15,000	5,500	40,000	10,000	2,000	54,000	1,800

Note: "–" means sample is too small to make a reliable estimate.
Source: Federal Reserve Board, Changes in U.S. Family Finances from 2004 to 2007: Evidence from the Survey of Consumer Finances, Federal Reserve Bulletin, February 2009, Internet site http://www.federalreserve.gov/pubs/oss/oss2/2007/scf2007home.html; calculations by New Strategist

Stock Values Fell between 2004 and 2007

The loss in the value of stocks deepened in 2008.

In 2007, the 51 percent majority of households owned stock either directly or indirectly through retirement accounts and mutual funds. The median value of the stock owned by the average household fell 2 percent between 2004 and 2007, to $35,000 after adjusting for inflation. The loss since then has been much greater. According to estimates by the Federal Reserve Board, the median value of the stock owned by the average household fell to $22,500 by October 2008—a 36 percent decline between 2007 and 2008.

The majority of householders ranging in age from 35 to 74 own stock, the value peaking among householders aged 55 to 64 at $78,000. Overall, stock accounts for the 53 percent majority of financial assets owned by the average household.

■ Much of the stock owned by households is held in retirement accounts, the value of which declined sharply in the financial turmoil of 2008.

Stock ownership peaks in the 45-to-64 age group

(percent of households that own stock directly or indirectly, by age, 2007)

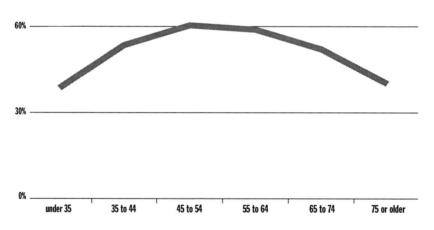

Table 11.6 Stock Ownership of Households by Age of Householder, 2004 and 2007

(percentage of households owning stock directly or indirectly, median value of stock for owners, and share of total household financial assets accounted for by stock holdings, by age of householder, 2004 and 2007; percent and percentage point change, 2004–07; in 2007 dollars)

	2007	2004	percentage point change
PERCENT OWNING STOCK			
Total households	**51.1%**	**50.2%**	**0.9**
Under age 35	38.6	40.8	–2.2
Aged 35 to 44	53.5	54.5	–1.0
Aged 45 to 54	60.4	56.5	3.9
Aged 55 to 64	58.9	62.8	–3.9
Aged 65 to 74	52.1	46.9	5.2
Aged 75 or older	40.1	34.8	5.3

	2007	2004	percent change
MEDIAN VALUE OF STOCK			
Total households	**$35,000**	**$35,700**	**–2.0%**
Under age 35	7,000	8,800	–20.5
Aged 35 to 44	26,000	22,000	18.2
Aged 45 to 54	45,000	54,900	–18.0
Aged 55 to 64	78,000	78,000	0.0
Aged 65 to 74	57,000	76,900	–25.9
Aged 75 or older	41,000	94,300	–56.5

	2007	2004	percentage point change
STOCK AS SHARE OF FINANCIAL ASSETS			
Total households	**53.3%**	**51.3%**	**2.0**
Under age 35	44.3	40.3	4.0
Aged 35 to 44	53.7	53.5	0.2
Aged 45 to 54	53.0	53.8	–0.8
Aged 55 to 64	55.0	55.0	0.0
Aged 65 to 74	55.3	51.5	3.8
Aged 75 or older	48.1	39.3	8.8

Source: Federal Reserve Board, Changes in U.S. Family Finances from 2004 to 2007: Evidence from the Survey of Consumer Finances, Federal Reserve Bulletin, February 2009, Internet site http://www.federalreserve.gov/pubs/oss/oss2/2007/scf2007home.html; calculations by New Strategist

Table 11.7 Stock Ownership by Household Income Percentile, 2004 and 2007

(percentage of households owning stock directly or indirectly, median value of stock for owners, and share of total household financial assets accounted for by stock holdings, by household income percentile, 2004 and 2007; percentage point change in ownership and share of finanacial assets and percent change in value, 2004–07; in 2007 dollars)

	2007	2004	percentage point change
PERCENT OWNING STOCK			
Total households	**51.1%**	**50.2%**	**0.9**
Below 20 percent	13.6	11.7	1.9
20 to 39.9 percent	34.0	29.6	4.4
40 to 59.9 percent	49.5	51.7	–2.2
60 to 79.9 percent	70.5	69.9	0.6
80 to 89.9 percent	84.4	83.8	0.6
90 percent or higher	91.0	92.7	–1.7

	2007	2004	percent change
MEDIAN VALUE OF STOCK			
Total households	**$35,000**	**$35,700**	**–2.0%**
Below 20 percent	6,500	8,200	–20.7
20 to 39.9 percent	8,800	11,000	–20.0
40 to 59.9 percent	17,700	16,500	7.3
60 to 79.9 percent	34,100	28,700	18.8
80 to 89.9 percent	62,000	60,900	1.8
90 percent or higher	219,000	225,200	–2.8

	2007	2004	percentage point change
SHARE OF FINANCIAL ASSETS			
Total households	**53.3%**	**51.3%**	**2.0**
Below 20 percent	39.0	32.0	7.0
20 to 39.9 percent	34.3	30.9	3.4
40 to 59.9 percent	38.3	43.4	–5.1
60 to 79.9 percent	52.5	41.7	10.8
80 to 89.9 percent	49.3	48.8	0.5
90 percent or higher	57.6	57.5	0.1

Source: Federal Reserve Board, Changes in U.S. Family Finances from 2004 to 2007: Evidence from the Survey of Consumer Finances, Federal Reserve Bulletin, February 2009, Internet site http://www.federalreserve.gov/pubs/oss/oss2/2007/scf2007home.html; calculations by New Strategist

Nonfinancial Assets Are the Foundation of Household Wealth

For the average household, nonfinancial assets are six times as valuable as financial assets.

The median value of the nonfinancial assets owned by the average American household stood at $177,400 in 2007, much greater than the $28,800 median in financial assets. Between 2004 and 2007, the value of the nonfinancial assets owned by the average household grew 9 percent, after adjusting for inflation. Rising housing prices were behind the increase, and the collapse of the housing market in the past few years substantially lowered the value of nonfinancial assets.

Eighty-seven percent of households own a vehicle, the most commonly held nonfinancial asset. The second most commonly owned nonfinancial asset is a home, owned by 69 percent. Homes are by far the most valuable asset owned by Americans, and they account for the largest share of net worth. In 2007, the median value of the average owned home stood at $200,000. The decline in housing prices since 2007 has lowered housing values. The Federal Reserve Board estimates that the median value of the average home fell to $181,600 by October 2008—still 3 percent higher than in 2004, after adjusting for inflation.

■ The drop in housing values is the primary cause of the decline in household net worth since 2007.

Median housing value peaks in the 45-to-54 age group

(median value of the primary residence among homeowners, by age of householder, 2007)

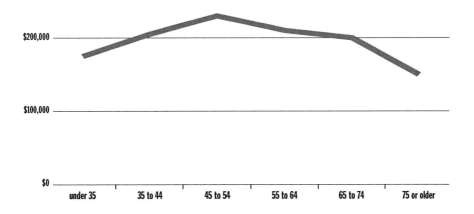

Table 11.8 Ownership and Value of Nonfinancial Assets, 2004 and 2007

(percentage of households owning any nonfinancial asset and median value of nonfinancial assets for owners, by selected characteristics, 2004 and 2007; percentage point change in ownership and percent change in value, 2004–07; in 2007 dollars)

	percent owning any nonfinancial asset			median value of nonfinancial assets		
	2007	2004	percentage point change	2007	2004	percent change
TOTAL HOUSEHOLDS	**92.0%**	**92.5%**	**−0.5**	**$177,400**	**$162,300**	**9.3%**
Household income percentile						
Below 20 percent	73.4	76.4	−3.0	40,000	24,600	62.6
20 to 39.9 percent	91.2	92.0	−0.8	77,200	78,000	−1.0
40 to 59.9 percent	97.2	96.7	0.5	139,000	145,300	−4.3
60 to 79.9 percent	98.5	98.4	0.1	246,300	216,500	13.8
80 to 89.9 percent	99.6	99.1	0.5	360,100	309,500	16.3
90 percent or higher	99.7	99.3	0.4	799,900	715,200	11.8
Age of householder						
Under age 35	88.2	88.6	−0.4	30,900	35,500	−13.0
Aged 35 to 44	91.3	93.0	−1.7	182,600	166,200	9.9
Aged 45 to 54	95.0	94.7	0.3	224,900	202,600	11.0
Aged 55 to 64	95.6	92.6	3.0	233,100	248,600	−6.2
Aged 65 to 74	94.5	95.6	−1.1	212,200	177,000	19.9
Aged 75 or older	87.3	92.5	−5.2	157,100	150,600	4.3
Education of householder						
No high school diploma	80.9	81.9	−1.0	84,400	59,900	40.9
High school diploma	92.2	92.4	−0.2	137,700	119,900	14.8
Some college	91.0	93.3	−2.3	157,300	150,900	4.2
College degree	96.6	96.5	0.1	289,400	264,900	9.2
Race and Hispanic origin of householder						
Non-Hispanic white	94.6	95.8	−1.2	203,800	181,000	12.6
Nonwhite or Hispanic	85.8	84.0	1.8	102,000	70,400	44.9
Region						
Northeast	84.2	90.3	−6.1	250,000	228,100	9.6
Midwest	93.4	94.2	−0.8	157,500	165,000	−4.5
South	93.8	92.1	1.7	145,800	131,400	11.0
West	94.1	93.4	0.7	251,600	191,600	31.3
Housing status						
Owner	100.0	100.0	0.0	253,500	221,400	14.5
Renter or other	74.5	75.9	−1.4	10,100	9,200	9.8

Source: Federal Reserve Board, Changes in U.S. Family Finances from 2004 to 2007: Evidence from the Survey of Consumer Finances, Federal Reserve Bulletin, February 2009, Internet site http://www.federalreserve.gov/pubs/oss/oss2/2007/scf2007home.html; calculations by New Strategist

Table 11.9 Percent of Households Owning Nonfinancial Assets by Type of Asset, 2007

(percent of households owning nonfinancial assets by selected characteristics of households and type of asset, 2007)

	any nonfinancial asset	vehicles	primary residence	other residential property	equity in nonresidential property	business equity	other non-financial
TOTAL HOUSEHOLDS	**92.0%**	**87.0%**	**68.6%**	**13.7%**	**8.1%**	**12.0%**	**7.2%**
Household income percentile							
Below 20 percent	73.4	64.4	41.4	5.4	2.5	3.0	3.9
20 to 39.9 percent	91.2	85.9	55.2	6.5	3.9	4.5	5.7
40 to 59.9 percent	97.2	94.3	69.3	9.9	7.4	9.2	7.4
60 to 79.9 percent	98.5	95.4	83.9	15.4	9.4	15.9	7.2
80 to 89.9 percent	99.6	95.6	92.6	21.0	13.6	17.0	9.0
90 percent or higher	99.7	94.8	94.3	42.2	21.0	37.5	14.1
Age of householder							
Under age 35	88.2	85.4	40.7	5.6	3.2	6.8	5.9
Aged 35 to 44	91.3	87.5	66.1	12.0	7.5	16.0	5.5
Aged 45 to 54	95.0	90.3	77.3	15.7	9.5	15.2	8.7
Aged 55 to 64	95.6	92.2	81.0	20.9	11.5	16.3	8.5
Aged 65 to 74	94.5	90.6	85.5	18.9	12.3	10.1	9.1
Aged 75 or older	87.3	71.5	77.0	13.4	6.8	3.8	5.8
Education of householder							
No high school diploma	80.9	73.7	52.8	5.8	2.6	5.3	2.2
High school diploma	92.2	87.5	68.9	10.0	7.3	8.7	5.1
Some college	91.0	86.7	62.3	13.2	6.5	10.7	7.0
College degree	96.6	91.9	77.8	20.6	11.8	18.2	11.0
Race and Hispanic origin of householder							
Non-Hispanic white	94.6	89.6	75.6	15.3	9.0	13.9	8.4
Nonwhite or Hispanic	85.8	80.9	51.9	10.0	5.9	7.4	4.3
Region							
Northeast	84.2	75.4	66.1	13.3	5.6	7.8	5.5
Midwest	93.4	89.5	71.3	13.7	8.4	13.1	6.4
South	93.8	89.2	70.2	11.3	8.8	11.4	7.2
West	94.1	90.5	65.4	18.3	8.7	15.3	9.3
Housing status							
Owner	100.0	93.8	100.0	17.5	10.8	15.4	8.0
Renter or other	74.5	72.3	0.0	5.6	2.1	4.5	5.3

Source: Federal Reserve Board, Changes in U.S. Family Finances from 2004 to 2007: Evidence from the Survey of Consumer Finances, Federal Reserve Bulletin, February 2009, Internet site http://www.federalreserve.gov/pubs/oss/oss2/2007/scf2007home.html; calculations by New Strategist

Table 11.10 Median Value of Nonfinancial Assets by Type of Asset, 2007

(median value of nonfinancial assets for households owning asset, by selected characteristics of households and type of asset, 2007)

	any nonfinancial asset	vehicles	primary residence	other residential property	equity in nonresidential property	business equity	other non-financial
TOTAL HOUSEHOLDS	**$177,400**	**$15,500**	**$200,000**	**$146,000**	**$75,000**	**$100,500**	**$14,000**
Household income percentile							
Below 20 percent	40,000	5,600	100,000	60,000	65,000	100,000	3,000
20 to 39.9 percent	77,200	9,200	120,000	57,500	60,000	25,000	6,000
40 to 59.9 percent	139,000	14,600	150,000	100,000	40,000	53,700	10,000
60 to 79.9 percent	246,300	20,400	215,000	120,000	71,000	81,000	15,000
80 to 89.9 percent	360,100	25,400	300,000	175,000	72,000	100,000	20,000
90 percent or higher	799,900	33,900	500,000	324,000	175,000	500,000	75,000
Age of householder							
Under age 35	30,900	13,300	175,000	85,000	50,000	59,900	8,000
Aged 35 to 44	182,600	17,400	205,000	150,000	50,000	86,000	10,000
Aged 45 to 54	224,900	18,700	230,000	150,000	80,000	100,000	15,000
Aged 55 to 64	233,100	17,400	210,000	157,000	90,000	116,300	20,000
Aged 65 to 74	212,200	14,600	200,000	150,000	75,000	415,000	20,000
Aged 75 or older	157,100	9,400	150,000	100,000	110,000	250,000	25,000
Education of householder							
No high school diploma	84,400	10,400	122,500	65,000	125,000	66,000	13,200
High school diploma	137,700	13,300	150,000	76,000	50,000	100,000	7,300
Some college	157,300	14,600	192,000	100,000	52,800	81,200	13,000
College degree	289,400	19,900	280,000	200,000	90,000	125,400	20,000
Race and Hispanic origin of householder							
Non-Hispanic white	203,800	17,100	200,000	136,500	75,000	112,500	15,000
Nonwhite or Hispanic	102,000	12,000	180,000	175,000	62,700	60,000	8,000
Region							
Northeast	250,000	14,500	275,000	190,000	112,000	150,000	20,000
Midwest	157,500	14,600	155,000	110,000	52,800	112,400	10,000
South	145,800	15,600	160,000	120,000	71,500	93,800	15,000
West	251,600	17,100	300,000	210,000	90,000	101,400	14,000
Housing status							
Owner	253,500	18,400	200,000	150,000	80,000	113,400	20,000
Renter or other	10,100	8,600	0	85,000	38,000	50,000	5,400

Source: Federal Reserve Board, Changes in U.S. Family Finances from 2004 to 2007: Evidence from the Survey of Consumer Finances, Federal Reserve Bulletin, February 2009, Internet site http://www.federalreserve.gov/pubs/oss/oss2/2007/scf2007home.html; calculations by New Strategist

Most Households Are in Debt

More than three of four households owe money on mortgages, credits cards, or other types of loans.

Seventy-seven percent of households have debt, owing a median of $67,300 in 2007. The median amount of debt owed by the average debtor household increased by 11 percent between 2004 and 2007, after adjusting for inflation.

Householders aged 35 to 54 are most likely to be in debt, with 86 to 87 percent owing money. Debt declines with age, falling to a low of 31 percent among householders aged 75 or older.

The most common types of debt are home-secured debt such as mortgages (49 percent of households have this type of debt), installment loans such as for vehicles (47 percent), and credit card debt (46 percent). Mortgages account for the largest share of debt. The median amount owed by the average homeowner for the primary residence stood at $107,000 in 2007.

Most households either do not have a credit card or pay off their cards in full each month. Among householders aged 35 to 54, however, most had a balance remaining on their credit card after they paid their last bill. Although horror stories about credit card debt abound, the median amount owed by the average household is a relatively modest $3,000.

■ As Americans attempt to pay down their debt following the collapse of the housing bubble and the downturn in the stock market, consumer demand has declined.

Home-secured debt accounts for the largest amount owed

(median amount of debt for debtors, for the three most common types of debt, 2007)

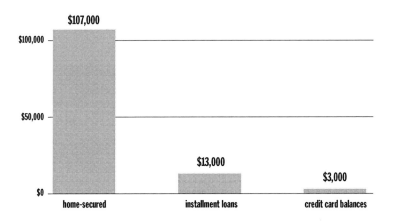

Table 11.11 Debt of Households, 2004 and 2007

(percentage of households with debt and median amount of debt for debtors, by age of householder, 2004 and 2007; percentage point change in households with debt and percent change in amount of debt, 2004–07; in 2007 dollars)

	percent with debt			median amount of debt		
	2007	2004	percentage point change	2007	2004	percent change
TOTAL HOUSEHOLDS	**77.0%**	**76.4%**	**0.6**	**$67,300**	**$60,700**	**10.9%**
Household income percentile						
Below 20 percent	51.7	52.6	–0.9	9,000	7,700	16.9
20 to 39.9 percent	70.2	69.8	0.4	18,000	17,600	2.3
40 to 59.9 percent	83.8	84.0	–0.2	54,500	48,800	11.7
60 to 79.9 percent	90.9	86.6	4.3	111,300	102,600	8.5
80 to 89.9 percent	89.6	91.9	–2.3	182,200	149,400	22.0
90 percent or higher	87.6	86.3	1.3	235,000	229,500	2.4
Age of householder						
Under age 35	83.5	79.8	3.7	36,200	36,900	–1.9
Aged 35 to 44	86.2	88.6	–2.4	106,200	95,800	10.9
Aged 45 to 54	86.8	88.4	–1.6	95,900	91,400	4.9
Aged 55 to 64	81.8	76.3	5.5	60,300	52,700	14.4
Aged 65 to 74	65.5	58.8	6.7	40,100	27,500	45.8
Aged 75 or older	31.4	40.3	–8.9	13,000	16,900	–23.1
Education of householder						
No high school diploma	55.5	53.4	2.1	19,500	13,200	47.7
High school diploma	75.1	73.2	1.9	40,000	34,000	17.6
Some college	80.8	84.2	–3.4	54,400	49,400	10.1
College degree	85.1	84.3	0.8	124,300	117,700	5.6
Race and Hispanic origin of householder						
Non-Hispanic white	76.8	78.0	–1.2	76,400	76,300	0.1
Nonwhite or Hispanic	77.7	72.5	5.2	43,900	33,500	31.0
Region						
Northeast	73.3	76.3	–3.0	66,600	60,100	10.8
Midwest	78.3	75.4	2.9	61,200	75,400	–18.8
South	75.3	75.0	0.3	60,900	44,300	37.5
West	81.6	79.9	1.7	95,500	85,200	12.1
Housing status						
Owner	82.4	82.3	0.1	111,100	105,200	5.6
Renter or other	65.4	63.4	2.0	9,200	8,600	7.0

Source: Federal Reserve Board, Changes in U.S. Family Finances from 2004 to 2007: Evidence from the Survey of Consumer Finances, Federal Reserve Bulletin, February 2009, Internet site http://www.federalreserve.gov/pubs/oss/oss2/2007/scf2007home.html; calculations by New Strategist

Table 11.12 Percent of Households with Debt, 2007

(percentage of households with debt by selected characteristics and type of debt, 2007)

| | | secured by residential property | | | | lines of credit not secured | |
	any debt	primary residence	other property	installment loans	credit card balances	by residential property	other debt
TOTAL HOUSEHOLDS	**77.0%**	**48.7%**	**5.5%**	**46.9%**	**46.1%**	**1.7%**	**6.8%**
Household income percentile							
Below 20 percent	51.7	14.9	1.1	27.8	25.7	–	3.9
20 to 39.9 percent	70.2	29.5	1.9	42.3	39.4	1.8	6.8
40 to 59.9 percent	83.8	50.5	2.6	54.0	54.9	–	6.4
60 to 79.9 percent	90.9	69.7	6.8	59.2	62.1	2.1	8.7
80 to 89.9 percent	89.6	80.8	8.5	57.4	55.8	–	9.6
90 percent or higher	87.6	76.4	21.9	45.0	40.6	2.1	7.0
Age of householder							
Under age 35	83.5	37.3	3.3	65.2	48.5	2.1	5.9
Aged 35 to 44	86.2	59.5	6.5	56.2	51.7	2.2	7.5
Aged 45 to 54	86.8	65.5	8.0	51.9	53.6	1.9	9.8
Aged 55 to 64	81.8	55.3	7.8	44.6	49.9	1.2	8.7
Aged 65 to 74	65.5	42.9	5.0	26.1	37.0	1.5	4.4
Aged 75 or older	31.4	13.9	0.6	7.0	18.8	–	1.3
Education of householder							
No high school diploma	55.5	26.0	1.9	33.3	26.9	–	5.3
High school diploma	75.1	45.0	3.2	46.0	46.8	1.4	6.4
Some college	80.8	46.9	6.4	54.3	51.0	2.2	9.3
College degree	85.1	61.6	8.7	49.1	50.2	1.7	6.5
Race and Hispanic origin of householder							
Non-Hispanic white	76.8	52.1	5.8	46.1	45.1	1.6	6.7
Nonwhite or Hispanic	77.7	40.4	4.8	48.9	48.4	2.0	7.0
Region							
Northeast	73.3	48.4	4.9	40.7	44.3	–	5.6
Midwest	78.3	51.0	5.2	47.9	45.5	1.9	7.0
South	75.3	46.6	4.6	48.5	43.4	1.7	6.9
West	81.6	49.9	8.1	48.4	52.4	2.7	7.5
Housing status							
Owner	82.4	70.9	6.9	46.1	50.1	1.3	6.8
Renter or other	65.4	0.0	2.6	48.6	37.3	2.8	6.9

Note: "–" means sample is too small to make a reliable estimate.
Source: Federal Reserve Board, Changes in U.S. Family Finances from 2004 to 2007: Evidence from the Survey of Consumer Finances, Federal Reserve Bulletin, February 2009, Internet site http://www.federalreserve.gov/pubs/oss/oss2/2007/scf2007home.html; calculations by New Strategist

Table 11.13 Median Value of Debt Owed by Households, 2007

(median value of debt for households with debt, by selected characteristics and type of debt, 2007)

	any debt	secured by residential property		installment loans	credit card balances	lines of credit not secured by residential property	other debt
		primary residence	other property				
TOTAL HOUSEHOLDS	$67,300	$107,000	$100,000	$13,000	$3,000	$3,800	$5,000
Household income percentile							
Below 20 percent	9,000	40,000	70,000	6,500	1,000	–	3,000
20 to 39.9 percent	18,000	51,000	42,000	9,800	1,800	1,300	4,000
40 to 59.9 percent	54,500	887,000	68,900	12,800	2,400	–	4,000
60 to 79.9 percent	111,300	115,000	83,000	16,300	4,000	5,100	5,300
80 to 89.9 percent	182,200	164,000	125,000	17,300	5,500	–	5,000
90 percent or higher	235,000	201,000	147,500	18,300	7,500	17,300	7,500
Age of householder							
Under age 35	36,200	135,300	78,000	15,000	1,800	1,000	4,500
Aged 35 to 44	106,200	128,000	101,600	13,500	3,500	4,600	5,000
Aged 45 to 54	95,900	110,000	82,000	12,900	3,600	6,000	4,500
Aged 55 to 64	60,300	85,000	130,000	10,900	3,600	10,000	6,000
Aged 65 to 74	40,100	69,000	125,000	10,300	3,000	30,000	5,000
Aged 75 or older	13,000	40,000	50,000	8,000	800	–	4,500
Education of householder							
No high school diploma	19,500	50,000	53,300	8,800	1,500	–	4,000
High school diploma	40,000	84,000	82,000	10,200	2,300	1,400	4,500
Some college	54,400	97,000	80,000	12,100	2,900	3,800	5,000
College degree	124,300	142,700	125,000	17,400	4,000	6,000	6,000
Race and Hispanic origin of householder							
Non-Hispanic white	76,400	106,000	90,800	13,400	3,300	5,000	5,000
Nonwhite or Hispanic	43,900	113,000	114,800	12,000	2,000	800	5,000
Region							
Northeast	66,600	107,000	95,000	12,100	3,000	–	6,500
Midwest	61,200	93,900	82,500	11,000	3,000	5,000	5,000
South	60,900	99,000	80,000	13,200	2,800	3,200	4,500
West	95,500	150,800	160,000	14,200	3,000	3,800	6,000
Housing status							
Owner	111,100	107,000	100,000	14,200	3,600	7,500	5,000
Renter or other	9,200	0	80,000	10,300	1,300	1,000	4,900

Note: "–" means sample is too small to make a reliable estimate.
Source: Federal Reserve Board, Changes in U.S. Family Finances from 2004 to 2007: Evidence from the Survey of Consumer Finances, Federal Reserve Bulletin, February 2009, Internet site http://www.federalreserve.gov/pubs/oss/oss2/2007/scf2007home.html; calculations by New Strategist

Two Out of Three Workers Have Access to a Retirement Plan

Among service workers, the figure is much smaller.

Retirement benefits have changed over the past few decades as the number of companies that offer defined-benefit pension plans has declined. Among workers with a retirement plan in 2006, only 31 percent said that a defined-benefit pension was their primary plan, down from 57 percent in 1988. The 67 percent majority of workers with a retirement plan in 2006 said that a defined-contribution plan (such as a 401k) was their primary type of plan, up from just 26 percent who said so in 1988.

Sixty-six percent of the nation's workers have access to a retirement plan at work, according to the Bureau of Labor Statistics' National Compensation Survey. Private-sector workers are much less likely than state and local government workers to have access to a retirement plan—only 61 percent of private-sector workers have access versus 89 percent of public-sector workers.

Not surprisingly, management and professional workers are more likely to have access to a retirement plan (80 to 83 percent) than service workers (44 percent). Unionized workers are more likely to have a retirement plan (90 percent) than those not in unions (61 percent). And workers at the top of the pay scale are more likely to have a retirement plan (88 percent) than those at the bottom (26 percent).

■ The stock market decline of 2008 depleted savings in defined-contribution retirement plans and raised the question of whether these plans will be adequate to support the nation's retirees.

Highly paid workers are more likely to have access to a retirement plan at work

(percent of workers with access to a retirement plan, by average wage percentile, 2008)

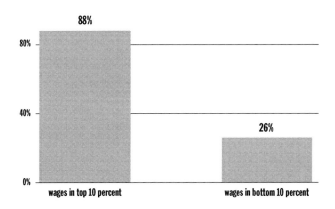

Table 11.14 Workers with a Retirement Plan by Type, 1988 to 2006

(percent distribution of nonagricultural wage and salary workers aged 16 or older who participate in a retirement plan at work, by type of plan considered primary, 1988 to 2006)

	total workers with a retirement plan	primary type of plan	
		defined benefit	defined contribution
2006	100.0%	30.9%	67.1%
2003	100.0	40.5	57.7
1998	100.0	46.3	51.5
1993	100.0	38.2	49.8
1988	100.0	56.7	25.8

Note: Figures do not sum to 100 because "other/don't know" is not shown.
Source: Employee Benefit Research Institute, Retirement Plan Participation: Survey of Income and Program Participation Data, 2006, Notes, February 2009, Internet site http://www.ebri.org/publications/notes/index.cfm?fa=notesDisp&content_id=4176

Table 11.15 Workers with Retirement Benefits, 2008

(percent of workers with access to and who participate in a retirement plan, and percent with access who participate [take-up rate], by selected characteristics and place of work, 2008)

	total workers			private industry			state and local government		
	access	participation	take-up rate	access	participation	take-up rate	access	participation	take-up rate
TOTAL WORKERS	**66%**	**56%**	**86%**	**61%**	**51%**	**83%**	**89%**	**86%**	**96%**
WORKER CHARACTERISTICS									
Management, business, and financial	83	79	94	82	77	94	–	–	–
Professional and related	80	73	91	73	64	88	91	88	96
Service	44	34	76	37	25	68	83	79	96
Sales and office	67	57	85	65	55	84	90	87	97
Natural resources, construction, maintenance	65	56	86	62	52	84	93	91	98
Production, transportation, and material moving	66	55	83	65	54	82	87	85	98
Full-time	75	66	87	71	60	85	99	95	97
Part-time	33	25	76	32	23	73	40	37	94
Union	90	86	96	85	80	95	97	94	97
Nonunion	61	51	83	59	48	81	83	80	96
Average wage within the following percentiles									
Less than 10.0	26	15	59	25	14	57	58	55	94
10.0 to 24.9	45	32	72	41	28	68	84	81	96
25.0 to 49.9	66	55	83	63	50	80	93	90	96
50.0 to 74.9	76	68	90	70	61	87	95	91	96
75.0 to 89.9	84	78	93	79	73	91	97	94	97
90.0 or greater	88	82	94	84	78	92	98	95	97
ESTABLISHMENT CHARACTERISTICS									
Goods producing	72	62	87	71	62	86	–	–	–
Service producing	64	55	86	59	49	82	89	86	96
Fewer than 100 workers	47	39	82	45	37	81	77	75	97
100 or more workers	82	72	88	79	67	85	91	88	96

Note: "Total workers" includes all workers in the private, nonfarm economy except private household workers and includes all workers in the public sector except those working for the federal government. "–" means 0 or sample is too small to make a reliable estimate.
Source: Bureau of Labor Statistics, Employee Benefits in the United States: March 2008, Internet site http://www.bls.gov/news .release/ebs2.toc.htm; calculations by New Strategist

Retirement Worries Are Growing

A record share of workers lack confidence in having enough money for a comfortable retirement.

Only 13 percent of workers are "very confident" in their ability to afford a comfortable retirement, according to the 2009 Retirement Confidence Survey—a record low since the survey was first fielded in the mid-1990s. The 13 percent figure is just half of the 26 percent who felt "very confident" in 2000.

Reality may be dawning on many workers. Since 2000, the expected age of retirement has climbed sharply. The percentage of workers expecting to retire at age 65 or older increased from 51 to 64 percent between 2000 and 2009. At the same time, the percentage expecting to retire before age 65 fell from 44 to 26 percent.

■ Only 20 percent of workers are very confident that they are doing a good job of saving for retirement, down from 30 percent who felt that way in 2000.

Most workers are not planning on an early retirement

(percentage of workers who expect to retire at age 65 or older, 2000 and 2009)

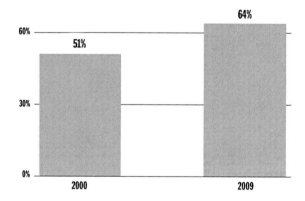

Table 11.16 Retirement Outlook, 2000 and 2009

(responses of workers aged 25 or older to selected questions about retirement, 2000 and 2009; percentage point change, 2000–09)

	2009	2000	percentage point change
Confidence in having enough money to live comfortably in retirement			
Very confident	13%	26%	−13
Somewhat confident	41	47	−6
Not too confident	22	18	4
Not at all confident	22	8	14
Confident that they are doing a good job of preparing financially for retirement			
Very confident	20	30	−10
Somewhat confident	49	49	0
Not too confident	16	13	3
Not at all confident	14	8	6
Confidence that the Social Security system will continue to provide benefits of at least equal value to the benefits received by retirees today			
Very confident	6	7	−1
Somewhat confident	26	21	5
Not too confident	28	39	−11
Not at all confident	39	32	7
Confidence that the Medicare system will continue to provide benefits of at least equal value to the benefits received by retirees today			
Very confident	5	6	−1
Somewhat confident	33	29	4
Not too confident	35	38	−3
Not at all confident	26	26	0
Expected age of retirement			
Before age 60	9	22	−13
Aged 60 to 64	17	22	−5
Age 65	23	28	−5
Aged 66 or older	31	19	12
Never retire	10	4	6
Don't know/refused	7	5	2

Source: Employee Benefit Research Institute, Retirement Confidence Surveys, Internet site http://www.ebri.org/surveys/rcs/

Glossary

adjusted for inflation Income or a change in income that has been adjusted for the rise in the cost of living, or the consumer price index (CPI-U-RS).

American Community Survey An ongoing nationwide survey of 250,000 households per month, providing detailed demographic data at the community level. Designed to replace the census long-form questionnaire, the ACS includes more than 60 questions that formerly appeared on the long form, such as language spoken at home, income, and education. ACS data are available for areas as small as census tracts.

American Housing Survey The AHS collects national and metropolitan-level data on the nation's housing, including apartments, single-family homes, and mobile homes. The nationally representative survey, with a sample of 55,000 homes, is conducted by the Census Bureau for the Department of Housing and Urban Development every other year.

American Indians In this book, American Indians include Alaska Natives (Eskimos and Aleuts) unless those groups are shown separately.

American Time Use Survey Under contract with the Bureau of Labor Statistics, the Census Bureau collects ATUS information, revealing how people spend their time. The ATUS sample is drawn from U.S. households completing their final month of interviews for the Current Population Survey. One individual from each selected household is chosen to participate in ATUS. Respondents are interviewed by telephone about their time use during the previous 24 hours. About 40,000 households are included in the sample each year.

Asian Includes Native Hawaiians and other Pacific Islanders unless those groups are shown separately.

Baby Boom U.S. residents born between 1946 and 1964.

Baby Bust U.S. residents born between 1965 and 1976, also known as Generation X.

Behavioral Risk Factor Surveillance System A collaborative project of the Centers for Disease Control and Prevention and U.S. states and territories. It is an ongoing data collection program designed to measure behavioral risk factors in the adult population aged 18 or older. All 50 states, three territories, and the District of Columbia take part in the survey, making the BRFSS the primary source of information on the health-related behaviors of Americans.

black Includes those who identified themselves as "black" or "African American."

Consumer Expenditure Survey An ongoing study administered by the Bureau of Labor Statistics of the day-to-day spending of American households. The CEX includes an interview survey and a diary survey. The average spending figures shown are the integrated data from both the diary and interview components of the survey. Two separate, nationally representative samples are used for the interview and diary surveys. For the interview survey, about 7,500 consumer units are interviewed on a rotating panel basis each quarter for five consecutive quarters. For the diary survey, 7,500 consumer units keep weekly diaries of spending for two consecutive weeks.

consumer unit *(on spending tables only)* For convenience, the term "consumer unit" and "household" are used interchangeably in the Spending chapter of this book, although consumer units are somewhat different from the Census Bureau's households. Consumer units are all related members of a household, or financially independent members of a household. A household may include more than one consumer unit.

Current Population Survey A nationally representative survey of the civilian noninstitutional population aged 15 or older. It is taken monthly by the Census Bureau for the Bureau of Labor Statistics, collecting information from more than 50,000 households on employment and unemployment. In March of each year, the survey includes the Annual Social and Economic Supplement (formerly called the Annual Demographic Survey), which is the source of most national data on the characteristics of Americans, such as educational attainment, living arrangements, and incomes.

disability The National Health Interview Survey estimates the number of people aged 18 or older who have difficulty in physical functioning, probing whether respondents could perform nine activities by themselves without using special equipment. The categories are walking a quarter mile; standing for two hours; sitting for two hours; walking up ten steps without resting; stooping, bending, kneeling; reaching over one's head; grasping or handling small objects; carrying a ten-pound object; and pushing/pulling a large object. Adults who reported that any of these activities was very difficult or they could not do it at all were defined as having physical difficulties.

dual-earner couple A married couple in which both the husband and wife are in the labor force.

earnings A type of income, earnings is the amount of money a person receives from his or her job. See also Income.

employed All civilians who did any work as a paid employee or farmer/self-employed worker, or who worked 15 hours or more as an unpaid farm worker or in a family-owned business, during the reference period. All those who have jobs but who are temporarily absent from their jobs due to illness, bad weather, vacation, labor management dispute, or personal reasons are considered employed.

expenditure The transaction cost including excise and sales taxes of goods and services acquired during the survey period. The full cost of each purchase is recorded even though full payment may not have been made at the date of purchase. Average expenditure figures may be artificially low for infrequently purchased items such as cars because figures are calculated using all consumer units within a demographic segment rather than just purchasers. Expenditure estimates include money spent on gifts for others.

family A group of two or more people (one of whom is the householder) related by birth, marriage, or adoption and living in the same household.

family household A household maintained by a householder who lives with one or more people related to him or her by blood, marriage, or adoption.

female/male householder A woman or man who maintains a household without a spouse present. May head family or nonfamily households.

foreign-born population People who are not U.S. citizens at birth.

full-time employment Thirty-five or more hours of work per week during a majority of the weeks worked.

full-time, year-round Fifty or more weeks of full-time employment during the previous calendar year.

General Social Survey A biennial survey of the attitudes of Americans taken by the University of Chicago's National Opinion Research Center. NORC conducts the GSS through face-to-face interviews with an independently drawn, representative sample of 1,500 to 3,000 noninstitutionalized people aged 18 or older who live in the United States.

Generation X U.S. residents born between 1965 and 1976, also known as the baby-bust generation.

Hispanic Because Hispanic is an ethnic origin rather than a race, Hispanics may be of any race. While most Hispanics are white, there are black, Asian, American Indian, and even Native Hawaiian Hispanics.

household All the persons who occupy a housing unit. A household includes the related family members and all the unrelated persons, if any, such as lodgers, foster children, wards, or employees who share the housing unit. A person living alone is counted as a household. A group of unrelated people who share a housing unit as roommates or unmarried partners is also counted as a household. Households do not include group quarters such as college dormitories, prisons, or nursing homes.

household, race/ethnicity of Households are categorized according to the race or ethnicity of the householder only.

householder The person (or one of the persons) in whose name the housing unit is owned or rented or, if there is no such person, any adult member. With married couples, the householder may be either the husband or wife. The householder is the reference person for the household.

householder, age of The age of the householder is used to categorize households into age groups such as those used in this book. Married couples, for example, are classified according to the age of either the husband or wife, depending on which one identified him or herself as the householder.

housing unit A house, an apartment, a group of rooms, or a single room occupied or intended for occupancy as separate living quarters. Separate living quarters are those in which the occupants do not live and eat with any other persons in the structure and that have direct access from the outside of the building or through a common hall that is used or intended for use by the occupants of another unit or by the general public. The occupants may be a single family, one person living alone, two or more families living together, or any other group of related or unrelated persons who share living arrangements.

Housing Vacancy Survey A supplement to the Current Population Survey, providing quarterly and annual data on rental and homeowner vacancy rates, characteristics of units available for occupancy, and homeownership rates by age, household type, region, state, and metropolitan area. The Current Population Survey sample includes 51,000 occupied housing units and 9,000 vacant units.

housing value The respondent's estimate of how much his or her house and lot would sell for if it were for sale.

iGeneration U.S. residents born in 1995 or later.

immigration The relatively permanent movement (change of residence) of people into the country of reference.

in-migration The relatively permanent movement (change of residence) of people into a subnational geographic entity, such as a region, division, state, metropolitan area, or county.

income Money received in the preceding calendar year by each person aged 15 or older from each of the following sources: 1) earnings from longest job or self-employment); 2) earnings from jobs other than longest job; 3) unemployment compensation; 4) workers' compensation; 5) Social Security; 6) Supplemental Security income; 7) public assistance; 8) veterans' payments; 9) survivor benefits; 10) disability benefits; 11) retirement pensions; 12) interest; 13) dividends; 14) rents and royalties or estates and trusts; 15) educational assistance; 16) alimony; 17) child support; 18) financial assistance from outside the household, and other periodic income. Income is reported in several ways in this book. "Household income" is the combined income of all household members. "Income of persons" is all income accruing to a person from all sources. "Earnings" are the money a person receives from his or her job.

industry Refers to the industry in which a person worked longest in the preceding calendar year.

job tenure The length of time a person has been employed continuously by the same employer.

labor force The labor force tables in this book show the civilian labor force only. The labor force includes both the employed and the unemployed (people who are looking for work). People are counted as being in the labor force if they were working or looking for work during the reference week in which the Census Bureau fields the Current Population Survey.

labor force participation rate The percent of the civilian noninstitutional population that is in the civilian labor force, which includes both the employed and the unemployed.

married couples with or without children under age 18 Married couples with or without own children under age 18 living in the same household. Couples without children under age 18 may be parents of grown children who live elsewhere, or they could be childless couples.

median The amount that divides the population or households into two equal portions: one below and one above the median. Medians can be calculated for income, age, and many other characteristics.

median income The amount that divides the income distribution into two equal groups, half having incomes above the median, half having incomes below the median. The medians for households or families are based on all households or families. The median for persons are based on all persons aged 15 or older with income.

metropolitan statistical area A large population nucleus with adjacent communities having a high degree of social and economic integration with the core, as defined by the Office of Management and Budget. In general, they must include a city or urbanized area with 50,000 or more inhabitants and a total population of 100,000 or more. The county (or counties) that contains the largest city is the "central county" (counties), along with any adjacent counties that are socially and economically integrated with the central county (or counties). In New England, MSAs are defined in terms of cities and towns rather than counties.

Millennial generation U.S. residents born between 1977 and 1994.

mobility status People are classified according to their mobility status on the basis of a comparison between their place of residence at the time of the March Current Population Survey and their place of residence in March of the previous year. "Nonmovers" are people living in the same house at the end of the period as at the beginning of the period. "Movers" are people living in a different house at the end of the period than at the beginning of the period. "Movers from abroad" are either citizens or aliens whose place of residence is outside the United States at the beginning of the period, that is, in an outlying area under the jurisdiction of the United States or in a foreign country. The mobility status of children is fully allocated from the mother if she is in the household; otherwise it is allocated from the householder.

National Ambulatory Medical Care Survey An annual survey of visits to nonfederally employed office-based physicians who are primarily engaged in direct patient care. Data are collected from physicians rather than patients, with each physician assigned a one-week reporting period. During the week, the physician or office staff record a systematic random sample of visit characteristics.

National Compensation Survey The Bureau of Labor Statistics' NCS examines the incidence and detailed provisions of selected employee benefit plans in small, medium, and large private establishments, and state and local governments. Each year bureau economists visit a representative sample of establishments across the country, asking questions about the establishment, its employees, and their benefits.

National Crime Victimization Survey The NCVS collects data each year on nonfatal crimes against people aged 12 or older, reported and not reported to the police, from a nationally representative sample of 42,000 households and 76,000 persons in the United States. The NCVS provides information about victims, offenders, and criminal offenses.

National Health and Nutrition Examination Survey A continuous survey of a representative sample of the U.S. civilian noninstitutionalized population. Respondents are interviewed at home about their health and nutrition, and the interview is followed up by a physical examination that measures such things as height and weight in mobile examination centers.

National Health Interview Survey A continuing nationwide sample survey of the civilian noninstitutional population of the U.S. conducted by the Census Bureau for the National Center for Health Statistics. In interviews each year, data are collected from more than 100,000 people about their illnesses, injuries, impairments, chronic and acute conditions, activity limitations, and use of health services.

National Hospital Ambulatory Medical Care Survey The NHAMCS, sponsored by the National Center for Health Statistics, is an annual national probability sample survey of visits to emergency departments and outpatient departments at non-federal, short stay and general hospitals. Hospital staff collect data from patient records.

National Household Education Survey The NHES, sponsored by the National Center for Education Statistics, provides descriptive data on the educational activities of the U.S. population, including after-school care and adult education. The NHES is a system of telephone surveys of a representative sample of 45,000 to 60,000 households in the U.S.

Native Hawaiian and other Pacific Islander The 2000 census identified this group for the first time as a separate racial category from Asians. In most survey data, however, the population is included with Asians.

net migration The result of subtracting out-migration from in-migration for an area. Another way to derive net migration is to subtract natural increase (births minus deaths) from total population change in an area.

nonfamily household A household maintained by a householder who lives alone or who lives with people to whom he or she is not related.

nonfamily householder A householder who lives alone or with nonrelatives.

non-Hispanic People who do not identify themselves as Hispanic are classified as non-Hispanic. Non-Hispanics may be of any race.

non-Hispanic white People who identify their race as white alone and who do not indicate an Hispanic origin.

nonmetropolitan area Counties that are not classified as metropolitan areas.

occupation Occupational classification is based on the kind of work a person did at his or her job during the previous calendar year. If a person changed jobs during the year, the data refer to the occupation of the job held the longest during that year.

occupied housing units A housing unit is classified as occupied if a person or group of people is living in it or if the occupants are only temporarily absent—on vacation, example. By definition, the count of occupied housing units is the same as the count of households.

outside principal cities The portion of a metropolitan county or counties that falls outside of the principal city or cities; generally regarded as the suburbs.

own children Sons and daughters, including stepchildren and adopted children, of the householder. The totals include never-married children living away from home in college dormitories.

owner occupied A housing unit is "owner occupied" if the owner lives in the unit, even if it is mortgaged or not fully paid for. A cooperative or condominium unit is "owner occupied" only if the owner lives in it. All other occupied units are classified as "renter occupied."

part-time employment Less than 35 hours of work per week in a majority of the weeks worked during the year.

percent change The change (either positive or negative) in a measure that is expressed as a proportion of the starting measure. When median income changes from $20,000 to $25,000, for example, this is a 25 percent increase.

percentage point change The change (either positive or negative) in a value which is already expressed as a percentage. When a labor force participation rate changes from 70 percent of 75 percent, for example, this is a 5 percentage point increase.

poverty level The official income threshold below which families and people are classified as living in poverty. The threshold rises each year with inflation and varies depending on family size and age of householder.

principal cities The largest cities in a metropolitan area are called the principal cities. The balance of a metropolitan area outside the principal cities is regarded as the "suburbs."

proportion or share The value of a part expressed as a percentage of the whole. If there are 4 million people aged 25 and 3 million of them are white, then the white proportion is 75 percent.

race Race is self-reported and can be defined in three ways. The "race alone" population comprises people who identify themselves as only one race. The "race in combination" population comprises people who identify themselves as more than one race, such as white and black. The "race, alone or in combination" population includes both those who identify themselves as one race and those who identify themselves as more than one race.

regions The four major regions and nine census divisions of the United States are the state groupings as shown below:

Northeast:
—New England: Connecticut, Maine, Massachusetts, New Hampshire, Rhode Island, and Vermont
—Middle Atlantic: New Jersey, New York, and Pennsylvania

Midwest:
—East North Central: Illinois, Indiana, Michigan, Ohio, and Wisconsin
—West North Central: Iowa, Kansas, Minnesota, Missouri, Nebraska, North Dakota, and South Dakota

South:
—South Atlantic: Delaware, District of Columbia, Florida, Georgia, Maryland, North Carolina, South Carolina, Virginia, and West Virginia
—East South Central: Alabama, Kentucky, Mississippi, and Tennessee
—West South Central: Arkansas, Louisiana, Oklahoma, and Texas

West:
—Mountain: Arizona, Colorado, Idaho, Montana, Nevada, New Mexico, Utah, and Wyoming
—Pacific: Alaska, California, Hawaii, Oregon, and Washington

renter occupied *See* Owner Occupied.

Retirement Confidence Survey The RCS, sponsored by the Employee Benefit Research Institute, the American Savings Education Council, and Mathew Greenwald & Associates, is an annual survey of a nationally representative sample of 1,000 people aged 25 or older. Respondents are asked a core set of questions that have been asked since 1996, measuring attitudes and behavior towards retirement. Additional questions are also asked about current retirement issues.

rounding Percentages are rounded to the nearest tenth of a percent; therefore, the percentages in a distribution do not always add exactly to 100.0 percent. The totals, however, are always shown as 100.0. Moreover, individual figures are rounded to the nearest thousand without being adjusted to group totals, which are independently rounded; percentages are based on the unrounded numbers.

self-employment A person is categorized as self-employed if he or she was self-employed in the job held longest during the reference period. Persons who report self-employment from a second job are excluded, but those who report wage-and-salary income from a second job are included. Unpaid workers in family businesses are excluded. Self-employment statistics include only nonagricultural workers and exclude people who work for themselves in incorporated business.

sex ratio The number of men per 100 women.

suburbs *See* Outside principal city.

Survey of Consumer Finances A triennial survey taken by the Federal Reserve Board. It collects data on the assets, debts, and net worth of American households. For the 2007 survey, the Federal Reserve Board interviewed a representative sample of 4,422 households.

unemployed People who, during the survey period, had no employment but were available and looking for work. Those who were laid off from their jobs and were waiting to be recalled are also classified as unemployed.

white The "white" racial category includes many Hispanics (who may be of any race) unless the term "non-Hispanic white" is used.

Bibliography

Bureau of Labor Statistics

Internet site http://www.bls.gov

—2000 and 2007 Consumer Expenditure Surveys, Internet site http://www.bls.gov/cex/

—2007 American Time Use Survey, Internet site http://www.bls.gov/tus/home.htm

—Characteristics of Minimum Wage Workers, 2008, Internet site http://www.bls.gov/cps/minwage2008tbls.htm

—Contingent and Alternative Employment Arrangements, Internet site http://www.bls.gov/news.release/conemp.toc.htm

—Economic and Employment Projections, Internet site http://www.bls.gov/news.release/ecopro.toc.htm

—Employee Benefits Survey, Internet site http://www.bls.gov/ncs/ebs/benefits/2008/ownership_civilian.htm

—Employee Tenure, Internet site http://www.bls.gov/news.release/tenure.toc.htm

—Employment Characteristics of Families, Internet site http://www.bls.gov/news.release/famee.toc.htm

—Labor Force Statistics from the Current Population Survey, Internet site http://www.bls.gov/cps/tables.htm#empstat

—*Monthly Labor Review*, "Labor Force Projections to 2016: More Workers in Their Golden Years," November 2007, Internet site http://www.bls.gov/opub/mlr/2007/11/contents.htm

Bureau of the Census

Internet site http://www.census.gov/

—2000 Census, American FactFinder, Internet site http://factfinder.census.gov/servlet/BasicFactsServlet

—2000 Census, Table DP-1: Profile of General Demographic Characteristics: 2000, Internet site http://www.census.gov/Press-Release/www/2001/demoprofile.html

—2007 American Community Survey, Internet site http://factfinder.census.gov/servlet/DatasetMainPageServlet?_program=ACS&_submenuId=&_lang=en&_ts=l

—2008 Current Population Survey Annual Social and Economic Supplement, Internet site http://www.census.gov/hhes/www/income/dinctabs.html

—2008 National Population Projections, Internet site http://www.census.gov/population/www/projections/2008projections.html

—American Housing Survey for the United States in 2007, Internet site http://www.census.gov/hhes/www/housing/ahs/ahs07/ahs07.html

—America's Families and Living Arrangements, 2008 Current Population Survey Annual Social and Economic Supplement, Internet site http://www.census.gov/population/www/socdemo/hh-fam/cps2008.html

—Educational Attainment in the United States: 2008, Detailed Tables, Current Population Survey Annual Social and Economic Supplement, Internet site http://www.census.gov/population/www/socdemo/education/cps2008.html

—Families and Living Arrangements, Historical Time Series, Current Population Survey Annual Social and Economic Supplements, Internet site http://www.census.gov/population/www/socdemo/hh-fam.html

—Geographic Mobility: 2007 to 2008, Detailed Tables, Current Population Survey Annual Social and Economic Supplement, Internet site http://www.census.gov/population/www/socdemo/migrate/cps2008.html

—Geographical Mobility/Migration, Current Population Survey Annual Social and Economic Supplements, Internet site http://www.census.gov/population/www/socdemo/migrate.html

—Health Insurance, Internet site http://pubdb3.census.gov/macro/032008/health/toc.htm

—Historical Health Insurance Tables, Internet site http://www.census.gov/hhes/www/hlthins/historic/index.html

—Historical Income Tables, Current Population Survey Annual Social and Economic Supplements, Internet site http://www.census.gov/hhes/www/income/histinc/histinctb.html

—Historical Poverty Tables, Current Population Survey Annual Social and Economic Supplements, Internet site http://www.census.gov/hhes/www/poverty/histpov/histpovtb.html

—*Historical Statistics of the United States, Colonial Times to 1970,* Part 1, 1975

—Housing Vacancy Surveys, Internet site http://www.census.gov/hhes/www/housing/hvs/hvs.html

—*Income, Poverty, and Health Insurance Coverage in the United States: 2007,* Current Population Report, P60-235, 2008; Internet site http://www.census.gov/hhes/www/income/histinc/h02AR.html

—Metropolitan and Micropolitan Statistical Areas, Internet site, http://www.census.gov/popest/metro/CBSA-est2008-annual.html

—*Metropolitan Areas and Cities*, 1990 Census Profile, No. 3, 1991

—National Population Estimate*s,* Internet site http://www.census.gov/popest/national/asrh/NC-EST2008-sa.html

—Number, Timing, and Duration of Marriages and Divorces: 2004, Detailed Tables, Internet site http://www.census.gov/population/www/socdemo/marr-div/2004detailed_tables.html

—School Enrollment, Historical Tables, Internet site http://www.census.gov/population/www/socdemo/school.html

—School Enrollment—Social and Economic Characteristics of Students: October 2007, detailed tables*,* Internet site http://www.census.gov/population/www/socdemo/school/cps2007.html

—State Population Estimate*s,* Internet site http://www.census.gov/popest/states/asrh/

—What's It Worth: Field of Training and Economic Status in 2004, Detailed Tables, Internet site http://www.census.gov/population/www/socdemo/education/sipp2004w2.html

Centers for Disease Control and Prevention
Internet site http://www.cdc.gov

—Behavioral Risk Factor Surveillance System, Prevalence Data, Internet site http://apps.nccd.cdc.gov/brfss/

— Cases of HIV/AIDS and AIDS, Internet site http://www.cdc.gov/hiv/topics/surveillance/resources/reports/2006report/

Department of Homeland Security
Internet site http://www.dhs.gov/index.shtm
—Immigration, 2008 Yearbook of Immigration Statistics, Internet site http://www.uscis
.gov/graphics/shared/statistics/yearbook/index.htm
—Estimates of the Unauthorized Immigrant Population Residing in the United States: January 2008, Internet site http://www.uscis.gov/graphics/shared/statistics/yearbook/index.htm

Employee Benefit Research Institute
Internet site http://www.ebri.org/
—2009 Retirement Confidence Survey, Internet site http://www.ebri.org/surveys/rcs/2009/
—"Retirement Plan Participation: Survey of Income and Program Participation (SIPP) Data, 2006," *Notes*, February 2009, Internet site http://www.ebri.org/publications/notes/index
.cfm?fa=notesDisp&content_id=4176

Federal Interagency Forum on Child and Family Statistics
Internet site http://childstats.gov
—America's Children in Brief: Key National Indicators of Well-Being, 2008, Internet site http://childstats.gov/americaschildren/tables.asp

Federal Reserve Board
Internet site http://www.federalreserve.gov/pubs/oss/oss2/scfindex.html
—"Changes in U.S. Family Finance from 2004 to 2007: Evidence from the Survey of Consumer Finances," *Federal Reserve Bulletin*, February 2009, Internet site http://www
.federalreserve.gov/pubs/oss/oss2/2007/scf2007home.html

National Center for Education Statistics
Internet site http://nces.ed.gov
—The Condition of Education, Internet site   http://nces.ed.gov/programs/coe/
—Digest of Education Statistics: 2008, Internet site http://nces.ed.gov/programs/digest/
— National Household Education Surveys Program, Parent and Family Involvement in Education, 2006–07 School Year, Internet site http://nces.ed.gov/pubsearch/pubsinfo
.asp?pubid=2008050
—Projections of Education Statistics to 2017, Internet site http://nces.ed.gov/programs/
projections/projections2017/tables.asp

National Center for Health Statistics
Internet site http://www.cdc.gov/nchs
—*Ambulatory Medical Care Utilization Estimates for 2006*, National Health Statistics Reports, No. 8, 2008, Internet site http://www.cdc.gov/nchs/about/major/ahcd/adata
.htm#CombinedRep orts
—*Anthropometric Reference Data for Children and Adults: United States, 2003–2006*, National Health Statistics Reports, Number 10, 2008, Internet site http://www.cdc.gov/nchs/
products/pubs/pubd/nhsr/nhsr.htm
—*Births: Preliminary Data for 2007*, National Vital Statistics Reports, Vol. 57, No. 12, 2009, Internet site http://www.cdc.gov/nchs/products/nvsr.htm#57_12

—*Complementary and Alternative Medicine Use Among Adults and Children: United States, 2007*, National Health Statistics Report, No. 12, 2008, Internet site http://nccam.nih.gov/news/camstats/2007/index.htm

—*Deaths: Preliminary Data for 2006*, National Vital Statistics Reports, Vol. 56, No. 16, 2008, Internet site http://www.cdc.gov/nchs/deaths.htm

—*Fertility, Contraception, and Fatherhood: Data on Men and Women from Cycle 6 of the 2002 National Survey of Family Growth*, Vital and Health Statistics, Series 23, No. 26, 2006; Internet site http://www.cdc.gov/nchs/nsfg.htm

—*Fertility, Family Planning, and Reproductive Health of U.S. Women: Data from the 2002 National Survey of Family Growth*, Vital and Health Statistics, Series 23, No. 25, 2005; Internet site http://www.cdc.gov/nchs/nsfg.htm

—*Health United States 2008,* Internet site http://www.cdc.gov/nchs/hus.htm

—*Summary Health Statistics for the U.S. Population: National Health Interview Survey, 2007*, Series 10, No. 238, 2008, Internet site http://www.cdc.gov/nchs/nhis.htm

—*Summary Health Statistics for U.S. Adults: National Health Interview Survey, 2007*, Series 10, No. 240, 2008, Internet site http://www.cdc.gov/nchs/nhis.htm

—*Summary Health Statistics for U.S. Children: National Health Interview Survey, 2007*, Series 10, No. 239, 2008, Internet site http://www.cdc.gov/nchs/nhis.htm

National Sporting Goods Association
Internet site http://www.nsga.org
—Sports Participation, Internet site http://www.nsga.org

Substance Abuse and Mental Health Services Administration
Internet site http://www.samhsa.gov
—National Survey on Drug Use and Health, 2007, Internet site http://www.oas.samhsa.gov/nsduh.htm

Survey Documentation and Analysis, Computer-assisted Survey Methods Program, University of California, Berkeley
Internet site http://sda.berkeley.edu/
—General Social Surveys, 1972-2008 Cumulative Data Files, Internet site http://sda.berkeley.edu/cgi-bin32/hsda?harcsda+gss08

Index

abortion, attitudes toward, 41, 44
adult education, 104–105
after-school activities, 288, 290
age
    abortion, attitudes toward, 41, 44
    adult education, participation in, 104–105
    AIDS, diagnosed with, 153–154
    alcohol use by, 123, 125
    alternative medicine use by, 147–150
    alternative work arrangements by, 314–315
    assets by, 538–548
    at first marriage, 372–373
    births by, 116–119
    blood pressure, high, 120–121
    business ownership, 12
    cholesterol, high, 120, 122
    cigarette smoking by, 123–124
    college enrollment by, 59, 90–91
    day care arrangement by, 289
    death penalty, attitudes toward, 41–42
    debts by, 549–552
    disabled by, 140–141
    divorce by, 380–381
    drug use, illicit, 126
    dual-earner couples by, 286–287
    educational attainment by, 49–51, 55–57
    evolution, attitudes toward, 30
    excitement in life by, 7
    foreign born by, 423
    gun permits, attitudes toward, 41, 43
    happiness, 4–6
    health care visits by, 142–145
    health conditions, 120–122, 132–139
    health insurance coverage, 127–129
    health insurance, percent without, 127, 129
    health insurance, reason for no coverage, 131
    health status by, 107–109
    homeownership by, 160–162
    hospital stays by, 151–152
    households by, 335, 338–341
    ideal number of children, 22–23
    income by, 206–210, 215–216, 219–223, 226–232,
        238–239, 248–250, 253–254
    job tenure, 304–306
    labor force by, 273–282, 286, 291–293, 305–308,
        322–323
    life expectancy, 157–158
    living arrangements by, 346–347, 303, 309, 311
    marital history by, 372–376
    marital status by, 312–313, 316, 370–371
    minimum wage workers by, 312–313
    mobility by, 11, 412, 414–415
    net worth by, 535, 542–544
    news sources, 38–39
    of children by parents' labor force participation,
        283–285
    of children in families, 360–362

    of husbands and wives, 377–379
    of retirement, 556–557
    perception of income by, 15–17
    political attitudes by, 38, 40–45
    population by, 385–390, 394–395
    poverty status by, 270–271
    premarital sex, attitudes toward, 35–36
    religion, attitudes toward, 28, 31–34
    right to die, attitudes toward, 41, 45
    satisfaction with financial situation, 16
    school enrollment by, 59–60
    science, attitudes toward, 29
    self-employed by, 307–308
    sex roles by, 25–26
    should government help the sick by, 27
    social class by, 14
    spanking children by, 24
    spending by, 433–443
    standard of living by, 18–21
    time use by, 519–522
    tolerance of same-sex relationships by, 35, 37
    trust in others by, 8
    unmarried partners by, 368, 370–371
    weight status by, 110–112
AIDS, people diagnosed with, 153–154
air conditioning, 182, 185
alcohol use by, 123, 125
alcoholic beverages, spending on
    by age of householder, 433–443
    by educational attainment, 497–507
    by household income, 444–463
    by household type, 464–474
    by race and Hispanic origin, 475–485
    by region, 486–496
    trends in, 430
allergies, in children, 184–185
alternative medicine use, 147–150
alternative work arrangements, 314–315
Alzheimer's disease, as a leading cause of death, 155–156
American Indians. See Race.
ancestry, 424
apartments, 176–178
apparel, spending on
    by age of householder, 433–443
    by educational attainment, 497–507
    by household income, 444–463
    by household type, 464–474
    by race and Hispanic origin, 475–485
    by region, 486–496
    trends in, 431
arthritis, 136–139
Asian language. See Language spoken at home.
Asians. See Race
assets, financial, 536–544
assets, nonfinancial, 536–537, 545–548
asthma
    in adults, 137–139
    in children, 132–135
attention deficit hyperactivity disorder, 132–135

attitudes
    how people get ahead, 10
    ideal number of children, 22–23
    political, 38, 40–45
    religious, 28, 31–34
    right to die, 41, 45
    satisfaction with financial situation, 16
    should government help the sick, 27
    toward abortion, 41, 44
    toward death penalty, 41–42
    toward evolution, 30
    toward gun permits, 41, 43
    toward life, 4–7
    toward medicare, 556–557
    toward news sources, 38–39
    toward premarital sex, 35–36
    toward retirement, 556–557
    toward same-sex relationships, 35–37
    toward science, 29
    toward sex roles, 25–26
    toward social security, 556–557
    toward spanking children, 24
    toward standard of living 18–21
automobile, as means of travel to work, 318–319.
        See also Vehicles.

back pain, 136–139
bathrooms, number of, 178
bedrooms, number of, 178
births
    by age, 116–119
    by birth order, 117–119
    by race and Hispanic origin of mother, 116–119
    by state, 351–352
    to unmarried women, 116, 118
blood pressure, high, 120–121
bonds, as financial asset, 536–537, 540–541
business
    equity, as nonfinancial asset, 536–537, 547–548
    ownership, 9, 12
    rooms used for in home, 178

cancer
    among leading causes of death, 155–156
    as health condition, 137–139
caring for household members, time spent, 510–532
caring for non-household members, time spent, 510–532
carpool, as means of travel to work, 318–319
carport, 184
cash contributions, spending on
    by age of householder, 433–443
    by educational attainment, 497–507
    by household income, 444–463
    by household type, 464–474
    by race and Hispanic origin, 475–485
    by region, 486–496
    trends in, 431
Catholic religion, preference for, 28, 31
central city. *See* Metropolitan status.
cerebrovascular disease, as a leading cause of death,
    155–156
certificates of deposit (CDs), as financial asset, 536–537,
    540–541

child care. *See* Day care.
children
    after-school activities, 288, 290
    AIDS, diagnosed with, 153–154
    asthma in, 132–135
    by age, 385–390, 394–395
    by parental involvement in school activities, 64–66
    drug use, illicit, 126
    drug use, prescription, 132–135
    foreign-born, 419–420
    health care visits by, 143–145
    health conditions of, 132–135
    hospital stays by, 151–152
    ideal number in families, 22–23
    in college, by family income, 85
    in day care, 288–290
    income of families with, 233–237
    labor force participation by presence of, 283–285
    life expectancy, 157–158
    living arrangements of, 352–359
    mobility, geographic, 412, 414–415
    number of, marital status by, 370–371
    of householder, 365–367
    participation in enrichment activities, 64–66
    population, 385–390, 394–395
    poverty status of, 270–271
    presence in families, 335, 337, 352–364
    presence of by characteristics of husbands and wives,
        354–364
    school enrollment of, 59–61, 69–72
    spending by households with, 464–474
    standard of living of, 21
    time spent caring for, 510–532
    working mothers and, 26
cholesterol, high, 120, 122
cigarette smoking, 123–124
cities. *See* Metropolitan status.
citizens, foreign born, 419–420
civic and religious activities, time spent in, 510–532
clothes dryer. *See* Clothes washer and dryer.
clothes washer and dryer in home, 184
clothing, spending on. *See* Apparel, spending on.
coal use, 180
cohabitation. *See* Unmarried partners.
college, children attending by family income, 85
college costs, 83–84
college degrees conferred, 95–103
college enrollment
    by age, 59, 90–91
    by family income, 85
    by full-time vs. part-time status, 87–89, 95–97
    by level of degree, 47, 94–103
    by parents' education, 86
    by race and Hispanic origin, 47, 79, 81, 92–94
    by sex, 47, 79, 82, 87, 96–103
    by type of institution, 82, 88–91
    by year of enrollment, 61, 85–86, 88–89
    private, 83–84, 89
    rate, 79–82, 85–86
    trends 79–82
community, amenities of, 192–193
commuting, 318–319
conservatives, 38, 40

contract workers, 314–315
contractors, independent, 314–315
cooking stove in home, 184
coronary, 136–139
couples, cohabiting. *See* Unmarried partners.
credit card debt, 536–537, 549–552
crime as neighborhood problem, 191

day care, 288–290
death, leading causes of, 155–156
death penalty, attitudes toward, 41–42
debt, 536–537, 549–552
deck, on home, 184
degrees conferred. *See* College degrees conferred.
dental insurance, as employee benefit, 321
diabetes
    among leading causes of death, 156
    chronic condition, 137–139
dining room, in home, 184
disability
    by age, 132–135, 140–141
    by type of disability, 140–141
    insurance, as employee benefit, 321
    learning, 133–135
dishwasher in home, 183
disposal in sink, 183
distance from home to work, 319
dividends, as source of income, 267
divorce, 372, 374–377, 380–383
doctor visits. *See* Health care visits.
drinking. *See* Alcohol use.
drug use, illicit, 126
drugs, prescription, 132–135, 321
dual-earners. *See* Households, married-couple.
duplexes, 176–178

earners, household income by number of, 206–208,
    233, 235
earnings. *See also* Income.
    as source of income, 266–267
    by educational attainment, 254–257
    by occupation, 258–262
    by sex, 254–262
    satisfaction with, 16
eating and drinking, time spent, 511–532
education, adult, 104–105
education, spending on
    by age of householder, 433–443
    by educational attainment, 497–507
    by household income, 444–463
    by household type, 464–474
    by race and Hispanic origin, 475–485
    by region, 486–496
    trends in, 432
educational activities, time spent, 510–532
educational assistance
    as employee benefit, 321
    as source of income, 266–267
    loans and grants for college, 83–84
educational attainment. *See also* College enrollment
    and School enrollment.
    abortion, attitudes toward, 41, 44
    adult education, participation by, 104–105
    alcohol use by, 123, 125
    alternative medicine use by, 146, 148–150
    assets by, 538–548
    business ownership by, 9, 12
    by age, 47–51, 55–57
    by race and Hispanic origin, 52–54
    by region, 55–57
    by sex, 47–54
    by state, 55, 58
    children's SAT scores by parents', 78
    cigarette smoking by, 123–124
    day care use by mother's, 288–290
    death penalty, attitudes toward, 41–42
    divorce by, 382–383
    earnings by, 254–257
    evolution, attitudes toward, 30
    excitement in life by, 7
    gun permits, attitudes toward, 41, 43
    happiness by, 4–6
    health care visits by, 145
    health conditions of children by parental, 133–135
    health insurance, reason for no coverage by, 131
    health status by, 107–109
    high school dropouts, 73–74
    high school graduates, projections of, 75–76
    homeownership by, 167
    hospital stays by, 151–152
    ideal number of children, 22–23
    income by, 201, 240–241, 254–257
    living arrangements of each sex by, 365–367
    marital status by, 370–371
    minimum wage workers by, 312–313
    mobility by, 11
    net worth by, 535
    news sources by, 38–39
    of husbands and wives, 377–379
    of parents by involvement in children's school
        activities, 64–66
    perception of income by, 15–17
    political attitudes by, 38, 40–45
    premarital sex, attitudes toward, 35–36
    religion, attitudes toward, 28, 31–34
    religious preferences by, 28, 31
    right to die, attitudes toward, 41, 45
    satisfaction with financial situation by, 16
    science, attitudes toward, 29
    sex roles by, 25–26
    should government help the sick, 27
    social class by, 14
    spanking children, attitudes toward, 24
    spending by, 497–507
    standard of living by, 19–21
    tolerance of same-sex relationships, 35, 37
    trust in others by, 8
    weight status by, 112
    working at home by, 316–317
educational enrichment activities, children's participation
    in, 64–66
electricity. *See also* Utilities, fuels, and public services,
    spending on.
    cost, 196
    use, 176–177, 180
emphysema, 137–139

employee benefits, 320–321
employment. *See* Labor force.
English, ability to speak, 425–426
entertainment, spending on
    by age of householder, 433–443
    by educational attainment, 497–507
    by household income, 444–463
    by household type, 464–474
    by race and Hispanic origin, 475–485
    by region, 486–496
    trends in, 427, 432
evolution, attitudes toward, 30
excitement in life, 7
exercise. *See also* Recreational activities.
    time spent in, 510–532

families, with children in college, 85
family type
    divorce by, 382–383
    health conditions of children by, 133–135
    marital status by, 370–371
fireplace, in home, 184
food, spending on
    by age of householder, 433–443
    by educational attainment, 497–507
    by household income, 444–463
    by household type, 464–474
    by race and Hispanic origin, 475–485
    by region, 486–496
    trends in, 428–430
footwear, spending on. *See* Apparel, spending on.
foreign-born population. *See also* Immigrants.
    by age, 423
    by citizenship status, 419–420
    by region/country of birth, 419–420
    by year of entry, 418, 420
    homeownership of, 165, 168
    size, 417–423
fuel oil. *See also* Utilities, fuels, and public services,
    spending on.
cost, 196
use, 180

garage or carport, 184
gas, natural. *See also* Utilities, fuels, and public services,
    spending on.
    cost, 196
    use, 176–177, 180
gated community, 192–193
gender. *See* sex.
gifts for non-household members, spending on
    by age of householder, 433–443
    by educational attainment, 497–507
    by household income, 444–463
    by household type, 464–474
    by race and Hispanic origin, 475–485
    by region, 486–496
    trends in, 432
gun permits, attitudes toward, 41, 43

happiness, 4–6
health care, spending on
    by age of householder, 433–443
    by educational attainment, 497–507

by household income, 444–463
by household type, 464–474
by race and Hispanic origin, 475–485
by region, 486–496
trends in, 431–432
health conditions. *See also* individual conditions.
    of adults, 120–122, 136–139
    of children, 132–135
health insurance. *See also* Health care, spending on.
    as an employee benefit, 320–321
    coverage, 127–128
    health care visits by status, 145
    hospital stays by status, 151–152
    people without, 127, 129–131
    reason for no, 127, 131
health status, 107–109
hearing impairments, 136–139
heart disease
    among leading causes of death, 155–156
    chronic condition, 136–139
heating fuels, 176–177, 181
high blood pressure, 120–121
high cholesterol, 120, 122
high school dropout rate, 73–74
holidays, paid, as an employee benefit, 321
home, as nonfinancial asset, 536–537, 545–548
homeownership status. *See also* Housing and Housing,
    spending on.
    air conditioning by, 185
    amenities of community by, 192–193
    amenities of housing unit by, 182–185
    by age, 160–162
    by educational attainment, 167
    by fuels used, 180
    by heating fuel, 176–177, 181
    by household type, 161, 163
    by income, 165–166
    by metropolitan area, 174–175
    by metropolitan status, 171
    by race and Hispanic origin, 159, 161, 164
    by region, 159, 169–170
    by size of unit, 176, 178
    by state, 172–173
    by type of unit, 176–177
    by year unit built, 179
    first-time, 198
    housing costs by, 194–196
    kitchen and laundry equipment by, 182–184
    neighborhood characteristics by, 189–190
    opinion of home by, 159, 186–187
    opinion of neighborhood by, 186, 188
    public services available by, 189, 191
    public transportation available by, 159, 189, 191
    schools, opinion of, 67–68
    trends, 159–161
homework, parents helping children with, 64, 66
homicide, as a leading cause of death, 156
hospital emergency department visits, 142–144
hospital outpatient visits, 142–144
hospital stays, overnight, 151–152
household services, spending on
    by age of householder, 433–443
    by educational attainment, 497–507
    by household income, 444–463

by household type, 464–474
by race and Hispanic origin, 475–485
by region, 486–496
trends in, 431
households
  assets of, 536–548
  by age, 335, 338–341
  by metropolitan status, 350–351
  by race and Hispanic origin, 342–343, 348–351
  by region, 348–349
  by size, 335, 344–347
  by type, 335–347, 352–367
  debt of, 549–552
  growth of, 348–349
  income of, 201–232, 263–265
  net worth of, 542–544
  spending by, 427–507
  trends, 335–339
households, family, female-headed
  by age of householder, 338–341
  by presence of children, 335, 337, 352–364
  by race and Hispanic origin, 342–343, 360–362
  growth of, 335–337
  homeownership of, 161, 163
  income of, 206–212, 215–218, 224–232, 236–239
  labor force participation by presence of
    children, 283–285
  poverty status, 271–272
households, family, male-headed
  by age of householder, 338–341
  by presence of children, 335–337, 352–364
  by race and Hispanic origin, 342–343, 360–362
  growth of, 335–337
  homeownership of, 161, 163
  income of, 206–212, 215–218, 224–232, 236–239
  labor force participation by presence of children,
    283–285
  poverty status, 271–272
  working fathers, 283–285
households, family, married-couple
  age of husbands and wives, 377–379
  by age of householder, 338–341
  by presence of children, 335, 337, 352–364
  by race and Hispanic origin, 360–362, 377, 379
  dual-earner, 233–235
  education of husbands and wives, 377–379
  growth of, 335–337
  homeownership of, 161, 163
  income of, 206–208, 215–218, 224–237
  income of husbands and wives, 233–235, 378
  interracial, 379
  labor force participation by presence of children,
    283–285, 363–364
  labor force status of husbands and wives, 283–285
  poverty status, 271–272
  spending by, 464–474
households, nonfamily. *See also* People living alone.
  by age of householder, 346–347
  by race and Hispanic origin, 342–343, 360–362
  growth of, 335, 346–347
  homeownership of, 161, 163
  income of, 206–210, 215–218, 224–232
housework, time spent, 510–532

housing. *See also* Homeownership and Housing,
    spending on.
  air-conditioning, 185
  amenities of, 182–185
  as nonfinancial asset, 536–537, 545–548
  by type, 176–178
  costs, 194–196
  fuels used, 176–177, 180
  kitchen and laundry equipment, 182–184
  mortgage characteristics, 200
  mortgage debt, 536–537
  number of rooms, 177
  opinion of unit, 186–187
  purchase price, 197–198
  size of unit, 176
  trends, 159–161
  value, 197–198
  year built, 179
housing, spending on
  by age of householder, 433–443
  by educational attainment, 497–507
  by household income, 444–463
  by household type, 464–474
  by race and Hispanic origin, 475–485
  by region, 486–496
  trends in, 430
hypertension, as leading cause of death, 156. *See also*
    Blood pressure, high.

ideal number of children, 22–23
immigrants. *See also* Foreign-born population.
  by state, 419
  trends, 417–420
  undocumented, 417, 420
income. *See also* Earnings and Poverty status.
  adult education, participation by, 105
  alcohol use by, 123, 125
  assets by, 538–548
  by age, 207–210, 215–216, 219–223, 226–232,
    238–239, 248–250, 253–254
  by educational attainment, 201, 240–241, 254–257
  by household type, 206–232, 263–265
  by metropolitan status, 263–264
  by number of earners, 206–208, 211, 215
  by occupation, 258–262
  by presence of children, 233–237
  by quintile, 204–208
  by race and Hispanic origin, 201, 206–208, 213–214,
    217–218, 221–223, 245–247, 253–254
  by region, 253–254, 263–264
  by sex, 201, 207–208, 215–218, 226–232, 236–239,
    242–262
  by state, 265
  change in, 17
  children in college by family, 85
  childrens' SAT scores by family, 78
  cigarette smoking by, 124
  debt by, 549–552
  health care visits by, 145
  health conditions of children by family, 133–135
  health insurance, reason for no coverage by, 131
  health status by, 107–109
  homeownership by, 165–166

hospital stays by, 151–152
household, 201–232, 263–265
housing costs by, 195
inequality, 204–205
net worth by, 542–544
of dual-earner couples, 233, 235
of full-time workers, 255–262
of husbands and wives, 233–235
perception of, 13–17
retirement benefits by, 553–555
satisfaction with, 13, 16
sources of, 266–267
spending by, 444–463
trends, 201–205, 209–214
independent contractors, 314–315
industry
    by occupation, 332–334
    projections, 332–334
    retirement benefits by, 553–555
influenza and pneumonia, as leading cause of death, 156
installment debt, 536–537, 549–552
insurance, health. See Health insurance.
insurance, personal. See Personal insurance and pensions.
insurance, property, 196
interest income, as source of income, 267
internet, as news source, 38–39

Jewish religion, preference for, 28, 31
job tenure, 304–306
journey to work, 318–319

kerosene use, 180
kidney disease, 137–139
kitchen and laundry equipment, by homeownership status, 182–184

labor force. See also Occupation.
    adult education, participation in by status, 104–105
    alternative work arrangements, 314–315
    by age, 273–282, 286, 291–293, 305–308, 322–323
    by industry, 332–334
    by race and Hispanic origin, 278–282, 294–302, 324–326
    by sex, 274–287, 291–295, 297–310, 324–326
    day care use by mother's status, 288–290
    dual earner couples, 286
    employee benefits, 320–321
    full-time workers, 291–292
    job tenure, 304–306
    journey to work, 318–319
    minimum wage workers, 312–313
    part-time workers, 291–293
    projections, 322–334
    self-employment, 307–308, 314–315
    status of husbands and wives, 286–287, 363–364
    trends, 273–275, 322–334
    unemployment, 283–287
    union representation, 309–311
    women in, by presence of children, 283–285
    work at home, 316–317
language spoken at home, 425–426
learning disability, in children, 132–135
leisure activities, time spent in, 510–532

liberals, 38, 40
life expectancy, 157–158
life insurance. See also Personal insurance and pensions, spending on.
    as employee benefit, 321
    as financial asset, 536–537, 540–541
liver disease
    among leading causes of death, 156
    as chronic condition, 137–139
living arrangements. See also individual household types.
    of adults, 365–367
    of children, 352–359
living room, two or more, 184

marital status. See also Unmarried partners.
    births by, 116, 118
    by age, 368–369, 372, 374–376
    by sex, 368–369, 372–376
    history, 380–381
    homeownership by, 163
    living arrangements of men by, 365–367
    median age at first marriage, 372–373
marriage
    age at first, 372–373
    interracial, 379
    percent dissolved, 372, 374–377, 380–383
Medicaid coverage, 127–129, 131
Medicare
    attitudes toward, 556–557
    coverage, 127–129
men. See Households, family, male-headed, people living alone and sex.
metropolitan status
    homeownership by, 171, 174–175
    households by, 350–351
    income by, 263–264
    population, 408–411
    retirement benefits by, 555
migraine headaches, 136–139
minimum wage workers, 312–313
mobile homes, 176–178
mobility
    by age, 11, 412, 414–415
    trends, 11, 412–413
moderates, 38, 40
mortgage. See also Housing, spending on.
    characteristics, 197–198
    debt, 536–537
mutual funds, as financial asset, 536–537, 540–541

neighborhood
    amenities, 189–193
    characteristics of, 189–190
    opinion of, 186, 188
    problems, 137, 139
    public services in, 189, 191
nephritis, among leading causes of death, 156
net worth, 542–544
newspapers, as news source, 38–39
news sources, 38–39
nonmetropolitan area. See Metropolitan status.

obesity. *See* Weight status.
occupation
    by race and Hispanic origin, 296–303
    by sex, 294–295, 297
    earnings by, 258–262
    employee benefits by, 320–321
    minimum wage workers by, 312–313
    participation in adult education by, 105
    projections, 327–334
    retirement benefits by, 320–321, 553–555
    union representation by, 309, 311
overweight. *See* Weight status.

parental involvement in childrens' education, 64–66
Parkinson's disease, as leading cause of death, 156
pensions, as source of income, 267. See also Personal
        insurance and pensions.
people living alone
    by age, 346–347
    by race and Hispanic origin, 360–362
    by sex, 335–337, 288–289, 346–347, 365–367
    growth of, 335–337, 346–347
    homeownership of, 161, 163
    income of, 206–208, 215–218, 226–232, 238–239
    spending of, 464–474
perception of income, 15–17
personal care activities, time spent, 510–532
personal care products and services, spending on
    by age of householder, 433–443
    by educational attainment, 497–507
    by household income, 444–463
    by household type, 464–474
    by race and Hispanic origin, 475–485
    by region, 486–496
    trends in, 432
personal insurance and pensions, spending on
    by age of householder, 433–443
    by educational attainment, 497–507
    by household income, 444–463
    by household type, 464–474
    by race and Hispanic origin, 475–485
    by region, 486–496
    trends in, 432
personal taxes, spending on
    by age of householder, 433–443
    by educational attainment, 497–507
    by household income, 444–463
    by household type, 464–474
    by race and Hispanic origin, 475–485
    by region, 486–496
    trends in, 432
physician visits. *See* Health care visits.
pneumonia and influenza, among leading causes
        of death, 156
police protection, 189, 191
political attitudes, 38, 40–45
population
    by age, 385–390, 394–395
    by ancestry, 424
    by language spoken at home, 425–426
    by metropolitan area, 408–411
    by metropolitan status, 408–409

    by race and Hispanic origin, 385, 391–397, 400–401,
        405–407
    by region, 398–401
    by sex, 386–387
    by state, 402–407
    citizenship status, 419–420
    foreign born, 419–420
    immigrant, 417–423
    mobility of, 412–415
    nativity status, 416, 419–420
    projections, 389–390, 396–397
porch, on home, 184
poverty status
    after-school activities by, 288–290
    by age, 270–271
    by family type, 271–272
    by race and Hispanic origin, 268, 270–272
    day care use by, 288–290
    trends in, 269
premarital sex, attitudes toward, 35–36
prescription medications. *See* Drugs, prescription.
projections
    of employment by industry, 332–334
    of employment by occupation, 327–334
    of high school graduates, 75–76
    of labor force, 322–334
    of population, 389–390, 396–397
    of school enrollment, 69–72
property insurance, 196
property taxes. *See* Housing, spending on.
Protestant religion, preference for, 28, 31
public assistance, as source of income, 267

race alone and race in combination, 391–393
race and Hispanic origin
    abortion, attitudes toward, 41, 44
    adult education, participation in, 104–105
    AIDS, diagnosed with, 153–154
    alcohol use by, 123, 125
    alternative medicine use by, 146, 148–150
    alternative work arrangements by, 314–315
    assets by, 538–548
    births by, 116–118
    business ownership by, 9, 12
    by age, 394–395
    by occupation, 296–303
    by region, 344, 346–347
    by state, 353–355
    cigarette smoking by, 124
    college enrollment by, 92–94
    college enrollment rate by, 79, 81
    day care use by, 288–290
    death penalty, attitudes toward, 41–42
    debt by, 501–503
    degrees conferred by, 95–97
    divorce by, 382–383
    educational attainment by, 52–54
    evolution, attitudes toward, 30
    excitement in life by, 7
    gun permits, attitudes toward, 41, 43
    happiness by, 4–6
    health care visits by, 143–145
    health conditions by, 132–139

health insurance, reason for no coverage, 131
health status by, 107–109
high school dropouts by, 73–74
homeownership by, 159, 161, 164
hospital stays by, 151–152
households of, 342–343, 348–351
husbands and wives, 360–362, 377, 379
ideal number of children, 22–23
income by, 201, 206–208, 213–214, 217–218,
    221–223, 245–247, 253–254
interracial marriage by, 379
labor force, 278–282, 294–302, 324–326
living arrangements by, 352, 356–359, 370–371,
    375–376
marital status by, 370–371
minimum wage workers by, 312–313
mobility by, 11
net worth of households by, 535
news sources by, 38–39
parental involvement in children's school
    activities by, 64–66
political attitudes by, 38, 40–45
population by, 385, 391–397, 400–401, 405–407
population projections by, 396–397
premarital sex, attitudes toward,35–36
religion, attitudes toward, 28, 31–34
religious preferences by, 28, 31
right to die, attitudes toward,, 41, 45
satisfaction with financial situation by, 16
Scholastic Assessment Test (SAT) scores by, 77–78
school enrollment by, 62–63
science, attitudes toward, 29
sex roles by, 25–26
should government help the sick, 27
social class by, 14
spanking children, attitudes toward, 24
spending by, 475–485
standard of living by, 18–21
tolerance of same-sex relationships by, 35, 37
time use by, 523–525
trust in others by, 8
union representation by, 309–311
weight status by, 110–112
radio, as news source, 38–39
reading, spending on
    by age of householder, 433–443
    by educational attainment, 497–507
    by household income, 444–463
    by household type, 464–474
    by race and Hispanic origin, 475–485
    by region, 486–496
    trends in, 432
recreational activities. See also Exercise.
    participation in, 113–115
    time spent in, 510–532
refrigerator, in home, 184
region
    assets by, 538–548
    day care use by, 288–290
    educational attainment by, 55–57
    health insurance, reason for no coverage by, 131
    homeownership by, 159, 169–170
    households by, 348–349

income by, 263–264
minimum wage workers by, 313
net worth by, 542–544
population by, 398–401
school enrollment projections by, 69–72
spending by, 486–496
religion, attitudes toward, 28, 31–34
religious
    activities, time spent in, 510–532
    attitudes, 28, 31–34
    preferences, 28, 31
Renters. See Homeownership.
rents, royalties, estates or trusts, as source of income, 267
respiratory disease
    among leading causes of death, 155–156
    as chronic condition, 137–139
retirement
    accounts, as financial asset, 536–537, 540–541
    attitudes toward, 556–557
    expected age of, 556–557
    income, 266–267
    plan, as employee benefit, 320–321, 553–555
    savings, 538
right to die, attitudes toward, 41, 45

same-sex relationships, attitudes toward 35, 37
satisfaction with financial situation, 16
savings bonds, as financial asset, 536–537, 540–541
Scholastic Assessment Test (SAT), 77–78
school activities, parental involvement in, 64–66
school enrollment. See also College enrollment and
Educational attainment.
    by age, 59–60
    by grade, 61, 70
    private, 70
    projections of, 69–72
school, satisfaction with local, 47, 67–68
science, attitude toward, 29
self-employment
    as independent contractors, 314–315
    as source of income, 267
    by age, 307–308
    work at home, 316–317
septicemia, as leading cause of death, 156
sex
    abortion, attitudes toward, 41, 44
    adult education, participation in, 105
    AIDS, diagnosed with, 153–154
    alcohol use by, 123, 125
    alternative medicine use by, 146, 148–150
    alternative work arrangements by, 314–315
    assets by, 538–548
    births, 116–119
    blood pressure, high, 120–121
    business ownership by, 12
    by age, 386–387
    by occupation, 294–295, 297
    cholesterol, high, 120, 122
    cigarette smoking by, 123–124
    college enrollment by, 47, 79, 82, 87, 96–103
    college enrollment rate by, 87, 96–103
    death penalty, attitudes toward, 41–42
    degrees conferred by, 95–103

earnings by, 254–262
educational attainment by, 47–51
evolution, attitudes toward, 30
excitement in life by, 7
gun permits, attitudes toward, 41, 43
happiness by, 4–6
health care visits by, 142–145
health insurance, reason for no coverage, 131
health status by, 107–109
high school dropouts by, 73–74
hospital stays by, 151–152
ideal number of children, 22–23
income by, 201, 242–262
job tenure by, 304–306
labor force by, 274–287, 291–295, 297–310, 324–326
life expectancy, 157–158
living arrangements by, 365–367
marital history by, 380–381
marital status by, 368–369, 372–376
minimum wage workers by, 312–313
mobility by, 11
news sources by, 38–39
political attitudes by, 38, 40–45
premarital sex, attitudes toward, 35–36
religious preferences, 28, 31
right to die, attitudes toward, 41, 45
satisfaction with financial situation by, 16
Scholastic Assessment Test (SAT) scores by, 77–78
sex roles by, 25–26
should government help the sick, 27
social class by, 14
spanking children, attitudes toward, 24
standard of living by, 18–21
time use by, 513–519, 521–522, 524–525
trust in others by, 8
tolerance of same-sex relationships by, 35, 37
union representation by, 309–311
unmarried partners by, 368, 370–371
weight status by, 110–112
working at home by, 316–317
working fathers, 285
working mothers, 26, 283–285
sex roles, 25–26
shopping
    available in neighborhood, 189, 191
    time spent, 510–532
should government help the sick, 27
sick leave, paid, as an employee benefit, 321
single-family detached homes, 176–178
Single parents. See Households, family, female- or
        male-headed.
single parents, spending of, 464–474
single-person households. See People living alone.
sleeping, time spent, 510–532
smoking. See Cigarette smoking and Tobacco products.
social class, 14
Social Security
    as source of income, 266–267
    attitudes toward, 556–557
solar energy use, 180
Spanish. See Language spoken at home.
spanking children, 24

spending
    by age of householder, 433–443
    by educational attainment, 497–507
    by household income, 444–463
    by household type, 464–474
    by race and Hispanic origin, 475–485
    by region, 486–496
    trends in, 427–432
sports. See Exercise and Recreational activities.
standard of living, 18–21
state
    educational attainment by, 11, 13
    homeownership by, 172–173
    immigrants by, 417, 420
    income by, 265
    population by, 404–407
    race and Hispanic origin by, 405–407
stock ownership, 537–538, 540–544
stroke, 136–139
suburbs. See Metropolitan status.
suicide, as a leading cause of death, 156
survivors' benefits, as source of income, 267

taxes. See Personal taxes, spending on.
telephone, availability by homeownership status, 184
television
    as news source, 38–39
    time spent watching, 510–532
temporary workers, 314–315
time spent commuting to work, 318–319
time spent volunteering, 510–532
time use
    by age, 519–522
    by race and Hispanic origin, 523–525
    by sex, 513–519, 521–522, 524–525
    percent reporting activity, 511–516
    weekdays vs. weekends, 526–532
tobacco products and smoking supplies, spending on
    by age of householder, 433–443
    by educational attainment, 497–507
    by household income, 444–463
    by household type, 464–474
    by race and Hispanic origin, 475–485
    by region, 486–496
    trends in, 432
tobacco use. See Cigarette smoking.
transaction accounts, as financial asset, 536–537,
        540–541
transportation, public
    as means of travel to work, 318–319
    available in neighborhood, 159, 189, 191
transportation, spending on
    by age of householder, 433–443
    by educational attainment, 497–507
    by household income, 444–463
    by household type, 464–474
    by race and Hispanic origin, 475–485
    by region, 486–496
    trends in, 427–431
trash removal cost, 196
travel to work. See Journey to work.

trends
>abortion, attitudes toward, 41, 44
>death penalty, attitudes toward, 41–42
>evolution, attitudes toward, 30
>excitement in life, 7
>family income relative to others, 15
>gun permits, attitudes toward, 41, 43
>happiness, 5
>happiness of marriage, 6
>homeownership, 159–161
>household, 335–339
>housing, 159–161
>how people get ahead, 10
>ideal number of children, 22–23
>income, 201–205, 209–214
>labor force, 273–275, 322–334
>mobility, 11, 412–413
>news sources, 38–39
>political, 38, 40–45
>premarital sex, attitudes toward 35–36
>religion, attitudes toward, 28, 31–34
>right to die, attitudes toward,, 41, 45
>satisfaction with financial situation, 16
>school enrollment, 59–63, 67–72
>science, attitudes toward, 29
>sex roles, 25–26
>should government help the sick, 27
>social class, 14
>spanking children, attitudes toward, 24
>spending, 427–432
>standard of living, 18–21
>tolerance of same-sex relationships, 35, 37
>trust in others, 8
trust in others, 8
tuition, college, 83–84

ulcers, 137–139
unemployed. See Labor force.
unemployment insurance, as source of income, 267
union
>representation, 309–311
>retirement benefits by status, 553–555
unmarried partners, 368, 370–371
utilities, fuels, public services, spending on
>by age of householder, 433–443
>by educational attainment, 497–507
>by household income, 444–463
>by household type, 464–474
>by race and Hispanic origin, 475–485
>by region, 486–496
>trends in, 431

vacation days, as an employee benefit, 321
vehicles
>as nonfinancial asset, 536–537, 547–548
>available by homeownership status, 184
vehicles, spending on
>by age of householder, 433–443
>by educational attainment, 497–507
>by household income, 444–463
>by household type, 464–474
>by race and Hispanic origin, 475–485
>by region, 486–496

trends in, 431
veteran's benefits, as source of income, 267
visual impairments, 137–139
volunteers
>parents, at children's school, 64–66
>time spent as, 510–532

wages and salaries, as source of income, 266–267
washing machines. See Clothes washers and dryers.
water, spending on, 196. See also Utilities, fuels, and
>public services, spending on.
waterfront property, 190
wealth
>assets, financial, 536–541
>assets, nonfinancial, 536–537, 545–548
>debt, 536–537, 549–552
>housing, 536–537, 547–548
>net worth, 542–544
>stock ownership, 542–544
weight status, 110–112
Whites. See also Whites, non-Hispanic.
widowhood, 372, 374–376
women. See Households, family female-headed and
>People living alone.
wood use, 180
work arrangements, alternative, 314–315
work at home, 316–317
worker's compensation, as source of income, 267
working, time spent, 510–532